RUSSIA

CHINA

HAMGYŎNGBUK-DO
• Ch'ŏngjin

HAMGYŎNGNAM-DO

P'YŎNGANBUK-DO

• Shinŭiju

• Hamhŭng

P'YŎNGANNAM-DO

P'YŎNG-YANG •

EAST SEA

HWANGHAE-DO

KANGWON-DO

• Haeju

KYŎNGGI-DO

• Ch'unch'ŏn

Ullŭngdo

■ SEOUL

INCH'ŎN •

• Suwon

YELLOW SEA

CH'UNGCH'ŎNG-
BUK-DO

CH'UNGCH'ŎNG
NAM-DO

• Ch'ŏngju

KYŎNGSANGBUK-DO

TAEJŎN •

• Chŏnju

• TAEGU

CHŎLLABUK-DO

KYŎNGSANGNAM-DO

Ch'ang-won •

• PUSAN

• KWANGJU

CHŎLLANAM-DO

CHEJU-DO

• Cheju

JAPAN

A HANDBOOK OF

KOREA

A HANDBOOK OF

KOREA

Korean Overseas Information Service

A HANDBOOK OF

KOREA

Published by
Korean Overseas Information Service
Copyright © 1993
All rights reserved.

Designed by
Yong Ahn Graphics
C.P.O. Box 7852, Seoul, Korea

First Edition: January 1978
Second Edition: November 1978
Third Edition: December 1979
Fourth Edition: January 1982
Fifth Edition: September 1983
Sixth Edition: January 1987
Seventh Edition: September 1988
Eighth Edition: December 1990
Ninth Edition: December 1993

Printed by
Samhwa Printing Co., Ltd.
C.P.O. Box 1307, Seoul, Korea

ISBN 89-7375-002-10 33910

PREFACE

We are happy to be able to publish this 1993 edition of the *Handbook of Korea*. Many students, businessmen and tourists have found earlier editions to be useful guides to the Republic of Korea. Korea is one of the fastest changing countries in the fastest growing region of the world, but is, nevertheless, rooted in traditions that stretch back to 2333 B.C., when Tan-gun—half divine and half human—founded a nation with lofty ideals from which all Koreans have drawn spiritual strength through the centuries.

The civilian, democratic Administration of President Kim Young Sam, inaugurated in 1993, immediately began sweeping reforms to create a New Korea—an economically thriving and corruption-free democratic society, providing a good life for its people. At the same time the nation began to look outward more earnestly than ever before, taking "internationalization" and "globalization" as watchwords for the future. As part of this process, Korea intends to make greater contributions to regional and international peace and prosperity and to make a greater presence felt on such global issue as free trade, human rights, the environment and the development of human resources.

This book will take the reader into the nation's misty past to provide a context to understand the dynamism of the present and its vision of the future—a future in which a peacefully unified country is able to play an even greater and more constructive global role. We hope that it will increase your interest in things Korean and strengthen the bonds of understanding and good will, helping to bring all peoples of the world closer together.

———————————————— • ————————————————

This book is published with the help of the Korea Press Center to promote international understanding and knowledge of the Republic of Korea.

CONTENTS

Romanization

The Romanization of Korean words in this book follows the government-approved McCune-Reischauer (Mc-R) system. Korean names are written with the family name first. In some cases, two spellings of a name are given: the Mc-R spelling and the person's preferred spelling. And in some cases, the names of people are given as they are best known; for example, Syngman Rhee. For the sake of clarity, there also is some repetition or redundancy in the English rendition of some Korean terms. For example, gang means river; san means mountain, and do means land or province. Because of common usage, and in an attempt to make for easier understanding, this work will repeat in English some of the terms stated in Korean. For example, it will refer to Chejudo Island or Namsan Mountain rather than adhering strictly to the usage of the purists.

LAND

"*Let us love, come grief, come gladness, this, our beloved land.*"
This line from the national anthem of Korea perhaps sums up the almost mystical affinity that bonds the Korean people and their land.

It is a land that has known the grief of warring tribes and warring neighbors, the grief of brutal colonial rule, fratricidal war, division and separation.

It also is a land that has known the gladness of family and clan, the gladness of nature and the seasons that give life to the earth, the mountains, rivers, coasts and seas. There is the gladness that springs from the traditions that have come to blend an ancient time with the modern world.

Geography

Location

Poised strategically in the northeastern part of the Asian continent, the Korean Peninsula thrusts in a southerly direction for about 1,000 kilometers.

To the north are regions of China and Russia, while the Chinese mainland lies directly to the west. To the east, the peninsula faces the islands of Japan. The shortest distance from the west coast of Korea to China's Shantung Peninsula is about 190 kilometers. The shortest distance from the southern port of Pusan to the Japanese island of Honshu is about 180 kilometers.

With its north-south elongation, Korea separates the Yellow Sea from the East Sea. The Korean Peninsula and all of its associated islands lie between 124° 11'00"E and 131° 52'42"E and between 33°06'40"N and 43° 00'39"N.

The land boundary between China and Korea is largely formed by two rivers: the Amnokkang River (Yalu River in Chinese) and the Tuman-gang River (Tumen River in Chinese). The last 16 kilometers of the Tuman-gang River also serve as a boundary with Russia. The Amnokkang River flowing southwest empties into the Yellow Sea; the Tuman-gang River first flows northeast and then southeast, emptying into the East Sea.

The Peninsula, contiguous to the two continental powers of China and Russia and adjacent to oceanic Japan, long acted as a land bridge over which continental cultures were transmitted to Japan. The peninsular location brought not only the advantage of easy access to adjacent cultures but also the disadvantage of furnishing a target for aggressive neighbors.

Area

The area of Korea is 221,607 square kilometers (about 85,563 sq. miles). At present, the land is divided into two parts: the Republic of Korea (South Korea) and the People's Republic of Korea (North Korea). The administrative area of the Republic of Korea is 99,237 square kilometers or about 45 percent of the whole of Korea. South Korea is slightly larger than Hungary or Portugal, and a little smaller than Iceland.

Administrative and Traditional Regions

Regional variations are greater than one might expect, partly because of topographical diversity and partly because of historical developments over a long period. From the early days of the Chosŏn Dynasty (1392-1910) up to the year of 1896, Korea was divided into eight administrative provinces: Hamgyŏng-do, P'yŏngan-do, Hwanghae-do, Kyŏnggi-do, Kangwon-do, Ch'ungch'ŏng-do, Chŏlla-do, and Kyŏngsang-do. These eight provinces were subdivided into 13 provinces in 1896, and eight of the 13 provinces currently are in South Korea. After 1945, Chejudo Island became an independent province, and Pusan, Taegu, Inch'ŏn, Kwangju, and very recently the Taejŏn metropolitan areas took on a status equivalent to provinces directly under the central government. Seoul, the capital of South Korea, is the only special city, which is administratively higher than a province. Thus, the Republic of Korea is comprised of one special city, five metropolitan

Percentage of Each Age Group

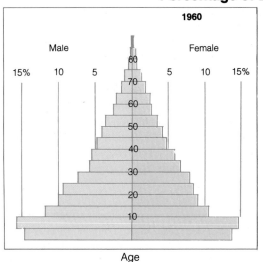

Age

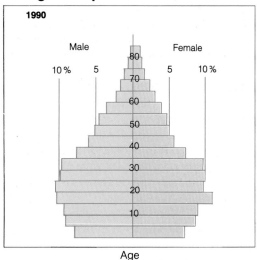

Age

areas, and nine provinces. The nine provinces are subdivided into 55 cities (*shi*) and 138 counties (*kun*).

Korea also may be divided into six larger traditional regions: Kwanbuk on the east and Kwansŏ on the west, now part of North Korea; Kiho, roughly the area of Kyŏnggi-do province, and a part of the Ch'ungch'ŏng-do province; Kwandong, a part of Kangwon-do province, east of the T'aebaek mountain range; Honam, the area comprising a part of the Ch'ungch'ŏng-do and all of the Chŏlla-do provinces; and Yŏngnam, the Kyŏngsang-do provinces. Minor

differences are found in dialects and customs among the six traditional regions.

Population

In mid-1992, South Korea had a population of 43,663,000, a density of 440 persons per square kilometer. The population of North Korea was estimated at 22,672,000 in 1992 according to a UN projection. As a whole, the population of the Republic of Korea increased rapidly after World War II. Before World War II, Koreans migrated to two major regions,

Population

(Thousand Persons)

Year	Census[1] population		Mid-year population		Annual rate of increase(%)	Density (Person/Km²)	Population of North Korea [2]
			Male	Female			
1960	—	25,012	12,551	12,462	—	254.1	10,600
1966	29,193	29,436	14,830	14,606	2.55	298.9	12,440
1970	31,466	32,241	16,309	15,932	2.21	328.2	13,890
1975	34,707	35,281	17,766	17,515	1.70	101.4	15,850
1980	37,436	38,124	19,236	18,888	1.57	385.1	18,030
1985	40,448	40,806	20,576	20,230	0.99	411.6	20,380
1990	43,411	42,869	21,568	21,301	0.99	431.8	21,733
1991	—	43,268	21,775	21,493	0.93	435.8	22,193
1992	—	43,663	21,979	21,685	0.91	439.8	22,672

Note: 1) Including foreigners 2) The results of a UN projection
Source: National Statistical Office

Manchuria and Japan. Today, there are more than two million Koreans in Manchuria and 600,000 Koreans in Japan. The close relationship between Korea and the United States after World War II resulted in a sizable number of Koreans moving to that country. It is estimated that more than 1.5 million Koreans now live in the United States. The most important internal migration in recent times occurred in the years of 1945 to 1953, especially during the Korean War (1950-53). It is estimated that about two million people have migrated from North Korea to South Korea since 1945. There are no significant racial minorities in Korea.

Since 1960, Korea has experienced a dramatic slowdown in population growth and consequently is undergoing rapid demographic transition. The birth rate had remained steady at a level of 40 births per thousand people every year, until 1960. This high fertility rate may be explained partly by little or no population control. There were also other causes for high fertility rate such as the early and universal marriage system prevalent in Korean society. With the nation's systematical pursuit of its socio-economic development in 1962 through its first five-year plan, measures for population control and family planning were incorporated as an integral part of its formal development plan. Owing to the successful implementation of the population control programs, the birth rate began to decline rapidly from about 42 per thousand people in 1960 to 30 by 1970, but leveled off during 1967-72 period, perhaps due to the threshold effect. The birth rate further declined to 22 per thousand people by 1982. Since the early 1980s, there was another sharp drop in the birth rate to 16.4 in 1985, and the rate remained at this level until recently. The total fertility rate in Korea has declined sharply, from 6.0 births per woman in 1960 to 4.5 births in 1970, to 2.7 births in 1980, and to the population replacement level of 2.1 births in the mid-1980s. The total fertility rate further declined and reached 1.6 births per woman in 1992.

The changes in mortality rate in Korea have been more moderate but have steadily declined over years. The death rate declined from 12.1 per thousand people in 1960 to 6.7 in 1980 and 5.9 in 1992.

Consequently, the rate of population growth has also shown a gradual and steady downward trend, to less than 1 percent in 1992 from 3 percent in 1960. Therefore, Korea has reached below its replacement level in the demographic transition, and the current low level of total fertility rate will remain within the range of 1.5 to 2.0. The Korean population is expected to grow at moderate rate to 46.8 million and 49.7 million in 2000 and 2010 respectively. The Korean demographic transition is expected to be completed in 2020.

Demographic changes in Korea have caused drastic changes in its population structure in the past three decades. During the past 30-year period, from 1960 to 1992, the proportion of the population aged 14 and less decreased from 42.3 to 24.8 percent while that of 15-64 increased from 54.8 to 70.0 percent, resulting in a decreased child dependency ratio, from 77.3 to 35.5 percent. The population between the ages 15 and 64 is expected to increase continuously, but slowly until around 2000, when the proportion will reach its peak at 72.2 percent, and decline slowly thereafter. At the same time, as a result of continuously declining fertility rates, the absolute size as well as the relative proporiton of the young population below the age of 15 will continue to decrease. The composition of the aged population over 65 has steadily increased over the years with prolonged life expectancy due to socio-economic development. The proportion of the aged in Korea remained around 3 percent in 1960 and 1970, and gradually increased to 3.8 percent and 5.2 percent in 1980 and 1992, respectively. However, this ratio is expected to rapidly grow in the next century reaching 6.8 percent in 2000 and doubling to 13 percent by 2020.

Settlements

Rapid industrialization in Korea since the early 1960s has accompanied drastic changes in the spatial distribution of human settlements. The urban population in Korea, which accounted for only 28.0 percent of the total population in 1960, doubled to 57.3 percent in 1980 and further increased to 74.4 percent in 1990, primarily due to rural-to-urban migration. The number of cities has also increased. There were only 12 major cities in 1945. Today there are six metropolitan areas, namely Seoul, Pusan, Taegu, Inch'ŏn, Kwangju, and Taejŏn, and 68 local cities.

Metropolitan growth and urbanization have been most pronounced in the two metropolitan cities of Seoul and Pusan. The population of the capital city of Seoul increased more than four-fold from 2.4 million in 1960, to 10.6 million in 1990 while in Pusan, the population increased from 1.2 million in 1960 to 3.8 million in 1990. From the early 1980s, the population concentration in the two metropolitan cities began to show a new trend: while the population decreased slightly in Seoul between 1985 and 1990, it increased in Pusan moderately throughout the 1980s. Seoul's surrounding satellite cities had experienced the most population growth. Consequently, the Seoul metropolitan area had 42.8 percent of the total population in 1990, and the Pusan metropolitan area followed with its approximately 17.3 percent. Altogether, 60.1 percent of the 1990 population lived in these two major metropolitan areas.

Rapid urbanization in Korea has resulted from rapid industrialization. The industrialization process strategy Korea employed since the early 1960s was that of outward orientation. The Korean Government promoted export-oriented light manufacturing in the initial stage of industrialization andheavy and chemical industries in the latter stage due to its weak agriculture base. In the process of transforming a typical agricultural society to industrial one, massive migration from rural areas to urban industrial centers resulted. To accomodate the influx of rural population, major cities expanded their boundaries; furthermore, industrial towns grew and evolved into new cities, accelerating urbanization.

Consequently, growth of cities become self-propelling with their continuously expanding employment opportunities and their concentrations of public and private institutions ranging from financial and commercial to educational and cultural. Such a concentration of nation's

Population of Major Cities(1990)

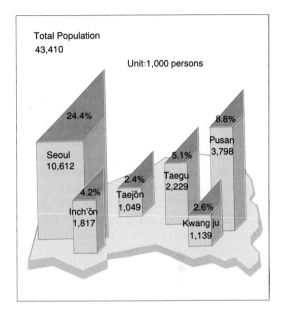

Total Population 43,410
Unit:1,000 persons

24.4% Seoul 10,612
8.8% Pusan 3,798
5.1% Taegu 2,229
4.2% Inch'ŏn 1,817
2.4% Taejŏn 1,049
2.6% Kwangju 1,139

best institutions in major cities was another important factor in rural-to-urban migration in Korea. Because of excessive concentration in the two Korean megalopolses, real estate prices have become prohibitively high and discouraged rural-to-urban migration in recent years. The absolute population size of Seoul thus decreased from 1985 to 1990. On the other hand, neighboring small cities and towns of Seoul and Pusan have recently experienced highest population growth rates.

As a result of the rapid urbanization after World War II, Korea has a small rural population, 25.6 percent in the 1990 census. As most of the rural population engages in agriculture, it is highly concentrated in the lowlands of the west and south coasts along the major river valleys. Agglomerated villages are common in rural areas with a few exceptions in mountainous regions and in areas of reclaimed land on the west coast. In agglomerated villages, farming activities, such as transplanting rice from seabeds, and harvesting and threshing rice are often carried out through the cooperative effort of the villagers. However, farm mechanization has resulted in changes in many agricultural activities, and recent farm labor shortages are arising mainly due to excessive rural-to-urban migration of young people.

Rural villages are usually located in the foothills and face southward. Such a location provides protection from the severe cold winter monsoons, and allows maximum use of the lowland for cultivation. The location of settlements and houses has also been influenced by geomancy, according to which the ideal site for a house or village has a hill behind it and faces a stream. Consequently, topographic maps usually show villages along the boundaries between hills or mountains and plains or river valleys.

The *Saemaŭl Undong* (New Community Movement) and the introduction of farm machinery have resulted in a gradual changing of the rural landscape. Farm villages are being developed into well-organized communities with a systematic arrangement of houses, increasingly constructed of cement and tile. Most straw-thatched houses disappeared during the 1970s. The use of wood fires for heating in the rural areas is decreasing rapidly with the increasing use of coal and in recent years gas. However, the most significant change in the rural areas had been a rapid decrease in population and a subsequent shortage of farm labor.

It is likely that the urbanization in Korea is anticipated to continue moderately in the near future. Evidence in the 1980s suggested that the net migration to metropolitan areas decreased rather sharply and that Kyŏnggi-do Province surrounding the capital city had attracted the most inter-province migrants during the same period. In view of the prevailing reasons for migration, the promotion of balanced regional development and the reduction of the urban and rural disparities in socio-economic conditions are necessary in order to alleviate the urbanization trend in Korea.

Land Forms

Korea is geomorphologically characterized by abundant hills and mountains, which occupy nearly 70 percent of its territory. Low hills, located mostly in the south and the west, give way gradually to increasingly higher mountains toward the east and the north. On the whole, the western and southern slopes of the Korean Peninsula are gentle with various types of plains, low hills, and basins developed along the rivers. The eastern slope is steep with no significant rivers or plains because high mountains are close to the coast. The western and southern coasts are highly indented with innumerable islands, but the eastern coast is generally smooth with few islands.

Mountains

The mountain ranges of Korea run in two major directions, north-to-south and northeast-to-southwest. The ranges of the north-to-south masses, the T'aebaek range in South Korea and the Nangnim range in North Korea, form the geological backbone of the Peninsula and constitute the drainage divide between the western and the eastern slopes. Many summits such as Mt. Nangnimsan (2,014m), Mt. Kŭmgangsan (1,638m), Mt. Sŏraksan (1,780m), and Mt. T'aebaeksan (1,546m) are located along the dividing ridge of the two mountain ranges. The Kŭmgangsan and Sŏraksan mountains are renowned for their scenic beauty. They have various spectacular land forms carved out of granite rocks, a series of rocky pinnacles piercing the sky, deep and narrow canyons bordered by nearly vertical granite walls and numerous waterfalls and rapids along the streams. The two mountain ranges, however, have been a great barrier to communications between the eastern and the western sides of the Peninsula since early times.

Smaller mountain ranges, originating in the Nangnim and the T'aebaek regions, run parallel to each other in a northeast-to-southwest direction. They are, from the north, the Kangnam, the Chogyu, the Myŏhyang, and the Myŏrak ranges, all located in North Korea. The Hamgyŏng range in North Korea and the Sobaek in South Korea also have their roots in the north-to-south ridge mountains and run in a generally northeast-to-southwest direction.

The parallel mountains on the western slope are mostly a series of continuous high hills, especially toward the west coast, offering no significant barriers to communications between

Hikers on Mt. Sŏraksan, which is ablaze with autumn colors.

the lowlands. However, the relatively high Sobaek range historically has obstructed free intercourse between the central and the southern regions and also between the eastern and the western districts in the southern region. Mt. Chirisan (1,915m) is the highest summit in the range.

It is believed that most of the Peninsula was an erosional lowland until the middle of Mesozoic era, when it began to undergo an uplift. The rate of uplift was increasingly greater toward the east, and the effect was even negative in the west. A periglacial and arid climate during the Pleistocene era is supposed to have accelerated erosion of the land surface. As a result, the land forms that have evolved show mature development with relatively large relief along the T'aebaek mountain range, but moving away from there, subdued hills with small relief become gradually prominent. In fact, low hills, which appear to be in the old stage, characterize most of the Peninsula. The so-called "roof of Korea," the Kaema Plateau, has an average elevation of about 1,500 meters above sea level, and Mt. Paektusan, the highest mountain on the Peninsula and located in the northwestern cor-

ner of the plateau, has an altitude of 2,744 meters above sea level.

The Peninsula is a rather stable land mass in spite of its proximity to Japan, so that Korea has neither active volcanoes nor strong earthquakes. There are a few extinct volcanoes that are believed to have been formed between the late Tertiary and early Quaternary periods. Mt. Paektusan is famous for a large crater lake called Ch'ŏnji, meaning "Heavenly Lake," which is located at its summit. Mt. Hallasan (1,950m) on Chejudo Island, the highest mountain in South Korea, has a record of minor volcanic activity during the middle of the Koryŏ Dynasty (918-1392 A.D.). It has a small crater lake called Paegnoktam and is peculiar in that it has more than 360 parasitic cones.

Volcanic activity during the geological past also developed several lava plateaus including the Shinge, Koksan, Ch'ŏrwon, and Kaema. Streams usually cut narrow channels with high and vertical walls in these flows due to the columnar joints in the lava, resulting in a picturesque landscape. Chejudo Island, especially, has numerous lava tunnels and sea cliffs.

Korea has a relatively wide distribution of

pre-Cambrian metamorphic rocks and Paleozoic sedimentary rocks and granite gneiss, of which limestone is one of the most common. Accordingly, there are many karstic areas, many of which are known for their caves. Tongnyŏng-gul, near Yŏngbyŏn on the southern side of the Ch'ŏngch'ŏn-gang River in North Korea, is the most famous cave. It is about 5 kilometers long and several of its chambers are nearly 150 meters wide and 50 meters high. There are also a number of limestone caves in South Korea. Among the most famous are Kossigul, Kosudonggul, Sŏngryugul and Hwangsŏnggul. All of these caves have stalagmites and stalactites, ponds, and streams.

Korea does not have mountains high enough to maintain glaciers or ice caps. However, during the Pleistocene era, when most of the continents of the northern hemisphere were repeatedly glaciated, some alpine glaciers developed in a few summit area of the Hamgyŏngsan and the Mach'ŏllyŏngsan mountains, leaving some erosional features such as small cirques. However, no depositional forms are found. Mt. Paektusan (2,744 m), Mt. Kwanmosan (2,541 m), and Namp'odaesan (2,434 m) show such forms. It is estimated that the snow line at the time of their development was approximately 2,000 meters. Recently, patterned soil and solifluction, which indicate strong periglacial phenomena during the Pleistocene era, have been found below the snow line.

Rivers

Most of Korea's major rivers flow into the Yellow Sea and the South Sea after draining the western and southern slopes of the Peninsula. Considering the size of its territory, Korea has a relatively large number of streams. Six rivers exceed 400 kilometers in channel length—the Amnokkang River (790 km), the Tuman-gang River (521 km), the Han-gang River (514 km), the Kŭmgang River (401 km) and the Naktonggang River (525 km). The first two rivers constitute international boundaries with China and Russia and flow into the Yellow and East seas respectively. The Naktonggang river flows into the South Sea and the rest into the Yellow Sea. Their flow discharges, which are to a great extent

The Han-gang River, which runs through Seoul, is lined with parks and recreation areas.

related to summer monsoons, fluctuate from season to season. In summer, the rivers swell with rainfall accompanying the monsoon, often flooding valley plains once or twice every year. In the other seasons, which are relatively dry, the water level becomes very low, and often much of the river beds become exposed. Typhoons normally hit South Korea along the coast of the South Sea, bringing heavy floods in late summer and early autumn

The gradient of longitudinal river beds is mostly low in the lower reaches of the major streams, permitting navigation for quite long distances from river mouths. Accordingly, rivers have played a significant role in life-styles since early times. Most historical capital cities such as Seoul, P'yŏngyang, and Puyŏ developed along major rivers as port cities. After the introduction of railroads and automobiles, the importance of rivers in terms of transportation decreased sharply. Rivers are now used extensively for irrigating rice fields. River irrigation has been much accelerated in recent years as a result of the introduction of modern technology. Previously only small tributaries could be dammed for the purpose of irrigation, but now more than 72 percent of rice fields depend on rivers for irrigation. Many large scale multipurpose dams for flood control, generation of hydroelectricity, irrigation, and etc. have been constructed or are under construction at various sites on all rivers in South Korea.

Plains and Basins

There are few large plains in Korea, but relatively wide plains are found on the west coast along the rivers. The overall elevation of these plains is low, and the effect of the sea level rise during postglacial times is noticeable, especially around river mouths. The plains have developed as a result of sedimentation after the sea level approached its present position. As a result, the plains appear wide compared with the associated rivers, but the alluvial deposits form relatively thin cover. These fertile plains are Korea's major rice-producing regions. The wide coastal plains near the river mouths change abruptly into narrow flood plains a short distance upstream. Large tidal ranges and funnel-shaped river mouths do not allow the formation of active deltas forming out into the sea, although rivers transport large amounts of silt during floods

Along the east coast, which has only small streams flowing from the T'aebaek mountain range to the coast, narrow strips of alluvial beaches can be found. The Naktonggang River flowing into South Sea has a relatively large delta at its mouth. Most of the delta is confined within the river valley, but is gradually advancing into the sea

Besides coastal alluvial plains, erosional basins formed at the junctions of large streams inland have been widely utilized as major agricultural regions since ancient times. Ch'unch'ŏn, Ch'ungju, and Wonju are examples of old towns developed in such places. The lowland of the basins is usually the site of erosionally weak granitic rock, and the mountains and hills on their periphery consist of highly resistant metamorphic rocks, such as gneiss and schist.

The wide range of temperature fluctuation and concentrated rains in summer induce intense weathering and erosion of rocks. Gentle slopes at the foot of mountains and hills around the basins are covered with thick deposits of weathered materials washed down from the steep upper slopes. Alluvial fans are seldom developed, even though rock fans covered with thin sediment are often discovered.

Coasts

There are about 3,000 islands off the coast of Korea, most of them in southern and southwestern coastal areas. The total length of coastline is estimated at 17,300 kilometers. The coastal length of the peninsular portion is about 8,700 kilometers and that of the islands about 8,600 kilometers. Korea's coastline is long compared to its total land area because there is much indentation.

The east coast has a relatively smooth coastline, except for the Yŏnghŭng and the Yŏngil bays, because of mountains running parallel and close to it. However, there are some variations in land forms. Where the mountains are close to the sea, the coast is rocky with few beaches. Sea cliffs and stacks characterize the coasts between Hŭngnam and Sŏngjin and between Kangnŭng and P'ohang. Haekŭmgang is one of the rocky coasts located adjacent to Mt. Kŭmgangsan. Beaches are found where small streams discharge into the sea. In many instances, they take the form of sand spits and bars enclosing coastal lagoons. Along the coast between Wonsan and Kangnung, there is a series of lagoons of which Kyŏngp'o and Hwajinp'o are among the most famous. With improved roads and transportation facilities, the east coast attracts many tourists in summer due to the lovely scenery and clean beaches. There are a few islands along the coast. Ullŭngdo, a volcanic island, is the largest.

In contrast with the east coast, the south and the west coasts are very irregular with innumerable islands, small peninsulas, and bays. The west coast facing the Yellow Sea has a large tidal range (6-9.3 meters at Inch'ŏn) and a shallow offshore bottom. Tidal flats, mostly composed of mud, are extensive, especially near the river mouths. As a result, water is murky throughout the year. Tidal flats are under extensive reclamation for agricultural land and salt pans.

The south coast is typically Riasic. The islands are the remnants of inundated hills, and the bays extend to the inundated valleys. The length of coastline is nearly eight times longer than its straight-line distance, and its indentation is far greater than that of the west coast. The tidal range of the south coast is between those of the west and the east. The tidal range is relatively small—1.3 meters at Pusan on the eastern side and 4.9 meters at Yŏsu in the center of the coast. Tidal flats are not as wide as on the west coast. Although mountains face the sea, there are few sea cliffs because innumerable islands prevent much erosive wave action along the mainland coast. Narrow tidal channels between islands are associated with extremely rapid tidal currents. At Ultolmok toward the western end of the south coast, the current reaches up to 7.5 knots, the highest recorded in Korea. The largest island in Korea is Chejudo, which is located about 140 kilometers south of Mokp'o.

Seas and Sea Currents

The depth of the Yellow Sea and the South Sea is less than 100 meters; therefore, their sea floors form a shallow continental shelf. These shallow seas are important for fisheries. Recently, explorations for petroleum in the continental shelf have been undertaken.

A branch of the warm Kuroshio Current, which comes from the east coast of the Philippines, splits into two near Chejudo Island, one current flowing into the Yellow Sea and the other into the East Sea. The Yellow Sea Current flows northward along the west coast and back southward along the east coast of China. It is a weak current due to the shallowness of the sea, with no significant influence on winter temperature. However, the Tonghan (East Korean) Current, which flows northward along the east coast after passing the Korea Strait, is very strong and has a high temperature gradient compared with adjacent waters. It flows in an eastward direction from near Chukbyŏn toward Ullŭngdo Island. In summer, however, its influence reaches a farther north to Tonghan Bay.

A cold current, the Pukhan (North Korean) Current, flows southward along the northeastern coast, and is a branch of the Liman Current coming from the Okhotsk Sea. Its strength becomes greater in winter and its influence reaches farther south, pressing the warm Tonghan Current to lower latitudes. Thus the East Sea near the coast, which has a seasonal interchange of cold and warm currents is excellent for fishing.

Most of the east coast has warmer temperatures in winter than the west coast due to the influence of the winter monsoon and warm current.

Climate

Continental Climate

The nature of Korea's climate is defined by its midlatitudinal location and peninsular configuration, as well as its position as an appendage to the world's largest continent, Asia, and is influenced more by the continent than the ocean.

Korea has a humid, East Asian monsoonal climate. The mean temperature during winter is generally below freezing. The mean temperature in January in Seoul is 3.5°C. below freezing, while that of London is 4.6°C. above freezing, and that of San Francisco is 10.1°C. Summer in Korea is hot. In most of the country, the mean temperature of hottest month is above 25°C. except in the northern interior. The mean temperature of the hottest month for Seoul is 25.3°C.

The annual temperature range between the coldest and hottest months for Seoul is about 28.3°C. The range of temperature is much greater in the north and in the interior than in the south and along the coasts.

Monsoon and Rainfall

Korea is located in the East-Asian monsoon belt. During the winter months, continental high pressure air masses develop over inland Siberia, from which strong northwesterly winds bring dry, cold air into Korea. The winter monsoon, usually stronger than the summer one, causes much hardship.

The summer monsoon brings abundant moisture from the ocean, and produces heavy rainfall. About 70 percent of the annual rainfall comes during June through September. Heavy showers with thunder and lightning are common. In addition, passing cyclonic storms add still more rainfall. Annual precipitation varies from 500 millimeters in the northeastern inland areas to 1,400 millimeters along the southern coast. The amount of rainfall decreases from the south to the north. The middle and upper parts of the river basins of the Sŏmjin-gang, Han-gang, and Ch'ŏngch'ŏn-gang are areas of comparatively heavy rainfall, partly because of the convergence of wet airflows along the river valleys and the orographic uplift of the air flows.

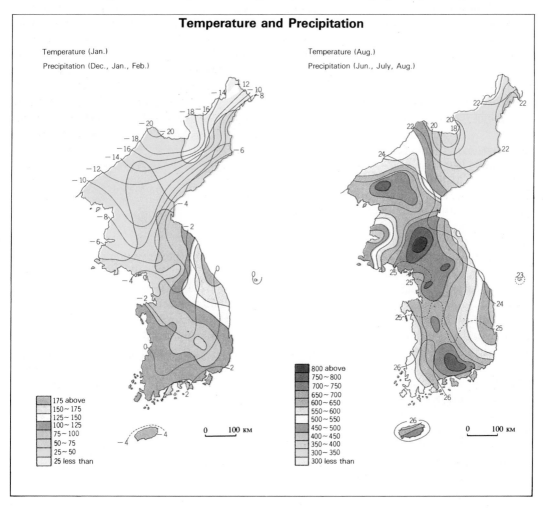

Temperature and Precipitation

The southern coastal belt and the islands of Chejudo and Ullŭngdo also are heavy rainfall areas which receive about 1,400 to 1,500 millimeters annually.

The winter monsoon, which originates in the interior of the Asian continent, is dry and low in temperature. It produces little precipitation except for a few winter snowfalls. The winter months normally receive less than 10 percent of the total annual precipitation. Seoul receives about 126 millimeters of precipitation during the winter months, December to March, which is less than one third of the amount of rainfall for July—383 millimeters.

There are great variations in precipitation from year to year. According to 178 years of precipitation records, the maximum annual precipitation in Seoul was 2,135, recorded in 1940; the minimum was 633.7 millimeters, in 1949. The statistics show that about once every eight years, annual precipitaion falls below the 1,000 millimeters mark, which is usually considered the minimum for rice cultivation where no irrigation is available. This explains why in the days of an insufficient irrigation system the Seoul area would have a rice crop failure once every eight years.

Cyclones

There are two types of cyclones which affect the climate of Korea. One originates in the Yangtze Valley and usually passes Korea in March and April and in the early part of summer, bringing abundant rainfall which is important for transplanting rice. The other type is the typhoon. Typhoons usually originate in the east Philippines, move toward the north and around Taiwan and shift direction mostly northeastward. The most common period for typhoons in Korea is July through August. The southern coast generally gets one or two mild typhoons a year, and a strong one every two or three years.

Spring

Spring comes with the arrival of the swallow, a migratory bird from the south, and the blooming of cherry blossoms in the last part of March or early April along the southern coast and nearby islands. It begins in the middle of April in

the central part of the country, and in the last part of April in the north. By April, a thaw sets in, and streams swell as ice breaks up, and spring rain comes in drizzles. Rainfall increases gradually during March, April and May. This rainfall is slight, but it is adequate for preparing seedbeds for rice, sowing spring vegetables, and planting summer crops such as barley and soybeans.

Spring winds are characterized by varied direction. The early spring has more gusty and dusty winds from the northwest, and as summer approaches, moist airstreams start blowing from the south. Spring is rather short, usually little

terized by heavy showers, often exceeding 200 millimeters of rainfall in a day, or sometimes more than 300 millimeters. This heavy concentration of rainfall occurs frequently in inland basins where airflows converge.

During the summer rainy season, rivers and streams throughout Korea are filled with runoff water from the upper reaches which often causes floods. Abundant rainfall and hot summers are necessary for growing rice. Inadequate rainfall or the late arrival of the rainy season is liable to cause failure of rice crops.

There is very little difference between north and south in summer temperature. Temperature differences are greater between the coast and the inland areas than between north and south. The highest temperature, 40°C, was recorded at Taegu and the inland basin on August 1, 1942.

Autumn

Autumn is rather short, lasting about two months from October to November. This is the season of transition from the hot and wet summer monsoon to the cold and dry winter monsoon. October brings a decided shift in air mass movements with a dry, continental airstream resulting in clear days. Nights are cool, particularly in the north, where frost normally occurs at this time. The clear autumn days are the most pleasant of the year. Dry and sunny weather is indispensable for rice to ripen and for farmers to reap it. In the central and southern parts of Korea, this is the season for planting winter crops such as barley and wheat.

more than two months, April and May, especially in the northern part of Korea.

Summer

Summer in Korea is hot and rainy. The season usually begins in June, when the temperature rises above 20°C, in most of Korea except the northern interior, and lasts about four months. The monthly rainfall is generally more than 100 millimeters.

Summer is the season of cyclonic storms and monsoonal rains. Especially in July there are many rainy days mingled with short clear spells and less cloudy days. Summer rainfall is charac-

Winter

During the winter the climate contrast between the northern and southern regions is most apparent. A January isothermal map shows that the minus 20°C. line passes the northern inland region while the 4°C. line passes the southern coast. Chunggangjin, North Korea, the coldest place on the Korean Peninsula, has a mean temperature of minus 20.8°C. and Chejudo Island has one of 5.2°C. during January, the coldest month. Thus, the north-south difference in January temperatures is about 26°C. In the winter of 1933, Chunggangjin had the lowest temperature ever recorded in Korea, minus 43.6°C.

Winter is characterized as cold and dry with the cold spell generally caused by the influence of the Siberian high pressure cell, a cold and dry air mass. However, due to fluctuations in the high-pressure cell, the northwest winter monsoon is not continuous, allowing calm periods when the weather is milder. Winter in Korea is long, lasting four months in the central and southern regions. Most rivers in North Korea are frozen over for several months.

The winter temperature has an important bearing on agriculture. Where the cold is not overly severe, two crops, usually rice and barley, may be grown.

Soil

The soil of the lowlands as well as the mountain areas is usually brownish with some varia-tion depending on the bedrock. Most soil is derived from granite and gneiss, with limestone and volcanic rocks in limited areas. Light brown and sandy acidic soils are common in those derived from granite, and clay brown to red soils are common in the granitic gneiss areas. In the areas of Kangwon-do and northern Hwanghae-do provinces, limestone-originated red soils are found. On Cheju-do and Ullŭngdo islands, and in northern Kangwon-do province, black volcanic soils are common. In the northern mountain areas, podzolic and ash-gray forest soils are found. Cultivated soils, especially paddy soils, are artificial surfaces developed through plowing, irrigation, and fertilizing over long periods. Silt from irrigation water and occasional flooding of rivers has changed the soil composition in many areas to a uniform silty loam unrelated to the natural soils of the vicinity.

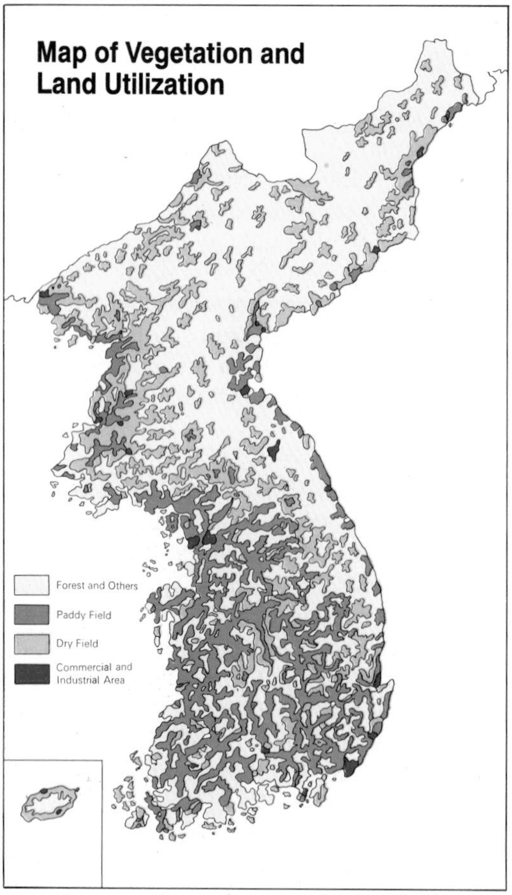

Map of Vegetation and Land Utilization

Forest and Others
Paddy Field
Dry Field
Commercial and Industrial Area

Flora

Due to the Korean Peninsula's long north-south stretch and topographic complexity, there are wide variations in temperature and rainfall. The mean temperature throughout the four seasons ranges from 5°C to 14°C and rainfall from 500 to 1,500 millimeters. Such an environment makes the land a diversified floral region. An enumeration of Korean plants, published in 1946 by Pak Man-kyu, listed 201 families, 1,102 genera, 3,347 species, 50 subspecies, 1,012 varieties and 168 formae of higher plants including pteridophytes. This means that more than 4,500 kinds of vascular plants, including about 400 endemics grow in the country. By comparison, there are about 1,500 species in Denmark and about 2,000 species in England. Many plants in northern Korea have elements in common with those growing in Manchuria. While in the north and high mountain areas many alpine plants are found, the central part and the western lowlands have the predominent vegetation of the temperate zone such as broad-leaved deciduous trees. The southern coast and the offshore islands of Chejudo and Ullŭngdo

Rose of Sharon

Amphicarpa

Forsythia

Cosmos Daisy

Lotus

Bellflower

Touch-me-not

Thistle

are regions where warm-temperate plants grow abundantly. Many evergreen plants growing in the southern parts are identical or similar to those found in the southwestern part of Japan.

While there are many plant species in Korea which have common elements with those growing in neighboring countries, the aforementioned environmental conditions have brought the emergence of a few endemic species.

Warm-Temperate Vegetation

Because of the high average annual temperature (14°C) prevailing over the southern part of the Peninsula and the offshore islands—Chejudo, Sohǔksando and Ullǔngdo—numerous plant species grow in those areas. On the shorelines of Chejudo Island, more than 70 species of broad-leaved evergreens grow; e.g., Camellia japonica Linne, *Cinnamomun camphora* Sieb., *Bladhia villosa* Thunb., *Quercus myrsinaefolia* Blume, *Ligustrum japonica* Koehne, *Biwa*

Vegetation Zones

Legend:
- Coniferous Forests
- Mixed Forests(northeast)
- Mixed Forests (northwest)
- Mixed Forests(central)
- Mixed Forests(south)
- Broadleaf Evergreen Forests

japonica (Thunb.) Gmelin, *Rhaphiolepis umbellata* Makino, *Neolistsea sericea* (Blume) Koidzumi, *Actinodaphne lancifolia* (Seib. et Zucc.) Meiss., *Euonymus japonicus* Thunb. *Euonymus fortunei* (Turcz.) Hand.-Mazz., *Trachelospermum asiaticum* Nakai var. *intermedium* Nakai, *Ficus pumila* Linne, *Machilus japonica* Sieb. et Zucc., *Daphniphyllum glaucescens* Blume, *Pittosporum tobira* (Thunb.) Aiton., *Citrus nobilis* Makino, ect. Also found are such herbal plants as Farfugium japonicum (L.) Kitam., *Pollia japonica* Thunb., *Crinum asiaticum* Linne var. *japonicum* Baker, and such broad-leaved deciduous trees as *Celtis Japonica* Planch., and *Elaeagnus macrophylla* Thunb.

The southeast slope of Mt. Hallasan on Chejudo Island is more abundant in warm-temperate vegetation than the northern side of the mountain. Such vegetation gradually diminishes in the number of species as the contour line of temperature moves northward to the southern shore of the peninsula via Kǒmundo, Sohǔksando and other islands. Near Pusan and Mokp'o, the number of natural broad-leaved evergreens is limited to fewer then 20 species, and these areas are the northernmost limits of the distribution of *Farfugium japonicum* (L.) Kitam

Ullǔngdo Island, located at 37°30' north latitude, has many plants of the warm temperate zone such as *Daphniphyllum glaucescens* Blume, *Camellia japonica* Linne, *Magnolia obovata* Thunb., *Ilex integra* Thunb., *Aucuba japonica* Thunb., *Neolitsea Sericea* (Blume) Koidzumi, and *Elaeagnus macrophyll* Thunb. Because of the high contour of the temperate zone, *Camellia japonica* Linne and *Neolitsea sericea* (Blume) Koidzumi are distributed as far north as Taech'ǒngdo Island off Hwanghae-do province. This distribution is caused by seed dispersal by sea currents.

Temperate Vegetation

The Korean Peninsula, except for the high terrains of Mt. Hallasan on Chejudo Island and the T'aebaeksan mountains, has a typical temperate zone climate.

It abounds in the type of vegetation natural to

the temperate zone, such as *Pinus densiflora* Sieb. et Zucc. and other deciduous broad-leaved trees. Typical deciduous broad-leaved trees found in Korea are *Quercus aliena* Blume, *Quercus acutissima* Carr., *Quercus serrata* Thunb., *Carpinus laxiflora* Blume, *Betula platyphylla* Sukat. var. *japonica* (Miq.) Hara, *Carpinus tschonoskii* Maxim., *Fraxinus rhynchophylla* Hance, *Salix gracilistyla* Miq., *Tilia amurensis* Komarov var. *barbigera* Nakai, *Styrax japonica* Sieb. et Zucc., *Forsythia koreanum* Nakai, *Lespedeza biclor* Turcz. var. *japonica* Nakai, *Rhododendron mucronulatum* Turcz., *Rhododendron yedoense* Maxim. var, *poukhanense* Nakai, and *Rhododendron schlipenbachii* Maxim. Herbaceous plants in this zone include *Miscanthus sinensis* Ander.,*Miscanthus sacchariflorus* (Maxim.) Hackel, *Calamagrostis arundinacea* (L.) Roth., *Chrysanthemum zawadskii* Herb., *Hylomecon vernalis Maxim.*, *Primula sieboldii* E. Morr., Platycodon *grandiflorum* (Jacq.) A. DC., *Adenophora triphylla* A. DC. var. tetraphylla Makino, *Codonopsis lanceolata* (Sieb. et Zucc.) Trautv., *Melanphyrum reseum* Maxim., *Elscholztia splendens* Nakai and *Gentiana chosenica* Okuyama

Among the endemic species of plants, there are Abeliophyllum distichum Nakai, *Hylomecon hylomeconoides* (Nakai) Y. Lee, and *Aconitum chiisanense* Nakai.

Cold-Temperate Vegetation

Cold temperate plants grow in the northern part of Korea and on high mountains, such as Mt. Sŏraksan, which is more than 1,000 meters high, Mt. Chirisan more than 1,300 meters high and Mt. Hallasan more than 1,500 meters high, where the mean annual temperature is 5°C. Typical of these locations are such needle-leaved trees as *Abies nephrolepis* Maxim., *Larix olegensis* Henry var. *koreana* Nakai, *Thuja koraiensis* Nakai, *Picea jezoensis* (Sieb. et Zucc.) Carr., *Pinus pumila* Regel, *Juniperus chinensis* Linne var. *sargentii* Henry, *Picea koraiensis* Nakai, *Abies Koreana* Wilson, *Taxus Cuspidata* Sieb. et Zucc. and broad-leaved deciduous trees as *Quercus mongolica* Fisher,

Quercus dentata Thunb., *Chosenia bracteosa* Nakai, *Betula platyphylla* Sukat.var. *japonica* (Miq.) Hara, *Betula ermanii* Chamiss, *Betula costata* Trautv., *Salix myrtilloides* Linne var. *mandshurica* Nakai, *Vaccinum ulginosum* Linne var. *krushianum* Herd., and *Syringa dilatata* Nakai.

As for endemic plants, there is a predominant growth of *Echinosophora koreensis* Nakai in Hamgyŏngbuk-do province and near Yanggu, Kangwon-do province. Myŏngch'ŏnkun, Hamgyŏngbuk-do province, is the native place of *Sasa coreana* Nakai and forms the northern limit for bamboo. Endemic herbal plants are *Terauchia anemarrhenaefolia* Nakai and *Hanabusaya asiatica* Nakai, which grow in the northern part of the country. *Rheum coreanum* Nakai is found in the range of the Changbaeksan mountains on the Pujŏn Plateau, Hamgyŏngnam-do province.

There are many kinds of plants common to Korea and Manchuria. Typical of these are *Astilboides tabularis* Engler, *Acerphyllum rossii* Engler and *Plagiorhegma dubia* Maxim.

Pinus pumila Regel grows abundantly in the northern mountains as well as on Mt. Sŏraksan, and *Thuja koraiensis* Nakai, which grows in the northern mountains, can be found on the higher part of the T'aebaeksan mountains. *Vaccinium ulginosum* Linne var. *krushanum* Herb., a plant of the northern element, grows on the summits of Mt. Sŏraksan and Mt. Hallasan. This is regarded as a relic species, its present location resulting from the climatic change which presumably occurred in the Tertiary Period.

Empetrum nigrum Linne var. *asiaticum* Nakai grows in the northernmost regions and the southern end of Mt. Hallasan, while *Diapensia lapponica* var. obovata Fr. Schm. is found on Mt. Hallasan and in Japan. Their distribution may suggest that the Korean Peninsula, Chejudo Island, and the Japanese archipelago were once a connected land mass.

Major flora in the cold-temperate elements of the northern forest are *Larix olgensis* Henry, *Picea jezoensis* (Sieb. et Zucc.) Carr., *Abies nephrolepis* Maxim., *Pinus koraiensis* Sieb. et Zucc., *Picea koraiensis* Nakai, and *Abies holophylla* Maxim.

The important needle-leaved trees growing on Mt. Kŭmgangsan are *Pinus koraiensis* Sieb. et Zucc., *Abies holiphylla* Maxim., *Picea jezoensis* Carr., *Larix olgensis* Henry, and *Thuja koraiensis* Nakai.

The predominant species growing on Mt. Chirisan are *Juniperus chinensis* Linne var. *sargentii* Henry, *Pinus koraiensis* Sieb. et Zucc., *Abies holiphylla* Maxim., *Abies Koreana* Wilson, and *Picea jezoensis* Carr. Near the summit of Mt. Hallasan on Chejudo Island are found *Abies Koreana* Wilson and *Juniperus chinensin* Linne var. *sargentii* Henry.

Flowering Periods

As for the patterns of flowering periods, July, the hottest month, is the time when flowering reaches its peak. The lower the temperature becomes, the fewer species bloom. Summer is the peak of the flowering season, although there are quite a few species blooming in spring and autumn. Woody plants tend to have their flowering peaks in May.

Flowers blooming in spring are *Forsythia koreana* Nakai, *Rhododendron mucronulatum* Turcz., *Lonicera praeflorens* Batalin, *Fraxinus ryhnchophylla* Hance, *Abeliophyllum disticum* Nakai, *Prunus ansu* Komarov, *Prunus yedoensis* Matsum., *Magnolia kobus* A. DC., *Sorbus alnifolia* (Sieb. et Zucc.) Koch., *Ginkgo biloba* Linne, *Iris rossii* Baker, *Pulsatilla cernua* Spreng var. *koreana* (Nakai) Y. Lee, *Erythronium japonicum* Decne, *Berberis amurensis* Rupr., *Cornus officinalis* Sieb. et Zucc., *Hylomecon vernalis* Maxim, and *Viola mandshurica* W. Becker.

Plants blooming in summer comprise *Paeonia japonica* Migabe et Takeda, *Paeonia lactiflora* Pazz., *Paeonia suffruticosa* Andrews, *Iris ensata* Thunb. var. *spontanea* (Kakino) Nakai, *Rosa rugosa* Thunb., *Sorbus commixta* Hedlund, *Magnolia sieboldii* K. Koch., *Majanthemum dilatatum* (Wood) Nelson et Macbride, *Lilium concolor* Salis., Lilium distichum Nakai, *Lilium hansonii* Leitch., *Morus alba* Linne, *Chenopodium centrorubrum* Nakai, *Syringa wolfii* Schneid, *Dianthus chinensis* Linne, *Rosa poryantha* Sieb. et Zucc.,

Hypericum ascyron Linne, *Cirsium maackii* Maxim. var. *koraiense* Nakai, *Platycodon grandiflorum* (Jacq.) A.DC., *Phytolacca insularis* Nakai, *Hanabusaya asiatica* Nakai, and *Anemone narcissiflora* Linne.

Plants which bloom in autumn are *Miscanthus sinensis* Ander, *Miscanthus sacchariflorus* Benth., *Sedum aizoon* Linne, *Gentiana scabra* Bnuge, *Elscholtzia splendens* Nakai, *Patrinia scabiosaefolia* Fischer, *Aster incisus* Fischer, *Chrysanthemum zawadskii* Herb., and *Lespedeza bicolor* Turcz. var. *japonica* Nakai

In winter, *Camellia japonica* Linne is seen blooming on Chejudo and the Hŭksando islands and also on the southrnmost coast.

Fauna

Zoogeography

Korea belongs to Palaearctic zoogeographical realm. Its geographical history, topography, and climate divide the Peninsula into highland and lowland districts. Included in the former are the Myohyangsan mountains, the Kaema Plateau and the more rugged terrain of the T'aebaeksan mountains, high in altitude and similar in climate to the Amur-Ussuri river region. Most of the district lies about 1,000 kilometers from Mt. Paektusan on the Korean-Manchurian border. Most of the area is covered with boreal forest and many of the higher mountains supported glaciers during the Pleistocene period.

Animal life in the district is closely related to that of the boreal zones of Manchuria, China, Siberia, Sakhalin and Hokkaido. Representative species are deer, roe deer, Amur goral, Manchurian weasel, brown bear, tiger, lynx, northern pika, water shrew, muskrat, Manchurian ring-necked pheasant, black grouse, hawk owl, pine grosbeak and three-toed woodpecker.

The remainder of the country is the lowland peninsular area which has a milder climate and includes the islands of Chejudo and Ullŭngdo. The fauna, closely related to that of southern Manchuria, central China, and Japan, include

White-bellied woodpecker

Magpie

Manchurian Crane

Hoopoe

Korean Wood Owl

White-naped Crane

White-tailed Sea Eagle

black bear, river deer, mandarin vole, white-bellied black (or Tristram's) woodpecker, fairy pitta and ring-necked pheasant.

Species

There have been 379 species of birds recorded in South Korea. Of these, 62 species are vagrants and Kuroda's Sheldrake has probably become extinct. Of the other 316 species, 50 are permanent residents and 266 are migrants. Of the migratory birds, 111 species visit the country in the winter, 64 in the summer and 90 in the spring and autumn. One hundred and fourteen species breed in Korea, 50 indigenous species and 64 species of summer visitors.

There are 18 other species of birds recorded in North Korea. Of these, five are boreal residents of the high terrain of Mt. Paektusan (black grouse, hawk owl, lesser-spotted woodpecker, three-toed woodpecker, and willow tit), and the remaining 13 are vagrants.

There are six orders, 17 families, 48 genera and 78 species of indigenous mammals in Korea. These include 28 species of Chiroptera, 18 Rodentia, 16 Carnivora, 11 Insectivora, two Lagomorpha, and seven Artiodactyla (even-toed ungulates). There are 28 endemic subspecies on record as inhabiting the Peninsula, but this is yet to be verified.

The large mammals are the tiger, leopard, lynx, leopard cat, wolf, badger, bear, marten, weasel, wild boar, roe deer, and Amur goral. A few species such as the bat, shrew, striped hamster, and muskrat are found only in North Korea. The tiger, lynx, two species of deer, Manchurian weasel, and northern pika are found only in the plateau regions of Mt. Paektusan in North Korea. Other wildlife species in South Korea include 25 reptiles, 14 amphibians, and 130 freshwater fishes.

Seventeen species of terrestrial mammals have been found on Chejudo Island. The wild boar, deer, and wild cat are now extinct and today the land is inhabited by roe deer, weasel, hamster, field mouse, house rat and two bat species. There are also 207 forms of birds, and eight amphibians and reptilians on the island.

Ullŭngdo Island is devoid of endemic mammals. The island's known mammals consist of six species (two species of bat, one shrew, and three house rats that are commensals of man), all of which are found on the Korean mainland. There are no amphibians or reptiles on the island except for frogs and snakes which have been introduced by man. As for birds, 54 species have been recorded on the island.

Natural Monuments

Twenty-three species of wildlife have been designated natural monuments, and 20 birds, two mammalians and several insect species have been designated endangered species. There are 17 localities designated as breeding grounds (eight egretries and heronries), passing or wintering grounds, or habitats for Tristram's woodpecker, fairy pitta, and loon. Also designated as monuments are the domesticated silky fowl, Californian grey whale, the endemic dog called *Chindogae*, and four fish species, the *Anguilla mormorata* Quoy and Germard, *Brachymystax lenox* Pallas, *Gonoprokopterus mylodon* Berg and *Siniperca scherzeri* Steindachner.

The following species of animals have been designated natural monuments by the Cultural Property Preservation Law under the auspices of the Ministry of Culture and Sports.

Species	Monument No.	Date Designated
White-bellied black woodpecker, *Dryocopus javensis richardsi*	197	May 30, 1968
Japanese crested ibis, *Nipponia nippon*	198	May 30, 1968
White stork, *Ciconia ciconia boyciana*	199	May 30, 1968
Black stock, *Ciconia nigra*	200	May 30, 1968
Whooper, whistling and mute swans, *Cygnus (cygnus, columbianus and olor)*	201	May 30, 1968
Manchurian crane, *Grus japonensis*	202	May 30, 1968
White-naped crane, *Grus vipio*	203	May 30, 1968
Fairy pitta, *Pitta brachyura nympha*	204	May 30, 1968
Black-faced spoonbill and Spoonbill, *Platalea (minor and leucorodia)*	205	May 30, 1968

Species	Monument No.	Date Designated
Great bustard, *Otis tarda dybowskii*	206	May 30, 1968
Japanese wood pigeon, *Columba janthina janthina*	215	November 20, 1968
Musk deer, *Moschus moschiferus parvipes*	216	November 20, 1968
Amur (Manchurian) goral, *Naemorhedus goral raddeanus*	217	November 20, 1968
Long-horned beetle, *Callipogon relichum*	218	November 20, 1968
Hooded crane, *Grus monacha*	228	October 30, 1970
Black woodpecker, *Dryocopus martius*	242	May 1, 1972
Black vulture, *Aegypius monachus*	243	June 20, 1973
Steller's sea eagle, *Haliaeetus pelagicus*	243	June 20, 1973
White-tailed sea eagle, *Haliaeetus albicilla*	243	June 20, 1973
Golden eagle, *Aquila chrysaetos*		June 20, 1973
Hawks, Harriers and Falcons (Goshawk, *Accipiter gentilis;* Chinese Sparrow Hawk, *Accipiter Soloensis;* Sparrow Hawk, *Accipiter nisus;* Han Harrier, *Circus cyaneus;* Peregrine Falcon, *Falco peregrinus;* and Kestrel, *Falco tinnunculus)*	323	November 4, 1882
Owls (Eagle Owl, *Bubo bubo;* Long-eared Owl, *Asio otus;* Short-eared Owl, *Asio flammeus;* Scops Owl, *Otus scops;* Collared Scops Owl, *Otus bakkamoena;* Brown Hawk Owl, *Ninox scutulata;* and Korean Wood Owl, *Strix aluco)*	324	November 4, 1982
Geese (Brent, *Branta bernicla* and Swan Goose, *Anser cygnoides)*	325	November 4, 1982
Oystercatcher, *Haematopus ostralegus*	326	November 4, 1982
Mandarin Duck, *Aix galericulata*	327	November 4, 1982

Egretries and Heronries	Number	Date
Chinch'ŏn, Ch'ungch'ŏngbuk-do Province	13	December 3, 1962
Haksŏm, Samch'ŏnp'o, Kyŏngsangnam-do Province	208	July 18, 1968
Shinjŏm-ri, Yŏju, Kyŏnggi-do Province	209	July 18, 1968
Pangchung-ri, Haenam, Chŏllanam-do Province	210	July 18, 1968
Yŏngwŏl-ri, Muan, Chŏllanam-do Province	211	July 18, 1968
Maep'o-ri, Yangyang Kangwon-do Province	229	November 5, 1970
Dosŏn-ri, T'ongyŏng, Kyŏngsangnam-do Province	231	November 5, 1970
Apkong-ri, Hoengsŏng, Kangwon-do Province	248	November 5, 1970

Water Birds and Sea Birds

Species and Habitat	Number	Date
The wintering ground for swans on Chindo Island, Chŏllanam-do Province	101	December 3, 1962
The Naktonggang River Delta colony for migratory birds, Pusan City and Kyŏngsangnam-do Province	179	July 13, 1966
The wintering colony of the Diver, *Gavia* around Kŏjedo Island, Kyŏngsangnam-do Province	227	September 13, 1971
The Han-gang River estuary for White-naped crane, *Grus vipio*	250	February 25, 1975
The breeding place for sea birds (Streaked Shear-water, *Calonectris leucomelas;* Swinhoe's Fork-tailed Petrel, *Oceanodroma monorhis;* and, White-rumped Swift, *Apus pacificus)* on	332	November 4, 1982

the islet Chilbaldo, Shinan-gun, Chŏllanam-do Province		
The breeding place for island birds (Streaked Shearwater, *Calonectris leucomelas* and Japanese Wood Pigeon, *Columba janthina*) on the islet Sasudo, Pukcheju-gun, Chejudo Island	333	November 4, 1982
The breeding place for the Black-tailed Gull, *Larus crassirostris* on Nando Island, Sŏsan-gun, Ch'ungch'ŏngnam-do Province	334	November 4, 1982
The breeding place for the Black-tailed Gull, *Larus crassirostris* on Hongdo Island, Tongyŏng-gun, Kyŏngsangnam-do Province	335	November 4, 1982
The breeding place for sea birds (Streaked Shearwater, *Calonectris leucomelas;* Swinhoe's Fork-tailed Petrel, *Oceanodroma monorhis;* and, the Black-tailed Gull, *Larus crassirostris)* on the islet of Tokdo, Ullŭng-gun, Kyŏngsangbuk-do Province	336	November 4, 1982
The breeding place for sea birds (Streaked Shearwater, *Calonectris leucomelas;* Swinhoe's Fork-tailed Petrel, *Oceanodroma monorhis;* and, Japanese Murrelet, *Synthliboramphus wumizusume)* on the islet Kuguldo, Shinan-gun, Chŏllanam-do Province	341	August 10, 1984

Land Birds

Species and Habitat	Number	Date
Kwangnŭng forest for the white-bellied black wood-pecker, *Dryocopus javensis richardsi*	11	December 3, 1962
The breeding place for fairy pitta, *Pitta brachyura nympha* at Haktong, Kŏjedo Island, Kyŏngsangnam-do Province	233	September 13, 1971
The feeding place for Japanese wood pigeon, *Columba janthina janthina* at Sadong, Ullŭngdo Island	237	December 14, 1971
The feeding and resting ground for transient migrants of Bunting group, *Emberiza rutila, E. tristrami, E. spodocephala,* and *E. aureola* at Chŏnt'ong-ri, Ch'olwon, Kangwon-do Province	245	July 10, 1973

Domestic Dogs and Fowls

Species	Number	Date
Sanctuary of *Chindogae,* primitive dog, in Chindo, Chindo-myŏn, Chindo-gun, Chŏllanam-do Province	53	July 10, 1973
The poultry farm of domesticated silky fowl "Ogolgae" at Wha'ak-ri, Yŏnan, Nonsan, Ch'ungch'ŏngnam-do Province	265	April 1, 1980

Freshwater Fishes

Species	Number	Date
Ch'ŏnjiyŏn Waterfall for *Anguilla marmorata* on Chejudo Island	27	December 3, 1962

The habitat of Manchurian trout, *Brachymystax lenok* in the Chŏngamsa Temple area, Kangwon-do Province	73	December 3, 1962
The habitat of Manchurian trout, *Brachymystax lenok* in Sŏch'ŏn, Pongwha-gun, Kyŏngsangbuk-do Province	74	December 3, 1962
Han-gang River, Kyŏnggi-do Province for *Siniperca scherzeri*	190	July 11, 1967
Kŭmgang River, Ch'ung-ch'ŏngbuk-do Province for *Gonoprokopterus mylodon*	238	May 1, 1972

Siberian Tiger

Amur Goral

Chindogae

Tristram's (or White-bellied Black) Woodpecker, *Dryocopus javensis richardsi*

Total length: 46 centimeters. A large black and white woodpecker with a crimson crown and crimson cheek patches. Upper parts, throat and upper breast, black; remainder of under parts and rump, white.

Tsushima, a large island in the Korea Strait, was known as one locality of the species. However, reckless hunting from 1898 to 1902 to export this rare species of bird to Western countries brought about virtual extinction. Belatedly, the Japanese designated it as a natural monument to protect and preserve the species. A specimen collected by the Japanese ornithologist Dr. Nagamichi Kuroda in 1920 was the last of this species seen on the island.

Tristram's woodpecker is a permanent resident of the Kyŏnggi-do and Kangwon-do provinces.

Old records indicate that such woodpeckers were collected a few times around Hwanghae-do (North Korea), Ch'ungch'ŏngbuk-do and Kyŏngsangnam-do provinces, but the only reported reliable breeding places are Kwang-nŭng and Kŭmnŭng in Kyŏnggi-do province.

Through two surveys of Mt. Sŏraksan in May 1966 and June 1976, the Ornithology Institute

of Kyunghee University established that the bird is found at an elevation of 1,000 meters in this range. This large woodpecker is a rare resident of what little heavy forest there is left in Korea. Nesting success in Korea was confirmed again in the forest of Kwangnŭng, and a pair of the birds breed there, changing their nesting site within a short distance each year.

White-naped Crane, *Grus vipio*

Total length: 119 centimeters. A pale grey crane with a white head and neck; the grey on the body continues up the sides of the neck in a narrow line to a little below the eye. Lore naked and red; legs red.

It is a regular winter visitor and passage migrant. The species is the most abundant of the cranes occurring in Korea, but its number has decreased in recent years. Flocks of about 2,000 birds concentrated in the estuary of the Han-gang River were observed in November 1975. This estuary is a bird sanctuary designated Natural Monument No. 250. The crane migrates to Korea in late October and November and winters here until the end of March.

Great Bustard, *Otis Tarda*

Length: male 102 centimeters, female 76 centimeters. Head and neck, grey; upper parts, buff with black bars; under parts, white. Male has a chestnut band across the breast; female lacks this band. Flies with neck outstretched and shows mostly white wings with black tips.

Until the end of World War II, it was common winter visitor in flocks of 40-50 birds throughout Korea. Hundreds were seen in paddies north of Seoul until the end of the 19th century. Today, few are seen wintering in Korea.

The bird has long been known as a game bird for the savory taste of its meat. As a species in danger of extinction throughout the world, its protection and preservation are urgently needed. This species is designated Natural Monument No.206 under the Cultural Property Preservation Law.

Vanishing and Extinct Species of Birds and Mammals

Kuroda's Sheldrake,
Tadorna cristata Kuroda

Today there are only three mounted specimens to testify to the existence of this bird. The last time this species was seen in Korea was in December 1916, when a female bird was shot on the lower reaches of the Naktonggang River near Pusan.

In April 1917, a female bird shot near Vladivostok was reported as a hybrid of two species of duck. A male bird was collected in the winter of 1913-14 at the Kŭmgang River estuary near Kunsan.

The female which was shot near Vladivostok is now in the National University Museum of Copenhagen, Denmark and the two specimens from Korea are preserved in the Yamashina Institute for Ornithology in Tokyo

This species is found in painting done by Japanese painter about 140 years ago. An old Japanese book on birds record it as a "Korean Mandarin Duck." It is therefore thought that the species was imported to Japan from Korea some 200 years ago.

Although the former exact range of this bird is unknown, it is generally believed that it bred in eastern Siberia and migrated to Korea and

Japan in winter.

The bird is in the *Red Data Book* of the International Union for Conservation of Nature (I.U.C.N.) but is believed to have become extinct. Two Russian students of ornithology claimed to have sighted three birds of this species in the Rimskii-Korsakov Archipelago in 1964, but there is no evidence to support their report.

Siberian Tiger, *Panthera tigris altaica* (Temminck)

This tiger is found in Korea, northeastern China and isolated regions of the Soviet Far East.

This species was once scattered widely in Korea, from Mt. Paektusan in the North to Chŏllanam-do province in the South. Many of these tigers were captured in all parts of Korea prior to World War II, including five tigers at Musan, Hamgyŏngbuk-do province in 1935; one female and one male at Kosan, Hamgyŏngnam-do province in 1924-29; one tiger at the Pulgapsa Temple in Chŏllanam-do province in 1911; one male on Mt. Karisan, Kangwon-do province in 1918; one male at Kyŏngju, Kyŏngsangbuk-do province in 1922, and one at Pukchin, P'yŏnganbuk-do province in 1930. There is no record showing the capture of a tiger after 1922 in South Korea, where the species probably is extinct. It is believed that any surviving Korean tigers make the rugged terrain of Mt. Paektusan, North Korea, their habitat.

Noteworthy Wildlife

Magpie, *Pica pica sericea Gould*

Length: 45 centimeters. Plumage, glossy greenish or purplish black and white with a long, graduated black tail. Scapulars, flanks and belly, white; remaining plumage, black.

Korea's national bird, the magpie lives in the lowlands, always in the vicinity of human habitation. It generally breeds in trees in the center of Seoul and other major cities as well as in or near villages.

The bird's call is a harsh "chak-chak-chak-chak" or "chat-chat-chat-chat." More varied or "conversational" chattering may be heard in the spring. It breeds in tall trees in late March and April and usually lays five to six eggs. The incubation period is 17-18 days. It feeds mostly on insects but also eats small mammals, birds, mollusks and vegetable matter.

Red Fox (Common Fox), *Vulpes Vulpes peculiosa* Kishida

Size: 60 centimeters or more long and 30 centimeters or more high at shoulders with a 45 centimeter long brush. Fur, sandy to reddish brown; under parts, white; and, legs and backs of ears, black. The muzzle is sharp pointed, the ears are large and erect and the eyes are large with vertical pupils.

The fox is mainly nocturnal but may be out during the day sunbathing or sleeping when the weather is good. It is a loner except during the mating season. It usually sleeps in a natural cavity or a burrow taken over from another animal, although it can dig its own burrow. It lives in almost any kind of area including gardens in small towns, but prefers woodlands. It feeds mainly on rats, mice and voles, but also eats all flesh, even carrion. It will eat poultry, game birds, lambs and any other bird or mammal it can catch. It also eats vegetables, fruits and grass.

The mating season is in January but may extend into February. Gestation is 51-63 days and the average litter is four. Cubs open their eyes at 10 days and leave the burrow when they are about a month old, at which time they are covered with soft, downy, chocolate colored fur and their tail is not a brush though it has the usual tag. The muzzle is blunt and the ears, small.

The male feeds the vixen as soon as the cubs are born and may continue to bring her food and to help feed the cubs for some weeks. The vixen teaches the cubs to forage later, and they leave their parents in August. The life expectancy of the fox is said to be about 12 years.

The red fox is rare in Korea and its number is said to be decreasing. One may be found in the Seoul Zoo.

Geology

Introduction

The first geological map of Korea, with a scale of 1:1,000,000, was published in 1928. In 1974, geological maps with a scale of 1:250,000 covering the whole of the Republic were published. The Geological Survey of Korea started to publish geological quadrangles with a scale of 1:50,000 from 1961, and by 1986, a total of 217 sheets covering 79 percent of the land area were published. The Geological Society of Korea was established in 1964, the Korea Institute of Mining Geology in 1968, and the Paleontological Society of Korea in 1984. The Geological Survey of Korea was renamed the Geological and Mineral Institute of Korea in 1973, and the name was changed again to the Korea Institute of Energy and Resources in 1981.

Topography

Physiographically, Korea is a mountainous peninsula extending south-southeast from the northeastern part of the China mainland. The north-northwest, south-southeast trend forms the T'aebaeksan Range, which is close to the east coast. The east coast is of an uplifted topography, showing a relatively straight shore line, whereas the west coast shows the features of a submerging shoreline. The mountains are not high, rarely exceeding 1,200 meters, but they are found almost everywhere and consequently the terrain may be said to be rugged and steep. Only near the west and southwest coasts are there extensive flat alluvial or deluvial plains and more subdued rolling hilly lands.

Geological Overview

Being a mountainous peninsula, Korea is of a diverse geologic make up. It is composed largely of Pre-Cambrian rocks, such as granite gneisses and other metamorphics. Two separate

Generalized Geological Sequence in Korea

Age	Period	System or Supagroup	Group of Formation
Cenozoic		Quarternary	
		Tertiary	Yŏnil, Changgi
Mesozoic	Cretaceous	Kyŏngsang	Pulguksa intrusions
			Shilla
			Naktong
	Jurassic	Taedong	Pansong
	Triassic	P'yŏng-an	Nogam, Mt. Kobangsan
Paleozoic	Permian		Sadong
	Carboniferous		Hongjŏm
	Devonian		(Absent)
	Silurian		Hoedong-ri
	Ordovician	Chosŏn	Great Limestone
	Cambrian		Yangdŏk
Proterozoic		Sangwon	Kuhyŏn
			Sadanggwi (in North Korea)
			Chikhyŏn
Archeozoic		Granite Gneiss	
		Yŏnch'ŏn	

Geological Map of the Korean Peninsula

Quaternary
Tertiary
Cretaceous
Jurassic
Carboniferous
Cambro-Ordovician
Metamorphic Sedimentary Rock
Gneiss
Basalt
Porphyrite-Diabase Granite
Porphyry - Diorite
Archaeozoic Proterozoic

Precambrian Sequence of South Korea

Kyŏnggi Massif	Yŏngnam Massif
Yŏnch'ŏn System	Granite
Granite Gneiss	Chirisan Gneiss
	Other Gneisses
Ch'unch'ŏn System Granite Gneiss	Yulli System
Kyŏnggi Metamorphic Rock Complex	Yŏngnam System

blocks of Paleozoic strata are found in South and North Korea. The one in the South covers the T'aebaeksan Range, and the one in the North is near P'yŏngyang. Mesozoic strata are found in the southeastern part of the Peninsula and Cenozoic strata are limited to some small areas scattered around the Peninsula. Jurassic and Cretaceous granites intrude through the older rocks in a northeastward-southwestward direction in some places, but show no specific trend in others.

Unlike nearby Japan, Korea is stable land with no active volcanoes and rare earthquake shocks, although the islands of Ullŭngdo and Chejudo are of volcanic origin. Mt. Paektusan in the North is capped with a caldera lake, and Mt. Hallasan on Chejudo Island has a small crater lake.

Tectonic and Geological Provinces

The Korean Peninsula lies within the Korea-China Heterogen. Basically the Pre-Cambrian basement of the peninsula is tectonically related to that of Manchuria and China. The P'yŏng-buk-Kaema Massif forms the southern part of Liao-Kaema Massif of southern Manchuria, and the Kyŏnggi and Mt. Sobaeksan massifs of the peninsula can be correlated with the Shantung and Fukien Massifs of China.

The Paleozoic sediments, lying on the Pre-Cambrian massifs in the P'yŏngan and Okch'ŏn basins, can be correlated with those in the Hwangho and Yangtze basins. On the other hand, the Mesozoic rocks of the Kyŏngsang Basin in the southeastern part of the Peninsula can be said to extend toward the Kwanmon Basin in the southwestern tip of Japan across the Korea Strait. The P'ohang Tertiary sedimentary rocks, distributed mainly in the southeastern corner of the land, lie on Mesozoic rocks.

Precambrian Geology

The Precambrian geology of Korea is yet to be fully explored. The earlier mentioned 1:250,000-scale geological maps published in 1974 offer a more detailed Precambrian stratigraphy of South Korea.

Subdivision of the Paleozoic Strata (Samch'ŏk Coal Field)

Classic			Proposed		Age
P'yŏngan System	Green Series			Tonggo Formation	Triassic
	Mt. Kobangsan Series (Mt. Kobangsan) Sadong Series	Hwangji Group Ch'ŏlam Group		Kohan Formation Tosagok Formation Hambaek Formation Changsŏng Formation	Permian
	Hongjŏm Series	Komok Group		Kumch'ŏn Formation Manhang Formation	Carboniferous

Hiatus: Late Ordovician Early-Carboniferous (Except Low Silurian)

Chosŏn System	Great Limestone Series	Tuwibong Formation Maggol Formation Tumugo Formation Tongjŏm Quartzite	Sangdong Group		Ordovician
		Hwajol Formation Taegi Formation			Cambrian
	Yangdŏk Series	Myobong Formation Changsan Formation	Samch'ŏk Group		

In general, the Kyŏnggi and Yŏngnam massifs belong to a low-pressure facies series, and the Okch'ŏn Metamorphic Belt to an intermediate pressure series.

Yŏnch'ŏn System

This system, belonging to the Kyŏnggi Massif, is distributed around Seoul City extending to Yŏnch'ŏn-kun in a northeasterly direction. The system is divided into upper and lower parts. The lower part is composed of biotite-quartz-feldspar schist, marble, lime-silicate, quartzite, and graphite schist, and the upper part is of mica-quartz-feldspar schist, mica schist, quartzite, augen gneiss, and garnet-bearing granitic gneiss.

Precambrian Granite Gneiss

This gneiss is also known as grey granite gneiss or Koguryŏ granite. Outcrops of it cover one-third of the surface of Korea, and are especially prevalent in the P'yŏngan-do provinces and in Hamgyŏngnam-do province. Intrusions of it are also found in the Yŏnch'ŏn System in the Kyŏnggi Massif.

Sangwon System

This system was first observed in the northern part of Korea, Sangwon, P'yŏngannam-do province, and Hwanghae-do province in central Korea, the main area of its distribution. *Collenia* fossils have been found in the limestone interbedded in the system. The presence of *Collenia* suggests that the system belongs to the Proterozoic.

Paleozoic Erathem

Paleozoic sediments in Korea are represented by the Lower Paleozoic Chosŏn System and the Upper Paleozoic P'yŏng an System. The Chosŏn System comprises the Cambrian to Middle Ordovician System, the P'yŏng-an System, the Middle Carboniferous to Permian, and the Unidentified Triassic System. Lower Siluria limestone was discovered from conodont fossils in 1980.

The Upper Ordovician, Devonian and Lower Carboniferous systems are not known to exist.

A stalactite cave near Yŏngwol, Kangwon-do on the east coast.

Cambro-Ordovician Strata

The Cambro-Ordovician Chosŏn System is widely distributed in the limestone plateau in northwest Korea. There are many other localities with scattered patches of the Chosŏn System. The Chosŏn System has been divided into two parts according to lithology, the Yangdŏk Series and the Great Limestone Series. These series are conformable to each other. The Yangdŏk Series overlies the Precambrian rocks unconformably. The Chosŏn System has recently been divided into two groups, the Cambrian Samch'ŏk Group, and the Ordovician Sangdong Group.

Yangdŏk Series

The Yangdŏk Series is divided into the Changsan and the Myobong formations in Kangwon-do province. The Changsan Formation consists mainly of white quartzite that is pebbly throughout, but it starts with thin basal conglomerates. The overlying Myobong Formation, which is predominated by greenish grey slates, follows the Changsan with alternating zones of quartzite and slate at its base. The average thickness of each of these two formations is about 200 meters.

Great Limestone Series

The Great Limestone Series, distributed in Kangwon-do province, in the east central part of Korea, is a sequence of thick limestone-rich sediments, as is the case with the series in northern Korea. The series has been divided into six formations. The lower part of the series, the Taegi Formation, consists mainly of a white limestone bed 350 meters thick. The Hwajŏl Formation is characterized by vermicular limestone showing a peculiarly weathered "worm-eaten" surface. The Hwajŏl Formation is covered over with Tongjŏm quartzite. The base of the latter seems to be in conformity with the base of the Ordovician System, the Sangdong Group. The Tumugol Limestone is of a lesser worm-eaten appearance. The Maggol and Tuwibong limestones consist of gray limestones. A bed of fossiliferous shale, known as Chigunsan shale, is intercalated between the two limestones. Trilobite, cephalopod, graptolite and other fossils are found in the limestones of the Great Limestone Series. Recently, a number of conodonts have been identified in the series.

Middle Paleozoic strata

Middle Paleozoic Strata from the Upper Ordovician to the Lower Carboniferous are not known to exist. However, the existence of the Lower Silurian Haedong-ri Formation has been established by the finding of Silurian conodont fauna. Some formations in the Okch'ŏn Supergroup are thought to be Middle Paleozoic in age by some geologists, though no substantive evidence has been found.

Carboniferous-Triassic Strata

Carboniferous-Triassic Strata of the P'yŏng-an System, distributed exclusively overlying the Middle Ordovician disconformably, are found roughly in four locations in North Korea, and in three areas in Kangwon-do province and Ch'ungch'ŏngbuk-do province in South Korea.

Hongjŏm Series

The main rocks of this series are slightly metamorphosed green, red, gray or mottled sandstones and shales with some light-colored limestone beds. Most shales are characterized by dark fine ottrelite. The limestone beds are fossiliferous with primitive fusulinids and other foraminifers, corals, brachiopods and others. The presence of fusulinids indicates the age of the series to be Moscovian of Middle Carboniferous. The Hongjŏm Series is about 220 meters thick on the average.

Sadong Series

The Sadong Series is characterized by somewhat metamorphosed gray to dark-gray sandstones, shales, coaly shales, coal beds, and dark grey limestone beds. Three or more coal beds are intercalated in the upper part of the series, and are an important source of anthracite. Upper Moscovian fusulinids are found in the Samch'ŏk and the Tanyang coalfields, while Sakmarian fusulinids are found in the Yongwol Coalfield. The thickness of the Sadong Series averages 150 meters.

Kobangsan Series

The series locally overlies the Sadong Series conformably, and is composed mainly of white quartzites intercalating some black shales. The age of the series is Middle to Late Permian but doubtfully Triassic. It is about 880 meters thick.

Green Nogam Series

It is composed mainly of green arkose sandstones with some conglomerate beds. The age of the series has not been clarified by fossils, though it has been thought to be Triassic because of its thickness. The series is 400-2,000 meters thick.

Mesozoic Erathem

The Lower Mesozoic is represented by the Green Series of the upper part of the P'yŏng-an System. The rest of the Mesozoic sediments in Korea are represented by the Middle Mesozoic Taedong System and the Upper Mesozoic Kyŏngsang System.

The Taedong System represents the Jurassic, and the Kyŏngsang the Cretaceous. In the Jurassic Period, a deformation known as Taebo Orogeny took place. This mountain forming process was the most intensive in Korea, which caused all earlier formations to fold, thrust and fault drastically.

Taedong System

The Taedong System is not widely distributed in Korea. Long, narrow, and patchy, it is scattered with or without distributional relationship with the P'yŏng-an System, though showing deformations as does the latter. It is subdivided into the Lower Namp'o, Upper Namp'o and Pansŏng groups in South Korea, which consist mainly of conglomerates, milky white pebble-bearing arkosic quartzose sandstones, black sandy shales, coaly shales, and coals. The Taedong System near P'yŏngyang in North Korea is subdivided into the Sunyŏn and Yugyŏng series, which consist of conglomerates, sandstones, and shales ranging up to 1,300 meters in thickness.

Plutonism in the Jurassic Period

Most of the granite bodies, except the Cretaceous ones, intruded during the Jurassic Period. In South Korea, granite batholiths show a characteristic distribution trend north north-

Paengnyŏngdo, an island off the west coast.

east-south southwest (so-called Sinian)

Most of them are biotite granites, and some are hornblende granites.

Kyŏngsang System

The Kyŏngsang Supergroup is distributed in a wide area in the Kyŏngsang-do provinces in the southeastern part of Korea. Animal fossils indicate that sediments were deposited in shallow water environments. They are of fresh to brackish water genera. No marine fossils have been found. The Kyŏngsang Basin was formed subsequent to the Taebo Orogeny and can be divided into three minor basins: the Yŏng-yang, Ŭisŏng, and Milyang basins.

The Kyŏngsang Supergroup is composed of the Naktong and Shilla groups and the Pulguksa Intrusives.

Plutonism in Cretaceous Period

The biotite granite intruded in the Kyŏngsang Supergroup is called Pulguksa Granite. The radiometris ages of intrusions are dated to be Late Cretaceous to Early Tertiary. A remarkable characteristic of the Plutonism of this period is that the granites are not of an orogenic production.

Naktong Group

This group is distributed in the western part of the Kyŏngsang-do provinces, and subdivided. It consists mainly of shales, sandstones, conglomerates, and one or two thin coal seams. The formations of the group have gentle monotonous eastward dip in contrast to the marked deformation of the Jurassic and Pre-Jurassic systems. Many ripple marks and sun cracks are found in many localities of the group, indicating that the group was formed in a shallow-water enviroment. Animal fossils indicative of the early Cretaceous age are prevalent. They include Viviparus, Hydrovia, Bulimus, Itometamia, Brotiopsis, Anisus, Trigonioides, Plicatounio, Nakamuranaia, Schistodesmus, and Estherites. Plant fossils include: group 1, Cladophlebis browniana, Onychiopsis mantelli, Ruffordia goepperti, and Nilssonia schaumbur gensis; group 2, Cladophlebis lobifolia, Coniopteris hymenophylloides, Dictyozamites falcatus, Ptilophyllum pecten, and Nilssonia compta. Group 1 indicates early Cretaceous and group 2 middle Jurassic. Because the Naktong Group overlies granite gneiss unconformably, its relationship to the Taedong System cannot be determined.

Shilla Group

This group, widely distributed in the Kyŏng-sang-do provinces, is subdivided.

The group consists of conglomerates, sandstones, shales, and volcanic rocks such as andesites, basalts, rhyolites, and tuffs, especially in the upper part of the series. The thick basal conglomerates form the criteria dividing the series from the Lower Naktong Groups. The Chŏkkang-ri Formation in South Korea and the Taebo Series near P'yŏngyang in North Korea are correlated to the Shilla Group. The former overlies the P'yŏngyang System, and the latter Taedong System unconformably. The Shilla Group has many more ripple marks and sun cracks than the Naktong Group, but the former is much more fossiliferous. Plant fossils found in this group indicating the whole range of the Cretaceous period are Filicales, Cycadales, Coniferales, and Angiospermae. Bones, eggs and tracks of dinosaurs are also evident in the Shilla sediments.

Cenozoic Geology

Neogene Tertiary Strata are found in some small area along the eastern coast of the Peninsula. They are, from north to south, the Kilchu-Myŏngch'ŏn Basin in North Korea, and the Pukp'yŏng, Yŏnghae, P'ohang and Ulsan basins in South Korea. The rocks are poorly lithified sandstones, shales, conglomerates, lavas, and sills. An alternation of land and marine deposits is characteristic of the strata.

Pongsan Series

This series is distributed in the Hwanghae-do and P'yŏngannam-do provinces of North Korea, and consists of an alternation of shales and sandstones, conglomerates, and coal beds. Fossils indicating the late Eocene include Colodon, Caenolophus, Desmatotherium and Portianotherium (animal fossils), and Populus, Platanus, and Vipurunus (plant fossils). The series is about 350 meters thick.

Yŏngdong Series

This series is distributed in Hamgyŏngbuk-do province, North Korea, and consists of sandstones, shales, interbedded coal beds, and alkali-basalts in the lower part of the series. Plant fossils indicating Middle to Late Oligocene include Pinus, Glyptostrobus, Sequoia, and Juglans. The series is 80 meters thick.

Changgi Group

This group is distributed in Kyŏngsangnam-do province, South Korea, and consists of conglomerates, volcanic rocks, sandstones, shales, and coal beds alternating with tuffs. Plant fossils indicating the early to middle Miocene include Sequoia, Salix, Carpinus, Alnus, Populus, Betula, Fagus, Fagophyllum, Castanea, Colylus, Zenthoxylon, Planea, Ficus, Uities, Acer, and Juglans. The series is approximately 1,400 meters thick.

Yŏnil Group

This is distributed in Yŏnil, South Korea and consists of conglomerates (200 meters thick) and thick shales (400 meters thick). Fossils indicating the Miocene include Turborotaria, Globigerina, and Globigerinoides, which are all foraminifers, Caridium, Solen, Lucina, and Potamides, which are all marine mollusks, from the sandstones; Leda, Cardium, Dosinia, Ostrea, and Pecten from the shales; and Salix, Quercus, Cinnamomum, Sapindus, and Aagus, which are all plant fossils, from the upper part of the shales.

Sŏgwip'o Formation

This formation is distributed in Chejudo Island off southwestern Korea. The formation consists of sandstones and mudstones. Fossils indicating the late Pliocene include marine mollusks and foraminifers.

General Tertiary Stratigraphy

	Pliocene	Sŏgwip'o Formation
Tertiary	Miocene	Yŏnil Group Changgi Group
	Oligocene Eocene	Yŏngdong Series Pongsan Series

Earthquakes

Nearly 1,800 earthquakes are recorded in various historical documents of past dynasties from 2 A.D. to 1907 and more than 200 have been scientifically recorded since 1905. Thus, the total number of recorded earthquakes in Korea is a little more than 2,000, of which only 48 were destructive—far fewer than those recorded in Japan but more than in Manchuria.

Frequency and intensity of earthquakes in these areas are directly related to their proximity to the Circum-Pacific Earthquake Belt. Japan is located on the belt, while Korea and Manchuria are some distance from it. Thus, seismicity in Korea is much stronger than in Manchuria and much weaker than in Japan.

In Korea, earthquakes occur mainly on faults or tectonic planes, which, viewed on the surface, are river courses. However, during this century, earthquakes have occurred frequently along mountain ranges such as Chirisan.

South Korea is a comparatively stronger seismic area than North Korea, and the west half of the Korean Peninsula has shown stronger seismicity than the east half.

The downstream basins of each of the main rivers flowing into the Yellow Sea, or Hwanghae, show a much denser distribution of earthquake epicenters than the middle and upper stream basins. However, both the Kŭmgang and Naktonggang rivers show a higher seismicity in both the lower and middle stream basins. The southwestern edge of the Kyŏnggi Massif, located in the central part of the Korean Peninsula or the northern margin of South Korea, has shown much stronger seismicity than the inland and northeastern coastal areas. Almost the entire area of the Okch'ŏn Zone has shown higher seismicity.

The northeastern part of the Yŏngdong-Kwangju trough has shown a relatively higher seismicity than the southwestern part. The southwestern part of the T'aebaeksan Block of the Yŏngnam Massif has shown a higher seismicity than the northeastern part, which is located in the eastern coastal area.

The northeastern edge of the Chirisan Block of the Yŏngnam Massif, a southwestern continuity of the Taebaeksan Block, and the central zone of the southern half along which the Chirisan mountain range runs, have shown relatively higher seismicity than other areas. The entire area of the Kyŏngsang Basin, occupying the southeastern edge of the Korean Peninsula, has shown high seismicity, and particularly both the eastern and western edges have historically shown an intensive seismicity with the southwestern edge of the Kyŏnggi Massif. The Ch'ugaryŏng Graben running through the central zone of the Kyŏnggi Massif in the north, northeast, south, and southwest directions, has shown a higher seismicity in both past and present times.

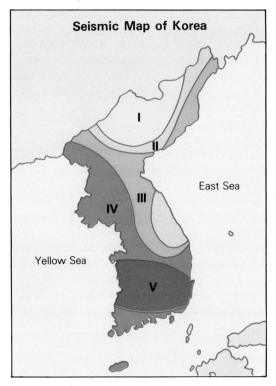

Seismic Map of Korea

I

II

III

IV

V

East Sea

Yellow Sea

PEOPLE AND LANGUAGE

People

Archaeological evidence indicates that the Korean Peninsula was inhabited by lower palaeolithic people at least as early as 500,000 B.C. Many archaeological sites, mostly located along rivers, have been excavated. The most famous are Sŏkchang-ri in Ch'ungch'ŏngnam-do province and Chŏngok-ri in Kyŏnggi-do province. Various stone tools, including hand-axes and chopper-scrapers, have been found at the sites, leading archaeologists to believe that their inhabitants engaged in hunting and fishing. These people are thought to have dwelt in caves, as the bones of many extinct animals and relics of their daily life have been unearthed in such places. The supposed connection between these palaeolithic people and today's Koreans is blurred at present by the lack of sufficient archaeological excavations and anthropological evidence.

It is the latecomers of neolithic culture that scholars generally agree are the direct ancestors of today's Koreans. According to anthropological and linguistic studies, as well as legendary sources, Koreans trace their ethnic origins from those who lived in and around the Altaic mountains in Central Asia. Several thousand years ago, these people began to migrate eastward until they finally settled in an area including Manchuria and the Korean Peninsula.

When these migrants entered the Korean Peninsula around the third millennium B.C., they were confronted by natives called Paleoasians, who were eventually driven into various areas outside the Korean Peninsula. The Ainu of the northern tip of Japan, the natives of Sakhalin and the Eskimos of the eastern coast of Siberia are all descendants of these Paleoasian tribes.

Archaeological studies have uncovered two different types of pottery of this period, which raises the possibility that there were people of two different cultural ages. The two types are comb pattern pottery of a Neolithic Age people and plain pottery of a Bronze Age people. The patterned pottery, believed to be the product of a food-gathering, hunting and fishing people,

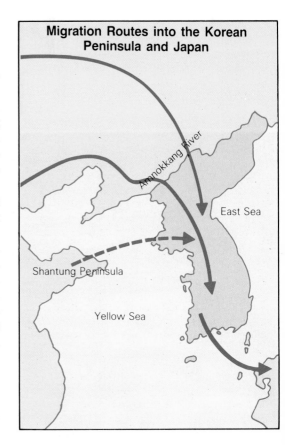

Migration Routes into the Korean Peninsula and Japan

Amnokkang River

East Sea

Shantung Peninsula

Yellow Sea

has been discovered near riverbanks and along the seashore, while the plain pottery, believed to have come from a food-producing people, has been unearthed mostly in the hilly regions of the country. Although these two people appear to have possessed different technologies, they shared the same culture, distinct from the Han Chinese.

As noted, most of the natives were subsequently driven north to Sakhalin, Kamchatka, and to the Arctic region by these newcomers, while a few were assimilated. Some of the migrants continued to move and eventually reached the southwestern shores of Japan. Therefore, there are cultural similarities in terms of beliefs, for example, shamanism, myths, and customs, as well as physical similarities among the ancient Koreans, Japanese and Siberian Eskimos.

Agriculture was introduced during the Bronze Age, which began around the 15th century B.C.

Increased food production and population growth led to social differentiation based on an unequal access to economic resources on the one hand, and clan or kin group formations on the other. Tribal societies of various sizes were established on the basis of clan relations, and some established chiefdoms and mini-states competing with each other. At the same time, people continued to migrate to Japan. Possessing more advanced civilization and culture, these migrants enjoyed ruling class status and even established their own small states. The southwestern part of Japan, in particular, offered easy access to culture from the Korean Peninsula. This region provides ample archaeological evidence of significant cultural and ethnic relations with Korea. More archaeological study is required to draw an exact map showing how widely Koreans were dispersed during this period. Based on Chinese records and archaeological reports, however, it is assumed that they were living not only on the Korean Peninsula but also in the vast area of Manchuria and even the region north of the Yellow River in today's People's Republic of China.

Cultural contact with the Chinese also was significant. Around the fourth century B.C., iron making was introduced through contacts with the Chinese. Inter-tribal competition as well as inter-ethnic contact with the Chinese became more frequent. The numerous Korean mini-states and tribal groups were integrated into several leading states, and resisted the military expansion of the Chinese. A strong sense of ethnic identity and cultural distinctiveness enabled them to remain ethnically and culturally different from the Chinese.

As the ancient history of Korea shows, various small states were composed of dialectal groups within the Altaic language family. In the latter half of the seventh century A.D., these early states were unified in the Shilla Kingdom, a significant event because this political unity was to consolidate the homogeneity of the Korean people, speaking one language and sharing the same culture.

However, the northern half of the Korean Peninsula and the whole of Manchuria, which had been the territory of another state called Koguryŏ, came under the reign of a new state called Parhae, established by a refugee group from defeated Koguryŏ. This state was highly heterogeneous both in ethnicity and in culture. The ruling class was composed exclusively of

Koreans, while the general public was made up of various non-Korean local ethnic groups including the Manchurian Tungus. The ruling Koreans failed to incorporate the non-Koreans, and as a result, their state was challenged and gave way to the largest of the native ethnic groups. From that time, Manchuria was inhabited by various groups of Tungusic people.

While there was a considerable mixing of races among the various peoples in Manchuria, the inhabitants of the Korean Peninsula maintained their ethnic identity with only minimal mixing with external groups. Although cultural contacts were extensive between Korea and China from the early stages of their history, ethnic assimilation did not occur. Koreans were (and still are) highly conscious of ethnic differences and cultural distinctions, which meant keeping their identity despite relations with China and Japan. Koreans exported their own culture and transmitted Chinese culture to Japan from ancient times, but they did not attempt any ethnic mixing with the Japanese. Many ethnic groups in Manchuria lost most of their ethnic identity and were even completely assimilated with dominant groups, but Koreans kept their ethnic identity and culture intact.

It is reported that approximately half a million Koreans live in Central Asia while more than two million Koreans reside in the vast areas of Manchuria, and that they have maintained their ethnic as well as cultural identity. Although they are minorities in their respective lands, they use their own language and letters and maintain traditional Korean social institutions and life styles. At the same time, they prefer ethnic endogamy so that retention of their own physical distinctiveness as well as cultural traditions is ensured.

According to a 1986 study by the Korean Institute of Science and Technology, the average height of a modern Korean is 167.7cm for men and 155.5 cm for women. In terms of height, this means that Korean males belong to the upper middle scale and Korean females to the medium scale, compared to other Asian people. The most distinctive physical features are almond-shaped eyes, black hair and relatively high cheek bones. It may also be noted that all Korean babies are born with blue spots on the lower part of the back, which is typical of Mongolians.

Language

Spoken by about 60 million people, Korean ranks among the major languages of the world. Although most speakers of Korean live on the Korean Peninsula and its adjacent islands, more than three million are scattered throughout the world on every continent.

The origin of the Korean language is as obscure as the origin of the Korean people. In the 19th century when Western scholars "discovered" the Korean language, this was the first question they raised. These scholars proposed various theories linking the Korean language with Ural-Altaic, Japanese, Chinese, Tibetan, Dravidian Ainu, Indo-European and other languages. Among these, only the relationship between Korean and Altaic (which groups the Turkic, Mongolian and Manchu-Tungus languages) on the one hand and between Korean and Japanese on the other have continuously attracted the attention of comparative linguists in the 20th century.

Altaic, Korean and Japanese exhibit similarities not only in their general structure, but also share common features such as vowel harmony and lack of conjunctions, although the vowel harmony in old Japanese has been the object of dispute among specialists in the field. Moreover, it has been found that these languages have various common elements in their grammar and vocabulary. Although much work remains to be done, research seems to show that Korean is probably related to both Altaic and Japanese.

History

According to early historical records, two groups of languages were spoken in Manchuria and on the Korean Peninsula at the dawn of the Christian era: the Northern or Puyŏ group and the southern or Han group. Around the middle

Articulation of Korean Consonants

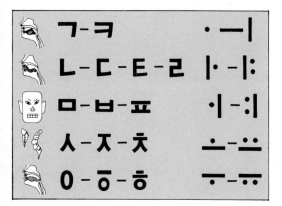

Rules of Spelling

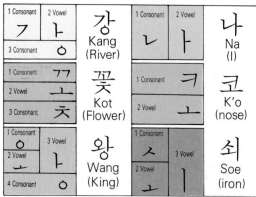

of the seventh century the kingdom of Shilla conquered the kingdoms of Paekche in the southwest and Koguryŏ in the north, and its language became dominant on the peninsula. As a result, the linguistic unification of the peninsula was achieved on the basis of the Shilla language.

After the peninsula was unified, the Koryŏ Dynasty was founded in the 10th century, and the capital was moved to Kaesong in the center of the Korean Peninsula. The dialect of Kaesŏng became the standard for the national language. When the Chosŏn Dynasty was founded at the end of the 14th century, the capital was moved to Seoul. However, since Seoul is geographically close to Kaesŏng, this had no significant effect on the development of the language.

Korean Script

The Korean script which is now generally called *Han-gŭl* was invented in 1443 under Sejong (r.1418-50), the fourth king of the Chosŏn Dynasty, who called it *Hunmin chŏng-ŭm* (proper sounds to instruct the people). However, the script was not promulgated until the appearance in a document which was also called *Hunmin chŏng-ŭm* in 1446.

The motivation behind the invention of Korean script, according to Sejong's preface to the above book, was to enable the Korean people to write their own language in their own way. Until the introduction of *Hunmin chŏng-ŭm*, only Chinese characters were used to write,

by the upper classes. There also seems to have been a secondary motivation behind the development of Korean script, that of representing the "correct" sounds of Chinese characters.

In producing the Korean script, Sejong and the scholars who assisted him probably referred to several writing systems such as Chinese old seal characters, the Uighur script and the Mongolian scripts, but the system of the Korean script is based upon their phonological studies. Above all, they developed a theory of tripartite division of the syllable into initial, medial and final, as opposed to the bipartite division of traditional Chinese phonology.

The initial sounds (consonants) are represented by 16 letters of which there are five basic forms. According to the explanations of the original *Hunmin chŏng-ŭm* text,

- (k) depicts the root of the tongue blocking the throat;
- (n) depicts the outline of the tongue touching the upper palate;
- (m) depicts the outline of the mouth;
- (s) depicts the outline of the incisor; and
- (g) depicts the outline of the throat.

The other initial letters were derived by adding strokes to the basic letters. No letters were invented for the final sounds, the initial letters being used for that purpose.

The original *Hunmin chŏng-ŭm* text also explains that the medial sounds (vowels) are represented by 11 letters of which there are three basic forms:

- (a) is a depiction of Heaven;

The Korean Alphabet

Vowels / Consonants	ㅏ [a]	ㅑ [ya]	ㅓ [ŏ]	ㅕ [yŏ]	ㅗ [o]	ㅛ [yo]	ㅜ [u]	ㅠ [yu]	ㅡ [ŭ]	ㅣ [i]
ㄱ [k,g]	가	갸	거	겨	고	교	구	규	그	기
ㄴ [n]	나	냐	너	녀	노	뇨	누	뉴	느	니
ㄷ [t,d]	다	댜	더	뎌	도	됴	두	듀	드	디
ㄹ [r,l]	라	랴	러	려	로	료	루	류	르	리
ㅁ [m]	마	먀	머	며	모	묘	무	뮤	므	미
ㅂ [p,b]	바	뱌	버	벼	보	뵤	부	뷰	브	비
ㅅ¹ [s,sh]	사	샤	서	셔	소	쇼	수	슈	스	시
ㅇ²	아	야	어	여	오	요	우	유	으	이
ㅈ [ch,j]	자	쟈	저	져	조	죠	주	쥬	즈	지
ㅊ [ch´]	차	챠	처	쳐	초	쵸	추	츄	츠	치
ㅋ [k´]	카	캬	커	켜	코	쿄	쿠	큐	크	키
ㅌ [t´]	타	탸	터	텨	토	툐	투	튜	트	티
ㅍ [p´]	파	퍄	퍼	펴	포	표	푸	퓨	프	피
ㅎ [h]	하	햐	허	혀	호	효	후	휴	흐	히

Note:(1) Generally 신문 is spelled in English as "shinmun," 소나무 as "sonamu," 설악산 as "Sŏraksan," and 안녕하십니까, as "annyŏnghashimnikka."

(2) The consonant ㅇ nowadays has double functions which were originally played by two different consonants. The initial consonant is a silent letter. For example, 아 is a vowel sound pronounced like "a" ; 야 is another vowel sound pronounced like "ya." The final consonant is pronounced like "ng." For example, 앙 is pronounced like "ang" while 양 is pronounced like "yang."

In addition to the original 14 consonants, five double consonants—ㄲ (kk), ㄸ (tt), ㅃ (pp), ㅆ (ss), ㅉ (tch)—are used for making initial consonant sounds. For example, Koreans use such wórds as 까, 떠, 뿌, 쓰, or 씨. Various compound consonants such as ㄲ, ㄳ, ㄵ, ㄶ, ㄺ, ㄻ, ㄼ, ㄽ, ㄿ, ㅀ, ㅄ, ㅆ are used for making final consonant sounds, For example, there are words such as 깎, 삯, 앉, 많, 밝, 젊, 넓, 돐, 읊, 잃, 없 or 있.

In addition to 10 vowels, the following vowels are used 애 (ae), 얘 (yae), 에 (e), 예 (ye), 외 (oe), 위 (wi), 와 (wa), 워 (wo), 왜 (wae) and 웨 (we). There are words such as 개 (kae), 얘 (yae), 네 (ne), 례 (rye), 되 (toe), 휘 (hwi), 촤 (ch'wa), 줘 (chwo), 쇄 (swae), or 췌(ch'we).

— (ŭ) is a depiction of Earth; and,

∣ (i) is a depiction of man. By combining these three signs the other medial letters are formed.

After the promulgation of the Korean alphabet, its popularity gradually increased, especially in modern times, to the point where it replaced Chinese characters as the main system of writing in Korea.

One of the characteristics of the Korean script is the syllabic grouping of the initial, medial and final letters. However, Korean script is essentially different from such syllabic writing systems as Japanese Kana. It is an alphabetic system which is characterized by syllabic grouping. Some examples are the following:

(na-mu) "tree."

(sa-ram) "man," and

(son-nim) "guest".

Standard Language and Orthography

Modern Korean is divided into six dialects: Central, Northwest, Northeast, Southeast, Southwest and Cheju. Except for the Cheju dialect, these are similar enough for speakers of the various dialects to understand each other. This is due to the fact that Korea has been a centralized state for more than a thousand years with the language of the capital exercising a steady influence on the language spoken throughout the country.

The language of the capital was established as the basis for modern standard Korean in 1936, as a result of the deliberations of a committee organized by the Korean Language Research Society. The language of the political and cultural center of a nation usually becomes the standard language through a gradual process. In Korea, however, the case was somewhat different, since the guidelines for the national standard language were determined by a small but dedicated group of scholars during the Japanese occupation. They worked to preserve their own language in the face of an oppressive regime which sought the eventual extinction of the Korean language.

Modern orthography was also determined by the Korean Language Research Society in 1933, rather than being the product of a gradual process of selection. Whereas 15th century orthography had been based on a phonemic principle, with each letter representing one phoneme, modern Korean orthography operates on a morphophonemic principle. That is, while a morpheme, or a minimum meaningful unit, may be realized differently according to its context, its orthographic representation is a single base form. The Korean word for "price," for example, is pronounced *kaps, kap*, or *kam* according to context; nevertheless, it is always spelled according to its base form, *kaps*.

Phonology

The Korean language possesses a rich variety of vowels and consonants with ten simple vowels and three series of stops and affricates: plain, aspirated, and glottalized. This gives difficulty to foreigners who are just starting to learn the language, and also complicates the task of Romanization.

Phonemes of the plain stop series are realized as unvoiced sounds in the word-initial position, voiced sounds in the intervocalic position and unreleased sounds in the word-final position, e.g. *kap [kap]* "case or small box" and *kap-e [kabe]* "in the case." The liquid phoneme is realized as "r" in the intervocalic position and "l" in the word-final position. For example, *tar [tal]* "moon," and *tar-e [tare]* "at the moon."

Another characteristic of modern Korean is that there are no consonant clusters or liquid sounds in the word-initial position. As a result, Koreans pronounce the English word "stop" in two syllables, as *[Swt'op]*, and change the initial "l" or "r" in foreign words to "n." Recently, however, there has been a tendency to pronounce initial liquid sounds in Western loan words.

Korean is similar to the Altaic languages in that it possesses vowel harmony. Evidence indicates that vowel harmony was rigidly observed in old Korean, but rules have been significantly weakened in modern Korean. Vowel harmony nevertheless continues to play an important role in modern Korean in the onomatopoetic and mimetic words so abundant in the language.

Romanization

Korean is a difficult language to Romanize, given the variety of vowel and consonant phonemes and the complex rules for their realization. Of the Romanization systems that have been in use since the 19th century, the most widely accepted have been the McCune-Reischauer System (1939), and the Ministry of Education System (1959). The former has been used mainly in the United States and other Western countries, while the latter has been used in Korea. In 1984, however, the Korean system was revised along the lines of the McCune-Reischauer System, with a few modifications, so that the two systems most widely used in Korea and the West are now, in effect, the same.

The system is a phonetic one, designed to faithfully represent modern Korean pronunciation with the Latin alphabet. Under this system, a single phoneme of Korean may be represented by more than one Latin letter, depending on how the Korean phoneme is realized in a given context. As explained above, plain stops and affricates in modern Korean are pronounced as either unvoiced or voiced sounds, and the liquid as "r" or "l," depending on the context. The 1984 Romanization system reflects these variants.

Morphology and Syntax

Korean is one of the so-called agglutinative languages which add suffixes to nominal and verbal stems in derivation and inflection. Suffixes agglutinate one after another and indicate different styles of speech, express moods and aspects, and function as case markers, connectives, etc. Vowel gradation, that is, the change of vowels to make morphological distinctions such as singular-plural in nouns (e.g.man-men) and present-past in verbs (e.g.sing-sang), is not found in Korean.

Korean is a verb-final language: the verb is always the last constituent of the sentence. Constituents other than verbs are relatively free to switch around, although the normal and preferred word order is subject-object-verb.

In Korean, modifying words or phrases precede the modified words without exception: adjectives precede nouns, adverbs precede verbs, etc. Since Korean has no relative clauses, the clauses precede the nouns they modify however long they may be.

One of the important characteristics of Korean grammar is the honorific system. Korean is perhaps the only language in the world which has honorific suffixes such as -shi-, exalting the subject of the sentence, and -supni-, showing the speaker's respect to the hearer. Although Japanese has a well-developed system of honorific expressions, it is different from that of Korean in that it utilizes auxiliary verbs instead of suffixes.

Vocabulary

The vocabulary of the Korean language is composed of indigenous words and loan-words, the latter being the result of contacts with other languages. The majority of the loan-words are of Chinese origin, often called Sino-Korean words, a reflection of several millennia of Chinese cultural influence on Korea. In modern Korean, native words are significantly outnumbered by Sino-Korean words. As about half the English vocabulary is said to be of Romance origin, most of which entered English during the three centuries following the Norman Conquest, the situation is by no means unique to Korea. for several millennia in the past.

As a result, a dual system of native and Sino-Korean words pervades the Korean lexicon, including two sets of numerals which are interchangeable in some cases but mutually exclusive in others. For example, native numerals are used with shi (the hour, i.e. ahop shi, "nine o'clock") but Sino-Korean numerals are used with pun (the minute,i.e. ku pun, "nine minutes").

The process of modernization has resulted in a steady flow of Western words entering the Korean language. Technological and scientific terms represent the majority of these loan-words, although Western terms have been introduced into almost every field.

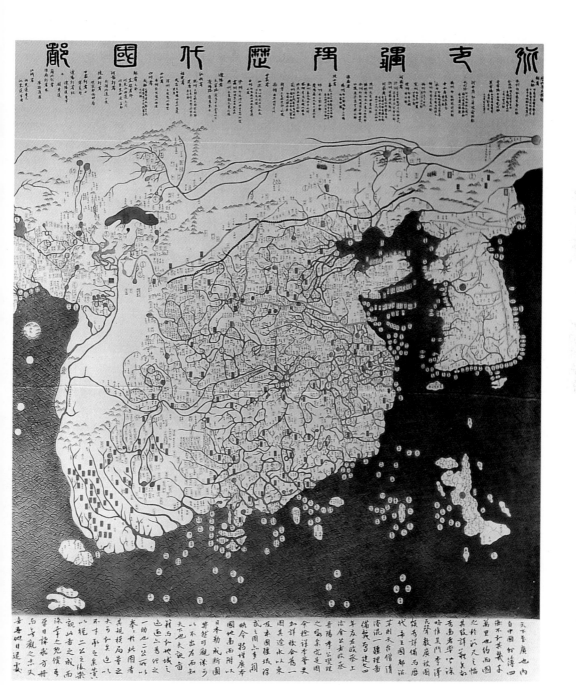

CHRONOLOGICAL TABLE

	KOREA	CHINA	JAPAN	THE WEST
B.C	Paleolithic Age			
5,000	Neolithic Age			
2,000		Bronze Age	Jomon Period	Early Mesopotamia Egyptian Kingdoms
1,000		Shang Dynasty (1766-1122) Chou (1122-256)		
	Bronze Age Ancient Chosŏn	Spring and Autumn Era (770-476) Iron Age		Greek Civilization Founding of Rome (735)
500	Iron Age Puyŏ	Warring States Era (475-221) Chin Dynasty (221-206) Western Han Dynasty (206B.C.-A.D.9)	Bronze Age Yayoi Period	Socrates (469-399) Alexander the Great (356-323) First Punic War (264-241) Second Punic War (219-201)
200	Confederated Kingdoms of Samhan (Three Han States)			Julius Ceasar (101-44)
100	Three Kingdoms: Shilla (57B.C.-A.D.935) Koguryŏ (37B.C.-A.D.668) Paekche (18B.C.-A.D.660)			Birth of Jesus Christ
A.D.	Kaya (42-562)	Hsin Dynasty (8-25) Eastern Han Dynasty (26-221)		
200		Three Kingdoms (220-280) Chin Dynasty (265-420)	Iron Age Tumulus Period	
300				Christianity established as state religion of Roman Empire (392) Roman Empire split in two (395)
400		Northern and Southern Dynasties (420-581)		Anglo-Saxons established in Britain (449)
500		Sui Dynasty (581-618)	Asuka Period (552-645)	Mohammed (570-632)
600	Parhae Kingdom (669-928) Unified Shilla Kingdom (618-935)	T'ang Dynasty (618-906)	Nara Period (645-794)	Hegira (622) and beginning of Islamic era
700				
800			Heian Period (794-1185)	
900	Koryŏ Kingdom (918-1392)	Five Dynasties (906-960) Sung Dynasty (960-1279)		Charles the Great crowned first Holy Roman Emperor (800)
1000				
1100			Kamakura Period (1185-1392)	First Crusade (1096-99)
1200		Yüan Dynasty (1279-1368)		Magna Carta (1215) Marco Polo (1254-1324)
1300	Chosŏn Kingdom (1392-1910)	Ming Dynasty (1368-1644)	Muromachi (Ashikaga) Period (1392-1568)	The Hundred Years' War (1334-1434)
1400				Gutenberg's Press (1438) Columbus discovered America (1492)
1500			Momoyama Period (1568-1615)	Martin Luther launched reform of the Church (1517)
1600		Ch'ing Dynasty (1644-1911)	Tokugawa Period (1615-1867)	The Thirty Years' War (1618-48)
1700				American Independence (1776)· French Revolution (1789-1793)
1800	Taehan Empire Proclaimed (1897)		Modern Period (1868-)	American Civil War (1861-65)
1900	Annexation by Japan (1910) Establishment of the Republic of Korea (1948)	Establishment of the Republic of China (1912)		World War I (1914-18) World War II (1939-45)

Prehistoric Korea

The habitation of early man in Korea appears to have started about half a million years ago.

In the past decade archaeological excavations have shed much new light on the prehistoric society of Korea. At Sŏkchang-ri near Kongju, Ch'ungch'ŏng-namdo, artifacts of lower Paleolithic industry consisting of chopper-scraper culture was unearthed in the lower most part of the site. Bifacial chopper or chopping-tool culture followed. Hand axes and cleavers produced by men in later eras were also uncovered. At Sangwon near P'yŏngyang, numerous fossilized faunal remains from dietary debris of early men of the Lower Paleolithic Age were discovered.

During the Middle Paleolithic Period, pre-Neanderthal and Neanderthal men dwelt in caves at Chŏmmal near Chech'ŏn and Turubong near Ch'ŏngju. From the two caves, fossil remains of the rhinoceros, cave bear, brown bear, *maccacus*, hyena, and numerous deer (Pseudaxi gray var.), all extinct species, were excavated. Some bones of dietary debris were engraved with delineations of human faces as well as animal figures such as tigers, leopards, fish, birds, etc. These findings led to the conclusion that Neanderthal man had the capacity to create art.

From Chŏmmal cave a tool, possibly for hunting, fashioned from the radius of a pre-Neanderthal man was unearthed along with hunting and kitchen tools of animal bones. The shells of nuts collected for nourishment were also uncovered.

In Sŏkchang-ri and elsewhere in the riverine sites, numerous chipped stone tools were found with definite traces of Paleolithic tradition, made of fine-grain rocks such as quartzite, porphyry, obsidian, chert, and felsite manifest acheulian, mousteroid, and levalloisian. Those of the chopper tradition are of much cruder shape and chipped from quartz and pegmatite. Sŏkchang-ri middle layers showed that early men hunted with these bola or missile stones.

There are more upper Paleolithic sites as well. From an interesting habitation site at Sŏk-chang-ri locality 1, some human hairs of Mongoloid species were found with limonitic and manganese pigments near and around a hearth, as well as animal figures such as a dog, tortoise and bear made of rock, radiocarborn dated to 20,000 years earlier. The living floor of compact clay was hollowed out in the shape of a whale. It is quite possible that was done to pray for good fishing and hunting. Obsidian microblades were used in this hut for carving and the scraping of fish. The people may have been the early *homo sapiens* of Mongoloid stock who were ancestral to modern Koreans.

A few Mesolithic sites have been discovered recently with microlits. Many of the Mesolithic sites in the coastal areas of the west seem to have sunk due to the rise of sea levels during the Atlantic Neolithic Period. Flat-bottomed unmarked pottery of the early Neolithic Period first appeared, and followed by pottery with geometrical marks, a sign of cultural relationship between the Ural-Altaic regions where similar pottery developed.

With a few deviations, this pottery with a geometric surface design is similar to kamm-keramic or comb pottery, which is widespread in Korea. The design is incised in a herring bone pattern or simple sets of slanted lines. This pottery is of a half-egg shape with a round bottom and straight lip. The pottery was produced of clay or sandy clay mixed with talc, shell, asbestos and steatite temper, built by the coiling method and fired at a low temperature in an open kiln.

There are numerous sites of neolithic habitation. Known for the cluster of dug-out huts of this era are Ch'ongho-ri along the Taedonggang River near P'yŏngyang; Misa-ri and Amsa-dong along the Han-gang River near Seoul; and Tongsam-dong in the Naktonggang River estuary near Pusan. These sites are of the early neolithic period, around six to seven thousand years ago. The people of this period lived on fishing, hunting and gathering of wild fruits. They had also started to grind acorns and wild grains on saddle querns.

In the late Neolithic Period, probably the fourth millennium B.C., there was a change in the surface design on pottery. Parallel wavy lines or sets of pit marks in the shape of light-

A human face incised on a dee bone found in Turubong Cave near Ch'ŏngju; a scraper end scraper with a serrated edge of the Upper Paleolithic Era found in Sŏkchang-ri village, Kongju; three stone daggers, 10th century B.C.; and combware pot, Neolithic Age, circa 3000 B.C

ening flashes were adopted. There are many sites with this type of pottery along the riverine areas of the western and southern coasts of the peninsula.

Incipient dibbling and planting were developed together with the breeding of cattle. Digging sticks made of animal horn and stone hoes were used in the incipient farming. At the Chit'ap-ri site, carbonized millet was found in the pottery. The early Neolithic peoples made spindles and spindle-whorls to spin and weave clothes and fishing nets. They gradually began to sew with bone needles; they also selected seeds and destroyed weeds to protect the crops. Their huts were built in a round or semi-rectangular dugout form with a hearth; one of these with five hearths has been uncovered.

They believed in animism, and thought all natural objects had spirits. Shamanism was prevalent as elsewhere in the northeastern Asian regions. Shamans were believed to have supernatural power enabling them to contact the heavenly spirit to protect the family and community from evil spirits.

The Bronze Age began around the 15th century B.C. Pottery without any surface design and with a flat bottom was made during this period, as well as some black pottery and burnished red pottery. Red beans, soybeans, and millet were cultivated, as indicated by the imprint of such grains found on the surface of the pottery at Yangp'yŏng, and some gray organic flour was found in pottery at Hogok-

dong, Musan. Agriculture during the Bronze Age included rice cultivation in the southern part of Korea, as evidenced by the discovery of carbonized rice grains at Hunam-ri, Yŏju. One of the dwelling sites of this period was radiocarbon dated 2760 B.C. A bronze ritual ornament unearthed near Taejŏn depicts a man ploughing the land, and semi-lunar knives of polished stone are found almost everywhere in the site of unmarked pottery. Rectangular huts and burial sites in the form of dolmen and stone cists are much larger than those of the previous era.

As agriculture developed, surplus was stored, and specialization of labor into peasant, artisan and bondman emerged, a change which brought about mutual influence between kinship groups. The increase of food production contributed to the rise of population and necessitated migration; some of the Neolithic people possibly migrated to Kyushu, southern Japan in this stage.

Clans of these communities came into contact and advances of technology in smelting bronze stimulated peaceful relations and the practice of exogamy. Metallurgy possibly started from firing at pottery kilns. The rise of smiths and miners of raw material contributed to the emergence of the ruling and the ruled. The distribution of dolmens and menhirs is pervasive in Korea, showing that the spread of megalithic-bronze culture developed extensively on the peninsula.

In this period the mastery of bronze technology served as a powerful weapon for the conquest of different clans, and thereby expedited the rise of larger units of tribal society.

Ancient period

Tan-gun and Ancient Chosŏn

The people of Ancient Chosŏn are recorded as Tung-i, "eastern bowmen" or "eastern barbarians." They spread in Manchuria, the eastern littoral of China, areas north of the Yangtze River, and the Korean Peninsula. The eastern bowmen had a myth in which the legendary founder Tan-gun was born of a father of heavenly descent and a women from a bear-totem tribe. He is said to have started to rule in 2333 B.C., and his descendants reigned in Chosŏn, the "land of morning calm," for more than a millennium.

When the Chou people pushed the Yin, the eastern bowmen moved toward Manchuria and the Korean Peninsula for better climatic conditions. They seem to have maintained unity, as China's great sages, Confucius and Mencius, praised their consanguineous order and the decorum of their society.

The eastern bowmen on the western coast of the Yellow Sea clashed with the Chou people during China's period of warring states. This led them to move toward southern Manchuria and the Korean Peninsula.

There were other tribes of eastern bowmen, Ye-Maek in the Manchurian area and Han on the Korean Peninsula, all belonging to the Tungusic family and linguistically belonging to the Altaic. When Yin collapsed, Kija, a subject of the Yin state, entered Tan-gun's domain and introduced the culture of Yin around the 13th century B.C.

Then came the invasion of Yen in the northeastern sector of China, and Ancient Chosŏn lost the territories west of the Liao River in the third century B.C. By this time iron culture was developing and warring states pushed the refugees eastward.

Among the immigrants, Wiman entered the

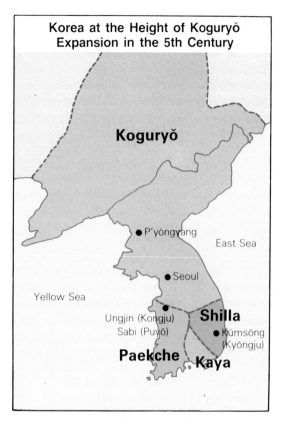

Korea at the Height of Koguryŏ Expansion in the 5th Century

Koguryŏ

P'yŏngyang

East Sea

Seoul

Yellow Sea

Ungjin (Kongju)
Sabi (Puyŏ)

Shilla

Kŭmsŏng
(Kyŏngju)

Paekche   Kaya

service of Ancient Chosŏn as military commander with a base on the Amnokkang (Yalu) River. He drove King Chun to the south and usurped power. But in 109 B.C. the Han emperor Wu-ti dispatched a massive invasion by land and sea to Ancient Chosŏn in the estuary of the Liao River. Ancient Chosŏn was defeated after two years and four Chinese provincial commands were set up in southern Manchuria and the northern part of the Korean Peninsula. Not long after the establishment of the four commanderies, however, the Korean attack became fierce and the last of the commanderies, Lolang (Korean: Nangnang) was destroyed by Koguryŏ in A.D. 313.

The Three Kingdoms

Ancient Korea in the last stage of bronze culture of Karasuk affinity saw the impact of the iron culture in China's state power. The rise of Puyŏ was seen in Manchuria along with China's development. In the southern part of

Korea, tribal leagues of the three Han gradually developed to the stage of state-building. Paekche and Shilla were prominent in the south, Koguryŏ in the north.

By the first century A.D., Koguryŏ was firmly established as a state power and destroyed the Chinese colony Lolang (Nangnang) in A.D. 313. In A.D. 342, however, Koguryŏ's capital fell before the Chinese Yen. Paekche amassed power while Koguryŏ was fighting against the Chinese, and came into conflict with Koguryŏ in the late fourth century. Then came the growth of Shilla with more fully organized state power.

Koguryŏ was the first to adopt Buddhism as royal creed in 372; Paekche, the second in 384; and Shilla, the last in A.D. 528. Buddhist scriptures in Chinese translation were also adopted. Koguryŏ established an academy to educate the nobility and compiled a state history consisting of 100 chapters before the introduction of Buddhism. Paekche also compiled its history in the early fourth century prior to A.D. 384. Only Shilla undertook compilation of its history immediately following the adoption of Buddhism.

Thus the three developed state organizations occupied the Korean Peninsula, adopting Confucian and Buddhist hierarchical structures with the king at the pinnacle. State codes were promulgated to initiate a legal system to rule the people. In this process, Koguryŏ annexed Puyŏ, and Shilla conquered Kaya. The three states were competing with each other in strengthening Buddhist-Confucian state power, in efforts toward serious territorial expansion.

At this juncture Shilla developed its *Hwarang*, (flower of youth corps), a voluntary social organization. The *Hwarang* members were trained as a group in the arts of war, literary taste and community life, partly through pilgrimages. The educational objectives were: 1) loyalty to the monarch, 2) filial piety to parents, 3) amicability among friends, 4) no retreat in war, and 5) aversion to unnecessary killing. These objectives were postulated by the famous monk Won-gwang, who consolidated Buddhist-Confucian virtues in the education of Shilla youths. This movement became popular and the corps contributed to the strength of the Shilla state.

With the youth corps, Shilla was able to amass state power in the cultural sphere as well. With the aid of a Paekche architect, it erected a huge temple, Hwangnyongsa, and a towering pagoda famous even in China. The 70m-high pagoda of Hwangnyongsa stood from A.D. 645 until the Mongol invasion of the 13th century. Shilla was ready to learn from Koguryŏ and Paekche, and also dispatched monks to China to learn about China's culture, especially through Buddhist doctrine, architecture and Chinese classics.

While Shilla was building amicable relations with T'ang China, Koguryŏ was in fierce conflict with Sui and T'ang. Sui Emperor Yang-ti, after successful campaigns against the northern nomadic tribes, invaded Koguryŏ with more than one million troops. In A.D. 612 Koguryŏ General Ŭlchi Mundŏk held the fortresses against Yang-ti's army and navy for several months and destroyed the Sui troops in retreat. An ambush at Salsu (Ch'ŏngch'ŏn-gang River) allowed only 2,700 Sui troops out of 300,000 men to escape. Sui fell from power partly as a result of the defeat by Koguryŏ.

After the rise of T'ang, T'ai-tsung contemplated revenge while protecting against invasion by building fortifications and walls along the Liao River. In A.D. 644, 648 and 655, T'ai-tsung attempted unsuccessful invasions. T'ang then turned to Shilla for assistance.

Shilla also persuaded T'ang China to come to its aid in the conquest of Paekche and Koguryŏ. Koguryŏ had earlier defeated Sui Yang-ti, and T'ai-tsung's hostile relationship drove T'ang Kao-tsung to ally with Shilla in the campaign against Paekche and then Koguryŏ.

The latecomer to statehood, Shilla was finally able to defeat the other two states, but unable to control the whole territory of Koguryŏ which extended to Manchuria. T'ang's intention toward Shilla was made clear in the aftermath of the unification by Shilla. The Paekche king and his family were taken to T'ang in 660 and a T'ang general appointed military governor to rule the Paekche territory. Koguryŏ's last king, his officials and 200,000 prisoners were also taken to China in 668 and Koguryŏ's territory

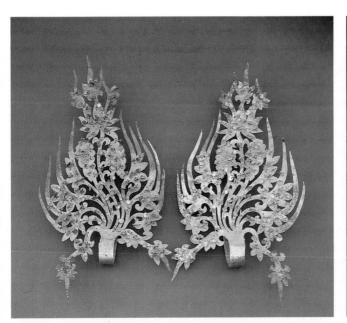

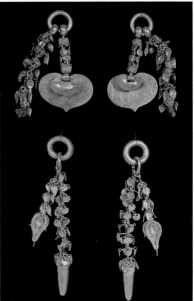

The brick tomb chamber of King Muryŏng (r. 501-523) of the Paekche Kingdom and his queen (bottom); the golden diadem ornaments in a flower-flame pattern, found in the tomb (top left); and the king's golden ear pendants with heart-shaped spangles and comma-shaped jade ornaments.

was administered by T'ang generals. T'ang Kao-tsung's desires were now evident, and Shilla was determined to fight against T'ang. The determination of Kim Yusin, Shilla's foremost general who led and marshaled Shilla's campaigns, counteracted the Chinese instigation of Paekche and Koguryŏ to rebel against Shilla. Shilla commenced active resistance against Chinese domination in T'ang-controlled territory. In 671 Shilla started its own operations against Chinese rule and took the Chinese administrative headquarters, thereby retaking all of the Paekche territory. China invaded again in 674 against Shilla, who had succeeded in quelling the T'ang army at Maech'o Fortress near Yanggu and the Ch'ŏnsŏng Fortress at the Yesŏnggang River near Kaesŏng. Shilla's army also successfully drove out the T'ang army from P'yŏngyang. Nevertheless, the Chinese army persistently claimed the territories of Paekche and Koguryŏ until A.D. 735 when they gave in to Shilla's claim of territory south of the Taedonggang River. Shilla became a unique state covering most of the Korean Peninsula and the majority of the people of the former three states.

One Koguryŏ warrior, Ko Sagye, who was taken by a T'ang general, joined the T'ang army. His son Son-ji had a successful military career in T'ang and conquered Tashkent in the mid-eighth century, transmitting paper-making technology to the Arabian countries. The Shilla monk Hye Ch'o in 727 visited India for pilgrimages to historic Buddhist sites in five Indian kingdoms, an account of which is preserved as an important historical record about eighth century India.

The Parhae Kingdom

Subsequent to the fall of Koguryŏ, Tae Choyŏng, a former Koguryŏ general, formed an army of Koguryŏ and Malgal (a Tungusic tribe) people, and led a migration to Chinese-controlled territory. They settled eventually near Kirin in Manchuria, and there founded a state which was at first called Chin, but in A.D.713 was renamed Parhae (P'ohai in Chinese). Parhae soon gained control of most of the for-

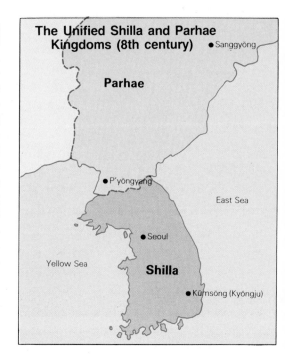

The Unified Shilla and Parhae Kingdoms (8th century)

Parhae

• Sanggyŏng

• P'yŏngyang

East Sea

• Seoul

Yellow Sea

Shilla

• Kŭmsŏng (Kyŏngju)

mer Koguryŏ territory. The ruling class of Parhae consisted mostly of Koguryŏ (i.e. Korean) people. Parhae declared itself the successor to Koguryŏ, and sometimes called itself *Koryŏ-kuk* (state of Koryŏ).

Parhae prosperity reached its height in the first half of the ninth century during the reign of King Sŏn. At that time, Parhae territory extended from the Sungari and Amur rivers in northern Manchuria all the way down to the northern provinces of modern Korea. Its capital was Tonggyŏng, in the Kirin area, where the state had originally been founded.

Parhae was to become a victim of the political confusion and violence which accompanied the fall of the T'ang Dynasty. In 926 the Khitan, who later came to dominate much of Manchuria and northern China, conquered Parhae. Many of the ruling class, who were mostly Koreans, moved south and joined the newly founded Koryŏ Kingdom, which replaced Shilla at that time.

While the Manchurian portion of the Parhae territory was lost, the area south of the Amnok (Yalu)-Tuman boundary was restored and the people migrated to Korea.

Pulguksa Temple in Kyŏngju was first built in 535.

Unified Shilla

Shilla (668-935) reached its peak of power and prosperity in the middle of the eighth century. It attempted to establish an ideal Buddhist country and constructed the Sŏkkuram cave shrine and Pulguksa Temple with splendorous masonic art. Extensive printing of Buddhist scripture was undertaken with woodblocks. The oldest imprint of the *Dharani* sutra, probably printed between A.D. 706 and 751, was brought to light during the recent restoration of a three-story pagoda at Pulguksa.

The nobility of Koguryŏ and Paekche were treated with some generosity. Scholars specializing in diplomatic correspondence, medicine, mathematics, and astronomy were installed to bring professional personnel into government service. The distribution of *chŏngjŏn* (equity land system) was put into practice in 722 for the peasants, and the people in the country then became eligible to cultivate allotted lands. In addition, reservoirs were erected for rice field irrigation. For the allotted land the peasants had to return in kind crops of rice, millet, barley and wheat. Taxation in kind was collected in accordance with the actual crops from the land. In addition, the peasants were bound to plant mulberry trees for silkworms, and walnut and pine nut trees as a side tax to the government and nobility. They raised cattle and horses, two to four head in each household. The Shilla people enjoyed an affluent life. The capital city prospered and there were streets of more than 10 kilometers distance.

During this period, a prominent monk, Wonhyo, started a new sect of Buddhism among the common people. By his creative thinking, Buddhism was brought to the public as a popular religion.

There was no more war in the eighth century and the desire for learning grew. *Idu*, a new transcription system of Korean words by the use of Chinese characters, was invented by Shilla scholars of the mid-upper class next to the upper-royal nobility, or *Chingol* (true bone). The growing need for scholarly work necessitated the recruitment of mid-upper class scholars, so a quasi-civil service examination system was instituted in 788 to meet the need.

The state cult of Buddhism began to deteriorate as the nobility indulged in easy luxurious lives. Buddhism began to establish a new *Sŏn* sect (generally known in the West by its Japanese name Zen) in the remote mountain area. In the cities, the state cult also encountered difficulties as conflict among the nobility in out-lying districts intensified, and the throne contin-ued to lose power as struggles within the *Chingol* clan also increased. King Hyegong was assassinated in 780. During this time, there were frequent, but futile, attempts to usurp the throne.

In the outlying areas there also were uprisings initiated by *Chingol* magistrates. King Aejang was killed by his uncle who succeeded to the throne. Thus Shilla in the ninth century was shaken by intra-clan conflict both around the throne and in district administration. Chang Po-go, a successful merchant, held sway in mar-itime commerce in the ninth century at Ch'ŏng-hae-jin (Wando), transporting goods to and from Chinese and Japanese ports. He was one among many local leaders to rebel against the Shilla throne.

The government prohibited the building of new temples and extravagant decorations alto-gether in 806.

One of the many prominent scholars, Ch'oe Ch'i-won, who had passed the T'ang civil examination and drafted a manifesto against Huang Tsao, returned to his own home country. However, his suggestions were not taken seri-ously, or put in practice. Although offered a high-ranking office, Ch'oe retreated to Haeinsa Temple to live as a hermit. Scholars and talent-ed persons from the mid-upper class wished for a change from Shilla's rule.

Koryŏ Period

Shilla was torn to pieces by rebel leaders such as Kyŏn-hwon who proclaimed Latter Paekche in Chŏnju in 900, and Kungye who proclaimed Latter Koguryŏ the following year at Kaesŏng. Wang Kŏn, the last rebel leader, the son of a gentry family, became the first minister of Kungye. Overthrowing Kungye for misde-meanors and malpractice in administration in 918, he sought and received the support of land-lords and merchants whose economic as well as political power overwhelmed the Shilla govern-ment.

Wang Kŏn easily raided Latter Paekche in 934, and received a voluntary surrender in 935. The following year he accepted the abdication of King Kyŏngsun of Shilla.

Wang Kŏn was at first content to leave provincial magnates undisturbed. He was partic-ularly careful to placate the Shilla aristocracy. He gave former King Kyŏngsun the highest post in his government, and even married a woman of the Shilla royal clan, thus somewhat legitimizing his rule.

Enthroned as the founder king of the Koryŏ Dynasty (918- 1392), the name of which was derived from Koguryŏ, he drafted ten injunc-tions for his successors to observe. Among the ten injunctions he predicted probable conflict between his state and the northern nomadic states with Koguryŏ's territory as the objective, and advised the strengthening of the state. He advised that Buddhist temples must not be interfered with, and warned against usurpation and internal conflict among the royal clans and weakening of local power.

King T'aejo's (Wang Kŏn's posthumous title) lenient policy plus his marriage ties made the rebellious local lords relatively obedient. To weaken the local power, King Kwangjong (r.949-975) instituted emancipation of slaves in order to restore the commoner status of those unjustly bonded in 956. This helped to increase revenue and was welcomed by the people unjustly forced into captivity.

Two years later, he installed a civil service examination system to recruit officials by mer-it. His successor King Kyŏngjong (r. 975-981), put into practice the allotting of land and forest lots to officials. These policies enabled the Koryŏ state to gain a foothold as a centralized government. King Sŏngjong (r.981-997) in 982 adopted the suggestions in the memorial writ-ten by Confucian scholar Ch'oe Sŭng-no and paved the way to rule by Confucian state model. District officials were appointed by the central government, and all arms privately owned were collected to be recast into agricultural tools.

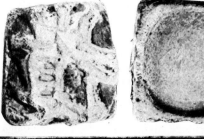

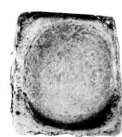

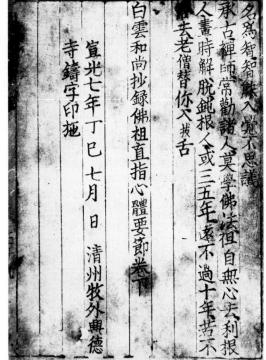

A map of the Koryŏ Kingdom, 11th century (top left); the earliest movable metal type was invented in Korea during the 12th century (top right); the earliest extant material in the world printed with movable metal type, printed in 1377 and now preserved in the Bibliotheque National Francaise, Paris (right); the wooden blocks for the Tripitaka Koreana, carved between 1237 and 1252, are preserved in a naturally ventilated storage room(bottom).

The government organization was set up after the T'ang system, but the power to make admonitions to the throne on the part of officials and censorship of royal decisions was instituted. With such internal order, Koryŏ was long able to withstand foreign invasion.

The Khitan rose to power and began to confederate, transforming their old tribal league into a centralized organization. They conquered Parhae in 926 and in 937 officially came to be called Liao. As noted earlier, the people of Parhae fled to Koryŏ, but Liao was now ready to strike, and Koryŏ tried in vain to open diplomatic relations. Liao initiated attacks in 983, in 985, in 989, and in 993, continuing to harass Koryŏ. However, in 993, Koryŏ's commanding general Sŏ Hŭi (940-998), facing a stalemate with the Liao army, convened peace talks with Liao general Hsiao to end the enmity with the recognition of the territorial rights of Koryŏ south of the Amnokkang River.

Diplomatic relations were opened between the two states in 994. But Liao attacked again in 1010 and the Koryŏ king fled to the south. The conflict became more complicated as the northern Jurchen tribes grew stronger in the Korean border area of Manchuria. As the conflicts continued to afflict war-weary Koryŏ, King Hyŏnjong (r.1009-31) ordered the carving of the Tripitaka, imploring Buddha's aid, which consisted of about 6,000 chapters.

However, in 1115 the Jurchen proclaimed the Chin empire and came into conflict with Liao. Chin conquered Liao in 1125, and turned to an invasion of Sung. By 1126 it conquered the Northern Sung which fled south of the Yangtze River. Two Sung emperors were captured by Chin, and royal as well as private Sung libraries came into Chin possession.

Koryŏ had its own calamity that year. In 1126, all of the palace buildings, including tens of thousands of books in the royal library and national academy, were turned into ashes when the palace buildings were set afire by the father-in-law of King Injong. Koryŏ lost the famed collection, and there was no way to obtain books from Sung. To print books with wood blocks was prohibitive in cost and time consuming. Then came the idea of typography and

the casting of bronze type began with the same technology that was used in coin-casting. Koryŏ printing with movable metal type was developed to print many titles in limited copies around the mid-12th century.

In 1145, King Injong (r.1112-1146) had a Confucian scholar, Kim Pu-sik, compile the Samguk Sagi (History of the Three Kingdoms). About one hundred years later, monk by the name of Iryŏn compiled the Samguk Yusa (Memorabilia of the Three Kingdoms), which records important history and traditions that are not found in the history.

Conflict increased between civil and military officials as the latter were degraded and paid poorly. In 1170, the military officials rose up against the civil officials and paid them back with bloodshed. Around this time the Mongols consolidated power, and the new Sung techniques of smelting iron with corks was utilized by the Mongols in the production of arms. With the new arms, the Mongols conquered Chin in 1215 and chased the diehard Liao refugees into the territory of Koryŏ, which was consequently plagued by consecutive Mongol invasions. As a result, the Koryŏ court and officials fled to Kangwhado Island in 1232.

Mongols invaded in 1238 and looted Koryŏ, destroying the splendid Shilla pagoda of Hwangnyongsa Temple. The Koryŏ court on Kanghwado carved the second Tripitaka Koreana consisting of over 80,000 wood blocks inscribed on both sides, which is now stored at Haeinsa Temple. This enormous task was also conducted with pious patriotism to secure Buddha's protection against the Mongols. The people of Koryŏ reached a consensus to resist the foreign invaders and safeguard the nation despite the incessant attacks and invasions.

From the middle of the 14th century, the Mongol power declined rapidly, with their own internal struggles for the throne, and in the 1340s, frequent rebellions broke out all over China.

Free at last from Mongol domination, Koryŏ began efforts to reform its government. King Kongmin (r.1351-74), first removed pro-Mongol aristocrats and military officers. These deposed people formed a dissident faction which plotted an unsuccessful coup against the king.

A second internal problem was the question of land holdings. By now the land-grant system had broken down, and Mongol-favored officials and military men, along with a handful of landed gentry, owned the vast majority of agricultural land, which was worked by tenant farmers and bondsmen. King Kongmin's attempt at land reform was met with opposition and subterfuge from those officials who were supposed to implement his reforms, being the owners of the land whose ownership was supposed to undergo a drastic change.

A third problem was the rising animosity between the Buddhists and Confucian scholars. Normally, and during most of the dynastic period, Buddhism and Confucian creeds coexisted with little conflict. It must be noted here that by this time Korean scholars had become imbued with the Neo-Confucian doctrine as advocated by Chu Hsi in the late 12th century, just before the advent of the Mongols. The new Confucian scholars did not agree with the idea that one should denounce one's family ties to become a monk because the very basis of Confucian philosophy was founded on strong family and social relationships. The wealth and power of the monasteries and the great expense incurred by the state for Buddhist festivals became the target of criticism.

Another problem was that Japanese pirates were no longer hit-and-run bandits, but organized military marauders raiding deep into the country. It was at that time that General Yi Sŏng-gye distinguished himself by repelling the pirates in a series of successful engagements.

Early Chosŏn Period

State Structure

General Yi Sŏng-gye seized political and military power, deposing King Ch'ang (r.1388-89) and placing Kongyang (r.1389-92) on the throne. He and his faction then carried out a

The Chosŏn Dynasty (15th century)

sweeping land reform. Neo-Confucian ideology became political capital in his fight against the declining Koryŏ monarchy and nobility.

The *Kwajŏnpŏp* (rank land law) was instituted, providing not only land for General Yi to distribute but also the power to rule the country. He and his group were well aware that the ability to bring order and to end the decadent Koryŏ Kingdom lay in the land tenure system.

Under the terms of the status land system, land was ordinarily distributed for life only, on the basis of one's status or rank. Recipients were given the right to collect rents, while the peasant was given the right to cultivate. The customary rent amounted to half the crop and was usually paid as rent-tax to the state.

Since the peasant, as tenant, was guaranteed land tenure in terms of cultivation rights not subject to confiscation, his livelihood was improved. In addition, the accumulation of land by the *yangban*, or office-holding aristocrats, was strictly controlled by the stipulation that status land would be granted only in the Kyŏnggi area around the capital, where the government could easily maintain supervision and surveillance.

By resolutely carrying out land reform. Yi Sŏng-gye and his followers grasped economic power. King Kongyang was forced to abdicate and Yi Sŏng-gye's followers placed Yi on the throne, bringing an end to the house of Wang. Yi Sŏng-gye renamed the kingdom Chosŏn and he was given the dynastic name of T'aejo. The establishment of institutions of Confucian learning was given first priority in order to institute a Confucian state. A college and five municipal schools were set up in Seoul, and local schools were established in all the magistracies. From these schools, Confucian-oriented scholar-officials were recruited for government office.

The *yangban* class acting in concert had power to interfere with the monarchial administration and decision-making procedures. Under Confucian precepts, the bureaucracy was to act as the agent of the monarch's will, since the monarch had a vested interest in benevolent rule. The monarch in turn had to heed the advice of Confucian scholars. In this connection the Office of Royal Lecturers and the Office of State Councilors (*Uijŏngbu*) were of prime importance. Below this were the six boards of administration—civil appointment, taxation, rites, military, punishment and public works— the principal government organizations in the capital. In provincial areas administrative divisions and magistrates under provincial governors carried out local administration.

The Censorate Offices submitted memorials and remonstrances to the monarch and had the authority to ratify and rectify the monarch's appointment of officials and his renovative decrees. The court historians, who were to record daily happenings in the court and make verbatim records of the royal conversation, were empowered to criticize and keep the monarch under surveillance.

In order to enhance Confucian learning, movable metal type was cast for the printing of Confucian classics and historical literature in 1403. Typography was developed and improved by the repeated casting of new fonts as a means of promoting Confucian studies for the welfare and prosperity of the state.

Sejong's Confucian Humanism

Chosŏn's fourth king, Sejong (r.1418-50), was noted for his mastery of Confucian learning. In addition to his internalization of Confucian values, he showed himself able to successfully deal with the *yangban* scholars. His rule in the mid-15th century was marked by progressive ideas in administration, phonetics, national script, economics, science, music, medical science and humanistic studies. He established the *Chiphyŏnjŏn* (Hall of Worthies) in order to promote research in institutional traditions and politico-economics.

Sejong showed great concern for the livelihood of the peasants, providing relief in time of drought and flood. He had Chŏng Ch'o compile the *Nongsa chiksŏl* (Straight Talk on Farming), a volume replete with information collected from experienced elder peasants throughout the country. The first of its kind in Korea, this became the classic work on Korean agriculture. He also put into effect a sliding tax scale which eased the peasants' burden. Sejong ordered the development of the pluviometer in 1442 and distributed duplicates to the Office of Astronomy in Seoul and to local magistrates to record precipitation. This preceded Gastelli's pluviometer of 1639 by almost 200 years.

One of his most celebrated achievements was the creation of the Korean alphabet, *Han-gŭl*. It was as awareness that his people must have a writing system designed to express the language of their everyday speech, and a desire that all his subjects be able to learn and use it that impelled King Sejong to have scholars of the Hall of Worthies devise the alphabet. The Korean alphabet, consisting of 11 vowels and 28 consonants possessing geometic beauty, simplicity, and scientific accuracy, is such that an uneducated man can learn it in a few hours.

Confucian scholars raised considerable opposition and protested that the use of Korean script would retard Confucian studies. Sejong persisted in his determination to promote *Han-gŭl* for the benefit of the people, and *Hunmin chŏng-ŭm*, or "The Correct Sounds for the Instruction of the People", was distributed in 1446.

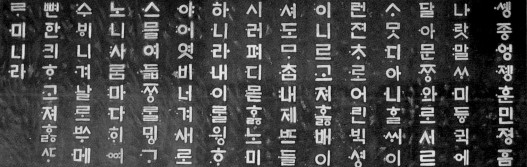

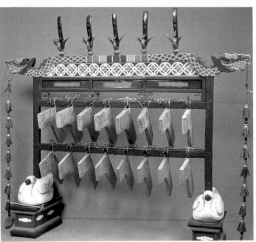

King Sejong is known for the creation of an alphabet for the Korean language, then called hunminchŏng-ŭm or "script for the people" and shown here in a monument celebrating its creation (top), and for his encouragement of scientific and musical invention which resulted in a water clock (center, left) and p'yŏn-gyŏng,a set of chimes (bottom). An illustration from the Samgang-haengshildo, a book about loyal subjects, filial sons and faithful wives edited by SŏlSun on the orders of King Sejong in 1431 (above).

The official written language continued to be Chinese, as was Latin in Europe, but now the Korean people had at their disposal a means of writing their own language. A bilingual poetic eulogy on the foundings of the dynasty *Yŏngbiŏch'ŏn ka* (Songs of Flying Dragons) was composed in Korean as well as in Chinese, and the *Sŏkpo sangjŏl* (Episodes from the Life of the Buddha) was translated into Korean. These works laid the foundation for practical use of the Korean script.

Sejong showed his concern for the health of the people by ordering the compilation of medical books. A 365-chapter compendium on Chinese medicine as well as the *Hyangyakchipsŏngbang* (A Compilation of Native Korean Prescriptions) in 85 chapters, was completed in 1433. This latter included 959 entries on disease diagnoses, 10,706 prescriptions, and 1,477 items on acupuncture therapy. Another book on how to collect local medicinal material was published in the vernacular language.

Sejong's interest in astronomical science was comprehensive and sun dials, water clocks, orreries of the solar system, celestial globes, astronomical maps, and atlases of the seven planets were produced at his instigation. He had a notation system for Korean as well as Chinese music devised or revised, and had one of his talented subjects, Pak Yŏn, improve musical instruments of various kinds and compose a sort of orchestral music.

In foreign relations, Sejong took strong measures against the Jurchen tribes. The territory in the northeastern frontier area was restored, and six fortresses were established after General Kim Chong-sŏ quelled the Jurchen invaders in 1434. In 1443 Sejong installed four counties on the northern border, and opened three ports to the Japanese to help trade. Sejong's land tax reform, health policy and invention of the Korean alphabet all contributed to the improvement of life and hence the awakening of the people.

Sejong was able to bring the Confucian state to realization in the true sense of the word, and to engender a modern national consciousness in the minds of the people. Although he had earlier confiscated temple lands and bondsmen and

otherwise restricted Buddhism, he later became especially devoted to that faith after the death of his beloved queen. His health declined in that period, and he abdicated the throne to his son Munjong (r.1450-52). Unfortunately, his legacy of stability and prosperity was not sustained by his short-lived successors.

Monarchy versus *Yangban*

King Munjong's death in 1452 brought an 11-year-old prince to the throne. State affairs were left in the hands of state councilors, and the monarchical power declined. In 1455, the unscrupulous Prince Suyang, uncle of the child-king Tanjong, usurped the throne by murder and regicide after quelling the opposition of officials and military officers, and ruthlessly suppressing attempts to restore Tanjong.

King Sejo (r.1455-68), as Prince Suyang is officially known, closed the Hall of Worthies, abolished some posts in the Censorate Offices, and crippled the Office of Royal Lecturers (*Kyŏngyŏn*), all measures designed to loosen the ideological restraints on the monarchy. The Office of Study Promotion was instituted, ostensibly as a means of promoting Confucianism. In fact, it was used merely as a royal library rather than an organization designed to promote and propagate Confucian ideals. Further, he initiated the practice of giving private audiences to individual officials, flouting the regulation which made the presence of historians and censorate officials mandatory at royal audiences.

An attempt to raise the status of the monarchy was, however, justified, as formerly the Korean monarch had been vulnerable to inordinate *yangban* pressure. Yang Sŏng-ji, a talented scholar under Sejong, advocated the monarch's cause in his memorials. Yang stressed Korea's unique position, asserting the need to preserve indigenous traditions—Tan-gun, according to him, was the "Son-of-Heaven Ruler." He formulated the proposition that Korea, like China, was a nation upon which the "Mandate of Heaven" was bestowed. This argument strengthened Sejo's hand vis-a-vis the bureaucracy.

None of the Yi kings had been strong enough to defy the *yangban* officials by praying in person at the Temple of Heaven, where the Son of Heaven alone was qualified to converse with the Heavenly God. Sejo, however, in his sacrificial ode to the Heavenly God at the Temple of Heaven, used the phrase "the founder of the dynasty, the imperial great-great grandfather, T'aejo (founder king Yi Sŏng-gye)."

Sejo ordered the compilation of a detailed map of Korea to provide further control of outlying areas. Census-taking of all soldiers and reserves in the various districts was enforced, and the Civil Register Act requiring all citizens to carry identification tags was reinforced. He installed large military garrisons in each province and ordered every town to produce arms.

By arranging generous land grants and medicine, Sejo showed his concern for the welfare of the army. He also ordered the migration of people to the sparsely populated northern border areas.

The monarch acted decisively in the matter of recruitment of new officials, increasing the number of military graduates to further strengthen the monarchial power. He also gave the title of "Meritorious Subject" to various officials on three different occasions to widen the base of loyal support. With the increase of inheritable land grants to meritorious subjects, however, land available for the newly-appointed officials decreased. To solve this problem and to limit the economic power of the officials and *yangban*, Sejo instituted the official land system, which allowed land grants in terms of rent for office tenure only. Thus the status land system by which the *yangban* enjoyed life-time tenure was discontinued, and those parties who refused to compromise lost their land holdings. This limitation of land grants to incumbent officials meant that the old landed *yangban* class changed to either an employed bureaucracy with land or landless *yangban* with prestige only.

Sejo offered interim civil and military service examinations more often, in addition to the time-honored examinations given every three years. Since the number of successful candidates in the interim examinations exceeded those from fixed examinations by a ratio of two to one, this virtually brought the civil examination system under the monarch's sway.

To divert the attention of the Neo-Confucian scholars, Sejo defied Confucian orthodoxy by supporting Taoism and Buddhism. An Office for Publication of Buddhist Scriptures was established, where the compilation of Buddhist literature and Korean translation of such literature became active. Fifty copies of the bulky Koryŏ *Tripitaka* were printed for distribution. To equip the often Sinocentric scholars with a comprehensive history of their own country, the compilation of *Tongguk T'onggam* (Comprehensive Mirror of the Eastern Kingdom) began in 1458 and was completed after the king's death.

During this time, the compilation of the Grand Code for State Administration was initiated. The *Kyŏngguk Taejŏn* (National Code), became the corner-stone of the dynastic administration and provided the monarchial system with a sort of constitutional law in written form.

Resurgence of Neo-Confucian Rule

The child-king Sŏngjong (r.1469-94) ascended to the throne and ruled under the regency of the dowager queen and minister-consultants. The anti-Sejo literati used the institution of the royal lecture to try to abolish Buddhist rituals and other anomalies in the life of the court, and the unfortunate child was subjected to a rigorous schedule of two to four royal lectures per day. The Office of Study Promotion was expanded to serve as a censorate in addition to providing royal lecturers. Heavy Confucian indoctrination was the order of the day, and state support of Buddhism gradually diminished. During Songjong's reign, officials' rights to collect tax and rent from official land as personal income began to wane.

Young scholars were treated well and given opportunities at the newly-established Hall of Leave for Study, and Confucianism once again found its place in the royal administration. An ambitious publication program was implemented, producing such works as a compendium of Korean historical geography; also issued were an anthology of Korean-Chinese literature, and an illustrated text on traditional music.

Such efforts to restore Confucian rule were not sufficient to satisfy the scholarly in general, however. Those among them who had suffered discrimination during Sejo's reign gained a foot-hold at court, but economic conditions were not greatly improved. Following the implementation of central collection and distribution of rent on the officials' land, the officials and *yangban* sought land control in terms of the right to cultivate, thereby encroaching upon the peasant's share of landed rights. Moreover, land area grew as a result of reclamation, and this contributed further to the growth of agricultural estates, a process which the dynasty attempted to prevent. Some agricultural estates gathered bondsmen and peasants, some of whom abandoned their free status in order to escape the heavy land tax, corvee, and tribute taxes.

The desire to hold landed interests became more intense, as the path to governmental appointment was open to the anti-Sejo factions but competition for such appointments became fiercer. Those who were already established as the owners of meritorious subject land, special land grants, reclaimed land, or accumulated landed rights to cultivate were becoming targets of criticism.

The literati upheld the family and clan rites and etiquette prescribed by neo-Confucian doctrine, but were impoverished by the costly rituals involved—marriages, funerals, and memorial ceremonies. To maintain themselves, the literati depended heavily on their kinship ties, relying on assistance given by an appointed official of the same kin group. These mutual assistance relationships affected both officials in the capital, and landed *yangban* in the outlying areas as well. This was also a key factor in the politico-economic life of each *yangban* during the Chosŏn Dynasty and was intensified during Sŏngjong's reign. Kim Chong-jik (1432-92) was a leading scholar-official with many followers, who advocated the Neo-Confucian rectification theory which implied condemnation of Sejo's usurpation. His success represented for a while the peak of the resurgent Neo-Confucian school.

Sŏngjong's successor in 1495 was Prince Yŏn-san, whose reign was noted for his unscrupulous suppression of the literati. In the initial period, he was hard pressed by that clamorous group which opposed Buddhist rituals observed at the death of the Queen Mother. Infuriated by the hundreds of memorials and protests made by the Neo-Confucian literati, Yŏnsan-gun lashed out at them. His first purge was based on an accusation of state crimes because one of Kim Chong-jik's students had implicitly criticized Sejo's usurpation in his historical notes. By this purge and another which followed in 1504, Yŏnsan-gun eliminated the checks exercised by historians, the censorate, and state councilors. Confucian statecraft almost collapsed. His extraordinary anti-Confucian and anti-Buddhist acts contravened the Grand Code for State Administration and dismayed the *yangban* as a whole until he was finally deposed.

It fell to Chungjong (r.1506-44), supported by the officials who had deposed Yŏnsan, to restore Confucian rule. The resurgence of the Neo-Confucian school made the enhancement of the economic status of the literati an urgent necessity. Some were rewarded with meritorious subject land, but others found a solution through securing charters for private schools endowed with some land and bondsmen. Such local private schools became intellectual training centers for schools of thought as well as for kin groups.

The increase of refugee peasants contributed to the ever increasing burden of taxes upon the remaining peasants. Cho Kwang-jo, an influential school official, advocated the recommendation system for recruitment of government officials and the organization of local guilds to improve the impoverished condition of the literati. The recommendation system was implemented and his group was recruited for official posts, but this alone did not satisfy them since they were not rewarded with appropriate land. In 1519, the year they achieved their goal of implementing the recommendation examination system, these Neo-Confucian scholars faced a spurious charge of treason.

The ministers and the literati were often embroiled in royal succession problems, and competed among themselves for places in the bureaucracy, especially since their numbers had rapidly increased with the expansion of private schools. Their common interests based on local school and kinship organizations were bound to spilt them into factions, all the more bitterly divided for being within the same status. The number of private schools exceeded one hundred in the late 16th century, and eminent scholars of the Neo-Confucian philosophy sheltered themselves in such institutions.

As for the people in general, they were hard-pressed by the levies of land tax, corvee, military tax, service and especially tribute tax, which was collected by authorized agents. The growth of agricultural estates accelerated, contributing further to the decline of the peasant economy. A righteous outlaw named Im Kkŏk-chŏng rose up against the greedy officials. Recruiting a large group of peasants, he confiscated the wealth of rich *yangban* officials and distributed it to the poor. He seized government granaries and gave relief to hungry people in the provinces of Kyŏnggi-do and Hwanghae-do. Although he was caught and beheaded in 1562, his chivalry and revolutionary ideas captured the admiration of the people and inspired the popular novel, *The Tale of Hong Kil-tong*.

Resistance Against Japanese

The founder-king T'aejo, as noted, distinguished himself in resistance against Japanese marauders. After the latter's depredations had ceased, Korea opened three ports for trade with Japanese feudal lords, giving investiture to the Tsushima lord who had been engaged in lucrative trade with other ranking Japanese. The Japanese liaison officers staying at these ports caused trouble at times, however, and the amount of Korea's grant was reduced.

After the assassination of Oda Nobunaga, who temporarily called a truce among Japan's warring lords, Toyotomi Hideyoshi rose to power in 1590. Hideyoshi's problem was to find a way to weaken the powerful feudal lords of the western part of Japan. In this explosive domes-

tic situation, he looked abroad and decided that an invasion of China would provide the outlet needed for a peaceful solution at home. When Korea rejected Hideyoshi's request for aid in attacking China, he ordered his generals to invade Korea in 1592. The Japanese army, armed with matchlock guns with which Korean soldiers were not familiar, reached Seoul within two weeks. They had attempted to invade the granary province of Chŏlla-do, only to meet the strong resistance of the people led by General Kim Shi-min at Chinju. They then turned back towards Seoul.

King Sŏnjo and the royal princes fled to the northern provinces and appealed to the Ming Emperor for aid against the invaders. The Japanese generals squabbled among themselves, while Korean Admiral Yi Sun-shin conducted a brilliant series of operations in the Korean Straits, destroying many Japanese ships. The ironclad *Kŏbuksŏn*,(turtle ships) which Admiral Yi improved with plated armor resembling a turtle shell, protected the sailors and marines, and were more than a match for anything else afloat.

With the appearance of Ming contingents, the Japanese were forced to fight a combined Ming-Korean army. Cut off from supplies and reinforcements owing to Admiral Yi's control of the sea, the Japanese were hard pressed. A Korean volunteer army organized in the southern provinces harassed them with guerrilla tactics, while disease and malnutrition took its toll. Peace negotiations were held between the Ming general and the Japanese, who had by then lost the will to fight and started to retreat, stalked by volunteer peasant forces and contingents of Buddhist monks.

Peace negotiations dragged on for five years but proved fruitless, and Hideyoshi sent his army to Korea again in 1597. The invasion this time encompassed only Kyŏngsang-do and part of the Chŏlla-do provinces, as the invaders were harassed by the volunteer army.

The Japanese retreated and Hideyoshi's death forced the evacuation of his forces. Admiral Yi, in his attempt to smash the Japanese retreat, was struck by a stray bullet and killed during a climactic naval battle. The war ended at long

A picture depicting a Kŏbuksŏn, *turtle boat, which successfully harassed the invading Japanese forces off the southern coast in the 16th century.*

last, with grave impact upon Korea, Ming China, and Japan.

Impact of the War

The results of the Hideyoshi invasion included destruction of governmental records, cultural objects, archives, historical documents and works of art, devastation of land, decrease of population, and loss of artisans and technicians. Arable land amounted to only one third of the prewar acreage, and the resulting decrease of revenue necessitated additional taxation of less devastated provinces such as Kyŏnggi-do and Ch'ungch'ŏng-do. The government resorted to selling official titles and *yangban* status, and on one occasion held an examination for government service open to the bondsman class. The loss of artisans brought a decline in handiwork quality, as well as in manufactured goods such as pottery and book printing. The Neo-Confucian norms and values were shaken, and the class distinctions which the *yangban* tried to uphold began to crumble.

The Japanese, on the other hand, achieved a peaceful, centralized feudal society under Hideyoshi's successor, Tokugawa Ieyasu. Importation of the political philosophy of Neo-Confucianism and the study of medicinal materials and therapy developed in Korea helped Japanese scholars to make significant contributions to their society. The introduction of typography with movable metal type expedited book printing, and Korean artisans captured by the Japanese army developed ceramic and textile products. After the Tokugawa takeover, Japan wanted peaceful diplomatic relations with Korea in order to benefit further from the

Korean version of Chinese culture.

For Ming China the results were catastrophic. The economic setback suffered in the campaign later led to the collapse of the dynasty.

Late Chosŏn Period

The postwar period of the 17th century in Korea witnessed a social and economic transformation. The rise of wealthy merchants contributed to the decline of the *yangban* society, while financial difficulty drove the government repeatedly to undertake tax reforms and sales of titles. Upward social mobility, almost unknown in the prewar period, began to take place. Rich peasants and merchants acquired *yangban* status, and *nobi* bondsmen were able to purchase freedom.

Neo-Confucian orthodoxy was called into question by a rising critical spirit which engendered distrust of the *yangban*. The impact of western culture entering through China gave further impetus to pragmatic studies which called for socio-economic reforms and readjustments. Factional strife intensified. Attention was drawn to agricultural problems as more *yangban*—dropouts from the struggle for power—became involved in cultivation of the land. As a result, agromanagerial techniques and production methods were steadily improved. Privately operated handicraft factories replaced government-operated ones, stimulating the production of goods for sale.

The increase in mercantile activities expedited the rise of commercial farming, which in turn began to transform rural life. The circulation of coin currency spread, providing a bridge between rural life and city economy. The rise of popular verse and fiction drew the attention of the people to abuses and encouraged participation in social reforms.

Postwar Readjustment

The urgent tasks of the postwar period were reorganization of the defense forces and increase of state revenues. The Border Defense Council (*Pibyŏnsa*) was elevated to the status of a *de facto* decision-making body. A national defense council consisting of state councilors, ministers of the six boards and military staff generals made important decisions ranging from war to selection of a crown prince.

The arts of war which had proved to be effective in defense against Japanese pirates on the south China coast were given first priority in the postwar defense activity. This system of army training, however, required an additional budget which had to be collected as taxes from the peasants. Privately-owned bondsmen, who had previously been exempted from military service, were recruited for training, and had a new reason to consider themselves equal to commoners.

The reconstruction of palace buildings and the printing of lost books, such as duplicate sets of the *Chosŏn Wangjo Shillok* (Annals of the Dynasty of Chosŏn), land ledgers, and census records, all required extra funds. Wooden printing type was carved because of the metal shortage brought about by arms production. Books were sold to pay for expenses, contrary to the prewar practice. Efforts were made to revive the peasant economy, the main source of revenue.

Medical care for the disease-stricken populace was an urgent need and gave impetus to the compilation of medical treatises such as *Tongŭi Pogam* (Exemplar of Korean Medicine), which was completed in 1610.

The system of recruitment for the bureaucracy by merit had long deteriorated, as both civil and military service examinations virtually became levers in the hands of powerful officials and the faction in power. The irregular special examination graduates created a pressing demand for land, at the same time the practice of holding unregistered land was draining state revenue. As some *yangban* sought control of tax-free school land, the number of private schools quadrupled during the 17th century alone, multiplying the school estates which sheltered an increasing number of literati and students.

The royal relatives and officials in power accumulated land deserted in wartime and converted it into tax-exempt holdings. Competition for office became intense, since a term in office could easily lead to economic advantage. The factional split in 1585 was between a younger and an elder group of scholars, called the *Tongin* (Eastern) faction and the *Sŏin* (Western) faction respectively and this rivalry was intensified under the postwar financial difficulties. Splits often occurred over issues such as the question of selection of the crown prince and rituals of royal mourning.

The *Tongin* faction divided again into the *Namin* (Southern) faction and the *Pukin* (Northern) faction, and the latter gained power during the reign of Kwanghaegun (r.1608-23), who made efforts to restore the Confucian state. When the Manchus rose up against Ming China, who asked Korea for assistance, Kwanghaegun, mindful of the assistance rendered by the Chinese in Korea's struggle against the Japanese, promptly sent an army of 10,000. However, when it became obvious the Manchus would be victorious, the Koreans quickly surrendered thus avoiding any retaliation.

In the aftermath of this switch, Kwanghaegun was deposed by the newly ascendant *Sŏin* faction which was pro-Ming. The insurrection which ensued demonstrated the necessity of strengthening the defense of the capital area. Accordingly, new camps were built around the capital city, and the fortress of Namhansansŏng was constructed for its protection.

The Manchus thus felt the need to eliminate any threat from Korea. The peace treaty concluded after the first Manchu invasion stipulated that Korea would come to the aid of the Manchus, not the Ming. Upon King Injo's (r.1623-49) refusal to acknowledge a suzerain-vassal relationship in 1636, the Manchu ruler, now enthroned as the Ch'ing Emperor of China, invaded Korea. King Injo fled to Namhansansŏng, then capitulated to the invaders on a bank of the Han-gang River. He agreed to break relations with the defeated Ming and to send princes as hostages.

This personal surrender of King Injo was a double blow to the monarchy and *yangban*, as the nation had to acknowledge subservience to the "pagan" tribes of the Manchu. Distrust of the orthodox Neo-Confucian *yangban* began to grow in the minds of the people, who had been denied an opportunity to resist the Ch'ing army.

A deep sense of humiliation and disgrace was felt, and sympathy toward Ming was strong. The peasants and bondsmen openly ridiculed the *yangban*, and offspring of interclass mating, mostly between *yangban* male and non-*yangban* female, became a serious social problem. These included sons of prominent officials, who nevertheless were considered outcasts and banned from governmental service.

Resentment of the rigid social stratification as described in the previously mentioned *Tale of Hong Kil-tong* spurred the rise of revolutionary ideas. The basic theme in the novel—that all men were created equal—gave encouragement to the people and undermined the prestige of the *yangban* society.

Tax Reforms

During this period, there was a gradual rise of subordinate agents of the tribute-tax collector who collected extraordinary additional amounts. This practice, started in the prewar period, became so rampant that peasants often turned over their land to powerful *yangban*, who would then help them to withdraw the land from registration so that the *yangban* could collect the tax themselves.

Attempts to convert the tribute-tax to an additional tax on land were partly successful. An additional tax on land, *Taedongbŏp* (Uniform Land Tax Law), was vigorously advocated by Kim Yuk, the chief minister of King Hyojong (r.1649-59). Its implementation proved highly advantageous both to state revenues and to the lot of the peasants. Such an outcome was especially valuable to King Hyojong, whose aim was to strengthen the army and increase national revenue so as to oppose the Ch'ing. As a further revenue measure, he decreed a universal tax in exchange for exemption from military service to be paid by all males, even monks.

Hyojong's anti-Ch'ing ideas came to naught, as in 1654 and 1658 he was forced to send trained military men at the request of Ch'ing

China to help them fight in Manchuria against Russian invaders. His economic policies were more effective and the population more than doubled in the ten years after his death.

The increase in the national population from 2,290,000 in 1657 to 5,018,000 in 1669 was remarkable. The Seoul population grew from 80,572 to 194,030 in the same period. The national increase was largely due to the enforcement of tax reforms and the improvement in agromanagerial and agricultural techniques. The increase in the Seoul population can be attributed to the influx of merchants dealing in goods no longer paid to the government as tribute-tax.

After the *Taedongpŏp* (Uniform Land Tax Law) was implemented in most parts of the country the governmental demand for local products in kind was met by merchants who became purchase agents for that purpose. Acquiring the privilege of monopoly, they set the pattern for the guilds which spread nationwide. The decline of government-operated workshops and manufacture stimulated artisans and technicians to create private workshops and to go into business as dealers in their own products, often forming into guilds.

In the provincial towns, markets were held every five days, serving as channels between producers and Seoul merchants. The licensed suppliers of local products in Seoul gradually accumulated capital with their lucrative and guaranteed transactions.

Thus a new notion of wealth came into being: that of mercantile wealth, consisting no longer of land and bondsmen but of commodities for quantitative trade in money. Commercial capital was given a foundation on which to grow, as trade flourished and currency circulated. However, these efforts, whose purpose was to preserve the Confucian *yangban* society, led to the erosion of that same society.

Rise of a Reformist School

With the death of Hyojong, the *yangban* no longer paid the universal military service tax, and were once again virtually exempted from military service. A critical attitude developed among the out-of-power *yangban* as an obstacle to social progress. Yun Hyu and Pak Se-dang were among the prominent scholars who attacked the idolized system of Chu Hsi. Conservative *yangban* branded them as heretics, but the time was ripe for the rise of a new school of thought committed to criticism of the traditional order.

To the new generation of scholars, the living conditions of the people meant more than the problems of legitimacy and ritual so dear to the literati of the Neo-Confucian bureaucracy. "No nation can survive without the well-being of the peasant, whereas the people can flourish even without a monarch." Such was the modern thinking that underlay the reformist school's pragmatic studies.

Yu Hyŏng-won in his *Pan'gye-surok* (Essays on Social Reform) suggested the following measures: the establishment of a land system under which benefits could be shared equitably by all; the institution of the recommendation system, replacing civil service examinations; the establishment of equal opportunities for all men; the reform of government organization; and the adoption of new learning. His proposals found no official acceptance, but his reformist school of thought became the mainstream of pragmatic studies. Emphasis was given to agriculture, since the success of the suggested reforms depended upon the solution of agricultural problems. The need for pragmatic studies was keenly felt by scholars who were removed from the bureaucracy. The latter, on the other hand was preoccupied with internal power struggles, and factions clashed over differing interpretations of Neo-Confucian rites.

During the latter half of the 17th century, the struggle for power among the factions became fierce and more factions split off, among which the *Noron* faction, or the elder group, and the *Soron,* the younger group, were prominent. Such factional strife had nothing to do with the life of the peasant or the national interests. The majority of the younger group began to show concern over the well-being of the peasants, whose condition was closer to their own, since many of the *yangban* engaged in farming and could not even afford to hold bondsmen.

It was in this process of social-economic change that the reformist school confronted the demands of society. Mercantile activities continued to grow with the development of government-licensed supplier guilds on a nationwide scale as, their transactions accounted for 60 percent of the total government revenue. Government revenues were constantly growing during this period, and some wealthy farmers converted their status to that of *yangban*. The population growth kept pace as well, increasing by almost two million in the 48 years from 1669 to 1717.

King Yŏngjo's Reforms

Realizing its detrimental effects on state administration, King Yŏngjo (r.1724-76) attempted to end factional strife as soon as he ascended the throne. To reinstate the short-lived universal military service tax, he even came out of the palace gate and solicited the opinions of officials, literati, soldiers, and peasants. He reduced the military service tax by half, and ordered the deficiency supplemented by the taxes on fisheries, salt, vessels, and an additional land tax. Yŏngjo also regularized the financial system of state revenues and expenses by adopting an accounting system. His realistic policies allowed the payment of taxes in grain in the remote Kyŏngsang-do province to nearby ports, and payment in cotton or cash for grain in mountainous areas. The circulation of currency was encouraged by increased coin casting.

His concern for the improvement of peasant life was manifest in his eagerness to educate the people by distributing important books in Korean script, including books on agriculture.

The pluviometer was again manufactured in quantity and distributed to local offices, and extensive public works were undertaken. Yŏngjo upgraded the status of the offspring of commoners, opening another possibility for upward social mobility. His policies were intended to reassert the Confucian monarchy and humanistic rule, but they could not stem the tide of social change.

Mercantile activities increased in volume at a rapid rate in the 18th century. There was accumulation of capital through monopoly and wholesaling that expanded through guild organization. Many merchants were concentrated in Seoul. The traditional divisions of government-chartered shops, the licensed tribute-goods supplier, and the small shopkeepers in the alleys and streets, were integrated into the fabric of a monopoly and wholesale system. The temporary shops were originally set up to meet the demands of the people on special occasions, such as civil service examinations, royal processions, and other national events, but they continued after the events to supply the general populace with groceries and sundry items. Operated by poor shop-keepers in temporary huts, they were for the most part dependent on the wholesale merchants. As a result, the wholesale merchant's price policies had direct impact on the life of the populace of Seoul.

The artisans often became self-employed producers. Some even developed into factory owners and obtained charters of monopoly for the sale of their products. In some cases, it proved more lucrative simply to be a wholesale dealer in certain commodities than to engage in the production of goods. It was becoming a fashion among merchants and artisans to obtain charters by creating a new commodity through minor refinement of goods already chartered. The charter ensured monopoly and the protection of the government.

The so-called estuary merchants monopolized commodities from the provinces of Kyŏnggi-do and Ch'ungch'ŏng-do, and other wholesale merchants had nationwide networks for the sale of ginseng. The merchants of Kaesŏng or Songdo competed vigorously with their Seoul counterparts in wholesale activities, conducting tripartite international trade between Japan and China; they traded ginseng and other Korean products for Japanese silver and Chinese books and silk. They even accompanied the envoy missions to China in their quest for gain. They went into the business of buying up paper for trade to China from the original producers in Buddhist temples, horse hair for hats from the remote southern island of Chejudo, and otter fur from hunters on the east coast.

The constant movement of trading ships

between and among these remote ports is described in Yi Chung-hwan's *T'aengnichi* (Ecological Guide to Korea) and depicted in Yi In-mun's painting, the *Inexhaustible Rivers and Mountains.*

The monopoly and wholesale activities created a larger demand for silver and copper, which in turn gave impetus to the mining industry. Under strict control of the government in pre-war times, mines were turned over to private operators. In the 17th century, 68 silver mines were in operation but copper mining was not well developed, as copper was supplied by Japan. In the 18th century, however, copper mines were also developed when the Japanese stopped exporting copper and Ch'ing demanded great supplies of it.

The constant rise in price of commodities would have threatened the livelihood of the populace of Seoul had they not been involved one way or another in mercantile activities. Regardless of status, many *yangban* and commoners engaged in some kind of merchant activity.

Thus Seoul made great strides as a commercial and industrial city in the 18th century. The popular demand for handicraft goods such as knives, horse hair hats, dining tables and brassware was ever increasing. Restrictions on the wearing of the horse hair hat, originally a symbol of *yangban* status, virtually disappeared.

The increase in the number of *yangban* had been the cause of their impoverishment, as their land-holdings had to be divided equally among the sons at the least, and often the daughter too, whether married or not. The *yangban* of declining fortunes had the choice of either engaging in agriculture as owner-cultivator, or in lucrative enterprises indirectly. Money-lending was another field they entered as trade and currency circulation expanded.

The notion that commerce and industry were marginal occupations needed changing, and the necessity for learning from Ch'ing China was urged. Pak Chi-won, Pak Che-ga, and others who had traveled to Ch'ing with the Korean envoy missions witnessed the development of commerce and manufacturing industry there. Upon returning to Korea they proposed positive

policies for the development of commerce, metallurgy, fishing, stock farming, horticulture, and mining.

Even the pirating of books became commercialized, as competition developed among well-to-do *yangban* in the publication of collected literary works of renowned ancestors. This led to the printing of popular fiction and poetry. The people especially appreciated satire and social criticism. *The Story of Ch'unhyang,* telling of the fidelity of an entertainer's daughter, was widely read as it was full of satire directed against the greed and snobbery of officials.

Development of Agriculture

The development of trade and manufacturing stimulated agricultural diversity. Commercial farming of ginseng, hemp, tobacco, and medicinal herbs was practiced in various parts of the country. Improved agricultural techniques increased yields. For example, transplantation of rice, which had been common only in the fields of Chŏlla-do, Kyŏngsang-do, Kangwon-do provinces, now spread northward to the provinces of Ch'ungchŏng-do, Kyŏnggi-do and Hwanghae-do. This technique not only yielded more rice, but allowed two crops a year, barley and rice.

The improved ratio between productivity and labor gave peasants incentive to revolutionize agromanagerial procedures, since it was possible for them to rise to wealth through managerial expansion. The wealthy *yangban* and peasants gradually enlarged their farm lands by renting other land. This drove the poor peasants elsewhere for employment in cities, mining, and manufacturing. Some became mountain recluses, living by slash-and-burn agriculture practices.

The land-tax burden was shifted to the tenant farmers. As in other decaying medieval societies, this sort of socio-economic change drove the poor peasant further into poverty. The well-to-do peasants on the other hand were able to purchase *yangban* titles which increased their prestige and power in the local society.

Rules were set for sale of titles, and there was

Genre painting by Shin Yun-bok (Hyewon) of the Chosŏn Dynasty: while men work in the field, women prepare food for them

a gradual rise in such sales as the government was often faced with a shortage of revenue. Bondsmen were emancipated and often became owners of land and other bondsmen. The increase of *yangban* from the 1690s to the 1850s was fantastic. In these years, the number in some sectors increased from 9.2 to 70.2 percent of the population, whereas the commoners, mostly peasants, decreased from 53.7 to 28.2 percent, and bondsmen from 37.1 to 1.5 percent. This upward social mobility was a result of the exploitation of newly created wealth by a chronically deficit-ridden government. The forging and purchase of genealogies conferring social recognition on members of the non *yangban* class was prevalent in the 18th century.

There was, however, another side to the picture. Some *yangban* actually descended to the status of commoner, and began to intermarry with peasants and other lower classes. Government offices, unable to afford the support of bondsmen, gradually freed them in return for tribute or a lump-sum tax payment. The number of office-owned bondsmen decreased from 190,000 in the 17th century to 27,000 in the mid-18th century. Bondsmen privately owned by *yangban* numbered 400,000 in 1623, but decreased sharply in the course of social change, and many of the *yangban* could not afford to hold even a single bondsmen. Under such conditions some private bondsman became part-tenant and part-free cultivators. Finally, in 1801, all bondsmen registers of government offices and palaces were destroyed by the government to assure their emancipation.

Pragmatic Studies

The urge to learn about Ch'ing China was basically oriented towards the well-being of Korea. The rise of pragmatic studies continued, as many scholars attempted to seek the solution to social problems by administrative reforms in land distribution and agricultural improvement, emphasizing limitation of landholding and application of egalitarian principles in land tenure. Yi Ik proposed the creation of an open society by abolishment of class distinctions and emancipation of bondsmen. Pak Chi-won wrote stories ridiculing the idle, unproductive and pretentious way of life of the *yangban*. For the social advancement of Korea, he advocated improvement of agricultural equipment, irrigation systems and new cultivation techniques. There were scholars like Pak Che-ga, Yi Tŏkmu and Hong Tae-yong who recommended that Korea import western techniques and participate in international trade along with Ch'ing China. They were the vanguard of a movement that was destined to destroy the traditional *yangban* attitude toward technology and commerce.

Even while absorbing western culture and techniques by way of China, concern for Korea's identity began to revive as Koreans began to study their own history, geography, language, and epigraphy. Painters departed from traditional China-oriented painting styles and began to paint the scenery and life of Korea. An Chong-bok asserted an independent Korean line in Korea's historiography by emphasizing Tan-gun and Kija as the first legitimate rulers. This reinterpretation can be seen as parallel to Chu Hsi's legitimation by Shu Han of China's three states period. An's contribution to the historiography of Korea was his emphasis on the role of the people who expelled foreign invaders. He reprimanded the ruling classes for having mainly concerned themselves with how best to exploit the people.

His book *Tongsa Kangmok* (Annotated Account of Korean History) made a lasting impression on such modern historians as Pak Ŭn-shik and Shin Ch'ae-ho. Han Ch'i-yun paid great attention to the states of Koguryŏ and Parhae, viewing the latter as an integral part of Korean history. In the same vein, Yŭ Tuk-kong, another historian, wrote a monograph on Parhae.

Historical geography kept pace with other branches of historical study, and wood block cartography developed. Chŏng Sang-gi's ingenious scaling device stimulated Korean cartography. Kim Chŏng-ho created a scale map of modern cartographic precision on the basis of his indefatigable travels throughout the peninsula.

Compilation of books increased in the 18th century. *Tongguk-munhŏn pigo* (Reference Compilation of Documents on Korea) was supplemented; *Taejŏn-t'ongp'yŏn* (Comprehensive National Code) and the *Compendium of Korean Music* were compiled, as were diplomatic archives. King Chŏngjo (r.1776-1800), himself a scholar, employed young scholars of mixed origin in his newly-established Inner Royal Library for such projects.

For the economical publication of fine editions, movable metal type was repeatedly cast, and the carving of wooden type continued. The printing of fiction developed into a business enterprise in the 18th-19th century.

Korean typographical enterprise gave stimulus to developments in Ch'ing. The famous Chinese encyclopedia *Kuchin Tushu Chich'eng* was printed for the first time with movable copper type in 1772. *Ssuk'u Ch'uanshu*, the great Chinese bibliography, was printed with wooden type when a Korean Manchu, Chin Chien, suggested this economical method to the Ch'ienlung Emperor.

The people were strongly motivated to learn and import things for practical use in response to felt needs.

Emergence of Modern Culture

The most significant change in this period was the rise of the critical spirit and a new philosophy, which made deep inroads into the traditional Confucian outlook. The rise of popular novels and mass participation in cultural activities presaged the decline of traditional society.

In his popular novel, *The Tale of Hong Kiltong*, Hŏ Kyun (1569-1618) advocated popular revolt against misrule. His hero Hong Kil-tong, like the virtuous outlaw Im Kkŏk-chŏng, was enraged by governmental corruption and rose up against it. Hŏ Kyun realized that the lower class, if provoked to action, would become a powerful force, particularly since the peasant class would join in struggle for social justice. In his vision of needed social change, he saw in

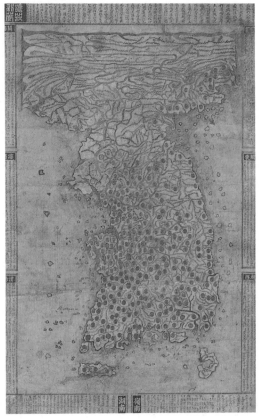

Two Korean maps, Tongguk-yŏ Chido, *circa 1720, and* Taedong-yŏ Chido, *circa 1861.*

passion between man and woman the dispensation of heaven itself, superseding the rigid relationships dignified as the Confucian norms.

Like the Renaissance philosophers, he made a bold departure from traditional norms and values, basing his morality on the true nature of man. It was Hŏ Kyun's conviction, eloquently expressed in his pioneer egalitarian novel, that every man was endowed with particular talents to survive, and ought not to be exploited by others. He found the class-divided, traditional society abominable.

In the *Tale of Ch'unhyang*, an unknown author exposes the corrupt magistracy and the decaying *yangban* ethos. Giving a happy ending to an interclass mating, he held out the promise of a brighter society characterized by equality and justice. This popular novel was also dramatized in quasi-operatic style.

Yi Su-gwang (1563-1628), probably the earliest Korean thinker to have contact with Catholic and European culture, stressed the idea that knowledge is of no value unless it results in action, just as enforcement is an essential part of the substance of law. His *Chibong-yusŏl* (Topical Discourses of Chibong) published in 1614, is an encyclopedic effort similar in inspiration to the work of French encyclopedists. It greatly expanded the knowledge available to Koreans of the countries of Europe and Southeast Asia, and explained the nature of Catholicism for the first time.

Pak Chi-won (1737-1805), a thinker comparable to Hŏ Kyun, declared that Heaven bestows unique talents on all men. His *Tale of the Yangban* describes a *yangban* who had done nothing but read while subsisting on government provender. To reimburse the government, the *yangban* sold his status to a merchant, but the latter discarded it when he realized that the essence of *yangban* life was idleness, corruption, and hypocrisy. The discrediting of the traditional *yangban* values left a void that was keenly felt, and it was in response to this need that pragmatic philosophy developed.

Hong Tae-yong (1731-83) in his scientific quest declared that "nothing is substantial without a sincere mind." He saw in natural science the essence of all spiritual activities, and refuted the traditional concept that science and technology were marginal branches of knowledge. The earth's rotation, the cause of eclipses and the nature of the rainbow were included among his scientifically valid findings, and his work in mathematics was no less noteworthy. He rated Western science and technology superior to anything T'ang or Sung civilization had to offer, and advocated the pursuit of such learning for the good of society.

Remarkable scientific achievement was made by Chŏng Yag-yong (Tasan, 1762-1836), who also was known for his deep concern for the peasants and people. His construction plan for the fortifications of Hwasŏng as Korea's emergency capital included the use of his own applications: cranes, windlasses, pulleys and specially designed vehicles. Yi Kyu-gyŏng as well compiled works on various branches of natural science. A collective work on astronomical and meteorological development in Korea was published in 1818.

Welfare Programs

The ideal of a Confucian welfare state was conceived and implemented by King Sejong in the 15th century, but it was Yi Su-gwang who elaborated on the philosophy of welfare in the period following the Hideyoshi invasions. He propounded the idea that the way was to be found among the people, and its noblest realization was to feed and clothe the people properly.

Pak Se-dang said he would go to the country and engage in manual labor, since Confucius endured labors more onerous than farming. Since such men espoused egalitarian principles, their concerns were more and more centered upon public welfare programs.

Yi Ik stated that learning or knowledge should not be sought unless it was of benefit to the daily life of the people in general. His sharp analysis of the causes of factionalism stemmed from a deep concern for a welfare policy.

Kim Yuk, who is known for his implementation of the *Taedongbŏp*, or Uniform Land Tax Law, recommended the increased use of vehicles. Hong Tae-yong and Pak Chi-won also saw increased vehicular traffic as promising great advantage for the national economy. Pak made a farsighted statement: "The ruler will be blamed by future generations for not having learned from pragmatic studies."

Chŏng Yag-yong was outstanding among the scholars who analyzed the evils of society and made positive proposals for reform. He saw the paramount importance of agriculture, stock-raising, fisheries, and sericulture. He advocated a system of land distribution based on egalitarian principles, and the placement of people in professions in accordance with their ability.

Exploitation continued, however, and distressed people sought salvation. Catholicism met the needs of many, since its tenets accorded with the new egalitarian principles in addition to stressing salvation. Some scholars were converted to Catholicism, and others benefitted from the scientific learning that accompanied the religion. The number of Catholics in Korea gradually increased.

Since Catholicism was opposed both to Confucian ancestral rituals and to rigid social stratification, Catholics were termed criminals by the state. Many of them, including prominent scholars such as Chŏng Yag-yong and his brothers, were punished or even executed.

Catholicism prospered secretly nonetheless, especially among artisans such as pottery makers. The negation of traditional values in a quest for salvation was an enigma to the Confucian-oriented *yangban* officials, and they resorted to various means of suppressing the alien faith. It was evident that the men in power were far behind the people in their social and

Two illustrations from the Dutchman Hendrik Hamel's Description du Royaume de Coree, Amsterdam, 1668: *the one on the left is of his boat drifting and the other depicts his landing on Chejudo Island. Hamel was one of the first Europeans to visit Korea.*

intellectual consciousness.

For the welfare of the people, medical jurisprudence was emphasized in order to ensure fair practice of medicine. Other significant studies relating to the welfare of the people included work on therapeutic practices based on the physical features of mankind. Yi Chema (b.1837) classified man into four different physical types and developed different therapeutic treatment for each.

Equality, human dignity, opportunity, public welfare, and the advancement of the national economy were conspicuous principles in the philosophy that emerged in this period. This development of the 17th-18th centuries is in some respects reminiscent of the Renaissance period of Western Europe.

In the literary scene, love stories were popular and sold well. Since books printed from metal type were too costly for commoners, readers, popular demand was met by the use of the cheaper clay-carved plates, in addition to wood-type printing. Anthologies of *sijo* poems by two intermediary class men were noteworthy. Kim Ch'ŏn-t'aek assembled 580 poems, from the Koryŏ period on, in his *Ch'ŏng guyŏngŏn* (Enduring Poetry of Korea), and Kim Sujang (b.1482) compiled a similar anthology entitled *Haedong kayo* (Songs of Korea). Chŏng Ch'ŏl (Songgang, 1534-1593) and Yun Sŏn-do (Kosan, 1587-1671) were talented *yangban* poets whose individual anthologies were also published.

Korea-centered painting also came into vogue. Chŏng Sŏn (Kyŏmjae, 1676-1759), unlike his predecessors, depicted the landscape of Korea, while Kim Hong-do (Tanwon, b.1740) and Shin Yun-bok (Hyewon, b.1758) concentrated on themes of the daily life of the masses. White porcelain with underglaze blue line-drawings was produced in quantity to meet public demand. Modern intellectuality dawned in all sectors of 18th century Korea.

Reform Attempts

In the early 19th century economic developments and improvements in social conditions increased. The people in general thought that foreign ideas and European commercial enterprise in particular should be taken seriously. Some officials advocated a thoroughgoing reform of national finance. The central government examined the proposal, but its implementation was thwarted by a struggle for power. There were numerous agrarian revolts which gradually led to political upheaval.

The powerful *yangban* officials, through their marriage ties with the royal family, were able to ensure for themselves a firm grasp on political power; every important national policy formulated in the early 19th century was for their interests. They were divided into numerous contending cliques, and did not pay any attention to the general welfare. Such was Korea's internal situation when, at the end of the 18th century, the British, in their quest for Asian markets, made their first problings into Korean waters. In the 1840s Russian and French vessels added their appearance, causing great excitement among the people.

The government carried out persecutions of Catholics in 1801 and 1839. This tended to disperse the converts to outlying districts, where Catholicism spread among impoverished farmers and *yangban* who came to depend more on religious salvation.

In 1863, Prince Yi Ha-ung, better known as the Taewon-gun or Prince Regent, put into effect a series of sweeping reforms encompassing national finance and government administration in order to strengthen the royal authority. He strongly opposed the increasing infiltration of foreign commercial interests into the country. In the spring of 1866, the government ordered rigorous persecution of Catholics. Aroused by this measure, the French fleet sailed up the Han-gang River and hostilities broke out on Kanghwado Island.

Economic and social developments drove the majority of *yangban* to bankruptcy, while the peasants and merchants were eager to throw off the traditional social constraints. As these trends developed, the government devised measures to suppress them. Another impetus to social dynamism was the increase in offspring of *yangban* and mothers of lower origin.

Although the elimination of bondsmen resulted in an increase in the number of taxable people, the exploitation of farmers by the ruling class caused the state's tax revenues to decline.

Peasant Wars of 1812 and 1862

In this period drought and flood alternately struck the country, causing a succession of bad harvests, which in turn generated a grim cycle of famine. Excessive tax collection and forced labor ensued. These adverse natural and social conditions ignited a series of agrarian revolts. Hong Kyŏng-nae in 1812 rose up with the peasants at Kasan in the northern part of Korea and held power in that district for some months. Frightened government officials dispatched the army, and only after a hard campaign were they able to suppress the revolt. In the south, all the way to Chejudo Island, as well as in the north,

the peasantry persevered in its struggle against oppression at the hands of the government, the local nobility and the wealthy landlords.

Half a century after Hong Kyŏng-nae's well-organized fight, the situation had not improved. A group of farmers in Chinju, Kyŏngsang-do province, rebelled against their oppressive overlords, the provincial officials and the wealthy landowners. This uprising of 1862 is directly attributable to the exploitation of destitute farmers by Paek Nak-shin, a newly-appointed military commander who had jurisdiction over the western half of Kyŏngsang-do province.

Yu Kye-ch'un, an intellectual native to the district who was outraged by Paek Nak-shin's rapacious conduct, led the farmers to riot, denouncing corrupt minor officials and wealthy landlords. The rebels killed local government functionaries, set fire to government buildings, and wrought considerable destruction. The startled Seoul government hurriedly sent an investigator to the scene. On the basis of his findings of fraudulent practices on the part of the local officials concerned, the government hastily revised the land, military and grain lending systems in an effort to eliminate such abuses. From the outset, however, it was unrealistic to expect the ruling class in the central government, which was itself deeply involved in such frauds, to make radical changes. But at least a superficial attempt at reform was made.

The agrarian revolt in Chinju served as a signal for similar uprisings elsewhere. In Kyŏngsang-do, Chŏlla-do and Ch'ungch'ŏng-do provinces, on faraway Chejudo Island in central Korea and in Hamgyŏng-do and P'yŏngan-do provinces in the north, groups of farmers rose up, attacking offices in principal towns and routing officials.

Under such social conditions, Ch'oe Che-u formulated the ideology of *Tonghak* (Eastern Learning) in order to rescue the farmers from prevalent poverty and unrest, and to restore political and social stability. His ideas rapidly gained acceptance, and he set his doctrines to music so that farmers would understand and accept them more readily. His teachings were systematized and compiled as a message of salvation to farmers in distress. The songs he sang

From Ernest Oppert's book on Korea Forbidden Land, *an illustration of the steamer "Emperor" at anchor at Kanghwado Island.*

were a mixture of traditional elements from Confucianism, Buddhism and Sŏn-gyo (teachings of Shilla's *Hwarang,* and to these he added modern humanistic ideas. Exclusionism was another characteristic of his religion, which incorporated an early form of nationalism and rejected alien thought.

Challenges of Modernization

Response to Capitalist Encroachment

During the late 19th century, insistent demands for commercial relations were made by the British, the Russians and other Europeans. The Prussian merchant Ernest J. Oppert in 1866 twice knocked on Korea's door and requested trade, but was refused. In the same year the American ship *General Sherman* made its memorable sortie into Korean waters with the objective of forcing the Korean government to enter into commercial relations. The vessel reached the Taedonggang River with a cargo of European merchandise and proceeded to P'yŏngyang, where they used unseemly force in dealing with Korean soldiers and civilians. The infuriated Koreans attacked the ship and set it afire.

The Taewon-gun's massacre of Catholics was a powerful stimulus for France, which had already established beachheads in Indochina, to move aggressively against Korea. Admiral Pierre G. Roze, commander of France's Indochina fleet, led his squadron to waters off Kanghwado on October 13, 1866 and landed troops on the island. They were repulsed, however, by Korean forces, and the French fleet was forced to withdraw.

From 1868, Japan, as a first step in its aggressive policy toward the peninsula, began pressing Korea to start negotiations aimed at revising traditional relations. From the American standpoint, such a revision also was highly desirable. The *General Sherman* incident stimulated the United States to intensify its efforts to force Korea to open its ports, and in 1871 Washington directed its Asian fleet to invade Kanghwado Island. The American troops were repulsed by the Korean garrison and their fleet retreated from Korean waters.

When Japan indicated its intention to terminate traditional diplomatic relations with Korea, the Taewon-gun expressed a different view. He was for restoring the time-honored procedure in which the ruling clan of Tsushima Island served as an intermediary between the two governments.

Because the Taewon-gun was adamant on the matter, Japanese leaders seized upon the "Korea problem" as an outlet to relieve domestic discontent, and made plans for an aggressive war. Japanese officials stationed in the area were instructed to spy on Korea's domestic situation. Japanese leaders proposed that 30 regiments should be sent to occupy the whole of the peninsula. Korea's natural resources and abundant rice production were important factors in Japan's aggressive designs. In pursuit of their objective, the Japanese fabricated a number of incidents. They sent their warships to raid points on Korea's coast, Pusan and Kanghwado Island, creating an atmosphere just short of actual war. The Japanese delegation which landed at Kapkot, Kanghwado Island on January 16, 1876, was fully equipped for combat, being escorted by 400 troops.

Such was the atmosphere in which a 12-article treaty was concluded. Presented unilaterally by the Japanese, this pact provided for revision of diplomatic relations. An addendum to the treaty, consisting of a trade accord and a customs agreement, all drafted by Japan, was signed in July. These instruments provided a legal basis for Japanese aggression by granting to the Japanese such privileges as extraterritoriality, exemption from customs duties, and legal recognition of Japanese currency in the ports to be opened to foreign trade. Creating a legal basis for Japanese aggression in Korea, these were unequal treaties, forced upon Korea just as Japan had been coerced years before by European powers and America.

In 1881, the scope of Japanese encroachment was broadened by the opening of Wonsan and Inch'ŏn ports. Another demand was that a Japanese consul be stationed in the capital. In the course of these events, there emerged among Koreans two strongly held opinions—one advocating the repulsion of "crooked" foreign powers, and the other calling for domestic reform.

Arguments for Repulsion

Korea's learned Confucianists, on the basis of information obtained through Ch'ing China, regarded the infiltration of European capitalist power as a potentially disruptive intrusion. They wanted to strengthen their alignment with Neo-Confucian ethics, and grew intolerant of new creeds. The closing of many local schools by the Taewon-gun in 1864 increased apathy. Deprived of their spiritual, political and financial strongholds, the Confucian literati felt a need to restore Neo-Confucian supremacy. Another factor conducive to xenophobia was the invasion of Korean waters by foreign fleets in 1866.

These factors stimulated Yi Hong-no (1792-1868) to strongly advocate repelling European capitalist encroachment. He called for political reform and stability, and reinforcement of Korea's national defense capability. His conclusion was that Europeanization of the country could be prevented by keeping capitalism out. He proposed the boycotting of European goods. His disciples and many Confucian scholars and thinkers affiliated with his school also called for the strengthening of national defense.

In 1881, many Confucianists raised objections to the policies of China and Japan. About that time, Paek Nak-kwan proposed that Korea should open up to foreign interests only after it had prepared fully for commercial competition. Some of these Confucianists were punished on charges of opposing state policy. Those Confucianists who advocated the repulsion of foreign influence were primarily oriented toward practical reform measures and not abstract ideas.

Reformists

A Korean "goodwill mission" was invited to Japan in 1876 and 1880, to inspect various new institutions Japan had installed on European models. On his return in 1880, Kim Koeng-jip (later known as Kim Hong-jip) brought to Korea a booklet titled *Chosŏn Ch'aengyak* (Korean Stratagem) written by a Chinese official of the Ch'ing legation in Japan. It advised Korea to accept European institutions and technology for the sake of economic development, and to strengthen its defense capability in collaboration with China, Japan and the United States in order to check Russia's southward expansion.

Once this "stratagem" became known in Korea, Confucian scholars, who in 1876 had advocated the expulsion of Japanese influence, launched a movement strongly opposed to the infiltration of foreign capitalism. The movement soon spread among Confucian students in Kyŏngsang-do, Kangwon-do, Kyŏnggi-do, Ch'ungch'ŏng-do and Chŏlla-do provinces. The government dispatched a group of young aristocrats to Japan in 1881 for a study of administrative, military, educational industrial and technological institutions. Meanwhile, at the request of Ch'ing China, another group of 60 young Koreans led by Kim Yun-shik visited China, where they studied chiefly the arts of manufacturing and handling Western weapons. This kind of reform attempt arose within the government itself, and the wave soon spread to engulf not only the *yangban* and middle classes but the society as a whole.

Opposition to Japan

The Japanese minister to Korea, Hanabusa Yoshimoto, forced the Korean government to introduce the Japanese army training system, and a separate training command was established for this purpose. Implementation of army reorganization and training was of itself an effective springboard for aggression. Japan monopolized the Korean market in 1876. Two years later, Japan's Daiichi Bank established a branch office in Pusan, encouraging Japanese merchants to infiltrate Korea *en masse*. The Japanese merchants could purchase rice, soy beans, cattle hides and alluvial gold at incredibly low prices, reaping exorbitant profits at home. Korea, on the other hand, was faced with the pressing need of devising some means of protecting its national economy.

Discriminatory treatment within the armed forces became an inflammatory issue. While the opposition movement was at its height, soldiers undergoing Japanese training in special units were paid and rewarded conspicuously better than the ordinary troops in traditional training. Infuriated by these injustices, the latter rose up in revolt. Giving vent to their anger at the Japanese aggressors, the Korean soldiers assaulted the Japanese legation, forcing the Japanese minister and his party to flee to Inch'ŏn at night. State administration was once again entrusted to the Taewon-gun in the hope that he might be able to save the situation.

Queen Min and her clique, having barely escaped the rioting army by fleeing the palace, asked China for a contingent of troops to help suppress the uprising. The Chinese responded by sending four warships and 3,000 troops to Korea. Moreover, they seized the Taewon-gun and took him to Peking. Minister Hanabusa, who had managed to escape to Japan, returned to Seoul on August 12, bringing 1,500 troops aboard four warships. Storming into the capital, Hanabusa pressed the Korean government to pay reparations for the damages and to agree to the stationing of Japanese troops in Korea.

In the Chemulp'o Treaty, concluded under Japanese exaction, Korea agreed to Japan's demands, which included Korea's promise to pay 500,000 won in reparations and gave permission for the stationing of Japanese troops in the capital for the defense of the Japanese legation. The treaty further broadened the scope of Japan's aggressive activities centering around such ports as Pusan, Inch'ŏn and Wonsan.

Meanwhile, the Chinese continued their interference in Korea's internal affairs. They reorganized the Korean government system at will, appointing to important posts members of the Min clique who had previously held high positions. China's powerful Li Hung-chang sent his emissaries, P.G. Moellendorff and Ma Chien-chung, to Korea to carry out the task of reorganizing Korea's diplomacy. Yüan Shih-kai of Ch'ing took command of the Korean army, providing it with Chinese-style training.

To reinstate Chinese control in Korea, China advised Korea to conclude a series of commercial treaties with European powers and America. The Korea-U.S. treaty of commerce was concluded on May 22 and signed on June 6, 1882. Korea signed revised treaties with Great Britain and Germany in Seoul on November 26, 1883. The two new treaties, together with the first international treaty concluded with Japan, were most disadvantageous to Korea. In addition, a treaty of commerce was signed with Russia on June 25, 1884, and was followed on August 8, 1888, by the conclusion of another agreement governing Korean-Russian overland commerce. A treaty of commerce with France was signed on June 4, 1886.

Japan concluded an agreement with Korea concerning commercial activities of Japanese residents in Korea. The tax rates fixed in the agreement with Japan were very disadvantageous to Korea. Moellendorff tried to introduce Russian influence into Korea with the purpose of engineering a secret treaty of protection between the two countries. His action, however, precipitated the British occupation of Kŏmundo (Port Hamilton) in order to check the Russian advance. Korea was plunged into a whirlpool of international rivalries.

With the British occupation of Kŏmundo on April 10, 1885, Korea lost control over one of the best ports on the south sea. After exacting, through Li Hung-chang, a pledge from Russia that it would not attempt occupation of any part of Korea, Great Britain withdrew its fleet from the port on February 27, 1887.

Political Upheaval of 1884

The conclusion of a series of commercial treaties with foreign countries intensified the encroachment of capitalist powers. A group of reformists denounced the leading politicians for their reliance on foreign influence and tried to introduce reforms that would improve social conditions, enrich the people and strengthen national power. The main concern of Kim Ok-kyun and Hong Yŏng-shik was to set modern reform in motion. The Min family's heavy reliance on China in the wake of the army revolt had resulted in the occupation of the capital by Chinese forces.

At the outbreak of war between China and France, Japanese Minister to Korea Takezoe Shinichiro talked with these reformists about plans for a *coup d'etat*. Although China had withdrawn part of its expeditionary forces from Korea, the Chinese maintained far superior military strength over the Japanese.

The reformists planned the assassination of prominent politicians affiliated with China at a reception to be given on December 4, 1884, but the plot was not fully carried out. The reformists first called on King Kojong (r.1863-1907) at the royal palace and pressed for his sanction of their reform plan. On December 5, they assassinated military commanders and ministers inside the palace gate on their way to a royal audience. The reformists were forced to flee, however, without proclaiming their comprehensive 14-point Reform Decree. Kim Ok-kyun and Sŏ Chae-p'il escaped to Inch'ŏn, where they boarded a Japanese ship for asylum in Japan.

Japan settled pending problems with China by concluding the Tientsin Treaty, in which the two sides agreed to: pull their expeditionary forces out of Korea simultaneously; not send military instructors for the training of the Korean army; and also notify the other side beforehand should one decide to send troops to Korea. However, Yüan Shih-kai remained in Seoul interfering in Korea's internal affairs, while Japan, not to be outdone, was ready to pounce upon any suitable opportunity for encroachment.

Japan had already consolidated its bases for economic aggression on the peninsula. The Japanese looked to Korea's production to meet demand for rice and soy beans, which was soaring commensurately with Japan's population growth. Korean rice was superior in quality to Japanese rice and also much cheaper. The Japanese started by usurious means to exploit Korean peasants by making them dependent upon Japanese capital. Through branch offices of the Daiichi Bank opened in Pusan, Wonsan and Inch'ŏn, Japan also made bargain purchases of cowhide for military use, and gold as a reserve fund for the Bank of Japan.

Japanese exports to Korea consisted, in the initial period, mainly of the resale of European, especially English, and American commodities. Japan later kept these European commodities for home consumption, gradually replacing export goods with Japanese products of low quality, mostly sundry merchandise for daily use.

There developed a great outflow of grain which eventually devastated the life of the Korean peasants. In 1889 and 1891, when the farmers of Hamgyŏng-do and Hwanghae-do provinces suffered crop failure, the Japanese government exacted exorbitant indemnities for losses allegedly suffered by Japanese merchants. Consequently most farmers were impoverished, and their indignation was directed at Korea's ruling class which they held responsible for their plight. The only recourse was to uprise, and during the period from the 1884 political upheaval to 1894, farmers struggles broke out repeatedly in all provinces.

Tonghak Struggle of 1894

Tonghak, or Eastern Learning, was based on the doctrine of the salvation of farmers from their destitute life. Although its preaching had a religious aspect, the main concern was for realistic national stability and security. Seeing that his teaching was gaining popularity, the government executed Ch'oe Che-u in 1864 on charges of confusing society. His movement lived on, however, and poverty-stricken farmers flocked to his standard. Large-scale *Tonghak* demonstrations took place in 1892 in Chŏlla-do and Ch'ung-ch'ŏng-do provinces. In 1893, *Tonghak* believers went to Seoul and staged a demonstration in front of the royal palace, but were dispersed by the army. About 20,000 *Tonghak* movement followers assembled at Poŭn, Ch'ungch'ŏng-do province, and proclaimed their determination to reject Japan and Europe. In 1894, Chŏn Pong-jun assumed leadership of the *Tonghak* movement in Chŏlla-do province, where cruel exploitation of the already hard-pressed farmers was in process after the construction of a new reservoir.

Their peaceful protests having proven fruit-less, the farmers resorted to violence. The government countered with draconian measures, and an inspector sent from Seoul ordered wholesale executions. Chŏn led a larger uprising and defeated the government army occupying the provincial capital of Chŏnju. There they agreed to a cease-fire and submitted a comprehensive reform plan. Unfortunately, however, the royal court, dominated by the Min family, decided to ask for Chinese intervention. Chinese forces, 2,000 strong, landed at Asan beginning June 8 and took Kongju, while government troops recaptured Chŏnju on June 11, and the peasant army dispersed. Japan landed 400 marines on June 10 and a mixed brigade on June 16, and Japanese forces soon entered Seoul.

The Japanese army turned its attention to the *Tonghak* only after they had expelled the Chinese forces from Korean territory. The *Tonghak* movement, facing combined government and Japanese troops, was dealt a crushing blow at T'aein, Chŏlla-do province. Chŏn Pong-jun was captured alive and beheaded in the capital. Countless *Tonghak* troops and farmers were captured and massacred by the Japanese.

Reform Attempts

The unsuccessful 1884 coup d'etat brought frustration to the reform efforts, but the need for reform still was keenly felt by the populace and some leaders of the government as well. The disintegration of traditional social order was accelerated by the peasant struggle. Such developments led Korea to implement institutional reform.

The conservative government had been compelled to accept the administrative reform proposals submitted by the *Tonghak* rebels at the time of the cease-fire in Chŏnju in 1894. This peasant struggle was utilized by the Japanese army for its aggressive purposes. Then, in the course of the Sino-Japanese War, Japan forced Korea to carry out reform by armed threat, while expelling the China-oriented conservative politicians from the government. The peace treaty ending the Sino-Japanese War was concluded on April 17, 1895, at Shimonoseki,

King Kojong with his senior ministers.

Japan. China's influence waned, and the Korean government was forcibly integrated into Japan's design of imperialistic aggression.

On July 27, 1894, a Supreme Council for Military and State Administration was established to function as the nation's highest executive and legislative organ. On July 29, it passed a 23-article reform plan, but this was not by any means autonomous, as it was accompanied by the aggressive intent of Japan. The reform movement was led mainly by politicians heavily Japan- oriented, but the Taewon-gun fought Japanese aggression by inciting *Tonghak* followers to engage in anti-Japanese activities.

The Supreme Council passed no less than 208 reform measures. These included: the use of the founding of the Chŏson Dynasty as a basis for the calendar; disciplinary action against corrupt officials; the liberalization of commercial activities; the establishment of a new currency system on the silver standard; unity in financial administration under the jurisdiction of the Ministry of Finance; the standardization of weights and measures; cash payment of all taxes; the establishment of joint stock companies; the separation of judicial power in accordance with the law of court reorganization; and the unification of police power. In spite of these measures, the reform could hardly be substantial. On December 17, the Kim Hong-jip cabinet was excluded from political circles and the Supreme Council for Military and State Administration was closed.

The new cabinet attempted a reform on the basis of the 14-Article Great Plan in an abbreviated version of those reform measures. The plan aimed at the following: national autonomy and independence; the separation of the royal court and the government; the introduction of the budget system to national revenue and expenditure under the jurisdiction of the Ministry of Finance; the observance of the statutory rates in collecting taxes; the education of military officers; the establishment of a military system on the basis of universal conscription; the reform of the local government system;

the protection of civil life and property; the enactment of civil and criminal codes; the employment of competent persons at government offices; and the provision of opportunities for talented young men to pursue advanced studies abroad to acquire modern knowledge and techniques.

Intensified Japanese Aggression

Japanese aggression in Korea was "a matter of life or death," as was earlier expressed by Hayashi Tadashi, one-time Japanese minister to London. As Japanese aggression intensified, the Min clique collaborated with Russian Minister Karl Waeber to force Kim Hong-jip to reorganize his cabinet, and pro-Russian figures such as Yi Pŏm-jin were given cabinet posts.

The government, reorganizing the military structure in April 1895, hired Japanese officers as instructors. They trained about 800 Korean officers and men who were then assigned to the royal palace as guards under training. It was under these circumstances of questionable palace security that militant Japanese Minister Miura Goro and other Japanese decided to assassinate Queen Min, the leading figure in the Min clique, as she was again making secret overtures to China and Russia. Taking advantage of the trainee-guards and those who opposed the Min family, Japanese troops, crushing resistance put up by the royal bodyguards, intruded into Kyŏngbokkung Palace at dawn on October 8.

Storming into the Okhoru Pavilion, the Japanese found and killed Queen Min, and burned her body with kerosene. The foreign missions were outraged by this atrocity. The Japanese government hurriedly repatriated those who had taken part in the action and detained them briefly at Hiroshima Prison as a subterfuge. Their trial, to borrow the words of a Japanese historian Yamabe Kentaro, was "a deliberate miscarriage of justice, designed to protect the culprits."

Despite the Japanese brutality, the European powers, in their apprehension over Russia's southward expansion, welcomed the overt Japanese aggression as a counter to the Russian threat. Germany saw the continued presence of the Japanese army as indispensable, while other powers maintained that a demand for its withdrawal would only produce more trouble. Great Britain believed the entrustment of Korea to Japan was a proper measure to check the Russian advance. The American government instructed its minister not to make any statement unfavorable to Japan.

Informed of the assassination of Queen Min by a mob of Japanese intruders, the nation was gripped with indignation. Confucian scholars mobilized volunteers to fight against the Japanese. The Kim Hong-jip cabinet, spurred greatly by the incident, expedited reform. It adopted the solar calendar, established primary schools in Seoul, introduced smallpox vaccinations, started modern postal service, and reorganized the military system, with the Royal Army Guards stationed in Seoul and other detachments in the provinces. During this reform, the Japanese forced the cabinet to issue a decree banning topknots. Citizens wearing topknots were arrested on the streets or at their homes, and were forced to cut them off. Ch'oe Ik-hyŏn defying the decree, was arrested and imprisoned, but he did not yield. With these attempts, the Japanese tried to wipe out Korean heritage, only to stimulate the armed resistance of the Korean volunteer "righteous armies."

Spontaneous "righteous troops" protesting the ban on topknots spread all over the country. The Royal Guards of Seoul were dispatched to suppress them. The resultant weakening of palace security was seen by Russia as an opportunity to extend its influence. From a Russian warship lying at anchor off Inch'ŏn, 100 sailors were summoned, ostensibly to protect the Russian legation. Shortly afterward, they were reinforced by an additional contingent of 120 sailors. Ex-minister Waeber, remaining in Seoul, plotted to persuade King Kojong to take refuge at the Russian legation. Home Minister Yu Kil-jun, meanwhile, conferred with Japanese Minister Komura Jutaro concerning counter-measures that might be taken against Russia. At dawn on February 11, 1896, Kojong and the Crown Prince went to the Russian legation to escape the Japanese menace, and were protected by guards provided by other legations as well. Japanese Minister Komura called on Russian Minister Speyer at the Russian Legation and requested that the emperor return to the royal palace, but Emperor Kojong refused, knowing that he had chosen the lesser of two evils.

At the same time the Korean government, following a proposal made by the Russian minister, appointed Russians as consultants for military training and financial administration. In May, a Korean delegation led by Min Yŏng-hwan and Yun Ch'i-ho concluded a treaty in Russia with Foreign Minister Lobanoff, agreeing to the following: Russia would protect the Korean monarch and, if necessary, would send additional troops to Korea; the consultants in question would be subject to the guidance of the Russian minister; the two governments would enter into a loan agreement when deemed necessary in view of Korea's economic conditions; and the Russian government would be authorized to connect its telegraph lines with the Korean telegraph network. With the Korean king in custody, Russia lost no time in implementing the aggressive provisions of the treaty.

During the king's stay at the Russian legation, Korea's foreign relations were aimed at protecting the royal family from the atmosphere of terror created in the royal palace by Japanese violence. This overriding concern was conducive to reliance on Russia despite its aggressive policy.

The United States, Great Britain, France, Germany and Japan competed for concessions. From its Russian refuge, the Korean government granted unconditional concessions without the usual stipulations as to the terms of lease or conditions of taxes. Korea was deprived of its properties by the world powers through such concessions.

Awakening of the People

Sŏ Chae-p'il (Philip Jaisohn) proceeded in 1884 from asylum in Japan to America and studied medicine. On his return to Korea in 1896, he resumed leadership of the nation's modern reform program. Appointed a consultant to the Privy Council, Sŏ was able to broaden his contacts with prominent government leaders. Obtaining a donation of 5,000 won from Home Minister Yu Kil-jun, he inaugurated the newspaper *Tongnip Shinmun* (The Independent) on April 7, 1896. Published in pure *Han-gŭl* (the Korean script) and in English, the journal was well received by the public.

Aimed at conveying both domestic and foreign news to the Korean people, the newspaper argued both for and against government policies in an impartial manner. It called for the nation's all-out effort to strengthen its autonomy and promote the public good. It reflected the needs of the time when the Korean government was being shaken to its foundations by the aggressive policies of Japan and Russia. Sŏ demanded that the government give top priority to the promotion of civil rights, and that it safeguard national sovereignty by combatting the growth of foreign influence. The publisher also did his utmost to introduce to his readers modern science and the ideology of the Western world.

The *Tongnip Shinmun* grew rapidly, from an initial circulation of 300 to 3,000. In his tireless efforts to enlighten the masses, Sŏ also availed himself of every opportunity to address the people on the streets on current topics. His newspaper awakened the citizenry to the urgent needs of the day: eliminating corruption, expanding education, solidifying national sovereignty and promoting civil rights.

The Independence Club, which Sŏ helped to found, was formally activated in July 1896, with Minister of War An Kyŏng-su as president and Foreign Minister Yi Wan-yong as chairman. Prominent government and civic personages who had led the country in modern reform and in the struggle for independence were counted among its members, as well as a number of important government leaders. The Crown Prince, as a token of cooperation, made a donation of 1,000 won to the club, thereby arousing great interest among people throughout the country.

Sŏ Chae-p'il did his best to awaken the public to the needs of modernization. He asserted that the following steps were vital to national development: mass education, road construction, commerce promoting national wealth, women's education, *Han-gŭl* for mass education, currency in domestic transactions, wide circulation of both domestic and foreign newspapers, exploitation of mining resources and establishment of a congress.

Voicing his strong opposition to government's delegation of it financial and military authority to Russia since February 1897, Sŏ made a protest to the government concerning Russia's demand for the concession of Chŏryŏng-do Island (present Yŏngdo) off Pusan, and for the establishment of a Korean-Russian Bank. Speaking at a mass rally in the heart of Seoul, Sŏ asked the government to dismiss the Russian military and financial consultants. Syngman Rhee (Yi Sŭng-man) and other speakers who took the rostrum at the same rally also drew enthusiastic applause from the audience by pointing out the absurdity of entrusting the financial and military authority of Korea to another country.

The Independence Club frequently presented to the government opinions concerning the reform of domestic administration and did not hesitate to register opposition. Its demands for the dismissal of ranking government officials guilty of irregularities and fraud were put in effect. Through "outside" sources the club also conducted an investigation of the government's concession of rights in lumbering, mining, and railway construction, and filed a protest with the government to correct abuses. The government thereupon imprisoned leading members of the club and by imperial edict ordered its dissolution, an oppressive action that stifled the club's movement for civil rights and national sovereignty. The club, albeit short-lived, bequeathed its spirit to subsequent national movements.

The people were united in condemning the king's flight to a foreign legation and the continuous granting of economic concessions to foreigners and their outrage coalesced in the Independence Club's campaign. As a result of this, Kojong moved out of the Russian legation to Kyŏngun-gung (today's Tŏksugung Palace) in February 1897, and changed his reign name to Kwangmu (Martial Brilliance) in August. He proclaimed to the nation and the world the establishment of an independent "Great Han Empire" in October, after which he was called by the title "Emperor." This was a significant victory for the pressure of Korean public opinion.

Russia-Japan Rivalry

On condition that Japan tacitly consent to Russia's 25-year lease of Port Arthur as a naval base and Talien as a commercial port, Russia agreed not to hamper Japanese commercial and industrial activities in Korea. Such was the substance of the Russo-Japanese Treaty III, concluded April 25, 1899, between Japanese Foreign Minister Nishi and Russia's Minister to Japan, Rosen. Russia thereby gave Japan a free hand for its aggressive operations in Korea.

As an anti-foreign movement erupted in Manchuria in the wake of the Boxer Rebellion, Russia threw a huge army of 180,000 troops into the area on the pretext of guarding its railways. Three-fourths of the Manchurian territory came under occupation by the Russians, where they watched for an opportunity to invade Korea.

Precisely such a proposal to invade was made to the Russian government in 1903 by the manager of a Russian lumber company operating on the Amnokkang River, a company owned by the imperial Russian foundation. Russian minister Pavloff proposed that Russia establish a sphere of influence south of the river and reject any interference by other powers in Manchuria. Accordingly, Russia assembled its fleet in Port Arthur and deployed ground forces in Fenghuang-ch'eng and along the Amnokkang River. In August 1903, Russia occupied Yongamp'o and hastily constructed military facilities, including fortresses, barracks and communication lines.

Through the Anglo-Japanese treaty of alliance in 1902, Japan, with the cooperation of Great Britain, obtained international recognition for its aggressive policy toward Korea. This treaty provided that in return for British support, Japan would assume the burden of checking the Russian southward advance in the Far East. Japan agreed to recognize the Russia occupation of Manchuria, on condition that Russia recognize its activities in Korea.

Russia and Japan stood face to face, each attempting to occupy both sides of the Amnokkang River as a preliminary step toward the occupation of both Korea and Manchuria. On February 8, 1904, Japan opened fire on the Russian fleets off Inch'ŏn and Port Arthur, thereby touching off the Russo-Japanese War (1904-05).

Colonial Consolidation

At the outbreak of the Russo-Japanese War, Korea proclaimed its neutrality to the world. Nevertheless, Japan sent troops into Seoul in large numbers and, on February 23, 1904, forced the Korean government to sign the Korea-Japan Protocol. This unilaterally exacted Korean concessions necessary for Japan's execution of the war. Japan stationed six and a half battalions in Korea, which laid military railways, seized Korean telegraphic and telephone networks by occupying the Central Telecommunications Office, and pre-empted land for military use. In September, Japan proclaimed military control over the whole territory of Korea, decreeing the death penalty for any Korean national caught trespassing on the military railway communications line.

By a revision of the military rule of January 6, 1905, Japan suppressed any anti-Japanese movement through assembly, associations, or the press, proclaiming on July 3 that those violating the military rule would be dealt with under Japanese law. In the first Korea-Japan Agreement concluded on August 22, 1904, it was stipulated that a financial consultant would be appointed from among the Japanese and a diplomatic consultant from among nationals of third powers recommended by the Japanese government. This provision was obviously designed to deprive Korea of its national rights.

The agreement was reinforced by the "Principles Concerning Facilities in Korea" concluded late in May 1904, which granted extensive privileges to Japan. These included the stationing of troops in Korea even after the Russo-Japanese War, expropriation of land for military use,

supervision of Korea's diplomacy and financial administration, seizure of Korea's transportation and communications facilities, and exploitation of concessions in agriculture, forestry, mining and fisheries.

Japan sent as diplomatic consultant an ex-official of its foreign office, an American named Stevens, and as financial consultant Megata Tanetaro, an official of its Ministry of Finance. The latter assumed full authority over Korea's financial administration, and by a currency reform, brought the Korean currency under the Japanese monetary system, devaluating it by from one fifth to one half in order to plunder Korean properties. Japanese officials further penetrated the Korean government to work in the Ministry of War, the Police, and the Ministry of Education, and in the Royal Household as consultants, thereby undermining the government's authority.

During the war with Russia, Japan and Great Britain revised the Anglo-Japanese Treaty of Alliance on August 12, 1905, obtaining British consent to the Japanese scheme for colonizing Korea under the guise of protection. In the secret Taft-Katsura agreement, Japan and the United States recognized Japan's prerogatives in Korea. At the Portsmouth Peace Conference, which was concluded in September 1905, Japan requested that "Korea be placed at Japan's free disposal" in accordance with the second Anglo-Japanese Treaty of Alliance and the U.S.-Japanese agreement.

The United States, Great Britain and Russia at last gave international acquiescence to Japanese aggression in Korea. Recognizing that Japan possessed superior political, military and economic interests in Korea, the U.S. president rejected Emperor Kojong's personal letter on the illegitimacy of the Korea-Japan treaty presented through the efforts of missionary-diplomat Homer B. Hulbert.

Immediately after the Portsmouth Treaty went into effect, Japan sent Ito Hirobumi to Korea and forced the Korean government to conclude the second Korea-Japan Treaty. By that time Seoul had already been invaded by a Japanese cavalry unit, an artillery battalion and a military police unit. On November 17, Ito pressed the Korean government to sign the draft treaty designed to isolate the Korean government by severing its foreign relations completely. Diplomacy was then taken from Korean control and placed under the control of the Japanese Foreign Office. The treaty also established the Office of the Resident-General in Korea to enforce colonial rule.

Resident-General and Resistance

Outright control by Japanese began on February 1, 1906. The Resident-General was invested with full authority in regard to Korea's diplomacy, domestic administration and military affairs. Through the Council for Improvement of Korean Administration, he pressed the Korean government to accept Japan's aggressive policy in the fields of finance, banking, agriculture, forestry, mining, transportation, education, culture, jurisprudence, internal security, local administration and the royal household.

In order to cover up their coercive actions, the Resident-General sent Stevens, paid by the Korean government, to the United States to advance Japanese propaganda. Upon his arrival in San Francisco, Stevens, who is said to have received several tens of thousands of dollars from the Japanese, made a false statement that the Korean people in general welcomed the Korea-Japan treaty. Infuriated by this canard, Korean emigrants Chang In-hwan and Chŏn Myŏng-un assassinated him in March 1907.

When Emperor Kojong dispatched an emissary to the Peace Conference at the Hague in June 1907 and exposed to the world Japan's aggressive policy, the Office of the Resident-General forced the monarch to abdicate the throne, and the third Korea-Japan Agreement of July was forced upon Korea, which provided a legal basis for Japan's appropriation of Korea. A large number of Japanese officials penetrated the executive and judicial branches of the Korean government, accelerating the Japanese scheme of taking the power of the Korean government. The Korean armed forces were disarmed and disbanded and the judicial system was reorganized to serve Japanese aggression.

Moreover, in a secret memorandum attached to the Korean-Japan agreement, it was stipulated that Korean military forces would be dissolved and that courts, newly-constructed prisons, and the police would be turned over to Japanese management. This enabled the Japanese to assume actual judicial and police authority.

The Korean Empire was now a nominal one. The Japanese aggressors exerted armed pressure upon the government through their military forces and police. In June 1910, Japan instituted a military police system by appointing the commander of the Japanese military police to the concurrent post of superintendent for police administration.

While carrying out the war against Russia, Japan promoted a puppet society, the *Ilchinhoe*. The people reacted with rage, and the *Daehan* Club, the *Hwangsŏng* (Seoul) YMCA and the National Education Research Association attacked the *Ilchinhoe* vehemently. When Chang Chi-yŏn, publisher of the *Hwangsŏng Shinmun*, assailed the protectorate treaty in an editorial, Japanese police arrested him and closed down his newspaper. Another newspaper, the *Daehan Maeil Shinbo*, published in Korean, Chinese and English, assailed Japan's agressive and oppressive policies and served as a guide for Korean national resistance.

Many leaders representing all walks of life committed suicide in protest of the forced treaty, and many attempts were made to assassinate ranking officials of the Korean government who had cooperated in bringing the aggressive treaty into being.

Emperor Kojong appealed unsuccessfully to both the united States and the Hague Peace Conference of 1907 for support in repudiating the treaty. Korean resistance to Japanese control intensified, but was ruthlessly suppressed by the Japanese military. Uprisings led by leading Confucian scholars flared in the provinces of Ch'ungch'ŏng-do, Chŏlla-do, Kyŏngsang-do and Kangwon-do.

Although the resistance fighters, mainly young peasants, were short of weapons, they fought bravely against the Japanese troops. The resistance assumed major proportions and developed into all-out war with Japan when the regular army joined in the fighting after its forced disbandment by the Japanese. Fighting spread to every part of the country, as not only farmers and soldiers, but also hunters and mine workers of northern Korea joined in the resistance. Commanders included Confucian scholars of the *yangban* class and a number of commoners.

Many pitched battles were fought between 1907 and 1909, but the resistance fighters were more active in guerrilla tactics, rescuing Koreans from Japanese captivity and destroying Japanese transportation and communications facilities. F.A. McKenzie, the only foreigner who visited the volunteer soldiers in their battle areas and personally observed their activities, wrote the following:

"As I stood on a mountain pass, looking down on the valley leading to *Inch'ŏn*, I recalled these words of my friend. The 'strong hand of Japan' was certainly being shown here. I beheld in front of me village after village reduced to ashes. Destruction, thorough and complete, had fallen upon it. Not a single house was left, and not a single wall of a house."

The situation of the volunteer army was extremely difficult, in that it had to supply itself as best it could with weapons and other necessities to fight against Japan, while the Japanese army and police could easily obtain war supplies from their country. The Korean armed resistance gradually grew weaker, and Japan reported that the Korean volunteer army had ceased to exist in November 1910 or in March 1912 with its last operation in Hwanghae-do province. McKenzie reported, however, that the volunteer army's resistance may have continued until 1915. At home the resistance took the form of underground organization, while a group of patriots crossed the Amnokkang and Tumangang rivers into Manchuria, where they organized the Korean Independence Army with it stronghold in Kando. This army became the main force in all subsequent struggles against the Japanese. The volunteer soldiers performed a duty as the vanguard in independence resistance both at home and abroad, demonstrating the nation's ability to resist Japan's colonial policy.

When the resistance army established a stronghold at Kando, Manchuria, the population of the Kando district as of 1909 consisted of 83,000 Koreans and 21,000 Chinese. The Resident-General, in order to destroy the Korean independence movement there, set up a branch office and stationed an army plus military and civilian police forces in Kando. A corps of Korean independence fighters under the leadership of Hong Pŏm-do had already moved to Kando, but Japan sought to oppress Korean residents in the district by demanding that China recognize Kando as Korean territory.

There was a change of policy, however, as a result of China's concession authorizing Japan's Southern Manchurian Railroad Company to lay branch lines and exploit mining resources in Manchuria. In return, Japan concluded a treaty with China on September 4, 1909, recognizing Chinese territorial rights over Kando.

Nevertheless, the Japanese consulate general newly established in Kando continued to exert pressure against Korean independence activities. A young Korean patriot, An Chung-gŭn, assassinated Resident-General Ito at the Harbin Railroad Station on October 26, 1909.

Under the treaty concluded on August 22, 1910, and proclaimed a week later, Japan gave the coup de grace to the Korean Empire and changed the Office of the Resident-General to that of Government-General. The proclamation of the treaty had been preceded by severe suppressive measures, including the suspension of newspaper publication and the arrest of thousands of Korean leaders, and the capital in particular was guarded tightly by Japanese combat troops. The treaty was the product of a conspiracy between treacherous Korean officials, who had been the target of national hatred, and Japanese officials of the Office of the Resident-General.

Economic Exploitation

Between 1905 and 1908, Japanese control of Korea's currency was secured with the rapidly growing volume of Daiichi Bank notes. Supported by generous loans from their home government, Japanese merchants could easily expand their activities and invade the Korean market. Japanese firms operated in Korea with a combined capital in excess of 10 million won. The number of Japanese residents in Korea in 1908 totalled to 126,000, and by 1911 the number had risen to 210,000.

The number of Japanese residents engaged in farming also grew rapidly as Japan's seizure of Korean land gathered momentum. Korean farmers controlled by the usurious Japanese capital became easy prey to expropriation. The Office of the Resident-General enacted a series of laws concerning land ownership to the decided advantage of the Japanese.

In the meantime, large Japanese capitalists coercively purchased land, mainly in Chŏlla-do and Ch'ungch'ŏng-do provinces, during the period from 1905 to 1910. The Honam plain in Chŏlla-do province, long known as the Korean granary, was rapidly becoming a Japanese farm, and such land seizures quickly spread to other provinces. Intruding into fertile and well-irrigated lands on a nationwide scale, the Japanese advanced toward the north, occupying first the Taegu and Choch'iwon areas along the Seoul-Pusan railway and the Hwangju area along the Seoul-Shinŭiju railway.

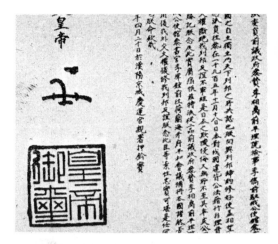

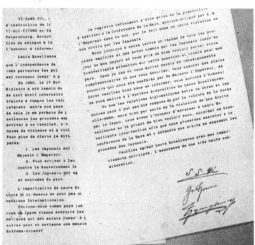

In order to carry out land expropriation on a broader and more systematic scale, the Resident-General began the practice of distributing to Japanese farmers unclaimed land and military farms of the Korean government. Having worked out a plan aimed at resettling Japanese farmers in Korea,he established the Oriental Development Company in 1908 and seized Korean land, reducing the royal property and its budget.

The Japanese plan called for the seizure of state-owned unreclaimed land, military farms cultivated by troops, and the mobilization of Korean laborers for their reclamation. Within a year, the company had seized 30,000 hectares (75,000 acres) of military farms and unreclaimed land. Property was removed from the royal household by means of removing the power of financial management. This was aimed at preventing Emperor Kojong from raising resistance funds.

Facing page: The imperial credentials bearing the seal of Emperor Kojong given to the Korean envoys to the Hague Peace Conference (top); petition submitted to the Hague Peace Conference by Yi Sang-sŏl, Yi Chun and Yi Wi-jong of the Hague mission, protesting the Japanese attempt to colonize Korea (middle); photograph of the three emissaries inset in a newpaper in Hague at the time (bottom).

Armed Koreans rose against the Japanese toward the end of the Chosŏn Dynasty (1392-1910) (top); a painting of the assassination of Ito Hirobumi by An Chung-gŭn at Harbin station in October 1909 (bottom)

Educational Change

The Independence Club's advocacy of modern reform raised popular consciousness of political participation. Schools founded by Christian missionaries introduced European style, modern education to Korea. In the face of intensifying Japanese aggression, the government worked toward resolving educational problems. It promulgated regulations for the Hansŏng Normal School, foreign language institutes and primary education in 1895, and those for medical colleges, middle schools and commercial and technical schools in 1899, thereby laying the foundation for modern education. In 1904, commercial and technical schools were expanded to include agricultural schools. Foreign language institutes for Japanese, English and French came into being in 1895, for Russian in 1896, and for Chinese and German in 1900.

Special schools were established to provide skilled workers for various government agencies. They offered curricula in such fields as mining, law, postal service and electricity. There were many other schools founded by private citizens and missionaries to encourage independence conciousness. The Ch'ŏngnyŏn Hagwon, founded in 1904 and operated by pastor Chŏn Tŏk-ki, provided education for young men in close liaison with the activities of the *Shinminhoe*, a secret independence organization. Its membership included prominent intellectuals and patriotic leaders. However, the school was forced to close by the Japanese in 1914.

Through the Office of the Resident-General, Japan assumed actual power over Korean education, effecting reorganization of the educational system by imperial edict. The Japanese attempted to bring all schools under government management, reduce the number of schools, subordinate the content of education to their colonial policy, and retard Korean education by lowering the level of academic content. Through the decree for private schools promulgated in 1908, the Japanese strengthened their control over private schools and shut many of them down.

Schools were, however, continuously established in the Maritime Province and in the Kando district across the Tuman-gang River. In 1919 the number of Korean schools reached 130 in Manchuria alone. Like their colleagues at home, patriotic leaders in exile in Manchuria laid emphasis on education as a prerequisite for the independence struggle.

In 1905, Chu Shi-gyŏng made a proposal to the government concerning studies of the Korean language and compilation of a dictionary. As a result of his efforts and those of the National Language Research Institute established in 1907, a new system was introduced for the national script. Under this system, the exclusive use of Chinese characters in official documents and communication was replaced by the mixed use of Chinese characters and *Han-gŭl*.

Newspapers and books used the new writing system in order to spread knowledge of European institutions more rapidly among the populace. Through his work on Korean grammar and phonology published in the years 1908-14, Chu Shi-gyŏng exerted a profound impact on scientific research of the Korean language. He also taught that language and script were the foundation of national spirit and culture.

On the basis of a modern understanding of the national language, a new literary movement began, aimed at arousing national consciousness among the masses. New-style poems, novels and travel accounts were published in *Han-gŭl*. These creative literary achievements were made possible by the translation and imitation of European and American literature, from the latter part of the 19th century to the 1910s. This early stage of the enlightenment movement provided a basis for the modern literature of the 1920s.

Further Moves Against Japanese Rule

The Japanese Government-General was constantly sensitive to the public awareness and education of Koreans. Thus, in a nationwide search conducted in 1910 for books on Korean history and geography, 200,000 to 300,000 were confiscated and burned. Included in the proscription were Korean readers, biographies of national heroes of earlier centuries, and Korean translations of foreign books relating to independence, the birth of the nation, revolution, etc.

The Japanese also re-interpreted Korean history for their own purposes. Historians employed at the Research Department of the Southern Manchurian Railroad Company were ordered to distort Korean history. *The Historical Geography of Manchuria, Historical Geography of Korea,* and *Report of Geographical* and *Historical Research in Manchuria* are products of such historiography. In the *History of the Korean Peninsula* (1915), the Japanese limited the scope of Korean history to the peninsula, severing it from relations with the Asian continent and brushing aside as fallacy judgments made by Korean historians.

This Japanese attempt to annihilate the Korean national consciousness was even more conspicuous in educational policy. The educational act promulgated in September 1911 was geared mainly to secure manpower for the operation of the colonial establishment. The Japanese also tightened their control of traditional as well as private schools. More than 90 percent of school-age children were denied the opportunity to learn, thereby keeping them illiterate. The 12 years between 1910 and 1922 saw a spectacular decrease in the number of private schools, from more than 2,000 to about 600. Such was the dire effect of the efforts of the Japanese colonial masters to extinguish Korea's national consciousness.

Early in 1907, when resistance against the Office of the Resident- General was at its height under the leadership of the "righteous armies," the *Shinminhoe* came into being. The aim of this secret organization was to recover independence. Led by An Ch'ang-ho, the association continued to grow, and by 1910 had a membership of more than 300, representing all the provinces.

On December 27, 1910, Governor-General Terauchi was to attend a ceremony dedicating the railway bridge over the Amnokkang River. On a false charge that *Shinminhoe* members had engaged in a conspiracy to assassinate him on his way to the ceremony, the Japanese arrested more than 600 of the society members and their sympathizers, of whom 105 were convicted under severe torture. Some were beaten to death and six members, including Yun Ch'i-ho, Yang Ki-t'ak, An T'ae-guk and Yi Sŭng-hun, were sentenced to prison terms.

This Japanese fabrication was exposed by such foreign missionaries as H.G. Underwood, G.S. McCune and S.A. Moffet. P.L. Gilette, secretary-general of the Korean Young Men's Christian Association, went to China and declared to the world that the incident was a fabrication. The same disclosure was made in a booklet entitled *The Korean Conspiracy Case* by A.J. Brown, secretary-general of the Presbyterian Missions in Foreign Countries, at the request of missionary organization in Korea. Brown criticized Japan's colonial policy, calling Korea "a well-regulated penal colony."

In spite of Terauchi's maneuvering to dissolve the *Shinminhoe*, commanders of the "righteous armies" organized the Independence Army Headquarters in 1913 under the leadership of Im Pyŏng-ch'an with the aim of redirecting popular opinion to the cause of restoring national sovereignty. The objectives of the Korean Sovereignty Restoration Corps, originally organized at Anilam, a Buddhist monastery in Taegu in 1915, included independence agitation through direct action and through diplomatic channels, and the supplying of military funds to the Provisional Korean Government in Exile in Shanghai. The corps planned an assault on Japanese military police stations in 1919, mobilizing thousands of villagers.

Land Survey and Other Forms of Oppression

At the time the Government-General was established, the Japanese embarked on land surveying for the consolidation of their colonial economic system. They concentrated all of their administrative resources on this project, mobilizing both military and civilian police forces.

Prior to this, in order to reorganize its financial administration in 1898, the Korean government had launched a land survey, and the Office of Land Survey of the Ministry of Finance issued land certificates in 1901 to farms that were surveyed. The project was not completed and in 1905 Japan forced the Ministry of Finance to carry out a land survey to provide an inventory of the Korean government's revenue sources, paving the way for seizure of land.

In 1908, the Japanese forced the Korean government to establish a land survey office to ascertain the amount of real estate owned by the royal household. On the basis of this survey, all immovables owned by the household, except the palaces, the royal mausoleum and royal tombs, were listed as government property. The land thus entered was later absorbed by the Japanese when they deprived Korea of its sovereignty. In 1912, the Government-General promulgated laws requiring real-estate owners to make reports on their of land within a prescribed period of time, empowering the Japanese financial office to endorse ownership of all land.

The land survey took eight years, beginning in 1910, and cost 20,400,000 yen. It laid the foundation for wholesale expropriation of land.

By utilizing the favorable new conditions, the Oriental Development Company was able to expand its ownership of land to 154,221 hectares. The number of tenant farmers subordinate to the company exceeded 300,000, tenant farmers who had already been deprived of their own right to cultivate land as a result of Japanese aggression.

The number of disputes concerning land ownership which arose as a result of the survey amounted to 34,000 cases. Most of these disputes came from Koreans who were deprived of their land by the survey, or by false accusations from Japanese in their attempts at illegal acquisition of land. The Government-General resolved the disputes by the application of the "enforced conciliation law."

In 1911 the Government-General enforced measures to provide the Japanese freedom to fell trees, and the authority of Japanese lumbering companies in Korea was expanded. In May 1918, the Japanese promulgated the Korean Forestry Ordinance, forcing forest owners to register with the colonial office. Through a survey separating state and private forests, the Japanese used the pretext of nationalization to transfer the ownership of 1,090,000 hectares of village forests and 3,090,000 hectares of grave forests to Japanese lumbering companies. Excessive felling of trees by the Japanese brought about devastation of Korean forests, and extensive erosion followed in the devastated mountains.

To impede the progress of existing Korean companies and prevent the creation of new ones, the Company Ordinance was issued in December 1910. This ordinance empowered the government to grant charters, resulting in great hindrance to the development of Korean capital. Even chartered companies were subject to suspension or dissolution by the Government-General at will, and heavy penalties were stipulated for violators.

The reduction of Korean capital was accompanied by rapid growth of Japanese investment in fundamental industries.

In the same vein, the Regulations for Fisheries Associations of 1912 enabled the Japanese to bring Korean fisheries under their control by enforcing joint sale of all that Korean fishermen caught. About 30,000 Japanese fishermen residing in Korea, and about 90,000 other Japanese fishermen, mostly poachers, devastated the Korean fishing grounds which had been providing a livelihood for 200,000 Korean fishermen.

Korean farmers fared no better, as the Government General controlled financial associations by means of usurious loans. In addition, the Oriental Development Company served as an agent of the Government-General in implementing a large-scale resettlement program that saw no fewer than 98,000 Japanese owner-families settled in Korea prior to 1918.

March 1st Independence Struggle

A nationwide uprising on March 1, 1919 was an outcry for national survival in the face of the intolerable aggression, oppression, and plundering by the Japanese colonialists. An apparent sudden change in the international situation in the wake of World War I stimulated a group of Korean leaders to launch an independence struggle, both at home and abroad. Among the activities of Korean leaders abroad, Syngman Rhee, then in the United States, planned to go to Paris in 1918 to make an appeal for Korean independence, but his travel abroad was not permitted by the U.S. government, which considered its relationship with Japan more important. As an alternative, Rhee made a personal appeal to U.S. President Woodrow Wilson, who was in Paris at that time, to place Korea under the trusteeship of the League of Nations.

In December 1918, Korean students in Tokyo discussed the question of Korean independence and selected a committee of 10 members, including Ch'oe P'al-yong, to put their plan into practice in January 1919. They convened a meeting of the Korean Student Association at the Korean Young Men's Christian Association building in Tokyo and declared Korean independence, but the students who gathered were dispersed by police after a brief clash. On February 23, they held a rally in Hibiya Park under the auspices of the Korean Youth Independence Corps, and staged demonstrations calling for Korean independence. Their aim was to stimulate independence resistance and make an appeal to the international society of nations.

The New Korea Youth Party was organized in China in 1918, and it was decided that Kim Kyu-shik would be sent to the Paris Peace Conference to appeal for Korean independence. The party broadened its contacts with leaders in China, the United States, Japan, Manchuria and the Maritime Province of Siberia to promote its cause.

At home, leaders of the *Ch'ŏndogyo* (formerly *Tonghak*) movement, the most prominent among them being Son Pyŏng-hŭi, decided that the independence movement should be popular in nature and non-violent. Under the leadership of Yi Sang-jae and Pak Hui-do, directors of the Young Men's Christian Association, students rallied to the banner of independence. The leaders of the movement also opened contact with Yi Sŭng-hŭn. The contributions of Ch'oe Nam-son and Kim To-t'ae were especially valuable in cementing ties between the *Ch'ŏndogyo* and Christian leaders.

On the Buddhist side, Han Yong-un had been carrying out a reform movement to rescue Buddhism from its decline caused by Japanese policy, and he also called strongly for an independence movement. Receiving an offer of cooperation from the *Ch'ŏndogyo* leaders, he immediately responded. The Confucianists had been constantly expressing antagonism to Japanese aggression, and some of them led the volunteer "righteous armies" in direct engagements with the Japanese.

The independence movement was planned also in close liaison with various organizations which had been operating in secret. The climax came on March 1, 1919, when, during a period of public mourning for the recently deceased Emperor Kojong, the Declaration of Korean Independence was publicly proclaimed at Pagoda Park in Seoul. The aroused citizenry then demonstrated in the streets, shouting for Korean independence. This ignited a nationwide movement in which many people took part, regardless of locality and social status.

The Koreans who were arrested by the Japanese and brought to trial represented all occupations and educational levels. Whereas the Koreans had no weapons at that time, the Japanese had stationed in their colony regular ground forces of one and a half divisions, in addition to a 5,402-man police force in 751 stations and a military police force nearly 8,000 strong. By mobilizing these armed forces, the Japanese perpetrated brutal atrocities in their effort to suppress the peaceful demonstrations of the Korean people. The Japanese side reinforced its police by throwing six infantry battalions and 400 military police troops into the suppression campaign. These forces killed about 7,500 Koreans and wounded nearly 16,000.

Defining any Korean taking part in the independence resistance as a criminal, the Japanese decided to cope with subsequent demonstrations by a policy of massacre. A case at Suwon, Kyŏnggi-do province, was typical. On April 15 that year, a squad of Japanese troops ordered about 30 villagers to assemble in a Christian church, closed all the windows and doors, then set the building

Launching the Independence Movement of March 1, 1919.

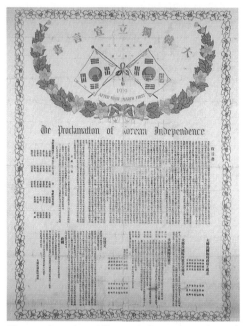

The proclamation of Korean independence issued in April 1919, the Korean Provisional Government in exile in Shanghai.

Prior to trying to assassinate a Japanese army general in Shanghai, Yun Pong-gil(1908-32) held up a written pledge to give his life in the cause of national independence.

The key members of the Korean Provisional Government in exile in Shanghai.

afire. While the church burned for five hours, the Japanese soldiers aimed a concentrated barrage at the confined civilians, killing all of them, including women and infants. The Japanese soldiers also burned 31 houses in the village, then set fire to 317 houses in 15 villages in the vicinity. Informed of the incident, F.W. Schofield, a Canadian missionary, and other American missionaries visited the scene of the incident on April 17, personally viewing the traces of Japanese atrocities, and informed the world of what they had seen.

The 33 signers of the Declaration of Korean Independence were taken before a Japanese court for trial, along with 48 others who worked in close cooperation with them for the independence movement. One of the prisoners, Han Yong-un, wrote "A Letter of Korean Independence," stating the reasons why the Korean people should be free. This writing ranks with the three-article Public Pledge attached to the Declaration of Korean Independence as one of the basic documents which laid the spiritual foundation of the 1919 independence movement. The Korean people in the course of the movement realized the necessity for both a government and armed resistance.

The Provisional Government of Korea

At the height of the independence movement, a provisional government of Korea was established in Vladivostok on March 21, in Shanghai on April 11, and in Seoul on April 21. The reason for such action in three different places almost simultaneously can be explained by the fact that the need for leadership was felt to be most urgent in the independence struggle.

The provisional government in Seoul, with all 13 provinces represented, proclaimed Korean independence, asking Japan to repeal its colonial system and withdraw its occupation forces from Korea. It called upon the Korean people to refuse payment of taxes to the Japanese government, not to accept trials by Japanese courts, and to avoid employment at colonial offices. A direct challenge was posed by the Seoul government against the entire Japanese colonial system.

The National Council of Korea in Vladivostok, when notified of the establishment of a provisional government in Shanghai, made efforts to integrate its activities with those of the Shanghai group. The latter passed a resolution calling for integration with the Seoul government. The first cabinet meeting was convened

Kim Ku, President of the Korean
Provisional Government in Shanghai,
returning to Seoul in 1945,
following liberation.(left).
A reply, dated April 28, 1944,
by Kim Ku to a letter from a Chinese
politician congratulating Kim on his
reelection as President of the Korean
Provisional Government in Shanghai.
(above).

on November 4, marking the start of the functioning of the Provisional Government.

As a representative of the Korean people, and as their only independence organization abroad, the Provisional Government, despite financial difficulties and attempts at infiltration and suppression, did its best to fulfill the international obligations of the Korean government. It declared war on totalitarian Japan and provided close cooperation with the Allied Powers during the World War II. For 27 years, until its return home on November 23, 1945, after the Japanese surrender, the Provisional Government strove to represent the Korean people.

The Independence Army

Various independence forces operating in Manchuria were unified and placed under the command of the Provisional Government. The independence armies underwent frequent reorganization, however, owing to changes in the international situation and differences of opinion among leaders of the Provisional Government. A group of leaders met in Peking in April 1921 to work out a plan for united military action, realizing that the most urgent task was to unite the independence armies active in Manchuria. The conference later developed into the all-inclusive Council of National Representatives that held its first meeting in Shanghai in January 1923. Armed resistance under the leadership of the Provisional Government was given a firm basis, and the Korean troops in Manchuria continuously fought the Japanese army, sometimes with spectacular success.

In October 1920 at Ch'ŏngsan-ri, a gallant force of about 400 men, in a fierce four-day battle, dealt a crushing blow to a Japanese force of brigade strength. It was only in Manchuria that armed struggle was carried on continuously. During the Bolshevik revolution, a brief invasion by the Japanese army drove the Korean independence fighters from the Russian Maritime Province. A Korean army of 3,000 men was besieged by the Red Army in the "free city" of Braweschensk in June 1921, and several hundred Koreans were killed. The survivors, numbering 1,700, were ordered by the Chinese government to abandon their weapons and taken to Irkutsk to be absorbed into the Red Army, putting an end to their fight for independence.

Changes in Japan's Colonial Policy

The Japanese counterattack against the Korean independence movement was typical of Japan's militaristic policy. The Japanese forced colonial-style education down to a minimum level. They banned the teaching of the Korean language and history while laying greater emphasis on the teaching of Japanese language and history. The deliberate policy of annihilation was hailed by Japanese propaganda as a "cultural policy."

Though absorbed into the ordinary police structure, the military police executed police administration as before under the protection of special laws. The police force expanded as a result of transfers and amalgamation of military policemen into the ordinary police.

A group of Korean educational leaders passed a resolution on June 22, 1920, calling for approval of their plan to establish a private university. The Japanese rejected the resolution, however, under provisions of the Korean Education Ordinance, and reacted with renewed oppression. Instead, they established Keijo Imperial University as a colonial institute in 1924-1926. Admission of Korean students to

that university was limited to one-third to one-fourth of the total number of students. Extreme limitation of fundamental education for Koreans was the most important basic "cultural policy" of Governor-General Saito Makoto.

In 1920 the Government-General permitted the start of two private newspapers besides those already in existence as its own organs for propaganda. The real intent of this permission was to spy on Koreans of anti-Japanese opinion. Enforcement of strict censorship was practiced on every word and phrase. Japanese colonial policy was geared as before to the oppression of the Korean people by expansion of the police, judicial and prison systems.

Having completed a land survey, Japan planned to meet its food grain shortage with increased rice production in Korea. In order to fill the deficit, Japan called for sharply increased rice production by soil improvement and modernization of farming methods. The plan fell short of its goals and was finally abandoned in 1934, but the increase in rice production was impressive, and large quantities were shipped to Japan.

The policy of increased rice production inflicted severe damage to Korean farmers. The drastic decline in per capita rice consumption by Koreans between 1912 and 1931 was due to an increase in the quantity of rice sent to Japan of more than 500 percent during the period. Having taken from Korea 48 to 50 percent of its total rice production, the Government-General attempted to supply a small part of the resultant grain deficit by importing millet from Manchuria, but the price was higher than the price Japan paid for Korean rice.

More and more farmers were downgraded by the colonial policy to either tenants or semi-tenants. In 1931, they numbered nearly 12 million, comprising 2,325,707 households under high farm-rents in a state of near starvation. The farm-rents, a principal means of exploitation, were as high as 50 to 80 percent of the annual income from farming.

The destitution facing Korean farmers before the harvest of summer barley periodically drove them to the verge of starvation. Some farmers (about 19 percent) emigrated to Manchuria,

Siberia, and Japan. Still others found employment as unskilled laborers in factories or did odd jobs to earn a small and uncertain income. Some families had to disperse, each member earning his own livelihood.

A considerable number of those who stuck to farming were burdened by usurious loans. According to statistics compiled in 1930, at least 75 percent of the 1,733,797 farming households were in debt. More than 70 percent of the debts were payable to Japanese financial institutions, at interest ranging from 15 to 35 percent a year.

Koreans living in urban areas fared no better than their rural countrymen. Nearly 80 percent of urban dwellers lived in grinding poverty. It was Japanese policy to keep the wages of Koreans at less than half the amount paid to their Japanese counterparts. The fact that 132 out of 170 disputes occurring in 1935 concerned demands for higher wages is clear evidence of the poverty which overwhelmed the colonialized people.

The devastating effects of the colonial agricultural policy finally weakened the very basis of colonial domination. Japan, seeing the importance of rural problems, tried to resolve them by establishing rational relations between agriculture and industry. Governor-General Ugaki Kazunari (1931-36) professed a desire to rejuvenate Korean rural villages, binding them into near feudal bondage.

In 1934 the Farmland Ordinance was enacted, ostensibly with a view to securing the position of tenant farmers. In fact, these measures resulted only in recognizing the exploitation of farmers through high-interest farm rents. An agency set up by the Government-General to settle the tenant disputes served only to protect the interests of landlords.

Governor-General Ugaki, who had advocated rural development, enforced cotton cultivation in southern Korea early in the 1930s when Japan's import of cotton was restricted for financial reasons. As a result, cotton output increased from 689,000 *kŭn* (1 *kŭn* equals about 0.6kg) in 1910 to 213,749,000 *kŭn* in 1934. In order to give a helping hand to Japan's import of raw wool as well, he forced the northern district of Korea to raise sheep, thereby subordinating Korea to Japan's textile industry.

As the 1930s dawned, the Government-General gave priority to the police in budget allocation, surpassing the outlay for general administration and education. The Japanese police were further armed with a set of oppressive laws designed to crush any national or social opposition: laws governing rebellion, riot, disturbance, publication, press and crimes against the Japanese royalty (*lese majeste*), political offenses and maintenance of public order. After 1919, the Korean criminal ordinances and the Korean civil ordinances underwent revision. In particular, the revised Korean census registration ordinance imposed strict surveillance and repression on the routine daily activities of Koreans.

Whereas the rate of increase in general crimes was relatively slow, that of political offenses showed a rapid increase, reflecting intensified ideological oppression. The strengthening of physical restraint measures was accompanied by strict enforcement of the colonial education policy.

The colonial university was given the task of the compilation of the history of Korea under the Korean History Compilation Society founded by the Government-General. Their objective was to negate the creativity, originality, and autonomous spirit of the Korean people in their cultural and historical traditions. In order to achieve such an aim, they kept historical documents and royal library collections from Korean scholars.

Colonial Policy in Action

The independence movement, meanwhile, improved in organization and methods. More militant, systematic, and diversified resistance was effected. Japan's colonial policy in Korea remained unchanged although fancy appellations such as "new administration" or "cultural administration" were used to gloss it over after the March First resistance movement.

The reorganization of the police brought about a rapid increase in the numbers of organization and in budgetary appropriations. The police budget quadrupled in the 1920s, comprising 12-13 percent of the total budget, In contrast educational outlays were less than 1.8 percent of the police appropriations.

The police did their utmost to suppress all spontaneous activities by Koreans. The depth of police penetration was evident in the number of inhabitants per policeman—one policeman for 722 persons in Korea, compared with one for 1,150 in Japan.

As a result of judicial reforms designed to crack down on political offenses, so-called "thought" prosecutors and "thought" judges were appointed and "special high police" squads were added to each police organization. Communist circles, which spread rapidly in Korea following the trend of the times, were among the main targets of the Japanese police. Strikes, labor disputes and tenant farmer protests were largely motivated by anti-colonial and nationalistic sentiments directed against the Japanese.

Various laws and ordinances were utilized to halt all critical expression and acts of sabotage or sedition against the Japanese colonial authorities. In enacting and promulgating the laws, Governor-General Saito expressed his determination to suppress all resistance movements.

By the 1930s, the peasants were on the verge of starvation. The only way out of such a condition was to desert the farm. Many went to Manchuria or Japan, only to find it no easier to settle there. According to the statistics of the Government-General for 1925, of all the farm deserters, 2.88 percent went to Manchuria and Siberia, 16.85 percent to Japan, and 46.39 percent were scattered in cities of Korea with marginal jobs.

A dwindling of the international market following the close of World War I had a decisive bearing upon the colonial policy of Japan. The Japan Nitrogen Fertilizer Co., Onoda Cements and Japanese textile businesses found cheap labor available in Korea. The invasion of massive Japanese capital gradually forced native landowners and tenant farmers to abandon farmland in return for nominal compensation. Korean-owned lands were bought or virtually expropriated at about one percent of the then current value to accommodate Japanese industrial plants. The Government-General granted eminent domain to Japanese capitalists in an arbitrary manner.

Expansion of Japanese colonial capital during the 1920s resulted in increased poverty and depression for the Koreans, and became a target of the resistance struggle. It also stimulated the rise of the socialist movement that was in vogue at that time throughout the world. Japanese laborers frequently joined Koreans in disputes over Japanese capital interests.

The exiled Provisional Government of Korea made efforts to appeal before the great powers at the League of Nations Conference in Geneva in 1932, but leading countries with colonies of their own refused to discuss the Korean problem. Nevertheless, some countries made persistent efforts to recognize the Provisional Government. The Moscow government of Lenin approved the granting of a loan in the amount of two million rubles, while the Canton government of Sun Yat-sen extended formal recognition to the Provisional Government.

Secret organizations continued to operate at home, attacking and destroying Japanese police stations and government buildings. Korean leaders were also active in supplying funds to independence fighters in Manchuria and Shanghai to promote their military and political activities. Along the northern border many small groups of Korean soldiers continued attacks against the Japanese troops. The Ŭiyŏltan, organized in Manchuria in November of 1919, as an independence organization, infiltrated its commandos into Seoul and Tokyo to carry out the mission of attacking Japanese government offices and assassinating officials. There were frequent explosion incidents in Korea and Japan, and even in China. Yun Pong-gil, a member of the Aeguktan (Patriotic Association), succeeded in killing several Japanese army commanders in China with a bomb at their gathering in Shanghai in April 1933. His success raised the morale not only of Koreans but also of the Chinese who were faced with mounting Japanese aggression.

Manchuria lay just across the Amnokkang River, so many loyal troops went there after

1906, and when Korea was overtaken by Japan, groups of patriotic leaders sought exile there. They engaged in reclaiming farmland, educating the children of exiled patriots and organizing military training centers. Manchuria was also an ideal military base for launching quick attacks on the Japanese, and the independence troops operating in eastern and southern Manchuria were gradually integrated under the leadership of the Provisional Government.

The independence army suffered severe financial hardship, while Japan tried to obtain the cooperation of the Chinese in an attempt to oust it from Manchuria or to annihilate it altogether. Despite such adversities, the Korean troops fought well and achieved significant results. The Ch'ŏngsan-ri Battle of October 1920, in which a Korean force outnumbered eight to one triumphed over the Japanese, will remain a landmark in the history of the Korean independence struggle.

Venting their rancor on the Koreans for that disastrous defeat, Japanese troops slaughtered many Korean residents in Manchuria. Some others were buried alive in random massacres, and other atrocities were committed in horrible scenes, as witnessed by a Presbyterian missionary from America.

As the independence army's resistance in Manchuria and its penetration into Korea intensified, the Government-General concluded an agreement designed to block Korean activities in that area with Chang Tso-lin, a strongman in Manchuria. In order to overcome the crisis, many separate units were incorporated into a 15,000-man force. The reorganized independence army continued its struggle even in 1933, when Japan succeeded in annexing Manchuria. But, by making use of mounted bandits, the Japanese troops slaughtered many Korean residents.

Most impressive among various activities at home after the 1919 independence uprising was the press movement aimed at promoting national consciousness by criticizing and attacking Japanese colonial policy. In 1920, three newspapers came into being, the *Dong-a Ilbo*, the *Chosun Ilbo* and the *Shisa Shinmun*. These dailies spread the use of the Korean language and made significant contributions in the traditional fields of literature, drama, films, music and fine arts, and also in the dissemination of information from abroad.

The educational movement began to awaken the masses on a broadscale to the necessity for anti-Japanese struggle. Private institutes and night courses for workers were established by the Koreans themselves. Youths and students who came to cities from rural villages could earn their school expenses through affiliation with organizations of self-supporting students. The determined effort to establish a private college in order to provide higher learning was repeatedly rejected by the government-general.

Prominent among social projects at that time were the movement for women's liberations, the juvenile protection movement and a movement designed to eliminate discrimination on the basis of class. These movements were carried out in close association with the national liberation movement, and at times were connected with the socialist movement which first made its debut in Korea in 1920, as well as with Christian churches.

A nationwide movement for a self-supporting economy was also launched in order to shake off the colonial economic shackles. The Korean YMCA began a rural enlightenment campaign on a nationwide scale, and the successors to *Tonghak* followed suit. These movements aimed at economic self-sufficiency, and called for the boycott of Japanese commodities.

A common front between nationalist and communist leaders mounted a vigorous campaign against the Japanese, and a nationwide student movement erupted on June 10, 1926. The Communist Party secretly sent Kwon O-sŏl home from Shanghai to lead the independence demonstration, a mass struggle as large in scope as the March First 1919 independence movement, by capitalizing on the masses gathered because of the demise of former Emperor Sunjong in April of 1926.

Preservation of Korean Culture

A group of about 10 teachers in private schools organized the Korean Language Society

(*Chosŏn Ŏhakhoe*) in December 1921, with the mission of "contributing to the education of our next generation by studying the principles of the Korean language." The *Dong-a Ilbo* and *Chosun Ilbo* dailies and monthly magazines rendered full cooperation to the Korean language movement. The *Chosun Ilbo* designated a *"Han-gŭl* Day, when the daily carried a special supplement presenting treatises by scholars specializing in the study of the Korean language.

A journal devoted to *Han-gŭl* was published and by 1932 had secured for itself a firm position as the organ of the Korean Language Society, which not only conducted research but also subsidized scholars faced with financial difficulty. The society fixed a new spelling system for the Korean language in 1933 and standardized Korean and the transcription system of foreign words. Also, the task of editing and publishing a Korean dictionary was undertaken in 1929 and continuously pursued by the society. *Ch'oe Hyŏn-bae's* works on Korean grammar and linguistic theory contributed immensely to the promotion of the national language movement under Japanese rule. Meanwhile, the daily newspapers launched a mass enlightenment campaign. The *Dong-a Ilbo* adopted the newly proclaimed spelling system April 1, 1933, and the *Chosun Ilbo* soon followed suit. Furthermore, the newspapers sponsored a literacy campaign, enlisting the participation of middle school students. The *Chosun Ilbo* upheld the slogan, "the movement toward the people." However, beginning in October 1942, leading members of the society were arrested and imprisoned, and only the Japanese surrender of August 15, 1945, ended the long ordeal of some of these patriots.

The Japanese embarked upon rewriting Korean history from a strongly Japan-centered viewpoint which tried to denigrate the nation. Korean historians in their struggle for independence had to refute and discredit the Japanese historiography on Korea, and describe the results of Japanese aggression as they witnessed it. Pak Ŭn-shik, Shin Ch'ae-ho, An Chae-hong and Chŏng In-bo made the most outstanding contributions by refuting the distorted history of the Japanese colonial scholars.

Pak Ŭn-Shik (1861-1926) attempted to find the means to convey to contemporary Koreans and future generations the reality of the nation's efforts to achieve overall reform, and to do justice to Korean experiences during the armed resistance against alien invaders. During his exile, he wrote two books with cooperation from his colleagues. These books, which were published at the same time, made a lasting impact upon the minds of Koreans.

Song Sang-do (1871-1946) was a unique researcher who compiled biographies of each of the independence fighters after gathering facts through on-the-spot inquiries. Undertaken under the shadow of Japanese surveillance and oppression, his work, concentrating on the period between 1919 to 1945, supplemented Pak Ŭn-shik's works dealing with activities abroad until 1919.

Shin Ch'ae-ho (1880-1936), who wrote on the early history of Korea, actively participated in the armed independence movement in Manchuria, Shanghai and Peking. He continuously made public the results of his studies on Korean history.

Modern literature, written in *Han-gŭl*, called upon the public to achieve social and national awakening, and sought to absorb the spiritual heritage of modern European literature. Two main streams developed in the process of absorbing foreign literature: one group of writers produced satirical works in an effort to stimulate a spirit of independence and patriotism, while another relied on foreign influence trying to transplant into Korea the modern transition that had taken place in Europe. Pak Ŭn-shik, Shin Ch'ae-ho and An Kuk-sŏn produced works belonging to the first category, and representative among writers of the second group was Yi In-jik. Spiritual downfall was the fate of both groups under Japanese domination.

The essence of modern Korean literature can be found in the literary activities of a group of writers who in the 1920s contemplated the colonial reality from a nationalist viewpoint and tried to overcome their dilemma through literary works. The move toward what was called "new literature," replacing the traditional literature, started as early as 1908. It was impossible for

Korean writers to produce enlightening works before 1919, because of the press law forced upon the Korean government in 1907. The Government-General allowed the Koreans publish their works only through the Maeil Shin-bo, the Japanese propaganda medium in Korean; thus it was difficult to create a literature reflecting the true Korean consciousness.

In 1919 Kim Tong-in and Kim Ŏk founded a literary magazine, *Ch'angjo* (Creation) marking the starting point of modern Korean literature. The magazine was followed by *P'yehŏ* (Ruins), published in 1920 by Hwang Sŏg-u and Yŏm Sang-sŏp; *Paekcho* (White Tide) published in 1922 by Yi Sang-hwa and Hyŏn Chin-gŏn; and *Kŭmsŏng* (Gold Star) published in 1923 by Yi Chang-hŭe and Yang Chu-dong. Through such literary works, these writers tried to grasp the dominant current of thought and show the future course Korea should take.

Other literary magazines which appeared during the 1920s and 1930s laid the basis for the future development of modern Korean literature. Almost all of these magazines were ordered to discontinue publication in the 1940s as the Japanese tightened their grip with the spread of their aggressive war to the Pacific and all of Southeast Asia. The important task of the 1920s was to work out ways of introducing foreign elements into literary works dealing with the reality of colonial rule in Korea.

Shim Hun's *Sangnoksu* (Evergreen Tree, 1943) was based on the theme of rural development pursued by the Koreans. Yi Ki-yŏng's *Kohyang* (The Home Country, 1932) described the process of infiltration of Japanese colonial capital into the rural areas. In these works and others, the poverty of Korean rural villages of the 1930s was delineated with a romantic touch. Hong Myŏng-hŭi's *Im Kkŏk-chŏng* described a confrontation between corrupt government officials and a group of bandits led by *Im Kkŏk-chŏng* and stirred the people's antagonism toward Japanese colonial rule.

There were many poets as well who appealed to the national sentiment. Perhaps the greatest pioneer of modern poetry was Han Yong-un. His *Nimŭi Ch'immuk* (The Silence, 1925) expressed his affection for a homeland deprived

of sovereignty. The beautiful spirit of another poet, Yi Sang-hwa, sang his boundless love of his homeland in a symbolic way, and Yi Yuk-sa, who was arrested, imprisoned and tortured to death by the Japanese military police, expressed his endless hope for the future of his fatherland. These were the main themes in the Korean literary spirit throughout the colonial period.

Yŏm Sang-sŏp was one writer who pursued national consciousness in historical perspective. He tried to describe the independence struggle in the 1920s in terms of the interaction between nationalism and communism. In *Samdae* (The Three Generations, 1932), a historical monument, he gave expression to the dilemmas and frictions faced by Koreans in the process of transition from a traditional to a capitalist society.

In deriving their themes from such transitional phenomena, writers of the 1930s had to part from Yŏm's naturalistic, realistic style and resort to satirical touches. One of these writers, Ch'ae Man-shik, made his debut late in the 1930s. His *Ch'ŏnha T'aep'yŏngch'un* (The Peaceful Spring on Earth, 1937) ridicules the outdated vestiges still found in colonized Korea, and his *T'akryu* (The Muddy Stream, 1941) satirizes Korean society in general, sharply criticizing Japanese capital for its devastating effect on Korean society.

Shinganhoe—a Unified National Organization

Founded on February 15, 1927, *Shinganhoe* (New Stem Association) was a unified national organization. The association attempted to form a joint front by combining leaders of the nationalist and communist camps. The plan to organize *Shinganhoe* was first proposed by nationalist leaders keenly realizing the necessity of combining leaders of the nationalists and communists into one of the various independence organizations. The communist camp, under a directive from the Comintern, also felt the need of forming a joint front in cooperation with the nationalist camp.

At the time of its founding, *Shinganhoe* was headed by Yi Sang-jae, president, An Chae-

The Korean Independence Army activated in China in 1940s.

hong, secretary-general, and Hong Myŏng-hŭi, in charge of organization. Yi Sŭng-bok distinguished himself in raising operational funds. From its foundation, the association was subjected to extreme oppression by the Japanese police. The declaration of the association proclaimed upon its inception, did not survive, leaving only its platform which called for political and economic awakening, unity of purpose and rejection of any compromise with Japan. The association flatly rejected an attempt made by some Koreans for autonomy under Japanese rule.

The association sponsored local meetings which were aimed at discussing such measures as: the exemption of school fees for children of proletarian families; demands for the teaching of the Korean language; opposition to the Japanese emigration policy; the denunciation of compromising political movements; abolition of the "Laws and Ordinances of 1919" and of special control laws against Koreans (laws aimed at oppressing the nationalist and communist movements); opposition to all county agricultural associations (Japan's exploitation agencies); enforcement of education for the benefit of Koreans; the acquisition of freedom for the study of social sciences; opposition to imperialistic colonial education policy; and the abolition

of *hyanggyo* and acquisition of the right to dispose of property.

The *Shinganhoe* was, however, plagued by disunity and pressure from the Comintern, which soon ordered the Korean Communists to work for its dissolution. Early in 1931 the leftist leaders of the *Shinganhoe* asked for its dissolution. The Pusan branch was disbanded, and at a Seoul meeting on May 16, 1931, the resistance organization finally disappeared, succumbing to maneuvering by its left-wing elements. Its nationalist leaders were arrested by the police, and there emerged no other resistance organization of comparable scale, as the Japanese intensified their harsh, oppressive policies.

Resistance Against Final Extinction

The beginning of Japan's war of aggression on the Asian continent and its spread into the Pacific brought further tightening of Japan's reins over Korea. The Japanese colonial policy was aimed at transforming Korea into a logistical base for continental aggression, the closing phase of Japanese colonial rule in Korea.

Invading Manchuria on the pretext of a fabricated provocation in Mukden, the Japanese soon took over the whole region. The venture was sparked by Japan's quest for an overseas solution for its economic depression at home.

Monopolistic capital from Japan flowed into Korea to create the arsenal for invasion of the continent. Cheap labor was available as the result of Korean impoverishment caused by Japanese exploitation. Rapid advances had been made in some manufacturing, but it was a "dependent" industrialization, geared to colonialism.

Japan carried on its war of continental invasion from Manchuria into mid-China. During the 1930s in Korea emphasis gradually shifted from foodstuff manufacturing to such heavy industries as machines, chemicals and metals. In 1939, heavy industry constituted more than 50 percent of all industrial sectors. Production of agricultural commodities steadily declined in value from 60 percent of the gross national product in 1931 to 32 percent in 1942.

Despite marked progress in industries, the native capital invested was minimal. As the war went on, the exploitation of Korean labor became ever greater. Koreans were excluded from positions of skilled work and forced to do heavy manual labor at wages less than half those received by their Japanese counterparts. The official enforcement of industrial development went hand in hand with the colonial agricultural policy of increasing rice production.

As the tide of the war turned against the Japanese, they squeezed more and more agricultural products out of the peasants by means of *kongch'ul* or "quota delivery." Farmers were compelled to grow rice with expensive fertilizers to fulfill their assigned quotas.

In March 1944, the Japanese placed production quotas on major mining and manufacturing industries for the purpose of securing military supplies, and medium and small enterprises were consolidated. Alignment of colonial industries was undertaken with emphasis placed on iron and light metal industries and production of raw materials. These economic restrictions were accompanied by further infringement upon freedom of thought and civil liberties.

For example, in the course of invading China in 1937, the Japanese began to suppress freedom of religion and faith, substituting compulsory worship at Japanese Shinto shrines, and in 1938, Korean language teaching was banned from secondary school curricula and from April 1941, the curricula of Japanese schools was imposed upon Korean schools. As the war intensified, the education of Koreans under the Education Decree of March 1943 was increasingly geared to the Japanese war establishment. No longer was the Korean language taught in primary schools.

But such high-handed oppression by the Government-General could hardly fail to bring about persistent resistance. Many were arrested on charges of "seeking to attain the ambition of liberating the Korean people." Nationalists were the most active group in the most oppressive period (1937-45). In 1941 a Thought Criminals Preventive Custody Law went into force, and a protective prison was established in Seoul, where almost all anti-Japanese activists were herded. The Government-General declared that preventive custody was intended to isolate from society these unruly "thought criminals" and to discipline them. It was the first step in a drive to uproot the will to independence from the minds of the Koreans.

In 1942, the Government-General came under the central administrative control of the Japanese government, and a massive mobilization of Korean manpower and materials was integrated into the war effort. From 1943, Korean youths were drafted into the Japanese army, and the Student Volunteer Ordinance of January 20, 1944, forced Korean college students into the army,

Moreover, under the National General Mobilization Act of Japan, Korean labor was subjected to forcible removal from the peninsula. The drafting of laborers began in 1939 and many were sent to Japan, Sakhalin or Southeast Asia. Statistics up to August 15, 1945, show that 4,146,098 workers were assigned inside Korea and 1,259,933 in Japan. Many Korean workers were put sent the coal mines in Japan; some of them remain in Japan and Sakhalin even to this day.

The course of the Sino-Japanese War forced the Chinese Nationalist Government to move to Chungking, and in 1940, the Provisional Government of Korea as well had to move

A special ceremony inaugurating the Republic of Korea Government on August 15, 1948.

Chŏng Han-gyŏng (Henry Chung) to go to Cairo to promote the cause of Korean independence. Upon the proposal of Generalissimo Chiang, the three powers agreed to include a call for Korea's self-determination and independence in the Cairo Declaration.

In February 1944, the Provisional Government brought some leftist personalities into its fold and formed a sort of coalition cabinet, with Kim Ku as chairman and Kim Kyu-shik as vice chairman. In February 1945, it formally declared war against Japan and Germany by taking part in active campaigns; altogether after 1943, more than 5,000 Korean troops joined the allied forces in military operations throughout the Chinese theater of war. Korean college students and youths drafted into the Japanese army deserted their units to join the ranks of China's anti-Japanese resistance war. In the United States as well, a number of Korean immigrants volunteered for the U.S. Army to fight against the Japanese in the Pacific. Korean Communists in Kando, northeast Manchuria, also joined the Soviet Russian or Chinese Communists.

there. On August 28, 1941, the Provisional Government, in response to the declaration by President Roosevelt and Prime Minister Churchill, issued a statement demanding recognition of the Korean government; military, technical and economic assistance for the prosecution of anti-Japanese campaigns; and Korean participation in deciding the fate of Korea after the war.

After Japan's surprise attack on Pearl Harbor, the Provisional Government of Korea set up a Euro-American Liaison Committee in Washington for the purpose of active diplomacy with European and American states. An aid agreement was concluded with the Nationalist government of China, and efforts were made to strengthen the internal organization of the government. When the three powers, the United States, China and Britain, met in Cairo in 1943, Kim Ku of the Provisional Government sought the aid of Chiang Kai-shek, while Liaison Committee Director Syngman Rhee ordered

Contemporary Period

Establishment of the Republic of Korea

For Koreans, who had long been denied independent development in all walks of life, the Japanese surrender in 1945 brought another confrontation—that of ideological conflicts such as many postwar colonial peoples have experienced, and the difficulty of overcoming and liquidating colonial conditions accumulated during the four decades of Japanese domination. Liberation did not bring independence for which the Koreans had fought so hard, but the inception of ideological conflict in a partitioned country.

The occupation of a divided Korea by the United States and Soviet Union frustrated the efforts of Koreans to establish an independent government. The transplantation of two conflicting political ideologies south and north of the 38th Parallel further intensified the national split. Among the Allies, the foreign ministers of the United States, the Soviet Union and Britain met in Moscow on December 15, 1945, and decided to put Korea under the trusteeship of the four powers—the U.S., the USSR, Britain, and China—as a provisional step to unite the divided country. Korea protested against the international decision, imposed only four months after liberation from colonial rule, since it cast a shadow over Korean hopes for establishment of an independent government. The determination to resist and defy foreign domination, no matter what form it might take, is shared by all formerly colonized peoples.

President Syngman Rhee of the First Republic.

Although the Communists changed their initial opposition to support, probably due to instructions from Moscow, the vast majority of the people determinedly opposed trusteeship as another form of colonial rule. This problem, together with conflict of ideologies, further accelerated the national division. In the Soviet-occupied area, the opposition to the trusteeship was suppressed, and Cho Man-sik, the prominent national leader, was put under arrest by the Soviet authorities.

Thus the partitioned occupation of Korea by the United States and the Soviet Union, together with internal conflicts, frustrated efforts for independence and unity. The series of post war international decisions made without regard for the Korean people left them far from their goal of national independence.

After the Soviet Union and the United States occupied Korea, each imposing its own system on the area under its jurisdiction, political conflict and social disorder became rampant. The internal disorder south of the 38th parallel worsened in proportion to the rigid regimentation of society under the communist system in the North until 1948, when two ideologically opposed governments were established.

On the basis of the realities of the Korean Peninsula, the Government of the Republic of Korea was proclaimed on August 15, 1948, inheriting the legitimacy of the Provisional Government in Shanghai. Without being able to eliminate the vestiges of colonial rule, the new Government of Korea faced the pressing task of reconstructing the bankrupt economy left by the Japanese, and the chaos of the three years of the post-liberation period. These, together with various other problems, were too demanding a task for a new and inexperienced government.

The ideological confrontation between the North and the South inevitably gave rise to a tense military confrontation, another major burden placed on the government. In 1948, the U.S. Military Government handed over to the ROK Government its administrative authority. This was followed by the conclusion between the Republic of Korea and the United States of a provisional military pact and the establishment of the Economic Cooperation Administration.

In 1948, the United States withdrew its occupation forces from Korea, leaving only a small group of military advisers. The Soviet Union had already done the same in the northern half of Korea, where the Democratic People's Republic of Korea was established. A number of agreements were concluded for the Soviet Union to provide North Korea with military, economic, technological, and cultural assistance. China also established diplomatic relations with North Korea. In 1949, the Communist army in North Korea provoked sporadic skirmishes along the 38th parallel.

The Korean War

Under such circumstances early on the Sunday morning of June 25, 1950, without any warning or declaration of war, North Korean troops invaded the unprepared South across 38th parallel. It was a well-prepared, all-out attack. South Korea's troops fought bravely, but proved no match for the heavily armed Communists and the Russian T-3 tanks, who were not checked until they reached the Naktonggang River near Taegu.

The Republic of Korea appealed to the United Nations. In response, the Security Council passed a resolution ordering the Communists to withdraw to the 38th parallel and encouraged all member countries to give military support to the Republic. U.S. troops soon began to arrive, and were subsequently joined by those from 15 other nations: Australia, New Zealand, Britain, France, Canada, South Africa, Turkey, Thailand, Greece, Netherlands, Ethiopia, Columbia, the Philippines, Belgium, and Luxemburg. The three Scandinavian countries sent hospitals along with medical personnel.

Under the command of Gen. Douglas MacArther, the allied forces began to take the initiative, and after a surprise landing at Inch'ŏn, pushed the Communists out of South Korea and advanced into the North.

But in October the Communist Chinese intervened, throwing such large numbers of troops into battle that the U.N. forces were forced to retreat. Seoul once again fell into Communist hands on January 4, 1951. The U.N. Forces regrouped and mounted a counterattack, retaking Seoul on March 12. A stalemate was reached roughly in the area along the 38th parallel, where the conflict had begun.

At this point the Russians called for truce negotiations, which finally began at Kaesŏng in July of 1951, and were transferred to P'anmunjŏm in November that year. The talks dragged on for two years before an armistice agreement was reached on July 27, 1953.

Democratic Revolution

In the aftermath of the war, the country was beset with many problems—economic, social and political. The old patriot, Syngman Rhee, unable to see that he had outlived his useful-

ness, clung tenaciously to power. This refusal on the part of Rhee and his associates to let democratic processes take their normal course was at least partly responsible for the social and political unrest that followed the war.

Social disorder and hostility to the government complicated the already staggering problems created by the war. There were many thousands of war-widows, more than 100,000 orphans, and thousands of unemployed, whose ranks were swelled by farmers leaving their land to seek work in the cities. Exact statistics are not available, but in 1961 it was estimated that there were about 279,000 unemployed, of whom 72,000 were university graduates, and 51,000 discharged soldiers and laid-off workers. This provided a powderkeg of anger and resentment that waited only for a spark to set it off.

The spark was provided by President Rhee and the Liberal Party in the course of the elections of 1960. Realizing its own unpopularity, the ruling regime used every means, legal and illegal, to rig the elections in its favor. Demonstrations broke out almost at once, especially among students. The first occurred in Taegu on February 28, 1960, protesting political interference in schools. On March 15, election day, there were student demonstrations against the election, and police fired into the crowds. In early April a riot followed the discovery at Masan of the body of a student who had been killed by police.

The most serious demonstrations were in Seoul. Responding to the Masan affair, practically all of the students in the capital poured into the streets. Again police fired on them as they near the presidential residence and there was bloodshed. Martial law was imposed and troops dispersed the crowds.

Rhee had no choice but to step down. His desire for power had overcome his patriotism in the end. The students had led the people into the first successful democratic revolution in Korea's history, showing that Korean democracy was alive and healthy.

On July 15, 1960, an amendment to the Constitution was adopted by the incumbent assembly providing for a cabinet system of government with a bicameral legislature. At the same time, the two houses of the newly elected assembly in a joint session elected Yun Po-sun President of the Second Republic, and he was sworn in on August 15. President Yun nominated Dr. Chang Myon (John M. Chang) as prime minister, whose nomination was promptly confirmed by the House of Representatives. At this time the Liberal Party was replaced by the Democratic Party as the majority party, and it immediately split into the New Democrats and the (Old) Democrats. The Prime Minister belonged to the former while the President belonged to the latter. Neither was strong enough constitutionally or personally to fill the gap created by the sudden ouster of the 12-year-old autocratic rule of President Syngman Rhee.

The new Government was unable to cope with the situation in which it found itself. For one thing, most members of the new cabinet, while without question honest people, had little experience in government. The leaders, tasting the long-denied fruits of political power, began to wallow in its corrupting effect. The national economy had been brought to the brink of bankruptcy due to unfair tax collection practices coupled with waste and mismanagement of foreign aid and domestic resources under the Rhee Administration. Prime Minister Chang's cabinet not only failed to muster the united support of the populace to cope with such problems, but helplessly stood by and watched daily demonstrations by students who thought they could sway national affairs by parading in the streets.

The North Korean Communists, having recovered from their disastrous adventure of 1950-1953, seized the opportunity of internal disorder in the South to subvert whatever effort the Chang Administration could put forth. Elements of doubtful allegiance began urging "peaceful unification" a familiar line of propaganda emanating from Radio P'yŏngyang daily at that time.

The Military Revolution and the Third and Fourth Republics

Before daybreak on May 16, 1961, the sound of sporadic rifle fire announced an uprising of military men. Battalions of soldiers, marines,

President Yun Po-sun of the Second Republic.

and paratroopers marched into Seoul, occupying the capital city in a lightning coup led by Maj. Gen. Park Chung Hee.

Later that morning, the Military Revolutionary Committee, headed by Army Chief-of-Staff Lt. Gen. Chang Do-yong, announced over the radio that it had taken over all three branches of the government and proclaimed a six-point pledge: strong anti- communism, respect for the U.N. Charter, closer relations with the United States and other free nations, eradication of corruption, establishment of a self-supporting economy, and efforts for national reunification. He also pledged transfer of the government to civilian rule as soon as the revolutionary missions were accomplished.

The Revolutionary Committee, later renamed the Supreme Council for National Reconstruction, set out implement its aims. A new constitution was approved in a national referendum and promulgated in December 1963, thus inaugurating the Third Republic. In the presidential election held in October the following year, Park Chung Hee, who had resigned from the army, ran for office, despite his original promise of retiring from politics, and was elected President. In the National Assembly elections held in November, candidates from Park's Democratic Republican party won an impressive victory, forming a stable majority force. With the stage thus set, Park formally took office in December.

In the 1967 presidential election, President Park, with 51.4 percent of the total votes, was

Prime Minister Chang Myon of the Second Republic.

e-elected to a second four-year term over his chief opponent Yun Po-sun. In 1971, he won a third term by defeating Kim Dae-jung.

Under President Park's leadership, the human and natural resources of the nation were effectively organized for the first time in modern history. The economy began to grow at an annual rate of 9.2 percent. Per capita GNP zoomed from a mere $87 in 1962 to $1,503 in 1980, and exports rose by 32.8 percent a year from $56.7 million in 1962 to $17.5 billion in 1980.

In the diplomatic area, relations were normalized with Japan in June 1965, putting an end to the hiatus of formal bilateral relations due largely to antagonism stemming from Japan's occupation of Korea from 1910 to 1945. It was also at the initiative of President Park that the first formal intra-Korean dialogue was begun. The Red Cross societies of the two parts of Korea began meetings in September 1971, to discuss the question of locating and exchanging information about relatives separated by the South-North division. Political contacts were started in May 1972, culminating in the historic South-North Joint Communique of July 4, 1972, in which South and North Korea agreed to work for peaceful reunification.

Perceiving grave implications for Korea in the rapidly changing domestic and international situation, the Park Administration decided that to compete more effectively with North Korea and meet other challenges, all national strength should be consolidated into one cohesive force. Constitutional amendments were proposed in

October 1972 and approved in a subsequent national referendum. With the promulgation of the revised Constitution in December, a new political order, referred to as the *Yushin* (Revitalizing Reforms) system was established and the Fourth Republic inaugurated.

In the ensuing years, Korea successfully weathered the oil crisis and continued to develop economically. The *Saemaŭl* (New Community) Movement brought increasing prosperity to rural and urban areas and provided experience in problem solving. Diplomatic relations continued to expand. Only the South-North dialogue floundered and then came to a standstill.

Successful as he was in developing a backward economy and in modernizing certain aspects of society, President Park relied on autocratic means in implementing his policies. The *Yushin* constitution made it possible for him to remain in office indefinitely through well-controlled electoral procedures and also ensured him a kind of built-in majority in the legislature.

People began criticizing the harshly repressive measures of the Government. There was also criticism of the injustices perpetuated in the wake of policies geared to rapid economic growth, particularly to the underprivileged. Trade union movements were severely restricted. The combination of pent-up dissatisfaction with the high-handed methods of the government and frustration in popular desire for political participation and economic redistribution led to Park's demise.

On October 26, 1979, President Park was assassinated by the chief of the Korean CIA, and Prime Minister Choi Kyu-hah became acting president under the Constitution. Shortly thereafter he was elected President by the National Conference for Unification, an electoral college set up as part of the *Yushin* system.

During the next several months, Korea went through a difficult period characterized by political, social and economic instability. Hanging in balance was Korea's development toward a fuller democracy or reversion to the autocratic past. Under such circumstances, another military leader, Chun Doo Hwan, emerged. It also was in the midst of this political upheaval that

President
Park Chung Hee
of the Third and
Fourth Republics.

*President
Choi Kyu-hah
who assumed
office after President
Park's
assassination
in October 1979.*

the tragic Kwangju incident took place. In May 1980, civilian uprisings in that southern city protesting the new military autocracy were harshly put down by troops, causing a large number of casualities and providing an anti-government issue that was to linger for years.

Chun was subsequently elected President in the electoral college set up under the *Yushin* Constitution on August 27, and in October, he promulgated a new revised constitution, which limited the presidency to a single seven-year term.

The Fifth Republic

Following the establishment of the Fifth Republic, events moved quickly. Political parties began to organize again in December 1980, and all political activities were resumed in January 1981; martial law was lifted at the same time. A presidential election was held in February along with National Assembly elections. On April 11, the opening session of the National Assembly, consisting of 276 members from eight political parties, was convened and the groundwork for the Fifth Republic was in place. On March 3, 1981, President Chun took office, promising to build a "Great Korea" in a new era.

Although it was virtually the same as the Third and the Fourth Republics in its autocratic governing, the Fifth Republic registered some remarkable achievements, including the first-ever surplus in the international balance of pay-

ments and a peaceful transfer of power at the end of the seven-year term of President Chun, no small feat considering Korea's past record of political upheaval at the end of every presidency. The period also was plagued by many political problems, however, that tended to overshadow the accomplishments. Questions included the legitimacy of the Government itself and pressure for constitutional change for the direct election of a president. The Sixth Republic was born out of the need to find a solution to these pressing issues which had grown to crisis proportions.

The Sixth Republic

The Sixth Republic began with the inauguration of Roh Tae Woo as president for the 13th presidential term and the simultaneous implementation of the revised Constitution. These events had been preceded by the June 29, 1987 Declaration of Political Reforms in which Roh acceded to all of the opposition's demands, thereby defusing the political crisis and providing for the first direct election of the president in 16 years. The Sixth Republic, unlike the Fifth, thus began on a positive note with the most serious political issues being resolved.

President Roh began his term of office promising that authoritarian rule would end and that the June 29 Declaration would continue to be faithfully implemented. Many steps were taken to change not only the appearance of the Government but the substance as well. These

*President
Chun Doo Hwan
of the Fifth
Republic.*

*President
Roh Tae woo
of the Sixth
Republic.*

ranged from the repeal or revision of non-demo-cratic laws after the entire legal code had been reviewed, to the use of a round table at presidential meetings to improve interaction with his ministers. A number of people who had been detained on political charges were released and had their civil rights restored. Institutional and non-institutional interference in press activities and labor-management affairs was discontinued.

The elections for the 13th National Assembly held on April 26, 1988, ended with surprising results. Not only was the ruling Democratic Justice Party unable to win a working majority in the Assembly, but Kim Dae-jung's Party for Peace and Democracy became the largest opposition party, with Kim Young Sam's Reunification Democratic Party and Kim Jong-pil's New Democratic Republican Party placing third and fourth respectively. In their first test of strength in the Assembly after the elections, the strengthened opposition rejected President Roh's first appointee for Chief Justice, although they later accepted his second choice.

The Assembly's first major work was the establishment of special panels to look into various aspects of the Fifth Republic, including irregularities of the government, the Kwangju pro-democracy movement of 1980, claims of election fraud, controversial laws, and the problem of regionalism.

The political environment was shaken in January of 1990 when the ruling DLP, in an effort to overcome its mere plurality-status in the Assembly, managed to bring in Kim Young Sam's RDP and Kim Jong-pil's NDRP. The three parties were merged into the Democratic Liberal Party (DLP), which now commanded a two-thirds majority in the legislative body.

The DLP won a landslide victory in local-council elections on March 26 and June 20, 1991. In the 14th National Assembly elections held on March 24, 1992, however, the ruling DLP fared much worse, failing to maintain its majority by a single seat. This setback was only temporary as the DLP managed to recruit several independent lawmakers to its flag, thereby regaining its simple legislative majority.

The Kim Young Sam Administration

The elections for the 14th presidential term were held on December 18, 1992. The three major candidates were the ruling DLP's Kim Young Sam, the opposition Democratic Party's Kim Dae-jung, and the newly founded United People's Party candidate Chung Ju-yung, founder of the Hyundai Group. Kim Young Sam was elected, winning 42 percent of the votes, far outpacing Kim Dae-jung, his former opposition party colleague and fellow participant in the fight against authoritarian regimes, as well as his intense political rival. Chung Ju-yung did not do as well as some had expected. Kim's election returned Korea to the hands of a democratically elected civilian President for the first time since the military coup d'etat of 1961.

In his inaugural remarks on Feburary 25,

President Kim Young Sam.

1993, President Kim Young Sam vowed publicly to build a "New Korea," pledging to fight corruption in the public and private sectors and to revitalize Korea's straining economy. President Kim called on the Korean people to join him in building a New Korea by increasing national discipline, cooperating more extensively and bearing a fair share of the load. He urged Koreans to recapture their evaporating industriousness, to stop the erosion of their values and regain their self-confidence.

One of President Kim's initial measures after taking office was to open the streets around Chong Wa Dae, the presidential office and residence complex, to ordinary citizens. Under the previous authoritarian governments, citizens had been barred access to the areas surrounding the Blue House for security reasons.

In his first few months in office, President Kim was more active in his fight against corruption than anyone could have ever imagined, unleashing a veritable whirlwind of reform. His cabinet almost immediately published a "100 Day Plan for the New Economy," a series of short-term measures designed to boost the economy; this was later followed by the announce-

ment of a New Five-Year Plan for the New Economy, a set of long-term economy policies. The President also announced the implementation of the real-name financial transaction system in August 1993, a major economic reform designed to eliminate corruption and irregularities in the economy.

Asserting that "no one should strive for power and money at the same time," President Kim also required the submission of financial statements by all major government, political and military figures, most of which were made public. Several of the initially appointed cabinet members were forced to resign when the public became aware of their past improperties. A number of DLP Assemblymen resigned or bolted from the party for similar reasons, and the prosecution moved to indict others. The opposition DP, after releasing its own round of public financial statements, also lost face when it could not agree on how to proceed against several of its own Assemblymen caught in the same snare. A common refrain emerged in the press— "There's no stopping Y.S."—as the press has nicknamed the new President, after his English initials.

President Kim has said he expects his reform campaign against corruption to continue throughout his five-year term, and at this point, no one doubts him. His anti-corruption efforts extended to not only the Administration and party, but also the military, universities, banks, and even traffic police. Some of these sectors were known as sanctuaries in past regimes. President Kim's reforms have amounted to a "quiet revolution" which is enormously popular. A nationwide poll released by the Korean Gallup Company in late September showed over 90 percent approval rating for his reforms.

History will rate the success of President Kim's five-year term on whether his quiet revolution succeeds. If the reforms continue with their success, President Kim's popular civilian government will set the precedent for what a clean and democratic government can and should accomplish in Korea.

BELIEF, PHILOSOPHY AND RELIGION

Traditional Beliefs

Koreans traditionally have shown an intense love of their land, an emotion felt so strongly that it has been reflected in their beliefs, philosophy and religion.

The mountains, rivers, coasts and seas, and the four seasons that nurture them, have played important roles in forming basic thoughts and relationships among the people of the peninsula since earliest times. Their ancestors migrated across the vast plains from Siberia and Manchuria, seeking to find homes in a warmer clime. Settling of their own free will, they came to shape a history distinctively their own.

Samguk yusa (Memorabilia of the Three Kingdoms) records that it was Tan-gun who founded the nation of Korea. Legend says his father, Hwanung, a heavenly deity, decided to settle on earth in response to the desire of earthlings. A bear was transformed into a woman, and Hwanung married her. Tan-gun was born of their union and began a reign in 2333 B.C. that was to continue for more than a millennium.

While some have dismissed the legend as an indication of the totemism of the Korean people, others have noted the significance of a belief in which a deity had, of his own volition, desired to become a human being. They held that the Korean people did not consider the earth a place of exile for heavenly beings, not a place the erring were sent to live in penance.

This view was that the land and country comprised a dream, so good that even the deities and animals wanted to live there, and that the Korean people felt gratified to have chosen such a place for their home.

Even the neighboring Chinese were said to have expressed wonder at the beauty of Korea, summing it up in one of their ancient verses: "Would rather live in Korea and see Mt. Kŭmgangsan (Diamond Mountains)."

Once known as the "Eastern Land of Courtesy," Korea in its long history, seldom cultivated overseas interests, never invaded its neighbors, nor sought development outside given boundaries. Ancient Chinese records say it was the custom of the Korean people, being so courteous to each other, to avoid walking on the road, fearing it would hamper the movement of another. Foreigners commonly were called barbarians.

This excessive adulation of their homeland, while being averse to the coveting of the territories of others, eventually invited aggression from outside, bringing the subjugation of the Korean people and a period of colonial suffering.

Among the many Korean proverbs is one declaring preference for "an earthly field of dung to the wonders of the afterworld." This demonstrates the choice of the life of the present, no matter how sordid it may be, to that of an imaginative, unknown heaven. Korean literature contains many tales reflecting such a psychological trend in thinking.

In traditional literature, a beautiful lady, called *Sŏnnyŏ*, would descend from heaven in search of a fuller life on earth, marry an earthling, become a mother and eventually fulfill the chores expected of every married woman. She would then go back to her former abode in heaven, but there is usually no reference to what became of her after her return to heaven.

The art of Korea is different in its lines and colors, clearly distinguished from the strong, bold strokes of the Asian continent, or from dazzling colorations and excessive refinement that mark the art of island nations. On the surface the pale colors reflect nothing strong or positive; often they are taken to have a negative meaning. Images of willows or clouds are painted not in bold, firm lines, but in pale, thin brush strokes. But these elements should not lead to a hasty interpretation that Korea ancestors were life-weary. The magical effect of these strokes and lines seem, at a close look, to reflect the ardent yearning for the life of the *sŏnin*, the hermit. The heavens, rivers, and other objects of nature are rarely painted in strong colors; the pale grayish colors have an attraction of their own.

Foreigners who have lived in Korea and acquired some knowledge of the Korean language may wonder at the frequent use of the phrase, "*aigo chukketta*," which literally means

A model of sŏnangdang, *a pile of stones at the entrance of a village to pray for good luck—a shrine of one of the oldest indigenous Korean faiths.*

"I could just die." They may also wonder at so many passages in popular ballads or lyrics in which people vent their sadness against the transience of life. One hearing a rendition of *ch'ang*, a style of folk singing, for instance, might even feel it is a voice crying in agony. Hearing and reading Korean songs and writings, foreigners may raise the question whether this is not the true characteristic of the people. This negative outlook on life was caused by the decline in the power of the state in succeeding chapters of history, and made all the more bitter by subsequent foreign invasions of Korea.

These views have now given way to the newly resurging vitality of youthful Koreans who want no more of this nihilistic attitude. No matter how much they "want to die," they ardently desire a good life on this earth. One proof of this way of thinking might be found in the way children are named in Korea. Many names take the meaning of stone and iron, such as *Ch'adori* or *Soedori*. Stone and iron are ageless, hard and able to withstand the test of time. These names

are given in the hope of bestowing long life on the bearers.

Koreans have a flair for decorating things with Chinese ideographs, the most common being *su*, meaning long life, and *pok*, bliss. Of these two characters, preference is for the former. First is long life, and then well-being. The two letters are always read *su-pok* and not *pok-su*. Wealth, a good career, health, and many children are considered factors of bliss.

In building a house or choosing a place for burial, Koreans have always considered the natural surroundings, such as the course of a river or shape of a mountain, important. There were criteria for choosing the most ideal place, which went by the name *myŏngdang*. Large amounts of money were often spent for the purpose of selecting a *myŏngdang* by means of geomancy. Without exception, powerful families concentrated their attention on securing such places for residences and burial grounds, not to speak of royal palaces and royal tombs. This observance of geomancy is evident in numerous graves that dot the Korean countryside. This practice flourished during the Koryŏ and Chosŏn periods.

Heaven has always been considered the source of both mercy and wrath. Periodic rituals with offerings to heaven were conducted for the benefit of farmers and fishermen. Believing in the power of heaven over the destiny of mankind, they prayed for bumper crops or safe voyages. Among the many exclamations in Korea are two which concern the subject of heaven: "Heaven" is shouted when some extraordinary emergency arises, and "learn to fear heaven" is uttered when someone does something unacceptable. Heaven was respected because of its vastness and light; it was neither a religious worship, nor a traditional folk custom. It was for this reason that human dignity was often associated with heaven. For example, a king was a "son of heaven." This creed eventually produced the *Tonghak* philosophy or Eastern Learning in the late 19th century, the essential concept of which equated the power of heaven with that of man.

There seems to be no single concept as far as the philosophy of Korea is concerned. Just as the life of a Korean could hardly be divorced from the currents of the world, so with philosophic tenets. Korean philosophy has progressed and became enriched through meetings, conflicts, and combinations with alien thoughts. At certain stages in history, Koreans learned to combine their own inherent philosophies with those of other countries. This process often produced a brilliant synthesis, disclosing the imaginative power and creative sense of Koreans. Thus, foreign philosophy as well benefitted from Korean influence.

Koreans rarely indulged in discussing abstract matters, for their interest was focused on the present. Some, of course, did theorize and brought forth solid philosophic theses, but always these were accompanied by calls for actual practice. Apparently the ancient sage did not stroll amid beautiful scenery, lost in meditation over abstract escapist thought. To many of them, it was important that their thoughts help cultivate their personality. The principles which guided members of the *Hwarang* corps during the Shilla Kingdom included matching body

with mind, and matching word with action. It was a demonstration of true Korean philosophy.

Through the expounding of Buddhism, theorizing upon Confucianism, and showing reverence for heaven and all the spirits that inhabit nature's creatures, Koreans shaped their philosophy.

Early Philosophers

In the history of Korean philosophy, no man has held the cause of national consensus as much as did Yi I (Yulgok) in the 16th century. National consensus is something gained only through spontaneous harmony of public opinions, and it must not be confused with ideological struggle. A national consensus in meaning more closely approaches national philosophy and is not achieved through coercion or seduction.

Yi's theory was that national consensus must come spontaneously from all sections of the population, for any enforced formation of a national consensus could only result in calamity. This national consensus in its true sense would not be attained if the true voice of dissent was stifled in favor of blind assent. A national consensus arrived at through suppression of true patriotic voices would not be a true national consensus. Yi insisted that this national consensus should follow the dictates of changing situations. Speaking of his own time, he expressed the fear that, because the true voice of dissent was being stifled, opinions of the ruled were seriously divided. He feared there would soon be national calamities. According to his theory, national consensus was the vitality of the state and he declared that survival of the kingdom depended on whether this public opinion or national consensus could be achieved.

Yi I made a serious distinction between national consensus and "idle prattle," or to put it into more modern terminology, "demagoguery." He held that demagoguery, once started, shakes the foundation of the kingdom if it is not checked in time, and soon becomes too big to control. No man, however high his stature, can survive once he is involved in demagoguery. No eloquence or courage can save the kingdom once it is enveloped in demagoguery. Public resentment is directly attributed to misrule by the leadership. The ruler should take the voice of the subjects more seriously. The poor are deprived of their true nature, morality crumbles and penal systems are rendered ineffective under such circumstances. A man who risks his life for something does so for legitimate reason. Any act of reform should have the sole purpose of bettering the life of the people. Injustice will not be eliminated if corrupt officials escape reform.

Po U, a Buddhist philosopher, advocated the Unitary Theory of *Ilchong-ron* in which he identified intellect, *il*, with heart, *shim*. According to his philosophy, the body of man must be identified with the body of the universe. By the same token, the heart of man is the heart of the universe, the vitality of man the vitality governing the universe. Hence, heaven should be considered the same as man, and vice versa.

The emergence of the *Tonghak* philosophy, which followed these assertions, was significant for it was based on the theory that man was equal to heaven, and that he should be served as heaven is to be feared.

Ch'oe Hae-wŏl (1829-98) further enriched the argument by claiming that as man is heaven and heaven is equal to man, the two concepts could not be considered separately. Following this theory, there should be no distinction as to class or origin.

Following the emergence of the philosophy of equality came the advocacy of sincerity in learning. It was thought that the ultimate purpose of learning was sincerity, and sincerity was the true way for people to become what they are.

In line with this philosophy, Yi Ik-chae (1287-1367) recommended to the king during the latter part of the Koryŏ Dynasty a series of measures aimed at correcting educational policies. Among these was one holding that all learning should emphasize "realism". Yi himself disdained metaphysical subjects, comparing empty talk to weeds.

A little later, Kwŏn Kŭn (1352-1409) dis-

Yi I (Yulgok, 1536-84), above, and Yi Hwang (T'oegye, 1501-70), two of Korea's most outstanding philosophers.

cussed the theme of *shilli* and *shilshim*, both of which could be translated as realistic reasoning and realistic mind.

But Yi Hwang (T'oegye, 1501-70) used the word *sirhak* or practical learning in the preface of his book, *Essence of Neo-Confucianism*. In his letter addressed to Hwang Chung-gǒ, he used the word *mushil* (endeavor to be realistic) to convey his philosophy.

According to Yi I, a "sincere man" was the "man who knew the realism of heaven." And, because the mind was the essence of the body, it was not the soul which was evil. Evil would merely surround the soul, and this was why an insincere man could not be restored to his original good self. The spirit of reverence is a weapon for defeating this evil; the spirit of reverence constitutes the essence of sincerity. Sincerity thus becomes the origin of reverence, and it is this factor that constitutes man's essence.

Yi I himself was a completely sincere soul. A composition he wrote at the age of 20 said a household could not sustain harmony unless every member in the family was sufficiently sincere; that when confronted with misfortune, one most undertake deep self-reflection to find and correct one's own mistakes. And most important of all, Yi said the reason for reading was to put into practice what one had learned. Reading for the sake of reading would not do, he said. Yi's stepmother enjoyed drinking wine, but Yi never tried to reprove her for this unfortunate habit. Every morning he would inquire after her comfort, offering her several cups himself. This continued for years until she was finally moved to desist from the drinking habit. When he died, his stepmother, in gratitude for his dedication, dressed in white mourning attire for three years. Yi seems to have practiced what he preached. His life was one of consistent sincerity.

Po U's theory of *ilchong* (one origin) contained similar tenets. Although he had been indicted several times for his Buddhist inclinations, his theory called for a simple observance of sincerity and faith. The way of heaven, he said, was one—the prevailing of sincerity. Man's true form of mind is clean, marred by no

private greed or prejudice, he insisted. To him righteousness was always unitary in structure. Although he differed with Confucian scholars, his essential position on sincerity was the same. He also declared that righteousness was to be gained through a spirit of reverence.

Certain aspects of the thoughts of the school of realism may coincide with those of Western existential philosophers. Kierkegaard, for example, said that man could stand before the absolute only when he had transformed himself to his original sincerity. Heidegger then assumed that only when man achieved sincerity could he transcend. According to Jaspers, only thus would man confront his reality.

Sartre summed it up by saying that only the true existential man can secure his freedom. At the core of existentialism lies the spirit of sincerity. Apparently such early existentialism was vigorously pursued by Korean philosophers, forming the basis of their cultural development.

Pak Chi-wǒn (1737-1805) claimed that *sǒng* (nature) caused the existence of sincerity. Being virtuous was the act of securing substance. Therefore, one must not expend energy in unrealistic fields but should occupy the mind only with realistic questions. A wise man prefers substance to surface, for it is in the nature of things that the brighter the surface, the less the substance.

Another proponent of the philosophy of sincerity was Chǒng Yag-yong (Tasan, 1762-1836). At the age of 40, when he was thrown into jail, he confessed that night and day his only thought revolved around this central theme. He sought consolation by reciting the *Sǒng* chapter in the ancient Chinese classic, *The Great Learning*. Life and death depended on heaven, and the only everlasting thing in life was sincerity, he said. Later, when he was exiled to Kangjin, he wrote letters to his two sons advising them to pin the *Sǒng* chapter on the wall and abide by its rule. Sincerity was his last conviction.

Tonghak, or Eastern Learning, also emphasized this aspect of sincerity. In proclamations and numerous songs composed for instruction and for extolling the virtue of learning and diligence, this major theme of sincerity was end-

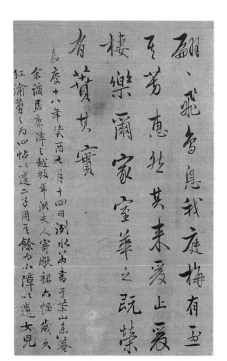

A calligraphic piece by Chŏng Yak-yong (Tasan, 1762-1836), the greatest of the Sirhak scholars.

lessly repeated. Reverence and sincerity were the basis of this Eastern Learning.

This philosophy of long tradition later saw further development through the educator-patriot An Ch'ang-ho's call to "practice with diligence." The word sincerity summarized his lifelong maxim. He taught students and practiced what he taught. He resented tricksters and avoided slandering others. In his dealing with others, pretension was meticulously excluded. The basis of this philosophy later became the core of *Hŭngsadan* or the Society for Raising Gentlemen, which he formed in 1913.

Along with the emphasis on action followed increased concern over the improvement of public welfare and the laying of foundations for understanding modern science and technology. Yi Hang-bok wrote that Yi I "personally manufactured his own hoes and worked bellows. A great man does not disdain this sort of work."

Another philosopher, Pak Yŏn-am went so far as to argue that vehicles would be machines of the greatest utility in the kingdom. Roads would be built naturally if there were vehicles available, he said, and he wondered aloud why vehi-

cles were not put to wider use. It was his idea to have many vehicles made and introduced to farmers. One needs a good machine to work better, he said, and warned that rulers would be blamed by future generations for not having learned the spirit of *sirhak* or realistic thinking. Chŏng Yag-yong was famous for his concern for public welfare. In his letters to his son, he not only warned that defense capability was important, but drew his son's attention to the importance of farming. "Planting fruit and vegetables in your garden would be far better than scribbling insignificant lines on your paper," he told his son. To him, farmers produced wealth, and nothing could equal the art of gardening, cattle-raising, fishing and sericulture. Men and women, old and young, each must possess professions befitting their abilities, he said. If the theory of sincerity concerned itself with moral issues, the problem of public welfare was connected with the development of economy and industry. The word "substance" has two edges to its meaning; morality and industry. This thinking is closer than any other idea to the philosophy behind Korea's endeavor for nation-building. It includes the question of rediscovery of the nation as well as economic development.

The scientific way of thinking became more and more associated with the problem of public welfare during the time of Chŏng Yag-yong. At the age of 28, Chŏng suggested that boats could be strung together to form a pontoon, and when he was 31 years old, he tried for the first time to use a crane to build a fortress wall in Suwon. He discovered the principle of the pulley. He was also interested in an early form of vaccination as demonstrated by notes on inoculation in his book.

Contemporary Thought

It is a hazardous task to attempt to deal with a subject like modern thought in Korea because there is no clear demarcation separating the thinking of the present-day Korean from that of his predecessors. Yet some explanation is in order since it is certain that the present-day

Korean's opinions of everything around him are far different from his ancestors. However different, his way of thinking in the modern world is colored by a national frame of mind centered for centuries on faith in such religious-philosophical beliefs as Buddhism, Taoism, and especially, Confucianism. A typical young modern Korean may express complete disinterest in Confucianism but he remains, all the same, bound by the Confucian approach to disciplinary habits of work and study, life and play. Such discipline is the core of the Confucian ethic.

In order to draw a line which may have marked the advent of the world of new ideas, the traditional thinking of the Korean people must be recalled. Generally the arbitrary line of 1894 can be assumed as the necessary demarcation. This was the year of the Kabo Reforms which brought reverberating shocks to the tottering feudalistic structure of Chosŏn. True, Korea had contacts with the West before this: Japan's Hideyoshi brought Western firearms to Korea in order to conquer; shipwrecked Dutchmen brought Western instruments; Catholic priests opened Korea's eye to Western achievements; and more substantially, foreign treaties from 1882 on brought in many foreigners with any number of new ideas. But it was the Kabo Reforms that shocked the Chosŏn Kingdom both politically and socially and gave rise to a stream of movements pressing for the modernization of society.

From 1894 on, Western nations and Japan began to pour capital into Korea to exploit Korea's market and natural resources. Along with these foreign investments came new ideas which inevitably replaced feudalistic ideas of politics and society. Confucianism was split into two schools under the impact. The positive school, forever admiring Chinese culture, stuck loyally by a declining dynasty to oppose all foreign influences, particularly Japanese militarism. The negative school retreated from everything, old or new. The political world became polluted with the domination of men who either followed Japanese policies or collaborated with representatives of the Japanese Government. At the same times, this process provided a basis for the introduction of new ideas and these opportunities, in turn, resulted in conflicting schools of thought on the best method to bring about modernization.

The movement to reform Korean society after 1894 was a movement aimed at modernization. However, this proved impossible at the close of the 19th century because of unfavorable political and economic conditions. Politicians, steeped in degenerate times, were simply not up to the task of meeting a bold and demanding challenge. Even assuming that there were enough men among them who understood the nature of the aggressive Japanese capitalism and opposed it fully, the internal feudal economy of the kingdom was too weak and the economy of Japan, allied with England, too strong. Not only economically but even spiritually, the power of the old ideas was tottering while there was no other ideological system prepared to stem the tides of corruption. Politically, Korea was bankrupt and Japan, certain in its aim of imperialistic expansion in an age of imperialism, meant to fill the vacuum.

From 1882 on, that is to say, when the "Hermit Kingdom" was at last opened by the signing of treaty with the United States, Koreans came into increasing contact with Westerners, especially American missionaries who brought not only the Bible but knowledge of Western medicine and education as well. Through such contacts and from the lessons of China and Japan, Korean leaders became convinced that their country had to be modernized. The obvious answer was to replace the agricultural economy, which was on the brink of collapse, with capitalism. Many wanted to effect this transformation at one bound as Japan had done.

This, of course, proved to be an impracticable task in the face of the circumstances. Impracticable or impossible, of more concern is what Koreans were thinking about the need for modern reforms. Many intellectuals urged a capitalistic solution during this critical period and even long after the Japanese domination.

Yu Kil-chun (1856-1916) lived at a time when capitalism was swiftly developing imperialistic wings throughout the world. Realizing the danger of Korea falling into the status of a colony directly from a court-dominated agricultural society, he sought a program that might save the land from this fate through modernization. Many Koreans would have none of this and he was continually hounded by conservatives who were anti-Japanese and pro-Chinese. At first, he strove for economic and political reforms, but after Korea became a colony, he turned his efforts to educational ends.

Yu's most outstanding work was a book entitled *Sŏyu Kyŏnmun* (Observations on a Journey to the West). Printed in Yokohama, Japan, it was a revolutionary work for the time, for its size (20 chapters, 555 pages), for its new style of mixing *Han-gŭl* letters and Chinese characters, and, above all, for its content. The purpose of the book was to contribute to the modernization of Korea by informing the reader of what the Western world was doing and accomplishing. Yu emphasized the rights of the people, nationalism, and international spirit. He stressed the contrast he saw between the West and his native country, saying that what he found at home was the poverty and weakness of an underdeveloped agricultural land, while what he found in the West were high standards of living under a highly developed system of commercialism. Yu's book was aimed at the persuading Koreans to accept a capitalistic system of society. It was the first work of modern tenor to reach the Korean reading public.

Like Yu, Paek In-gyu tried to introduce a capitalistic spirit into Korea. His main work, *The Economic History of Korea*, was published in San Francisco in 1920. It was long overdue, but as a development of Korean modern thinking, it was still monumental. In the preface, he made the following point: "If we study the economic history of Korea more deeply, we may be able to foster an education in economics which may prove to be the key to the economic independence of Korea. Economic independence will accelerate political independence." An overseas student with a master's degree from the University of Southern California, Paek was absorbed in the cause of national independence throughout his foreign travels. By showing the interrelation between economic and political independence, he reemphasized the meaning of the sweeping independence movement that erupted in 1919.

Korean movements for national independence and resistance to Japanese domination may be difficult to understand. Too many emotions were involved over too long a period of time to present a clear picture other than the spontaneous stream symbolized by the independence movement or the joyous liberation of 1945. At one extreme, it might be said that the Korean people achieved nothing. After all, the independence movement was a failure, and liberation was incidental to the settlement to World War II. At the other extreme, one might conclude that every Korean who retained his national identity successfully earned his independence and liberated himself, since the open aim of the enemy was to erase that identity. Clearly, such extreme conclusions will not do, for Koreans are not all heroes or all cowards but a people like every other people, loving peace and hating tyranny. The true picture lies somewhere in between. Such a picture, however, is far from clear as the history of the Korean fight for independence has yet to be studied thoroughly. There is no literature comprehensive enough to give a good grasp of the ideology behind it.

Despite the Japanese, the process of modernization begun in 1894 continued throughout the colonial period. Numbers of Koreans pioneered in modern thinking to pave the path to national democracy. To be a modern thinker was to stimulate the spirit of nationalism in the people. This was the lifelong task of men like Chang Chi-yŏn and Shin Ch'ae-ho. Chang (1861-1921) was a prolific writer who reflected the spirit of modern times in numerous newspaper articles and a number of books. Shin (1880-1936) began as a student of ancient Korea, devoted his life to the cause of Korean independence, and died in a Japanese prison cell. His fate was by no means exceptional.

Another name that cannot be omitted is Chu Shi-kyŏng. As the pioneer of a scientific approach to the Korean language and the individual responsible for the systematization of Korean grammar, Chu played an important role in reawakening the national consciousness of the people. The Korean language was an anathema to Japanese imperialism, and the linguists who followed in his footsteps were incarcerated for years. How this resistance through language relates to direct political action remains to be fully described. Consciously or otherwise, the linguists must have seen in this a means to foster the national spirit that would speed the day of national independence. One of them, Ch'oe Hyŏn-bae, suggested as much. The viewpoint of the linguists themselves may have been biased, but to preserve and uphold one's mother tongue was to resist an enemy which was bent on eliminating it. At the very least, by championing the language issue, Chu and his successors reminded the people of their national birthright.

American Protestant missionaries who began arriving after 1884 were also instrumental in reawakening the national consciousness. It was in Protestant churches that Koreans first heard about democracy and human rights. Korean Protestants formed the Independence Club, and from Korean Protestant ranks came the spearhead for the independence movement. The leading work reflecting the Korean spirit of nationalism through Protestant inspiration was *The Spirit of Independence* by the man who later became the first President of the Republic of Korea, Dr. Syngman Rhee. The importance of this book cannot be overestimated. It must be carefully read against a proper Korean background to be appreciated properly. Only such a correct appreciation can lead to an understanding of the political trends of Korea after 1945.

Under the mounting pressures of the long period of Japanese imperialism, the nationalistic and democratic yearnings of the Korean people found a new logic to resolve the intolerable situation. That logic was related directly to social thinking in modern Japan.

Many Koreans may have accepted new trends of thinking directly from the West but the main thrust came via Japan. It was mostly under the influence of Japanese thinkers that anarchist or socialist thinking were born. The only counterbalance was the spread of communism that flowed in from the Soviet Union rather than Japan. The route travelled from Siberia through the Chientao province of Manchuria with its large Korean community and over the northeastern border into the Hamgyŏng-do province, traditionally a stronghold of opposition to government in Seoul. All these social theories were accepted unconditionally by Korean as tools for national liberation before being fully studied, and for that reason, they have never really been thoroughly understood.

Voluntary movements against Japanese domination began toward the end of the 19th century. At first, they were based largely on Confucianism. After the downfall of Chosŏn, many Koreans, living either in exile or studying at home or in Japan, adopted social or political theories that seemed to offer the most likely prospects of defeating the designs of Japanese imperialism. The search continued despite the clutch of Japanese colonialism.

Meanwhile, the national economy was crumbling. Save for the landlord class which collaborated with the Japanese colonizers, farmers were reduced to a state of virtual bankruptcy. Many quit the country altogether, some going to Japan and others to Manchuria. Those who remained were at the mercy of arbitrary Japanese exploitation. Increasingly, Korean intellectuals, who saw the plight of the farmers firsthand, became preoccupied with the land problem. Most of them found the answer in socialism or communism, thereby splitting Koreans into socialists and nationalists.

Under Japanese rule, the two camps shared a common goal of anti-Japanese resistance and national liberation. With liberation, the split became acute and the conflict fierce and open. Ideological confusion was superimposed on an atmosphere of a joy-drunken liberated state. Almost immediately, too, the Soviet-American cold war sharpened the conflict and drove the opposing sides apart. Confusion was ended and in its place stood the confrontation of two hostile, uncompromising ideologies, separated by a line neither side would acknowledge. The North went Communist, and the South adopted the model of American democracy.

The Republic of Korea, which is the official English name for the southern state, adopted liberalism as its guiding principle. From the day of its birth in 1948, however, the Republic was to experience for more than a decade the untold sorrow of ideological confrontation, fratricidal war, devastation, destitution, self-doubt, and despondency. The society went through unchanging stagnancy with vestiges of feudalism and remnants of Japanese imperialism all piled together in a sea of contradictions. Also present were the fears and insecurities created by the unprovoked attack from the North in 1950 and the continuing threat of its recurrence.

These were serious elements that had to be corrected in order to clear away enough of the contradictions for a liberal climate to prevail. The problems were basically political but the mood, even in college lecture-classes, was escapism from politics and, indeed, from all reality, save for the perusal of Western authors. Yet these were Korean problems and as such, had to be weighed and studied by Koreans themselves in or out of school. The clarification had to be sought not only from scholars of the social and humanistic sciences but, more importantly, from students of philosophy. The last subject of interest for those enmeshed in an escapist mood was philosophy; yet all problems must, first and last, be explained philosophically. Not all problems were the result of internal divisions. Many stemmed from the division of the country into two zones by outside powers, compounding the task of the Korean student of philosophy. He had to choose one out of many and diverse currents of thought in the world order to find the key that would unify the conflicting ideas at home.

One tradition Korea inherited from the Japanese years and which must be held in high esteem is the literary spirit that was born. Many patriots expressed themselves in literary creation. The trends of this literature have yet to be analyzed sufficiently to link its spirit with the spirit of social and political movements.

What is seen clearly in the creative literature of the era is the spirit of transition from feudal to modern society. The proletarian literature which reflected the sufferings of the Korean people under Japanese imperialism and colonialism, even before developing to a full-fledged stage, transmogrified itself into an activist movement of political resistance. The overall literary trend was a search for harmony of realism with romanticism. It did not merely reflect social condition but expressed national aspirations. A third school wanted to escape from everything. Men of letters suffocated by the reality of the harsh conditions in which they were living sought escape from social conditions, even to the point of suicide. The poet, Yi Sang, for instance, spent his entire life in a stifling atmosphere. One of his poems, entitled "Fatigue," may be considered a striking description of the anxiety and unrest of his day. It was a prayer for salvation by the Creator and as such not merely the prayer of a young man of 29 in the year 1927, but the prayer of many a young man of the 1950s.

Korean youth yearned for deliverance from the difficulties caused by the political and economic deficiencies of society. This was as it should have been, but only if they remembered never to succumb to isolation, despondency, or cynicism. Their deliverance would come not from their negativist dissension but from their positive search for a future.

To find a new philosophy that may clear the path to a bright future requires a backward gaze. The point of departure for Koreans today lies in a searching review of their own history.

Religion

The primitive Korean, a hunter-fisher, was bewildered by the way in which things around him behaved. He wondered if, like humans, other things had spirits.

As the family grew larger and larger, clans and then tribes gradually developed. The sense of wonder was shared by tribe members and they attempted to understand, and if possible, to come to terms with their environment. Their search eventually evolved into a nature-belief that powerful spirits resided in natural forces and animate and inanimate objects surrounding them. Thus, when the hunter had to kill an animal for food, he performed a rite invoking the approval of the spirit of the victim. When the farmers wished for a good harvest, they held

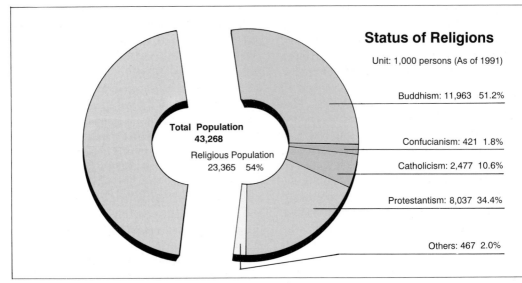

Status of Religions

Unit: 1,000 persons (As of 1991)

Total Population
43,268

Religious Population
23,365   54%

Buddhism: 11,963   51.2%

Confucianism: 421   1.8%

Catholicism: 2,477   10.6%

Protestantism: 8,037   34.4%

Others: 467   2.0%

Source: National Statistical office.

ceremonies which were intended to propitiate the local gods of field and forest.

For personal as opposed to social needs, individuals of such primitive societies required an intermediary with the spirit world who could avert bad luck, cure sickness and assure passage from this world to the next when the time came. Such a priest-like individual, known as a shaman, would be called upon to perform the requisite rituals. This system of belief, or shamanism, still persists in obscure corners of Korea today.

The tribal communities gradually developed into kingdoms. By the first century B.C., three kingdoms, Koguryŏ, Paekche and Shilla, dominated the Korean Peninsula. Religious rituals common to these tribal states included a service directed at propitiating heaven. When this service was over, villagers spent the night dancing and singing.

This tribal rituals were conducted by chieftains, who were regarded as "messengers of the Heavenly Emperor." In southern Korea, however, the Sam Han tribes, or three Han tribes, had separate officials for this function performed at sodo or holy places. These were regarded as so sacred that a fugitive could seek sanctuary there without fear of molestation.

As tribal communities achieved statehood, each kingdom required a system of worship which could bind the numerous constituent communities. This brought the system of the "founder's altar." Upon taking over, the chieftain or king would visit this altar and offer prayers. These altars developed into shrines. Some were dedicated to the king's forebearers and others to *sajik*, or the gods of land and harvest. As late as Chosŏn, the founder-king, T'aejo, built an altar, *sajiktan*, in 1394 to honor the gods of land and harvest with prayers four times a year. This site is commemorated today in the name of a city block in Seoul called Sajik-dong, located to the west of Kyŏngbokkung Palace and the National Museum.

During the Three Kingdoms era more organized religions began to flow into Korea from China. Taoism, Confucianism and Buddhism came one after another, were readily accepted, and remained with the Koreans until modern times.

The introduction of these religions did not result in the abandonment of animistic beliefs and practices. When Buddhism and Confucianism entered Korea from continental Asia, neither considered itself in conflict with the other, nor in opposition to rites relating to local nature-spirits. Christianity was the only imported religion to proclaim its exclusive possession of the truth. However it has not been able to make much headway against the long-ingrained habit of religious syncretism, at least among the simpler rural people.

This is not to say that Koreans are fickle when it comes to religion, nor that they are especially gullible. Rather, in religion as in much else, Koreans tend to be pragmatic. They will try anything once, and the criterion for evaluating a system of belief or a course of action is whether it works in a pinch. It might be more appropriate to say that the fundamental Korean character of incessant search for harmony transcends all existing forms and systems of religion. This is exemplified in the tenets of the *Hwarang* spirit—the national spirit that eventually led Shilla, one of the three kingdoms, to unify the peninsula. To the *Hwarang*, or the elite of Shilla youth, as it was to some of the modern nationalist thinkers of turbulent 19th century Korea, the truth lay, or was to be sought, in a combination of traditional beliefs and newly introduced established religions.

Early Myths

Korea's oldest religion, other than nature worship, is *Taejonggyo*. Called *Koshindo* until the early 20th century, it embodies a myth of national foundation comparable to other nations. There are few adherents of this belief today, but it has obviously influenced later religious developments.

Taejonggyo is a belief about 4,000 years old and embodies the concept of a triune god: creator, teacher, and temporal king, whose name is Hanŭl. This god took human form in the person of Tan-gun, the father, teacher, and king of the Korean people, who was born of a heavenly deity father and a bear-totem tribe woman. This event supposedly happened in 2333 B.C., and until recent times Korean calendars and dates were reckoned from that year. Tan-gun became the great teacher and law-giver of the tribes living on the Korean Peninsula, reigning over them until he ascended to heaven.

In order to propagate worship of Hanŭl, Tangŭn established rituals for offering prayers of praise and propitiation to heaven. These rituals became established among nobles and commoners alike by the time of the Three Kingdoms

period, but with the introduction of foreign religions, purity in the practice of *Taejonggyo* gradually declined. By the 15th century, this cult had practically disappeared. However, the resurgence of Korean nationalism and a spirit of independence in the late 19th and early 20th centuries led to the appearance of several sects claiming to represent a revival of this ancient cult.

Taoism

It is difficult to pinpoint the exact date when Taoism, as philosophy and religion, came to influence Korea. Murals found in Koguryŏ tumuli near Kangsŏ, P'yŏngan-do province, show Taoist influence. Records indicate that the teachings of Lao Tzu and Chuang Tzu were brought to Korea in the 7th century A.D., and that there were some active effort to study them.

The introduction of Taoism underminded an already weak Buddhism which lacked popular appeal but was supported by the court. Buddhist temples were gradually converted into Taoist temples during Koguryŏ.

In Paekche, too, there was a trend towards a belief in Taoist spirits. But the strongest imprint of Taoist influence can be discerned in the guiding principles of the *Hwarang* of Shilla, who were trained in patience, simplicity, contentment, and harmony—all part of Taoist ethics—along with the Confucian doctrine of loyalty, filial piety, righteousness, and good faith, and the Buddhist teaching of compassion.

Although Taoism failed to proliferate as an independent cult, it continued to permeate all strata of the Korean populace. For one thing, Taoism's syncretic worship of a multiplicity of gods fitted in readily with Korea's animistic beliefs. For another, Taoism freely borrowed from Confucianism and Buddhism in its institutions, temples, ceremonies and canon.

The most apparent trace of Taoist influence among Koreans is the search for blessings and longevity, the strongest of Taoist features. The fact that the indelible Taoist mark in the two Chinese characters *su* (longevity) and *pok* (bliss) decorate so many everyday articles, such as spoons and pillow cases, shows that Taoism

Buddhists at Pongwonsa Temple in Seoul on Buddha's birthday.

permeated the everyday life of the Korean people. Also, the number of peaks and valleys throughout the country bearing such Taoist-related names as "Immortal's Peak" or "Fairy's Valley" indicates a strong Taoist influence.

Buddhism

Buddhism in its original form was an esoteric philosophical formula for personal salvation through renunciation of worldly desires. Avoiding rebirth in the endless cycle of reincarnations which is a feature of India's Hindu religion, it sought to bring about the absorption of the soul of the enlightened into Nirvana.

Buddha taught that certain enlightened, compassionate souls, called bodhisattvas, would voluntarily delay their union with Nirvana in order to remain on earth teaching truth and enlightening others, presumably until every human soul had achieved Nirvana. Rebirth would cease completely, all souls would become absorbed into Nirvana, and the world

would come to an end, all of which would take incalculable eons.

Buddhism originally was a religion without a god, consisting of a set of premises on how to avoid earthly suffering by following the proper procedures of what might be called spiritual mechanics or discipline.

With the spread of Buddhism from its point of origin in India, however, all sorts of local superstitions and theological systems were introduced into it, producing an elaborate array of deities, saviors, saints, heavens, and hells that the founder of the religion, Prince Gautama, had never mentioned. It was this type of Buddhism, called Mahayana or the Greater Vehicle, that appeared in Korea around A.D.372, brought by missionary monks from India and China. In Korea, as elsewhere, it adopted regional peculiarities and predilections as it became firmly established.

No doubt Buddhism had to devise a system of rewards, punishments, and rules that would appeal to the simple and uneducated more than the esoteric, ascetic doctrines of the founder could. In a sense, Pauline Christianity with its neo-Platonic influences did the same thing for Christianity. But the Greco-Roman world in which Christianity spread was a more culturally homogeneous region in many respects than the East Asian area penetrated by Buddhism. Despite the fragmentation of Christianity, the diversity of beliefs in that religion does not approach the bewildering array of ideas and creeds that crop up under the title of Buddhism.

For example, almost every Korean Buddhist temple complex has a side chapel near the main worship hall containing a shrine to the mountain spirit, or tutelary deity of the site. This is usually depicted as an old man with a pet tiger. The symbol is derived both from Chinese Taoist tradition and its union with local animistic beliefs. The shrine is venerated along with the ceremonies in honor of Buddha that are performed at the temple, lest the local mountain spirit on whose land the temple stands should become angry.

At the time Buddhism entered the peninsula in the fourth century A.D., Korea was nearing the middle of the Three Kingdoms period and was soon to be unified as a single nation under Shilla. Primarily for geographical reasons, Shilla was the last of the three to be penetrated by the foreign religion. Koguryŏ, the northern kingdom, was visited by a Chinese monk named Sundo in the year A.D.372, and a dozen years later, neighboring Paekche, was a host to an Indian missionary, Marananta, who had come by way of China. Shilla was not exposed to Buddhist influence until about half a century later, and it was only in A.D.528, after the martyrdom of the saintly monk Ich'adon, that it became legal to preach Buddhism openly.

Meanwhile, the new religion must have spread rapidly in the two western and northern kingdoms, apparently under royal patronage. Many temples and monasteries were constructed, and hordes of believers converted. So deeply rooted did Buddhism become in Paekche and Koguryŏ, that by the sixth century priests, scriptures, and religious artisans and artifacts were being sent to Japan, forming the basis of the early Buddhist culture there. Much of the prestige

attached to the new cult in Korea, and its eventual adoption as the state religion in all of the three kingdoms, may be traced to Korea's respect for Chinese learning.

By the time Shilla unified the peninsula under one government in A.D.668, Buddhism had been embraced as the state religion, though governmental systems were already being run along Confucian lines, with no conflict between the two.

Royal patronage during this brief golden age of Unified Shilla produced a magnificent flowering of Buddhist arts and temple architecture. The rapid fragmentation of the kingdom after less than 200 years did not harm the position of the Buddhist church, however. The succeeding dynasty which took power in A.D.936 and founded the Koryŏ Kingdom was even more enthusiastic in its support of the imported doctrine.

Of the many famous monks and theologians of the shilla era, possibly the most influential was Wonhyo, the only clerical leader of that day who did not study in China. Wonhyo tried to unify the various Buddhist sects and sought to make the religion popular and applicable to the daily lives of the people. He wrote many books, and legend ascribes to him a brief love affair with a royal princess—the son of their union supposedly the scholar who invented the system of writing Korean in Chinese ideographs called *idu*.

In contrast to that of Koguryŏ and Paekche, Buddhism in Shilla was not confined to the royal court. It was a religion of the people, expected not only to solve the fundamental problems of life, but also to promote the national interest. It flourished and led to the development of a brilliant culture. Most of Korea's tangible cultural assets are Buddhist-related, and Kyŏngju, the capital of Shilla, is virtually an open-air museum of Buddhist relics and art objects.

During the Koryŏ Dynasty, monks became politicians and courtiers, some of them corrupt or worldly in their interests. In the 13th century, the Mongols invaded Korea, conquering and ravaging the entire country except for the Hangang River estuary island of Kanghwado, where the king and the court took refuge. The reaction of the court was to implore divine assistance by undertaking the immense project of carving the entire bulk of Buddhist scriptures onto wooden blocks for printing. This is the so-called *Tripitaka Koreana*, still extant today and on display at the Haeinsa Temple. The set of 81,258 wood blocks, which took 16 years to complete, is considered one of the most outstanding masterpieces in the history of Buddhism. Nevertheless, this act of piety did not result in the defeat of the Mongols, who made Korea a vassal state.

Naturally, because of the power that Buddhists held, they shared some of the blame for the national disaster, and from that era may be dated a definite and rapid decline in Korean Buddhism. To make matters worse, King Kongmin in the mid-14th century appointed a totally corrupt monk, Shindon, to a high official post, touching off protests among the Confucian literati of the court. The corruption of the temples and abuses of the monks were reflected in the earthy satire of village mask dance dramas, as well as in lofty essays such as "Anti-Buddhism" by Confucianist Chŏng To-jŏn, which declared: "The Indian religion is one which destroys morality and harms the country."

Though the Mongols had by then given up actual occupation of Korea, their influence on the government was still great. Since Buddhist power in the court continued unabated, the Buddhists were rightly or wrongly identified with the pro-Mongol faction. As a result, when Gen. Yi Sŏng-gye staged a revolt and had himself proclaimed king in 1392, his policy was both anti-Mongol and anti-Buddhist. Though the new king, his family, and most of his successors were devout believers in Buddhism, all influence of the religion was removed from the government. Vast wealth and land holdings of temples were seized.

Throughout the history of Chosŏn (1392-1910), the dynasty Yi Sŏng-gye founded, Buddhism seemed to revive whenever politically powerful members of the royal family were Buddhists. However, efforts for Buddhist revival met with strong opposition from Confucian scholars and officials. Buddhist

monks organized armies of monks to help defend the country during the Japanese invasions of Korea between 1592 and 1598 and won a number of decisive victories. Despite such contributions to national defense, official oppression of Buddhism continued until the last years of the Chosŏn period. Buddhist monks were ranked in the lowest social class and were not permitted into the capital. The severe oppression drove the temples into remote mountainous areas, making Buddhism a monastic religion rather than a religion for laymen. This historic background accounts for the fact that major Buddhist temples are in a relatively inaccessible areas.

Confucianism was the state cult or national religion during that entire era, and in an effort to prune and control Buddhism, several kings forcibly reformed and consolidated the various sects. When the Japanese took over as colonial rulers in 1910, there was some attempt to infiltrate Korean Buddhist sect or amalgamate them with Japanese Buddhist sects. The attempts by and large failed, and may even have resulted in a revival of interest in native Buddhism on the part of Koreans.

Japanese monks could marry, while the entire Korean Buddhist tradition had been one of clerical celibacy. Under Japanese influence, some Korean monks adopted the custom of marrying, and, after liberation in 1945, there were bitter legal battles for many years over the legitimacy of ownership of certain temple properties by the married and celibate sects. The celibates eventually won.

Buddhism has the largest following of all Korea's religions. As of 1991, there were 26 Buddhist sects and 9,231 temples with more than 11 million followers in Korea.

Chogyejong is the largest of the sects. It is headquartered in Chogyesa Temple in Seoul and has 24 regional centers across the country.

Buddhism in Korea is undergoing a sort of renaissance stemming from a conscious attempt to adapt to the changes of industrialization, an increased interest among Koreans in traditional thought, and stricter standards for monks. Buddhist orders have set up urban centers for the propagation of the faith. The *Tripitaka*

Koreana is being translated into modern Korean, foreign monks are receiving training at Korean temples and temples are being built in foreign countries.

Confucianism

Confucius, the Chinese sage who is assumed to have lived during the sixth century B.C., set up an ideal ethical-moral system intended to govern relationships within the family and the state in harmonious unity. It was basically a system of subordinations: of the son to the father, of the younger to the elder brother, of the wife to the husband, and of the subject to the throne. It inculcated filial piety, reverence for ancestors, and fidelity to friends. Strong emphasis was placed upon decorum, rites, and ceremony. Scholarship and aesthetic cultivation were regarded as prerequisites for those in governing or official positions.

Confucius bequeathed to posterity several books regarded as the essential classics, some of which he reputedly wrote himself, and others which he edited in definitive form from earlier versions. To these were added many volumes of commentary, some of them purporting to be dialogues between the master and his disciples, though in some cases these can be dated centuries after the sage's death.

Confucius himself never obtained a government post to test his theories, living most of his life as a wandering scholar-teacher. However, his successors were instrumental in creating a form of imperial government in China based on Confucian principles. This type of government, and the socio-political institutions it presupposed, lasted thousands of years. Although many alterations were introduced by later philosophers, Confucianism can lay claim to being the most influential system of human thought ever devised.

Confucian thought embraced no consideration of the supernatural, except for an impersonal divine order referred to as heaven. It left human affairs alone as long as relative order and good government prevailed on earth. In this sense, Confucianism was like early Buddhism, a religion without a god. But as ages passed, the sage and his principal disciples were canonized by later followers as a means of spreading their doctrines among simple, lesser educated people.

In both cases, the argument is endless as to whether either Buddhism or Confucianism was actually a religion in the Western sense. However, since they jointly or mutually filled the social functions of religion in Korea, it may be proper to admit them into this category for purposes of historical consideration.

Over the ages, wherever Confucianism spread within the vast Chinese sphere of influence, it worked in tandem with any local religion that provided a supernatural framework and cosmology. It did not come into conflict with Buddhism necessarily, except perhaps as a rival for royal patronage and political power on the temporal level.

The date Confucianism became established in Korea is so early it cannot be even approximately pinpointed. No doubt, Confucian classics entered the peninsula with the earliest specimens of written Chinese material well before the beginning of the Christian era. Koguryŏ, Paekche and Shilla all left records that indicate the early existence of Confucian influence. In Koguryŏ, for example, there was a central Confucian university functioning by the fourth century A.D., showing a long and deeply-rooted tradition already in existence. The provinces had scattered private Confucian academies called *kyŏngdang*.

The neighboring kingdom of Paekche established similar institutions at about the same time. As usual, the southern kingdom of Shilla was later in importing the foreign influence. However, when it conquered and absorbed the other kingdoms in the seventh century A.D., its interest in Confucianism and other aspects of Chinese culture increased rapidly. Delegations of scholars were sent to China to observe the working of Confucian institutions firsthand, and to bring back voluminous writings on the subject. Though Buddhism was the state religion of Unified Shilla, Confucianism formed the philosophical and structural backbone of the state.

In Korea, Confucianism was accepted so eagerly and in so strict a form that the Chinese themselves regarded the Korean adherents as

A ritual celebrating Confucius's birthday.

more virtuous than themselves. They referred to Korea as "the country of Eastern decorum," a reference to the punctiliousness with which the Koreans observed all phases of the doctrinal ritual.

With the passage of centuries, this literal or fanatical adherence to Confucian thought gave rise to many factions, heresies, and hair-splitting disputes, even more pronounced, perhaps, than in China. Divergence in interpretation of Confucian doctrine naturally became associated with political power struggles and clan feuds, which eventually weakened the government.

Confucianism in Korea meant a system of education, ceremony, and civil administration. With the passing of the monarchical system in the early 20th century, only the first function remained important. However, the deeply ingrained Confucian mode of manners and social relations is still a major factor in the way Koreans think and act.

The static and traditional aspects of Confucian philosophy have been considered by some an obstacle to the modernization of Korea, at least until fairly recently, although the stability and security encouraged by the system may have much to recommend them.

Unified Silla lasted only about two centuries, giving way to the Koryŏ Kingdom in the 10th century. The form of government did not materially change, except that the influence of Buddhism became more marked.

The institutionalization of Confucian principles of government proceeded with the adoption of the *kwagŏ* or civil service examination. Thus, in theory at least, the government would be of a meritocratic system run by the best scholars selected through regional and national examinations held at regular intervals. These examinations were open to all, except for certain classes regarded as menial such as butchers, actors, musicians, and doctors. Those who passed the examinations were awarded posts commensurate with their abilities in either civil or military fields. The civil servants included magistrates, provincial governors, and courtiers, while the military naturally consisted of army and navy officers.

In theory, each man had to pass the examinations on his own merits. In practice, there was a system of hereditary nobility or *yangban*, holders of landed estates from the throne, who, because of their wealth and influence, could get official preferment without actually taking the exams.

Subject matter of the exams consisted entirely of Confucian classics and commentaries, plus the writing of poetry and essays on a given subject. Skill in the calligraphy of Chinese characters counted strongly in evaluations.

It may be argued that this type of rote learning was remote from the practical aspects of administration, but the effort necessary to learn the difficult Chinese material presupposed a rather high degree of intelligence. The time devoted to study did not leave much leisure for the development of bad habits.

However, things did not always work out ideally. The provincial administrator was underpaid by the central government and was thus tempted to accept bribes or to squeeze the poor. The courtiers in the capital, far from attempting to advise the king on the best way to run the country and earn the continuing approval of heaven, all too often squabbled bitterly for personal or factional advantage.

The most brilliant philosophers of Confucianism, while perhaps paragons of virtue themselves, usually devoted most of their efforts to devising highly abstract metaphysical systems to explain the universe and man's place therein, without the slightest attempt at empirical observation or experimental methodology.

When Buddhist influence in the Koryŏ court was blamed for Korea's surrender to the Mongols, and the dynasty that ruled Koryo was overthrown by the Yi, who banished Buddhism and restored political ascendancy to the Confucianist, the latter had a golden opportunity to achieve a renaissance. In the 15th and 16th centuries, under rulers who were generally enlightened or themselves scholars, there was considerable progress in social reform, modernization, and justice. It was an era of inventions, as represented in the development of an exact phonetic system for transcribing the Korean language, called *Han-gŭl*.

Confucianism produced a new crop of philosophers starting in the 17th century with the *Sirhak* or Practical Learning school, whose concerns were less academic than utilitarian. Perhaps under the influence of Western ideas filtering into Korea indirectly via Jesuit missionaries then active in China, there arose a new interest among the literati in such matters as national productivity and defense, agriculture, trade, and the welfare of the people.

Unfortunately, shortsighted factionalism was still rampant in the royal court. When the Japanese invaded in 1592 and again in 1598, Korea was nearly defenseless and during the rest of the dynasty never recovered from the devastation. Instead, the nation adopted a policy of isolationism until the late 19th century. During these stagnant centuries, the dogmatic Confucian sects continued complacently to pick the dry bones of doctrine and suck the thinning blood of the country, while isolated reformers of the *Sirhak* group could only remonstrate and rage ineffectually.

Every year, the royal examinations were held in Seoul for those seeking high posts, and twice yearly the solemn spring and autumn rites honoring Confucius were held. The latter are still held at the Confucian university of Sungkyunkwan.

Then suddenly, with the usurpation of power by the Japanese in 1910, the Confucian system virtually disappeared, a process repeated in China two years later with the end of the last royal dynasty there.

While Confucius' teachings may have disappeared as a basis for government and administration, after so many centuries of indoctrination in these tenets, Koreans could hardly be said to have discarded the customs, habits, and thought patterns derived from the system. On one hand, there is reverence for age, social stability, and a respect for learning and cultivation. On the other there is idolization of the past, social rigidity, and an abstract unworldliness that prefers to see things as they ought to be rather than as they are.

Although there is no organized confucian church, there are Confucian organizations. Ancestral rites and memorial ceremonies in honor of outstanding Confucians are held regularly. Sungkyunkwan University in Seoul is the country's center of Confucianism and the site of a shrine to Confucius, where memorial ceremonies are held annually in spring and autumn. There are also over 200 *hyanggyo*, or Confucian

A Catholic mass at the Myŏng-dong Cathedral in Seoul.

academies with shrines, in Korea that teach young people traditional values and manners. They seek to make Confucian values more relevant to a modern, industrial society.

Catholicism

The surge of Christian mission activity began to reach Korea as early as the 17th century, when copies of Catholic missionary Matteo Ricci's works in Chinese were brought back from Peking by the annual tributary mission sent there to exchange gifts with the Chinese emperor.

Along with religion doctrine, the material included aspects of Western learning such as a more accurate calendar system and other matters that attracted the attention of the *Sirhak* or Practical Learning School. By the 18th century, there were several converts or potential converts to the Western doctrine. No priests entered Korea until 1785, however, when a Jesuit, Father Peter Grammont, crossed the border

secretly and began baptizing believers and ordaining clergy.

Another foreign priest, a Chinese Catholic called Father Chu Mun-mo in Korean, followed 10 years later, though the propagation of foreign religion on Korean soil was still technically against the law. A tolerant or lackadaisical administration resulted in a rather liberal view of the Catholic movement, though there were sporadic persecutions.

By the year 1863, there were 12 Korean priests who presided over a community of about 23,000 believers. At that point, with the coming to power of the xenophobic prince regent called the Taewon-gun, who blamed all Korean's problems on outside encroachments, persecution began in earnest. It continued until 1876, when the prince regent lost power, and Korea was forced to sign treaties with Western powers guaranteeing the safety of foreign missionaries and their freedom to engage in proselytizing.

In 1925, a total of 79 Koreans who had been martyred during the Chosŏn Dynasty persecu-

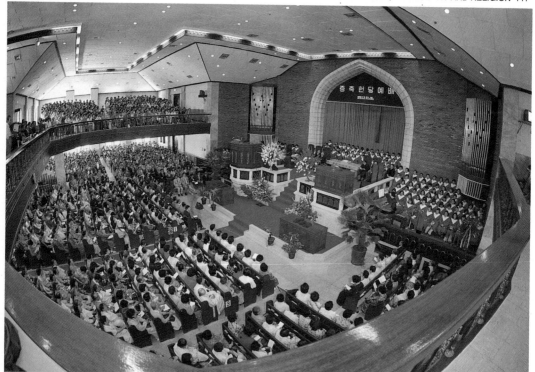

Dedicating a newly-enlarged Christian church.

tions were beatified at St. Peter's Basilica, and in 1968 an additional 24 were beatified. During and following the Korean War (1950-53), the number of Catholic relief organizations and missionaries increased and the Korean Catholic Church grew quickly. In 1962, a Korean church hierarchy was established. By 1986, there were three archdioceses and 14 dioceses in Korea. The year 1962 was also significant for the Korean church because of the reforms authorized by the Second Vatican Council. The right to say mass in Korean and a joint Catholic-Protestant translation of the Bible contributed to the rapid growth of the Roman Catholic Church and its adaptation to Korean culture.

The Roman Catholic Church in Korea celebrated its bicentennial with a visit to Korea by Pope John Paul II and the canonization of 93 Korean and 10 French missionary martyrs in 1984. It was the first time that a canonization ceremony had been held outside the Vatican, and it gave Korea the fourth largest number of Catholic saints in the world.

Protestantism

After treaties with foreign powers were signed, Protestant missionaries of several persuasions began to stream into Korea, the first being Dr. Horace N. Allen, who arrived in 1884. The Presbyterians and Methodists from the outset appeared most successful in gaining converts, and still have the most members among Korean churches. For some time around the turn of the century, evangelical churches felt that Korea was the best mission field in the world, and that with various emotion-filled revival movements sweeping the peninsula, it would not be long before Korea became a preponderantly Christian nation.

Dr. Spencer Palmer in his monograph *Korea and Christianity* pointed out the contrast between the missionary approaches in China and Korea. The first Jesuits who went to China noted the government was highly centralized and the mass of the people controlled from above. Therefore, their strategy was designed to convert the court and emperor to their beliefs, and thereby spread salvation to the whole country as if it were by fiat from above. The Chinese court respected the scientific learning of the Western missionaries, used the Jesuits as consultants or advisors, but politely declined, in most cases, to take the Catholic theology seriously.

When the Protestants arrived in China some time later, they did no better, for they came in conjunction with gunboat diplomacy and commercial exploitation. Few lasting converts are made at the point of a gun. The sincerity of missionaries can be doubted when many of them were observed getting rich in exploitative business dealings, including in some cases even supporting the notorious opium trade.

In Korea, through a combination of luck and astuteness, the situation was completely different. The missionaries, especially the late-arriving Protestants, came as bearers of modern knowledge in many fields filling a vacuum which the isolated, indrawn Korean nation desperately needed filled if it was to attain the modernization that might assure its continued independence.

The missionaries arranged for the advanced education abroad of many of Korea's young potential leaders and stood shoulder to shoulder with patriotic resistance to Japan's encroachments upon Korean sovereignty.

After annexation in 1910, many foreign missionaries gave direct and indirect assistance to the Korean independence movement, whose leadership—by no coincidence—was predominantly made up with Christian graduates of their own schools. These efforts continued until the Japanese expulsion of the missionaries in 1940 on the eve of World War II. There were innumerable cases of persecution of Korean Christians after 1910, as much for political as for religious reasons, since the Japanese regarded the Korean church as subversive to its own dominance over the peninsula.

Koreans have not forgotten the aid and comfort afforded them in their darkest hours by foreign missionaries, Protestant and Catholic alike, and the help provided by mission-sponsored modernization movements in everything from

Taejonggyo followers bow before Tan-gun's portrait.

agriculture to sanitation.

Since the Korean War, Protestant churches have experienced such phenomenal growth that today there are 70 denominations in Korea. The year 1985 was the centennial of Protestantism in Korea and more than 20 denominations and 24 organizations set up a Council for the 100th Anniversary of the Korean Church to plan various programs in memory of church pioneers and to bring the Protestant churches together as one church. Having been dependent for much of the first century of its existence, the Protestant churches placed new emphasis on service to others, both to Korea's poor in the form of such services as free eye operations and blood donations and to the rest of the world by sending out missionaries.

New Religions

Korea's flourishing modern movements, grouped under the heading of "New Religions," number more than 240 throughout the country. Most of them have small memberships and have developed primarily from the *Tonghak* Movement of the 1860s. The largest such sect boasts as many as 600,000 followers, and some of the smaller ones consist of groups of 10 or so members only. A total overall figure would probably give a membership of 1,600,000 for all these recent sects taken together.

The *Tonghak* Movement arose in the mid-19th century in response to many complex social factors. In a sense it was a reaction against Catholicism, which was called "Western Learning" whereas *Tonghak* was "Eastern Learning." It also was inspired by the political decadence of the period and the plight of country people, ground under the heels of city aristocrats or idle rural gentry. In these respects it was a reform movement, including anti-foreign elements in the realization that Korea was threatened by outside domination as well as inner decay.

The founder of the *Tonghak* Movement, Ch'oe Che-u, readily admitted the syncretic nature of his theology, typical of Korean religions throughout the ages. "Our Way is originally not Confucianism, Buddhism, or Taoism," he wrote, "But our Way is a combination of the three."

The immediate appeal of Ch'oe's doctrine was its optimism and belief in a better future—though whether in this world or the next was rather vague. As Ch'oe wrote in a poem: "Heaven told me, `For 50,000 years since the world began, you are the first person to have penetrated into the Fathomless Great Way'."

The people believed in and followed Ch'oe, a country scholar and minor aristocrat, and the result was a rural-based revolution which upset the weak and vacillating central government in Seoul. Between 1862 and 1864, parts of southern Korea were under the control of *Tonghak* armies, but in the latter year, government forces won a decisive victory. Ch'oe was captured and executed for heresy. However, his movement survived under other leadership, changing its name to *Ch'ŏndogyo* and its nature from a political to a purely religious nationalist approach. The March 1, 1919 Independence Movement issued its public declaration against Japanese dominance with 33 signatures of nationalist leaders. Many of these were Christians, and several Buddhist, but the head of the group was Son Pyŏung-hŭi, the leader of *Ch'ŏndogyo*.

Most of the other new Korean religions adopted this attitude too, each espousing veneration of a different divine leader or savior sent down from heaven to redeem the world. Some are still active, while some are legendary figures such as Tan-gun. Others have been martyred, like Ch'oe, or have passed on.

A few of the sects are ultra-nationalistic and proclaim that Korea will be the next great world empire, that Korean is the coming world language, and that a Korean will be sent to as the divinely appointed savior of all mankind.

Though syncretism had been a normal process in Korean religion through the centuries, the *Tonghak* Movement was the first to attempt to rationalize this process systematically. The founder, Ch'oe, aimed at a religious system, in his own words, "fusing into one the ethics of Confucianism, the awakening to nature taught in Buddhism, and Taoist cultivation of energy." He even introduced the idea of the personal God of Catholicism, the intrusion of which he had been battling all his life.

Syncretism in one degree or another can be found in all the denominations belonging to Tonghak and allied Chungsan sects. The same trend may be noted in the creeds of almost all the newer religions, such as *Ilshimgyo*, *Taejonggyo*, *Muryŏng Ch'ŏndo*, the *Pongnam*, *Todŏkhoe* and *Chŏngilhoe*. Most of these religions are Confucian in ethics, follow Buddhist-type rites, and adopt Taoist methods in religious practice.

The new religions have mushroomed in times of social instability, but their number and influence have been reduced in recent years as Korean society has become more stable. Either stressing the worship of Tan-gun, the legendary founder of the Korean nation, or offering doctrines similar to those of the established churches, the new religions have gradually become accepted, with some becoming well established (*Ch'ŏndogyo, Wonbulgyo, Taejonggyo*, the Unification Church, etc.) and others being absorbed by the older religions. There are also some Japanese religions and Christian-based religions which are being propagated with the assistance of foreign religious groups. Although most of the new religions began in the rural

The central Islamic mosque in Seoul.

areas, they spread to the cities and, like the more established churches, sought to make themselves relevant to the needs of an industrialized society.

Islam

The first Koreans in modern times to be introduced to Islam lived in Manchuria, where they had moved between 1895 and 1928 under Japanese colonial policy. After World War II, many Koreans returned to the peninsula from Manchuria and among them were converts to Islam. They were not organized, however, and had no place of worship until the Korean War when Turkish troops came to Korea as part of the 16-nation United Nations Command and brought with them an Imam as chaplain. Korean Muslims were granted permission to worship with the Turkish troops and the Islamic faith grew.

In September 1955, the inaugural service of Korean Islam was held, followed by the election of the first Korean Imam, the organization of the Korean Islamic Society and the establishment of a mosque in Seoul. In 1966, the Korean Islamic Society was expanded and reorganized as the Korean Muslim Federation and in 1967, Korean Islam was officially registered with the Ministry of Culture, giving it legal status. The central mosque was dedicated in Seoul in 1976 and subsequently seven other mosques were built including one in Pusan and one in Kwangju. Today there are more than 20,000 Muslims in Korea and cultural and religious contact with Moslem countries is brisk.

CUSTOMS AND TRADITIONS

Family Customs

The vast changes that have swept Asia, along with the rest of the world, in recent decades naturally have been reflected in a different life style for many Koreans. Moves toward modernization of society have been accompanied by alterations and adjustments in customs and traditions.

Despite the changes, there are those who maintain that Korea—for all the high-rise buildings, superhighways and technological advances—still is one of the most Confucian of all countries, holding beneath the surface to a long cherished approach to the proper way of life.

In early times, the typical Korean family was large. Several generations often lived together, and many children were desired for stability and security. It was not unusual for the number of sharing one house to total a dozen or more. In recent years, the movement to urban areas and the spread of apartment-type housing have meant that newly married couples tend to live in their own quarters instead of living with other family members, giving rise to an increasing number of nuclear families.

Traditionally, in a Korean home the head of the family was regarded as the source of authority. All family members were expected to do what was ordered or desired by the family head. Strict instructions were to be obeyed without demur. It would have been unthinkable for children or grandchildren to place themselves in opposition to the wishes of their elders.

Obedience to the superior was regarded as natural and one of the most admirable virtues. On the other hand, it was understood that the patriarch of the family would be fair in dealing with the family members.

The adage that a man must first seek his own development and manage his family properly before he could govern the nation reflects the Confucian idea of order. This holds that if a man is unable to control his family, he could hardly be qualified to govern a country.

Under this system or order, man traditionally has been given the responsibility of representing, supporting and protecting the family as well as the power to command. If he cannot wield this power and exercise this responsibility, he loses face as the head of the family. Order at home is maintained through obedience to superiors, that is, children obeying parents, the wife the husband, the servants the master. It is a long social tradition that Koreans respect and obey elders in accordance with social decorum.

There are many monuments throughout Korea commemorating loyal subjects, filial sons, and faithful women. Though often costly, these monuments were erected to honor such people as models for society. Community service and spirit were nurtured through the acknowledgment of the importance of family, social order, loyalty, filial piety, and fidelity.

The Korean people have always attached importance to the concept of fidelity. Women, even if their husbands died young, were encouraged to be faithful by serving his parents and not remarrying. In some cases, girls whose husbands-to-be died during the engagement period never married. Such behavior was admired and many communities erected stone monuments recognizing certain people for displaying such attributes.

Monuments to, and stories about, filial sons and daughters abound as well. Filial piety is considered the basic component and premise in the forming and shaping of personality. The traditional family consciousness expresses itself in filial piety, attaching the most importance to the father-son relationship. Parents are the absolute authority, to be accorded strict obedience and respect. However, filial piety concerns not only one's parents, but one's conduct toward others and one's conduct in society. The value of a man emanates from the achievement of filial piety and if he violates the norm he is censured.

Traditionally, this concept of filial piety is even reflected in speech. There are complicated, elaborate sets of honorific words, depending on position. If not correct in speech and deportment, it is difficult to gain and maintain respect. Thus there are strict rules of conduct both within and out of the home.

In earlier days, a common type of Korean house was a rectangular, L or U-shaped single-

Bowing to parents and elders is an age-old New Year's custom.

story structure, built chiefly of wood and clay. The roof was not high and was mostly thatched with straw. The simplest form of the Korean house consisted of a living room, another room, and a kitchen, with the toilet set apart and away from the living quarters. The structure and size differed according to the size of the family, the range of social intercourse, and wealth. A larger house would consist of the main family quarters at the center, a closet, a maid's room, a barn, and a toilet at the side. At the front part of the inner yard were quarters for the master of the house and for male guests, and adjoining the gate was a room for servants.

Today it would be difficult to point out a "typical" Korean house for nearly all recent structures are of concrete or ferro-concrete construction. Though not widely recognized, this change, from predominantly wood structures to largely concrete structures, entails a subtle yet far-reaching change in the lifestyle of Koreans.

The individual Korean house, old or new, is built to protect its inhabitants from cold weather. Generally, it is somewhat low, with rooms relatively small and not many doors or windows, the greater part being walls. Some of the rooms will have *ondol* floors which are heated via under-the-floor flues. This system of heating is so ingrained in Korean life that even the most fashionable, Western-style houses built in recent years are, with few exceptions, provided with a few rooms with concrete floors heated by means of a heat-radiating network of pipes. Many Koreans still prefer to sit and sleep on cushions and thick mats on the floor.

In a traditional Korean home, there is little furniture and seating is on the floor. Bedrooms and dining rooms are not specially provided, so usually a living room also functions for sleeping and eating. The room used by the housewife is a place for family gatherings and the center of household management. Therefore, this room is equipped with wardrobes, bedding, and other paraphernalia. The front quarters are used exclusively by the master of the house, and if he is an educated man, are equipped with a desk, shelves, books, and a few cushions. Normally, the master retires to the housewife's room for

Kanggangsuwŏlle, *a traditional circle dance, performed under the full moon to celebrate* ch'usŏk *(the Harvest Moon Festival).*

the night.

Again, in a traditional home, the *hanbok* or Korean dress is worn as it is more convenient and suitable to the *ondol* oriented lifestyle, and Western-style dress is usually worn outside the home, as it is more practical for work. However, on holidays like New Year's Day, *Hanshik,* and *Ch'usŏk,* the entire family, regardless of age or sex, often wears Korean traditional dress.

Mealtime at home brings the entire family together. The main dish is rice to which *chap-gok* or grains such as barley and millet and or a variety of beans are often added. Soup is always served and *kimch'i,* a spicy, fermented cabbage, is invariably a side dish. Soy sauce, dried pepper, red pepper paste and *toenjang* or bean paste are used for seasoning.

Koreans like wine and enjoy drinks before meals. Entertaining guests with wine is customary. Of course guests who do not drink are excused from this custom with a great show of regret. Westerners, when asked to drink repeatedly, often exchanging cups, might think the request is a nuisance. Koreans who are not

asked in the same situation would think of it as rude or stingy on the part of the host and might even protest at such an impolite omission. Reciprocity in sharing wine in a convivial atmosphere is important to Koreans.

At home, where hierarchical human relations should be maintained, younger members or inferiors were not allowed to drink or smoke in front of superiors or older people. Ignorance of this rule distinguished an uncultured man, and he was censured as such. Especially in the case of smoking, censure could be severe.

Sentiment, love, and duty between family members are normally strong and cannot be severed. Relations among family members are not merely self-serving ones, but extend far beyond. Family members are conscious of their bondage of blood, and have established a tradition of cooperation and mutual assistance.

Customs among Clan Members

Among Koreans there is a strong bond between relatives and clan members. This goes beyond personal interests or hopes of gain, adhering to traditional principles regarding mutual cooperation as a solemn duty. Because of this, the family system is one of security in which people in trouble can count on support from relatives.

In the past, brothers often lived in the same house after marriage and, in some cases, even cousins occupied the same house. Such large families are rare these days as families have branched into smaller units. Still, they often reside in the same neighborhood and maintain contact. Those who live far away tend to get together on special occasions such as marriage, the 60th or 70th birthday, the birthday of a child, and on traditional holidays. At such times everyone pitches in to assist with preparations and to entertain.

Respect for ancestors as symbolized in family rituals is central to the clan system. Special memorial services for great-great-grandparents are conducted in the home on the anniversary of their deaths, between 1 a.m. and 2 a.m. For the fifth generation and beyond, services are held once a year on *Ch'usŏk* (the Harvest Moon Festival), the 15th day of the Eighth Moon, or on a selected, supposedly auspicious day. On this day descendants gather at the ancestral tomb to perform ceremonial rites. This memorial service is such an important duty that descendants travel long distances to participate.

Often on these days, clan members take advantage of the gathering to hold an annual conference. A clan that has many branches and members may divide into smaller units, each establishing a common coffer and property. The conference is organized to decide and implement policies of common interest such as the maintenance of ancestral tombs and the management of clan properties.

Koreans regard tradition highly and maintain records dozens of generations long. Genealogies minutely record official ranks, achievements, royal citations, the localities of tombs and other information. They also include maternal genealogies and the names of male and female children. Thus, genealogies graphically show the history and tradition of the clan and its members.

When meeting for the first time, Koreans of the same family name first decide if they are members of the same clan. If so, they must consult the genealogy to find how closely related. If one belongs to an older generation, respect must be shown through the use of honorifics and certain respectful words that imply family.

Society

Social Order

The relationship between old and young is one of five human relationships upon which the Confucian concept of social order is based, and it is this concept that long dictated Korean behavior to a large extent. In traditional Korean society, older people are respected for their knowledge and experience and young people must conduct themselves accordingly.

The importance of social order can be observed especially on New Year's Day when, after the usual memorial services for ancestors, family members bow to grandparents, parents, older brothers, relatives, and so on in accordance with age. Young people may even seek out the village elders to pay due respect by bowing to them, even though they are not related.

At meetings, social gatherings, or drinking parties, social order becomes an immediate question: who should greet whom first, who should sit where, who should sit down first, who should pour wine for whom first. Among close friends, those born earlier are treated as elder brothers and sisters. Among acquaintances, one is expected to use honorifics to those 10 years older than oneself. However, if the difference is less than 10 years, people address one another as equals. Care must be taken not to disturb social order for to do so is to be viewed as uncouth and lacking in social decorum.

Social Relations

Under Confucianism, the proper relationship between the sexes was based on one of the five human relationships—that of husband and wife. This does not aim at discrimination, but holds that both men and women have certain duties to perform and a set of ethics to observe vis-a-vis the other. In its practical application, this ideal, learned from an early age, affected not just husband and wife, but virtually all relations between the sexes.

From early childhood, children played and grew up segregated by sex as illustrated in the adage, "Boys and girls at the age of seven should not be allowed to sit in the same room." This was adhered to except in the case of brothers and sisters who followed another set of ethics governing family relations.

The strict application of these rules resulted in severe restrictions on women while relative freedom was allowed for men. For women there was the law of three obediences: obeisance to the father before marriage, to the husband upon marriage, and to the son after the husband's death. This female submission was not due to any supposed weakness or inadequacy on the part of the female, but simply the organization of society. The woman's role was "within," that is within the home, which was her domain. The man's role was "outside," that is in all the affairs of society and life beyond the confines of the home.

It was the woman's duty to care for the children, to help her husband with the farmwork, to prepare the meals, to make the family's clothes, and to maintain an atmosphere of peace so that her husband would be more capable of handling the larger issues of society. The female role was firmly established and women were expected to adhere strictly to that role.

Although strict observance of Confucian inspired ideals now is a rarity, Korean men and women still are conscious of their positions as expressed not only in their behavior but speech as well. Love and affection were not to be expressed openly, not even between husband and wife. And, just as there are special words and honorifics for use with family, friends, and elders, so there are for husband and wife as well.

Cooperative Activities

Kye, meaning agreement or bond, is a social organization based on the principle of mutual cooperation and aid with a specific objective. All *kye* collect dues and manage a fund and, depending on the objective and program, are classified into many kinds. One type is the *wich'in-gye*, literally meaning *kye* for the parents. This *kye* is organized by those who have aged parents in order to provide for their *hwangap* or 60th birthday celebration. This is a special celebration, for in the past few people lived to be 60. With the increased longevity of the modern day, the 70th birthday anniversary often is observed. Children must honor their parents at this time with a large party. As it usually involves many guests and feasting, it is quite costly. To prepare for this time, funds or rice are collected each month or annually to help each member in turn to defray the cost of the celebration.

Traditionally, people prepared splendid funerals as expressions of filial piety, and these tended to be costly. To prepare for a parent's funeral, some form a *sangjo-gye*. In such a *kye*, not only are there monetary benefits, but the *kye* members all pitch in to carry the bier, to serve as messengers, to dig the grave, etc.

Weddings also are expensive as they not only entail the exchange of gifts and dowry, including bedding, furniture, and household utensils, but also several large parties to entertain guests. This is often more than one household can afford so the wedding *kye* is popular.

The village *kye* is characterized by the admission of all villagers. It collects an agreed-upon sum of money from each family and sometimes raises funds through collective work such as *ture* (cooperative farming). The village *kye* has no specific purpose other than helping villagers through unexpected times of need or building and repairing facilities for the community.

Lately, *kye* characterized by monetary interests are becoming very popular among housewives in large cities as they not only provide

A nong-ak*(farmers' dance and band music)* perfomance to celebrate a good harvest resulting from the village-wide pooling of labor.

extra cash but also opportunities for getting together, exchanging gossip and partying. The conventional *kye*, however, is based on mutual aid and cooperation with each member performing his duties as if it were his own business. As it is difficult to maintain if a member does not pay his dues or reneges on his duties, solidarity is a must. Through such a system many families have prospered and many villages developed.

Besides the *kye*, there are other cooperative activities—planting, the building of bridges and roads, the digging of wells, shamanistic rites, etc. Whatever the case, people participate with a spirit of cooperation and cheerfulness. During celebrations not only relatives and neighbors but all the people of the community pitch in with the preparations and work, as well as with the celebration. Planting, weeding, the building of bridges and their repair, and the digging of wells are tasks that are usually done through the collective labor of the entire community. Farm work by such collective labor is called ture and historical records show that this custom appeared as early as the Shilla Kingdom. In

Shilla villages, women and girls would gather on moonlit nights in groups with a leader and compete in weaving. The *ture* weaving is a good example of combining work with play.

With the development of the textile industry, *ture* weaving disappeared, but in rural areas the custom still exists and is associated with such tasks as transplanting, weeding, and rice harvesting. As this work needs to be done quickly and at a proper time, the village leaders decide priority projects and the composition of the ture. It is usually one working man from each family but sometimes a woman may be admitted or a family may be exempted for some reason upon the consent of the village leaders.

When the *ture* is underway, pennants and banners planted around the field identify the work area. Music, the rhythm aiding in the collective movements of the workers, usually accompanies transplanting and weeding. Going to and from the fields is accompanied by much singing and often a farmers' band.

When the work is completed, the total mandays and amount of work are calculated and

Ch'ajŏn Nori *is played not only for fun, but also to foster village teamwork.*

payment is made by the landowners. With this payment, a sum of money is added to the village welfare fund, and a certain amount is usually set aside for a day of drinking and relaxing.

Some of this fund, as well as donations, may be used for the financing of shamanistic rites as it is believed that certain gods control certain functions of the community. It is most important that all villagers take part in these rites, whether through actual performance or observance. In some ceremonies, such as the rain rite, all the adults participate but in others only selected officers who are regarded as ritually clean perform the rites.

Highly illustrative of the Korean spirit of cooperation are games and dances, such as *Kanggangsuwŏllae*, mask dances, and tug-of-war, performed at festivals and on special occasions. Many of these require not only performers but other people to prepare the necessary props and equipment.

One such game is the *Chajŏn Nori* or "juggernaut battle" which requires wooden vehicles upon which people can ride and be pushed

about. The preparations that go into these are extensive, with much time and labor going into the cutting of wood and the making of the vehicles.

Another is the tug of war requiring all-out cooperation and skill. An entire township composed of many townships, may participate, dividing into two groups to stage the tug of war. Each village or township must make a straw rope of a prescribed thickness and length. On the day of the contest, the team representatives, sometimes numbering as many as a hundred, bring the rope to the site. All of the ropes are then connected and the tug of war begins. One side of the rope is considered female and the other side male. It is hoped that the female side will win as it is symbolic of a good harvest.

Although many of these customs are disappearing, or are revived solely for their recreational or aesthetic value, they are representative of the Korean people, their customs and ideals.

Annual Customs

For thousands of years, Koreans have reckoned time according to the lunar calendar. Contrary to common belief, the lunar calendar has always been adjusted to correspond to the solar year by intercalation or adding a whole lunar month, or Moon, to the lunar year twice every five years. This can be demonstrated by the fact that the solar calendar is divided into 24 equal portions, or *chŏl*, of which the equinoxes and solstices are used as fixed points. Even before the solar calendar was introduced to Asia, the lunar calendar showed these *chŏl* or seasonal nodes, which are important dates especially in agriculture. Give or take one or two days, these nodes fall more or less on the same day by the solar calendar but not on any regular day when reckoned by the lunar calendar. The most important of the *chŏl* are of course the equinoxes and solstices, but *ipch'un* (the advent of spring) is given more weight than others because it is the first node of the year, marking the approaching spring. Several special holidays are reckoned by the lunar calendar even today.

The first day of the first month, New Year's Day, or *Sŏl*, one of the biggest holidays of the year. In observing it, people traditionally dress their best, take off from work and the family gathers to observe the ancestral ceremonies. A feast is spread and the younger members of the family make New Year's obeisance to the elders. Then the young go around the neighborhood to offer New Year's greetings to older relatives and acquaintances.

Another important date by the lunar calendar is *Ch'usŏk*, or the Harvest Moon Festival, which falls on the 15th day of the Eighth Moon or usually in September or October by the solar calendar. As this date marks the harvest time, it is regarded as a thanksgiving day, and is celebrated as enthusiastically as New Year's Day.

There are a few other important days in the lunar year. The 15th day of the First Moon is regarded as important since it is the first full moon of the year. People crack various kinds of nuts and set off firecrackers to exercise harmful spirits, insects and animals. In the evening a variety of traditional games takes place under

National and Public Holidays

New Year's holidays (January 1-2)
Sŏl holidays (Last day of Twelfth Moon through the second day of the First Moon)
Independence Movement Day (March 1)
Arbor Day (April 5)
Buddha's Birthday (8th day of the Fourth Moon)
Children's Day (May 5)
Memorial Day (June 6)
Constitution Day (July 17)
Liberation Day (August 15)
Ch'usŏk holidays (14th to 16th days of the Eighth Moon)
National Foundation Day (October 3)
Christmas (December 25)

the moonlight. Tug of war, stone fights, and mock fights with torches are held between neighboring villages. These are staged by youths and middle-aged men before hundreds of spectators who come from far and near. These games are played to win or lose, and tradition has it that the winning village will be blessed with bumper crops. Such games perhaps were started to determine priority in drawing farming water from a common source.

Sometime during the First or Second Moon is a day called *Hanshik*. This is the 105th day after the winter solstice, falling about the fifth of April by the solar calendar. On this day, rites for ancestors are observed early in the morning, when the whole family visits the tombs of their direct ancestors to pay respects, tidy up the tombs, and plant more turf if necessary.

The fifth day of the Fifth Moon is called *Tano*, which is another big holiday. According to ancient records, people on this day rested from work, dressed up in their best, and feasted as they did on New Year's Day. Special events include wrestling matches for men in which the

On special occasions like New Year's Day, playing yut(a game like parcheesi)(top), seesawing(left) and kite-flying(right) are popular.

champion receives a bull as a prize, and swinging competitions for women in which the winner gets a gold ring.

The Tenth Moon is the month for *kimjang*. During this month kimchi or pickled vegetables, an indispensable subsidiary food for Koreans, is prepared to last the three months of winter, so that every household is busy with this important work. During this month a set phrase of greeting is, "Have you finished *kimjang*?"

The Twelfth Moon, called *Sŏttal*, is a time when people set things in proper order and settle accounts, to prepare for welcoming in the new year. An honorable man is not supposed to carry his debts over to the next year.

By tradition one must stay awake on the night before New Year's Day. Records tell that in the old days the court held exorcising ceremonies, called *narye*, to expel evil spirits. Ten dancers of *narye* in *ch'ŏyong* masks danced to the accompaniment of music. In rural areas a musical performance of *nong-ak* or farmers' music is used to also expel evil spirits and usher in good fortune.

Buddha's Birthday recently has been designated a national holiday. This is the eighth day of the Fourth Moon of the lunar calendar, which generally falls in April or May.

Beliefs

Divination

Divination developed from the desire to know and control one's destiny, a desire that has been characteristic of man for ages. There is mention of divination in Korea as early as the Three Kingdoms period (37 B.C.-A.D. 668).

In the beginning, people wanted to know the how, why, and what of such natural phenomena as comets, solar and lunar eclipses, rainbows, flowers, and the migration of birds. Such phenomena were thought to be symbolic of things to come.

In the Shilla Kingdom (57 B.C.-A.D. 935) there was a position called *Ilgwan* or solar officer whose job was to divine and report to the king when unusual phenomena occurred in nature. During the Koryŏ Dynasty (918-1392) a similar official was called the doctor of divination. He observed and interpreted meteorological phenomena and divined the future of the dynasty and the fortunes of individuals. At first, divination was concerned mainly with natural phenomena and important problems of life, but soon it was extended to small affairs and events of daily life.

Divination based on natural phenomena judges the fortunes and misfortunes of life and its future through the sun, the moon, the stars, clouds, rain, rainbows, and wind. Natural phenomena resulting from the interactions of these elements are thought to have certain relations with human life and, therefore, symbolize what is to come. Each man is believed to have his own star, and the stars of heroes, sages, and great men are especially large. The brightness of a star or the falling of a star are thought to have a bearing upon the fate of a man.

The appearance and disappearance of certain animals, the manner, nature and time of their crying, their behavior, all are seen as signs of what is coming. The cow, the horse, the dog, the hen, the cat, the magpie, the crow, the spider, the ant, and the snake were major subjects for observation in ancient Korea.

Plant divination is based on unusual plant phenomena. For example, a tree may dry up, a withered tree may put forth new buds, a flower may blossom or a tree put forth leaves at an unusual time. All of these are considered significant in regard to human life.

Dreams also are believed to foretell the future. According to legends and historical records, good dreams usually signify a happy event such as a promotion, even ascension to the throne, while bad dreams forecast disaster. The number of books on dream interpretation is indicative of the interest in this form of divination.

Another method of divination deals with physiognomy and phrenology. The nose, the eyes, the mouth, the ears, the complexion, the hair, the feet, the hands, the voice, the deportment, the surface and hue of the body, the lines on the palms, and birthmarks are believed to reflect future events. Parallel systems of prediction in Western cultures often do not agree with traditional Asian divination.

The results of games are also thought to forecast the future. During the First Moon, the *yunnori* game is played in homes, employing four round backed, flat-faced sticks. The sticks are thrown in the air and the score depends on how they land, back up or face up. The result of the four-stick game is used to divine the farming results of the year. Players are divided into two sides, the mountain and the plain. If the mountain wins, it means a year of bad crops. If the plain wins, a good harvest is guaranteed. In the tug of war game, a male side and female side are formed, and the victory of the male side is thought to mean a year of bad crops. If the female side wins, it foretells the opposite.

Yin-yang divination is based on the principles of *yin* (negative force) and *yang* (positive force). Through the laws governing the *yin-yang* interaction, the five elements—metal, wood, water, fire and earth—are produced and destroyed.*T'ŏjŏng-pigyŏl*, a popular form of fortunetelling, is based on the yin-yang principles and elements.

With the beginning of the new lunar year, everyone calculates their fortune and future for the coming 12 months. This is done using the book of *T'ojŏng-pigyŏl*, and the date and time of birth by the lunar calendar. This fortune telling is a popular pastime on New Year's Day and the following two weeks. During this time, an old man with a book of *T'ojŏng-pigyŏl* is a common sight in marketplaces and on street corners, where people are likely to gather.

Not only older people, but young people as well rely on the various forms of divination. Quite often students will consult a fortune-teller about examinations, college entrance and other school matters, business, etc. Of course, consultation is a must before marriage to ensure the appropriate partner. Young children try to find lost articles by spitting into the palm and hitting the spittle with one finger. Supposedly the direction the spittle takes is indicative of the direction one should take to find the article.

Divination remains popular and fortunetellers are a common sight. Competition in Korean society is strong, and it is believed divination can help to ensure success.

Geomancy

In Korea, geomancy is a method of divination for locating favorable sites for cities, residences, and burial grounds. This belief holds that happiness and prosperity will prevail over house built on an ideal site. The site of the ancestral grave must be ideal as well, as the location is believed to exert a lasting and decisive influence over the destinies of the entire family.

The basic theory of geomancy stems from the belief that the earth, being the mother, is the producer of all things, and the fever or energy of the earth in each site exercises a decisive influence over those who utilize the land. The theory asserts that where male and female, that is heaven and earth, are in concord and communicate with one another, the inner fever or energy will spring out and the outer energy will ferment, thereby producing wind and water. The Korean word for geomancy is *p'ungsu*, literally meaning wind and water.

Topography is the essential factor in geomancy for it is these points, where the energy flows and is stored, that are considered *myŏngdang* or propitious sites. The ideal site is ground surrounded by mountains—a high, rugged range to the north, flanked by hills folded in many ranges called the blue dragon to the left, and the white tiger to the right. The building or tomb must face a low hill in the south and the center of the site should command a relatively wide expanse of plain to the front. A river flowing through the plain makes it an even better location.

Such requirements are met precisely by the capital city of Seoul. The location was selected about 550 years ago after much research and consideration by King T'aejo, the founder of the Chosŏn Dynasty.

The city is surrounded by mountains—the high, rugged Pugaksan (the turtle) to the north, Naksan (the blue dragon) to the east, Mallidongsan (the white tiger) to the west, and Namsan to the south. Through the basin flows the Han-gang River and the Chŏng gyech'ŏn Stream, making the site the perfect seat for the government. As it was, the Chosŏn Dynasty prospered for some 500 years.

If a person or family experiences one misfortune after another, it is attributed to the disadvantageous location of the residence or ancestral tomb. If the site of a village has been selected well geomantically, villagers should receive many benefits with filial sons, loyal subjects, and faithful wives abounding. The modern cemetery has frustrated the attempts of urban dwellers to locate the ideal burial ground, but many rural people still are preoccupied with the principles of geomancy, going to great length to find the choice *myŏngdang*.

Folk Medicine

In ancient times illness was thought to be due to something entering the body, and recovery meant ridding oneself of this contamination. Shamans, usually female, were employed to drive away the evil spirit.

The original function of the shaman was not just to drive evil spirits from the body, but to charm away all the spirits that bring unhappiness. The shaman also performed rites invoking the gods' blessings for good fortune, the birth of a male child, a good harvest, rain, etc.

To cure the sick, the shaman made offerings of food and wine, and sometimes even sacrifices of animals, symbolizing the ill person. In return for the offerings, the shaman would request the spirits to leave the body and home of the sick person and never return. Making the entreaty, the shaman would sing, chant, dance, and pray.

If this was not effective, a more active and hostile approach was made. The locality of the spirits would be sought out and if found, beaten, shut up in a bottle, floated down the river, buried in the ground, or wounded with a sharp knife or stick through a performance symbolic of such actions. These performances, lasting anywhere from an hour to a week, were accompanied by music, chanting, singing, dancing, and praying.

Fortunetellers were often consulted in the treatment of sickness. Through divination it was believed they could determine the causes of illness and advise an appropriate treatment.

Not only sickness, but also misfortune, and calamities of various kinds were attributed to evil spirits. To protect against these, Koreans would often post *pujŏk*, or talismans, at certain places in and around the house such as the gate, the ceiling beam, over the door, and in the barn.

Most talismans were painted in red ink on yellow or white mulberry paper. Red has traditionally been thought to possess the power to suppress evil, and for this reason, red beans, red clay, red gowns and other red items are often used in shamanistic rites.

Korean talismans range in style from highly structured, geometric patterns to free-form swirls and doodles. Some consist of a single Chinese ideograph and others incorporate lines of Chinese or Sanskrit into a maze of effigies, figures, star charts, and religious symbols. These are not only for exorcising evil spirits, but also there are talismans for inviting good spirits in requesting assistance in almost any circumstance. Talismans were commonly used to:

drive out diseases,
fulfill the desire for a good job,
secure safe travel either on land or sea,
make a clean sweep of the "three calamities,"
secure a harmonious conjugal life,
guarantee non-invasion by evil spirits,
pray for the safe birth of a child,
eliminate calamities,
maintain a peaceful household,
terminate misfortunes in official careers,
achieve the 100 things desired,
repel the concubine of one's husband,
secure the birth of a male child,
sell or buy a house or move into a new house,
expiate sin by hearing Buddhist scriptures,
calm an apprehensive mind,
secure peaceful living,
secure longevity,
assure many children,
expel thieves,
produce high officials in the family,
expiate sins and achieve nirvana,
dream a happy dream that brings fortune and luck,
avoid sudden death,
maintain harmonious relations between father

and son,
and maintain a flourishing business.

The employment of such talismans is an involved process requiring rites of purification, orienting oneself psychologically, performing chants, painting the talisman, and posting it in the appropriate place. At the beginning of the lunar year, Buddhist monks often prepare talismans and send them to their followers for posting.

The beginning of spring is also an important time and, by custom, families usually post a talisman requesting that spring bring happiness and harmony to the family. Many of these customs and practices are still in practice today.

Village Rites and Rituals

Not only are talismans used but certain ritual rites and ceremonies are performed as well to ensure a prosperous, harmonious life. There are many, and most are influenced strongly by the elements and environment which affect the livelihood of the villagers. For example, those living in mountains and valleys tend to make offerings to the mountain spirit while fisherman honor the dragon spirit of the sea. There are rites for the home and rites for the village, and all of these vary with each part of the country.

The most commonly performed rites are those for the mountain spirit who watches over the village and influences the harvest. According to legend, upon his death Tan-gun, the founder of Korea, became the mountain spirit of Asadal, the ancient capital of Korea. Each village has its own special mountain, usually to the north, where the shrine of the mountain spirit is located. Offerings are made to this spirit often but especially during the 15 days after the lunar New Year's Day.

Also protecting the village is the *sŏnang* spirit. It looks after the welfare of all the villagers, bringing happiness and goodness, and warding off evil, disaster, and misfortune. The *sŏnang-dang*, or shrine, to the spirit *sŏnang*, is usually near the entrance to the village or on a hill overlooking the village. The shrine and the surrounding area are regarded as holy ground.

Villagers express their reverence for the spirit by keeping the area clean, and placing tree branches and rocks around the shrine.

Ruling the waters is the dragon spirit, who is believed to live in a palace under the sea. Often referred to as the dragon king, Korean literature abounds with stories of his exploits. As this spirit is thought to control the flow of water, its quality, and the waves of the sea, special care must be taken to ensure his happiness.

In time of drought, a special ceremony is conducted imploring the spirits for rain to nourish the crops and ensure a plentiful harvest. At such times, women climb to the mountain shrine to pray, sing and dance. To and from the shrine the women carry two bottles of water, sprinkling it along the way as a gift to the spirit.

During the first month of the lunar calendar, ceremonies and events are held imploring the spirits for peace and fortune in the coming year. Some of the rites are performed only by wives while some rites, such as the offerings to the earth spirit involve the entire village.

On New Year's Day of the lunar calendar, after respect had been shown family members and the ancestral tomb had been visited, villagers would gather to enjoy a farmers' band and to pay respect and tribute to the earth spirit. First they would visit the home of the wealthiest villager, where they would be entertained with food and drink. They would then dance around the yard and through the house and barns singing songs to the earth spirit, asking that the family and home be blessed in the coming year. Afterward, they would move on to the next house and the next until all the homes had been visited. With such merrymaking activities, the earth spirit was supposed to be pleased and would endow the people with many rewards throughout the year.

Most villages have special officers to perform certain duties and acts connected with the village rites. These people must be of impeccable reputation, commanding the general respect of the villages. Some are elected permanently and others for certain periods. Some of the duties are the reading of prayers, the obtaining of shamans to perform certain rites and exorcism and the preparation of special offeratory foods.

Before the ceremonies, the officers must purify their minds and bodies through cold baths and prayers as it is believed that careless handling of the ceremony will bring the wrath of the spirits on the entire community.

The preparing of sacrificial food must be done with great care to avoid contamination. It is usually done at an officer's house after the premises have been purified. To do this red clay is scattered inside the house and straw ropes are hung to frighten away evil spirits. Red clay is put around the well from which water is drawn for cooking, and the cover is placed over the well. No word can be uttered while preparing and cooking the ritual foods so a piece of white cloth or a chestnut is held in the mouth to prevent speaking.

The village rite is usually performed in the early dawn with the proffering of wine, the reading of a prayer, and the burning of a hand-made piece of white paper. If, as the ceremonial officer is burning the paper, the ashes drift up to the sky, it is a happy omen for the village. If the unburned paper falls to the ground it signifies trouble.

After the paper burning, the shaman performs a ceremonial dance for receiving, entertaining, and sending off the spirit. The shaman coaxes the spirit into making an appearance and pleads with him to render the coming year one of happiness, prosperity and freedom from disease. To entice him into accepting the plea, the shaman entertains the spirit with wine and food and then sends it away. This is done to the accompaniment of much music and dancing.

While the rites are underway, not only the officers but the entire village must remain at home observing certain rules and taboos. Around the shrine are hung straw ropes intertwined with paper to prevent the admittance of unclean people: those who are in mourning, those who have killed living things, and women who are menstruating. A villager traveling in other areas who has seen a corpse or committed an unclean act is prohibited from entering the village until the rites are completed. If such a person enters during the ceremony, it is believed the spirits will become angry and nullify the effects of the rites.

In some villages a tree that is considered sacred is used as the centerpiece for the ceremony as it is thought that the spirits will reside there temporarily. With the completion of the rites, the tree is moved to the entrance of the village and carved into guardian figures. It can then protect the village by repelling evil spirits.

Some of these ceremonies can be quite large and last several days. One is the *Pyŏlshin-gut*, a ceremony to the mountain spirit, held in Kangnŭng, Kangwon-do province on *Tano*, the fifth day of the Fifth Moon. Ancient records of the 16th century report 100 shamans attending the services and even today Kangnŭng is known for the large shaman festivals held there every *Tano*.

The Life Cycle

Birth

From ancient times, Korean women have been encouraged to produce male children. In the past, prosperity was judged by the number of male offspring and social institutions did much to encourage such beliefs. No matter how many daughters were born, the absence of a male child was grounds for divorce, and men often took concubines with the hope of fathering a son.

The idea of son preference is rooted deeply in the Confucian patriarchal system. It was the women's duty to produce a male heir to ensure the continuance of her husband's bloodline and to perform important ancestral rites.

As the birth of a son was considered a blessing from various spirits, many prayers and rituals were undertaken by women with the hope of receiving such a blessing. Women often prayed and made offerings at certain Taoist shrines, and to the *Samshin Halmŏni* (grandmother spirit), the Big Dipper, the mountain spirit, Buddha, and to certain rocks and trees considered sacred. According to the legend of Korea's founding, such an offering was made under a large tree before the birth of Tan-gun. These shrines were usually visited and prayers offered in the dead of night or in the early dawn after certain ablutions had been undertaken. A women might make such offerings for a period of anywhere from 21 to 100 days.

Of these spirits, *Samshin Halmŏni* is the most involved with childbirth, for not only does she provide for the birth of the child, but for its growth and rearing as well. She is usually represented by a piece of folded white paper or some clean straw hung in a corner of the house, and it is to this shrine that offerings and prayers are made. It is through her intervention that birth occurs and the mother recovers quickly. The Mongolian spot, or blue mark, found on the buttocks of Asian infants is thought to be the place where *Samshin Halmŏni* slaps the infant to bring it to life.

When pregnancy occurs, there are many rules and taboos that must be observed to ensure a healthy child and a safe delivery. The woman must not approach nor do anything considered unclean. She must not kill anything. She must be careful where she urinates and must not step over a straw rope, steal or do other mischievous things. If the woman does any of these things it is believed she will have a difficult delivery, the infant may be born retarded or diseased, or some other misfortune might befall the family. Also, there are many foods such as rabbit, squid, crab, eggs and peaches that are considered harmful to eat. It was thought, for example, if the mother ate chicken, the skin of the child would be prickly like a chicken or if she ate duck, the child would walk like a duck. For the health of the child and the mother, all of the family must cooperate to see that these taboos are observed.

As the time of delivery approaches, the fireplace and holes in paper doors should not be repaired, and the family should not see a burning house. All of these are considered bad luck and will adversely affect the unborn child. To ensure an easy delivery, the laundry rope is loosened, all doors are kept open, the husband's clothes are used as quilts, and clothes are borrowed from a woman who had an easy childbirth to cover the woman at the time of birth.

There are various ways of trying to determine the sex of the unborn child. Some involve the physical appearance of the pregnant woman, some involve dream interpretation, and some involve complicated calculations based on the ages of the parents. If the mother dreams about horses, cows, dragons, tigers, bears, or other large animals, she will deliver a male child. If she dreams of flowers or toys that girls play with, she will deliver a female child.

Upon the birth of a child, a straw rope, or *kŭmjul*, is hung across the gate to the house. These is to frighten away evil spirits and to warn people not to enter, as a child has recently been born. The rope, twisted in a leftward spiral, is usually intertwined with pine branches and red peppers, signifying a male, or pine branches and charcoal indicating a female. This custom varies from region to region with seaweed, small rocks, and pieces of paper often intertwined in the rope. The *kŭmjul* is usually posted for 21 days. If more children are desired, the placenta and afterbirth are burned under the eaves of the house. If no more children are desired, these are burned or burned some distance from the house, usually in a clean sunny place on the side of a mountain. The ashes are often scattered to the winds or in a river.

For seven days after childbirth, rice and seaweed soup are offered to the *Samshin Halmŏni* in the morning and evening. These foods are then eaten by the mother to help with her recovery. Special offerings are made on the 14th and 21st days after birth.

Family members are careful not to show their happiness over the birth of a child and do not speak of its beauty or health as such behavior and speech are thought to make the spirits jealous and thereby cause harm. To ensure that this does not happen, children are often given lowly names like Dog's Dung, Straw Bag, and Stonehead. Also to keep the spirits happy, no animals are killed and people in mourning and those who have seen a funeral are not permitted to enter the house. It is feared such behavior will bring the wrath of the spirits on the family and especially on the newborn child.

A tol, or first birthday celebration.

Birthday Celebrations

On the 100th day after a child's birth, a small feast is usually held to celebrate the child having survived this difficult period. If the child is sick at this time, the family passes the day with neither announcement nor party for to do otherwise is considered bad luck for the infant.

At this time the *Samshin Halmŏni* is honored with offerings of rice and soup for having cared for the infant and mother, for helping them to live through a difficult period. The family, relatives, and friends then celebrate with rice cakes, wine, and other delicacies such as red and black bean cakes sweetened with sugar or honey.

To prevent disaster and to bring the child luck and happiness, red bean cakes are customarily placed at the four compass points within the house. If the steamed rice cakes are shared with 100 people, it is thought the child will have a long life. Therefore, rice cakes are usually sent to as many people as possible to help share the happiness of the occasion. Those receiving rice cakes do not return the serving vessels empty, but with skeins of thread expressing the hope of longevity, and of rice and money symbolizing future wealth.

Such customs are part of the *tol*, or first birthday, celebration as well. Because of the high infant mortality rate in the past, this celebration is considered even more important. Like the 100th day celebration, it begins with offerings of rice and soup to the *Samshin Halmŏni*. However, the highlight of this celebration is when the child symbolically foretells its future.

For this ritual the child is dressed in new traditional Korean clothes. A male child wears the traditional headgear of the unmarried youth, and the female wears make-up. The child is seated before a table of various foods and objects such as thread, books, note-books, brushes, ink, and money which have been given by friends and relatives. The child is urged to pick up an object from the table, as it is believed the one selected foretells the child's future. If the child picks up a writing brush or book, he is destined to be a scholar. If he picks up money or rice, he will be wealthy; cakes or other food, a government official; a sword or bow, a military commander. If the child picks up the thread, it is believed he will live a long life.

This is followed by feasting and enjoying the antics of the toddler. Often at this time guests will present gifts of money, clothes, or gold

A traditional marriage ceremony.

rings to the parents for the child. Upon departing, guests are given packages of rice cakes and other foods to take with them, for, as with the hundredth day celebration, this sharing of rice cakes is thought to bring the child long life and happiness.

Although smaller than these celebrations, the birthday celebration of any member of the family calls for ample food, wine, and other delicacies. These parties are usually celebrated with only family members.

The *hwan-gap*, or 60th birthday, has been considered especially important, for this is the day when one has completed the zodiacal cycle. Even more important is the fact that in the past, before the advent of modern medicine, few people lived to be 60. *Hwan-gap* is a time for great celebration when children honor their parents with a large feast and much merrymaking.

With the parents seated at the main banquet table, sons and daughters, in order by age, bow and offer wine to their parents. After the direct descendants have performed this ritual, the father's younger brothers and their sons and then younger friends pay their respects in the same manner. While these rituals are being car-

ried out, traditional music usually is played and professional entertainers sing songs urging people to drink.

The family members and relatives indulge in various activities to make the parents feel young, often dressing like small children and dancing and singing songs. In the old days guests would compete in composing poetry or songs to celebrate the occasion.

In the past, years after the 60th birthday were regarded as extra years and each would be celebrated but not as lavishly as the *hwan-gap*. Upon the 70th birthday, or *kohi* meaning old and rare, another celebration on the scale of a *hwan-gap* was celebrated.

Marriage

Similar to the *hwan-gap* celebration is the celebration for the 60th wedding anniversary. This is a time of especially great fanfare for not only is it symbolic of a long life but it represents a long life shared by two people. One might wonder how this is possible, but in the past people usually married at an early age. During the Chosŏn period, marriage at the age of 12 was not uncommon, but women generally married at the age of 16. The wife tended to be a couple of years older than the husband, especially among upper-class families. For financial reasons, males of the lower classes tended to marry at a later age. Nevertheless, people usually were married before the age of 20.

As noted earlier, from the age of seven boys and girls traditionally were not even allowed to sit in the same room. This left little chance for love to develop and, if by some chance, there was the igniting of a romantic spark, this was never shown. In Confucian society the repressing of one's emotions was regarded as a sign of culture.

In the past affection or love played no part in the choice of a spouse. The young couple had little or nothing to say in the matter since marriage usually was arranged by the parents with the aid of a fortuneteller. The couple generally did not meet until the day of the wedding. Times have changed, however, and there are now two paths leading to marriage. One, yŏnae, or a love match, involves the meeting, falling in love, and marriage of two people. The other, chungmae, or arranged marriage, involves the arranged meeting of two people by a go-between and, upon agreement of the two parties, marriage.

Chungmae includes several complicated traditional procedures. One is the examination by the two families of the so-called "four pillars" of the young couple. As the four pillars—the year, month, day, and hour of birth, supposedly influence one's fortune, these require careful examination. For example, if the four pillars are good one will be successful in government service, but if one's hour pillar is bad, one will be poor and die young, etc.

After the examination of the four pillars, it must be determined if the two can live harmoniously as a married couple. Called kung-hap, this is usually divined by a fortuneteller and is considered especially important. Even though the four pillars are good, if the kung-hap predicts difficulty, the two parties may lose interest. As outright rejection for any reason is difficult, the four pillars and kung-hap are often used as excuses to cancel.

When the four pillars and kung-hap are acceptable, things generally progress smoothly to the next step—the engagement ceremony. For this the two families get together at the girl's house, or sometimes at a hotel or restaurant, but never at the boy's house. The two young people exchange gifts, and a piece of handmade white paper on which the man's four pillars have been written is ceremoniously presented to the girl's family. A discussion follows and the marriage date is selected.

A few days before the scheduled marriage ceremony, the man's family usually sends a ham or box containing gifts or yemul for the bride. These normally are yards of red and blue fabric for a traditional dress and jewelry. In the past a servant usually carried the box but nowadays friends of the bridegroom generally perform the honor.

The box was usually delivered at night and upon approaching the house, the carrier, with much frolicking and joking, would shout, "Buy a ham! Ham for sale." The ham would not be given to the parents of the bride until wine and food and a sum of money had been given as bribes. Upon receiving the money, the carrier would then present the ham to the bride's father. For his service the carrier would be treated to a feast at which time the bride's father would open the ham and examine the contents.

The traditional wedding ceremony normally was held at the bride's house, either in the front room or the courtyard. It began with the bride and groom exchanging bows and drinks. This was done facing each other with the wedding table between them. On the table were red and blue threads, burning candles, and a pair of wooden ducks symbolizing conjugal affection. During the bows the bride was usually assisted by an elderly female servant or a woman well versed in wedding procedures.

The wedding ceremony was followed by another ceremony called p'yebaek. This was the bride's first greeting to her parents-in-law and the other members of her husband's family. During this ceremony the bride would bow to her husband's parents, who were seated before a table of cooked chicken, jujubes, chestnuts, and fruits. Also at this time the bride would present the groom's parents with gifts of silk, and greetings were exchanged between the two families.

With the approach of night, the newly married couple would retire to their prepared room. It was considered great sport for relatives to peep into the room by making holes in the paper doors. The bridegroom would first take off the bride's headgear, undo her coat string, and remove only one of her socks. he would then put out the candle, being careful not to blow it out as it was thought to do so was breathing out one's luck. He would extinguish it with a stick he prepared for this purpose. Once they entered the room, they could not leave until sunrise, when the young husband would then visit with his in-laws.

The newly married couple, accompanied by the bride's father or uncle and a small procession carrying various articles and gifts would travel to the bridegroom's home. The bride usually rode in a palanquin while the bridegroom led the procession on horseback. After staying a few days at the groom's house, the couple would again travel to the bride's home to report to her parents. At such a time there would be a large party to familiarize the groom with the bride's family, especially with the young men of the bride's clan. This was characterized by much boisterousness and rough handling of the groom. If he was not witty and generous, he would be forced to drink beyond his capacity and be hit with dried fish or sticks.

These days, weddings are usually held in public wedding halls. Amid music played on a piano or tape recorded, the bridegroom, wearing a Western-style suit, enters the hall where guests are seated and stands before the presiding person. The bride, dressed in a Western wedding dress, enters and escorted by her father, takes her place by the groom. Facing each other before the officiator, the bride and groom exchange vows and gifts. The officiator usually gives a lengthy homily on love, social duty, and life in general. Then the bride and groom bow to the guests and the ceremony is over except for the picture taking.

Although the marriage ceremony itself has changed, many of the traditional practices and ceremonies leading to the marriage ceremony are still observed, although modified for today's lifestyle.

Funerals

As with other customs and beliefs, funeral services also have been dictated by Confucian tradition. Respect for ancestors being one of the basic teachings of Confucianism, utmost care had to be taken in connection with everything related to the funeral service of parents.

In the past, it was most important that a person be with his family at the time of death, preferably in his own home. Even today a dying person often is rushed from the hospital to the home so that he might die happily. In earlier times, if the dying person was male, his last moments could not be observed by any female, and if female, they could not be observed by any male.

With the confirmation of death, the body was covered with a quilt, and formal wailing, or *kok*, announced the passing. On hearing this long, drawn out wail, the family members would join in and these sounds informed the villagers of the death.

At the same time the coat of the dead would be carried to the roof of the house by a male member of the family, crying loudly for the soul of the dead man to return to the body. After this ceremony, called *ch'ohon*, the body was arranged so that it faced south and the coat was placed over it.

The *yŏm*, or preparation of the corpse, followed. This required bathing the body in perfumed water and dressing it in specially prepared clothes. These clothes, made of fine hemp cloth, were often prepared in advance by the deceased. The hair would then be combed, the finger and toe nails trimmed, and the clippings put in a small bag and placed under the quilt. This bag would be put in the coffin later.

The corpse, bound in seven places with hemp cloth, would then be placed in the coffin, which was often prepared well in advance. Made of wood, the coffin usually consisted of six planks about eight centimeters thick—the heaven plank, the earth plank, and the east, west, south, and north planks. The Chinese character for heaven would be inscribed on the inside of the coffin top and the character for sea added at each of the four corners. The top was then nailed down and the name of the deceased written on the top while the family members wailed loudly.

Having placed a banner of red, on which the name and rank of the deceased were written, and the coffin in the place of honor, the family members would don mourning clothes of coarse, handwoven hemp and prepare to receive guests. Obituary notices were sent to clan members, acquaintances, and friends. These days the newspapers and postal service are often utilized for this purpose, but in the past servants or hired messengers delivered them. When receiving an obituary notice it would not be taken into the house, but put into a chink in the outside of the wall or the front gate. Those receiving obituary notices would travel to the house of the deceased to pay their respects. As master of the house, the eldest son received each guest with much wailing. Often, gifts of money were presented to the eldest son to help with funeral expenses. The names of the guests were recorded in the condolence book and they were entertained with food and drink. This conveyance of condolences, called *munsang*, is considered highly important. Not to follow such practice was considered a great offense to the family and the deceased and often led to the termination of friendship and relations.

During the wake, lasting three, five, seven, or nine days, breakfast and dinner meals were offered and a bed prepared for the deceased, as though the person were still living. This was accompanied by chanting and the burning of incense.

The *ch'ulssang* or carrying of the bier to the grave site was done with much fanfare. Leading the procession were persons carrying funeral flags, and burning incense, and there was usually a person ringing a bell and singing in a deep, mournful voice. The coffin, decorated with banners and paper flowers followed, was carried on the shoulders of relatives or members of the funeral *kye*. The eldest son came next, followed by other family members, relatives, and friends.

Arriving at the grave, which had already been prepared to the exact specifications as divined by a geomancer, incense was burned and the grave cleansed of so-called evil spirits. After formal bows and the appropriate wailing, the coffin was lowered into the pit. Clay was packed around the coffin, and, to prevent water seepage, the earth covering the top was packed tightly by men stamping to the accompaniment of singing and music.

Often stone monuments and tablets were erected at the grave site. The larger these monuments, the more filial the children were thought to be. In the home, an ancestral tablet, usually of wood, was made and placed in the family shrine. Those not attending the funeral could express their sorrow by wailing in front of this tablet.

As it was believed that the soul of the deceased remained at home with the family, every day for a month meals were prepared and offered to the deceased before the tablet. After a month, only the morning meal was offered on the first and 15th days of every month for a year. The offering on the first anniversary of death was called *sosang*. On the morning of this day, after certain ablutions, ritual vessels and special food were made ready and at dawn the rites performed, involving the ceremonial feeding of the dead amid much bowing and chanting.

On the second anniversary, a similar rite called *taesang*, was performed, signifying the end of mourning. It was not until that time that the mourning clothes were discarded and the temporary shrine removed. One month later another ceremony called *tamjye* was held and only then did the life of the family return to normal. In the past, children wore mourning clothes and refrained from any type of merrymaking, singing, and drinking during the entire two-year period of mourning. Children often regarded the death of a parent as proof of their own failure.

Many of these practices have disappeared and others have been modified and simplified. Nowadays mourners tend to wear black garments with armbands of ramie fabric. For the three-month mourning period, women often wear bows of white hemp cloth in their hair or pinned to their clothes and men pin bows of hemp cloth to their clothes, evidence that filial piety still is important.

Rites

Like the wearing of hemp bows and armbands, many families still observe special ancestral rites. During the harvest season, they reserve the best grains and fruits for ceremonial offerings and time and money are spent in the preparation of the ritual foods. Foods that were favorites of the deceased usually are prepared as well.

Rites for the fifth generation and above are performed at the ancestral tomb on *Ch'usŏk*, the harvest festival. Those for others are usually performed in the home between midnight and four a.m. on special days such as birthdays, *sosang*, and *taesang*. Before the ceremony, family members gather and talk about the ancestors and the deceased, nurturing family pride.

According to traditional rules, the ritual foods are arranged on a table in front of the ancestral tablet and the ceremony begins. The eldest male first offers a cup of wine to the ancestors and bows twice. The next eldest follows the same procedure and then the chopsticks and spoons are moved around the table to different foods in the manner of eating. After a short time, scorched-rice tea is offered to the ancestors and a prayer is read. The ceremony ends with all of the participants bowing twice. The food is then removed to the kitchen to be served to the family members. These procedures may differ from region to region and family to family, but the reason for following them remains the same and still is strong in Korean culture.

CULTURE AND
THE ARTS

The Origin of Korean Culture

Korea's rich culture is often described as unique. Despite Korea's distinctive, intrinsic characteristics, this adjective may sometimes be overworked or applied too loosely. An understanding of the culture of Northeast Asia is a prerequisite to any study or serious discussion of the origin of Korean culture. The early influence of other Asian countries on the Korean Peninsula can be seen, for example, in the comb-pattern pottery of the Neolithic Age, and in the lute-shaped daggers, twin-knobbed mirrors and geometric patterns of the Bronze Age.

The early growth and development of the Korean people was not uniform, but was generally characterized by active contact, and sometimes struggle, with the Chinese people. From the time the Korean people developed an agricultural society, centering around the cultivation of rice, their culture gradually became identified with that of China. Korea produced iron tools and weapons, and developed politically, economically, philosophically and culturally under a strong Chinese influence.

But an understanding of cultural exchange alone cannot fully explain Korean culture. A proper understanding of the characteristics of the Korean people is also essential, and these characteristics must be explained in the context of the nation's historical development. Consider how Buddhism and Confucianism were introduced into Korea. Although Confucianism slightly preceded Buddhism, Buddhism rather than Confucianism was first embraced by the Korean people. This occurred because Buddhism was more conducive than Confucianism to the building of an aristocratic, centralized state bent on expansion.

Some attribute the Five Secular Commandments followed by the youth of Shilla (57 B.C.- A.D. 935) to Buddhism, while others attribute them to Confucianism. Won-gwang, the man responsible for teaching these commandments in the early 600s, was a Buddhist priest who was also well versed in the teachings of Confucius. Thus the commandments' roots may be attributed to either source.

However, another side of the picture should also be considered. As society was in need of moral codes for the development of royal authority and a patriarchal family system, the promotion of the youth corps called *Hwarang* and the protection of property such as domestic animals would, in any case, have been held in high esteem even if Buddhism and Confucianism had not been introduced into Korea at that time.

The same may be said of the *Sŏn* (Zen) sect of Buddhism. It was introduced into Korea long before Shilla absorbed the other two kingdoms of Paekche (18 B.C.- A.D. 660) and Koguryŏ (37 B.C.-A.D. 668), but it did not become popular until late in the Unified Shilla (668-935) period when powerful local landlords rose against the centralized ruling system. In other words, *Sŏn* Buddhism gained acceptance and importance as a religion of the local landlords.

Neo-Confucianism began to attract attention during the late Koryŏ (918-1392) period and eventually became the prevailing ideology of the Chosŏn Dynasty (1392-1910). It is believed to have been introduced to Korea through cultural exchanges with Yüan China. However, the acceptance of Neo-Confucianism can be better explained in relation to the rise of the middle class, a group of medium and small landlords with the status of local gentry, who entered officialdom not through hereditary right but through a civil service examination. These were men of probity, critical of the pro-Yüan ruling families that had come to possess large-scale holdings through illegal means. This new middle class welcomed Neo-Confucian moral principles as a spiritual support.

These people, who subsequently took up the leadership of a new dynasty, were not, as is commonly believed, worshipers of a powerful China. On the contrary, they tried to rediscover the historical tradition of the nation, traced the beginnings back to the Tangun era, and supported King Sejong's (r. 1418-50) new Korean alphabet, *Han-gŭl*.

A new interest in improving Korean technology and the economy prevailed among Chosŏn scholars of the 17th and 18th centuries.

Transplanting, double cropping and constructing reservoirs greatly facilitated agricultural development in this period. A nationwide commercial network was organized with Seoul and Kaesong as its two centers. Merchants promoted foreign trade at Ŭiju, and independent handicrafts flourished. In this social milieu, *Sirhak*, or the "Practical Learning," school of Confucianism developed. *Sirhak*, which aimed at reforming society through the promotion of an awareness of native historical traditions, also reaped unprecedented benefits in terms of the influence of Western culture and the Ch'ing Chinese methodology of historical research.

The development of Korean art also paralleled the general development of Korean culture. The powerful style of mural paintings of Koguryŏ reflects the temperament of the Koguryŏ people. Although a study of the stylistic development of Koguryŏ murals can aid in dating the ancient tombs and shed light on the cultural exchanges, it cannot fully explain the historical significance of these art works.

The same may be said of the stone cave-temple, Sŏkkuram, of the Shilla Kingdom. The structure of this artificial cave-temple with its magnificent Buddha in the center represents a unified universe. The grotto seems to idealize the harmonized world. The same may be said of the two stone pagodas, Sŏkkat'ap and Tabot'ap in Pulguksa Temple, perhaps the best stone works of the Unified Shilla period. They were products of an aristocratic temperament which, under the ruling system of absolute monarchy, took harmony as its ideal. As memorials to *Sŏn* priests they are examples of the *Sŏn* Buddhist art that appeared toward the end of the Unified Shilla period. Their swirling spiral patterns express the complex spiritual attitude of the period that defied the centralized ruling system.

The beauty of celadon of the Koryŏ dynasty symbolizes the taste of its ruling aristocracy. Although Koryŏ celadon emerged under the strong influence of Sung Chinese celadon, the delicate Koryŏ celadon was obviously unique to the Koryŏ aristocracy. In contrast, the simple and staid beauty of the Chosŏn white porcelain is directly linked to the lifestyle and attitudes of the Chosŏn military and civilian upper class,

A Shilla period stoneware figure of a man playing a musical instrument.

who placed stronger emphasis on practical use than luxury.

Although Chosŏn painting has generally been regarded as a mere imitation or a regional school of Chinese painting, it is original, with the composition, brush work and colors reflecting Korean tastes. During the 17th and 18th centuries, some painters executed realistic paintings of the Korean landscape with bold brush strokes. Genre paintings also flourished in this period. These paintings invariably had a typical Korean flavor, depicting scenes of elegant young *yangban* (aristocrats) flirting with *kisaeng* (trained entertainment girls similar to Japan's *geisha*), or showing farmers and artisans practicing their trades.

While the foreign influence on Korean art cannot be ignored, it is almost impossible to appreciate the real value of Korean art without properly understanding the underlying context of Korean history and culture. This obvious truth has more often than not been overlooked.

Although a work of art will have its own independent and intrinsic value once it is freed from the hand of the artist, the historic background that generated the work must not be forgotten. In this sense, works of art are historic products that transcend individual taste.

Literature

Poetry

In old Korea, skill in poetic composition was a practical business. It was one of the major indicators of a man's ability to serve his country well as a public servant, and at the same time it was the yardstick of a man's personal cultivation. This approach to poetry had some interesting consequences.

First, poetry tended to be "I" centered, confessional. In the hands of anyone less than a consummate artist, this sort of subjective tradition labors within severe limitations, but in the hands of great masters, the reader discovers his own experience, and consequently that of all men, in the experience of the poet, moving in the process from the particular to the universal. This is the mark of good poetry indeed.

Second, poetry was characterized by a pervading movement toward transcendence, reflecting not only the Buddhist tradition of freedom and liberation, but also the Confucian tradition which, while aspiring toward order and control, still seeks the ultimate in wisdom. Buddhism and Confucianism have had an enormous influence on all facets of Korean literature. Buddhism was dominant during the Koryŏ Dynasty when *hansi* (poems in Chinese characters) developed to maturity; Confucianism was dominant throughout the Chosŏn Dynasty when the *sijo* and the *kasa*, the two literary genres deemed as best expressing the Korean sensibility, reached their fullest development. Personal cultivation is integral in both systems. The transcendent man to which Buddhism aspires and the sage man to which Confucianism aspires share common ground.

Third, composition tended to be spontaneous: a visit to a temple, meeting a friend, celebrating the arrival of spring, a gift of wine. A concrete emotion prompted the writing of a poem.

Fourth, poets tended to take a particular attitude toward nature. Nature was seen conceptually. The appreciation of nature led to contemplation, which in turn led to rapture, not over the physically beautiful but over the morally beautiful. The poet did not see this mountain or this section of mountain. He did not see this flower or this individual petal. He saw the universal essence of a mountain, the universal essence of a flower. It is an approach that is primarily symbolic, with the emphasis always on the inner landscape of the heart. This remains the core of the Korean tradition to this day.

The earliest Korean poetry consisted of songs of ritual worship and songs designed to accompany work. These songs were invariably linked with music and dance. Unfortunately, there was no writing system in Korea until Chinese characters were introduced, thought to be in the second century. Chinese characters quickly became popular with the elite in Korea, leading to the development of a tradition of *hansi* poetry, that is, poems in Chinese, following all the rules of Chinese prosody, but written by Korean poets. Ch'oe Ch'i-won (857-?) of Shilla is the first flower of this tradition. Ch'oe passed the T'ang state examination in 874 at the age of eighteen and quickly gained a reputation in China as an outstanding poet. Despite his great success in China, he was obviously a man acquainted with sadness as revealed by this representative poem:

Autumn winds are blowing;
I chant a sad song.
So few people in this world
have ever understood me.
It is the third watch;
rain splatters the window.
I sit in front of the lamp,
my spirit 10,000 *li* away

During the Shilla period a system of recording Korean sounds in Chinese characters, called *idu*, was developed, thus making it possible to record the vernacular *hyangga* which flourished during Unified Shilla and the early part of Koryŏ. At this time, twenty-five *hyangga* are still extant.

The *changga* (literally meaning long song)

replaced the *hyangga* during the Koryŏ Dynasty. There were two divisions of *changga: kyŏnggich'ega* which were recorded in Chinese and reflected Confucian thought, and *sogyo*, exquisite little popular lyrics, which were passed on orally. The term *sogyo*, meaning vulgar or common, shows the sense of disapprobation with which Confucian norms greeted the genre. Nevertheless, these little lyrics are delicate and subtle.

The pattern of Korean poetry had been solidly established by the time Yi Kyu-bo (1168-1241) began to write his *hansi* in the middle of the Koryŏ Dynasty. Yi Kyu-bo's poems are intensely personal, very often dramatic vignettes from the poet's own life. He describes an external landscape—a temple, a posthouse, an inn—and then he moves to an inner landscape of the heart. The poems are brief, song-like and revelatory. They describe moments of personal illumination. The reader meets the poet in the more intense moments of the daily grind; it may be a problem on the job, a problem with one of his children or with his wife; it may be a visit to a temple or to a friend; it may be an occasion of sorrow or joy. However, the occasion is always intimately connected with the poet himself. The poem is his reaction to the situation, his personal experience:

Desolate the monk's room
    beside the ancient tree;
one lamp burns in the shrine,
    one incense burner smokes.
I ask the old monk
    how on earth he spends his days:
a chat when a guest comes;
    when the guest goes, a nap.

With a few deft strokes—tree, lamp, incense burner—the speaker paints the hermitage, before moving on, almost casually, to an intense zen landscape of the heart. The monk represents that ideal of transcendence which cultivated men strove to attain. However, central to the poem is how the light generated by the monk touches the speaker. Thus the focus of the poem is on the speaker; his experience, not the monk's, is dominant.

The tradition of *hansi* flourished from Shilla through Koryŏ and Chosŏn, and boasts many fine poets. Here is a quatrain by the 16th century poet Chŏng Chak, showing the tradition at its very best:

At first I wondered if the figure
on the distant sands were a white heron,
but to the sound of piping on the wind
the vast expanse of sky and
river faded into evening.

Sijo are quite different from *hansi* poems in the feeling they engender. This difference in sensibility may derive from the fact that *hansi* were written in Chinese, the language of literature and official business, whereas *sijo* were written in *Han-gŭl*, the language of the home and of the common people. At any rate, *sijo* are even more private and more personal than *hansi*. An image is introduced, developed, and the poet presents a statement of his own experience, all within the narrow confines of three lines and 45 syllables. Nothing is allowed to get between the poet and his subject.

The first use of the term *sijo* occurs in a record written by Shin Kwang-su (1712-1775) which states that the *sijo ch'ang* (song) began with Yi Se-ch'un, a well-known contemporary singer. This reference is to the music rather than to the lyric and the term itself seems to be a shortened version of *sijŏlgayo*, meaning popular seasonal songs. The term *sijo*, as used today, came into use early in the 20th century in order to distinguish the traditional verse form from the flood of new poetry, free verse etc., from the West which had begun to sweep the literary stage.

Scholars still debate the origin of the *sijo* form. Theories abound: a development of Shilla *hyangga* or of Buddhist songs imported from Ming China; a form that developed naturally in the course of translating Chinese poems into Korean; a development of the Koryŏ *tan'ga*; or a form that goes back to the shamanistic chants of antiquity. The difficulty in unraveling the history of the *sijo* is compounded by the fact that *Han-gŭl* was not invented until 1446, so that sijo written prior to this date were either recorded originally in Chinese and only later on translated or retranslated into Korean, or transmitted orally from the beginning. The problem is further compounded by the fact that the first of the great anthologies, *Ch'ŏnggu yŏn-gŏn,* was not published until 1728, and texts of individual poets are contained in posthumous collections of their writings, many produced long after their deaths.

The *sijo* is a three-line poem (song), 14 to 16 syllables in each line, distributed through four distinct breath groups with the total number of syllables not being more than 45. This is the regular or ordinary form of sijo, called *p'yŏng-sijo.*

> The tree is diseased;
> > no one rests in its pavilion.
> When it stood tall and verdant,
> > no one passed it by.
> But the leaves have fallen,
> > the boughs are broken;
> not even birds perch there now.

Notice the intensity of focus in this Chŏng Ch'ŏl (1536-1593) *sijo.* We see the tree as it is now, ragged and broken, and we see it as it was when it was tall and verdant. The final line "not even birds perch there now" penetrates right to the bone in its depiction of the fate of those who fall from political favor.

There are two variations of the basic form; the *ŏt-sijo,* in which the first or the second line may be somewhat extended; and the *sasŏl-sijo,* in which all three lines may be extended, the first two lines without restriction, and the third line within certain limits. The *sasŏl-sijo* is distinguished by a wider range of subject than the *p'yŏng-sijo* and by a marvelous sense of humor:

> Rip your black robe asunder;
> > fashion a pair of breeches.
> Take off your rosary;
> > use it for the donkey's crupper.
> These ten years studying
> > Buddha's Pure Land,
> > invoking the Goddess of Mercy
> > and Amithaba's saving hand,
> > let them go where they will.

> Night on a nun's breast
> > is no time for reciting sutras.

Chŏng Ch'ŏl was the first of the great *sijo* poets. Royal Inspector, governor of a province, personal secretary to the king, second prime minister, general of the army—these are some of the positions held by him during a career which was punctuated by periods of voluntary retirement, dismissal and exile. He was by nature a brilliant but rather stubborn man, and his career was marked by continuous controversy.

Whatever the ambivalence in Chŏng Ch'ŏl's personality, it is at least certain he was a poet of the first rank. In his work we see that versatility in the use of language— the startling phrase, the spare elegant expression, the density of meaning, the use of irony— which are so much a part of the *sijo* tradition:

> What happens if you pull down
> > beams and supports?
> A host of opinions greet
> > the leaning skeleton house.
> Carpenters with rulers and ink
> > keep milling around.

There is nothing quite like this in the previous history of the *sijo.* The images are startlingly clear, precise, and incisive, beams and supports being qualified and extended by the use of skeleton with all the connotations of that word. The final image of carpenters running around with rulers and ink lends comedy, irony, indeed the surgeon's scalpel to the poem. The poem supposedly reflects the confusion of the court at the time of Japanese warlord Hideyoshi's invasion in the 1590s.

Yun Sŏn-do (1587-1671), regarded by most Korean commentators as the greatest of the *sijo* poets, is another in the long list of poet-ministers who had turbulent political careers. Seventy-six of his *sijo* are still extant.

Yun Sŏn-do's most notable achievement, *The Fisherman's Calendar,* is a cycle of 40 poems, describing the four seasons in one of the poet's favorite retreats. The fisherman is a time honored symbol of a wise man who lives simply in nature. There is a solid tradition of poems treating this theme both in China and Korea. Yun Sŏn-do was inspired to write his poem when reworking the earlier *Fisherman's Song* by Yi Hyŏn-bo (1467-1555) which itself was a reworking of an anonymous poem from Koryŏ.

The *Fisherman's Calendar* shows some differences in syllable count from the regular *sijo* pattern. In addition, it features two refrains not customary in *sijo*: the first refrain, varying in a regular pattern through the verses, describes various tasks on the boat, pushing off, raising sail, lowering sail, rowing, etc.; the second refrain is onomatopoeic, *chigukch'ŏng*, *chigukch'ŏng* representing the winding of the anchor chain, and *ŏsawa*, the rhythm of the oars. The first poem in the Winter cycle gives the flavor of the series:

Winter sunlight falls thick
    after the clouds have cleared.
    Push away, push away!
Ice binds heaven and earth,
    yet the sea remains unchanged.
    Chigukch'ŏng, chigukch'ŏng, ŏsawa!
Billow after billow,
    rolls of silk unfurled.

Kim Su-jang (1690-?) is the third of the great *sijo* poets. A *chungin* (neither commoner nor aristocrat) as opposed to a *yangban*, the road to official preferment was effectively blocked to him, and this may have prompted him to take early retirement from the minor post he held in the military ministry. At any rate, he lived to extreme old age, spending his time in the company of his friends, savoring the delights of nature at his villa in Hwagae-dong in Seoul. Apart from a few documented facts, we know next to nothing about Kim Su-jang, except that he edited a famous anthology of *sijo*, called *Haedong-kayo* (Songs of the Eastern Country).

Kim Su-jang's poems are distinguished above all by a wonderful sense of humor. This sense of humor may have been typical of the time in which he lived because many of the best anonymous poems, which account for a sizable proportion of the *sijo* canon and presumably also date from the 18th century, reveal a comparable wit. However, no other poet has left his name to the kind of poem for which Kim Su-jang is justly famous. The descriptive method of these poems reflects the change that had occurred in literary circles under the influence of *Sirhak* (Practical Learning), a change away from poetry to prose as the popular literary genre, and the consequent reactionary effect of this on the writing of poetry:

Look at that girl in blouse
    and patterned skirt,
    her face prettily powdered,
    her hair as yet unpinned.
Yesterday she deceived me,
    and now she's off to deceive another,
    fresh cut flowers held firmly in her
    hand, hips swinging lightly as the sun
    goes down.

Of course, humor is not the only distinguishing quality of Kim Su-jang's poetic world. He also reveals a fine sensibility, which is apparent particularly in the untrammeled joy he experiences in the simple life of nature. Harmony with oneself and with nature has always been the distinguishing characteristic of the wise man. The great poets have all sought this harmony, even though the task has been arduous and the results sometimes wanting.

Toward the middle of the 15th century a new genre of vernacular verse called *kasa*, more descriptive and expository than earlier Koryŏ songs, made its appearance. The *kasa* has no stanzaic divisions. Designed to be sung, the kasa adheres to certain patterns of composition. Chŏng Ch'ŏl is the finest master of the *kasa* form and his "*Kwandong-pyŏlgok* (1580)" describing eight famous scenes in the *Diamond Mountains* represents the tradition at its best.

Chinese remained the language of government and of literature until the 19th century. In 1884 the Western powers and Japan forced the opening of Korean ports, an event which marked the end of the isolation of the "Hermit Kingdom" and the beginning of a flood of Western influence. Following annexation in 1910, an increasing number of young Korean intellectuals began to go to Japan for university education, where they came into contact with current trends in Japanese literary circles. Within Korea the period was marked by a surge of nationalist sentiment which culminated in the March First Independence Movement of 1919.

The rise in nationalist sentiment was accompanied by a rejection in literature of Chinese and the Chinese tradition in favor of *han-gŭl* and the Western tradition. Working with Western models—Baudelaire, Verlaine, Yeats and Symons—young writers began to create a new literature. Symons's *The Symbolist Movement in Literature* was translated into Japanese quite early in the 20th century. In Japan it became a sort of bible of criticism. The young Korean poets had some English and less French. Most of their translations seem to have been made from Japanese texts, sometimes with an eye on the English. Most of the theory came from Japanese translations of English sources. The result of this complex skein of influence was a poetry full of pre-Raphaelite colors, characterized by a *fin-de-siecle* atmosphere of world weariness, decadence and pessimism, with Symons perhaps as the dominant influence.

Imitation was inevitable in this new poetry. The poets, all young men in their 20s, set out consciously to write a new Korean poetry based on their understanding of Western models. The approach was one of trial and error. Kim Ŏk (1893-?) in his article "Rhythm and Breath in Poetic Form," (1919) notes the lack of an educated reading public and the lack of an articulated criticism.

Kim So-wol (1902-1934) was the first of these young poets to move away from imitation and create something new on the basis of assimilated influences. So-wol was much more than a writer of pretty lyrics. His essay *Sihon* (1925) is the first manifesto of mysticism in modern Korean poetry. Perhaps his most significant achievement was the flexibility and versatility he achieved in the use of the Korean language. He incorporated the saltiness and bite of the vernacular into a modern idiom which contrasts sharply with the more formal Chinese tradition. "Azaleas" is perhaps So-wol's most anthologized piece:

If you grow so sick of me

that you would wish to go,
I'll let you go gently, without a word.
On Yaksan, Yŏngbyŏn
I'll pluck an armful of azaleas
and strew them in your path.
Tread gently
on these flowers
that deck your parting steps.
If you grow so sick of me
that you would wish to go,
though I die, I'll shed no tears.

Chŏng Chi-yong (1902-?) and Kim Ki-rim (1908-?) ushered in the second stage of modern poetry. Both steeped in the imagist mode, they were part of a literary movement coming to grips with modernism. In them we see the discarding of the Pre-Raphaelite tints, which dominated the first stage of 20th century Korean poetry, in favor of a more modern idiom. Chŏng Chi-yong generates a special kind of excitement in his work: "Sea" reveals his mastery of imagist effects:

The channel flaps like a tent
now that the whale has crossed.
White water bundling up; *paduk* stones
tumbling, tumbling down.
The sea skylark soars: silver drops its flight;
vigilant half the day
to claw, to scavenge red flesh.
A shell, azalea hued, takes the sun
in a seaweed smelling rock crevice,
while a sea swallow on wing slide
glides in a plate-glass sky.
Sea—see right, right down.
Sea
green as bamboo leaves.
Spring.
What does it look like?
Little hills, lines of flower bud lanterns lit?
What does it look like?
Thick thickets of pine and bamboo?
What does it look like?
A crouching tiger
draped in a blanket.
spotted yellow and black?
And you, my friend, take some such scene,

a white
smoke like
sea,
and voyage far, far away.

The technique here is new; the conception of the poem (the point of view, for example), the way the images are organized and the quality of the images—flapping sea, *paduk* waves, scavenging skylark—are all new. Chŏng Chi-yong and Kim Ki-rim represent Korea's first experiments with modernism, an influence that has been continuously significant as the history of the modern idiom has unfolded.

The forced dissolution of the Korean Artists Proletarian Federation (KAPF) in the mid-1930s introduced a period of intense Japanese repression. However, following the tradition of Han Yong-un (1879-1944)—monk, poet, and patriot, a towering light in the 1920s—the defiant note continued to ring out in the work of Yi Yuk-sa (1904-1944) and Yun Tong-ju (1917-1945), who remain symbols of undying resistance to foreign domination. The Blue Deer Group, Pak Tu-jin (1916-), Pak Mok-wol (1919-1978) and Cho Chi-hun (1920-1968), sought to sublimate the harsh reality of Japanese oppression in nature poetry . All three are recognized as masters of lyrical language. Indeed the elegance and harmony of Cho Chi-hun's "Monk Dance" has never been surpassed.

The Korean War made the idiom of the pre-war period seem dated and unrelated to contemporary problems. The post-war era was characterized by a poetry that was experimental in form and highly critical of the contemporary scene in content. Beginning in the 1960s, the process of industrialization bred a profound sense of alienation, isolation, and dehumanization which was increasingly reflected in poetry. A new radical political-social consciousness awakened, and the more radical committed poets, the celebrated Kim Chi-ha (1941-),for example, or the man who assumed his mantle as leading dissident in the 1980s, Kim Nam-ju, paid for their dissent by spending long periods in jail. Furthermore, the old battle of accusation and counter accusation between adherents of pure literature and a more committed revolu-

tionary approach erupted once again. The violence of the Kwangju uprising which ushered in the 1980s, led younger intellectuals to lash out in anger against the poetry establishment, represented for the most part by the older generation of poets, for their failure to find a poetic voice to prevent or even confront such tragedy. The young intellectuals reacted forcefully, both in form and content, asserting the failure of the humanist stance to find adequate solutions. It is of more than passing interest that four pillars of the older poetry community, Cho Byŏng-hwa (1916-), Sŏ Chŏng-ju (1915-), Pak Tu-jin (1916-) and Kim Ch'un-su (1922-) all produced new collections in the spring of 1990.

The 1980s also were characterized by the vigorous reemergence of the genre of workers' poetry, a genre which traces its roots back to the KAPF literature of the 1920s and early 1930s, and possibly even has roots that go as far back as Chŏng Ta-san (1762-1836).

Despite some seesawing of his popular image, Sŏ Chŏng-ju was generally recognized as the best Korean poet of this century until Chŏng Chi-yong's recent rehabilitation swung the pendulum back the other way. The appeal of Sŏ Chŏng-ju's work rests first, in his use of language, so distinctively that of his native Chŏlla province; second, in the sensuality particularly apparent in his earlier work which has evoked comparisons with Baudelaire and Yeats; and third, in his return to the mainly-Buddhist spirit of Shilla to find values that should enlighten the new Korea which will replace the tragic Korea of the recent past. His approach is that of a poetry of revelation. His lyrics are short, with an intense Zen style illumination. "Untitled" is typical:

So hushed
the sky
an orchid
wondering
why
opened
its petals
wide

There is obviously a plethora of poetic talent in Korea, but how the moderns will measure up to the great poets of the past in the litmus test of time remains uncertain. In particular, the literary quality of much of the committed poetry remains undetermined; admittedly, objective judgments are extremely difficult from such close quarters. There are literally hundreds of poets publishing work in authoritative literary magazines and academic journals, all introduced with suitable encomiums by name writers, all vying annually for a large number of lucrative literary prizes. The enormous success in the 1980s of To Chong-hwan's *My Hollyhock Love*—a linked series of love poems dedicated to his recently deceased wife which sold more than a million copies—has introduced a new note to poetry creation: the possibility of enormous commercial success. These various factors contribute to creating a somewhat unique environment for the writing of poetry in Korea. Poets and readers alike look to the future with a mixture of optimism and a certain trepidation.

Narrative Tradition

The sources of Korea's narrative tradition can be traced to a rich storehouse of myths, legends, and folk tales, the oldest surviving examples of which are recorded in *Samguk sagi* and *Samguk yusa* (1285?). *New Stories of the Golden Turtle*, written in Chinese by Kim Si-sŭp (1435-1493), is usually regarded as the beginning of fiction in Korea. Only the first book, containing five stories, survives today. The stories are marked by Korean settings and tragic endings, in contrast with the Chinese settings and romantic happy endings that characterized earlier works.

Korean fiction in the vernacular begins with Hŏ Kyun's (1569-1618) celebrated *The Story of Hong Kil-tong*, which describes how the hero becomes the leader of a band of thieves and ends up establishing a classless utopia on Yul island. The novel advocates the abolition of the class system, the eradication of corruption, and the elimination of the abuse of power by greedy bureaucrats.

The Nine Cloud Dream (1689) by Kim Man-jung (1637-1692) marked the coming of age of the Korean novel. The story concerns a Buddhist monk who dreams that he is reincarnated as a successful Confucian bureaucrat. *The Nine Cloud Dream* employs a sophisticated symbolism to explore the tensions between the Buddhist and the Confucian approaches to life. The theme of the novel is in the title, "Nine Cloud Dream" or *kuunmong*: in the cloud-dream state the true face of reality is hidden, thus implying a state of human imperfection. *The Story of Lady Sa* (1690), also by Kim Man-jung, is a satire on the institution of concubinage, directed at King Sukjong's treatment of Queen Inhyŏn.

During the 17th century, *Sirhak* (Practical Learning), emphasizing empirical knowledge and practical living, came into prominence. With it came a movement away from poetry to prose as the mode of literary expression, and a new, more realistic kind of fiction satirizing the social prejudices of the day made its appearance. The writing of Pak Chi-won (1737-1805), with its incisive satire on the hypocrisy of *yangban* (aristocratic) life, is representative of the new realism.

The Story of Ch'unhyang is by far the most popular of the Chosŏn Dynasty novels. Originally a popular tale, it was developed by travelling entertainers into *p'ansori* (a folk opera genre). The novel describes a love affair between the son of a nobleman, Yi Toryŏng, and the daughter of a *kisaeng*, Ch'unhyang. After the young couple's secret marriage, Yi Toryŏng is ordered to accompany his father to the capital. The provincial governor tries to make Ch'unhyang his concubine. She refuses on the grounds that she is a married woman. Enraged the governor throws her in jail and inflicts the most severe torture on her. Ch'unhyang remains faithful. In the meantime, Yi Toryŏng returns disguised as a beggar. He is, in fact, a royal inspector, and he duly punishes the cruel governor and restores Ch'unhyang to happiness. The novel presents a satirical treatment of corrupt officials, a sensitive delineation of social problems, a finely modulated humor centered in the minor characters, an extraordinary depiction of the ideal of faithfulness, and a lovely, playful picture of young love.

The historical novel is a distinct type of

Chosŏn Dynasty fiction. *Imjin nok*, author unknown, records the exploits of famous generals who fought against the Japanese warlord Hideyoshi. *Kyech'uk Diary*, by an anonymous court lady, records the sufferings endured by Queen Mother Inmok (1584-1632) under the tyrant Kwanghaegun (1556-1622). *Hanjungnok*, by Princess Hyegyŏng (1735-1815), is an elegant account of court life in diary form. The princess relates the death of her consort Prince Sado (1735-1762) at an early age, her own subsequent life of sadness in seclusion and her personal suffering at the hands of slanderers. The *Tale of Queen Inhyŏn* recounts court intrigue during the reign of Sukjong. The childless Queen Inhyŏn (1667-1701) brought in Lady Chang to bear Sukjong an heir. After giving birth to a son, Lady Chang plotted intrigues until she finally succeeded in having Inhyŏn removed from the court, and afterwards, had many of Inhyŏn's followers killed. Eventually Sukjong, out of feelings of remorse, killed Lady Chang and restored Queen Inhyŏn to her rightful place.

The 19th century marked a decline in the classical novel. Toward the end of the century Korea entered a period of profound political and social change. The opening of the ports in 1884 and the treaties with the great powers which followed marked the end of the Hermit Kingdom and the beginning of a veritable flood of Western influence. An incident in Ch'ae Mansik's (1902-1950) story *Ready-made Life* (1933) illustrates the scale of these changes. The scene is a public monument in Seoul. A western couple, armed with camera, alights from a car and proceeds to take in the sights. The narrator comments: "If Taewon-gun saw this... and automatically a smile came to his lips... Taewon-gun was the last Korean Don Quixote: he tried to stop a thunderbolt with a gourd." Taewon-gun, of course, is a symbol of everything in Korea that opposed the relentless advance of Western influence. Prior to 1876, Western influence had been restricted to contacts with Western art and science between the annual tribute legations to Beijing and the Catholic missionaries working there and to contacts with priests who actually began to work in Korea. After 1876 the wave of Western influence grew to tidal proportions, with Protestant missionaries, working particularly in education, forming the vanguard.

At this time a new national consciousness began to emerge, its first dawning signaled toward the end of the century by the *Tonghak* (Eastern Learning) Movement, an unprecedented popular revolt against corruption and injustice. In the years immediately before and after annexation in 1910, this new national consciousness began to be expressed through the medium of a literature written in *Han-gŭl* called *sinmunhak* or "new literature". These were crisis years, years of alternating hope and despair. Modernization had begun, and with it came new ideas, new fears. U.S. President Woodrow Wilson's declaration of the rights of small nations became a rallying cry for young Korean intellectuals educated in Japan and recently returned.

The new literature was a reaction against Chinese characters and the Chinese literary tradition in favor of a literature written in *Han-gŭl* along European lines. The modern novel was a new concept in Korea, and the work that appeared under its title was something in between the old Chinese romances and the modern Western novel. *Tears of Blood* (1906) by Yi In-jik (1862-1916), the first of these new novels, is a romance of the familiar formula of rewarding good and punishing evil which assigns a significant role to dreams. Although it had not fully developed an acceptable realistic language, it was the first of its kind and it expressed the ideas that were the rallying cries of the age: freedom to pick one's partner in marriage, the need for education, the call for enlightenment, and the urgency of the task of modernization.

In 1908 Ch'oe Nam-sŏn (1890-1957) produced *Sonyŏn,* the first semi-literary magazine. This magazine and a series of others published between 1908 and 1928 provided a forum for young writers to express their ideas. Ch'oe Nam-sŏn worked closely with another fervent young nationalist, Yi Kwang-su (1892-?), who used the novel as a vehicle to promote his ideas. Yi Kwang-su's *The Heartless* (1917) was the first Korean modern novel. It is a romantic story with a complicated combination of love versus arranged marriages, a great emphasis on the value of overseas education, the need for sacrifice for one's country, and the conflict of values of the old world and the new. The interests of both Ch'oe Nam-sŏn and Yi Kwang-su were not primarily literary, but centered in the promotion of nationalism and enlightenment. Young men rallied to the cause, bright-eyed with revisionary hope. The dark days that had followed annexation were over. Hope was viable again.

However, the failure of the March First Independence Movement in 1919 shattered all of the hopes that had been built up in the preceding decade. It bred a climate of intellectual pessimism and disillusion that limited the roads an intellectual might take. One could take the escapist route and ignore the situation altogether; one could adopt the nationalist platform of "Strengthen the Nation," or one could take the Marxist option which developed in literature from the New Direction Group and culminated in the organization of KAPF or the Korean Artists Proletarian Federation.

While the failure of the March First Independence Movement was traumatic, the movement did produce significant positive results, in particular the policy of appeasement which the Japanese government subsequently adopted. Under the new policy the publication of Korean newspapers and magazines was permitted, organizations could be formed and meetings could be held. All such activities, of course, took place against a background of strict police surveillance.

One of the lessons learned from the March First Movement was that independence was not going to be won by emotional appeals alone. This realization gave considerable impetus to the "Strengthen the Nation" approach. Yi Kwang-su was one of those who threw his weight behind this program. Up until 1919 Yi Kwang-su had been a radical idealist preaching independence through education, modernization and popular demonstrations, but he became more of a realist, thinking in terms of what was immediately feasible, with independence as a long range goal. He called for a greater emphasis on morality and education and used his novels to propagate his ideas.

A reaction against this kind of doctrinaire literature was inevitable, and it came in the form of Korea's first purely literary magazine, *Creation* (1919). Written by a group of young men studying in Japan under the leadership of the brilliant, if eccentric, Kim Tong-in (1900-1951), it stated that the purpose of literature lay not in political propaganda but in depicting life as it is. Art for art's sake was the imported catchword.

Young Korean students in Japan had been introduced, by Japanese translations for the most part, to Zola, Maupassant, Tolstoy, Turgenev, Dostoevsky, and Wilde; an exposure which opened up new worlds. Life as it appeared was their model, and life at the time presented a rather grim aspect. Not surprisingly, the negative, pessimistic side of what they read seemed to influence them most. They felt trapped by a whole range of historical, social, economic, and biological forces which they regarded as fate, and as a result wrote their fiction with a kind of hyper-realism close in end-product, if not in theory, to the determinism of French naturalism.

Kim Tong-in, Hyŏn Chin-gŏn (1900-1943), Yŏm Sang-sŏp (1897-1963) and others began to write about Korea as they saw it: a dark, gloomy, sordid world. Kim Tong-in was the foremost of the new generation, an Oscar Wilde type figure complete with morning coat, carnation and cane. His stories run the gamut of all the "-isms" current at the time, from naturalism to aestheticism.

Hyŏn Chin-gŏn was arguably the best short writer of the generation. In style and technique his work was reminiscent of Maupassant and Chekhov. *A Lucky Day* (1922), a particularly fine depiction of the tragic fate of a poor rickshawman in Japanese times, is typical of his approach. Many commentators feel that the Korean modern novel came of age with Yŏm Sang-sŏp's *Before the Hurrah* (1923) and *Three Generations* (1931). These novels are remarkable for the realistic picture they give of life in colonial Korea, the cruelty of the oppression, the backwardness of the people.

From 1923 onward, the New Direction Group

heralded a change in the literary hegemony: a change from pure literature to a propaganda literature dedicated to spreading socialist principles. In 1925, KAPF was formed and consequently absorbed the New Direction Group. Pure literature was forgotten and once again literature entered a period of political propaganda. The literary world became a battlefield between Marxists and nationalists, where theoretical disputes without any real literary creativity were held. The proletarian groups remained in the ascendancy until the mid-1930s when they were rooted out by the Japanese police.

For the rest of that decade there was no real dominating influence in literature. There was, however, a good deal of experimentation, notably the work of Yi Sang (1910-1938), who tried to plumb the depths of the subconscious mind in a series of stories set in red light areas. The mind being analyzed is his own, helpless as he gradually sinks into inevitable degradation.

During this period Ch'ae Man-sik wrote his inimitable *Peace Under Heaven* (1937). There is nothing quite like it in fiction anywhere. It seems to be almost a new genre, reminiscent of Dickens in the vividness of the hero's character; of Fielding with its intrusive narrator, and of *p'ansori* in narrative technique. It represents the marriage of realism to the classical romance, a novel full of hilarity whose hero, Master Yun, is the most best characterized character in all of Korean fiction. Greedy, vain, unscrupulous, philandering, stingy, Master Yun manipulates and is manipulated by the family of wastrels, ne'er-do-wells and incompetents with which he has surrounded himself, but manages nevertheless to preserve an almost childish innocence so that it is impossible to stay angry with him. Through this genial monster, Ch'ae Man-sik is satirizing the foibles of the Korean people under the Japanese.

During the 1930s another group of writers, notably Kim Tong-ni (1913-), Hwang Sun-won (1915-) and Yi Hyo-sŏk (1907-1942), began writing a completely new type of story. The whole trend of literature had been to deemphasize the past, because the past represented all that was opposed to enlightenment, modernization and nationalism. These writers began to examine what was uniquely Korean, writing in lyrical prose of the real spirit of Korea they had looked for in the past.

Hwang Sun-won is Korea's premier short story writer. Using a classical approach, his stories usually focus on an emotion. In *Cranes* (1953), a representative piece, two childhood friends find themselves in the role of captor and captive during the war. The story delineates the subtle changes of emotion experienced by the captor: rage, anger, shame, responsibility, compassion; until finally the roles of the two men in effect become reversed; psychologically, captor becomes captive and captive becomes captor. The story ends with the captor letting the captive go. The theme is obvious: feelings of humanity triumph over the absurdity of the exposition, and the change of mood is suggested through a glance or a gesture rather than through direct statement. Hwang Sun-won, also a novelist with a formidable reputation, always addresses interesting issues: *Sun and Moon* (1966), for example, deals with the butcher class, widely discriminated against in old Korea, and *Moving Castle* (1973) is a study of shamanism.

The 1940s brought renewed oppression by the Japanese, and an unproductive decade in literature. Liberation in 1945 was followed by great social and political confusion, and 1950 found the country in the throes of war again.

The 1950s saw the emergence of new generation of writers, young writers who had experienced the horrors of civil war and who were now looking for meaning amid the cruelty and corruption of post-war society. Existentialism, introduced before the war, had come in vogue, exerting a marked influence on the literature of the period. Chang Yong-hak (1921-) and Son Chang-sŏp (1922-) are typical of the new generation in their search for meaning in a society where all order has broken down. The prison camp in Chang Yong-hak's *The Poetry of John* (1955) is a symbol of a postwar society which denies the individual his most basic rights. This society which defeats man in all his aspirations is also the backdrop for Son Chang-sŏp's grotesque characters, people without morality, people buried in a maze of inhibitions and complexes.

The quest for freedom was central. Post-war intellectuals were concerned with discovering or rediscovering the self, the value of the individual self, in effect, a romantic objective. *The Square* (1961), by Ch'oe In-hun (1936-), is representative of this quest for freedom. The story deals directly with the consequences of the war and a dilemma which must have faced many prisoner-of-war intellectuals: whether to choose south, north, or a neutral country after the armistice. In *The Square,* two seagulls follow the vessel *Tagore* on its voyage from Korea. On board are a group of Korean POWs who chose to go to a neutral country after the Korean War rather than live in the South or the North. For one of them, Yi Myŏng-jun, the birds symbolize two lost loves, a girl from the South and a girl from the North.

Myŏng-jun recalls his life as a young introspective philosophy major in pre-war Seoul: politically and socially unaware at that time, he was searching for an understanding of life. His quest was to find the square, a symbol of space, light, meaning, and understanding. While forming an uneasy relationship with Yun-ae, his first girl, he is taken in for questioning by the police because his father is an active, ranking figure in the Communist party in the North, and is beaten in the course of interrogation. Disillusioned and alienated, he takes up a chance offer of smuggled passage to the North, where in his encounters with his father and the party he again finds nothing but disillusionment and alienation.

Myŏng-jun meets the second girl in his life, Ŭn-hye, a dancer and a free spirit, quite free of political posturing. Ŭn-hye loves Myŏng-jun but does not share his intellectual melancholia. Myŏng-jun becomes dependent on her and demands that she refuse a chance to dance in Moscow. She agrees but ends up breaking her promise. Myŏng-jun is left once again with a sense of ultimate betrayal.

Myŏng-jun returns to Seoul as an intelligence officer during the Communist occupation of the city during the war. He meets Yun-ae again only to discover that she has married his old friend, Tae-sik. Tae-sik is in trouble with the occupying authorities and Yun-ae pleads with

Myŏng-jun to save his friend's life. Myŏng-jun humiliates Yun-ae, but relents, just stopping short of subjecting her to the ultimate degradation of rape. In the end he arranges the escape of both Yun-ae and Tae-sik.

Back at the battle front, Myŏng-jun is reunited with Ŭn-hye, who has become a nurse. They snatch whatever human warmth fate allows them within the harsh reality of life at the front until finally Ŭn-hye is killed. Myŏng-jun is left once again with a complete disillusionment. He has nothing to live for, in the South or the North. He is taken prisoner and when offered the choice of South, North or a neutral place of residence, he chooses to go to a neutral country. However, he disappears overboard before the boat reaches its destination. He chooses the ultimate disillusionment.

The Square reflected the existential mood that was dominant in European literature in the 1950s. It was a towering best seller, and interestingly enough, returned to the bestseller charts during the democratization crisis of recent years. As a depiction of a young Korean intellectual under stress, no better work has been written. *The Square* combines the best qualities of Camus and Hemingway. Yet, it is a difficult book. The philosophical asides are distracting, and the theme is extremely dark and pessimistic. The characters seem unable to go outside themselves, to attain any sort of vision of a world that does not turn within the confines of their own private experience. Yi Myŏng-jun is unabashedly self-centered; his quest for meaning is totally personal and selfish. When he is also shown to be diabolically cruel, the reader unfamiliar with Korea finds it virtually impossible to empathize with his dilemma.

The mid-1960s and early 1970s saw another new generation of writers begin to make their mark on the literary scene. These were writers who had either been children during the Korean conflict or had been so young that they had no vivid memories of the horror of war. As a consequence, the war and its aftermath began to lose their place of dominance in the subject matter of literature. Kim Sŭng-ok's (1941-) *Seoul: Winter 1964* is a brilliant satire of a society where all order has broken down and human relationships have become meaningless. Highly experimental in form, it is a horrifying tragi-comic depiction of alienation and the absurdity of human existence. There is no plot worth speaking of, just the conversation between the narrator Kim, a graduate school student, An, and a middle-aged man they happen to meet in a roadside drinking stall. The conversation is banal at best, and at times totally absurd, but the story is remarkably successful in creating an effect of ultimate futility.

During this period a new awareness of social and political issues came to the fore, and brought a consequent concern about corruption and the abuse of power. The characters of Hwang Sŏk-yŏng (1943-) come mostly from the lowest levels of society, people who find themselves in conflict with an unjust society and who face inevitable defeat. *Chang Kil-san* (1975), which has attracted considerable critical attention, provides a panoramic picture of the 18th century while depicting the tragic life of a legendary rebel hero. *A Strange Place* (1971) shows management and corrupt overseers cruelly exploiting the workers on a reclamation project. *The Road to Sampo* (1975), one of Hwang Sŏk-yŏng's finest stories, is a delicate mood piece told almost entirely through dialogue, without the overt social message of *A Strange Place*, though the inferences are there for the reader to make. Two laborers who meet on the road go into a village winehouse, where the madam tells them about Paekhwa, the winehouse girl, who has absconded without paying money she owes. It is obvious that Paekhwa is a victim of exploitation. The madam offers a reward to the two men for information as to her whereabouts. As the two men travel the snow covered road they meet Paekhwa, who turns out to be a simple, sensitive girl, not the hardened prostitute one might have expected. She has run away because she cannot bear the degradation of winehouse life. Fundamentally she remains a victim of exploitation without any real hope for the future.

The Kwangju uprising in 1980 brought the anomalies of contemporary society into even sharper focus. There was a growing sense of the urgent need to solve the problems that beset Korean society, in particular, the gaping wound of national division. A "division" literature has emerged in recent years which traces its roots back to Ch'oe In-hun's *The Square*, but with a slightly different emphasis. *The Age of the Hero* (1984), by Yi Mun-yŏl (1948-), depicts a hero who has freely chosen the Communist way of life. The book emphasizes personal responsibility in choices. Cho Chŏng-nae's (1942-) *Taebaeksan* (1986) asserts that division was part of an inevitable evolutionary process inherent in the class struggle between landowners and tenants.

The 1980s also were marked by a wave of "novels of the masses" (*minjung*) and "novels of workers" (*nodongja*) which focus on the entire gamut of social problems associated with industrialization and see the working class as pivotal in social reform and the future development of the nation. The part played by workers in the events leading up to the establishment of the Sixth Republic in June 1987 provided a strong impetus to the production of workers' literature.

Recently the magazine *Wolgan Chosŏn* surveyed 107 novelists, asking them to evaluate contemporary fiction. Yi Mun-yŏl was selected as best novelist, with Hwang Sŏk-yŏng second. Pak Kyŏng-ri's (1927-) monumental novel *The Land* (1970) was chosen as the outstanding contemporary novel.

Yi Mun-yŏl has written a series of significant novels and novellas: *The Son of Man* (1979), *The Age of the Hero* (1984), *Our Twisted Hero* (1987), *Even Fallen Things Have Wings* (1989). All were bestsellers. *Our Twisted Hero*, an allegory about the abuse of power, delineates the latent tendency in man toward dictatorship against the background of an elementary school. Ŏm Sŏk-dae, monitor of the sixth grade, rules his class with an iron fist. A sinister, shadowy figure, he terrorizes the class into abject submission, reducing them to cringing, fawning pawns. He beats them, takes their money, uses them to cheat on exams, collects "dues," sells preferment, and in general insists on being treated as a king.

A transfer student from Seoul challenges Sŏk-dae's dictatorship, leading to a long, lonely struggle which ends in the capitulation of the

Seoul boy. However, in capitulation he discovers a new side to Sŏk-dae's corrupt regime. He begins to taste the sweets of special favor and power. The Seoul boy becomes Sŏk-dae's reluctant lieutenant.

A new teacher takes over the class and immediately becomes suspicious of Sŏk-dae. An investigation reveals that Sŏk-dae has been cheating on his exams. The teacher gives him a severe beating in front of the class, humiliating him in the process. Seeing their king reduced to a sniveling weakling, the boys, once such loyal supporters, now turn on him like snakes. The only exception is the Seoul boy.

After Sŏk-dae's departure, the long process of restoring democratic procedures in the class begins. Boys are elected to positions of responsibility and are deposed just as quickly. Some groups act recklessly, some groups do not act at all. In the end, after much pain and toil, dignity is restored to all.

There is fairly general consensus among critics that Pak Kyŏng-ri's *The Land* is the most significant novel of our time. *The Land* is a massive historical chronicle portraying a traditional landowning family before, during and after Japanese colonization against a panorama of cultural conflict between old world values and the values of the emerging new world. Pak Kyŏng-ri displays a marvelous historical sensivity in creating a detailed, totally convincing world, and cast of finely realized characters moving around the central heroine, Ch'oe, the commanding presence throughout the novel.

Pak Kyŏng-ri made her debut in the 1950s, quickly attracting attention with stories like *Faithless Generation* (1956), an incisive analysis of the basis of faith in one's fellow man in postwar society,which won an award in*Hyŏndae Munhak* in 1956. The publication of the first part of *The Land* in 1970 brought her national fame, a fame which has grown with the appearance of each new volume in the sequence and the great popularity of the TV series based on the novel.

Korea has an abundance of talented novelists and a great variety of outlets in magazines, journals and "mooks" for the publication of fiction. Daily newspapers feature serial novels, and,

while this may have the effect of lowering literary standards, it does present the possibility of instantaneous fame and larger monetary rewards. Add to this a plethora of valuable literary prizes to be won every year, and the result is a ready-made formula for a vibrant market in fiction. Korean fiction has had to struggle to develop its own distinctive voice, and the full fruits of the struggle have perhaps yet to be reaped.

Painting

Traditional

Korean painting has developed steadily throughout its long history, from the Three Kingdoms period (c. 1st century B.C. to 7th century A.D.) to modern times, despite the frequent disasters and invasions that have swept the country. Having absorbed foreign influences, particularly Chinese, on a selective basis, Korean painting has achieved an independent style and has to some extent influenced the evolution of Japanese painting. Because of its characteristic features and the active contact it has maintained with foreign art, the work of Korean artists can be distinguished from those of other East Asian countries.

It presents a series of cultural achievements typical of the creative vigor and aesthetic sense of Koreans. Thus it is in itself a reliable catalogue of the changing fortunes of the country's culture, and a glance at the development of Korean painting may serve as a shortcut to the understanding of Korean art and culture as a whole.

Painting is believed to have appeared in Korea probably around the fourth century A.D., at the latest, about the middle of the Three Kingdoms period. It developed mainly under Chinese and other foreign influences, but evolved different styles in each kingdom.

The Kingdom of Koguryŏ was situated on the northern part of the peninsula bordering Manchuria, within easy reach of China, and its painting naturally evolved under Chinese influ-

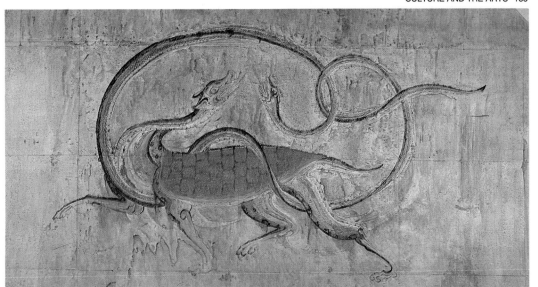

This turtle of the north, one of four shamanist deities that guard the universe(top), dancing scene(middle), and hunting scene(bottom) are all wall paintings from Koguryŏ tombs.

ence. Koguryŏ paintings were marked by vitality and rhythmic forms. These are clearly traceable in extant murals found in more than 50 chambered tombs scattered in the T'ungkou plain across the Amnokkang River in Manchuria and in the vicinity of P'yŏngyang, Koguryŏ's southern capital.

The chief subject of the early Koguryŏ murals was the occupant of the tomb. There were also Buddhist elements with scenes depicting the customs of the period in which the occupant lived. An outstanding example is the mural of Tomb No. 3 in Anak, which, from an inscription, is known to have been built in the year 357. Painted in ancient style, it is arranged in a triangular composition in which the portrait of the occupant is flanked by servants. The rudimentary method of shading used in depicting the drapery illustrates the early adoption of foreign techniques in the fourth century. A similar portrait has been found in the mural of the recently discovered Tŏkhŭng-ri Tomb, built in 408.

Koguryŏ paintings began to show remarkable strength and movement in the sixth century. For instance, the hunting scene on the left wall of the Tomb of Dancers captures the vigorous movement of the hunters, who are depicted riding at full gallop in a valley separated by a range of mountains. It is noticeable that the mountains here are stylized in the form of wavy strips, while the human figures and animals are rendered realistically. This seems to suggest that landscape painting was less developed than figure painting in the sixth century. The characteristic Koguryŏ style exemplified by this painting is common in the murals of the period between the sixth and seventh centuries: for instance, in later ones such as those of the Tomb of the Four Cardinal Deities in T'ungkou and Tomb No. 1 in Chinp'a-ri, near P'yŏngyang.

A wall painting in the Tomb of Four Cardinal Deities at T'ungkou depicts a fierce engagement between an entwined tortoise and a snake, with extraordinary vigor. The heads of the tortoise and snake face each other in a heraldic design and are surrounded by shapes resembling raging waves or flying clouds. Such dynamic forms may have developed under the influence of the art of the Six Dynasties (A.D. 265-589) in China, typified by the carving on the surface of a stone sarcophagus in the collection of the Nelson Gallery of Art in Kansas City. The murals of the Koguryŏ Tomb are, however, more vigorous, a characteristic of Koguryŏ painting that was fully developed in the seventh century. The colors became more vivid and the landscape more realistic and refined. Thus, while absorbing foreign influence, Koguryŏ artists at the same time were still able to achieve a forceful and rhythmic style of their own which culminated in the tomb murals of the seventh century.

The Paekche Kingdom developed its elegant and refined styles by combining artistic influence from Koguryŏ and the southern dynasties of China, especially the Liang Dynasty (502-557). Although there is not much left today to testify to the brilliant achievements of Paekche painting, there are some relics that reflect its taste and refinement, such as the mural depicting the Four Cardinal Deities in Tomb No. 6 in Songsan-ri in Kongju and the mural of a lotus flower and flying clouds on the ceiling of the Painted Tomb in Nŭngsan-ri in Puyŏ. As examples of this style, there are also ornamental wall tiles with landscape designs in relief, fish and dragons painted on a headrest and a mountain landscape carved on a silver vessel discovered in the Tomb of King Muryŏng.

Paekche artists portrayed the Four Cardinal Deities on the walls of chambered tombs following the influence of Koguryŏ. In the tomb in Nungsan-ri in Puyŏ, they were painted directly on the stone wall, just as in the murals of Koguryŏ of the late sixth and seventh centuries, while the flying clouds and lotus blossoms on the ceiling are floating in almost the same way as in the Koguryŏ mural of Tomb No. 1 in Chinp'a-ri. As the rendering of the clouds and lotus show, however, the Paekche paintings are more elegant and refined in taste than Koguryŏ works, presenting a contrast to the vigorous Koguryŏ style.

The features of Paekche painting are evident in some of the eight ornamental wall tiles with landscape designs, discovered in 1938 at the site of an old temple in Kyuammyŏn, Puyŏ. They

Buddha's Discourse on the Avatamsaka Sutra, 1343-67, gold and silver on indigo paper, 20 x 36.5cm.

illustrate the refined Paekche style, in which scenery consists of stylized rounded mountains, rocks, cliffs, trees and clouds, revealing a new development in composition. The mountains are arranged in such a way that one can feel distance and depth. Believed to have been painted in the seventh century, the wall tiles are some of the earliest landscape painting known and represent an important landmark in East Asian art.

Old Shilla (57 B.C.-A.D. 668) painting was little known until the excavation of Tomb No. 155 (Heavenly Horse Tomb) and Tomb No. 98 in Kyŏngju. The excavated paintings of a white horse (which gave its name to Tomb No. 155), mounted horsemen, phoenix and cattle provide a glimpse of the Old Shilla style. The first three paintings are rendered on birch bark, the fourth on the surface of a lacquered vessel.

Although the painting excavated from the Heavenly Horse Tomb is inferior to the Koguryŏ murals, this does not necessarily mean that Old Shilla painting is generally poorer than that of Koguryŏ, for the work from the Kyŏngju tombs is believed to have been executed not by professional painters but by artisans.

The Old Shilla paintings so far discovered differ in style from Koguryŏ, and Paekche paintings. While the Koguryŏ style is marked by dynamic and rhythmic qualities and the Paekche style reflects elegant and relaxed tastes, Old Shilla painting is somewhat gloomy in feeling.

As has been noted, painters of the Three Kingdoms developed their own styles despite strong influence from China and in turn played an important role in the development of Japanese art. Japanese culture during the reign of Empress Suiko (593-628), for example, was inspired and nurtured by the Paekche court, and early institutions were generally shaped with help from Koguryŏ and Paekche scholars, architects, priests and artists who were active in Japan during the sixth and seventh centuries. According to literary sources, among the representative Korean painters who contributed to the evolution of Japanese art during the Three Kingdoms period were Paekga, Prince Ajwa, and Insaraa from Paekche, and Tamjing, Kasoil and Jamaryo from Koguryŏ.

The Unified Shilla period (668-935) followed the unification of the peninsula by Shilla, resulting in the development of a single homogeneous culture. Like Buddhist sculpture and handicrafts, painting may have developed remarkably in this harmonious atmosphere. Since there is but one example dating from this period, the development of painting of that time can only be deduced from fragmentary records.

The Office of Painting, Ch'aejŏn, continued to function during the Unified Shilla period and produced such eminent painters as Solgŏ, Chonghwa and Honggye, who specialized in Buddhist painting, and Kim Ch'ungŭi, who was active at the T'ang court. As a result of active cultural exchanges with T'ang China, it is known from their literary sources that portraiture, landscape and Buddhist painting developed during this period.

Solgŏ was the principal figure on the artistic scene of Unified Shilla. He is reputed to have executed the legendary painting of an old pine on one of the walls of Hwangyongsa Temple, the image of Bodhisattva Avalokitesvara in Punhangsa Temple, and the image of Vimalakirtin in Tansŏksa Temple. The old pine painted on a wall of Hwangyongsa was said to have been so realistic that birds attempted to perch there. Solgŏ's paintings, including those with Buddhist themes, are said to have been at once scrupulously realistic and full of spirit.

By chance, a Buddhist painting of the Unified Shilla period was discovered several years ago. Executed on the wrapping paper of a Buddhist scroll, it is worn out along the central axis and separated into two fragments. It dates back to 754, according to the inscription on the accompanying scroll of the *Avatamsaka Sutra*, and depicts a Buddhist sermon held in a temple. Buddhist figures and architecture are represented in extremely fine and elaborate gold lines on blue-brown paper. In general, the figures in this painting have the same features as the Buddhist statues of the mid-eighth century. It may be assumed that in general painting was consistent with Buddhist sculpture in the Unified Shilla period.

The Koryŏ period had more varied subjects and styles of painting. Paintings were produced to meet practical demand and also for the spiritual satisfaction of artists for whom painting was an avocation and not a profession.

The Academy of Painting was founded at the beginning of the Koryŏ period and produced Yi Nyŏng and many other outstanding painters. It was not only academy men who painted, but also priests and members of the royal family and the nobility. The themes included figures and portraiture, landscapes, birds and flowers, bamboo and plum trees and other plants, all done usually in ink only. Portraits of kings, ranking officials and members of the upper class were in great demand, and buildings were constructed to enshrine the royal portraits.

Painters began to produce landscapes that may have been based on actual scenes. Yi Nyŏng, for instance, painted such landscapes as *Yesŏng River View* and *South Gate of Ch'ŏnsusa Temple*. In addition to Yi's paintings, such works as *Diamond Mountains, Landscape of Chinyang* and *Eight Views of Songdo* were produced by anonymous artists. This style of landscape may not be directly linked to the later school of Chŏng Sŏn (1676-1759), who based landscapes upon actual Korean scenes and subjects, but it nevertheless formed a tradition of depicting actual Korean scenery.

It is noteworthy that many ink paintings of popular plants such as bamboo, plum and orchid were done by scholar-painters and Sŏn priests during the Koryŏ period, when religious themes, such as Buddhism, Confucianism and Taoism, also formed subjects of paintings. The paintings of Buddhist themes were especially elaborate and reflected the aristocratic taste of the period, as did the refined celadon vessels in blue-green glazes.

Painting styles became more varied after contacts with Sung and Yüan China. There are, however, few examples of Korean paintings of the period, and the development of Buddhist painting during the Koryŏ period must be traced from the Korean Buddhist paintings remaining in Japan. The painters of Buddhist themes had been closely associated with the royal household, which favored Buddhism as the state religion. One outstanding example of Koryŏ Buddhist painting is *Avalokitesvara Holding a Willow Branch* by the Korean priest Hyeho, now preserved in the Asakusa Temple in Tokyo. This image is characteristic of the Koryŏ period, with its slim and elegant lines rendered in rich

A Dream Visit to Peach Blossom Land *by An Kyŏn (1418-?)*

colors on silk, the graceful movement, transparent drapery, the long narrow eyes, small mouth, and the delicate branch of willow. The image is elaborately executed in every detail.

The Chosŏn period saw remarkable progress in Korean painting. Scholar-painters and prominent members of the Academy of Painting developed traditional styles to a high degree, while the activities of priest-painters waned under the government policy of neglecting Buddhism in favor of Confucianism. Paintings became more diverse and distinctly Korean in terms of composition, brushwork, and treatment of space. While absorbing the styles of Chinese masters of the Sung, Yüan, Ming, and Ch'ing periods, Korean painters were able to evolve their own styles which played an important part in the development of Japanese *sumi-e* (ink painting) of the Muromachi period (1392-1573), evident in the work of Shubun and his followers.

The paintings of the Chosŏn Dynasty may be divided into four smaller periods: early (1392-1550), middle (1550-1700). late (1700-1850), and the final years (1850-1910). The most important part of the early Chosŏn period was the 15th century, during which time King Sejong (r.1418-50) reigned. To it belong such

great masters as An Kyŏn (r.1418-?) and Kang Hŭi-an who exercised a profound influence on later painters. The Korean tradition in painting was firmly established during the later reigns of King Sŏngjong (r.1469-94), King Chungjong (r. 1506-44), and King Myŏngjong (r. 1545-47). As a result of frequent contacts with China, Korean painters adopted Chinese styles. They included the Li-Kuo or Kuo-Hsi school; the Ma Yuan and Hsia Kuei school of Southern Sung; and the academy style and the Che school of the Ming Dynasty (1368-1644).

An Kyŏn may be taken as a representative painter of 15th century Korea. Chinese paintings in the collection of Prince Anp'yŏng, the younger brother of King Sejong, played an important part in the development of An's style. After studying the many excellent Chinese paintings in the prince's collection thoroughly, he then evolved his own personal idiom. His painting *A Dream Visit to Peach Blossom Land,* now in the Tenri Central Library in Japan, demonstrates not only his virtuosity based on the Chinese Kuo Hsi manner, but the achievement of his own personal style as well. It is characterized by such elements as the additive arrangement of echoing shapes and forms, the use of two deferent perspectives to emphasize

Cats and Sparrows *by Pyŏn Sang-byŏk, a court
painter of the early 18th century.*

sage in meditation on a rock, now in the
National Museum of Korea in Seoul, is typical
of his refined style, showing his outstanding
artistic talent and scholarly spirit, despite the
strong influence of the Che school.

The influence of the Chinese Ma-Hsia school
is apparent in *A Stroll under the Moonlit Pine
Tree*, attributed to Yi Sang-jwa, a 16th century
artist. Frequently reproduced in various publications, Yi's landscape features a "one-corner
composition" dominated by a gnarled pine tree,
and a sage strolling with an attendant in the
moonlight.

The style of the Chinese Mi Fu school, followed by such masters as Kao K'o-kung of the
Yüan Dynasty (1280-1368), can also be detected in the landscapes of Ch'oe Suk-ch'ang, Yi
Chang-son, Sŏ Mun-bo, and other members of
the Academy of Painting. This style, one of the
main streams of scholar-painting, thus continued in 15th century Korean paintings.

Chosŏn period artists did not merely imitate
Chinese painting. They studied Chinese styles
selectively and successfully developed a distinctly Korean character in their work. Taking
root during the reign of King Sejong in the 15th
century, these native styles continued to grow,
and by the 16th century a tradition of landscape
painting with Korean flavor and technique was
flourishing. This is apparent in a number of
landscapes, including those of the Diamond
Mountains and Samgaksan, based on real
Korean landscapes and done by members of the
Academy of Painting and based upon actual
Korean scenes.

The middle period (1550-1700) was an era of
disaster and political disorder resulting from the
Japanese invasion of Korea in 1592-1597, partisan dissent, and a series of internal revolts.
Nevertheless, painting in distinctly Korean
styles flourished. These may be summarized as
follows: the style of the Che school, followed in
the early period by Kang Hŭi-an and taken up
by Kim Chae, Yi Kyŏng-yun, Kim Myŏng-guk,
and many others; the style of An Kyŏn, pursued
by Yi Chŏng-kun, Yi Sung-hyo, Yi Ching, and
others; traditional Korean themes including
birds, flowers, and animals, painted by Yi Am,
Kim Shik, and Cho Sŏk; and ink paintings of

the height of mountains and the spaciousness of
the Peach Blossom land, the use of diagonal
movement, and the creation of strange fantasy.
With these techniques, he was able to handle
complex and imaginary subjects with striking
deftness. As an academy painter, An Kyŏn continued to be active at the courts of kings Sejong,
Sejo, and Sŏngjong. Painters of later generations, such as Yang P'aeng-son, continued to
follow his style.

Kang Hŭi-an, an important contemporary of
An Kyŏn, travelled to China, where he was able
to see and study Ming paintings of both the academic and the Che school. His painting of a

bamboo, plum trees and grapes, done by such masters as Yi Chŏng, O Mong-yong, and Hwang Chip-jung. Scholar-painting of the Chinese Southern school also was introduced to Korea.

Thus, despite frequent political upheavals, painting flourished and the artistic tradition of the early Chosŏn period continued to develop. Painters based new styles on the tradition established by An Kyŏn and his followers. One important aspect of the painting of this period was the widespread popularity of native birds, flowers, and animals as subjects. Some outstanding examples include *A Dog with Puppies* by Yi Am, who was active at the end of the early and beginning of the middle Chosŏn periods; a painting of a cow by Kim Shik; the ink paintings of birds and flowers by Cho Sŏk and his son, Cho Chi-un; and the ink paintings of bamboo by Yi Chŏng; the ink paintings of a plum tree by O Mong-yong, and the ink paintings of grapes by Hwang Chip-jung. This genre was continued in the paintings of cats and sparrows by Pyŏn Sang-byŏk, who worked in the tradition of the middle Chosŏn period even though most of his work was produced in later years.

Although painters of the middle Chosŏn period developed their own distinctive styles based on the earlier tradition, they were not sufficiently active to pursue the Chinese Southern style then being introduced into Korea. This task remained for painters of the later period.

Korean painters of the later Chosŏn period were inspired by Chinese painting of the Yüan, Ming and Ch'ing periods, and by Western styles brought to China during the reigns of emperors K'ang Hsi (1662-1722), Yung Cheng (1723-35), and Ch'ien Lung (1736-95). Despite the pervasive influence of those Ming and Ch'ing masters, however, Korean painters also used new techniques and drew inspiration from their environment. The result was that Korean characteristics in their work became even more clearly defined. With the advent of the movement for Practical Learning, which encouraged progressive ideas of independence, more and more painters based their landscapes on Korean scenes and subjects. This trend was especially apparent during the reigns of the 18th century kings Yŏngjo and Chŏngjo, when scholars of the Practical Learning school played a vital role in the development of learning and art.

The new developments in technique and style may be summarized as follows: the Chinese Che school style, favored during the middle Chosŏn period, was replaced by the style of the Chinese Southern school; Chŏng Sŏn and his followers adopted and transformed the techniques of the Chinese Southern school for use in the painting of Korean landscapes; Kim Hong-do, Shin Yun-bok, and their followers produced a large number of genre paintings depicting scenes of daily life, and Western methods of painting gained their first introduction into Korea.

The Chinese Southern school style, already introduced during the middle Chosŏn period, attained great favor during the later period. The major artists who advocated this style were also eminent scholars, such as Kang Se-hwang, Shin Wi, and Kim Chŏng-hŭi.

Although landscape painting based on actual scenes had been done as early as the Koryŏ period and was continued by painters of the early and middle Chosŏn periods, the landscapes of Chŏng Sŏn and his followers proclaimed a distinctly new style indigenous to Korea. Founded on the techniques of the Chinese Southern school, the style refined by Chŏng Sŏn took on a truly native character, as can be seen in the painting *Clearing after the Rain on Inwang Mountain*. Such landscapes are visually exciting because of their composition, brushwork, and coloring.

Genre painting also proved to be remarkably Korean in character. Some painters of the preceding periods had depicted scenes of everyday life, but the potential of genre painting, in the true sense of the term, was not fully explored until the work of Kim Hong-do, Shin Yun-bok, and Kim Tŭk-shin during the later Chosŏn period. Kim Hong-do and his follower Kim Tŭk-shin painted many humorous scenes from actual life, as exemplified in *Village School*. Unlike the literati paintings of the earlier periods, their paintings came from direct contact with the life of the common people. Their subjects were ordinary folk in typical Korean dress such as the

Clearing after the Rain on Inwang Mountain *by Chŏng Sŏn (1676-1759)*

*ch'im*a and the *chŏgori*, straw-thatched houses, farm scenes, and blacksmiths, etc.

Shin Yun-bok liked to paint romantic love scenes of men and women of his time, as seen in *Party by the Lotus Pond*. The subjects of his genre scenes were not common people, but members of the upper class, usually shown enjoying themselves. Not only did depict light-hearted and romantic scenes might have been offensive to conservatives in that Confucian-oriented society, but he even dared to paint scenes which included women of doubtful virtue. Shin's paintings, rendered with a lively, refined brush and fresh colors, differ in theme, composition, brushwork, and coloring from those of Kim Hong-do and Kim Tŭk-shin. All three, however, shared a common interest in depicting everyday scenes in a whimsical manner. Without such painting the popular customs of that time would hardly be known.

Another important aspect of the later Chosŏn period was the introduction of Western methods of painting from China. Western techniques of shading and perspective were brought to Ch'ing China by Jesuit missionaries, and were, in turn, introduced to Korea by members of the Korean mission who travelled to Yenching. Painters such as Kim Tu-ryang, Yi Hŭi-yŏng, and Pak Che-ga experimented with these new methods, which were increasingly adopted by painters of succeeding periods and even by artisans who produced folk paintings. Although Western techniques of ink painting exerted little influence on Korean painting at the time of their introduction, they later came to play an important part in the development of new styles in the 19th century.

During the final period of the Chosŏn Dynasty (1850-1910), the types of landscape and genre painting done in the middle and late Chosŏn periods began to disappear, giving way to the Chinese Southern school style followed by Kim Chŏng-hŭi and his followers. *The Orchid* by Kim shows the highly spiritual world of a scholar, portrayed in a simple and condensed style. His calligraphy, too, is unique and impressive, the strokes reminding one of broken bones.

The final period saw the development of fresh, new styles: one followed by Kim Chŏng-hŭi and his adherents Cho Hŭi-ryong, Hŏ Ryŏn, and Chŏn Ki, who together constituted the Ch'usa school (so named for Kim's sobriquet); another followed by Yun Che-hong, Kim Su-chŏl, and Kim Ch'ang-su, who formed the Haksan school (after Yun's sobriquet); and one

Wrestling Match *(top left)and a* Mask Dance *(top right) by Kim Hong-do, and* Lovers under the Moon*(bottom) by* Shin Yun-bok.

Korean brush paintings: Bamboo *by Cho Hui-ryŏng (1789-1866), a member of the* Ch'usa *School;* In Search of Plum Blossoms across the P'agyo Bridge *by Shim Sa-jŏng (done in 1766)*

led by Hong Se-sŏp. While the Ch'usa school kept alive the scholarly style of the Chinese Southern school, the artists of the Haksan group developed new styles based on Western techniques, as shown in landscapes by Kim Su-ch'ŏl. The simplified forms and watercolor effects are particularly remarkable in Kim's paintings. One may also observe the use of a new and striking composition, emphasized by the bird's-eye-view and bold brushwork of wet ink washes, in Hong Se-sŏp's *Swimming Ducks*. Despite continuing influence from Ch'ing China, these artists worked in distinct styles that led to modern Korean painting. On the whole, however, painting declined during the final Chosŏn peri-

od, probably because of political disorder.

The sole figure who stands out in that period of relative artistic stagnation is Chang Sŭng-ŏp. Excelling in a wide range of objects including landscape and flowers, he exercised profound influence over later painters, and was followed by his two students, An Chung-shik and Cho Sŏk-jin. Although he was endowed with outstanding skill, Chang lacked the lofty spirit of a learned man, for he had no opportunity to study the theories of eminent scholars such as Prince Anp'yŏng and Kang Se-hwang, with which earlier masters like An Kyŏn, Chŏng Sŏn and Kim Hong-do were familiar. Chang's style was characterized by powerful brushwork and vivid coloring that are apparent in his landscapes, but his paintings remained inferior in spirit to the work of earlier masters.

As can be seen, Korean painters, while selectively absorbing Chinese styles throughout, continued to create their own styles, suited to their own tastes. However, the traditional styles of Korean painting tended to deteriorate in the late 19th and early 20th century, especially following annexation by the Japanese in 1910.

Contemporary

The problem of dating of Korean contemporary art accurately remains a yet to be resolved. This may sound strange to general readers, but in drawing a clear line to declare when a new age has set in for the art of any country, art historians must have considerable patience as well as excellent insight.

In Europe and America, the term contemporary art is usually employed to indicate the specific schools of art which have evolved since the end of World War II. A similar "post-war" conception is applied in defining contemporary art in Korea. It seems to be the general opinion of the nation's art historians and critics that the Korean War (1950-53) marks the beginning of the contemporary age in Korean art history. However, there is no appropriate historical justification for this. From a purist view of art history, the birth of contemporary Korean art, unlike that of Europe, appears to have lacked the necessary momentum. Korean art experienced a period of unhappy discontinuity in the stream of its modern history. What is now called contemporary art is believed to have developed as a sort of reaction to or a social need resulting from the political and psychological situation of the Korean people following the devastating internecine war.

The artists of the 1950s were obviously encouraged by their harsh postwar environment to pursue the common objective of giving expression to their unhappy situation. Such a social background may explain why these young artists of the so-called "Korean War generation" were attracted to the school of expressionism which had developed in postwar Europe in a similarly unfortunate situation.

It is easy to imagine the psychological and ethical motivation of these artists of the Korean War generation, who responded hastily to the popular aesthetics of French abstract art. They plunged into exploring a new concept of art without acquainting themselves with the basic techniques of geometric stylization which constituted its primary idiom of expression. Such a reckless attitude may be attibuted to the desperateness of those suffering artists. They had to give vent to their inner urges and impulses and doubts about the future in the years of extreme chaos following a war of horrible destruction.

As is widely known, expressionism came into vogue in the early 1950s in Paris. Artists of this movement refused to comply with traditional concepts of art and their creative endeavors went so far as to lead painting "to cease to be painting," as Dubuffet once put it. They opposed all images and theories of form and denounced the futility of everything manmade and unnatural. What they advocated was an art of existentialism.

Expressionist paintings were produced in great quantities by avant-garde artists toward the end of the 1950s, especially between 1958 and 1959. In view of Korea's geographical location and its cultural and social environments, it was only natural that there would be a considerable interval before the waves of a new art movement in Europe or America would be embraced by the country's art circles. The works displayed in the Modern Art Exhibition in the late 1950s showed that Korean artists were experimenting with a new sense of direction rather than simply exploring randomly as they had done earlier. The works in the exhibitions in the early 1960s showed that the artists appeared to be on the right path to discovering new values and concepts of art.

Another event of unmistakable significance in this budding period of contemporary Korean art was the creation of the Contemporary Korean Art Exhibition for Invited Artists by the major daily newspaper *Chosun Ilbo* in 1957. As the first independent exhibition in Korea, it contributed greatly to encouraging creative activity among artists. This was in contrast to the gov-

The White Bull by Yi Chung-sŏp(1916-1956). *(above)*
The Rhythm of Aak (Court Music), by Kim Ki-chang
(1913-   ). *(right)*
Mountains and the Moon, 1952 by Kim Whan-ki.
(facing page left)
Water Drops SH 87006 by Kim Tschang-yeul(1929-   ).
(facing page right)

ernment-sponsored National Exhibition of Fine Art which was extremely academic and conservative. While it is true that this state-organized contest was of primary importance for many years, it should also be admitted that it discouraged experimentation and the development of new art forms and new trends with its conservative guidelines. The Contemporary Korean Art Exhibition for Invited Artists was established with the aim of invigorating the nation's fine arts by providing an exposition venue for the majority of independent artists who were being neglected by the state-organized contest. The exhibition appears to have fulfilled its goal for some time.

Abstract art in Korea rejected traditional order and values in pursuit of direct expressions of man's free spirit. Accordingly, abstract artists tried to avoid repetition in their new methods of expression. However, this proved to be paradoxical. Since abstraction was meant to be a means for the artistic expression of man's unconscious instincts, then a repeated execution of the same methods and styles would be unavoidable, as

man's basic instinct seldom change.

The great zeal Korean artists showed for abstract expressionism began to diminish in the latter half of the 1960s, as they were faced with the problems of repetition and lack of inspiration. The artists of the abstract school thus had to struggle to find a means to revitalize their art.

Appearing around 1968 was a new generation of artists, known to some as the "April 19 generation," so-called because they were mainly educated after the April 19, 1960 Revolution, when the authoritarian government of Syngmann Rhee was overthrown in the wake of fierce student demonstrations. Among the group exhibitions initiated by the artists of the April 19 generation, two are of particular significance: the Young Artists' Exhibition, which was organized by graduates of Hongik University, and the Exhibition of Contemporary Painting '68, organized by graduates of Seoul National University.

The two shows were very different, and within each was evident a number of different styles and trends. Nonetheless, the artists participating

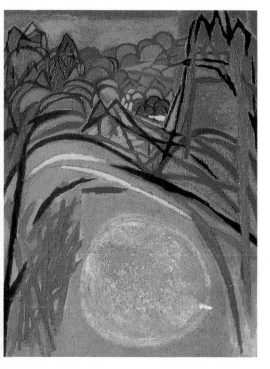

in the two shows shared a common ideal: a resistance to tradition. The two groups also showed an inclination towards geometric abstraction in reaction to the anti-formal art which had been most popular in the nation's art circles. Another common tendency noticed in the works of these young artists was that they were showing a keen interest in found objects, or "*objet trouvé*," and the possibilities they offered.

As noted art critic Clement Greenberg has pointed out, pictures by the Abstract Expressionists still maintained the original "painterly" nature of painting. From an etymological viewpoint, the words "plastic" and "painterly" convey opposite meanings. These etymological definitions may aid an understanding of the historical significance of the serious attempts made by the artists of this new generation to restore the basic order of forms in painting, protest against the popular conception of Abstract Expressionists who advocated destruction of forms. In the early 1970s, contemporary Korean painting began to explore geometric

compositions with a view towards re-establishing the original value of forms. At the head of this movement was the Origin Group, which was formed in 1966.

At the same time, some young artists in other sections of the art community were challenged by in extending the concept of fine art to an appreciation of various objects in nature, in which they seemed to discover new aesthetic qualities. Their interest was not only in achieving artistic imagery but, more basically, in seeking a significant encounter between man's consciousness and surrounding objects as well as a successful union of humanity and the natural world. They endeavored to change or expand the general concepts of fine art. Leading this movement were two prominent groups called the A.G. Group (or the Korean Avant-Garde Art Association) and the S.T. (Space and Time) Group, both of which were organized in 1969.

It should be pointed out that such an extended concept of fine art was not totally foreign to the majority of Korean artists. Rather, they seemed to recognize that the idea had its roots in the traditional perspective of nature and the universe held by all Asian cultures, including Korea's. Traditionally, Koreans have seldom viewed humanity and nature from two separate perspectives. They have instead tried to identify with nature, and even with the whole universe. It was through this age-old tradition that the young experimentalists discovered a valuable source of artistic inspiration.

A similar creed of pan-naturalist philosophy is detected in monochromatic pictures of a minimalist tendency, which constituted an important style of Korean painting in the late 1970s. These paintings of a simple color scheme, which are often described as representing the "reductionist" concept in its crystallized form, attempted to avoid all illusions possibly attainable from images and composition. Some viewers may see some resemblance to American art of the minimalist school in these paintings. Be that as it may, it is certain that the Korean artists of this time were less interested in expressions of their emotions. Instead, they intended to visualize fundamental truths of the universe that superseded all art theories.

Korean painting since the 1960s has been guided for the most part by abstractionism, which is further classified into abstract expressionism, post-painterly abstract painting of geometric stylization and abstract monochromatic painting. The 1980s witnessed the birth of a powerful movement directed toward issuing messages of social consequence, signaled by the birth of the Reality and Speech Group early in the 1980s which technically divorced itself from all trends of modernist painting including abstraction.

The artists of this group, who apparently banded together with the primary goal of highlighting social evils, have chosen painting as a visual language to give voice to their opinions. This tendency of young artists to seek an active role in society can be understood as a Korean adaptation of the worldwide trend of "new painting." But in the context of Korea's political and social circumstances in recent years, this movement for the so-called "art for the masses" takes on a particular historical significance, though whether or not its value as art deserves unequivocal praise is questionable.

Folk

The rediscovery and re-evaluation of a great wealth of long-forgotten Korean folk paintings has been one of the most exciting cultural events of recent years.

Conventionally, Korean painting has been grouped into two major categories—pure painting and "functional" painting. Yet, although there is no such thing as a really pure, academic form of painting any more than there exists an exclusively "functional" painting, this classification still often dominates the thinking of artists, art historians, connoisseurs and art dealers. The traditional Confucian scholar's scorn of popular paintings that were colorful and contained folk motifs was at the basis of the idea that unsigned "functional" paintings were a low form of art.

"Functional" in this context has a wide sense. Among "functional" paintings were included those used in accordance with old Korean customs for specific seasonal festivals, such as New Year's Day, the first day of spring, and the fifth day of the Fifth Moon. Old records as well as those paintings that remain indicate that most of these paintings included longevity symbols, happiness symbols and guardian images to ward off evil spirits and in this sense fulfilled a useful, even magical function

The old Confucian-oriented Korean scholars classified as folk painting virtually everything outside the elitist areas of literati and Sŏn painting and calligraphy, created for the intellectual diversion of the scholar class. Yet a great deal of this painting was not folk painting at all in the sense that this term is used elsewhere in the world, meaning a simple form of painting executed by amateurs, with no reference to the rules of any school of art.

Korean folk painting, therefore, developed as an art of an entirenation, of all classes, directly related to a particular lifestyle; and although in many cases the individual names of these painters are unknown, the type of people in each group is known. They ranged from wandering craftsmen to court painters, all of whom participated in this popular art.

The first group consisted of painters known as "passing guests," wanderers who travelled from one village to another producing domestic paintings at individual households. Most of them were naive peasant craftsmen, but some skilled artists were found among them, usually those who had failed to become court painters.

The second group was made up of painter-monks. Talented monks who received severe training from a master usually became professional painters and produced various Buddhist ritual paintings for temples. Those who failed to survive the severe regimen often turned to the life of wandering painter-monks, travelling from one temple to another and earning their living by painting murals on temple walls.

The third group consisted of court painters. In terms of social position, a court painter was the highest rank obtainable in Korea for an artist. It is often thought that the works of these men were only in the classical style, but they were also hired to decorate palaces and to provide ornamental designs.

Folk paintings were to be found in the royal court, Buddhist temples, shaman shrines, *kisaeng* drinking houses, altars and private houses. Some themes were reserved exclusively for the court while others were used only in temples, shrines and upon altars. The remainder were used by ordinary folk to decorate their homes and to enrich everyday life.

In a Korean home certain works of art can be installed permanently while others are brought out only during certain seasons or on special occasions. A few themes are suitable anywhere within the house, but others are intended to be placed in one particular location in order to produce felicitous results. For example, the door painting of a tiger to repel evil belongs at the front entrance, while a painting or print of a dog is intended for a storage room door. Screens with representations of flowers and birds or babies belong to bedroom walls.

Korean folk painting is often classified in terms of its relationship to the concepts of Confucianism, Taoism, Buddhism or shamanism. This classification is valid when there is a clear religious identification: paintings on the

A folk painting of an evil-repelling tiger.

theme of Buddha's life are Buddhist painting, those of the Taoist immortals are Taoist painting, illustrations of Confucian teaching are Confucian painting and those of the Mountain Spirit are shaman painting. However, at times these religious motifs are so complexly interwoven that it becomes impossible to determine to which specific religioneach belongs. The end result is a general impression that in Korea there is Taoist Buddhism, Buddhist shamanism, and Taoist shamanism. One finds that the thought behind religious ritual painting is actually the shamanisticfolk content of each religion rather than its academic aspect.

Analysis of Korean domestic paintings containing various symbols reveals a common denominator which interlocks these religious ideas tightly together. This common denominator is an inborn desire for a long and happy life and protection against evil spirits. Thus, these works of art are no more than the Korean expression of a universal aspiration. Though there are a certain number of paintings which may be grouped as ethnographic, such ethnic themes do not characterize Korean folk paintings as much as do universal ones.

A striking characteristic of Korean folk painting is the extent of stylization, which leads to abstract art, expressing man's dreams, imagination, symbolism, life, humor, satire, and sense of fantasy. There is no attempt at realism, and there is a filling in of space thatcon trasts with the aesthetics of open space typical of classic Asian painting. Another aspect is animism, which is positively expressed in all kinds of animal, rock and tree paintings and which is in fact a reflection of shamanistic animism. A third characteristic, usually referred to as the "naive style," is developed by a combination of abstraction and animism which portrays a genuine, childlike world where a man's heart is more important than his name.

The whole range of these paintings deals with the life of the masses, often in a most unconventional and unorthodox manner. Dating back to ancient Korea, some of these paintings are serious and others are frivolous, some deal with imaginary things and others with real objects. Some have religious overtones; some of them were done by expert hands, such as those of professional court painters, and others were done by amateurs.

Whatever the subjects and whoever the artists, there is one thing common to them all— they are uniquely Korean and inseparably tied to the actual lives of the people of the time.

Calligraphy

In Korea, as in China and Japan, calligraphy has long been considered a form of art. Korean calligraphy derives from the written form of the Chinese language, in which each character is composed of a number of differently shaped strokes within an imaginary square and is intended to convey a specific meaning. Koreans have used Chinese characters for writing since around the second or third century A.D., although their own language is of an entirely different system. Even after the invention of the Korean alphabet *Han-gŭl* in 1446, Chinese continued to be used as the official script until the late 19th century. Traditional Korean calligraphers wrote in Chinese rather than in Korean. Under the influence of Chinese culture, calligraphy was always closely connected with painting in Korea, and some believe that painting was influenced by calligraphy in terms of the vitality, rhythm, and economy of strokes. A calligraphic work would be hung on a wall like a painting and admired in the same way, each stroke being praised for its own attributes, the ink for its tone, and the whole composition for its strength, individuality, vitality and so on. A piece of fine calligraphy is not a symmetrical arrangement of conventional shape but, rather, something like the coordinated movements of a skillfully choreographed dance—impulse, movement, momentary poise, and the interplay of active forces combining to form a balanced whole.

Technically speaking, the art of calligraphy depends on the skill and imagination of the writer to give interesting shape to his brush strokes and to compose beautiful structures from them. This is done without any retouching or shading and, most important of all, with well-balanced spaces between strokes. Such spacing is acquired only through years of practice and training. But dexterity of brushwork and cultivation of aesthetic sensitivity do not constitute the only elements essential to understanding the basic nature of the art of calligraphy. Among the fashionable classes of old Korea, the art was regarded as a necessary process of mental discipline for a cultured gentleman. The practical function of calligraphy as handwriting or a means of communication was often overshadowed by the philosophical implications attached to the act of executing it.

The fundamental inspiration of calligraphy, as of all other arts which flourished in ancient Korea, is nature. Each stroke in a character, even each dot, suggests the form of a natural object. Like the ancient Chinese masters, Korean calligraphers recognized that, just as every twig of a living tree is alive, every tiny stroke of a piece of fine calligraphy must be made to live. This is the very property of calligraphy that distinguishes its strokes from those in a printed word. Chinese ideograms have an abstract, pictorial quality which further adds to the visual attraction of calligraphy by permitting a writer of accomplished artistry to enjoy almost unlimited possibilities inexpressing himself as would a great painter in his paintings.

Like the tools of a traditional ink-and-brush painter, the tools of a calligrapher are few— good ink, an ink stone, a good brush and good paper (some prefer silk). These items were called affectionately the "four stationery treasures" (or sometimes the "four friends of a scholar"). Great care was taken in selecting and maintaining them because they often served as a measure of the owner's aesthetic taste and eye for beauty.

Korea boasts a long tradition in calligraphy, dating to the early years of the Three Kingdoms period, when Chinese literature is known to have been taught for the first time at royal academies and state-run institutions for higher education. In spite of such a long history and the prominent efforts rendered by numerous aristocratic noblemen and artists to promote the art through many centuries, few pieces of ancient calligraphic works have survived the many foreign invasions and internal conflicts. The seven-year invasion by the Japanese warlord Toyotomi Hideyoshi in the late 16th century, in particular, caused serious damage to historic monuments and cultural objects, not to mention a tremendous loss of humnan lives, across the peninsula. Thus the number of existing fragments of calligraphy dating to the years preceding that war is less than 20.

Satisfying the academic curiosity of modern students of Korean calligraphy are many works in stone which have outlived the vicissitudes of history and destructive fires of war. Among several inscribed stone monuments from the ancient Three Kingdoms period, an object of unsurpassed historic significance is a huge stone monument erected in A.D 414. in southern

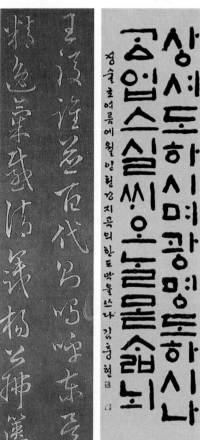

A fan featuring a drawing of an orchid with a poem by Ch'usa (1786-1856); a scroll (left) by Han Ho (1543-1605) and one (right) by Kim Ch'ung-hyŏn (1921-).

Manchuria in honor of military achievements of King Kwanggaet'o of Koguryŏ. This stone monument, which is 6.4 meters high, carries an epitaph of some 1,800 Chinese characters engraved in an angular, epigraphic style. Most epigraphists and specialists in ancient Korean calligraphy note that the style is expressive of the bravery and vigor of the people of the ancient military state which ruled a considerble portion of Manchuria and the northern half of the peninsula.

Even more scarce are references to the standard of calligraphic art achieved in the southwestern kingdom of Paekche. In view of the high level of scholarship and refinement of the artistry, it is most likely that this kingdom enjoyed a notable degree of maturity in calligraphy. The accidental discovery of the tomb of King Muryŏng and his queen in the ancient Paekche capital of Kongju in central Korea in 1972 yielded many important archaeological finds, including a rare treasure for calligraphers and epigraphists in the form of a square stone tablet. Placed at the entrance to the sixth century burial chamber, it was a sort of certificate of proof that a plot of land was purchased from underground deities in order to build the tomb. The Chinese characters engraved on the stone slab show great elegance and dexterity of technique, apparently influenced by the contemporary Chinese writing of a noncursive style.

In the following Unified Shilla period, devotion and adherence to the T'ang culture of China gave birth to such great masters of calligraphy as Kim Saeng and Ch'oe Ch'i-won. Their styles or writing basically followed those of famous Chinese masters Ou Yang-hsun andYu Shinnan. Wang Hsi-chih, another Chinese master, was also greatly admired, and his semi-cursive style was widely copied. But the squarish, regular style of Ou Yang-hsun, which was inherited from the Shilla Kingdom, continued to prevail in the Koryŏ period until around 1350. About this time the supple and graceful style of the Chinese calligrapher Chao Meng-fu of the Yüan Dynasty was introduced and came into vogue. Since that time the Chao style has remained the basic undercurrent in Korean calligraphy.

The early rulers of Koryŏ adopted the Chinese example of employing a civil service examination to recruit officials which required applicants to compose verses on given topics. Handwriting was naturally included in the criteria for judgement, and such a system gave impetus to the interest in improving handwriting among the upper classes. The court administerd a seperate examination for scriveners to serve in lower positions. From this period, when Buddhism thrived as the state religion, have come a wealth of examples through which the standard of calligraphy can be understood. The existing objects include tombstones, woodblock prints and handwritten copies of Buddhist scriptures, epitaphs on memorial stupas for revered priests, and temple monuments. Among the master calligraphers of celebrated fame from this period are Yi Am, Yi Che-hyŏn, Ku Chokt'al and Han Yun.

The calligraphy of the Chosŏn Dynasty first followed the elegant supple touch of the Chao Meng-fu style. Prince Anp'yŏng (1418-53), the third son of King Sejong, was unrivaled in his style and his dexterous hand. He wrote a commentary on the previously mentioned painting, *A Dream Visit to Peach Blossom Land*, by An Kyŏn, one of the greatest painters of his time. Han Ho, who is better known by is pen name Sŏkpong, is another important name in the history of Korean calligraphy. But he merely remained a faithful student of Wang Wsi-chih who fully mastering that style, and failed to develop an individual style his own. Early in the 16th century, a weakened, unimaginative style became more and more evident and Korean calligraphy entered a period of sterility.

The 19th century saw, however, the emergence of individual styles related to those of Chinese calligrapher Wen Cheng-ming of the 16th to the early 17th century. The new trend resulted from Korea's close cultural contacts with Ch'ing China. Such contacts were pursued ardently by a group of scholars and intellectuals eager to follow the Ch'ing model of seeking practical approaches to better the lives of the people and to build a modern state.

The greatest master of the Chosŏn period was Kim Ch'ŏng-hŭi who belonged to the group called *Sirhak*, or "School of Practical Learning." A distinguished calligrapher, painter and scholar, Kim established the so-called *"ch'usa"* style. His calligraphy is derived from the *li shu* script of China, but his sense of pictorial composition, harmony within asymmetry, and animation wrought by unmatched, forceful strokes led to the creation of a dynamic style of his own.

A few Chosŏn calligraphers continued in their

work in the early decades of the present century. However, the influence of Japanese calligraphy began to be felt around 1920. Since World War II, traditional calligraphy has survived only as a minor art. A new trend since the 1960s has been calligraphy employing the Korean alphabet.

Sculpture

Ancient

Sculpture in the most primitive sense of the word must have started in the Paleolithic Age, although no example that can be attributed to that time has been found. The earliest examples of sculpture known are some rock carvings on the Pan-gudae Cliff in Ulchu-kun and some clay figurines of men and animals dating from the Neolithic Age. The Bronze Age saw the active production of bronze, earthen-ware and clay figurines, but it was not until the introduction of Buddhism that sculpture in Korea began to develop in both quantity and quality. Any sculpture worth mentioning falls in the category of Buddhist sculpture.

Koguryŏ Period (37 B.C.-A.D. 668)

Buddhist images were brought into the country when Buddhism was introduced to Koguryŏ in 372. It is believed that not until several decades later did Korean artisans begin to make Buddhist images. Although there is no tangible proof, it is quite plausible that Koguryŏ was the earliest of the three kingdoms to make Buddhist images, as it was the first to be exposed to the religion. The construction of temples such as Ch'ŏmunsa and Ibullansa three years after Buddhism reached Koguryŏ supports this assumption. Murals in tombs and many historic records also indicate that Buddhism greatly influenced the culture of Koguryŏ.

Nevertheless, no Buddhist images made by Koreans have been found that date before A.D. 500. A gilt-bronze image of a seated Buddha of the fourth or fifth century was recently found in Ttuksŏm in Seoul, which was part of the Paekche Kingdom, but it is believed to be a Chinese import as its style is strongly suggestive of the Northern Wei sculpture. If proven to be a Korean imitation of a Chinese Buddha, it would be the earliest example of a Korean-made Buddhist sculpture. As it is, the earliest Koguryŏ Buddhas-or indeed the earliest Korean Buddhas—with definitive inscriptions of date appear only after the sixth century.

The rugged terrain and the harsh climate of Koguryŏ's vast territory are reflected in its arts, which were influenced by the temperamental and vital style of Northern Wei bordering the country on its continental side. The unrealistic and geometric quality of the Northern Wei style, resulting from efforts towards an independent form of expression free from the imported styles that accompanied the introduction of Buddhism, and the ascetic spirituality characteristic of the early stages of any religion blended with the ruggedness of Koguryŏ's native arts to produce a straightforward style. It is not easy to define the style of Koguryŏ Buddhas from the few extant diminutive gilt-bronze or clay figurines. Nevertheless, assuming these to be representative of the general sculptural trends of the time, a number of identifying characteristics can be drawn. The Koguryŏ Buddhas have lean elongated faces, prominent usnisas (a protuberance on top of the head symbolic of the marks of a Buddha) on mostly shaven heads, rigid cylindrical bodies draped by thick robes that have "fish-tail" folds at the hem on both sides, and hands that are disproportionately large. The boat-shaped nimbuses encircle not only the heads but also most of the length of the bodies and are decorated with crude but meticulously depicted flames. The pedestals, which are cylindrical, are finished with lotus petals carved with a masculine feel.

Embodying these characteristics best is a gilt-bronze standing Buddha with the inscription "*Yongga seventh year*," which corresponds to 537. Made at Tongsa Temple in P'yŏngyang, it was found in 1967 in Hach'on-ri, Kyŏngsang-nam-do. The archaic smile of its elongated face, the rigid body draped in a thick robe and the hem of the robe that is pointed like feathers at the sides, all work together to produce a spiritual quality.

Gilt-bronze Standing Buddha with inscribed date of 539, Koguryŏ. Ht. 16.2cm.

Buddhism became firmly established, sculpture experienced many stylistic changes and a truly Koguryo style developed around 560.

Paekche Period (18 B.C.-A.D.660)

Buddhism was introduced to Paekche via Eastern China by an Indian monk named Maranant'a in 384, 12 years after it was introduced to Koguryŏ. The production of Buddhist images in Paekche is believed to have begun no later than the fifth century, because the aforementioned diminutive gilt-bronze Buddha excavated in Seoul implies that local imitations of the Chinese and Indian Buddhas could have been made by that time, and because ancient records show that a temple was built in 385 in Hansŏng, today's Seoul. However, Paekche images inscribed with fifth century dates have not yet been found. The earliest examples date from the sixth century and include a stone triad and some clay images from Chŏngnimsa Temple, a gilt-bronze standing Buddha from the site of Powonsa Temple, some Buddhas carved around a boulder in Yesan, and a gilt-bronze Buddha with the name Chŏng Chi-won inscribed on it. Though retaining the traditions of Wei and the Koguryŏ style exemplified by the Wono-ri Buddha in their refined faces, thick robes and graceful forms, these Buddhas show signs of Paekche modifications.

Characteristics unique to Paekche sculpture are clearly evident in all the Buddhist images of the late sixth century, including an agalmatolite seated Buddha and a gilt-bronze bodhisattva from Kunsu-ri, and stone reliefs of Buddhist triads in Sŏsan and T'aean.

As it is recorded that artisans and painters were invited to Paekche from Liang China in 541, the arts of the southern dynasties of China must have influenced Paekche sculpture from the mid-sixth century. Whatever their influences were, Paekche Buddhas of the time are characterized by warm, human attributes. The small usnisa, the stately but relaxed body, the voluminous curvature under the thick robe, the diminished side-flare of the hems of the robe, the folds of the robe of the bodhisattva that cross each other in the shape of an "X," the simple but refined rendering of the lotus petals of the

A gilt-bronze Buddhist triad with the inscription "*Kyemi year*" (Editor's note: it is not known what year this corresponds to) as its casting date also shows the same characteristics. However, a relaxing of the tension and rigidity is seen in a triad bearing the inscription "*Shinmyo year*," or 571. Though basically of the style influenced by Northern Wei, as illustrated by the symmetrical folds of its thick robe, a slight change in modeling is apparent in the fullness of its face and the much softer rendering of the hems of the robe that fluctuate in an M-shape. This is probably attributable to the influences of Eastern and Western Wei or even the early Northern Ch'i or Chou which resulted in a new phase in the evolvement of a style very much Koguryŏ's own. A number of clay Buddhas of the same style found in Wono-ri, P'yŏngannamdo (North Korea) are believed to have been made in the mid-sixth century, though they are without inscribed dates.

As Koguryŏ's artisans improved and

Rock-cut Buddha Triad, 7th century, Paekche. Ht. 2.8m.

pedestals are definitely local traits Paekche artisans developed from the Chinese styles of the late Northern Wei, Ch'i and Chou. What makes a Paekche Buddha truly its own is the unfathomably benevolent smile that graces the round pleasant face. That expression, often labeled the "Paekche smile," is unique.

Influenced by the Sui and T'ang dynasties of China, Buddhist images became elongated and slender around 600. The modeling of the bodies became much fuller and some bodhisattvas were depicted slightly twisted with S-shaped postures rather than in upright, static positions. These traits are best illustrated by a gilt-bronze standing bodhisattva in the Ch'a Myŏng-ho collection, a gilt-bronze standing Buddha from Kyuam in Puyŏ, and a seated stone Sakyamuni in Yŏndong-ri, Iksan, Chŏllabuk-do.

Paekche sculpture can be described as being more refined and subtle, a result of its more temperate climate and fertile land.

Shilla Period (57 B.C.-A.D. 668)

It took time for Shilla to officially accept Buddhism because of the kingdom's conservatism and geographical remoteness, but when it finally did in 527, the production of Buddhist images began. A Buddha about 5 meters tall was made in Hwangnyongsa Temple within two or three decades of the recognition of the religion. Buddhist sculpture developed so rapidly that by 579, Shilla artisans were exporting their works to Japan. This growth was made possible by the originality of Shilla's artists and the cultural influences of the neighboring Paekche and Koguryŏ kingdoms.

Examples of early Shilla sculpture include a gilt-bronze standing Buddha which is believed to have come from Hwangyongsa, a stone relief of a group of Buddhas on Tansŏksan Mountain in Kyŏngju, a Maitreya seated half cross-legged (National Museum collection), and a gilt-bronze standing bodhisattva excavated from Koch'ang (Kansong Museum collection). Of these, the

The main image of Buddha in Sŏkkuram, 8th century, Unified Shilla.

Gilt-bronze Maitreya, early 7th century, Three Kingdoms.

relief on Tansŏksan Mountain best represents the techniques and style of early Shilla. The giant Buddha of Hwangnyongsa, which unfortunately was destroyed, must have been of great artistic value as it is recorded to have been one of the three most important treasures of Shilla.

The seventh century saw drastic changes in both the quantity and quality of Buddhist sculpture. The seated stone Buddha of Inwang-ri of Kyŏngju; the headless figure seated half cross-legged in a posture of meditation on Songhwasan Mountain; a Buddhist group in T'apkok; a part of a stone figure in a half-seated meditation posture and a stone relief of Buddha, both from Mulya in Ponghwa; and a standing copper bodhisattva (the former Tŏksugung Museum collection) are some examples of this period that share the same stylistic traits. Some of them are portrayed in geometric abstraction, with some indication of Ch'i and Chou influenes, and some with Sui and T'ang Chinese influences evident in their round, full faces, relaxed bodies and the realistic rendering of the garments.

The stone relief of T'apkok and the triad of Samhwaryŏng best illustrate the Shilla sculpture of the time. The Buddha, the central figure of the triad, is seated on a low stool in a rather awkward pose. With a low usnisa, a round, chubby face with a smile, the plastic rendering of the body under the thin robe, the shallow relief of the sparse folds which make a whorl on the knee, the Buddhist swastika on the forehead, the decorative knot of the belt, and the simple halo, it is a definite departure from the style of the previous period. Chinese influences of Ch'i, Chou and especially of Northern Chou are quite obvious. The triad is believed to date from around 600, antedating slightly a triad in Pae-ri which is believed to have been made in the early 600s.

Unified Shilla Period (668-935)

Following Shilla's unification of the peninsula, the regional differences of the three kingdoms were integrated gradually and, with the assimilation of T'ang Chinese elements, a new style unique to Unified Shilla emerged around

700. Examples of the early Unified Shilla period are the Buddhist guardian gods of Sach'ŏ nwangsa and Sŏkchangsa temples, the Buddhist triad of Kunwi, the stone relief of Buddha in Kahŭng-ri of Yŏngju, a group of relief images of Buddhas and bodhisattvas from Yŏngi, and two gold Buddhas from Kuhwang-ri. Each reflects the confusion of the transitional era while retaining some regional elements. For instance, in the case of the triad of Kunwi, which is similar to the gold Buddhas of Kuhwang-ri except for the facial depiction, traditional abstraction is combined with the new realism. This is seen in the modeling of the shaven head with a prominent usnisa, the solemn face with thick eyelids and elongated ears, and the dignified but rather crouched body that is supported by an angular pedestal.

Realism became more prevalent in the early eighth century around 710, but as can be seen in the Amitabha and Maitreya images of Kamsansa, it is mixed with idealistic elements. The curvilinear lines and the voluminous, elastic bodies of these two images are encountered repeatedly in the Buddhas of Kulbulsa Temple, the seated Sakyamuni of Poriam Hermitage, the stone relief of Ch'ilburam Hermitage, and the Buddhist group of Sŏkkuram Grotto Shrine.

Needless to say, the Sŏkkuram images are the masterpieces of the sculptural art as well as the supreme embodiment of the religious spirituality of the time. The image of the Sakyamuni Buddha in the rotunda of the grotto is the culmination of Korean sculpture with its superb rendering of the round, plastic face with long brows, perfect nose and ethereal smile, and the magnificent, lifelike body clothed in a thin robe that falls in shallow folds.

These idealized and realistic features of plastic forms and sensual resiliency disappeared gradually after Sŏkkuram. By 800 there emerged a neo-realistic style emphasizing a solemness of facial expression and human proportions, thus producing a sense of emaciation in place of the former monumentality. Buddhas of this period are characterized by subdued expression and a lack of vitality in lines and form. This style is most evident in the stone relief of Pangŏsan Mountain, which was made in 835, and the triad

of Yunchigok Valley of Namsan, Kyŏngju, which was made in 801. A number of Vairocana and Bhaisajyaguru Buddhas were made in the mid-ninth century in many temples throughout the country including Tonghwasa, Porimsa, Top'iansa, Ch'uksŏsa, Pusŏksa and Pŏpchusa, all in variations of this style. In the later years there appeared a tendency to exaggerate the upper part of the body. Buddhas of magnificent proportion were also made occasionally.

Koryŏ (918-1392) and Chosŏn (1392-1910) Periods

A great number of Buddhist images were made, many of them of excellent artistic quality, in the Koryŏ period as the kingdom that succeeded Shilla proclaimed itself to be a Buddhist nation. The iron Buddha of Kwangju, the stone Buddha of Kaet'aesa Temple, the gilt-bronze Buddha of Munsusa Temple and the wooden Buddha of Pongnimsa Temple represent the best of the extant Koryŏ works.

The quality as well as the quantity of Buddhist sculpture declined rapidly with the beginning of the Chosŏn Dynasty when Buddhism was suppressed as a national policy. Most of the existing Chosŏn images were made after the Japanese invasions of 1592-98 when Buddhism recovered some of its former vitality and splendor. Buddhas of this period have their own unique qualities and merits.

Modern

Most art historians agree that the year 1919 marks the genesis of modern Korean sculpture. In that year, a young art student of a pioneering spirit enrolled in a prestigious Japanese art school in order to study the still unfamiliar art of European sculpture. Several other students soon followed in his footsteps, leading eventually to the opening of an age of modern sculpture in Korea.

The country was under the colonial rule of Japan at the time. Not only in the fine arts but also in all academic and cultural fields, the nation was experiencing a state of extreme stagnancy and deprivation. Japan's colonial regime was wielding unchecked power in all spheres of

Jiwon's Face, *1967 by Kwon Jin-kyu.*

Monumental Yoon-Mok, *1987 by Chung Kwan-mo.*

life. Even in literature and the arts, Japan was the only window to the world for Koreans and this window was usually stained with a strong Japanese coloring. It is from this general perspective that the overall background and the development of sculpture as a major aesthetic movement in modern Korean history should be viewed.

Sculpture is not the only art form that underwent an unhappy disruption of development during this tragic chapter of Korean history at the turn of the century, characterized by the decline of an old dynastic government and the intrusions of foreign powers. Unfortunately, the immediate predecessors to early pioneers in modern sculpture cannot be named, as is the case with most other fields of arts, especially pottery. Moreover, the birth of modern Korean sculpture was unthinkable without the predominant influence of European sculpture. However, this does not mean that Korea has a meager history of sculptural art. As shown in the previous

section, there is a brilliant tradition of stone and bronze carving that goes back to the ancient Three Kingdoms period. It also is significant to note that, in spite of the differences in style and material as well as in the time of creation, the Buddhist images cast by ancient Korean sculptors more than a millennium ago and the abstract forms envisaged by their remote successors in modern times often give similar message in their profound spiritual dimension. The message would best be interpreted as an aspiration to accomplish the utopian idealism which is expressed in the same placid and modest manner. This yearning, possibly born of the unique course of Korea's national history, may have further been intensified by the inherent spiritual and aesthetic disposition of the people.

The pioneering student mentioned earlier, Kim Pok-chin, renowned artist in the history of modern Korean sculpture, entered the Tokyo School of Fine Art in 1919. He returned home to become the first Korean ever trained in the

Dream of a Spring Day, *1961 by Kim Kyŏng-sŭng.*

Columba & Agnes, *1954 by Kim Se-choong.*

sculptural art of the West. A few other students then enrolled in the same Japanese institution for art education. Those artists, including Kim Chong-yŏng, Kim Kyŏng-sŭng and Yun Hyo-jung, soon joined Kim Pok-chin in introducing sculpture influenced by European traditions to Korea. They were mostly absorbed with sculpting portions of the human body such as heads and torsos in a realistic manner, which they had learned in Tokyo where academic realism prevailed. These sculptors were active in presenting works at national art exhibitions held annually under government sponsorship both in Seoul and Tokyo. This early stage of modern sculpture suffered from a lack of creative inspiration despite the pioneering zest of early artists, who were largely obsessed with imitating Western sculpture and transplanting it to Korea's cultural soil. The national circumstances were far from conducive to lively activity among artists as Japan was pulling its colonial reins ever more tightly in preparation for

World War II. In 1945 Korea was liberated, but the overall situation did not improve and became even more hostile for artistic creation as the country headed into ideological conflicts and military confrontation between South and North Korea.

Admiration of Western sculpture breathed some life into the activities of Korean sculptors during this unstable period, however. Yun Hyo-jung met Marino Marini in Venice in 1952, and was greatly influenced by the famous sculptor and his works. Another occurrence worth mentioning from those dark years was the first showing of abstract works in the National Exhibition of Fine Art in 1954.

After an armistice brought the three-year Korean War to a cease-fire in 1953, art circles began to regain some vitality. A few large-scale exhibitions were organized by private organizations, and these helped encourage a remarkable diversity in style and technique most visible in the fields of painting and sculpture. Among the exhibitions of notable significance were the annual membership show sponsored by the Korean Fine Art Association, and the Contemporary Korean Art Exhibition for Invited Artists sponsored by the leading daily newspaper *Chosun Ilbo*. The latter deserves special note for providing emerging artists of avant-garde tendencies the chance to display their works.

Modern Korean sculpture had become firmly established by the end of the 1950s. The conflict between the opposing schools of realism and abstractionism was increasing and sculptors were employing a greater diversity of materials, including assorted metals and stone breaking with their traditional reliance on plaster and wood.

From the 1960s to the 1970s, Korean sculpture made impressive progress due to the country's rapid economic development as well as to political and social changes. Dominating the Korean sculptural arts in this period of dramatic transitions were two major international modern art movements. The first of these was the so-called "anti-formal abstractionism," first introduced to Korea from the late 1950s to the early 1960s. The movement, which acquired major impetus with the creation of the Korean Avant-Garde Art Association, breathed new life into the world of Korean sculpture throughout the 1960s. Sculptors of this vein repudiated all natural forms respected in the traditional school of academic realism. They sought to give spontaneous expression to their emotions through non-representational shapes. In the following decade of the 1970s, this emotional abstractionism faced a strong challenge from another new art movement that opposed conception and style, called "sculptural conceptualism."

Sculptural conceptualism pursued "pure" abstraction, free from all emotional binds and connotations. In terms of style, artists of this movement favored simple and daring forms in contrast to those of the previous generation of anti-formal vanguardism which tended to be complex and intricate. The 1980s experienced an unprecedented burgeoning of sculptors and sculptural activity. A number of young artists became nostalgic about past trends of a more humane nature, in reaction to the cold intellectualism of the previous decade.

Crafts

Ancient

One of the best ways to understand life during the prehistoric ages is to study the dwelling sites and the tools and other relics the people of those times made and used. Of course, the more tools and relics, whether stone, bone, earth or other materials, there are available, the more accurate the information.

A great number of relics of the Paleolithic, Neolithic and Bronze ages have been found in Korea. Traces of conscious efforts to beautify the tools are obvious even from those times. Though prehistoric stoneware and earthenware are basically of the same kind and nature all over the world, they have their own regional climatic differences.

Of the staggering amount of handicrafts that flourished during the last five or six thousand years, those that are considered most intrinsic to Korea are discussed here with the hope of increasing the reader's understanding of Korean handicrafts.

Metalcraft

Bronze relics including mirrors, axes, knives, vessels, bells, belt hooks and various kinds of ornaments and ritual ware, all dating from the Bronze Age, have been found all over Korea. Of these, the belt hooks deserve special notice for, decorated with handsome animal figures, they bear traits of the northern nomadic tribes. Many of the bronze artifacts show complex links to the cultures of Minusinsk, Scythia and Ordos.

The art of metalcraft made such steady progress through the early Iron Age that by the time the three kingdoms of Koguryŏ, Paekche and Shilla emerged to dominate the peninsula in the first century B.C., a high level of sophistication had been reached as evidenced by relics recovered from tombs of that time. Thanks mainly to the ingenious construction of the

Shilla tombs, many valuable relics have been recovered from them intact. Unfortunately, most Koguryŏ relics have been lost or destroyed. Gold crowns and other objects have been found in Paekche tombs, but most of the extant metalware of any importance is from the Shilla tombs.

A golden crown (National Treasure No. 87) dating back to the fifth to sixth century is an example of Shilla's metalcraft art at its best. One of several Shilla crowns hitherto excavated, it is of two parts, an inner and an outer crown. A forked gold piece symbolizing the feathers of a bird stems from the inner part and is slanted slightly backward. Across the front of the outer crown are upright tree-like ornaments in a repetitive design that looks like the Chinese ideograph "ch'ul" 出. At the back of it are two antler-shaped uprights. A string of pendants hangs from each side near the front of the crown. The inner part of the crown is decorated in open-work of continuous patterns of many different designs. Linear engraving and repousse work festoon the erect ornaments, the diadem and the pendants, which are further embellished with gold beads and comma-shaped pieces of jade attached with gold wire. The crown ornaments oscillate in a golden brilliance at the lightest vibration.

A mastery of goldsmithing in this period is evident in the gold belts with gold ornamental pendants, as well as in the gold necklaces, earrings, bracelets and sword ornamentations. Most notable are a pair of ear pendants and an agate-inlaid sword handle and sheath of a geometric symmetrical design showing a highly accomplished art of filigree combined with granulation. The granulation and filigree techniques, which originated in Egypt, are believed to have reached Korea via India and China sometime before Christ, for the techniques were employed in some of the golden ornaments excavated from the tombs of Nangnang (108 B.C.-A.D. 313).

With the flowering of Buddhist culture, metalcraft flourished. The bronze bells of Shilla were famed for their size, elegance and sonority. A mastery of craftsmanship is exemplified in the ornate gold and gilt-bronze reliquaries for

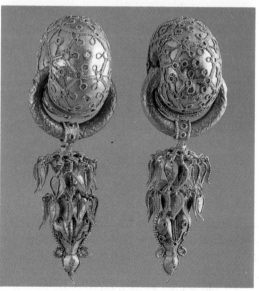

A golden crown with gold spangles and commashaped jades(top) and a pair of gold and giltbronze ear pendants excavated from Shilla tombs and believed to date from the 5th or 6th century.

Ash-glazed gray stoneware vessel in shape of warrior on horseback 5th-6th century ancient Shilla. Ht. 23.3cm.

sari, the cremated remains of prominent priests that have been retrieved from the country's many stone pagodas. Incense burners, small bells, bronze mirrors and other ornaments of excellence exist in quantity.

In discussing metalcraft of Korea, one may also note that metal printing was undertaken as early as 1240 in Koryŏ, preceding Gutenberg's invention of printing type by some 200 years.

Pottery

Earthenware, which dates to the prehistoric age, diversified in form and decoration during the Three Kingdoms period. Glazed pottery appeared in Shilla and developed into an early form of celadon during the last years of the kingdom. Influenced by the highly developed ceramic arts of T'ang, Sung and the Five Dynasties of China, celadon glazed porcelain

and other porcelain ceramics as we now know them emerged in the early Koryŏ period. Celadon ware is reported to have been introduced to Koryŏ in the 10th century from the T'zu-yao kiln of China's late Chou period, and local celadon production might have been attempted by the end of that century. A passage praising the refined beauty of the celadon glaze appears in *Kao-li T'u-ching* (Illustrated Account of Koryŏ), a travelogue by a Chinese man who visited Koryŏ in the early 12th century.

During the 11th century, when the art of celadon had already achieved a remarkable level, artists concentrated on the perfection of forms and a glaze which was bluish green. The early pieces are called plain celadon because of their lack of colorful decoration. Floral designs were sometimes engraved or carved in relief on the surface of the pieces, which were often made in the shape of men, animals, or fruit. For instance, a lion crouches on the lid of an incense burner designed so that the smoke would float out through the lion's mouth. There also are tea kettles with spouts shaped like a turtle's mouth. Slip painting using white clay appeared at this time.

The technique of inlaying developed in the mid-12th century. This involved incising designs into the clay and filling the incisions with white or black slip. Excess slip was smoothed away prior to the firing. In later years, designs and patterns were painted on the pieces in underglaze iron.

Inlaid celadons declined from the end of Koryŏ through the early Chosŏn period, gradually giving way to a ware made of the same greyish clay as Koryŏ celadon but decorated with a method employing white slip called *punch'ŏng* It was a popular method of decoration because of the rich variety of patterns possible. With *punch'ŏng*, they could be inlaid or stamped, painted in iron pigment, or even made by scratching designs into the slip coating on the vessels or cutting away the slip to create a design. Slip was simply brushed on with a coarse brush sometimes to create a design exuding a feeling of spontaneity. Compared to the dignified simplicity of the plain or inlaid celadons with their perfectly balanced forms and linear patterns, *punch'ŏng* ware was characterized by spontaneous artlessness and carefree cruse forms. The decorations on them were also marked with a singular lack of restraint. The transition to a warmer and more humble taste in pottery perhaps was analogous to that of the society in general of the Chosŏn Dynasty.

Celadon ware, white porcelain and iron-glazed ware continued to be made while *punch'ŏng* was enjoying its heyday, but from the mid-Chosŏn period of the 17th-18th centuries white porcelain became the most popular. It was produced in bulk by numerous public and private kilns all over the country. The public kiln in Punwon by the Han-gang River was the most active because of an abundance of good clay and firewood.

Plain white porcelain was made at first but soon this began to be decorated with designs of

A mid-12th century inlaid celadon vase (top) and a 16th century white porcelain jar with underglaze iron decoration.

A traditional four-story chest covered with thin sheets of ox horn.

underglaze blue cobalt, copper oxide and iron oxide. White porcelain ware with underglaze blue decoration which had appeared briefly in the mid-15th century was rediscovered and produced vigorously. Plum tree and bird combinations, landscapes, grapes and grapevines, pine trees, bamboo, and orchid were most often painted on the Chosŏn white porcelains. Designs of stylized waves, fish, dragons and clouds, and *shipjangsaeng* (ten objects symbolizing longevity) appeared in the later years. Many of the paintings were done in the contemporary literati style. All Chosŏn porcelain ware was noted for its clear luminosity, whiteness, the simple elegance of its curved forms and the thickness of the walls.

Woodcraft and Lacquerware

Wooden furniture designs in Korea developed as a result of the custom of sitting and sleeping on cushions and mats on the floor. Korean furniture is characterized by simple, sensitive designs, compact forms, and practical-ity.

Chosŏn woodcraftsmen were noted for the attention they paid to even the parts hidden from view and their ingenuity in blending practicality and beauty. Artisans sought to achieve pieces that were both sturdy and aesthetically pleasing. The use of glue and nails was avoided wherever possible by fitting parts into each other by ingenious methods.

The grain and texture of the wood, which varies from one kind to another, was regarded as a major decorative element and was presented in a pleasing arrangement. The wood was polished with oil to maximize the natural effect of the grain and no paint was applied.

Metal hinges and ornaments were used on chests and other wooden furniture not only to reinforce their structure but also to enhance their beauty. White bronze, bronze, copper, and iron were most frequently used for making hinges, padlocks and decorations. Iron ornaments blackened with perilla oil and soot were admired for their simplicity and practicality.

The history of lacquerware inlaid with mother-of-pearl goes back to Shilla. Judging from the Chinese praise bestowed on elaborate lacquerware in the *Kao-li T'u-ching,* the art must have been highly developed in the Koryŏ period. A special lacquerware studio was set up in 1272 to produce mother-of-pearl inlaid cases to contain the woodblock-printed manuscripts of the *Tripitaka Koreana.* Some of the cases are in museum collections in Japan, the United States and Europe.

Lacquerware of Koryŏ was generally decorated with dainty mother-of-pearl chrysanthemums or other floral patterns in continuous arabesque designs. Tin or bronze wire was used to depict the vines, and sometimes pieces of turtle shell, very thinly cut and tinted red or yellow, were used for variety.

Analogous to the decline of the sophisticated techniques of inlaid celadon ware, the exquisite daintiness gradually disappeared from inlaid lacquerware toward the end of the Koryŏ period. Mother-of-pearl designs became bolder and larger, and sometimes rather coarse. Peonies, grapes, phoenixes and bamboo took the place of the delicate arabesque patterns. *Shipjangsaeng* also became popular in time and remains so today.

Hwagak is a woodcraft form involving a technique that employs ox horn to decorate chests, boxes and small objects for women. It is not known when this technique first came into use, but furniture decorated with ox horn long has been popular in women's quarters for its colorfulness. The use of ox horn is reminiscent of Koryŏ's penchant for turtle shells.

To make a *hwagak* piece, horns are boiled to remove the cartilaginous center and then sliced thin and ironed flat. The slices are then polished until they become translucent. Designs are painted on the pieces of horn in bright colors mixed with glue made of ox hide, and the pieces are glued on to the wooden surface with the painted side downward.

In a country where light and neutral colors were most popular, items of such colorfulness were unusual, and it is understandable that *hwagak* decorated chests were used only by women.

It is inevitable that the durability of ox horn work is limited in a climate of drastic seasonal changes such as Korea. With the development of horn preparations and the improved quality of glue, however, more durable ox horn pieces are expected to emerge.

The above touches on only a few of Korea's handicrafts. Many artisans who have devoted their lives to pursuing traditional handicrafts have been recognized as "human cultural treasures" in an effort to ensure survival of Korea's traditional arts and crafts.

Modern

Handicrafts and their makers have been appreciated in the western world, but in Korea artisans responsible for a wealth of excellent handicraft items have traditionally been dismissed as of humble origin and trade. Today, even though Korean eyes have been opened to the beauty of traditional handicrafts, some of which have been designated national treasures, the names of the craftsmen remain unknown. Occupational and class discrimination was so severe in the past that craftsmen, though they made pieces of unsurpassed skill, function and beauty, were never remembered.

For an easier understanding of modern Korean craft arts, their development since the modernization of the country is divided into two phases: modern crafts of 1910-45 and contemporary crafts of 1945 to the present. The period of modern crafts coincides with the Japanese colonization of Korea. It was a relatively dark age for traditional arts and only a very few pieces of notable value were produced as Koreans were endeavoring to maintain a national identity under a brutal foreign domination.

It also was a time of change brought about by the emergence of a new generation educated in the ways and thoughts of the West. With the introduction of Western arts, people began to look at crafts in a different way and to re-evaluate them. It was with this new outlook that Kim Pong-yong opened a studio for mother-of-pearl inlaid lacquerware in 1925, where he was to train numerous artisans over the next 20 years. The year 1928 was marked by the one-man design show of Yi Sun-sŏk, the first of its kind in the country. Craftsmen responded eagerly to the inclusion of handicrafts in the annual Chosŏn Arts Exhibition in 1932, the most prestigious public art exhibition in Korea. From then until its last show in May 1944, a year before the country's liberation from Japan, the exhibition provided many opportunities for craftsmen to show their works to the public. Chang Ki-myŏng, Kim Chin-gap, Kang Ch'ang-won, Kim Pong-yong, Kim Sŏng-kyu and Kim Chae-sŏk are some of the names that became well-known through the exhibition. However, it should be noted that Kim Pong-yong and Kim Sŏng-kyu had already won a silver prize and a copper prize, respectively, for the mother-of-pearl inlaid lacquerware work they submitted to the Paris World Fair in 1925.

Despite the appearance of a new breed of craftsmen educated abroad in modern craft arts, many dedicated themselves to preserving and passing on the traditional arts of ceramics, mother-of-pearl lacquerware and cabinet making. It is through the efforts and dedication of these craftsmen that traditional Korean handicrafts have survived.

With national liberation in 1945 came an age

Flower Vases, *1984 by Kwon Soon-hyung.* From the Earth Surface *(top), 1988 Won Kyŏng-hwan and* White Porcelain for Water Pot *(bottom), 1987 by Kim Yik-young.*

of confusion and turmoil. Political unrest caused by factional strife between the right and the left was detrimental to artistic activity. Nevertheless, the Chosŏn Industrial Association was organized in 1945, and the Association of Chosŏn Craft Artists was formed in 1946. Many universities and colleges set up courses in fine arts and crafts, and art exhibitions were held more frequently.

Artistic activities suffered another setback with the outbreak of the Korean War in 1950. The country was ravaged by war for three years and many artists were either killed or taken to North Korea.

The National Art Exhibition was reopened in 1953 after the government moved back to Seoul from Pusan, where it had sought refuge during the war. As it more or less marked the official resumption of artistic activities, contemporary craft arts as well may be said to have begun in that year. As the exhibition was held over the years, the opportunities for craft artists to reassert themselves increased and led to the development of a new image of Korean craft arts. The number of craftsmen increased as more universities and colleges opened courses in craft arts. The Korean Industrial Artists

Association, which had replaced the Chosŏn Industrial Artists Association, continued to grow and still holds annual exhibitions.

From the end of the 1960s through the early 1970s, there emerged a number of craft artist groups which, through innovative techniques, experimentalism and camaraderie, exerted a strong influence on the world of craft arts. Through their incentives, galleries, art magazines and other publications specializing in craft arts were launched, and in turn motivated more creative activities.

Contemporary crafts, including the industrial arts which are constantly exposed to new ideas and trends, made a distinct departure from the traditional handicrafts of folk art character.

The Korea Industrial Design Exhibition, established in 1968 to coordinate education in crafts with industrial needs and to upgrade the designs of craft products, has produced many artists and designers through exhibitions with three departments: commercial designs, craft arts and industrial arts. The Medium and Small Industry Promotion Corporation has been backing a nationwide folk arts and craft contest for a number of years. It also staged exhibitions for Olympic souvenirs three times to encourage creative participation of craft artists in the Olympic Games held in Seoul in 1988.

Many artists work and exhibit actively through the organizations they are associated with such as the Korean Designers Association, the Korea Craft Artists Association, the Tojŏn Exhibition, the Korean Metalcraft Association, the Korean Ceramic Artists Association, the Colorist Group, and the National Craft Artists Association.

Meanwhile, the Traditional Handicraft Exhibition has introduced highly skilled craftsmen in metal crafts, ceramics, jade carving, woodcraft, bambooware and lacquerware, rush products, textiles, paper making and other areas. It also has been instrumental in promoting public appreciation of the craftsmen known as human cultural properties and their works.

Besides these exhibitions, opportunities abound for craftsmen to introduce their works to the public as numerous exhibitions are held in Seoul and other major cities year round. Many are backed by influential newspapers and broadcasting systems. There are many universities and colleges and junior colleges in the country that offer craft courses that range from design to production.

International exchange shows and overseas training programs for craft artists are also becoming much more numerous.

Decorative Patterns

A Western scholar once observed that Korean patterns are characterized by continuous, repetitive arrangements, delineation, and a flattening of mass uniquely rendered with a spontaneity, vitality and unconcern for technical perfection. The repetitive arrangement is most evident in *punch'ŏng* ceramics and mother-of-pearl inlaid lacquerware, and the penchant for delineation in inlaid celadonware and early bronzeware.

While this observation is quite true, it should be noted that there were periods during Korea's history when little or no decoration was employed in artistic works. More often than not, Koreans favored monochromism and avoided lavish decorativeness. The comb patterns on the earthenware of the Neolithic Age are among the earliest patterns. Though suggestive of a cultural link with Karelia of northwest Russia, Finland, Denmark and northern Germany, the comb patterns are evidence of an early Korean preference for delineation. European earthenware of the same age, while being basically of the same nature as that of Korea, is decorated with dots. Abstract delineation became increasingly naturalistic with time so that by the early years of Koguryŏ, motifs inspired by animism appeared, as seen in tomb murals. A typical example is the Four Spirits—the blue dragon of the east, white tiger of the west, red phoenix of the south and black tortoise of the north—found in several Koguryŏ tombs. These four creatures appear again and again in all forms of Korean art as symbols of auspiciousness and authority. Linear renderings of quasi-abstract phoenixes and dragons symmetrically arranged can be seen in many Shilla ornaments.

Trees, antlers and bird wings, evidence of Siberian shamanistic traditions, are central to many motifs found in the crowns and pottery of Shilla. Swirling clouds of Han China origin decorate numerous Shilla ornaments as well as the walls of Koguryŏ and Shilla tombs. Honey suckle motifs are featured on the crowns of Paekche and, like the pendants on Shilla belts, probably came from the southern dynasties of China.

Buddhist designs combined with shamanistic, Taoist and Confucian elements are found in the arts of all the periods. Lotus flowers, clouds, lightning, and swastikas can be found in nearly every Buddhist structure or painting, either singly or in various configurations. One of the earliest signs of Buddhist influence is a simple 12-petaled lotus flower encircled by a border of honeysuckle vines and lotus buds painted on the ceiling of a Koguryŏ tomb.

A time-saving technique of stamping decorative designs developed during the Unified Shilla period when the flourishing of Buddhism led to a great demand for burial urns to contain cremated remains and other Buddhist objects. Flowers, beads, clouds, birds and knots are the most common stamped designs. Clouds and

Traditional Korean motifs.

chrysanthemums can be seen stamped on the surfaces of low-quality celadonware and mother-of-pearl inlaid lacquerware of the late Koryŏ period and the *punch'ŏng* ware of the early Chosŏn period. The rendering of patterns with stamps usually appeared during a time of cultural decline.

The simple, sedate harmony that marks Koryŏ celadon pieces and the well-balanced designs that decorate them perhaps can be attributed to Taoist influences. Naturalistic themes of leisurely, idealized life decorate many Koryŏ ceramics, lacquered items, incense burners and bronze *kundika* bottles used in Buddhist rituals. Line drawings of water birds floating on willow-lined streams, carefree children frolicking among lotus leaves or in pools and wild geese flying through a clear autumn sky are some of the most common scenes decorating

Koryŏ works.

Other motifs found in Koryŏ handicrafts include pomegranates, plum blossoms, bamboos, parrots, fish, and, of course, the ever present Buddhist themes of lotus petals and flowers, and a dragon with a jewel in its mouth.

With the emergence of the Chosŏn Dynasty, which suppressed Buddhism in favor of Confucianism around 1392, Confucianism permeated every facet of Korean life and thought. A preference for the simple and monochromic is evident in the arts of this period. The "Four Gentlemen"—plum, orchid, chrysanthemum and bamboo—are the dominant theme in the works of scholar-painters of Chosŏn because of their so-called noble attributes.

The "Four Gentlemen" painted in cobalt characterize much of the Chosŏn ceramics from the 15th century. Birds, especially in combination with plum blossoms, grapevines and evanescent grasses, are found in many forms of Chosŏn handicrafts.

Taoist influence is felt in one of the most popular themes of the time, *shipchangsaeng,* ten animals and objects that symbolize longevity. Rocks, mountains, water, clouds, pine trees, the fungus of immortality, tortoises, deer, cranes and the sun, the *shipchangsaeng* make appealing landscape paintings. In the same Taoist strain are designs of the Chinese ideographs *su* (longevity) and *pok* (good fortune). Rendered in cursive or other non-orthodox artistic styles, these two ideographs adorn various articles of everyday use such as pillow cases and spoons, as well as porcelain ware and woodcraft of Chosŏn. Down-to-earth themes rendered in a humorous way are found in the woodcraft, lacquerware and porcelain of the 19th century.

Nŭnghwap'an (diamond and flower) are the most commonly found patterns in traditional as well as modern Korea. They are found on book covers, wallpaper, and cloth. A typical *nŭnghwap'an* motif is of latticed lightning and chrysanthemums. The lattice invariably is done in a continuous diamond pattern and contained in each diamond is a chrysanthemum. The chrysanthemum is often replaced with the design of a tortoise shell, pomegranate, butterfly, cloud, or other object. These patterns are usually impressed on the material by using woodblock techniques.

Interesting lattice work of the same motifs found in *nŭnghwap'an* often adorn the mulberry papered doors and windows of Korean structures. While simple cross or fret designs are most commonly found, the doors of palatial structures and temples are often decorated with intricate combinations of lattice and flower patterns.

Another interesting group of Korean designs is found on rice-cake molds. These are interesting, invariably simple, and often indecipherable designs, mostly made up of lines and circles.

Despite a predilection for monochromic simplicity, Koreans are sometimes extremely lavish in the decorative arts as is evidenced by the brilliant coloring of the wooden structures of palaces, shrines and temples. The bracketing system of the eaves, the beams and the ceilings of such structures are intriguing studies of almost all patterns imaginable, rendered in the five cardinal colors of red, blue, yellow, white, and black. Dragons and phoenix motifs adorn the ceilings of the throne halls of palaces symbolizing the king's supreme authority, and designs meant to wish him longevity and prosperity decorate other parts of the halls. Colorful cloud and flower designs were adopted for their auspicious symbolism and are bordered by imaginative patterns symbolizing fragrance emanating from flowers. Controlling the configuration of these patterns is the revered theory of *yin-yang* harmony and the philosophy of the five cosmic elements.

Architecture

Traditional

Art produced by the Korean people traditionally has shared aesthetic concepts, motifs, techniques and forms with the art of their neighbors, China and Japan. Yet it has developed a distinctive style of its own. Korean art has seldom displayed the grandeur and aloofness of the Chinese nor the decorative sophistication of the Japanese. In terms of technical perfection and precision, Korean artists have generally been considered inferior to their immediate neighbors. Their strength lay rather in simplicity, spontaneity and a great respect for nature that usually leads to a sensation of modesty and serenity. Architecture provides an excellent example of this characteristic of Korean art. Aside from Buddhism, which was the main inspiration for many outstanding architectural feats, the Chinese philosophies of *yin* and *yang,* the five elements of the universe, geomancy, Taoism and Confucianism were the most evident influences in Korean architecture. As believers in a life of harmony with nature, Koreans readily accepted these naturalistic philosophies and applied their own interpretation of them to architectural plans and placement of buildings.

Excavated prehistoric pit dwellings.

Natural environment has always been regarded as an element of utmost importance in Korean architecture. Numerous Buddhist temples scattered across the country attest to Korea's outstanding tradition of Buddhist art, and frequently were located in mountains noted for their scenic beauty. What is unusual about ancient Korean architects is that they never attempted to resist the magnificence of the natural environment or to compete with it. They unanimously attempted an ideal harmonizing of their structures with the natural surroundings or tried to maintain attitudes of humble compliance. In the popular scheme for temple building in ancient Korea, sanctuaries, chapels and lecture halls were most often arranged in a compound at the foot of a mountain or in a valley in such a way that they were practically hidden by trees and shrubs. Conspicuousness was avoided in architecture much as extremes were in most other fields of figural arts.

In selecting the site for a building of any function, whether private dwellings or public facilities such as palaces and temples, Koreans tended to attach special meaning to the natural surroundings. They never considered a place good enough for a building of any type unless it commanded an appropriate view of "mountains and water." This pursuit of a constant contact with nature was not based only on aesthetics. Geomancy taught that man could not develop properly, intellectually or emotionally nor could expect a life of good fortune without the help of nature. Its principles were applied in selecting dwelling sites for both the living and the dead. A structure was invariably positioned to face south with a mountainous area at its back. Ideally, the mountain had to have "wings" at both sides so that it could embrace the structure which, in keeping with yin-yang considerations, had to have a stream flowing in front. Efforts were made to avoid having manmade construction disrupt the natural contour of the terrain, thereby disrupting the highly revered harmony of nature.

Traditional Korean architecture was seldom inclined towards ostentatiousness in scale or ornamentation. Rooms were of relatively small size and simply decorated. Korean architects favored the natural patterns of wood grains, just as potters were concerned with bringing out the inherent or natural characteristics of clay. Typifying this long-cultivated preference was the *sarangch'ae* or master's salon in the outer quarters of a scholar-official's house built in a Chosŏn period style. A cultured gentleman of respectable demeanor was never supposed to be superfluous in decorating his room. A few pieces of wooden furniture in simple design would suffice to adorn the room which was used mainly for reading and scholarly discussion. His taste for simplicity would often be emphasized by a small landscape painting rendered in ink and some pieces of pottery.

Prehistoric Period

Though the Chinese history *Samkukchi* and other records note the existence of three types of prehistoric dwellings in Korea—pit houses, log houses and elevated houses—only the remains of pit houses have been identified. Pit houses consisted of a 20-150cm-deep pit and a superstructure of grass and clay supported by a tripod-like frame made of logs to provide protection from wind and rain. Pit houses of the Neolithic period had circular or oval pits about

Twin pagodas and plinths mark the site of Kamŭnsa Temple.

5-6 meters in diameter with a hearth at the center. Most of the early ones were located on hills. As these dwellings were moved down nearer to rivers, the pits became rectangular and larger with two hearths.

Log houses were built by laying logs horizontally on top of one another, overlapping at the corners and filling the interstices between the logs with clay to keep the wind out. Similar houses are still found in mountainous areas.

Elevated houses, which probably originated in southern regions, are believed to have been first built as storages to keep grains out of the reach of animals and to keep them cooler. This style still survives in the two-story pavilions and the lookout stands erected in melon patches and orchards.

Three Kingdoms Period

Koguryŏ was not only the first of the three kingdoms to be influenced by Han China but also the one most influenced as evidenced in the construction style of its palaces, temples and tombs. Melding Chinese elements with their original type of construction, the people of Koguryŏ developed their own style. It was characterized by powerful expression and sturdiness,

necessitated by the rugged terrain and harsh climate of the country.

A Chinese writer noted, "The Koguryŏ people like to build palaces well." Patterned tiles and ornate bracket systems were already in use in many palaces in P'yŏngyang, the capital, and other town-fortresses in what now is Manchuria.

The construction of Buddhist temples was enthusiastically undertaken after Buddhism was introduced in 372 by way of China. A series of excavations in 1936-38 unearthed the sites of several major temples near P'yŏngyang, including those in Ch'ŏngam-ri, Wono-ri and Sango-ri. The excavations disclosed that the temples were built in a Koguryŏ style known as "three halls-one pagoda," with a hall in the east, west and north, and an entrance gate in the south. Palace buildings appear to have been arranged in this way also.

Murals in tombs dating from Koguryŏ are important to the study of the architecture of that time as many of them depict buildings which have pillars with entasis and have capitals on the top. The murals show that the bracket structures and coloring on the timbers characteristic of Korean architecture were already in use at the time.

A stone pagoda from the Paekche period (7th century A.D.) at Mirŭksa temple.

Paekche was influenced by Koguryŏ and also by China across the Yellow Sea. As it expanded southward, moving its capital to Ungjin (modern Kongju) in 475 and to Sabi (modern Puyŏ) in 538, its arts became richer and more refined than that of Koguryŏ and its architecture became more flexible with the use of curvilinear designs. Though no Paekche buildings are extant—in fact, no wooden structure of any of the three kingdoms now remains—it is possible to deduce from the Horyuji Temple of Japan, which Paekche artisans and technicians helped to build, that Paekche's architectural arts came into full bloom after the introduction of Buddhism in 384. What remains of the building sites, patterned tiles and other relics, as well as the stone pagodas that have survived the ravages of time, testifies to the highly developed techniques of Paekche.

Many palaces are recorded as having been built in Paekche but no traces of them remain except for the site of Kungnamji Pond, which is mentioned in the *Samguk sagi* (History of the Three Kingdoms). Kungnamji means "pond in the south of the palace."

The site of Mirŭksa, the largest of the Paekche temples and located in Iksan, Chŏlla-buk-do province, was excavated in 1980. The excavation disclosed many hitherto unknown facts about Paekche architecture. A stone pagoda at Mirŭksa is one of two extant Paekche pagodas and the prototype of all Korean pagodas. Mirŭksa had an unusual arrangement of three pagodas erected in a straight line going from east to west, each with a hall to its north. Each pagoda and hall appear to have been surrounded by covered corridors giving the appearance of three separate temples of a style called "one hall-one pagoda." The pagoda at the center was found to have been made of wood, while the other two were of stone. The sites of a large lecture hall and a middle gate were unearthed to the north and south of the wooden pagoda.

When the site of Chŏngnimsa Temple, the

The interior of Sŏkkuram.

site of the other existing Paekche pagoda, was excavated in 1982, the remains of a main hall (Taeungjŏn) and a lecture hall arranged in a line one behind the other were unearthed to the north of the pagoda. The remains of a middle gate, a main gate and a pond arranged in a line one in front of the other were discovered to its south. It was found that the temple was surrounded by corridors from the middle gate to the lecture hall. This "one pagoda" style was typical of Paekche as can be seen at a temple site in Kunsu-ri, Puyŏ and in Kŭmgangsa, also in Puyŏ, that was excavated in 1964. The buildings of Kŭmgangsa, however, were arranged in a line going from east to west rather than from north to south.

Shilla came under Buddhist influence after 527. Since it was separated from China by Koguryŏ and Paekche, China's cultural influence on it was much diluted. This accounted for the delayed but more independent and original cultural development of Shilla.

One of the early Shilla temples, Hwang nyongsa was systematically excavated and studied in 1976, and found to have been of considerable magnitude. It stood in a square walled area, the longest side of which was 288 meters. Just the area enclosed by corridors was about 8,800 *p'yŏng* (19,040 square-meters). The *Samguk yusa* (Memorabilia of the Three Kingdoms) records that there was a nine-story wooden pagoda built here in 645 that was 225 *ch'ŏk* high, or about 80 meters by today's scale. A large image of Sakyamuni Buddha is also recorded to have been enshrined in the main hall with the stone pedestal still remaining. Constructed in the middle of the sixth century, Hwangnyongsa flourished for more than 680 years during which the halls were rearranged many times. In its prime, immediately before Shilla's unification of the peninsula in 668, it was arranged in the "three halls-one pagoda" style, quite unlike that of the "three halls-three pagodas style" of Paekche's Mirŭksa.

Anapchi, a recently restored pond in Kyŏngju, was part of a detached palace.

Another major Shilla temple was Pun-hwangsa, on the site of which still stands three stories of what is recorded to have been a nine-story pagoda. As the remains show, the pagoda was made of stones cut to look like bricks. A set of stone flagpole supports and other stone relics also remain.

The Unified Shilla Period

Shilla defeated Paekche in 660 and Koguryŏ in 668 to unify the peninsula for the first time under what is known as Unified Shilla. As it had provided the moral strength to defeat the other two kingdoms, Buddhism flourished and along with it architecture and the arts. Many architectural masterpieces were created during the period, Pulguksa Temple and its grotto shrine Sŏkkuram the best examples. The development of Buddhist architecture brought the development of other forms of architecture, including palatial and residential types. An example of palace architecture of the time is Tonggung Palace in Kyŏngju, where a garden pond called Anapchi has been excavated and restored.

More than 50 major temples are mentioned in historical records. More than 10 of them,

including Pulguksa, are still in operation though their wooden structures are of more recent construction. The most artistically constructed is Pulguksa, which was completed in 752 with Kim Tae-sŏng as the master builder. Located on the western slope of T'ohamsan Mountain, the temple sits on tall terraces of natural and dressed stones of varying sizes that fit together beautifully. Stone railings run the length of the terraces. There once was a lotus pond in front of the temple, symbolically separating it from the secular world. The temple proper is approached by four staircases called bridges. The bridges in the east lead to the Tabot'ap and Sŏkkat'ap pagodas and Taeungjŏn, the main hall where an image of Sakyamuni Buddha is housed. Those in the west lead to Kŭngnakjŏn, the hall in which an image of Amita Buddha is housed. With Tabot'ap and Sokkat'ap, the two most beautiful Shilla pagodas, the temple is an example of the "two pagodas" style prevalent at the time and shows that stone pagodas replaced the wooden ones that had been favored in the "one pagoda" style.

The wooden structures now visible at Pulguksa were mostly constructed in the latter

Constructed before 1362, Muryangsujŏn of Pusŏksa Temple is one of Korea's oldest wooden structures.

part of the Chosŏn period (1392-1910), as the originals were destroyed in the course of frequent foreign invasions. Musŏljŏn, the Hall of Meeting; Pirojŏn, the Hall of Vairocana; Kwanŭm jŏn, the Hall of Avalokitesvara Bodhisattva, and the corridors were restored in 1972.

Sŏkkuram, a man-made grotto higher up on Mt. T'ohamsan, is the greatest artistic masterpiece of Korean grotto construction, with a perfect image of Buddha enshrined in it. An annex of Pulguksa, it was deliberately located to look out over the East Sea. It is comprised of an anteroom connected by a small passageway to a large rotunda and is like a complete temple in that it contains all of the elements and features generally found in the halls that compose a temple. Eight guardians of Buddhism are carved in relief of the walls of the antechamber and four Lokapalas on both sides of the door to the rotunda. The Sakyamuni Buddha is seated at the center of the rotunda, and images of 11 bodhisattvas and 10 disciples of Buddha are carved in relief along the wall. Statues of bodhisattvas are housed in niches in the upper part of the wall under the domed ceiling, and the ceiling is decorated with relief work. The wooden supper-

structure in ront of the grotto was added in 1964 when the grotto was repaired.

Shilla's palace construction is best represented by Tonggung, the palace of the crown prince. The site of the palace was excavated in 1976 to reveal the location of a hall called Imhaejŏn and Anapchi Pond.

Koryŏ Period

Inheriting Shilla culture, including Buddhism, and being influenced by the architectural trends of Sung China, Koryŏ in its early years developed an architectural style of brackets with curved bracket arms on top of columns called columnhead bracketing. With brackets placed only on the column heads, the framework was rather simple, and the ceiling was left bare with no covering panels or canopies, and roofs were mostly gabled. Kŭngnakjŏn, the Nirvana Hall of Pongjŏngsa Temple; Muryangsujŏn, the Amita Hall of Pusŏksa Temple both in Andong; Kyŏngsangbuk-do, Taeungjŏn, the Sakyamuni Hall of Sudŏksa Temple in Yesan; Ch'ungch'ŏ ngnam-do and the entrance gate of the Kaeksa Guest House in Kangnŭng, Kangwon-do, are representative of column-head styling. The

Kŭnjŏngjŏn, the throne hall in Kyŏngbokkung Palace in Seoul was built in 1394 and rebulit in 1867.

Nirvana Hall of Pongjongsa is the oldest wooden structure extant in Korea, having been reconstructed in 1363, as was determined when the building was dismantled for renovation in 1971.

Another style involving multi-cluster brackets influenced by Yüan China emerged after the mid-Koryŏ period and continued into the Chosŏn period. With clusters of brackets placed not only on the column heads but also on the horizontal beams between columns, this style was much heavier. A building thus constructed was sturdier and had a more imposing appearance. The roof was usually hipped and gabled and, unlike the column-head style, the ceiling was covered with panels, creating a checkered appearance.

During this period, Buddhism became tinged with Taoism, shamanism and other beliefs. The traditional styles of "one pagoda" or "two pagodas" for a certain number of halls disappeared from use as such shrines, as Ch'ilsŏnggak for the spirits of the Seven Stars, and Sanshin-gak for the *Sanshin*, or "Mountain Spirit," were

added to temple facilities. The placement of structures became more complicated with the introduction of geomancy into temple planning by a highly esteemed monk named Tosŏn-kuksa.

The best temples of the period were Hŭng wangsa, Purilsa and Manboksa. Though none still survive, the way in which they were arranged has become known through excavations of the temple sites.

Chosŏn Period

Under Chosŏn's suppression of Buddhism in favor of Confucianism, construction of temples declined drastically, while construction of Confucian shrines and private and public Confucian academies flourished. A simpler system of column-head bracketing was generally favored in the highly Confucian society, though the multicluster bracket style was still used in some Chosŏn structures. Kŭngnakjŏn of Muwisa Temple, Kuksajŏn and Hasadang of Songgwangsa Temple and Haet'almun Gate

Namdaemun, Seoul's South Gate, was bulit in 1396 and reconstructed in 1948.

of Togapsa Temple are examples of the column-head bracket style, and Namdaemun Gate of Seoul, Taeungjŏn Hall of Pongjŏngsa and Namdaemun Gate of Kaesŏng represent the multicluster bracket style of the early Chosŏn period.

In the aftermath of a series of foreign invasions, a new architectural style with wing-like brackets emerged in the mid-Chosŏn period. Simpler and more economical than the column-head style, it was well suited to the difficult financial situation the nation was experiencing caused by the wars. However, palace structures and important temple facilities continued to be built with the more ornate multicluster brackets as shown in the Myŏngjŏn Hall in Ch'anggyŏng-gung Palace, Taeungjŏn of T'ongdosa Temple, P'alsangjŏn of Pŏpchusa, and Kakhwangjŏn of Hwaŏmsa. Public buildings built in the wing-like bracket style include the main hall and Yongnyŏngjŏn Hall of Chongmyo, the royal ancestral shrine.

Toward the end of the 17th century, the *Sirhak* or "Practical Learning" school of Confucianism came into being. It greatly influenced the arts, encouraged scientific studies and inspired an awareness of nationalism through out the 18th century. Western thought and culture surged into the country, and architecture as well as other fields of art underwent a period of decline characterized by redundancy and superfluous decoration. Structures from this latter Chosŏn period are the Injŏngjon Hall of Ch'angdŏkkung, Chunghwajŏn Hall of Tŏksugung, and Tongdaemun, the East Gate of Seoul.

Chosŏn period town walls are best represented by one constructed around Seoul in 1396 and rebuilt in 1422, and one around Suwon completed in 1796 employing techniques highly influenced by Western methods. The Seoul wall had four major gates at each compass point and four smaller ones in between.

The greater part of the Chosŏn palaces were all but destroyed during the Japanese invasions of 1592-98. Most of the wooden palace structures now extant in Seoul were reconstructed in the middle and late Chosŏn periods. The multi-cluster bracket style was employed in most of the major palace structures, such as the audience halls and entrance gates, and the winglike bracket style in minor structures such as houses and pavilions. Few palace structures were built in the column-head style.

The roofs of the palace gates are hipped while the roofs of the main structures are hipped and gabled. Decorative ceramic figures in the shape of dragon and other animal heads are at each end of the ridges and rows of *chapsang*, which are clay figures derived from a popular Chinese story, line the sloping ridges to guard against evil spirits.

The ceilings of the major structures are finished with checkered panels or with highly decorated canopies that hide the framework of the roofs. Brackets and ceilings are colorfully painted, and the areas where the tie beams and pillars meet are decorated with carved corbels.

Residential Structures

Simple houses with a rectangular floor plan divided into a kitchen and one other room, common in mountainous areas as well as some farming areas, are reminiscent of the prehistoric pit houses. The *ondol* system of heating by channeling smoke through under-the-floor flues, used throughout Korea's history and still used today, developed from the hearths of the pit houses.

The rectangular floor of the earliest houses developed into an L-shaped plan and then into a U-shaped or square plan with a courtyard at the center. Upper-class houses consisted of a number of separate buildings generally with one to accommodate women and children, one for the men of the family and their guests, and one for servants, all enclosed within a wall. A family ancestral shrine was built behind the house. Ideally, a lotus pond and sometimes a pavilion were positioned in front of the house outside the wall.

Upper-class houses had a sturdy framework and many decorative elements, though the use of the colorful *tanch'ŏng* patterns found on temples and palaces was prohibited. The roofs were elegantly curved and accentuated with slightly uplifted eaves. Some had decorative round tiles at the edges of the roof along the eaves.

Houses of the lower class were usually made of logs and had little decorative wood-work. They were usually thatched. No ordinary house, neither upper-or lower-class, could be larger than 99 *kan*, a term referring to the square space inside four pillars that was used for the size of traditional structures.

It was toward the end of the last century, when Korea opened its doors to the world, that Western architecture was first introduced, signaling an era of rapid changes and diverse styles.

Modern

Any new visitor to Seoul will recognize that the teeming capital city is a fascinating showcase of architectural trends and styles. They represent not only Korea's indigenous cultural background, but also various designs, schemes and techniques of foreign artists of universal influence from different ages. The city's ever-changing skyline speaks for the speed with which Korea has developed in recent decades as well as its struggle to accomplish modernization amid the tides of Western culture and civilization. The city offers a kaleidoscopic view of the works of innumerable architects and engineers from both ancient and modern periods. Modern high-rises stand side by side with ancient royal palaces, private houses, temples, shrines, and gates.

The impact of Western architecture began to hit Korea during the last decades of the 19th century when Korea started to enter into treaties with foreign governments. In 1900, a British architect, at the request of the ruling family of the Chosŏn Dynasty, designed a royal residence of a Renaissance revival style in the Tŏksugung palace grounds in downtown Seoul. The two-story stone edifice, which was completed in 1909 and later used as the National Museum, was one of many Western-style buildings erected by foreigners in Seoul and major provincial cities around the turn of the century. Architecture was a segment of Korean life that

The Art Gallery of the Seoul Arts Center.

underwent the most obvious transformations during this period of turmoil when construction was fueled by the needs of foreign powers in Korea to build new structures of both a practical and symbolic nature. Buildings from that time include the Gothic-style Myŏngdong Cathedral (1898), the Renaissance-style Bank of Korea's main building (1912) and Seoul Railroad Station (1925), the Romanesque Seoul Anglican Church (1916) and the Seoul City Hall (1925).

Western-style buildings continued to emerge in Seoul, impressing its residents with their novel appearances and unfamiliar conveniences, until the 1930s. Western architects and engineers built many of them, especially churches and offices for foreign legations, but the Japanese gradually took over construction as their political power increased. The Japanese put up a number of new buildings for public offices, banks, schools and businesses, mostly in classical Western styles modified to suit their taste. The most important of the remaining structures from this colonial period is the building that housed the offices of Japan's government-general, though the interest it holds as an architectural monument for Koreans was overshadowed by the political implications of its design and location. The four-story, Renaissance-style granite structure, designed by a German architect, was completed in 1926 after 10 years of construction. It was used for the central government offices after national liberation in 1945 until 1983. It was renovated extensively from 1983 to August 1986, when it became the home of the National Museum of Korea.

The late 1930s to the 1950s was a dark period in the history of modern architecture in Korea. Japan was engaged in prolonged warfare and Koreans were suffering from extreme economic deprivation and harsh political control. Architectural activity was stagnant until after the 1950-53 Korean War.

In the early years of modern architecture's development, Koreans gained new ideas and skills from Western architects and engineers while they worked on important construction projects. Some young engineers were employed by the Japanese government and a few were successful enough to open their own firms later. Among these early pioneers were Pak Kil-yong, who designed the Hwashin Department Store building, and Pak Tong-jin, who designed the main building of Korea University. These architects, who were active in the early 1930s, are two of the most significant figures in the history of Korean architecture as they were the first Korean designers of important structures about whom there is any recorded history. Traditionally, Korean architecture relied on apprenticeship, and carpenters and masons were trained under master technicians. Formal education in Western architectural concepts and engineering was first introduced in Korea to 1916.

Korean architecture entered a new phase of development during the post-Korean War reconstruction with the return of two ambitious young architects of great talent from overseas universities—Kim Chung-ŏp from France and Kim Su-gŭn from Japan. They led Korean architecture to universalism in the following years. The office-residence of the French Embassy in Seoul designed by Kim Chung-ŏp, and the Liberty Center designed by Kim Su-gŭn, both constructed in the early 1960s, were a refreshing addition to Seoul's architectural environment. Both artists were influenced by the brutalism of Le Corbusier, but their different approaches have contributed greatly to the development of Korean architecture and have been a point of continuing academic debate.

Some structures of special note in Seoul include Kim Chung-ŏp's Samillo Building, significant because it introduced new technology in the 1970s; Ŏm Tŏk-mun's Sejong Cultural Center; Pak Chun-myŏng's 63-story Daehan Life Insurance Building; and Kim Su-gŭn's Kyongdong Methodist Church and the Olympic Stadium, showing the influence of the lines of Chosŏn ceramics.

Music

Traditional

Korea is rich in musical culture, and its music is distinctive despite tremendous influences from China. The same is true for Japanese music despite Korean influence. Evidence of these influences can presently be found in the existence of Koreanized-Chinese music called *tang-ak* in Korea and of Japanized-Korean music called *komagaku* in Japan. The Korean term *tang-ak* literallymeans music from T'ang Dynasty China. Similarly the Japanese term *komagaku* signifies music from the Koryŏ Dynasty in Korea.

Korean traditional music can be roughly divided into two major categories, *chŏng-ak* and *sog-ak*: music for the ruling class and for the common people, respectively. Within these two major types are various subcategories that make up the whole of Korean music. Thus, in *chŏng-ak* there are two different, but somewhat related meanings. In this broader sense the term refers to the elegant musical style that was considered "right" for the Korean ruling class in terms of Confucian philosophy, and within this broader meaning it also refers to ensemble music for men of high social status outside of the court. In this category, three important terms are *a-ak, tang-ak*, and *hyang-ak*. *Chŏng-ak* and *a-ak* can be used interchangeably, in their broader sense, referring to music for the ruling class, which includes *tang-ak, hyang-ak*, and Confucian ritual music. In its narrower sense *a-ak* refers to ritual temple music, of which at the present time only one example remains, *Munmyoak*. *Munmyoak* is music performed at *Munmyo*, the shrine where Confucius and his disciples are honored. *Tang-ak* refers to secular music of both the Chinese T'ang and Sung dynasties, which was altered to become court music after its introduction to Korea. *Hyang-ak* simply means native Korean music, a noted example of which is *Sujech'ŏn*, a piece of instrumental music often claimed to be at least 1,300 years old, which would predate the first compilation of Gregorian chants. Court music, a subcategory

A classical orchestra performs Sujech'ŏn *(top), a singer performs* Kasa *(long narrative song) to the accompaniment of a traditional ensemble (middle), and a kayagŭm orchestra performs* Kayagŭm Pyŏngch'ang *(bottom).*

of *chŏng-ak,* includes three types: ritual, banquet, and military music. Ritual music includes Confucian music and royal shrine music, while banquet music is of course music for courtly banquets. *Sujech'ŏn* is one of the most famous pieces of banquet music.

Music for the upper class consists of a type of ensemble music, *p'ungnyu,* the most sophisticated Korean lyric song genre; *kagok,* and the indigenous Korean popular song, *sijo. P'ungnyu* is an archaic word that formerly meant music in general. Its present literal meaning denotes the state of being in which a man at leisure physically and mentally removes himself from the everyday world into a harmonious mood suitable for the appreciation of poetry, music, and female companionship. When the term is used in the context of Korean classical music, however, it refers to a type of ensemble music for the nobility. One variety of this music, called *chul-p'ungnyu,* consists mainly of stringed instruments. A second variety, *taep'ungnyu,* consists mainly of wind instruments, and a third is a combination of the first two. *Kagok* uses a rhythmic pattern of either a 16-beat *changdan* (which literally means "long-short") or its varied form, a 10-beat *changdan.* Any *kagok* selection is based on the *ujo* or *kyemyŏnjo* mode, or sometimes on both. Instruments used for accompaniment are the *kŏmungo, kayagŭm, yang-gŭm, haegŭm, p'iri* and *changgo.*

Sog-ak, music for the commoner includes shaman music, Buddhist music, folk songs, farmers' music called *nong-ak,* a form of dramatic song called *p'ansori,* nd an instrumental solo music called *sanjo.* In shaman music, the role of an inspired female shaman priest called a *mudang* is very important. The *mudang* plays the part of a medium between the visible world and the supernatural. Singing, dancing, and instrument playing are always involved. One of the most important types of Buddhist music is called *pŏmp'ae,* a song of praise to Buddha, and today preserved by only a few priests. To promote this music, the government has designated *pomp'ae* as an intangible cultural asset and is taking steps to encourage new devotees of the art.

Since Korea traditionally has been an agricultural nation, the life of the farmer has always had significant influence on the musical history of the country. The most interesting characteristic of farmers' music is its 12 different rhythmic patterns called *shipich'ae,* which are led by a small gong called *kkwaenggwari.* One of the more appealing types of *sog-ak* is the *sanjo,* an instrumental solo piece originally in improvisational style for various instruments: the *kayagŭm, kŏmun-go, taegŭm, haegŭm, tanso,* and *p'iri. P'ansori* is another musical treasure of leading importance in Korea and can be defined as song in drama, an indigenous opera-like production with one singer storyteller. Within the *p'ansori, aniri* is the spoken description of the dramatic content between songs, and *pallim* is the physical motion of the drama.

Musical Instruments

Korea has developed a large number of musical instruments, and a total of 60 different kinds now are preserved at the National Classical Music Institute. Fifteen of these are no longer in use, some because of changes in musical fashion, others because of the discontinuance of ceremonies, associated with the royal court. The remaining 45 are all played today, though with varying degrees of frequency.

Following is a brief introduction to the most frequently used of the 14 chordophones, 17 aerophones, 13 idiophones, and 16 membranophones.

Kŏmun-go

The *kŏmun-go* is representative of zithers with six strings of twisted silk. The second, third, and fourth strings are stretched over 16 fixed frets and tuned by round pegs, while the other strings are stretched over movable bridges and tuned by moving the bridges to the left or right. The strings are plucked with a bamboo rod (*sultae*) which is held between the index and middle fingers of the right hand, while the left hand presses on the strings to produce microtones.

Kayagŭm

The *kayagŭm,* which is related to the Chinese

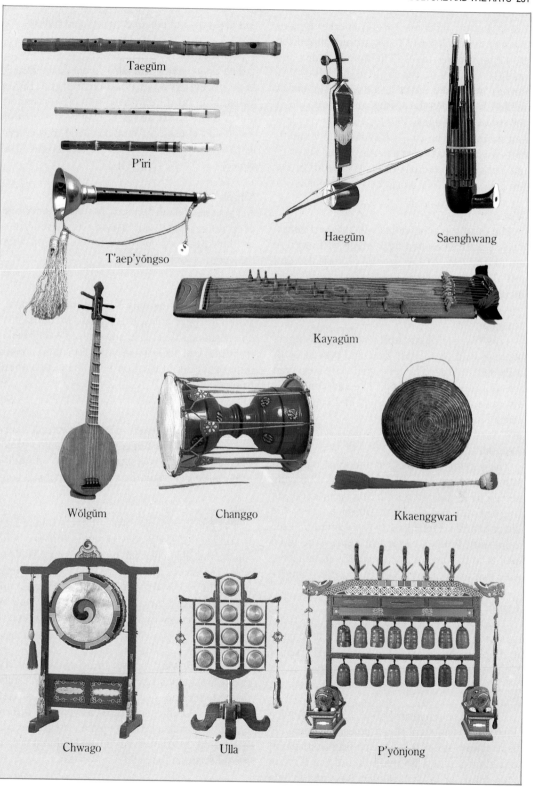

Taegŭm

P'iri

T'aep'yŏngso

Haegŭm

Saenghwang

Kayagŭm

Wŏlgŭm

Changgo

Kkaenggwari

Chwago

Ulla

P'yŏnjong

cheng and the Japanese *koto*, is another type of Korean zither. It has 12 silk strings supported by 12 movable bridges. The thumb, index and middle fingers of the right hand pluck the strings, while the index and middle fingers of the left hand touch the strings on the left side of the movable bridges. The tone quality is clear and delicate. The *sanjo Kayagŭm* is a small, narrow type of *kayagŭm* patterned after the original *kayagŭm* called *pŏpgŭm*. It is used for the fast fingering of folk music and *sanjo* music.

Ajaeng

The *ajaeng* is a bowed seven-stringed zither. Played with a resined bow made of forsythia wood, the tone of the *ajaeng* is majestic and full. The instrument is used primarily in court orchestras to reinforce the bass instruments.

Haegŭm

This two-stringed fiddle without a fingerboard is held on the left knee and played vertically with a bow. The tone quality is nasal and the sound is penetrating. The instrument is always found in Korean court and folk music ensembles.

Taegŭm

The *taegŭm* is the largest and most representative transverse flute of Korea. It has a blowing hole, a hole covered with a thin membrane, six finger holes and five non-finger holes at the lower end, for a total of 13. The vibration of the membrane lends a beautiful, expressive tonal quality to the music. The *taegŭm* is an indispensible instrument in any Korean music ensemble.

Tangjŏk

The *tangjŏk* is the smallest transverse flute, similar to the piccolo of the west. The tone quality is pure and clear, particularly in the upper register. It is only played with the *taegŭm*.

P'iri

The *p'iri*, a cylindrical oboe, has a long, wide double reed and eight finger holes, including the back thumb hole. It is the leading instrument and always takes the main melody in Korean court music or folk ensembles. Its sound is loud and has a distinctive tone quality and timbre.

T'aep'yŏngso

The *t'aep'yŏngso*, literally "great peace flute," is a conical wooden oboe with eight finger holes, a metal mouthpiece, and a cup-shaped metal bell. It produces a loud and piercing sound and is used for farmers' band music, traditional military band music and some folk music.

Nagak

This conch shell trumpet, producing only one deep note, is used exclusively as a drone in a military processional band in alternation with the *nabal*, a long trumpet.

Nabal

The *nabal* is the only Korean metal trumpet. Without finger holes, it is used to produce only one sustained tone. It is now played exclusively in military processional bands to sound a one-note drone in alternation with the conch shell trumpet.

Tanso

The *tanso* is a small, notched, vertical bamboo flute with five fingerholes, one on the back. The tone quality is exceedingly pure and delicate, making it a favorite solo instrument.

Pak

The *pak* is a clapper shaped like a folded fan. It consists of six pieces of wood loosely held together at the upper end by a cord made of deer skin. The pieces of wood are thicker at the loose ends. The *pak* is clapped once to start a piece of music and three times rapidly to mark the end of a piece. It is used by court and ritual orchestras.

P'yŏnjong

The *p'yŏnjong* is a set of 16 chromatically tuned bronze bell chimes hung in an elaborately decorated frame. The bells are the same size and shape but the thickness of their walls are different, giving each a different pitch. The player sits behind the instrument on the ground and uses a mallet to strike the bells.

P'yŏn-gyŏng

The *p'yŏn-gyŏng* is a set of 16 L-shaped slabs of jade stone. The counterpart of the bell chimes, it has played an essential role in court ceremonies since the 12th century. The stone slabs are the same size and shape but vary in thickness so that each has a different pitch. The thickest produces the highest pitch while the thinnest one, the lowest.

Kkwaenggwari

The *kkwaenggwari*, the smallest gong, is struck with a wooden mallet to produce a sharp, attention-commanding sound. It is used for farmers' band music (*nong-ak*) and shaman music. In farmers' band music, it is played by the leader to signal rhythmic patterns for the other musicians.

Changgo

The *changgo*, or hourglass drum, is the most frequently used accompaniment in almost all forms of Korean music. The thick skin of the left side is struck with the palm and produces a soft, low sound, and the thin skin of the right side is struck with a bamboo stick to produce a hard, crisp sound. The pitch of the right side can be made higher or lower by tightening or loosening the tension of the drum head. This is done by moving the central belts encircling the V-shaped laces to the right or to the left.

Chwago

The *chwago* is a medium-size barrel drum hung from a frame. Its sound reinforces the hourglass drum. It is used mainly in court music to accompany wind ensembles or full orchestras.

Classical Western

Among the many theories about the introduction of Western music to Korea, the most commonly accepted is that it was the teaching of hymns taught by foreign missionaries. Accordingly, 1885, the year American missionaries Horace G. Underwood and Henry G. Appenzeller arrived in Chemulp'o Port (today's Inch'ŏn), may be regarded as the beginning of Western music in Korea.

From that time, music from the West began to permeate Korea's musical culture. It flourished so well that around the turn of the century, conflicts between pro-Western and pro-Korean musical viewpoints began to arise. Many asked why Koreans should indulge in Western music.

There was not much development not refinement during the Japanese colonial rule, but some pioneer musicians did sow the seeds for future growth.

While traditional Korean folk songs formed the musical mainstream from the 1920s to the 1945 liberation, Western-style songs like "Pongsŏnhwa," composed by Hong Nan-p'a in 1919, enjoyed increasing popularity. Some of the most popular composers during that time were Ch'ae Tong-sŏn, Hyŏn Che-myŏng, Yi Hung-yŏl, Kim Se-hyŏng, Kim Tong-jin, Cho Tu-nam, and Kim Sŏng-t'ae. Many of their songs remain popular.

In 1948 Chŏng Hoe-gap presented a composition of his own entitled String Quartet No. 1 at a concert commemorating the graduation of the first class of the Music College of Seoul National University. Two years later an opera composed by Hyŏn Che-myŏng called *Ch'un hyangjŏn*, based on a traditional love story by the same name, opened and was enthusiastically received. These two events gave rise to expectations of active production of new works in composition; however, the Korean War (1950-53) brought a brutal halt to any new development.

Korea's music world was introduced to modern compositional techniques in 1955 when the country began to recover from the devastation wrought by the war. Around that time, composer Na Un-yŏng began to present to the public works based on a 12-tonesystem and soon other musicians began to join the mainstream of world music. In 1958 the members of the Composition Department of the Music College of Seoul National University formed a composers club that played an important role in the creation of new music in Korea. Composers like Yun Yi-sang residing in West Germany, and the late Ahn Ik-t'ae, composer of the national anthem of Korea, won worldwide fame for their distinctive musical talents in composition.

The KBS Symphony Orchestra performing at the Sejong Cultural Center in downtown Seoul.

More and more composers turned to chamber music during the 1970s, increasingly employing the techniques of their Western contemporaries. Leading musicians at this time included Chŏng Hoe-gap, Yi Sŏng-jae, Kang Sŏk-hŭi, Paek Pyŏng-dong, Kim Yong-jin, Pak Chae-yŏl, Na In-yŏng and Yi Yong-ja. A group of young composers centered around Kang Sok-hui won prizes in competitions sponsored by the World Association of Modern Music, demonstrating the level to which composition in Korea had risen.

Korea's first symphony orchestra was established in September 1945 under the name of the Korea Philharmonic Orchestra Society. The Seoul Philharmonic Orchestra was inaugurated in 1957 and the KBS (Korean Broadcasting System) Symphony Orchestra was formed in 1956. There has been a rapid growth of orchestras in the provincial cities as well in recent years: the symphony orchestras of Pusan, Taegu, Inch'ŏn, Kwangju and Suwon hold regular concerts, and the Korean Symphony, a privately operated orchestra, held its inaugural concert in 1985.

The quality of music performed in concerts, however, has been weak, given the large number of orchestras, ensembles and other groups. This is due in part to the interruption of musicians' instrumental training caused by the Korean War. In addition, only since the mid-1960s have there been quality performances by musicians who have returned home following musical training abroad.

The first opera performed here was Verdi's *La Traviata* in January 1948. Since that time, many opera groups have emerged and disappeared in the past 40 years. The National Opera Group, the Kim Cha-kyŏng Opera Group and the Seoul Opera Group led by Kim Pong-im are

Opera is one of the popular musical forms in Korea.

the most active. The National Opera Group opened in 1965 with a performance of Puccini's *La Boheme*. The Kim Cha-kyŏng Opera Group opened in 1968 with *La Traviata*.

Several Korean operas have been performed, including *Ch'unhyangjŏn* by Hyŏn Che-myŏng, *Prince Hodong* by Chang Il-nam, *Shim-ch'ŏngjŏn* by Kim Tong-jin, *Non-gae* by Hong Yŏnt'aek and *Ch'obun* by Pak Chae-yŏl, as well as many foreign operas including *La Traviata, Tosca, Madam Butterfly, Aida, Manon* and *Le Nozze di Figaro*. Church choirs have long led chorus activities. The first professional chorus came into being in 1973 with the formation of the National Chorus, followed by the Seoul City Chorus in 1978 and the Daewoo Chorus, a privately operated chorus, in 1983. Na Yŏng-su, one the nation's foremost chorus conductors, contributed greatly to raising the level of choral music.

An increasing number of Korean musicians are performing in concerts and other fields abroad. Many have won highest acclaim from foreign critics and audiences. A number have taken top awards in international competitions, and some have assumed prestigious posts as conductors or in other functions.

Among them are Chŏng Kyŏng-hwa (Chung Kyung-hwa), one of the world's foremost violinists; violinist Kang Tong-sŏk, a prize winner at the Elizabeth Concours; and violinist Kim Yŏng-uk, who is based in New York. Pianists performing abroad include Han Tong-il, who resides in the United States, Paek Kŏn-u, who resides in Paris, and Sŏ Hye-gyŏng and Sŏ Chuhŭi. Baritone Ch'oe Hyŏn-su won top honors in the voice section of the Ninth International Tchaikovsky Musical Competition in July 1990 in Moscow. He also received the Tchaikovsky Award, a prize for the best interpreter of

Tchaikovsky's music. Conductors working abroad include Chŏng Myŏng-hun who was appointed as the music director and principal conductor of the French National Bastille Opera.

The Yewon School and the Seoul Arts High School are two well-established schools that provide training in the arts for talented young people. Numerous graduates from these schools have gone on to study at music conservatories of international fame, including the highly regarded Juilliard School of Music. The students of these schools are expected to contribute much to the development of music in Korea.

Dance

Traditional

Korea's six varieties of traditional dance include: shaman, Buddhist and Confucian rituals, court entertainment, country or folk dances, and the mask-dance drama. Characteristic Korean movements are the heel walk, and turning on the heels; raising the body gently and lightly from the bent knee position; slight vibrations from the hips up; pulses from the shoulders; economy of action; and improvisation. The most distinctive of Korean movements is the suspended position, balancing on one foot with the free leg extended while the shoulders softly rise and fall. This conveys a deep sense of ecstatic power. Ecstasy permeates all of the types of dance, not only the shaman and farmers' folk dance, but even the extremely formal limited court dance in its shoulder pulsations.

Korean expression, as is true of Asian dance in general, differs from that of the West. The West defines the personality, the sex, the body of the dancer. The Korean dancer is impersonal, with sexuality de-emphasized. While Western dancers like to dominate space and play with light, sound, texture and dynamics, Korean dancers are not interested in external aspects of acrobatic physical motion but rather in expressing metaphysical joy. The Korean body, concealed in voluminous silks, with full sleeves,

becomes the image of some idealized flower or bird inhabiting a pure and abstract landscape, reflecting several thousand years of influence from surrounding cultures.

The origins of Korean dance are sacred, magical and ritual in character. Of Korea's three ritual forms, shaman, Buddhist, and Confucian, shamanism is the most highly developed of all and pervades all the others. In Confucianism, where the dancing is minimal, the ceremony is everything. Twice a year at Sungkyun-kwan University on Confucius' birthday, the second day of the Ninth Moon, and on the 21st day of the Third Moon, eight rows of eight students honor Confucius and several other Chinese and Korean scholars, by rhythmically bowing left, right and center. In the first half they hold a flute in one hand and a dragon-headed stick in the other, and in the second half they beat wooden hammers on wooden shields. Graded rows of jadeite stone gongs, and bronze bells are part of the antique musical accompaniment for the reverent slow-motion bowing, the ritualized incantation of poems and the libations of "divine wine." No one is so inconsiderate as to walk down the center path, which is left free to welcome the spirits. No such ceremony exists in China; Korea alone preserves this celebration.

Attending the grand ceremony at Chongmyo (Royal Family Shrine) on the first Sunday of May, when reverence is paid to the spirits of 20 Chosŏn kings and queens, music and dance designated Intangible Cultural Asset No. 1 by the Korean Government is performed. Court dignitaries make an imposing spectacle officiating before the 20 individual shrines. The special music, composed by King Sejong, using the same graded-by-thickness jade-stone gongs, bells and other ancient instruments, has a richer texture than that for the Confucian rites. The *Ilmu* (line dance), again eight rows of eight students in purple-lined cerise robes and courtier hats, is again a little more elaborate than the Confucian rites. They circle their arms and forearms, and bending one knee, lift the other leg from the ground three times, in addition to repeated bows facing the shrine, the west and the east. This was introduced to Korea from China's Sung Dynasty in 1114. Performed in

A court dance performance.

slow motion, the viewer feels a sacral reverence for the ancestral spirits.

Confucian influence on dance has been mainly repressive, but Buddhism—with a more permissive attitude—has contributed a positive influence, as some of the most beautiful court dances and many shaman rituals, especially those for the dead, demonstrate.

Korean court dance has ancient roots. Four hundred years before the emergence of Western renaissance court ballets in Italy, in the middle Koryŏ period (11th century), women court performers created elaborate poetic spectacles. These had sung verses as prelude and postlude, symbolic properties, magnificent costumes and special music. The boating dance for example, was performed by 32 maidens, six of whom pulled a boat with two children aboard. After dropping anchor, the craft was made to circle, pulled with ropes by four dancers. As many as 200 performers grouped in highly formalized patterns participated in other magnificent royal entertainments. Some, dating from King Hŏngang's reign (r.876-886) of the Shilla Kingdom, such as *Ch'ŏyong* Dance, or the

Dance of the Dragon of the Eastern Sea, indicate the cross-cultural exchanges of music and dance with T'ang China.

Korean art was highly prized at the T'ang court. Three Koguryŏ dances were included in the classic repertory, and two of them were immortalized by poets. Yi Po wrote:

Crowned in a golden hat the dancer
Like a white colt turns slowly,
The white sleeves fluttering against the wind
Like a bird from the Eastern Sea.

When it was performed in China, Yi Po's lines were sung with the dance.

Far more than just a passive go-between or cultural transmitter of Chinese arts to Japan, Korean artists created much of the best music and many of the dance forms given to both countries. Japan's artistic debt to Korea is enormous. As early as A.D. 285, Korean artists introduced what became the beginning of Japanese music, and in 548, more musicians were sent to Japan. During the Paekche Kingdom, the Korean Mimaji, returning from

The Ch'ŏyongmu.

the T'ang court, introduced China's masked comedy pantomime to Japan in A.D. 612 Known as *gigaku*, it was popularly sustained at the court in Nara.

The *Ch'ŏyong* or Dance of the Dragon of the Eastern Sea is a remarkable Korean classic. Originally a solo, later a duet, and by the time of the early Chosŏn period, a quintet, it was performed as an exorcism of all evils at the court before the New Year. The men, each wearing a brown faced mask and having individual costumes of blue, white, red, black and yellow signifying the five directions or four cardinal points and center, perform solo turning sequences. Then each dances in duet with the center figure, and all turn in unison. The music is a shaman song; the masks may have a link to Tibet; and the use of long white sleeves may derive from China.

Titles of the Korean court dances project images of birds and flowers: *Beautiful People Picking Peonies, the Coming of the Phoenix, the Nightingale* and the *Crane Dance*. The *Sword Dance*, performed today only by women, is a weapon dance which makes no pretense to swordsmanship, being a playfully percussive

spectacle. These genteel subjects reflect sophisticated delicacy of taste and quiet humor, as in the *Bellgame Dance*, where two teams of women compete throwing wooden balls through holes in two flower-bedecked gates. Those who succeed in making a goal receive a peony flower. Those who fail receive a black line painted on one cheek by a "brush girl." The tossing, awarding of prizes and penalties are all executed in flowing rhythmic movement, the whole preceded by ushers with standards, who sing opening and closing songs.

The classical *Nightingale Dance* requires the greatest control, for it is performed in the least space and is slowest of all. The main interest is the succession of accents with the rainbow-banded long flowing sleeves.

King Sejong, the great Chosŏn monarch who ascended the throne in 1418, gave himself over to music and dance as much as he did to literature, astronomy and the fine arts. He classified music and dance into three sections and made changes in the costumes of the court musicians and dancers. His grandson King Sŏngjong sponsored the writing of the comprehensive book on Korean music and dance, the *Akhak-kwŏebŏm* (Standard of Musical Science), which describes the dances, costumes, properties, procedures and instruments still used in recreating these ancient works of art.

Korea is fortunate to have these glories from the past and artists who can reconstruct them at the National Classical Institute of Music. Early records show that the noble court youths, the *hwarang* (elite youth corps of Shilla), came before the women court dancers. At one time the male corps danced only for the king and his ministers, while women dancers appeared only before the queen and her court.

The court *Hangmu* (Crane Dance) displays two lotus buds on a rear platform and has two dancers costumed as enormous cranes. As the dance evolves, the giant birds peck at the lotus buds with their long bills, the petals unfold and child dancers appear. A similar piece has the same emerging-from-lotus-bud children and two large storks as bird-principals. Peonies and lotus flowers are, of course, Buddhist-derived symbols.

The Lion Dance. (left) Hangmu, or Crane Dance. (right)

The performers of the court dance repertory today, trained and active at the National Classical Music Institute, present exquisite appearance in magnificent costumes with small flower crowns of gold, glistening with pendants. The necklines are high, the voluminous skirts are gathered over flattened breasts, the hands are concealed in rainbow-banded long sleeves which trail on the ground. The stockinged legs and Korean turned-up-toed-slippers are rarely seen unless the skirts swing away from the ankles in occasional turns. These are depersonalized, asexual images, more like flowers than humans. The control, the splendid carriage of the body, the quiet grace and always that lilting pulse from the chest into the shoulders with the arms outstretched suggests birds winging through the air without effort: art which conceals art.

Buddhism, the most liberal of religions, came to Korea from India, via China, in 372 A.D. The Shilla monk Chin Kam, who learned Buddhist chanting known as *Pŏmp'ae* in T'ang China, returned to Korea in 830, bringing that music and four dances associated with it. These dances can be observed at certain ceremonies in the temples of married monks. Designed to "supplicate Lord Buddha so that the souls of the departed may be permitted entrance to Nirvana," the first three are known as *Chak-pŏp* (Making the Law).

Serenely beautiful is the *Nabich'um* (Butterfly Dance) performed by Buddhist nuns. The *Parach'um* (Cymbal Dance) performed by two or four monks, requires strength and agility, for the large heavy brass cymbals must be swung rhythmically up and behind the head. The *Pŏpkoch'um* (Law Drum Dance) solo involves playing the large temple drum with two sticks. Since 1950 the secular version exploits almost acrobatic movement: the body wings in half-circles at first then in full circles of the upper body from a complete back-bend position. At the same time the dancer builds up an ecstatically frenzied rhythmic development while beating the drum.

The fourth Buddhist dance, also called the *Pŏpkoch'um*, is thrilling solo for a dancer using two sticks, but the drum is considerably smaller than the largest Buddhist drum. It begins with a dramatic rolling of the sticks around the ridges of the drum's circumference, invoking the spirit, and gradually builds to a crescendo of passionate drumming.

It is this dance, popularized and completely separated from the temple and religious connotation, which is now performed with five, nine, or as many as 12 dancers. Many small drums each within a stand, make a grand batterie *tour de force* of rhythmic dexterity combined with acrobatic movement to sensational effect. Buddhism has thus contributed highly effective dance to the professional art stage. Performed by glamorously made-up young women it now is secular, decorative, and usually the high point of most dance performances. A dramatic legend is sometimes associated with this dance, called *Sŭngmu* (Monk's Dance). A 16th century *kisaeng*, renowned as a poet, musician, dancer and irresistible paramour, was determined to seduce a particular monk of irreproachable celibacy. She visited his temple, donned Buddhist robes and hat, performed the thrilling drum patterns with the two sticks and at the end, disrobed completely. The poor monk, overwhelmed, capitulated. In the hands of a skillful performer, the tension between the erotic power of the dancer and the conflict with the drum symbolizing Buddhist law, can become a powerful experience for the spectator.

While kings, princes, courtiers, and professionals have all danced at court, and the monks in temples, historically one of the oldest forms of all is the strenuous outdoor farmers' dance. As an expression of folk culture, this has astonishing vigor and rhythmic verve. Leading a procession of men and boys, a bearer carries a pole with pheasant feathers at the top (the ghost or spirit symbol) and a banner proclaiming: "Farming is the Mainstay of the Nation." The dancers' hats are decorated with huge pompons of white paper flowers of Buddhist influence. They accompany themselves with hand-held drums, gongs, a piercingly loud reed instrument, and several *changgo* (double-barreled drums) beaten with two kinds of bamboo sticks. Following the leader's running, hopping, turning, they move counterclockwise and the exuberance never wanes. Each one in turn dances solo with his particular instrument. They circle in union and the high point is reached when smaller boys

rotate their heads producing long eccentric spirals with the white ribbons attached to the special swivel in the crown of their hats. They gyrate standing up and lying down and the flowing streamers' parabolas in the air make a joyous ending.

The farmers' dance, typically virile, is performed by both men and women today, but the circular *Kanggang-suwŏlle* is purely feminine. It is performed on the full moon of the first and eight lunar months by a large group of girls to their own singing of solo verse and chorus. It starts slowly, moving clockwise then counter clockwise and accelerates to a rapid whirling ecstatic climax.

Though the farmers' dance may include Buddhist-type hats, it is more a shaman-connected rite. In the villages, the bands of players go from house to house, performing a shaman *kut* (exorcism), with their exuberant rhythms and ear-splitting noise to drive away evil spirits and invoke good ones.

The term folk dance must be understood to mean any dance which represents the tradition of the Korean people, exclusive of the court. The intermingling of Buddhist with shaman forms, and Shaman rites with Buddhist rites, with some slight tinge of Confucianism over all, is to be accepted as natural, since Korea is rich in all three ancient traditions.

In early days ritual-dance-drama was an entity inseparable man, relating him to powers greater than himself. Masks were sacred, essential and needed for many purposes both magical and practical, and later artistic. Dr. Yi Tu-hyŏn, an expert on traditional dance and theater, noted a third century Ye tribe performed a religious service to tigers (who are gods of mountains), and the *Homu* (Tiger dance) was performed until late in the Chosŏn period. Among the 10 different mask dances surviving today, one is the lion dance, performed by two dancers under one cloth. Originally the lion—an avatar of Buddha—appeared as a threat to eat the bad characters, but now the depraved monks entertain him by dancing, so he is satisfied. The Korean lion is singularly relaxed with a shaggy and coat and sometimes an extra pair of goggle eyes wobbling on a spring. A monkey is includ-

Sŭngmu, *or Monk's Dance (left) and* Pyŏlsandae Nori (*a traditional masked dance-drama) of Yangju county (right).*

ed to imitate the other characters.

In the Koryŏ Dynasty (918-1392) the beginnings of verse drama, originally performed by a single dancer, developed into grand dancing dramas for end-of-the-year ceremonies. Gradually, five plays were integrated into a whole. These pastoral-comical-satirical farces of ancient origin open and close with rituals to the gods. In between are the episodes with masked shamans, monks, farmers, wives, *kisaeng*, concubines, *yangban* (aristocrats) and servants—the whole spectrum of feudal society's inevitable conflict between ages, sex and class dramatized. Pantomime, comic dialogue, intermittent singing and dancing, together with the extraordinary stylization of the masks, all serve to create a strong impression.

In one scene a midwife helps deliver a baby. The mother abandons it, and the father gives it a cautionary sermon. Corrupt lecherous monks, not very bright *yangban*, quarreling husbands, wives, and concubines receive the most humorous commentary.

At first the rhythms are heavy in slow six beats. These change to faster 12-beat patterns, with the same intense vigor and strength of the farmers' dance. From deep knee bounds, also like the farmers' dance, there is much flinging of one leg upward, making the long sleeves fly in the air. The male characters vibrate their bodies from the hips upward, shake their shoulders, protrude their heads, step and leap or hop with enormous gusto.

Important in themselves, Korean masks represent a link in the development of the ultimate Japanese masks of *Noh.* Two of them relate to the earlier masks of *gigaku*: the *Hahoe* man's mask with movable jaw, and the *Kakshi*, the strongly modeled woman's face with braided hair looped on the side. *Gigaku* masks, made of paulownia wood, cover the entire head. Korean masks made of wood, or gourds, sometimes paper and fur, cover the face only and the players first don a black cloth to conceal the back and sides of the head and neck.

As in the ancient *Ch'ŏyong* dance, the colors

of the costumes symbolize the five directions: blue-east, red-south, white-west, black-north and yellow-center. Thus the black-masked old monk's defeat by the youthful prodigal red-faced *Ch'wibari*, or the black-faced old first wife's defeat by the young white-faced concubine are symbolic of the victory of summer over winter. Comically appealing are the young girl's Picassoesque lopsided nose and simpering smile on one side of her face; the old nobleman's small white-fur-tufted eyebrows and whiskers. Equally repellent are the old woman's black face with red-and-white polka dots, and the bumps and ridges on the "Boil Monk's" face, a renegade from holy vows and the sly villain in seduction scenes.

The best place to see the mask dance drama is in the country, where the actors first file through the village streets, pausing at every house for blessing. Then they proceed along a rice-paddy ridge to the open hillside against the mountain background, making a primordial dramatic procession with the masks worn on top of their heads like figures out of a European fairy tale. The mask dance drama group from Yuyang-ri, Yangju-gun, Kyŏnggi-do, which has been named a Korean Cultural Treasure, preserves a strong tradition. They perform on Buddha's birthday, at *Ch'usŏk* and other festival times. The players, most of them men, have been doing this for years, and their style has authority and ease.

A good performance depends upon the improvisational ability of the players who banter with each other, arouse the audience to answer questions, shout comments, clap their hands rhythmically and sometimes join in the satirical refrains of the songs. General revel concludes the performance, with most of the audience pouring in the space and everyone dancing in robust dance-drama style to the shrilling trumpet. The Yangju masks are burned in a final ritual, one more proof that this expression goes deeper than casual amusement. The masks are considered sacred and must be recreated for each performance.

Modern

Until the 1920s, the Korean dance community had few opportunities to become familiar with the dance traditions of the West. In 1921, however, an event occurred that was to be of great importance for dancers in Korea who wanted to learn of the modern school. A group of Korean students residing in Vladivostok visited their homeland to give performances of European classical music and dance in Seoul and in Wonsan, a port city along the east coast of what is now North Korea. The Korean Students Music Company, which consisted of 11 college and high school students, provided Korean audiences with their first opportunity to glimpse the dance of the Western world. The program consisted of some Cossack, Hungarian and Spanish folk dances and classical music and ballet numbers.

An event of more importance in the history of modern Korean dance took place the next year. Baku Ishii, a pioneer of modern dance in Japan who had once studied under Isadora Duncan, visited Seoul in 1922 to present his *Dance Poem*. His performance created a stir among the Korean audience, especially the young students who had longed for a chance to appreciate the new dance of the time. The impact of Ishii's Seoul performance was so great that some young dance students left immediately for Tokyo to study under the famous Japanese master. Among them were Cho T'aek-won and Miss Ch'oe Sǔng-hi, who would later make distinguished contributions to the development of modern dance in Korea. Another memorable artist from this budding period of modern dance movement was Pae Ku-ja. Miss Pae organized her own dance company and experimented in creating ballet pieces using Korean folk themes and stage settings and opened a dance studio in Seoul in 1929. It was not until 1939, however, when Russian ballerina Eliana Pavlova visited Seoul to give a performance that Korean dance lovers were provided the opportunity to enjoy classical ballet of international standards.

An increasing number of people were becoming interested in Western dance about this time as part of the fascination with the Western arts

Every movement of Pak Myŏng-suk, a core member of the second generation of Korean modern dancer, is a forthright expression of the life force.

and humanities of various disciplines, including literature, philosophy, music and fine art. They were discovering that Western dance could appeal as much to Korean aesthetic sensibilities as their own dance legacy in spite of different methods of expression and history of development. Proof of this growing fascination with Western dance was the ever increasing number of students going to Japan to study. Many trained under Ishii, so his influence on Korean dance was naturally strong for a considerable period of time, until World War II.

Of all the dancers who studied in Japan around this time none were more instrumental in the development of new dance forms than Cho T'aek-won and Ch'oe Sŭng-hi. Both were devoted to creating their own dance expressions by incorporating the modern Western dance techniques they had learned in Japan and the spiritual motifs they drew from Korea's traditional dances. A number of dance pieces of outstanding creativity were composed by the two

artists. They successfully combined the subtle lyricism inherent in Korean emotion and the indigenous atmosphere of Korean folklore with fresh stage idioms borrowed from contemporary dances of the West. In 1937, Ch'oe Sŭng-hi embarked on a tour of the United States, Latin America and Europe under the sponsorship of Solomon Hurok, a world-renowned manager of performing arts at that time. She gave more than 100 performances during the tour, which continued until 1939, drawing favorable reactions from audiences and critics.

From 1945, when Korea was liberated from Japanese colonial rule, artists of all fields enjoyed increased freedom in their creative activities. However, dance circles were not given sufficient impetus to recover from the stagnation they had suffered during the last years of the colonial period. Political turmoil and economic hardship in the ensuing years destroyed the hope of many artists to bring a flourishing of the arts in the liberated country.

Scenes from The Nutcracker Suite *performed by a Korean ballet company.*

The Seoul Ballet Company, led by Han Tong-in, was among the groups which maintained a fairly impressive level of activity during the period between liberation and the outbreak of the Korean War in 1950. Despite various difficulties, the company struggled to continue to give performances. Its repertoire included such classical favorites as *Les Sylphides*, and its own creations inspired by ancient Korean folk tales.

Im Sŏng-nam, a leading male dancer, returned home in 1956 after studying ballet in Japan. He established a studio in Seoul soon afterward and organized a performing group of his own. He distinguished himself as a leading choreographer, teacher and lead dancer in male roles of Korean ballet, which was suffered from a chronic shortage of male dancers. He was named director of the National Ballet Company upon its inauguration in 1973. Under his leadership the National Ballet grew steadily and expanded its repertoire so that it now includes *Swan Lake, the Nutcracker, Coppelia, Scheherazade* and a number of original pieces employing themes from popular Korean legends and tales such as *The Pae Pijang Story.*

In this modern age of multiple interests and electronic media that provide people with easy access to popular culture, ballet in Korea has had to accept the status of an art with a limited audience, as in many other countries. The National Ballet has endeavored to raise the artistic level of its presentations and to enlarge and refine its repertoire in an effort to increase public interest. The Universal Ballet Company, a private professional performing group organized in 1984, helped to invigorate the local ballet scene. The company employed American dance teachers and invited foreign performers, most often male principal dancers, to perform with the company. The Universal Ballet toured Southeast Asia in 1985.

Another major stream of modern Korean dance has been led by a group of artists of more innovative vein. Yuk Wan-sun, a leading dancer and professor at Ewha Woman's University, introduced the techniques of Martha Graham. She achieved remarkable success with the modern dance drama, *Jesus Christ Superstar*. She was chief choreographer and lead performer in this dance piece which was performed in various cities across Korea for many years.

Miss Hong Shin-ja was another leading artist in the world of Korean contemporary dance. Formerly an English literature major at Sookmyung Women's University in Seoul, she went to the United States in 1963 and studied avant-garde dance. She attempted to express Korean spiritualism through contemporary Western dance techniques.

Korea's history and cultural heritage have been explored as a valuable source of inspiration by many other dancers. Numerous small dance groups have been organized, not only in Seoul but also in major provincial cities. Many sought to rediscover the value of Korea's indigenous dance culture and translate it into modern dance expressions to achieve an effective communication with audiences in Korea as well as with those of the world. Ch'ang Mu Hoe, or the Creative Dance Company, led by Miss Kim Mae-ja, was one of the most active groups in this line of experimentalism. The Korean Dance Festival, sponsored by the semi-government Korean Culture and Arts Foundation, encouraged the activities of these small private groups by offering them annual forums for joint presentations.

Another movement in Korean dance in the modern period has been masterminded by those artists who have maintained the original style of traditional Korean dance. They often rearrange the formats of the performance, however, to suit the modern stage. This has been necessary in view of the nature of traditional Korean dances-which have been handed down either as a kind of salon art for the entertainment of aristocrats or as communal rituals of village people. Kim Paek-pong and Kang Sŏn-yŏng ranked among the senior dancers who have excelled in this field.

Drama

Drama of Early Days

Korean drama had its origin in the religious rites of prehistoric days. Apparently simple Shilla (57 B.C.—A.D. 935) dance movements with musical accompaniment were developed into a kind of drama called the *Ch'ŏyong*. The *Ch'ŏyong* was not drama in the strict sense that is understood today, even though it had dramatic elements that followed a definite story line with a hero. It was a series of dramatic dances rather than actual drama. Besides *Ch'ŏyong*, there were several other shows performed for royal and popular entertainment, but again their primary emphasis on dance movements with music accompaniment disqualified them as true drama.

Dancing with musical accompaniment has always been important in Korean classic shows of all kinds regardless of their official designation as dance or drama. The *sandae* drama of the Koryŏ Dynasty (918-1392) contains more definite dramatic elements than the *Ch'ŏyong*. It was performed on stage by masked actors following a script with a story and occasional spoken lines. Dances and songs dominated the play. The *sandae* was further developed during the Chosŏn Dynasty (1392-1910), when it became one of the official functions of the court. Eventually, it lost royal patronage and became entertainment for the common people. This most representative of Korean classic dramas found wide popular acceptance, as the subjugated masses of agrarian Korean society found solace in a humorous, satirical masque that ridiculed the privileged classes—Buddhist priests and the *yangban* aristocrats.

Besides the shows described above, there were other dramatic forms of popular entertainment, such as puppet plays, acrobatic clowning, the *Ogwangdae*, the *Pyŏlsin-gut* (in the nature of a shamanistic ritual), and the Pongsan mask dance. All such classic entertainments, however declined with the introduction of Western culture in the 1900s.

Western Influences

The introduction of Western-style productions on the classic scene became a definite trend in 1908 when the Wongaksa Theater opened in Seoul under the auspices of the state. Until that time, entertainers had been without a theater and had to present their works either on a makeshift stage or in any village square large enough to accommodate a crowd.

The introduction of Western-style shows produced increasing interest in the "new drama" which, in contrast to the traditional "old drama" and its stress on music and dancing, relied almost exclusively on spoken dialogue. Less serious in its artistic standards but more popular with less sophisticated audiences were the "new-school plays" with their romantic stories of handsome heroes and beautiful heroines.

Drama became so popular in the 1930s that many amateur groups competed with the professionals. Especially noteworthy was the contribution of college groups.

World War II caused a temporary setback, followed by the Korean War of 1950-53, which proved even more disastrous for all segments of Korean society. A postwar boom in the motion picture industry brought further discouragement to attempts of theater performers to stage a comeback. Then came the rapid spread of television and its popular appeal. As a result, dramatic works for the most part recently have featured performances in small theaters or restaurants with limited audiences. In the 1980s, however, experimental drama made a comeback and was highly popular, especially among younger people.

Puppetry

No description of Korean drama could be complete without a word about puppet shows. From several references on the subject in Chinese classical books, it is believed they were performed from the outset of the Three Kingdoms era. Apparently the repertoire of the dramas was quite extensive, but only three plays have survived. There is no information available about the others.

Of the three, two cannot truly be called dramas because they consist of nothing more than simple manipulation of dolls with musical accompaniment and lack both script and storyline. The third, the *Kkoktukakshi*, is a drama in every sense of the word. It has a scenario which can be followed clearly and a definite cast of characters. It has inevitably declined with the great changes in modern taste but it is still played occasionally in village marketplaces. It is a typical example of the ridicule to which the leading classes of ancient Korea were subjected by Korean performers.

The *Kkoktukakshi* was presented by itinerant troupes of six or seven members, three of them usually musicians. The *dramatis personae* consisted of Pak Ch'ŏm-ji, the hero; his wife, Kkoktukakshi; his concubine; his younger brother; two young shaman women; a nephew; four Buddhist monks; the governor of P'yŏng-an-do province; the governor's butler; a hunter, and a serf. The musicians were included in the cast as villagers. It had eight acts, each more or less independent of the others, giving the whole play an distinct feeling.

As the curtain opens to the raucous beat of a drum, the hero, Pak Ch'ŏm-ji, is shown starting out on a countrywide tour of scenic spots. At dusk, he goes into a village inn for the night. At supper time, he hears a commotion outside and goes out to ascertain the source of the noise. There are several men beating on the ground in their excitement over a heated gambling game. It is music to the hero's ears, and he begins to dance in sheer delight, singing a song about the natural beauties of the eight provinces.

The second act opens with a young Buddhist monk dancing with two young female shamans. Pak Ch'ŏm-ji joins in, but after the merrymaking, he is chagrined to find that the two shamans he has tried to seduce are his own nieces. The hero pleads with the monk to stop dancing, but his pleas fall on deaf ears, whereupon he summons his nephew, the village strongman, who breaks it all up. Act Three depicts a ferocious, hungry monster devouring every bird that alights in a rice paddy. As the hero watches the hapless birds, the monster pounces upon him.

Along comes the nephew to his rescue. He grapples with the monster in a long and furious fight that is accompanied by a great deal of clamorous music. In the end, the monster is slain.

In Act Four, the hero searches in vain for his missing wife, Kkoktukakshi. Finally, he gives up the search and flirts with his concubine, at which time his wife shows up. A quarrel flares between the two women and is settled only when the hero agrees to divide his fortune equally between them. In the distribution, the concubine gets all the valuable property in the house, leaving the wife nothing but trash. There is a good deal of theatrical gesturing on the part of the tearful Kkoktukakshi to express her sorrow and rancor, but in the end she leaves the stage, her destination being a Buddhist temple deep in the Diamond Mountains where she intends to become a nun.

In Act Five, the hero is spurned by the concubine and, upon the unanimous advice of the villagers, sets forth on a journey in search of his wife.

Act Six introduces the governor of P'yŏngan-do province, who arrives at the provincial capital and immediately goes pheasant hunting.

Act Seven opens to the march of a funeral procession for the governor's mother. The governor shows no signs of mourning but seems only too glad to be rid of her, much to the scandalized surprise villagers. The coffin carrier has a sudden pain in his legs and drops the coffin, thus bringing the procession to a halt. Again, the hero's nephew saves the day. He appears half-naked, his huge muscles exposed, and lifts the coffin easily.

In the final act, a Buddhist temple is built on a holy mountain to console the spirit of the governor's deceased mother with 49 days of prayer.

The stage of this show was set up in any village square capable of holding a crowd. Four poles were erected to cover about 2 square meters of ground. Curtains were draped around the poles to hide the puppeteers from public view.

The puppets were carved of wood and clad in appropriate costumes, some with long beards according to the characters. The dolls were of varied heights, from 49 to 90 centimeters. The show was presented in the evening and the stage was illuminated by burning cloth soaked in oil tied to the ends of sticks.

Masque

The earliest authentic reference to the masque play appears in the *Samguk sagi* (History of the Three Kingdoms) which mentions three types performed during the ninth century of the Unified Shilla period. That the masque continued to be played during the Koryŏ period is indicated by the *Koryŏsa* (History of Koryo which refers to masque as one of the plays offered in the 31st year of the reign of King Kojong (1244). During the Chosŏn Dynasty, an official post was created for the express purpose of handling masque shows, which accordingly prospered as an official function of the court. In 1634, however, this post was abolished, and the masque had to cater to the common people.

The masque shows fall into four distinctive categories, three named after the localities where they were played.

The *Sandae* Masque

Of the four masque shows, *Sandae*, named after the royal nomenclature for the office responsible for handling masque shows, is the best known. It consists of 10 acts and 13 scenes, each named after the main role in each act and scene. Thus, Act One is "The High Priest;" Act Two, "The Pock-Marked Monk;" Act Three, "The Dark-Faced Monk;" Act Four, "The Monk with the Blinking Eyes" and so forth. Like the *Kkoktukakshi* puppet show, the *Sandae* brought out the triangular affair of the typical yangban, his wife and his concubine. It satirized the Chosŏn nobility and mocked the apostate monks.

The *Sandae* had an all-male cast, playing and dancing to the accompaniment of traditional Korean drums, strings, and winds blaring tunes based on folk songs, Buddhist invocations, shamanist invocations and the like. It also had one puppet and a set of 24 masks, one for each of the cast. It was performed on a makeshift open-air stage in the village square on holiday occasions, such as the *Tano* festival on the fifth

Pongsan mask dance.

day of the fifth month of the lunar calendar, or shaman prayer-days for rain. Starting after sunset, the show continued deep into the night.

This unique Korean drama has lost much popular support. Only one troupe continued to perform it in a Yangju village, Kyŏnggi-do province. A group was organized in Seoul about 90 years ago as the only authentic performers of the *Sandae* in latter-day Korea, but was disbanded after 50 years. The drama has been revived with government support and is designed an intangible cultural asset.

The *Haesŏ* Masque

The *Haesŏ* masque, performed in the Haeju area of Hwanghae-do province in the North, was also performed during the *Tano* festival. Its origin cannot be traced, but it is believed to have been created at about the same time as the *Sandae*. It was a seven-act play. The roles varied slightly according to the locality in which it was played, but the overall cast of characters was about the same as in *Kkoktukakshi* and the *Sandae*.

The *Hahoe* Masque

The *Hahoe* masque in the Hahoe district of Kyŏngsangbuk-do province was performed on the occasion of village festivals on the second day of the first lunar month. According to the old men of the village, its origin goes back more than 500 years.Unlike the two previous masque plays which were staged for public entertainment, the original purpose of the *Hahoe* was to appease the spirits of two departed women who were believed to possess potent spiritual powers over the village. The masque was part of a ritual observed to exorcise the village of evil spirits.

The *Ogwangdae* Masque

The fourth type, appearing in Kyŏng sang-nam-do province, was an acrobatic affair known as the *Ogwangdae*, or Play of the Five Clowns. The clowns apparently were the "Generals of the Five Directions," that is the generals who guarded positions in the north, south, east, west, and center. It was performed on the 15th day of the First Moon by village amateurs under the direction of the village elders versed in the play.

A Madang Nori *(a newly developed genre of traditional musical comedy),* entitled, A Tale of Yi Ch'un-P'ung .

Modern Drama

Western drama was first staged in Korea in 1908 at the newly opened Wongaksa Theater in Seoul. The advent of "new drama," as it was known, as opposed to the traditional dramas of the masque and puppetry, was perhaps inevitable at a time when the powerful influence of Western culture and civilization entered Korea

The pioneer of the "new drama" movement was Yi In-jik, who had returned from studying in Japan. It was Yi who made the Wongaksa a success. He not only wrote the plays for Korea's first theater proper, but managed, supervised and directed them. He was followed in 1911 by Im Sŏng-gu whose works were greeted with standing ovations from the outset. Im, however, turned to less-serious drama later, catering to popular romantic sentiments in what became known as "new-school plays." In 1912, another modernist, Yi Ki-se, appeared with two more troupes, and the world of theater became crowded. By then, a considerable number of profes-

sional actors, actresses, stage directors and playwrights were available to put the "new drama" on a solid footing.

A more serious group, calling itself the Drama Arts Society, was organized in 1921, mostly by students who had returned from Japan. A significant contribution to this Western-inspired movement was the formation of the *T'owŏlhoe* (Earth-Moon Society) in 1923 by a group of students then studying in Japan. Such figures as Pak Sŭng-hi and Kim P'albong, who later became an eminent writer, came home during school vacations to play major roles in "realistic" plays.

Though its members were amateurs, the T'owolhoe surpassed any other professional group with its high artistic standards and the introduction of "realistic" themes. The society's repertoire consisted mostly of original works written by its own members, but it also included translations and adaptations of world's masterpieces. Popular approval was so great that in its 10 years existence it presented a total of 180 performances—a record-breaking feat for that

Modern plays put on in Korean theaters : A Whistling Bird *(left) and* Princess Nangnang *and* Prince Hodong.

time. Its influence has been felt ever since in Korean dramatic circles.

Besides the *T'owolhoe,* a professional group called *Ch'wisŏngjwa* turned out a substantial number of good actors and actresses throughout the 1920s.

The most significant landmark in the next decade of development was formation of the Society for the Study of Dramatic Arts in 1931. Organized by the elite of Korea's theatrical and literary circles, this society presented numerous world masterpieces as well as original works by its members. Unfortunately, the Japanese Governor-General forced it to disband soon after its establishment because of its nationalistic tendencies, but its individual members carried on by organizing another body, the Drama Study Troupe. Under this name, it lasted until the end of the decade when the Japanese again forced its dissolution. The 1930s brought a period of socialistic thought that was reflected in the theatrical world by the Modern Theater, New Construction, and several other groups, all sympathetic to the leftist cause. The early 1940s was

a period of concentrated Pacific War efforts, and the theater came to a standstill under intensified Japanese pressure.

The tragic post-liberation division of the land and the ensuing political cleavage brought chaos in Korean dramatic circles. Numerous groups, each with its own political color, sprouted one after another and folded as quickly. With the establishment of the Republic of Korea Government in 1948 and the laying down of a definite political ideology, confusion ended and a National Theater was formed in 1950.

Following the Korean War, the New Drama Society, an organ of the National Theater, revived interest chiefly in Shakespeare and Yu Ch'i-jin, one of the foremost Korean dramatists. The boom of motion pictures and TV, however, deprived the stage of both talent and an audience, and decline set in.

Nevertheless, several groups courageously carried on, creating what is known as a "small theater" movement. They emphasized artistic presentations as opposed to the professional endeavors that sought large theater and better financial returns for the producer. The more serious-minded organized the Korean National Center of International Theater Institute in 1958, and engaged in international cultural exchanges. A number of other theater groups that where active and serious in purpose included the *Minchung* (Populace), *Yŏin* (Woman), *Shilhŏm* (Experimental), the *Chayu* (Freedom), the *Kakyo* (Bridge) and the *Kwangjang* (Plaza) theater groups.

Movies

Historical Sketch

The first showing of a motion picture in Korea was in 1903. The first Korean-made film, entitled *Righteous Revenge*, was shown to the general public in 1919 and directed by Kim To-san. It was a so-called kinedrama, designed to be combined with a stage performance. The first feature film, *Oath Under the Moon*, appeared four years later. Directed by Yun Paek-nam, the 1923 production was a prelude to the era of the silent movies in Korea. In 1926, the classic *Arirang,* a protest against Japanese colonial oppression, was produced by actor-director Na Un-gyu. It was followed by a few other films on the same subject.

With the great success of *Arirang*, the production of Korean films increased in number to about 10 per year until the film industry was stifled by the Japanese colonial government in 1930. Production dropped to only two or three films a year. The first sound film, *Ch'unhyangjŏn,* based on an old love story of the same name, was produced during this period by director Lee Myŏng-u.

Cinema activities in Korea were in the hands of the Japanese until Korea's liberation at the end of World War II in 1945. More than 140 films were produced from 1919 to 1945, mostly of a propagandist nature. After liberation, the film industry was reborn and the first color film, *The Diary of a Woman*, directed by Hong Sung-ki, was made in 1949. The Korean War (1950-1953) dealt a severe blow to the fledgling film industry, and only a few war documentaries were produced during that period.

In 1955, the government exempted all domestic film-makers from taxation in an effort to promote further development of the movie industry. This led to a rapid increase in the number of film-makers, and a golden age in Korean cinema. The number of films produced in the late 1950s reached approximately 100 annually, and about 200 a year in the 1960s. In 1969, The History of Korean Motion Pictures was published to celebrate the 50th anniversary of the introduction of cinema to the country.

Struggle for Revival

Korea's movie industry has been in a slump since 1970, due largely to the rapid development of television and a sudden decrease in the number of moviegoers. During the period of 1985-1988, domestic movie production averaged 83 films annually. However, encouraged in part by increased recognition at international film festivals, the Korean movie industry produced 96 films in 1992.

The number of moviegoers, which registered a record high of 173,043,272 in 1969, has declined continuously since 1970 and stood at 48,098,235 in 1985. This decline was halted and turned gradually around thanks to an increase in the number of foreign films resulting from import liberalization. The number of moviegoers reached 52,196,650 in 1991, and 47,110,000 in 1992.

On the other hand, the number of television sets increased from 879,564 in 1970 to 12,000,000 in 1991, or almost 14 times the 1970 figure. As the movie industry began regaining its vitality in the late 1980s and the number of foreign imports increased rapidly, the number of cinema houses at first grew at a rapid pace, then leveled off, standing at 762 in 1991 and 712 in 1992, while the number of multiplex cinemas with more than two screens in the same complex began to increase.

In 1971, the government, in a renewed effort to help the movie industry, launched a program of financial assistance for film production and script writing, and established the Motion

A scene from the movie, Sŏp'yŏnje.

Picture Promotion Corporation to support cinema circles both in financing and in dealing with technological problems. The government also provided outstanding producers with permits to import foreign films, subject to an annual quota.

With film production, Korea's film exports also declined steadily during the last two decades. Its export of 201 films in 1971 dropped to 86 in 1972, 24 in 1983 and 6 in 1984. This decline was halted, and a slight upturn started with 11 exports in 1992 and 18 in 1992. The increase was partly due to international recognition of Korean films at various film festivals.

Films showing encouraging signs in the form of international recognition in the past few years include: *Kipko-p'urŭnbam* (The Deep Blue Night), which was awarded the grand prize at the Tokyo Film Festival in 1985; *Why Bodhi Dharma Went to the Orient,* deemed the Best Picture at the Locarno Film Festival in 1989; *Our Twisted Hero,* which won both the East-West Center Award (The Grand Prize) at the Hawaii International Film Festival and the award for Best Producer at the World Film Festival in Montreal in 1992; *White Badge,* given the awards for both Best Picture and Best Director at the Tokyo International Film Festival.

Korean individuals have also fared well at these international competitions; director Yi Tu-yong received a special prize, the ISDAP Award, at the Venice Film Festival in 1981 for the movie *P'imak,* while Kang Su-yon won the award for Best Actress at the Venice Film Festival for her role in *Surrogate Woman* in 1987, and also at the Moscow International Film Festival in 1989 for her performance in *Aje, Aje, Bara Aje* (Come, Come, Come Upward). This was followed by Lee Hye-sook being awarded the prize for Best Actress at the 15th Montreal Film Festival in 1992.

The latest Korean movie to earn international acclaim was *Sŏp'yŏnje* a film about musicians from one school of *p'ansori,* a genre of Korean traditional folk music. This 1993 hit, directed by Im Kwon-taek and starring Oh Jong-hae, won the awards for Best Director and Best Actress at the 1st Shanghai International Film Festival in

September 1993.

This resurgence in the domestic film industry has also shown in box office gates. in 1991, the biggest box office turnout was for the movie *General's Son, II*, directed by Im Kwon-taek, which drew more than 350,000 viewers in Seoul's first run cinemas. Other outstanding films of 1991 included Fly High Run Far (*Kae Byok*) which won the Grand Bell Award (Korea's highest film award) for that year, *Silver Stallion, Death Song, Passion Portrait*, and *Camels Don't Cry Alone*. In 1992, the biggest gate attraction was *A Wedding Story*, which drew over 500,000 viewers. Other big hits of 1992 included *Our Twisted Hero, White Badge, The Road to the Race Track, and Kim's War*

The biggest hit of 1993 was the above-mentioned *Sŏp'yŏnje*, which shattered Korean box office records by drawing over 1 million viewers. Other popular movies included *A Woman and a Man, The Blue in You*, and *The 101st Proposal*.

Foreign Films

Foreign films rarely run at a loss when screened in Korea, and they served as an effective fund raising strategy for Korean film-makers until the mid-1980s. The American film *Die Hard* attracted an audience of more than 700,000 at Seoul's first-run cinemas.

In 1985, a law was put in force designed to separate film-making from film-importing. It required companies wishing to engage in either to register with the Ministry of Culture and sports in each category. Previously, only licensed film-makers who produced at least four motion pictures a year were permitted to import foreign films.

However, the promulgation of a new cinema law in January 1987 allows foreigners to engage in the film production business in Korea and to distribute foreign films here. This direct distribution includes activities by such major international distributors as United International Pictures, offering stiff competition to local movie makers and distributors. As a result, the Korean movie industry faces the reality of stiff foreign competition, and will have to find the

way of survival through technological and artistic improvements and the accumulation of capital. In 1992, a total of 319 foreign films were imported of which 201 films were shown to the public. It is yet to be seen whether the opening of the domestic film market will stifle the Korean film industry or stimulate it to improve in quality and compete with foreign films.

Magazines and Books

Historical Sketch

With its long history of modern printing methods, Korea has seen the publication of books, magazines and periodicals, along with newspapers, play an influential role. This has held true not only in the academic and cultural areas, but also in the political and entertainment fields.

The use of movable metal type is credited to the mid-12th century in Korea, about 200 years before such printing was developed in Europe by Johann Gutenberg. In 1973, Korean scholars found in the French National Museum a Buddhist classic bearing a colophon stating that it was printed in 1377 with metal type at the king's printing house in Korea's Ch'ungch'ŏng-do province, during the reign of U-wang of the Koryŏ Dynasty, 918-1392 .

It was in November 1896, however, that the country's first modern magazine, the *Bulletin of the Independence Society*, was published with the purpose of enlightening the masses through the dissemination of information, education and opinion. The *Bulletin* was issued as a bi-monthly along with the *Tongnip Shinmun*, which was the daily periodical of the society.

There were two English-language magazines already published prior to that first magazine, however. They were *Morning Calm* (July 1890-October 1936) and *Korean Repository* (1892; 1895-1898), both monthly publications. The former was published by the Church of England Korean Mission and the latter by the American Methodist Church under the editorship of Dr. F. Ohlinger. Even though both English-language

One of Korea's largest book stores, downtown Seoul.

magazines were church oriented, the former was also intended for broader distribution. The latter was chiefly addressed to its supporters at home, carrying cultural material, short descriptive articles on Korea, and news items on the Seoul foreign community.

In 1900, the Hansŏng Club published the Hansŏng Monthly Bulletin in both Korean and Japanese editions with the purpose of fostering Korean-Japan friendship, for which the club had been organized. As the annexation of Korea by Japan became imminent, a number of other magazines came into being. Some of the more successful ones included the monthly *Bulletin of the Korea Self-Support Society, Monthly Education, Home Magazine, Korean Peninsula, Ladies Instruction*, and *Lads*. Many scholastic and social organizations were formed at that time which published their own periodicals for the purpose of resisting the Japanese intrusion and fomenting social change. The monthly journals of the Sobuk Scholastic Society and the Kiho Educational Society were two prominent examples.

After annexation, no magazines except for a few innocuous publications were allowed to be published until 1920. That year, the Japanese colonialists introduced the Newspaper Law. In 1922, for the first time in a decade, a Korean periodical, the *Kaebyŏk* (The Beginning of the Universe) was permitted to print literary works and commentaries under strict Japanese censorship.

Kaebyŏk was followed by other magazines such as the *Shinch'ŏnji* or New World, the *Chosŏn-ji-kwang* or Light of Korea, the *Shinsaenghwal* or New Life and the *Tong myŏng* or Eastern Light. However, all these managed to incite anti-Japanese sentiments, and so the Japanese Government resorted to stricter censorship and suppressive measures once again. Four members of the *Shinsaenghwal* editorial staff were imprisoned and their press confiscated after only two months of publishing.

Kaebyŏk enjoyed an existence of 72 months, the longest of all the magazines in that period, but it too was forced to shut down in August 1926. After that, censorship and other restric-

About 7,000 periodicals are published in Korea.

Information. This total breaks down to 114 dailies, 1,847 weeklies, 2,910 monthlies, 667 bimonthlies, 1,001 quarterlies and 240 semi-annuals, and 176 annuals. There has recently been a notable trend toward proliferation of specialized magazines, ranging from housekeeping, sports, and leisure activities, to science and technology, health care, literature and art. In addition, more and more business firms are publishing in-house magazines. With the exception of student textbooks, 24,783 titles, totaling 136.7 million copies, were published in 1992. Topping the list was literature with 4,654 titles, followed by juvenile interest books with 4,149. Next came science and arts with 2,948 titles, followed by social sciences with 2,874, religions with 2,044, arts with 1,130, history with 953, languages with 938, philosophy with 608, pure science with 328, and general works with 232. School reference books came to 3,925 titles. As of the end of 1992, there were about 7,381 publishing companies in operation and the number of bookstores came to 5,371. During 1992, Korea imported 2,075 foreign periodicals totaling 11.09 million copies and 204,299 titles of foreign books totaling just over 3.58 million copies. The imported periodicals and books were valued at US$ 54.6 million.

tions together with the penetration of Japanese journals added to the attempted suppression of the vernacular language and halted interest in magazine journalism.

There can be no doubt, however, that magazines played an important role in enlightening the general public during a period when even scraps of information about the outside world were badly needed. Korean magazines also contributed greatly to the formation of a systematic Korean syntax and wide dissemination of the Korean alphabet, paving the way for literary and journalistic development in later days. The nation's liberation in 1945 unleashed a torrent of publishing businesses that have persisted, though with extreme ups and downs. Press freedom, which was restored with liberation, was one of the most important impetuses to this active trend.

Present State

As of the end of 1992, a total of 6,955 periodicals were registered with the Ministry of

Cultural Facilities

Korea offers a wide range of cultural facilities of all levels and categories. These places give real glimpses of the cultural and artistic achievements of Koreans of past and present, of both traditional and modern trends and tastes. They provide opportunities for cultural adventure not only for Koreans but also for foreign visitors and residents. From full-scale museums of international standards to small theaters where performers and spectators can intermingle for face-to-face communication, they vary in type and scale so as to satisfy the diverse interests and penchants of the communities they serve. Following is a selection of some of special interest.

The National Museum of Contemporary Art, in suburban Seoul (top). Art lovers at the National Museum of Contemporary Art located in the outskirts of Seoul (middle).The Hangaram Gallery of the Seoul Arts Center (bottom

Museums and Galleries

National Museums

There are eight museums financed and operated by the central government. The National Museum of Korea and the National Folklore Museum are in downtown Seoul and the National Museum of Contemporary Art is in Kwach'ŏn, Kyŏnggi-do Province, a suburb of Seoul. The other five are located in provincial cities that once were the capitals of ancient kingdoms. These cities are storehouses of remains and relics that shedlight on the cultural past of the particular region. Each museum has its own distinctive historical flavor.

The art collection of the royal court of the Chosŏn Dynasty (1392-1910) was turned into the seed collection of the present National Museum of Korea in 1908. Since then its collection has grown greatly and it has been housed in several different places. Its last home was in a modern structure influenced by Korea's past architectural traditions on the grounds of Kyŏngbokkung Palace. The building in which the museum is now located once housed the offices of the central government. The exhibition space in the renovated building is nearly 10,000 square meters, twice that of the previous museum building. A children's museum is housed in an annex.

Exhibition halls are located mostly on the 2nd, 3rd, and 4th floors. There are separate galleries for prehistoric artifacts: relics from the Koguryŏ and Paekche Kingdoms; relics from the Kaya Kingdom; artifacts from the Shilla Kingdom; relics from the Unified Shilla era; Buddhist sculpture; metal works; Koryŏ ceramics; Chosŏn pottery; calligraphic works; and Buddhist paintings. There is an outdoor exhibition area, a room for specially programmed exhibition area, a room for specially programmed exhibitions, and two rooms honoring two art connoisseurs who donated their private collections to the museum.

Exhibits of Korean artifacts and relics are put in cultural perspective when compared with those from Korea's neighbors which are displayed in the China room, Japan room, Central Asia room, Lolang room, Shinan room and the room for Western arts.

The total exhibition space can only show less than one tenth of the museum's collection which numbers about 110,000 pieces, and so there are no more than 10,000 items on permanent display.

The National Folklore Museum came into being in 1945, but was burned down during the Korean War. It was restored in 1966 and moved to its present site on the grounds of Kyongbokkung Palace in 1975. It has show rooms for manufacturing, food, architecture and furniture, wearing apparel, religions and belief, performing arts and entertainment, and social customs plus a special exhibition room.

The museum provides a look at traditional Korean lifestyles, customs and traditions as well as the paraphernalia used in everyday life. Visitors are advised to read the explanatory notes accompanying the exhibits to understand the Korean way of life.

The National Museum of Contemporary Art was reopened in 1986 at a huge new building in Kwach'ŏn in the southern suburbs of Seoul. Originally established at the Kyŏngbokkung Palace in 1969, the museum was moved to the Tŏksugung Palace near Seoul city hall in 1973 and remained there until it was relocated to a newly developed park in Kwach'ŏn.

The new museum complex occupies a 66,000 square meter site within the scenic park. The rectangular three-story building contains a horseshoe-shaped exhibition hall, a circular display area, a rectangular hall and circular corridors in which works are also displayed. The total display area covers 14,512 square meters. In addition, there is a 33,000 square meter sculpture garden.

The museum also has an education center, an auditorium, a seminar room, and several rooms specifically designed for paintings, ceramics, and handicraft classes.

The Kyŏngju National Museum dates to 1913 when the Kyŏngju Historical Association renovated an old Chosŏn-period guest house to display some 100 ancient relics. Its present building was constructed in 1975. Its collection has grown to around 12,000 items.

The museum boasts many bronze items excavated from the area as well as other remains from the Shilla period. Many of the objects in its collection have been unearthed in massive excavations conducted in Kyŏngju and the vicinity. Relics found in ancient royal tombs including Ch'ŏnmach'ong and Tumulus No. 98 are housed in Annex I. Annex II is filled with objects recovered from Anapchi, a pond on the site of a royal Shilla garden. Korea's largest bell, the bell of King Sŏngdŏk or the Emille Bell as it is better known, hangs in a pavilion on the grounds of the museum.

Buddhist art objects including images of Buddha, pagodas, pagoda and stupa parts and various other stone relics are scattered throughout grounds of the museum. The Kyŏngju Museum is a must for anyone interested in the art and culture of the Shilla Kingdom.

The Kwangju National Museum was constructed in 1978 to store and display the many ceramic vessels that have been recovered since the early 1970s from an ancient sunken ship of Yüan Chinese origin on the seabed off the coast of Shinan in Chŏllanam-do Province. It also houses other artifacts recovered from the Kwangju area, and includes of Paekche origin.

The Kongju National Museum dates to 1940 when a local association called the Society for the Exaltation of the History of Kongju moved an old Chosŏn-period office building to the site of·the present museum to provide a place to display Paekche artifacts uncovered in and around Kongju, a capital of the Paekche Kingdom. Some Paekche relics housed in the National Museum in Seoul were moved there in 1946. The discovery and excavation of the tomb of Paekche's 25th king, Muryŏng (r. 501-523), in 1971 made the present museum building a necessity. Most of the museum's collection is made up of items recovered from the royal tomb.

The Puyŏ National Museum's building was constructed in 1967. As Puyŏ was the last capital of the Paekche Kingdom, most of the museum's 6,200-piece collection consists of Paekche relics recovered from the Puyŏ vicinity.

Chinju was once the center of an ancient kingdom called Kaya that flourished in that area, and the Chinju National museum houses many Kaya artifacts including bronzeware as well as some prehistoric artifacts. The museum's 2,000-piece collection includes many items recovered from the lower and middle reaches of the Naktonggang River. Most of the items from the neolithic and bronze ages in its collection were found in the southern sections of Kyŏngsangnam-do Province.

Local Museums

Local museums are supported and operated by provincial and municipal administrative entities, not by the central government. They have been established in areas rich in archaeological finds and cultural remains that are distinct from other areas but have no national museum. They are usually dependent on the enthusiasm and devotion of local historians and art lovers who work to find things of historic and cultural value in their areas. Some of the more interesting once are listed below.

The Chŏngju Municipal Museum's collection is made up mostly of articles excavated in and around Chŏngju, formerly part of the Paekche kingdom. A total of 754 earthenware and copper pieces are on display in the museum.

Relics from the Paekche period account for most of the Kwangju Municipal Museum's collection. This city-run institution has been in existence since long before the Kwangju National Museum was built. The museum's collection includes 3,674 items.

A total of 1,111 items including many metalware objects are displayed in the Inch'ŏn Municipal Museum. Inch'ŏn, a major port of entry, was the first port opened to foreign trade.

Opened in 1984, the Cheju Folklore and Natural History Museum preserves, exhibits and studies the cultural heritage and folklore of the relatively isolated subtropical island of Chejudo, located off Korea's south coast, as well as its flora, fauna and geology.

The collection of the Pusan Municipal Museum is comprised of 2,079 relics which, for the most part, were collected from shell mounds and ancient tombs dating back to prehistoric times in the Pusan area once part of the Kaya Kingdom. Of particular interest are the earthen-

The interior of the National Museum of Contemporary Art in the suburbs of Seoul.

ware and articles made of bone.

As Koryŏng, Kyŏngsangbuk-do, was once a capital of the Kaya Kingdom, it is rich in historical sites such as ancient tombs. The Koryŏng Country Museum has a 1,500-piece collection that includes many earthenward pieces. The Koryŏng area is famous for pottery.

The Ch'unch'ŏn Museum is rather small but its collection includes a variety of art works, household items and utensils, and many excavated items.

College and University Museums

A total of 73 colleges and universities have their own museums. Those which have departments of archaeology and history often participate in the exploration and excavation of archaeological and historical remains. At times, they also undertake such activities on their own, frequently recovering objects of value which are preserved and displayed in their own museums.

By and large, the historical relics kept at these museums differ in character from region to region. Many of the relics at the Kyungpook and Yeungnam universities in Taegu, formerly part of the Shilla Kingdom, are remains from that kingdom. Collections of the museums of the Chŏnam, Chosun, and Jeonbug universities as well as the Kongju National Teachers College, all situated in what was the territory of the Paekche kingdom, consist predominantly of Paekche relics.

However, some university museums feature a collection of historical objects in one particular category that reflect the emphasis the schools place on certain studies. The Suk Joo-sun Memorial Museum of Korean Folk Art attached to Dankook university is renowned for a comprehensive collection of costumes and accessories of the Chosŏn period, donated to the school by Dr. Suk Joo-sun. These items are valuable to the study of the history of Korean apparel and ornaments. Soongjun University Museum is noted for an elaborated collection of objects and data related to the history of Christianity in Korea. Ewha Woman's University Museum and Kyunghee University Museum boast well-sorted collections of fauna, flora, and minerals in Korea.

Private Museums

There are more than a dozen private museums in Korea, most of them established by private citizens, religious organizations or business enterprises. In many cases, the collections consist of historical remains which took private collectors almost a lifetime to gather.

Some private collections are of folk culture, while others consist of books, religious objects, furniture, ornaments, embroidery and other valuable relics and artifacts. The size of the private museums vary according to the kind and content of collections. A few private museums far surpass local national museums in size and content.

The oldest private museum in Korea is the Kansong Art Museum. It was established by Chŏn Hyŏng P'il, a private collector, in 1938. The collection of the Kansong Art Museum comprises approximately 12,000 objects, including more than 10,000 volumes of books of 2,200 titles, more than 500 paintings and drawings, and 200 ceramic works. Among the collection are four ceramic pieces, two gilt-bronze Buddhist figures, three original books of immense value including the *Hunmin chŏng-um*, the original description of the Korean alphabet, and a painting, all of which have been designated national treasures. The collection also includes six ceramic pieces, two gilt-bronze Buddhist images and a book that have been designated treasures.

At the Yong-in Farm Land southeast of Seoul, the Ho-Am Art Museum is one of the most outstanding museums in both size and the scope of its collection. It includes not only a variety of ancient Korean works but also a number of major modern Korean art works. It also has a number of art pieces done by European artists such as Rodin, Bourdelle, Maillol and Henry Moore.

The museum was opened to the public in 1982 with a total of 6,104 objects. Its collection, however, has grown rapidly since then as it continues to purchase more and more works of art, both ancient and modern pieces.

The collecting of modern Korean art works was begun quite early when most Korean modern artists were little recognized. This collection, which includes the works of many famous artists who are no longer living, is particularly valuable to the study of Korea's modern art history.

The museum's collection includes a calligraphic work, a painting, four ceramic pieces, and eight metalwork pieces designated national treasures and a metalwork piece and two earthenware pieces designated treasures.

The Horim Art Museum was established by Yun Chang-sŏp with his private collection in 1982. Its collection is of high quality and includes many widely acclaimed masterpieces. Among these are 21 objects which were included in the highly celebrated exhibition "5000 Years of Korean Art," displayed both at home and abroad.

The 1,188-piece collection includes 111 metal art objects, five precious stones, 240 pieces of earthenware, 673 ceramic pieces, 18 ornamental roof tiles, three wood carvings, four paintings, and 134 miscellaneous items. The museum is especially noted for its excellent collection of ceramics and Buddhist art works.

The ceramics include a slip-covered porcelain flask decorated with an incised and graffito decoration, designated National Treasure No. 179. The Buddhist objects in the collection shed light on the history of Korea's Buddhist arts and some of them have helped solve puzzling questions about Buddhist art in Korea.

The Onyang Folk Museum is one of several museums of its kind established in provincial areas. It is almost comparable to the National Folklore Museum in size and variety. Originally begun as a private collection, many visitors have donated items to it.

The current collection includes 14,000 objects. Displayed in a systematic fashion, the items help the viewer to readily understand many aspects of local culture including tradi-

The Independence Hall Complex in Mokch'ŏn-myŏn, Ch'ŏnwon-kun, Ch'ungch'ŏngnam-do province.

tional lifestyle, industry, folk arts, folk beliefs, forms of amusements, scholarly pursuit, and local institutions.

Recently relocated to a site near a fabled pine tree that stands in the vicinity of Pŏpchusa, a renowned Buddhist temple on Mt. Songnisan, the Emille Museum is noted for its collection of works done by proverbial folk painters. Valued for their rustic simplicity and rich sense of humor, these paintings have been frequently exhibited in many cities in Korea and abroad. The 1,400-piece collection includes 800 folk paintings and 300 ancient roof tiles.

Specialty Museums

A number of other museums in Korea have been founded by business firms and various other organizations. These specialize in the collection and exhibition of historical data and related objects pertaining to the activities of the founders.

The Bankers Museum and the Securities Museum contain historical materials concerning Korea's financial institutions. The Handok Pharmaceutical Museum and the T'aepyŏngyang Chemicals museum are a rich source of data concerning the history of the chemical industries in Korea. The Textbook Museum serves as a useful guide to Korea's printing and publishing history. The Communications Museum has a comprehensive collection of historical items, especially items related to the postal service. A look at the nation's military history, including weaponry, can be taken at the Military Academy Museum and the Naval Academy Museum. Or, for a glimpse into the history of beer brewing in Korea, one may go to the OB Beer Museum.

Independence Hall Complex

The Independence Hall Complex stands on a 3,993,936 sq.m. site in the city of Mokch'onmyŏn, Ch'ŏnwon'gun, Ch'ungch'ŏngnam-do Province. Close to the Seoul-Pusan Expressway, the complex includes Independence Hall, seven display rooms, and a huge granite memorial.

Adjacent to a 142,000 square meter parking lot is a 46,200 square meter plaza where stands a towering 51.2 meter-high stone structure erected as a symbol of resolve toward progress and reunification of the divided land.

Behind the tower is the Independence Hall, a 46 meter-high, 126 meters-long building constructed in a traditional Korean style. In the center of the hall is a 15 meter-high stone sculpture named "The Korean Image." The hall functions as a library, as archives, an exhibition center, a theater, and a research facility.

The first display room features materials depicting the struggle to overcome national crises and ordeals of the past. The second display room exhibits materials concerned with the modern cultural movement and the Tonghak Movement as well as the Korean campaigns against foreign invaders prior to Japan's annexation of Korea in 1910. The third display room contains a 6 meter-high structure entitled "The Spirit of the Samil Independence Movement" and materials related to the period of Japanese rule.

Exhibited in the fourth display room are more materials on the Independence Movement. The fifth display room has a large movie screen that encircles the viewers. Films depict various campaigns waged by Korean independence fighters and militia. In the sixth display room are materials related to the activities of the Korean Independence Army and the Provisional Government of the Republic of Korea established in Shanghai, China in the wake of the March First Independence Movement.

On the hill behind these six display rooms is a 2-to-5 meter-high, 110 meter-long granite memorial with relief carvings and an eternal flame.

Galleries

Korea has a number of art galleries, many of them located near drama theaters, concert halls and dance theaters. Some of the largest are operated by the central and local governments. While they are concentrated in Seoul, there also are many fine galleries in other areas, especially in the provincial capitals and cities. The galleries frequently host individual and group exhibitions, both Korean and foreign. Some specialize in contemporary paintings, prints, sculpture, and crafts.

Dozens of art galleries are concentrated in the neighborhoods around the National Museum in Seoul. A narrow street a few blocks from the museum in Insa-dong and its side alleys are lined with galleries as well as shops specializing in antiques, curios, paintings, ceramics, and other art works, as well as frames for paintings and calligraphy.

Galleries in that area and in the areas to the immediate east and west of the museum include Hyundai Gallery, Jean Art Gallery, Sun Gallery, Tongsan-Bang, the French Cultural Center, Dong Duck Gallery, Kwanhun Gallery, the Arab Cultural Center, and Kyŏngin Gallery.

A street in Tongsung-dong lined with mini-theaters and art galleries known as Daehangno (University Street) is a mecca for many art lovers. Along one section of it is the Korean Culture and Arts Foundation. The institute's main building houses a fine arts hall that has a 468.6 square meter exhibition room on the first floor and a 464 square meter one on the second floor. Mostly international exchange exhibitions and exhibitions of local art groups are held in the hall.

The center's reference library offers cultural and art information about Korea and other countries and data for use by the general public. Works of Korean sculptors are located throughout the grounds of the institute.

The Duson and Saem-teo galleries are among the most popular in the Tongsung-dong area. Also of interest is the Korea Design and Packaging Center on the south side of Taehangno, which mostly works of visual design and industrial arts.

In the Shinch'on area, the location of Yŏnsei,

The Sejong Cultural Center in downtown Seoul.

Sŏgang, Hongik, and Ewha Woman's universities, there are a number of small art galleries as well as some small theaters. These galleries, including the Hangang Gallery, the Jun Gallery, and the Hu Gallery, exhibit mostly experimental works by young avant-garde painters.

The newly developed Kangnam residential area south of the Han-gang River is fast becoming a fashionable site for small theaters and art galleries. Some have moved to the plush new region from other traditional areas north of the river. The Ye Gallery and the Park Young Suk Gallery are among the most popular.

Most major department stores and shopping centers in the metropolis have art galleries. Because of their location, these galleries are constantly visited by large numbers of viewers. They include the Shinsegae Gallery, the Lotte Gallery, the Midopa Gallery, the Dongbang Gallery, and the Hyundai Gallery.

The 1,650 square meter Sejong Cultural Center Gallery in downtown Seoul is one of the largest in Korea. Because of its size and loca-tion, the gallery attracts many art lovers who can also enjoy excellent performances by world-renowned musicians, vocalists, and ballet dancers, at the Sejong Cultural Center's main auditorium.

Just down the street in the Press Center Building is the Seoul Gallery. It frequently hosts group exhibitions and international exhibitions, including world-famous masterpieces from Europe and the United States.

The two-story Ho-Am Gallery in the Joongang Ilbo Building, the headquarters of the *Joongang Ilbo* newspaper, is one of Seoul's new galleries. Part of the 924 square meter exhibition area on the first floor is 8.7 meters high to accommodate large exhibits. The second-floor exhibition area has a floor space of 396 square meters. There is also a 330 square meters outdoor display area for sculptural works. The gallery is one of the most frequently visited because of its high quality exhibits, as well as because of the Ho-Am Art Hall which is located within the same building.

The National Theater in Seoul.

Theaters

There are about a dozen all-purpose theaters in the country. Of course, the largest were built and opened during the 1970s. One has more than 4,000 seats, six have more than 2,000 seats each, and five have seating capacities of 1,000 or more. Although some college and university theaters have less than perfect stage facilities such as lighting and acoustics, they are spacious enough to stage large-scale performances.

The largest of its kind in Korea, the Sejong Cultural Center was opened in 1978. Housed in it are the Seoul Philharmonic Symphony Orchestra, the Seoul City Orchestra for Traditional Music, the Seoul Municipal Dance Company, the Seoul Municipal Choir, and the Seoul Municipal Junior Choir.

Many of the center's facilities including lighting, acoustics, stages, and curtains are computerized. The computer system can automatically shift the tone and color of the lighting 500 dif-

ferent ways. The Center's pipe organ is the largest in Asia.

The center's main theater can seat 4,000 spectators and its smaller one, 530. The center also has an annex theater, located close to the City Hall, which has a seating capacity of 1,236.

Equipped with world-class facilities including stages, lighting, and sound equipment, the National Theater consists of a 1,518-seat main theater, a smaller 454-seat theater, an experimental theater, and an open-air stage for traditional folk plays. The theater's performing groups include the National Drama Company, the National Traditional Opera Company, the National Dance Company, the National Ballet Company, the National Choir, and the National Opera Company.

Located on the grounds of the Korean Culture and Arts Foundation in Tongsung-dong, the Mun-ye Center is used mainly for drama and dance performances. It has a 709-seat main theater and a 250-seat one.

The 1,000-seat Ho-Am Art Hall in the

Joongang Ilbo Building is operated by the *Joong-ang Ilbo* newspaper. The hall features a computerized stage and equally sophisticated lighting, acoustical equipment and other stage facilities. Performances range from concerts, dramas, and dance to operas and musicals. Movies are also shown occasionally.

The Ryu Kwan-sun Memorial Hall on the grounds of the Ewha Girls High School in downtown Seoul was dedicated in 1974 as a memorial to Ryu Kwan-sun, a student of the high school who was imprisoned and tortured by the Japanese police for her active role in the March First Independence Movement, later dying in prison. With a seating capacity of 2,023, the hall is used primarily for concerts and musicals. *Jesus Christ Superstar* and *the Sound of Music* are two of the musicals that have been staged here.

The 1,990-seat Soong-eui Music Hall is favored for concerts, especially chamber music. Among the many groups that have performed here is the Los Angeles Ballet Troupe. The hall is near Myŏng-dong, Seoul's fashionable downtown shopping district.

Named after a renowned Korean composer, Hong Nanp'a, the Nanp'a Music Hall consists of a main concert hall with 786 seats, a smaller one with 330 seats, and various other facilities including classrooms and practice rooms. It is located on the grounds of Dankook University.

The Heritage Hall of Intangible Cultural Assets in Samsŏng-dong, Kangnam-gu, Seoul, was built with the specific aim of preserving "intangible cultural assets," that is, arts and handicrafts traditional to Korea. Attached to the hall are six Korean performing arts groups, including a court music group, a traditional dance troupe, *p'ansori* (operatic songs interspersed with narrative) performers, and mask dancers. The 300-seat hall is used both for performance and classes.

The Little Angels Performing Arts Center near the Children's Park in Seoul is the home of the Little Angels Troupe whose singing and dancing have been widely acclaimed. The troupe was organized in 1962, mostly of talented teen-agers. The arts center was dedicated in the early 1980s after eight years of construction.

The five-story building with a basement houses a large auditorium with a seating capacity of 1,500. Equipped with world-class facilities, the hall stages performances by top class Korean foreign musicians, vocalists, and dancers.

In addition, there are 42 auditoriums in Korea with more than 500 seats each, which are used for concerts and various other performing arts programs. Some of the more noted are the Ewha Woman's University Auditorium (3,500 seats), Yŏnsei University Auditorium (2,300 seats), Sookmyung Women's University Auditorium (1,200 seats), Chungang University Auditorium (800 seats), Sŏgang University Auditorium (728 seats), and Hanyang University's Paeknam Music Hall (800 seats).

Of special interest is the Seoul *Nori Madang* located within the Sŏkch'on Lake Park near the Olympic Park in southeastern Seoul. This traditional amphitheater was built in an effort to preserve Korean folk plays and at the same time provide the public with a traditional form of entertainment. Performances of traditional music, dance, dramas and martial arts and given here often, mostly on weekends.

The *Nori Madang* consists of an arena and a traditional Korean-style pavilion for musicians. There are also rooms for dressing and rehearsing. Spectator seating is on an embankment surrounding the 561 meters arena where performances are staged.

Many small theaters have emerged in Korea in recent years in response to the increasing popularity of plays. Some are attached to large theaters, and others are designed so that they become part of the audience. There are many mini-theaters with few than 200 seats each, as well as a number of outdoor stages. Some in Seoul. Listed below are some of these theaters.

The 430-seat Drama Center was founded in 1962 by Korea's pioneering dramatist, Yu Ch'i-jin. The oldest private modern drama theater of its kind in Korea, it has contributed importantly to the development of modern dramas and stage plays in the country.

The theater, which resembles an ancient Grecian amphitheater with rising tiers of seats around the stage, is equipped with excellent lighting and acoustical facilities as well as stage

The Mun-ye Center in Tongsung-dong, Seoul.

costumes and props. Situated within the premises of the Seoul Institute of the Arts at the foot of Mt. Namsan, it is easily accessible from downtown Seoul. The theater primarily presents theatrical programs produced by the Tongnang Repertory Company and the Tongnang Junior Drama Group.Close to the Korean Culture and Arts Foundation in Tongsung-dong, the Pat'anggol Theater is part of a complex which also includes a small art gallery, a cafe, and a coffee shop. It is noted for its relaxed ambience.

The 200-seat Saem-teo P'arangsae Theater is also located in Tongsung-dong. It has variable stage and seating system. It usually presents puppet shows for children in the daytime and plays for adult audiences in the evening.

Set up in 1984 in Taehyŏn-dong, western Seoul, where several universities are situated, the tiny Citizen Theater is used exclusively by the Citizens Theatrical Group. It can accommodate only 100 spectators but has excellent stage facilities. A slightly larger theater called the Shinsŏn Theater is located nearby. Its facilities include a variable stage.

In the same general area is the 200-seat Minye Theater which was founded by the Folk Art Puppet Theater. It offers special programs of traditional performing arts at least six times a year. It also holds folk drama workshops twice a year. Occasionally, the theater sponsors poetry recitations and presents poetic dramas. In addition, it provides the stage for excellent new drama selections.

In the nearby area, the small Malttugi Theater features both a variable stage and variable spectators' seating. Complete with lighting, acoustical and other stage facilities, the theater can seat up to 200 persons. Drama programs are often presented free of charge.

The 130-seat Sanulim Theater specializes in stage plays. Its architectural design is such that its acoustics are excellent.

The 280-seat Cecil Theater, which opened in January 1981, specializes in its own drama productions. It is located beside the Anglican Church, which is behind the Sejong Cultural

The Seoul Arts Center.

Center Annex.

The 130-to-170-capacity Salon Theater Ch'u, which was established in 1985 by Ch'u Song-ung, a noted Korean comedian and drama actor, is located in the Myŏng-dong area. It offers a French salon-type atmosphere in which performers and audience mingle after performances.

The 134-seat Shilhŏm Theater, located in Chong-no, was established in October 1960 for the exclusive use of the Shilhŏm Theatrical Group. It has a proscenium and is equipped with good stage facilities.

The Mirinae Theater in Chong-no has a variable stage with rows of spectators seats around it. The name of the theater, Mirinae, is an ancient Korean word denoting the Milky Way, a favorite theme of Korean folklore.

Of special interest is the Space Gallery, located near the Secret Garden in Chong-no. With a variable stage and variable seating arrangements for up to 200 spectators, it offers a wide range of performing arts such as traditional Korean plays, chamber music, poetry recitations, modern dance, traditional Korean dance, and even jazz. The theater is highly selective in its presentation of performing arts.

The 250-seat Hyundai Cultural Center in the Hyundai Department Store presents only its own theatrical productions. It was opened in December 1985.Other small playhouses with around 200 seats in Seoul include Pagoda Drama, Ch'angmu Dance, Minjung, Crystal Culture, King & Poetry, Elcanto Art, Yŏnu, T'emen malttugi, Aeogae, New Core Art, and Shinch'on "Pierrot."

Seoul Arts Center

One of the more recent, major arrivals on the cultural scene is the Seoul Arts Center. It is the first multi-disciplinary arts center and cultural park in Korea. Parts of the center were completed and put in use in the late 1980s, and with the opening of the main venue of the complex, the Seoul Opera House, in February, 1993, the center became completely ready for multi-disciplinary cultural activities.

Located in southern Seoul on the slope of Wonmyon Mountain, the center includes Seoul Opera House, Concert Hall, Calligraphy Hall, Arts Gallery, Arts Library and Cultural Theme Park. The total land space covers over 234,385 square meters and the total floor space 120,951 square meters.

The Seoul Opera House includes the Opera House, the Towol Theater, the Chayu Theater and numerous other facilities. The Opera House, which is complete with the latest technical equipment, is capable of staging five-act operas. It holds 2,340 seats and is equipped with three supplementary stages which make simultaneous rehearsals possible even during a performance. The Towol Theater, with 710 seats, is used mainly for drama, but is also available for dances, musicals, opera buffe and operettas. It has almost the same stage capabilities as that of the Opera House, although smaller in scale. The Chayu Theater is designed for the production of small-scale and experimental projects, and it has an adjustable capacity ranging from 300 to 600 seats. Free from any strict separation between stage and audutorium, the theater can be easily reshaped into an arena, proscenium, a typical apron, or other arrangement, according to the director's desires.

The Concert Hall was opened in February, 1988, with the aim of the presenting a wide variety of musical performances, including symphony orchestras, choral concerts, chamber groups and recitals, as well as offerings from the field of lighter entertainment. The Concert Hall already has provided the setting for the works of many outstanding musicians and has gained an international reputation for its superb acoustics.

The main auditorium of the Concert Hall has seats for 2,600 people. There also is a Recital Hall that can seat 400. Practice rooms, instrument areas and dressing rooms can accommodate two full-size orchestras at the same time.

Also opened in 1988 was the Calligraphy Hall, which adjoins the Korean Classical Music Institute, the Korean garden and market place at the center. Combining modern architecture with traditional Korean forms, the Calligraphy Hall was designed as a place to preserve and develop the national heritage in the calligraphic arts.

The Arts Gallery has a total floor area of 15,642 square meters and was planned to exhibit all forms of visual arts in two-dimensional or three-dimensional form. Exhibition space provided on three floors accommodates three types of galleries.

The nearby Arts Library, with a total floor area of 11,719 square meters, is intended to improve the knowledge and understanding of arts through reference materials and technological aids. In addition to printed materials, it includes various forms of audio-visual facilities with film archives and two small cinemas.

Atriums are featured in a number of the center facilities, and the natural-setting environment is carried further in the Cultural Theme Park that links and borders various cultural activity hubs. Gardens, trees, bushes, flowers, plants and lawns combine with plazas and water cascades to blend into the effort to make the Seoul Arts Center an important part of a move toward an era of the arts and culture.

CONSTITUTION AND GOVERNMENT

The Korean national flag, the *T'aegŭkki*, and the national flower, the *Mugunghwa*.

Historical Background

The concept of government in the Korean tradition is based principally on the Confucian socio-political doctrine that became official state philosophy during the Chosŏn Dynasty (1392-1910).

In the Confucian tradition, government is a reflection of *Li*, or a worldly authority conferred by the mandate of heaven. A good government, therefore, must assure a proper elite-mass relationship based on an authoritarian hierarchical social order, not on a contractual arrangement or "rule of law."

The culturally pervasive authoritarian submissiveness of Korean political attitudes and behavior patterns supported a government of the elite selected through the competitive *kwagŏ* or higher civil service examination. The Chosŏn government was an organic, unitary, centralized pyramid with the king at the apex of state institutions and major policy-making organs—the State Council (*Ŭijŏngbu*), the Royal Secretariat (*Sŭngjŏngwon*), and the six ministries — Personnel, Finance, Rites, War, Justice, and Public Works. Local government was divided into eight provinces (*do*), which in the main still exist today, and several types of counties. There was no separate judicial system, and administrative, legislative and judiciary functions were ultimately concentrated in the all-powerful monarch.

Governing functions were carried out exclusively by *sadaebu*, or scholar-officials of the *yangban* class. They prepared administrative timetables, supervised public works, established laws and regulations, and manned the court system. The scholar-officials, as generalists with diverse functions, constituted the ruling class, embodying the power of the state in a paternalistic and, at times, tyrannical manner.

It was not until 1910 that this traditional government structure was officially abolished by the Japanese, who annexed the country. Japan's colonial government (1910-45) attempted to integrate the Korean Peninsula and its people into the political, cultural, and economic systems of Japanese imperialism; a stern, central-ized, authoritarian administration, devoid of constitutional or popular restraints, and politically despotic and economically purposeful.

Generally, Japan's colonial government in Korea had three stages: 1) military dictatorship (1910-20); 2) conciliatory reforms (1920-39); and 3) integration (1939-45). During the first decade of annexation, political activity was looked upon as a dangerous nuisance by the Japanese military autocrats, and neither interest groups nor political parties were encouraged. Koreans were denied all access to political power, had no franchise, and were not even allowed voluntary association in nonpolitical activities.

Subsequent to the March First Independence Movement of 1919, restraints on socio-political activities were somewhat relaxed. Local administration was reorganized with prefectural advisory councils in which Koreans were allowed to participate, but the function of these councils were limited to consultation. During the last stage of occupation, the Japanese colonial bureaucracy sought to mobilize the Korean people for war preparations, while widening the scope of participation by Koreans in government. Even with that, the highest level a Korean could reach was head of a county (*kun*).

The Governor-General ruled Korea through the Government-General consisting of a secretariat and seven departments: home affairs, finance, industry, agriculture and forestry, education, justice, and police. Besides these departments and sections, there were a number of bureaus and institutions under the direct jurisdiction of the Governor-General. Local government was divided into 13 provinces, each ruled by a provincial governor. Each province exercised jurisdiction over municipalities, counties, towns, and townships. In comparison to the Chosŏn administrative structure, the colonial bureaucracy was highly specialized or differentiated, and even a cursory survey of its institutions shows a high degree of centralization.

After Korea's liberation from Japanese colonial rule, the American Military Government in Korea (1945-48) administered that part of the country south of the 38th parallel. It retained the Japanese bureaucratic administrative structure as a temporary measure, however, because

Koreans lacked experience in government and because the vacuum had to be filled quickly. As a result, the military government was neither popular nor effective.

Modern Korean government may be divided into six periods: 1) the Rhee Government under a presidential system (the First Republic, 1948-60), led by Syngman Rhee; 2) the Democratic Party Government under a parliamentary system (the Second Republic, 1960-61) led by Chang Myŏn; 3) the Third Republic (1962-72) and the Fourth Republic (1972-1980) led by Park Chung Hee and following his death, by Choi Kyu-hah; 4) the Fifth Republic (1980-88) led by Chun Doo Hwan; and 5) the Sixth Republic (1988-93)led by Roh Tae Woo; 6) the Kim Young Sam Administration (1993-).

The Rhee regime largely retained the pre-independence administrative apparatus of ministries, bureaus, and sections, but they were expanded somewhat in size and functional scope. Under Korea's first Constitution, the President appointed heads of ministries, who were also members of the State Council. Several agencies, such as the Offices of Monopoly, Legislation, Supply, and Marine Affairs, were created under various ministries. In addition to these ministries and offices, there were four agencies directly responsible to the President: the Board of Audit, the Office of Atomic Energy, the Office of Public Information, and the Inspection Commission. Local government had little autonomy because the President held the authority to appoint provincial governors and the mayor of Seoul.

Following the April 19th student uprising in 1960, the Second Republic was established by the Democratic Party on August 23, 1960, marking the beginning of the Chang Myŏn Administration. The Democratic Party instituted a parliamentary-cabinet type political system similar to the British system. The power of the President was to be symbolic or ceremonial, while the executive power was vested in the cabinet, headed by a prime minister and collectively responsible to the lower house. Local government was reorganized to decentralize many of its functions.

By law, local autonomy was provided for each local government unit with a representative assembly based upon popular elections. Because of extreme political crises, however, the Democratic Party Government was given to instability and was in no position to implement the local autonomy law. As a result of the military revolution on May 16, 1961, the Supreme Council for National Reconstruction headed by General Park Chung Hee took over the combined legislative, executive, and judicial functions of the government. After amending the Constitution, the general elections of 1963 made Park the President in a system based upon centralized government. Under this, the Third Republic Constitution, executive functions were concentrated in the President, who headed the State Council as Chief Executive.

Rapid social and economic change, U.S. President Richard Nixon's trip to Peking in February 1972, and the opening of the South-North dialogue led President Park to the conclusion that the central government had to be strengthened. The Constitution was amended by referendum in November 1972, ushering in the Fourth Republic. The *Yushin Hŏnpŏp*, or Revitalizing Reforms Constitution, as it was called, was aimed at insuring political stability, and at completing the historic task of national revival through socio-economic progress under strong presidential leadership.

The assassination of President Park on October 26, 1979, brought the disintegration of the *Yushin* system and the end of a political era. The transition period under martial law was headed by President Choi Kyu-hah, who had been prime minister under President Park. The Choi Administration established the Special Committee for National Security Measures, headed by General Chun Doo Hwan, to act as liaison with the martial law authorities and to effect reforms to solve the root causes of the social unrest, economic decline, increasing student demonstrations, and labor disputes following Park's death.

President Choi resigned on August 16, 1980, and Chun Doo Hwan was elected president by the National Conference for Unification on August 27.

One of the chief tasks of the interim administration was the preparation of amendments to the Constitution to meet demands for political reform. This work was begun in March 1980 and the amended Constitution was overwhelmingly endorsed on October 22, 1980. The Fifth Republic under President Chun Doo Hwan was officially established under the new Constitution promulgated on October 27, 1980. The chief significance of this constitution was its stipulation of a single seven-year term of office for the President, which President Chun saw as the basis on which democracy could be established. Its main failing was its otherwise authoritarian character highlighted by a weighted presidential election system.

Following the National Assembly elections in February, 1985, the opposition parties began to increase their demands for an amendment to the Constitution to provide for the direct election of the President. The ruling party at first opposed revising the Constitution, saying there should be at least one peaceful change of administrations before an amendment was considered. Later it changed its attitude when it became clear that there was sweeping public support for direct elections. On June 29, 1987, Roh Tae Woo, then chairman of the ruling Democratic Justice Party, made a declaration accepting broad political reforms, especially an amendment to the Constitution. This brought about a dramatic compromise settlement between the opposition and ruling parties, resulting in the first supra-partisan agreement on constitutional revision in Korea's history.

These efforts led to the birth of the Sixth Republic. In the presidential election held in December 1987, Roh Tae Woo was elected and in the following February, President Chun became the first Korean president to turn over the reins of government in a normal, constitutional procedure.

Demands for wider freedoms restrained by years of authoritarian government surfaced in many social sectors during the Roh Administration. Many of these demands were accommodated.

The Korean economy generally stagnated during the five years of the Roh Tae Woo regime, due mainly to a decrease in competitiveness fueled by widespread strikes, rapid wage increase, and growing protectionism overseas. Democratic institutions, however, were greatly strengthened in the Roh years. Labor union activities expanded dramatically, local autonomy was restored as citizens elected local councils throughout the country, and the press exercised freedom to the full extent.

The democratic advances achieved during the Roh administration set the stage for the return of civilian government after a 32-year hiatus. Kim Young Sam was elected President in December, 1992, and his inauguration on February 25, 1993, reopened civilian rule in Korea.

The Constitution

The Constitution of the Republic of Korea was first promulgated on July 17, 1948. It was amended in 1952 and 1954 during the First Republic, in 1960 following the Student Revolution, in 1962 and 1972 during the Third Republic, in 1980 during the Fourth Republic, and in 1987 during the Fifth Republic. The 1960 version provided the basis for the Second Republic; the 1962 version is known as the Constitution of the Third Republic; the 1972 version was the Yushin Hŏnpŏp, meaning Revitalizing Reforms Constitution of the Fourth Rebulic; the 1980 version, the Constitution of the Fifth Republic; and the 1987 version, the Constitution of the Sixth Republic. These revisions centered mostly on the form of government, methods of electing the President and his powers and term of office.

Under the *Yushin* Constitution, Korea's governmental system was more highly centralized than ever. The alleged purposes of the constitutional change were: first, to cope with the pre-emptive tasks of national defense and socio-economic development in the midst of international power politics; second, to open a South-North Korean dialogue looking to the peaceful unification of Korea; and third, to develop a democracy suitable for Korea, instead of following the practice of imitating the Western model of liberal-pluralist democracy without considering

Korea's possibilities and limitations.

With the death of President Park, it was generally agreed that the Constitution would have to be amended to take into account past grievances, especially the prolonged rule of one man, and the fact that Korea had developed to a new level of economic, social and political sophistication. The Constitution of the Fifth Republic purportedly aimed at the realization of a genuine democracy guaranteeing social justice and the well-being of all citizens, but in fact it retained the authoritarian character of the *Yushin* system.

The Constitution of the Sixth Republic, designed to eliminate all vestiges of authoritarianism, was especially significant because it was the first revised constitution to grow out of an agreement between the ruling and opposition parties which participated in its creation. It was unanimously approved by the National Assembly and received wide public support in a national referendum.

The most striking change is the adoption of the direct election of the President for a single five-year term and the curtailment of his powers through the abolition of presidential emergency powers and the presidential authority to dissolve the National Assembly. The Constitution also extends fundamental human rights, restores the right of the National Assembly, with a four-year term, to inspect government offices, creates a more independent judiciary, and applies democratic principles to the economy.

The Constitution consists of a preamble, 130 articles, and six supplementary rules. It is divided into 10 chapters: General Provisions, Rights and Duties of Citizens, the National Assembly, the Executive, the Courts, the Constitution Court, Election Management, Local Autonomy, the Economy, and Amendments.

The Constitution declares in Article I that the nature of the Republic of Korea is defined as democratic, and sovereignty is vested in the people. It respects international obligations, ratifies treaties, and the generally recognized rules of international law.

The Constitution guarantees the basic rights and freedoms of the Korean people, setting limits in the exercise of governmental powers, while making provisions whereby civil rights may be restricted by law only when necessary for the maintenance of national security, public order or general welfare. Political rights include: equality before the law regardless of sex, religion, or social status; freedom from arbitrary arrest; freedom of residence; the right to vote and to hold public office; the right of the accused to prompt assistance of counsel and to a speedy trial, and the right to request the court for a review of the legality of arrest or detention.

There are also other guarantees such as the privacy of correspondence and freedom of religion, conscience, speech, press, and assembly. The Constitution more explicitly emphasizes the right to a clean environment and the right to seek happiness, optimum wages, fair compensation, and protection of privacy. Freedom and rights of citizens may not be neglected simply because they are not enumerated in the Constitution.

The Constitution recognizes economic rights, including the right to own property; the right as well as the duty to work; freedom of choice of occupation, and the right to collective bargaining. Where public interest dictates, laws can limit the economic rights of citizens.

Among the social and cultural guarantees are those providing for the freedom of scientific and artistic pursuits, equal educational opportunities, lifelong education and improvement of teachers' status, welfare benefits for citizens incapable of earning a livelihood, and protection for working women and children. The basic law also declares that all citizens have the duty to pay taxes and the duty to defend the nation in accordance with the provisions of law.

A motion to amend the Constitution may be proposed either by the President or by a majority of the National Assembly. The National Assembly shall decide proposed amendments within 60 days of the public announcement of the amendment by the concurrence of two thirds or more of the members. Proposed amendments to the Constitution must be submitted to a national referendum not later than 30 days after passage by the National Assembly and shall be determined by a majority of the votes cast representing more than half of all voters.

The National Assembly

Legislative power is vested in the National Assembly, a unicameral body. The Assembly is composed of 299 members elected by popular vote for a four-year term. Assemblymen elected by popular vote comprise two thirds of the membership with the remaining seats distributed proportionately among parties winning five seats or more in the direct election. It is expected that the parties will appoint Assemblymen who can represent the national interest in contrast to local interests and thus they are called Chŏngukku Ŭiwon or National Constituency Assemblymen.

To be eligible for election, a candidate must be at least 25 years of age. One candidate from each electoral district is chosen by a plurality of votes. The present National Assembly has 224 seats for those elected by popular vote and 75 seats for proportionate distribution.

An Assemblyman is entitled to the usual privileges as a legislator. He is not held responsible outside the Assembly for any opinions expressed or votes cast in the legislative chamber. During the session of the Assembly, no Assemblyman may be arrested or detained without consent of the Assembly except in cases of *flagrante delicto*. In case of apprehension or detention of an Assemblyman prior to the opening of the session, he must be released during the session upon the request of the Assembly except in case of *flagrante delicto*. Aside from these privileges, an Assemblyman is subject to certain limitations. No Assemblyman may concurrently hold any other office proscribed by law, nor is he to abuse his position and privileges. However, with the exception of a few categories specified by law, Assembly members may pursue remunerative occupations outside parliament. They are required to maintain high standards of integrity.

Two types of legislative session are provided for, regular and extraordinary. A regular session is convened once every year in accordance with the provisions of law, and extraordinary sessions may be convened upon the request of the President or a quarter or more of the members of the Assembly. The period of a regular session is limited to 100 days, of extraordinary session to 30 days.

If the President requests the convening of an extraordinary session, he must clearly specify the period of the session and the reasons for the request. During an extraordinary session convened at the call of the President, only bills submitted by the chief executive will be deliberated within the stipulated period. Except as otherwise provided in the constitution or law, the attendance of more than one half of the Assembly members duly elected and seated, and the concurrent vote of more than one half of the Assembly members present, are necessary to make decisions of the National Assembly binding. In case of a tie vote, the matter is considered to be rejected by the Assembly. Legislative sessions are open to the public, but this rule can be waived with the approval of more than one half of the members present or when the speaker deems it necessary to do so in the interest of national security.

The National Assembly is vested with a number of functions under the Constitution. The foremost is that of lawmaking. The Assembly has the power to deliberate and act on all legislative bills introduced either by members of the Assembly or by the administration. A second function of the Assembly pertains to the approval of the national budget. The executive branch must formulate the budget bill for each fiscal year and submit it to the National Assembly at least 90 days before the beginning of a new fiscal year. The Assembly is required to decide upon the budget bill at least 30 days before the beginning of a new fiscal year. Issuance of national bonds and entering into contracts chargeable to the national treasury other than those authorized in the budget require the prior approval of the Assembly.

A third function of the legislature is in the area of foreign policy. The Assembly has the right of consent to the ratification of treaties pertaining to mutual assistance or mutual security, treaties concerning international organiza-

The National Assembly Building in Seoul.

tions, treaties of commerce, fisheries, and peace, treaties which cause a financial obligation to the state or people, treaties concerning the status of foreign armed forces on Korean territory, and treaties related to legislative matters. A fourth function is related to war. The Assembly has the right to approve a declaration of war, the dispatch of armed forces abroad or the stationing of alien forces within the country.

A fifth function of the Assembly is that of inspecting affairs of state or investigating specific matters of state affairs. When requested by the Assembly or its committees, the Prime Minister, State Council members, and representative of the executive branch must appear before the Assembly and answer questions. The legislature has the power to adopt a motion recommending to the President the dismissal of the Prime Minister or any member of the State Council. A motion for removal of executive officials may be introduced by one third or more

members of the Assembly, and passed with the concurrence of more than one half of the members of the Assembly.

A sixth function of the Assembly is impeachment. Should the President, the Prime Minister, cabinet members, heads of executive ministries, members of the Constitutional Court, judges, members of the Central Election Management Committee, members of the Board of Audit and Inspection or other public officials designated by law be deemed to have violated the Constitution or any other law in the performance of their duties, the National Assembly has the power to initiate motions for impeachment.

A motion for impeachment must be proposed by one third or more of the membership of the Assembly. The vote of a majority of the Assembly is necessary to carry an impeachment motion. A motion of impeachment against the President must be proposed by a majority of the members of the Assembly.

A person against whom impeachment proceedings have been instituted is suspended from exercising power until the end of the impeachment process. The effect of impeachment is limited to dismissal from public position. However, this does not exempt the impeached person from civil or criminal liability.

The Assembly elects one speaker and two vice speakers, who serve for two years. The Speaker presides over plenary sessions and represents the legislature, supervising its administration. The vice speakers assist the Speaker and take the chair in the absence of the Speaker.

The Assembly is divided into 16 standing committees with the following functional designations: House steering, Legislation and Judiciary, Foreign Affairs and National Unification, Administration, House Affairs, Finance, Economy and Science, National Defense, Education, Culture, Sports and Information, Agriculture, Forestry and Fisheries, Health and Social Affairs, Labor, Transportation and Communications, and Construction. In addition, special committees may be established whenever necessary.

Chairmen of the standing committees are elected from among members of the respective committees. The number of members of a standing committee is determined by Assembly regulations. Members serve for two years, and concurrent membership on more than one standing committee is prohibited. The committee chairman is authorized to control the proceedings, maintain order, and represent the committee. Bills and petitions are referred to the standing committees for examination. The committees constitute the chief forum for reconciling differences between the ruling and opposition parties.

Under the present National Assembly Act, each political group having 20 or more. Assemblymen may form a negotiating group which acts as a unit in inter-party negotiations in the Assembly. Assemblymen without party affiliation can form a separate negotiations group if their number is 20 or more. The negotiating groups name floor leaders and whips, who are responsible for negotiating with other groups. The floor leaders meet to discuss matters relating to the operation of the Assembly, meeting schedules, and debating orders of the items on agendas for plenary sessions and committee meetings.

A bill may be introduced by an Assemblyman with the concurrence of 20 or more Assembly members, or by the administration. When a bill is proposed or submitted, the Speaker refers it to the pertinent committee for consideration. For extensive examination, a committee may establish subcommittees under its authority. With the approval of the Speaker, a committee may hold public hearings to examine budget bills and other important bills or matters requiring professional knowledge, and solicit opinions from interested persons or experts.

Once a bill is acted upon, the committee's actions are reported to the Assembly floor. A bill voted down may not be referred to a plenary meeting unless the Speaker requests that it be dealt with at a plenary session. On the floor, the bill voted upon may be amended, rejected, approved, or sent back to the committee.

Each bill passed by the Assembly is sent to the executive branch and the President promulgates it within 15 days or may return it with his veto and explanatory statement to the legislature for reconsideration. The Assembly can, however, override the veto with the attendance of more than one half of the membership and with a two-thirds majority-vote of the members present. The bill in question then becomes law.

The President

Standing at the apex of the executive branch, the President functions as the head of state and represents the state in matters concerning foreign states. The President is elected by universal, equal, direct and secret ballot.

The presidential term is five years, and no one is allowed to seek a second term. This single-term provision is a safeguard for preventing anyone from holding the reins of government power for a protracted period of time. In case of presidential disability or death, the Prime Minister or the members of the State Council will temporarily act as President as determined by law.

The President holds supreme power regarding all executive functions. In the present political system, he plays six major roles. First, the President is head of state, symbolizing and representing the whole nation both in the governmental system and in foreign relations. He receives foreign diplomats, awards decorations and other honors, and performs ceremonial and pardoning functions. He has the duty to safeguard the independence, territorial integrity, and the continuity of the state and to protect the Constitution, in addition to the unique duty to pursue the peaceful unification of Korea. Second, the President is chief administrator, and thus enforces the laws passed by the legislature and issues orders and decrees for the enforcement of laws. The President has full power to direct the State Council and a varying number of advisory organs and executive agencies. He is authorized to appoint public officials, including the Prime Minister and heads of executive agencies. Third, the President is commander-in-chief of the armed forces. He has extensive authority over military policy, including the power to declare war. Fourth, the President is the leader of the major political party with a nationwide organization. He frequently appoints the top-level personnel of the executive branch, based on recommendations from his party. Fifth, the President is the chief diplomat and foreign policymaker. He may conclude treaties, accredit, receive or dispatch diplomatic envoys, and conclude peace with foreign nations. Finally, the President is chief policymaker and chief lawmaker. He may propose legislative bills to the National Assembly or express his views to the legislators in person or by written message. The President cannot dissolve the National Assembly, but, conversely, the National Assembly can hold the President ultimately accountable to the Constitution by means of the impeachment process.

In addition, the President is vested with extensive powers to meet national emergencies in time of internal turmoil, external menace, natural calamity or a grave financial or economic crisis. In such cases, the President can take the minimum necessary financial and economic actions or issue orders having the effect of law, only when it is required for the maintenance of national security or public peace and order, and there is no time to await convocation of the National Assembly. However, the President must subsequently notify and obtain the concurrence of the National Assembly. If he is unable to do so, the measure will be ineffective.

The President is also empowered to declare a state of martial law in accordance with the provisions of law in time of war, armed conflict, or similar national emergency. The exercise of such emergency power is, however, subject to the approval of the National Assembly.

State Council and Executive Agencies

The President performs his executive functions through the State Council made up of 15 to 30 members and presided over by the President, who is solely responsible for deciding all important governmental policies. The present State Council is composed of the President (chairman); the Prime Minister (vice chairman); two Deputy Prime Ministers, who are concurrently the Minister of the Economic Planning Board, and the Minister of National Unification Board respectively; 18 heads of executive ministries; and two ministers of state.

The State Council is to provide a forum for deliberation on major government policies and to advise the President accordingly. Constitutionally speaking, the council is a consultative body and in that capacity it has no decision-making power. The Constitution provides in Article 89 that the following matters are to be referred to the State Council for deliberation:

Basic plans on state affairs and general policies of the executive;

Declarations of war, conclusions of peace treaties and other important matters pertaining to foreign policy;

Draft amendments to the Constitution, proposals for national referenda, proposed treaties, legislative bills, and proposed presidential decrees;

Proposed budgets, closing of accounts, basic plans for disposal of state properties, conclusion of contracts which involve major financial obligations for the state, and other important financial matters;

Presidential emergency orders and emergency financial and economic actions or orders, proclamation and termination of martial law;

Important military affairs;

Matters pertaining to requests for convening extraordinary sessions of the National Assembly;

Awarding of honors;

Granting of amnesty, commutation and rehabilitation;

Matters regarding the determination of jurisdiction between executive ministries;

Basic plans concerning delegation or allocation of powers within the executive branch;

Evaluation and analysis of the administration of state affairs;

Formulation and coordination of important policies of each executive ministry;

Action for the dissolution of a political party;

Examination of petitions pertaining to executive policies submitted or referred to the executive branch;

Appointments of the prosecutor general, the presidents of the national universities, ambassadors, the chief of staff of each armed service, and such other public officials and managers of important state operated enterprises as are specified by law; and

Other matters presented by the President, the Prime Minister or a member of the State Council.

The Prime Minister is appointed by the President with the approval of the National Assembly. As the principal executive assistant to the President, the Prime Minister supervises the executive ministries under the direction of the President. Under his direct control, he manages the Office of Planning and Coordination. The Prime Minister has the power to deliberate major national policies and to attend the meetings of the National Assembly. He also has the

right to act on behalf of the President on such matters as may be delegated by the President, as well as the power to issue ordinances in his own name. Other authority vested in the Prime Minister includes the right to recommend to the President the appointment or dismissal of the members of the State Council.

Members of the State Council are appointed by the President upon recommendation by the Prime Minister. They have the right to lead and supervise the executive ministries under their administration, to deliberate major state affairs, to act on behalf of the President and to appear in the National Assembly and express opinions. The members are collectively and individually responsible to the President only.

In addition to the State Council, the President has two presidential agencies under his direct control to formulate and carry out national policies: The Board of Audit and Inspection, and the Agency for National Security Planning. Heads of these organizations are appointed by the President, but the presidential appointment to the Board of Audit and Inspection is subject to the approval of the National Assembly.

To aid the President and the State Council, the National Security Council, the Economic and Scientific Council, and the Administrative Reform Committee were established in 1964. But due to a drastic reshuffling of government structure, the former institutions were abolished and their functions were integrated into related ministries in November 1981.

The Board of Audit and Inspection, inaugurated in 1963, has the authority to audit the accounts of central and local government agencies, government corporations, and related organizations. The board is also vested with the power to inspect abuses of public authority or misconduct by public officials in their official duties. The findings are reported to the President and the National Assembly, although the board is responsible only to the chief executive.

The Agency for National Security Planning, originally established in June 1961 as the Central Intelligence Agency, is authorized to collect strategic intelligence of internal as well as external origin. It plans and coordinates the intelligence and security activities of the government, and engages in anti-communist activities.

Ministries

The Economic Planning Board

The Board takes charge of matters concerning the establishment of overall plans for development of the national economy, formation and execution of the government budget, mobilization of resources, investment, technical development, and economic cooperation with foreign countries and international organizations. The Minister of the Economic Planning Board is concurrently Deputy Prime Minister, and coordinates business among ministries related to economy and finance. The Board has Bureaus of Economic Planning, Price Policy, Project Evaluation, Post Evaluation and Coordination, Economic Research and Statistics; and Offices of Planning and Management, Budget, and Fair Trade. The Supply Administration is under the control of the Board.

The National Unification Board

The Board undertakes surveys and researches issues concerning national reunification, and works out measures and plans for national education and public information in preparation for the eventual reunification of the country. The Minister of the National Unification Board is concurrently Deputy Prime Minister.The board has Offices of Planning and Management, Unification Policy, and Information Analysis; and Bureaus of Intra-Korea Interchange and Cooperation, and Education and Public Information. It runs the Institute of Political Education for National Unification and oversees the Office of the South-North Dialogue.

The Ministry of Foreign Affairs

This Ministry has jurisdiction over matters concerning diplomacy, trade and treaties with foreign countries, other international agreements, and the protection and guidance of Korean nationals abroad. The Ministry is responsible for Korean missions to other countries, headed by ambassadors, consul-generals, and consuls, and maintains relations with the diplomatic and consular representatives of foreign states in Korea. The Ministry is also responsible for matters concerning economic and financial relations with other countries. The Ministry has Bureaus of Asian Affairs, American Affairs, European Affairs, African and Middle Eastern Affairs, International Organizations, Treaties, Information and Cultural Affairs, Economic Affairs, Consular and Overseas Residents Affairs, and Telecommunications and Documents; and Offices of Planning and Management, and Protocol. The Foreign Affairs and National Security Institute is under the control of the ministry.

The Ministry of Home Affairs

This Ministry is chiefly responsible for local administration, management of referenda, naturalization, civil emergency planning, the protection of lives and property of citizens, and national registries. The Ministry has a Planning and Management Office and Bureaus of Local Administration, and Local Finance, and Bureaus of Civil Defense and Fire-Prevention under the Direction of the Civil Defense Headquarters. The National Police Headquarters is under the direction and supervision of the Ministry.

The Ministry of Finance

This Ministry is responsible for the central government's financial affairs, including finance bills, currency, national bonds, accounts, taxation, customs, foreign exchange, and control of state-owned and vested properties. The Ministry controls and supervises the Office of National Tax Administration, and the Office of Customs Administration. The Ministry has Bureaus of Treasury, Finance, Securities and Insurance, International Finance, Tax Systems, and Customs, and Offices of Planning and Manegement, and National Tax Assessment. It also directs and supervises private banks in which the Government is the largest stockholder and the special banks set up by the Government.

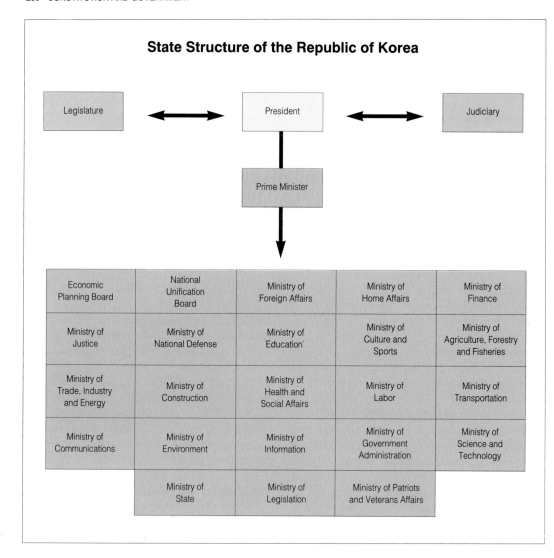

State Structure of the Republic of Korea

Economic Planning Board	National Unification Board	Ministry of Foreign Affairs	Ministry of Home Affairs	Ministry of Finance
Ministry of Justice	Ministry of National Defense	Ministry of Education`	Ministry of Culture and Sports	Ministry of Agriculture, Forestry and Fisheries
Ministry of Trade, Industry and Energy	Ministry of Construction	Ministry of Health and Social Affairs	Ministry of Labor	Ministry of Transportation
Ministry of Communications	Ministry of Environment	Ministry of Information	Ministry of Government Administration	Ministry of Science and Technology
	Ministry of State	Ministry of Legislation	Ministry of Patriots and Veterans Affairs	

The Ministry of Justice

This Ministry is responsible for prosecution, penal administration, control of exit from and entry into the country, protection of human rights, administration of civil and criminal justice, and other legal affairs. It is further responsible for the prison system, immigration, and supervision of prosecutors. The Ministry has Bureaus of Prosecution, Social Protection and Rehabilitation, Correction Administration, and Immigration Control; and Offices of Planning and Management, and Legal Affairs. The Ministry controls and supervises the Office of Public Prosecutions Administration.

The Ministry of National Defense

This Ministry deals with every aspect of the country's military affairs. The Armed Forces—Army, Navy, Air Force, and Homeland Reserve Forces—are placed under the control of this Ministry. Besides this, it is responsible for military registration. The functions of the Ministry include planning and management, budget, personnel, reserve forces, logistics, installations, medical affairs, defense industry, and information and education. The Ministry has a subordinate Office of Military Manpower.

The Ministry of Education

This Ministry is responsible for formulating and supervising the nation's educational and scientific policies and programs. The Ministry has Bureaus of Elementary and Secondary Education, Higher Education, Teacher Education, International Education, Non-formal Education, Vocational Education, and Educational Facilities; and Offices of Planning and Management, Supervision and Textbook Compilation, and Educational Policy. The Ministry controls and supervises the History Compilation Committee, the Central Educational Research Institute, the National Institute of Education, and the Executive Office of the National Academy of Science.

The Ministry of Culture and Sports

This Ministry is responsible for promoting and managing matters related to culture, arts, publications, policy on spoken and written Korean, religion, national sports and youth. It has Offices of Planning and Management, Religious Affairs, and Youth Policy, and Bureaus of Cultural Policy, Culture and Leisure, Arts Promotion, Language and Publications, Sports Policy, Sports Support, and International Sports. The Ministry controls and supervises the Cultural Property Preservation Office, the Korean Consolidated Arts school, the Executive Office of the National Academy of Arts, National Museums, the National Korean Language Institute, the National Library , the National Theater, the National Museum of Contemporary Art, the National Institute for Classic Music and the National Folk Museum. In addition, the Ministry is in charge of supporting and guiding the following specialized groups: in the culture and art field, the Korean Culture and Arts Foundation, the Seoul Arts Center, the Motion Picture and Arts Foundation, the Motion Picture Promotion Corporation and the Independence Hall; in the sports field, the Korea Amateur Sports Association, the Korean Olympic Committee and the Seoul Olympics Commemorative Sports Promotion Foundation; and in the youth development field, the Korean Institute for Youth Development.

The Ministry of Agriculture, Forestry and Fisheries

This Ministry is concerned with agriculture, horticulture and fruit-growing, sericulture, farmland irrigation, fisheries, and rural development. It administers loans for land improvement, promotion of plant culture and stock breeding, prevention of plant diseases, and guidance and assistance in the marketing of farm products. The Ministry is responsible for veterinary matters, land registration and agrarian rights. The Ministry has Bureaus of Agricultural Policy, Agricultural Production, Farmland, Special Crops and Sericultural Production, Livestock and Food Grain Policy, and Office of Planning and Management. Under its control and supervision are the Office of Rural Development Administration, the Office of Forestry and the Office of Fisheries Administration.

The Ministry of Trade, Industry and Energy

This Ministry is responsible for commerce, foreign trade, industry, and patents, and standards of manufactured products as well as the exploration, production, import, and all other matters related to energy and other resources. The Ministry also takes charge of trademarks, brands, cases of unfair competition, and import & export regulations. Its constituent bureaus are Trade, International Trade Promotion, Trade Cooperation, Industrial Policy, Small and Medium Industry, Basic Industry, Machinery Industry, Electronics and Information Industry, Textile Consumer Goods Industry, Energy Policy, Petroleum & Gas, Electronic Power, and Resources Development. The Office of Industrial Advancement Administration, the Office of Patents, and Korean Trade Commission are under the control and supervision of the Ministry.

The Ministry of Construction

This Ministry is responsible for establishing and coordinating plans for national land development and control, conservation, utilization, development and renovation of land and water resources, and construction of cities, roads, highways, ports, harbors, and housing. It is also concerned with building materials production, preparation of construction budgets, coordination of requirements, availability of materials and labor, and measures to stimulate construction, including building research and construction legislation. It has Bureaus of National Land Planning, Housing and Urban Planning, Water Resources, Public Roads, and Construction Industry and an Office of Planning and Management.

The Ministry of Health and Social Affairs

This Ministry deals with matters related to public health, epidemic prevention, public hygiene and sanitation, medical and pharmaceutical administration, public relief, emigration, women's and children's welfare, family planning, and various social welfare programs. It has Bureaus of Public Health, Medical Affairs, Drug and Food Affairs, Social Affairs, Social Insurance, and Home Welfare, and an Office of Planning and Management. It controls the National Health Institute, and the National Medical Center.

The Ministry of Labor

This Ministry is responsible for managing and coordinating matters related to standardization of working conditions, occupation stability, job training, insurance and social welfare for workers, and labor disputes. It has Bureaus of Labor Cooperation, Occupation Stability, and Job and Labor Insurance, and an Office of Planning and Management. Under its control are the Offices of Local Labor Administration, Rehabilitation and National Labor Science Research, the National Job Training Center, and the Central Labor Commission.

The Ministry of Transportation

This Ministry controls affairs concerning land transportation, marine transportation, air transportation, and tourism. It has Bureaus of Transport Coordination, Land Transport, Civil Aviation, and Tourism and an Office of Planning and Management. The Ministry also supervises the Office of National Railroads, which administers the national railroad services, and the Korea Maritime and Port Administration, which administers the construction and management of ports, excluding the construction of ports in the coastal industrial estate areas.

The Ministry of Communications

This Ministry controls postal affairs, postal exchanges, postal savings, postal pensions, and national life insurance. It has Bureaus of Posts, Telecommunications Administration, Radio Regulation Accounting, and Finance and Accounting; and Offices of Planning and Management, Postal Giro Remittance Ledger, Supply and Maintenance, Building Construction, and Radio Regulation; Institutes of Telecommunications Research, Communications Officials Training, and Postal Service Research; and a Computer Center.

The Ministry of Environment

This Ministry is responsible for preserving the natural environment and preventing environmental pollution. The Ministry includes the Coordination and Assessment Office, the Air Quality Management Bureau, and the Science and Technology Bureau. The Ministry supervises the National Institute of Environmental Research and the Regional Environmental Offices.

The Ministry of Information

This Ministry is responsible for collecting and disseminating information on national and international affairs and surveying national opinion. It handles matters related to the press and broadcasting. The Ministry includes the Planning and Management Office, Public Relations Office, Press Administration Bureau, Broadcasting Administration Bureau, and Advertisement Promotion Bureau. The Korean Overseas Information Service, the National Film Production Center and the Government Publishing Office are under its control.

The Ministry of Government Administration

This Ministry takes charge of administration of the State Council, the national archives, personnel management of public officials, improvement and evaluation of administration work, merits and awards, pensions for public officials, and other matters which do not come under the jurisdiction of other central administration agencies. It has Bureaus of General Affairs, Personnel, Administrative Management, and Welfare; and an Office of Planning and Management. The Central Public Officials Training Institute is under its control.

The Ministry of Science and Technology
This Ministry handles matters related to development and application of science and technology and management of industrial and technical manpower. It has Bureaus of Technology Promotion, Technical Cooperation, Atomic Energy, and Planning and Information Industry; and Offices of Planning and Management, and Research and Development Policy and Coordination. This Ministry supervises the National Science Museum, the Central Meteorological Service, and the National Astronomical Center.

The Ministry of State
There are two Ministers of State who are ex-officier members of the State Council. The First Minister of State is charged with national security, foreign and domestic policies and other state affairs. The Second Minister of State performs duties regarding social and cultural affairs with an emphasis on women, children, minors and the elderly.

The Ministry of Legislation
This Ministry is in charge of reviewing bills of laws, regulations and treaties; interpreting laws and regulations in answer to inquiries from the administrative branches of government; operating the Administrative Appeal Commission under the jurisdiction of the Prime Minister; research, study and publication of the statutes of the Republic of Korea in Korean and English; and other general affairs relating to legislation. It has one office and four bureaus.

The Ministry of Patriots and Veterans Affairs
This Ministry takes charge of veterans affairs including relief, loans, compensation, employment and insurance for disabled war veterans

and policemen; bereaved families of soldiers, policemen, and anti-Japanese independence fighters; students disabled in the Student Revolution of April 19, 1960; and defectors from North Korea. It has Bureaus of Management, Relief and Assistance, and Operation.

The Judiciary

Judicial power is vested in the courts, constitutionally an independent branch of the government. The court system functions on three levels: the Supreme Court; appellate courts; district courts (including branch courts) and the Family Court. The courts judge civil, criminal, administrative, election, and other judicial litigations, and manage and supervise affairs concerning registration of real estate, census registers, deposits, and judicial scriveners.

The Supreme Court, located in Seoul, is empowered to make a final review of the legality of administrative decrees, regulations, or dispositions. As the highest judicial tribunal, the Supreme Court hears appeals against the decisions of appellate courts, district and family courts, and courts-martial. Its decisions, final and binding, form judicial precedents for all lower courts. The Supreme Court may establish, within the scope of law, procedures pertaining to judicial proceedings and internal regulations of the courts.

The Chief Justice and Justices of the Supreme Court must be 40 years old or over, with more than 20 years of experience as judges, prosecutors or lawyers. Judges other than those of the Supreme Court must pass the Judicial Civil Service Examination and complete the prescribed in-service training courses, or must be duly qualified prosecutors and lawyers. The Chief Justice of the Supreme Court is appointed by the President with the consent of the National Assembly. Other justices are appointed by the President upon the recommendation of the Chief Justice. The term of office of the Chief Justice is six years and he cannot be reappointed. The term for other Justices is six years

The Seoul Court House

and they may be reappointed in accordance with the provisions of law, but must retire from office when they reach the age of 65.

The Constitution provides that the judges will act independently according to their consciences and in conformity with the Constitution and law. No judge can be dismissed or suspended from office, have his salary reduced, or suffer other unfavorable measures, except by impeachment, criminal punishment, or through the process of disciplinary action.

An appellate court consists of a presiding judge and usually three associate judges. It hears appeals against verdicts of district and family courts in civil and criminal cases, administrative cases, and special cases designated by law. There are four appellate courts in the country—Seoul, Taegu, Pusan and Kwangju. They hold their own trials to reach decisions for or against the verdicts of the lower courts. Only appellate courts can dispense justice on all administrative litigations filed by individuals or organizations against any government decision, order, or disposition.

District courts which have primary jurisdiction over most cases are set up in Seoul and 11 provincial cities: Inch'ŏn, Suwon, Ch'unch'ŏn, Taejŏn, Ch'ŏngju, Taegu, Pusan, Masan, Kwangju, Chŏnju and Cheju. The district court of Seoul is divided into two separate courts: the Seoul Civil District Court and the Seoul criminal District Court. District court trials usually are conducted by a single judge, but a three-judge panel is mandatory in serious cases such as civil cases in which the value in question exceeds ten million won, and criminal cases in which the defendant can be sentenced to death, penal servitude or imprisonment of more than one year. A district court can be assisted by one or more branch courts with single judges for the purpose of dealing with a part of district court business.

The Family Court is empowered to hear all cases involving matrimonial, juvenile, and other domestic matters. Court sessions are closed to the public to insure the privacy of the individuals concerned. At present the only family court is located in Seoul. In other places, the appropriate district court handles such matters.

Courts-martial are military courts which exercise jurisdiction over offenses committed by members of the armed forces and their civilian employees. These offenses include treason, disobedience, desertion, and other crimes as defined in the Military Penal Law. Civilians can come under the jurisdiction of a court-martial if implicated in cases of military espionage, interference with the execution of military duties, and certain other specified offenses.

Under the control of the Ministry of Justice, there is a system of public prosecutor offices. The prosecutors are empowered to conduct investigations into violations of law and to institute legal actions against suspected law-breakers, directing and supervising the judicial police under their control. As protectors of the public interest, they attend and address court hearings to insure due application of laws and decrees. The state's highest prosecuting agency is the Supreme Prosecutors Office headed by the Prosecutor General. It supervises and controls all subordinate offices: the high prosecutors offices, district prosecutors offices, and branch prosecutors offices. The high and district prosecutors offices are located in cities where their judicial counterparts sit. All these offices, including the Supreme Prosecutors Office, are under the direction of the Minister of Justice, who is, however, not authorized to assume control over prosecutor's disposition of justice, except when authorized by pertinent law. The Prosecutor General is appointed by the President from among experienced prosecutors, judges, and lawyers who have practiced law for more than 15 years. Other prosecutors are appointed by the Minister of Justice.

The Constitution Court

The Constitution Court's function is to adjudicate the constitutionality of a law upon the request of a court; impeachment; the dissolution of political parties; and jurisdictional disputes among state agencies, between state agencies and local governments and among local governments and petitions relating to the Constitution as prescribed by law.

The court is composed of nine adjudicators qualified to be court judges, who are appointed by the President. Among the adjudicators, three are appointed from among persons selected by the National Assembly, and three are nominated by the Chief Justice. The head of the Constitution Court is appointed by the President from among the adjudicators with the consent of the National Assembly.

The tenure of the adjudicators of the Constitution Court is six years, during which they may not join any political party, nor engage in political activities. No adjudicator of the Constitution Court can be dismissed except by impeachment or a sentence of imprisonment or heavier punishment. A decision of the Constitution Court on constitutionality, impeachment, dissolution of a political party or a petition relating to the Constitution requires the concurrent vote of more than six adjudicators.

The Election Management Committee

The Election Management Committee was established for the purpose of ensuring fair management of elections and national referenda, and to deal with affairs concerning political parties. The Central Election Management Committee is composed of nine members appointed by the President. Among the members, three are appointed from among persons selected by the National Assembly, and three are nominated by the Chief Justice. The chairman of the committee is elected from among its members. Membership of subordinate committees is to be made up of those with educational or legal backgrounds and other persons of learning and experience. Committee members serve a six-year term, which may be renewed. To ensure impartiality, election committee members are barred from joining political parties or engaging in any political activities. They cannot be dismissed except through impeachment or criminal conviction.

The central committee has the power to control and manage all matters related to elections, and to change, reverse or affirm decisions made by subordinate election committees. Election campaigns are conducted under the management of the election committees of each level within the limits determined by law. Election committees, subordinate to the central organ, are set up in Seoul and Pusan, in each province, and in each electoral district.

The Central Election Management Committee may, within the limits of laws and ordinances, establish regulations pertaining to the management of elections and national referenda, or regulations concerning political parties. The Election Management Committee of each level has the power to supervise the preparation of an electoral roster by each administrative organ under the control of the Ministry of Home Affairs and the President.

Citizens attaining the age of 20 are given the right to choose public officials by universal, direct, and secret ballot irrespective of sex, religion, or social status.

Local Government

The Constitution states in Article 117 that "local governments shall deal with matters pertaining to the welfare of local residents, manage properties, and may establish within the limit of laws and decrees, rules and regulations regarding local autonomy." Traditionally, however, the country has been ruled by a strong central government with no local autonomy in the true sense of the term.

The Local Government Act of 1949 provided each government unit with a representative local council. But it was not until 1952, while The Korean War was still going on, that local councils were first elected in the six southern provinces. The Special City of Seoul and Kyŏnggi-do and Kangwon-do provinces elected local councils in 1956. Local governments were of two types. On the one hand was the provincial government and on the other city (*shi*), county (*kun*), town (*ŭp*) and township (*myŏn*) governments. Unlike the provincial governments, the other governments originally had the authority to elect its executive officer and the right to carry out a nonconfidence vote against him. However, many instances of abuses of this right caused many problems for local governments which were compounded by financial and other difficulties. Therefore, the Local Government Act was amended several times to experiment with both the direct election and appointment of the chief executive officer. During the Second Republic (June 15, 1960- May 16, 1961), local autonomy was fully guaranteed, but it was suspended with the administration's collapse in 1961. Afterwards, local governments operated under the Law Concerning Temporary Measures for Local Autonomy, adopted by the military government of 1961 and amended in April 1981. According to the temporary law, the functions of all local assemblies were suspended and the administrative heads of local units were appointed. Since the beginning of the Third Republic, local governing functions have been performed by the Minister of Home Affairs and the respective provincial governors. Under the Constitution of the Fifth Republic local councils were to be established incrementally, taking into account the degree of financial self-reliance attained by local governments, but none were actually established.

Rapid regional development during the 1970s, and 1980s has increased the revenues of many local governments, and at the same time has strengthened the demand for increased services. In order to meet this demand more efficiently, the central government began in the

A session of the Seoul Metropolitan Council.

mid-1980s to encourage feasibility studies and to make plans for the resumption of local autonomy. Many public hearings and symposiums were held, beginning in about 1985, and books and articles began to appear on the subject.

As a result of a political compromise between the ruling and opposition parties in 1984, local autonomy was scheduled to be partially put into practice as of the first half of 1987. In October 1986, the Government put an amendment to the Local Government Act before the National Assembly, and it was approved on March 8, 1988, and promulgated on April 6. In this way the legal base for local autonomy was restored after 27 years.

According to the new act, the Special City of Seoul, five direct control cities (five metropolitan areas) and nine provinces are established as higher local governments, and as lower local governments, kus are established in the Special City of Seoul and five direct control cities, and cities (*shi*) and counties (*kun*), are established in provinces. Local community heads manage and supervise the administrative affairs of the state in their respective city, town, or township except as otherwise provided by law. The local executive functions include those delegated by the central Government, management of public properties and facilities, assessment and collection of local taxes, various fees, services, and goods, and other administrative affairs of the local community. Each level of local Government has a Board of Education which carries out matters related to education and culture in each community.

Korea's first local-council elections in 30 years took place on March 26, 1991, for small administrations (small cities, counties, and large-city wards) and on June 20, 1991, for large administrations (large cities and provinces). The revised law empowered these local councils to inspect and audit local government, giving the new bodies enhanced power.

The ruling DLP won over 70 percent of the seats in the 260 small-administration councils and 65 percent of those in the 15 large-administration councils, including a majority of seats in 11 of these 15. Independents fared better than expected, but opposition parties performed dismally in the elections. With the councils in place, the Government is moving to complete local autonomy by holding mayoral and gubernatorial elections.

Civil Service

Traditionally government officials had great prestige associated with their rank, power, and responsibility. The civil service was once regarded as the only honorable profession with the sole exception of scholarly pursuit. It embodied the highest sociopolitical aspirations of an individual because it usually entailed wealth, power, and social status. Since 1945, however, the civil service has no longer been the only socially respectable occupation, and the traditional deference accorded officialdom has diminished substantially.

The contemporary civil service system was introduced in August 1949, when the National Assembly enacted the Civil Service Law which was amended in 1950, 1961, and 1962. In 1963 a new act known as the National Civil Service Act was promulgated and continues in force today. The civil service is made up of national

and local government employees who are recruited, selected, and appointed by competent executive agencies of the central and local government. Officials of the central government generally have more prestige than their local counterparts. The national civil service is divided into two types, career and non-career, according to official function. The non-career category includes virtually all the top-ranking positions in the Government: members of the State Council, vice ministers of executive ministries, directors of other ministerial level offices, ambassadors and ministers, judges, secretaries to political appointees, military personnel, civilian employees of defense establishments, provincial governors, and mayors of Seoul and the five metropolitan areas. Presidents, deans, and faculty members of the national universities, and teachers in all secondary and elementary schools are collectively known as educational civil servants and are subject to a separate law called the Educational Civil Servant Act. The Ministry of Foreign Affairs Personnel Act was enacted to strengthen the career diplomat system in March 1981. The career category is divided into nine grades, and most government officials come under this classification. Officials of grades 1 to 5 are appointed by the President on the recommendation of the ministers concerned. Those of grades 6 to 9 are appointed by ministers.

The civil service comes under the Ministry of Government Administration, headed by a presidential appointee of cabinet rank. This office handles recruitment of candidates through open, competitive examination. Promotions are, according to the Civil Service Act, based on efficiency ratings, experience, merit, and competitive examination. The Central Officials Training Institute of the Ministry of Government Administration offers short-term, intensive, technical instruction to civil servants, including judicial personnel. A civil servant may not be discharged without cause as provided in the basic statute, and aggrieved parties may appeal to the Civil Service Board of Appeals. Officials in local government are also classified into career and non-career categories. The Local Civil Service Act promulgated in 1963 provides for the conditions and procedures of recruitment selection, appointment, job classification, promotion and other related matters. In general, the law is similar to that of the national civil service. As of December 31, 1992, there were 553,104 national civil servants and 286,297 local civil servants

Political Parties

Following the 1945 liberation from Japanese colonial rule, during which Koreans had no political rights whatsoever, the country attempted to introduce a modern political party system based on democratic ideals. Due to a lack of political training and experience, this proved a haphazard experiment.

By mid-1947, there were about 40 political parties of varying size and shades, including the South Korean Workers Party, a descendant of the pre-1945 Korean Communist Party, and the Korean Democratic Pary, a forerunner of the late Democratic Korea Party. These hurriedly formed parties were little more than political clubs, each with an insignificant number of followers attracted by regional, kinship, school, and personal ties. They had no clear platforms, adequate political dialogue, grass-roots support or organization.

The turning point in the development of the party system was the advent of Syngman Rhee's Liberal Party in December 1951. Rhee's subsequent use of the party as a means of hanging on to personal power stimulated the formation of an opposition Democratic Party. It was a conglomeration of political aspirants whose one objective was to challenge Rhee's personal rule and that of his party. The immediate post-Rhee years were marked again by the emergence of numerous parties including the new faction of Chang Myŏn and the old guard of Yun Po-sun, who later organized the New Democratic Party. After the military coup of 1961, party politics were banned temporarily by the military junta on the grounds of corruption and lack of discipline among party politicians.

In January 1963, the military government lifted the ban, restoring partisan activities. Kim Jong-pil and other military government leaders organized the Democratic Republican Party (*Minjukonghwadang*, DRP), which emerged victorious in general elections later that year. It was composed of retired military officers, former bureaucrats and former members of the Liberal Party. Opposition parties began to mushroom again, among them the Civil Rule Party (*Minjungdang*), and the reconstituted Democratic Party (*Minjudang*). In 1964 these rival oppositions were merged to form the People's Party (*Kukminŭidang*), but Yun Po-sun and his followers seceded in 1965 to form the New Korea Party (*Shinhandang*). In February 1967, the two were integrated into a united opposition party under the name of the New Democratic Party (*Shinmindang*).

In the general elections from 1967 through 1978, the Democratic Republican Party retained its position as the government ruling party led by President Park Chung Hee. The New Democratic Party, the main opposition party, drew its strength from the urban areas, especially benefiting from the protest vote cast against the government by many intellectuals and students. All political parties were influenced by several interest groups such as the press, business circles, intellectuals, students and labor unions.

Although not a political party, the *Yujŏng-hoe* (Revitalizing Reforms Political Fraternity) performed a significant political role in public policy-making. It was formed under the *Yushin* Constitution by the National Conference for Unification, basically an electoral college, which elected one third of the Assemblymen at the recomendation of the President. These Assemblymen were expected to focus their attention on national issues and they usually voted with the ruling party.

Following the assassination of President Park on October 26, 1979, latent social unrest burst to the surface in the form of labor disputes and student demonstrations. This was exacerbated by the presidential campaigning of the "three Kims"—Kim Dae-jung and Kim Young Sam of the New Democratic Party and Kim Jong-pil, who had taken over the leadership of Park Chung Hee's Democratic Republican Party. The caretaker government could neither control the situation which was threatening the economy nor carry out effective political reforms because real power was in the hands of a group of army officers who had seized power after Park's assassination.

On May 17, 1980, on the advice of military leaders, martial law, which had been declared in the Seoul area following the assassination, was extended throughout the country and opposition politicians, including Kim Dae-jung, were arrested on charges of subversion and corruption. Fierce resistance erupted in Kwangju and quickly escalated into bloody clashes which took martial law troops 10 days to put down. Kim Dae-jung was subsequently tried and convicted of sedition. He was later released but not amnestied.

Late in May, the Special Committee for National Security Measures was formed as a liaison to the martial law authorities and to assist the President. Headed by General Chun Doo Hwan, it prepared for a new government.

The subsequent Constitution of the Fifth Republic introduced a single seven-year presidential term but retained the electoral college.

All political parties were abolished and many politicians were banned from political activities. When political activities were resumed with the promulgation of the new Constitution, 15 new parties competed in the March 25, 1981, general elections and three won enough seats to form floor negotiating groups: the Democratic Justice Party (*Minju-jŏnguidang*, DJP) led by President Chun Doo Hwan; the Democratic Korea Party (*Minjuhangukdang*, DKP) formed by members of the New Democratic Party; and the Korea National Party (*Hangukkukmindang*, KNP) made up of the former members of the Democratic Republican Party.

Until the February 12, 1985, general elections, the opposition parties made little attempt to challenge the ruling party. The political ban was lifted for many shortly before that election and a number of the released politicians formed the New Korea Democratic Party (*Shinhanminjudang*, NKDP) which won a surprising 67 seats. The DKP won 35 seats and the KNP 20. The NKDP strength soon swelled to 103 seats and then was reduced to 91 when 12 younger members bolted.

The NKDP, controlled behind the scenes by Kim Young Sam and Kim Dae-jung—both still under the political ban—chose direct presidential elections as its first priority and allied itself with dissident organizations and students to pressure for constitutional revision. During the next two years, the political parties took up sides and confusion reigned. The ruling party first pushed for a parliamentary form of government and then decided to postpone any discussion of constitutional revision until after the 1988 Seoul Olympics. The opposition pushed for the direct election of a president and then split over the question of compromise with the Government, with Kim Young Sam and Kim Dae-jung (who still had not been amnestied and thus had to remain in the background) forming the Reunification Democratic Party (*T'ongilminjudang*, RDP). The public became increasingly frustrated and anxious with many middle class workers swelling the ranks of the student demonstrations. In early 1987, public discontent intensified with the disclosure of the torture-death of a university student and a subsequent police cover-up.

On June 10, 1987, Roh Tae Woo was nominated as the DJP presidential nominee and on the 29th of that month, he broke the political deadlock and cleared the air with a declaration of political reforms that accepted all of the opposition demands, including direct presidential elections, amnesty for political prisoners, including Kim Dae-jung, and other democratization measures. Roh said he would retire from public life if his proposals were not accepted and President Chun quickly endorsed the measures and turned over the presidency of the DJP to Roh.

Constitutional revision to implement the reforms of the June 29 Declaration was quickly worked out through ruling camp-opposition collaboration, and the Constitution of the Sixth Republic was approved in a national referumdum on October 27, 1987. Meanwhile, the rivalry between Kim Young Sam and Kim Dae-jung intensified, resulting in the latter leaving the RDP and forming the Party for Peace and Democracy (*P'yŏnghwa Minjudang*, PPD). The two Kims and Roh, along with Kim Jong-pil of the New Democratic Republican Party (*Shinminju Konghwadang*, NDRP) and several other minority candidates, all campaigned hard for the presidency, but in the end, the split in the opposition combined with public support for the June 29 Declaration gave Roh the victory with 36.6 percent of the vote. The election was noteworthy in that it was the first normal constitutional transfer of administrations in Korea's history.

Negotiations resumed on the National Assembly Members Election Act and once again the ruling DJP acceded to opposition demands, this time for one candidate from each district. The final outcome of the April 26, 1988 elections was surprising because for the first time the ruling party did not have a working majority in the Assembly. Also, Kim Dae-jung's PPD became the largest opposition party. Of the 299 seats in the 13th National Assembly, the DJP had 125 seats, the PPD 71, the RDP 60,

the NDRP 35 and independents 8. The character of the Assembly had changed; the opposition was able to exert much more pressure than in the past, and the ruling party needed to compromise or form coalitions to effect its policies. This situation was short-lived, however, as it was announced in January 1990 that the ruling DJP, the RDP and the NDRP had agreed to merge to form a single political party, the Democratic Liberal Party (*Minjadang*, DLP). The new ruling party would thus hold more than two-thirds of the seats in the Assembly. A number of Assemblymen opposed to Kim Young Sam's merger with the ruling party bolted from the RDP to form the Democratic Party (*Minjudang*, DP) under Lee Ki-taek in June 1990. Later in that year, another minority party, the progressive People's Party (*Minjungdang*, PP) was also formed.

As 1991 dawned, Korean politics were already gearing up for the 14th National Assembly elections scheduled for early 1992. In an effort to strengthen the opposition, Kim Dae-jung's PPD absorbed the New Democratic Union and renamed itself the New Democratic Party (*Shinmindang*, NDP) in April of 1991. Then, to unite the opposition, the NDP merged with Lee Ki-taek's DP in September 1991, also calling itself the Democratic Party (*Minjudang*, DP).

Other smaller parties emerged in quick succession as the Assembly elections neared. Chung Ju-yung, founder of the Hyundai group, one of Korea's largest conglomerates, established the United People's Party (*T'ongil Kungmindang*, UPP) in February 1992. That same month, Park Chan-jong formed the New Political Reform Party (*Shinjŏngdang*, NPRP).

The DLP won landslide victories in local-council elelctions on March 26 and June 20, 1991 but fared worse in the much-anticipated 14th National Assembly elections held on March 24, 1992. The ruling DLP fell one seat short of a majority, although later it recruited seven independents to retain its working majority in the legislature. The major opposition DP won 97 seats and the new UPP did surprisingly well, winning 31. The splinter parties did much worse; the NPRP won only one seat, that held by its founder, and the People's Party failed to win any and as a result was disbanded.

The elections for the 14th presidential term were held on December 18, 1992. The major candidates were Kim Young Sam, Kim Dae-jung, Chung Ju-yung, and Park Chan-jong, with several minority candidates running as well. In the end, Kim Young Sam won a plurality, garnering 42 percent of the vote, far outpacing Kim Dae-jung, who won 34 percent, and embarrassing Chung Ju-yung, with 16 percent.

After the election, Kim Dae-jung retired from politics and turned the leadership of the Democratic Party over to Lee Ki-taek. Chung Ju-yung also withdrew from politics, resigning from both the UPP which he had founded and funded and the National Assembly. After Chung left the UPP, many of the other members followed suit and left the party, leaving the party short of the minimum 20 seats required for negotiating group status on the Assembly floor.

With the inauguration of Kim Young Sam as the first democratically elected civilian President in three decades, a new age in Korean politics was ushered in. In his inauguration remarks, President Kim vowed to build a New Korea, one marked by clean and honest government and true democracy. Thus far, the President has kept true to his word, initiating a far-reaching anti-corruption campaign which has done much to restore government integrity. With his efforts, the future of Korean politics and democracy has never looked better.

FOREIGN RELATIONS

President Kim Young Sam holding a joint press conference with President Bill Clinton following their summit talks at the White House, Washington, D.C., November 23,1993.

U.S. President Bill Clinton
visiting President Kim Young Sam
for summit talks on July 10, 1993.

Some of the participants
at the APEC Leaders Economic
Meeting. A total of 14 national
leaders met on November 19 and
20, 1993, on Blake Island, Seattle,
to discuss further cooperation
and development of the Asia-
Pacific region.

President Kim Young Sam
and French President
Francois Mitterrand raising
a toast at a state dinner at Chong
Wa Dae on September 14, 1993.

Overview

Since its founding in 1948, the Republic of Korea has been continuously committed to the concepts of liberal democracy and free-market economics, but its foreign relations have undergone significant changes. As the East-West confrontation evolved into a state of cold war after World War II, the Republic of Korea pursued its foreign relations in concert with the nations of the West who advocated liberal democracy. In the years following the Korean War (1950-1953), the international community viewed Korea as a devastated, poverty-ridden state, but that image began to change in 1962 when the Republic adopted a policy of export-driven economic development and began to actively pursue international commerce worldwide.

As East-West confrontation sharpened during the Cold War, the Republic of Korea, regarded as a member of the Western bloc, began to expand its foreign relations by improving ties with traditional allies and by building cooperative relations with Third-World nations. The scope of its foreign relations expanded as trade ties and other economic links with these nations matured. Although Korea's total trade in 1962 amounted to a mere US$500 million, less than three decades later, Korea was the world's 13th largest trading nation, recording an astounding US$158.4 billion in two-way trade at the end of 1992. The Republic today is recognized around the world not only for the scale of its merchandise trade, but also for its success in international construction projects and for expanding overseas investments.

Since the 1970s, the diplomacy of the Republic has been designed to promote the independent and peaceful unification of the peninsula, which was tragically split in two as a result of World War II. Its diplomats have labored hard to build a climate conducive to maintaining dialogue with North Korea. At the same time, however, the Republic has fortified ties with allies and actively participated in international organizations. With its diplomatic foundation firmly in place, the Republic continued throughout the 1980s to pursue cooperative partnerships with all

countries in every field.

In the late 1980s and early 1990s, epochal changes in Eastern Europe and the Soviet Union brought an end to the Cold War, and the Republic of Korea moved swiftly to exploit the situation by actively promoting a "Northern Diplomacy." In 1988, Korea hosted the 24th Olympiad, revealing a new image formed by 30 years of rapid economic expansion. The Seoul Olympics provided an opportunity for the nations of the East and West to compete harmoniously for the first time in 12 years. Korea's energetic pursuit of a Northern Diplomacy contributed to the enhancing of its ties with former socialist countries, with whom relations had languished due to ideological and structural differences. Relations with most of them, including the former Soviet Union and China, were normalized in short order, and thus Korea's foreign relations became truly global.

South and North Korea joined the United Nations simultaneously in September 1991, crowning the success of the Northern Diplomacy. Furthermore, the foundation for peaceful coexistence between the South and the North was laid in December 1991, when they concluded the Agreement on Reconciliation, Nonaggression and Exchanges and Cooperation (the Basic Agreement) and the Joint Declaration of the Denuclearization of the Korean Peninsula. These historic documents planted the seeds of peace on the peninsula and in Northeast Asia and represented a strong first step toward the peaceful unification of the divided nation.

Today the Republic's diplomacy focuses on boosting the nation's international contributions and expanding its role on the international stage. The nation maintains relations with virtually every country and works actively to improve cooperative ties with them all. As of April 1993, the Republic had diplomatic relations with 171 nations and maintained 98 embassies, 38 consulates and four missions. It is a member of 52 international organizations, 16 of which are United Nations agencies, and a multitude of non-governmental international bodies. The number of foreign diplomatic missions permanently located in Seoul has jumped sharply, to more than 80. Since its admission to the United

Nations in September 1991, Korea has pursued membership in U.N.-sponsored organizations and in the various U.N. specialized agencies. Korea is very active in these bodies and has been selected to serve on the executive or governing boards of 22 of them.

In the 1990s, the diplomatic policies of the Republic of Korea will be aimed at securing international support for peace and stability in Northeast Asia and laying a foundation for the unification of the peninsula. Economic diplomacy will also be actively pursued so that Korea can join the ranks of the advanced countries and play a global role commensurate with its enhanced standing.

A Firm Security Structure

Exploiting a vacuum of power, North Korea invaded the Republic of Korea in 1950 in an attempt to extend the sway of Communism throughout the Korean Peninsula. In this, P'yŏngyang had the military support of the Soviet Union and China, its ideological allies. The Republic of Korea and the United Nations Command, led by the United States and composed of troops from 16 nations, contained the invading forces. Combat ceased when an armistice agreement was concluded in 1953, but the threat of invasion from the North continued to hang over the Republic. North Korea has persistently taken an aggressive stance, maintaining absolute military superiority over the South, despite its larger population and more advanced economy.

Economic growth in the 1970s and 1980s created an economy in the South far stronger than that of the North and boosted the people's confidence in the face of the continuing South-North confrontation. The Republic's democratization and social and political reforms have not only strengthened public confidence but improved its international image as well. The world community now sees Korea as a country blessed with democracy and a marked degree of freedom.

The Republic of Korea endeavors to develop diplomatic policies that will help win international support for its security posture and for the peace and stability of the Korean Peninsula. At the same time, however, South Korea works incessantly to neutralize international support for North Korea so as to temper the North's belligerent stance. In particular, the Republic has, over the years, maintained and strengthened a structure of security cooperation with the United States designed to sustain a credible military deterrent. South Korea has recently normalized relations with the republics of the former Soviet Union and with China. These new ties with the North's former military allies have triggered vast changes in the international situation. China and Russia no longer automatically support North Korea's positions.

The Republic of Korea has increased its national defense capability by emphasizing self-reliance. This increased military strength, coupled with the stationing of U.S. military forces in the South, has helped to somewhat diminish the threat of the North Korean conventional military forces. There is renewed concern, however, in the international community about North Korea's belligerency—a concern centered on its suspected development of nuclear weapons. If this threat is real, it will adversely effect not only the Korean Peninsula but the peace and stability of all of Northeast Asia. It was against this backdrop that the Republic's president, Roh Tae Woo, announced a serious initiative to pressure North Korea to abandon its nuclear development program. In November 1991, he issued the Initiative for Denuclearization and Peace on the Korean Peninsula, which was followed a month later by his Special Announcement on a Nuclear-Free Korean Peninsula. These initiatives resulted in an agreement on December 12 to hold working-level meetings on the nuclear issue. A Joint Declaration of the Denuclearization of the Korean Peninsula was initialed at the third working-level meeting on December 31, 1991, and brought into force in February 1992.

These developments led North Korea to sign a Nuclear Safeguard Agreement with the International Atomic Energy Agency (IAEA) in January 1992. The IAEA conducted its first inspection under that Agreement in May 1992. The South Korean Government, however, is continuing its efforts to negotiate with the North to realize the South-North mutual nuclear inspections stipulated in the Joint Declaration of Denuclearization. The South Korean Government will continue these and other efforts until suspicions over North Korea's nuclear weapons development program are completely cleared up.

North Korea made a startling and dismaying announcement on March 12, 1993, that it was withdrawing from the Nuclear Non-Proliferation Treaty (NPT). It was the first nation ever to make such an announcement. Its abrupt decision followed a demand by the IAEA to conduct special inspections of two facilities in the North which are widely suspected of being linked to its nuclear weapons development program. The North had previously refused to allow IAEA inspectors onto the two sites. South Korea is working in concert with the United Nations and with such countries as the United States, China and Japan to solve this issue. On June 11, 1993, following four high-level meetings with the United States and just one day before its withdrawal was to be final, North Korea announced that it had decided to "suspend as long as it considers necessary the effectuation of its withdrawal from the Treaty on the Non-Proliferation of Nuclear Weapons." Nevertheless, international suspicions will remain until the North allows the IAEA to inspect the two sites in question and any other facility without restriction, and agrees to South-North mutual inspections under the Joint Declaration of Denuclearization.

Ultimately, it is the Republic of Korea which must shoulder the responsibility for guaranteeing its own national security, and with this in mind, Korea has implemented a series of force improvement plans designed to enhance the self-reliance of its military. This has triggered a gradual reversal in the American and South Korean defense roles, with Korea increasingly asserting itself as leader and the United States providing support. Based on the ROK-U.S. security relationship, it is anticipated that the United States will continue to play a balancing role in the region, helping to ensure the peace and stability of Northeast Asia, including the Korean Peninsula. The assessment that U.S. forces may be necessary in Korea even after the unification of the Peninsula is based on a recognition of the long-term balancing role of the U.S. military in the region.

Relations with Traditional Allies

The keystone of the Republic of Korea's diplomacy is its traditional friendly relationships with Western nations, such as the United States, Japan and the nations of Western Europe, who share the values of liberal democracy and free-market economics. As a new world order emerges in the wake of the demise of the Cold War and the disintegration of the Soviet Union, South Korea is rapidly transforming its cooperative ties with these traditional allies into equal partnerships.

Despite the end of the Cold War and the on-again-off-again dialogue between the South and the North, the reality is that the Korean Peninsula remains divided and that confrontation continues. In view of this reality, South Korea regards close cooperation with its traditional allies, especially the United States of America, in the key areas of security, the economy and trade to be important for the continued progress of the country.

ROK-U.S. Relations: Toward a Mature Partnership

For the more than a century since the signing of the Treaty of Peace, Amity, Commerce and Navigation in 1882, Korea and the United States of America have maintained amicable relations. As the Republic of Korea's most important ally, the United States made enormous contributions to the nation when the Republic was established in 1948, during the Korean War (1950-1953) by coming to the defense of the nation against Communist aggression and again during the period of economic recovery after the war.

The relationship between the two nations has certainly not been static. Fueled by Korea's economic growth and increased national strength, it has consistently grown, developing into today's mature partnership. The process has not always been free of friction, but the two nations have worked to overcome problems in trade and other fields and have continued to refine their amicable ties. Relations today are not restricted to the security and economic spheres, but are broad and deep, encompassing every field of human endeavor.

A crucial diplomatic task facing Korea and the U.S. is the bilateral cooperation needed to establish peace on the Korean Peninsula and fulfill the conditions for unification. The Governments of the two nations basically share the same positions on these issues and are cooperating closely to achieve mutual goals. Korea will continue to assume the lead in the quest for peace and the unification of the peninsula, including the direction of the South-North dialogue, while the United States and other concerned nations remain strongly supportive.

Two-way trade between the Republic of Korea and the United States reached US$36 billion at the end of 1992. America is Korea's largest export market, purchasing 23.6 percent (US$18.1 billion) of Korean exports in 1992. Korea is the eighth largest trading partner of the United States, its seventh largest export market and fourth largest market for agricultural exports. Korea began to realize a trade surplus with the United States in 1982, and by 1987, Seoul's trade with Washington was US$9.6 billion in the black. This surplus triggered friction, but the two nations agreed on the need for more balanced trade and took the steps needed to redress the situation. Korea's market-opening measures have been particularly helpful in gradually reducing the trade surplus. The two countries today employ the offices of a variety of joint consultative bodies, including the Trade Action Group, to prevent trade strife and solve outstanding issues smoothly at both the policy and working levels, resulting in generally satisfactory economic and trade relations.

As the most important source of foreign capital and advanced technology, the United States contributed substantially to the Republic's economic growth during the period from 1962 to 1979 when the Korean economy developed rapidly. South Korea not only maintains cooperative political, economic and trade links with the United States but also pursues active exchanges in the cultural and social fields as well. The sheer breadth of the links between the two countries promotes an exceptionally active exchange of people. Over a million Korean-Americans now live in the United States and have earned an exemplary reputation. They provide an unseen impetus to friendly ties between the two countries.

Symbolic of the close ties between the two countries and of the seriousness of the challenges they face together, President Kim Young Sam and Bill Clinton have held two summit talks during their first year in office. Following the Group of Seven meeting in Tokyo, President Clinton first met with President Kim in Seoul July 10-11, 1993. They reaffirmed the U.S. commitment to the security of the Republic , agreed to continue to cooperate closely on the North Korean nuclear issue and launched a bilateral forum for economic consultations named the "Dialogue for Economic Cooperation." In an address at the Korean National Assembly, President Clinton also called for the creation of a Pacific community and for regional security dialogues.

Following the APEC Leaders Economic Meeting, President Kim made an official visit to Washington, D.C. on November 21-24, 1993. He and President Clinton continued the economic and security discussions begun in Seoul but concentrated especially on the North Korean nuclear issue. They agreed to make a thorough and broad effort to bring about a solution to this problem.

The Republic of Korea and the United States both value liberal democracy, human rights and market economics. Adhering to the principles of mutual benefit and equality, they have built upon a firm foundation in diplomacy and security to develop a mature partnership in all fields.

ROK-Japan Relations: Building a Relationship Oriented Toward the 21st Century

The Republic of Korea and Japan are neighboring countries, separated by the Strait of Korea. The two nations have had close cultural ties and active exchanges since ancient times. In the present century, however, the two nations experienced a deterioration in relations when Japan colonized Korea.

Fortunately in 1965, however, the two countries were able to exploit their geographic proximity and cultural similarity to reestablish diplomatic relations and have since then actively pursued the development of friendly relations through exchanges of people and goods in many fields. The expansion of these exchanges has served to further enhance understanding and cooperation. Japan and Korea exchange some 2.5 million visitors each year, and two-way trade now totals more than US$30 billion annually. These figures clearly reveal the interdependence of their relationship.

As part of the evolving new world order, the leaders of the Republic of Korea and Japan began to meet more frequently as illustrated by President Roh's visits to Japan in May 1990 and November 1992, the first working meeting between the two top leaders, and Prime Minister Miyazawa's visit to Seoul in January 1992. This trend has continued with the new Administrations of President Kim Young Sam and Prime Minister Morihiro Hosokawa. Shortly before the APEC Leaders Economic Meeting, Prime Minister Hosokawa made an official working visit to Korea November 6-7, 1993, emphasizing the importance of bilateral relations in shaping the post-Cold-War order in Northeast Asia. At the meeting in Kyŏngju, the Prime Minister admitted that Japan had in the past inflicted "unbearable suffering" on the Korean people and sincerely apologized, saying that he understood that there could be no genuine friendship between the two peoples until Japan came to terms with the past. The two leaders agreed to cooperate more closely to help resolve regional and global issues, promote

bilateral relations and solve the North Korean nuclear issue. They also agreed to institute a New Initiative for an Economic Partnership.

Cooperation with Japan is not limited to bilateral issues but includes concern for the stability and prosperity of Northeast Asia and extends to global issues as well. The foreign ministers of the two countries hold regularly scheduled annual consultations and generally meet four or five times on an ad hoc basis. Furthermore, there are numerous channels through which the two countries confer with each other on every possible topic—both outstanding issues of the day and historic issues that from time to time upset the bilateral relationship.

Trade between Korea and Japan reached approximately US$31 billion at the end of 1992, making each nation the other's second largest trading partner. The two nations also promote cooperation in investment, technology and other economic fields.

Even as bilateral ties develop to a degree unknown in the past, the fact remains that there are still elements of discord plaguing the relationship. For example, in 1992, the trade imbalance between the two countries hit a record US$7.9 billion in favor of Japan. Other issues resulting from the legacy of Japan's colonial rule of Korea also crop up from time to time.

In the 21st century, there will be even more active exchanges and cooperation between Korea and Japan. The two nations will not only work together to promote the prosperity of the Asia-Pacific region but also to address global issues. In the meantime, they are cooperating closely to bolster the peace and stability of Northeast Asia. For example, Japan works with the Republic of Korea to help set conditions for the normalization of relations with North Korea. It insists that the North must first clear up suspicions about its nuclear weapons development program, ensure progress in the South-North dialogue and sincerely implement the already concluded South-North agreements.

As the world's second largest economic power, Japan is also increasing its contributions and enhancing its political role in both the Asia-Pacific region and the world community. One element of this enhanced political role is Japan's decision to allow its Self-Defense Forces to take part in United Nations peacekeeping operations. In view of its experience with Japan in the past, Korea has expressed its deep concern over the decision to allow Japanese forces to be sent overseas. Korea maintains that Japan's international role should be restricted to the non-military field.

There is every indication that the 21st century will be a time of vitality for the Asia-Pacific region as a whole. In this new age, Korea and Japan will continue to cooperate in contributing to the international community and will work to enhance their mutually beneficial partnership.

ROK-Western Europe Relations: New Emphasis on Old Friendships

The Republic of Korea's traditionally close ties with the states of Western Europe, especially the nations of the European Community, are based on the shared ideals of liberal democracy, free trade and market economics. Britain, France and other Western European nations participated in the Korean War under the United Nations flag, and helped in the recovery after the war. Their relationship with Korea encompasses not only trade but other economic and technological areas.

In recent years, the Republic of Korea has strengthened relations with Britain, France and Germany via summit diplomacy, and since his inauguration, President Kim Young Sam has held summit talks with German Chancellor Helmut Kohl in March and with French President Francois Mitterand in September 1993. The Republic is pursuing ever closer and more practical ties with all the nations of Western Europe, especially with the members of the European Community, who as a group form Korea's third largest trading partner. This relationship will grow as the EC realizes its dream of economic integration and emerges as one of the three pillars of the world economy. The Republic will also seek to expand ties with individual European countries both within and outside of the EC. It will also participate fully in such organizations as the Korea-EC High-Level Consultations.

Cooperation in the Asia-Pacific Region

For the past decade, the Pacific region has had the highest economic growth rate in the world and in the 21st century, it is expected to be the driving force behind world economic development. Korea, Taiwan, Singapore and Hong Kong have already achieved significant industrialization. As nations like Thailand, Malaysia, Indonesia and China join the newly industrializing countries, the Asia-Pacific region will become one of the three pillars of the world economy, along with North America and the European community.

The Republic of Korea has diligently sought to expand cooperative ties in trade, economics and other fields not only with countries of ASEAN—Brunei, Indonesia, Malaysia, the Philippines, Singapore and Thailand—but with all the nations of the Asia-Pacific region. The increase in Korea's national strength has triggered a gradual expansion in its role in the region.

The nations of Southeast Asia are rich in natural resources and manpower and their economies are complementary to the economy of the Republic. Korea's trade with Southeast Asian nations has grown over the past several years at an annual rate of about 30 percent. This is a strong indication that the region will emerge as one of Korea's most important trading partners, along with the United States, Japan and the European Community. Two-way trade between the Republic of Korea and the ASEAN states broke the US$13 billion mark in 1991 and, in 1992, soared to US$15.8 billion. Korea's investment in Southeast Asia, meanwhile, has increased markedly in the past two to three years, reaching US$1 billion at the end of July 1992. Increased economic ties have triggered a flood of visitors; some 325,000 persons traveled between Korea and the ASEAN countries in 1992 and the number is increasing rapidly.

The Republic of Korea's expanded involvement in the region resulted in an invitation in

1991 to join Japan, Australia, New Zealand, the United States, Canada and the European Community as a dialogue partner of ASEAN. Since then, Korea's foreign minister has taken part in the ASEAN Post-Ministerial Conferences on regional and global issues.

In 1992, Korea and Vietnam put the past behind them and set up full diplomatic relations based on a future-oriented spirit of cooperation. This improved relationship will not only increase substantial bilateral cooperation but will contribute to the peace and stability of the entire region.

The Republic of Korea has also worked to preserve its traditionally friendly ties with Australia and New Zealand and to strengthen economic cooperation based on active trade relations and the development of resources.

The Republic of Korea played a major role in the creation of the Asia-Pacific Economic Cooperation (APEC) forum, which provides a useful channel for regional discussions at the ministerial level of trade and investment issues. The "Seoul Declaration," which was adopted at the third APEC Ministerial Meeting hosted by the Republic, laid the foundation for the institutionalization of APEC. Korea is particularly proud of its diplomatic role in bringing China, Taiwan and Hong Kong, three key regional economic powers, into the APEC fold, giving the forum a new impetus. Subsequently, the Republic played a leading role at the first APEC Leaders Economic Meeting in Seattle in November 1993, which was convened along with the fifth APEC Ministerial Meeting, to work toward a new economic community in the Pacific Rim, now emerging as the global economic center.

Northern Diplomacy

After his inauguration in 1988, President Roh Tae Woo adopted "Northern Diplomacy" as the key element of his foreign policy. Korea had enjoyed diplomatic relations with most Western countries, but its contacts with the former and current socialist states located mostly to the north of the Peninsula, which were friendly with North Korea, were limited. The aim of this policy was to create an international environment conducive to the peace and stability of the Korean Peninsula and to smooth the way for the eventual peaceful unification of the South and the North. The success of the Northern Diplomacy resulted in the normalization of relations with the former Soviet Union, the states of Eastern Europe, and finally China.

The stunning success of the Northern Diplomacy led to the simultaneous entry of South and North Korea into the United Nations and to the signing of several agreements, including the Basic Agreement and the Declaration of the Denuclearization of the Korean Peninsula, making peaceful unification of the peninsula less of a dream and more of a real objective.

On July 7, 1988, President Roh Tae Woo made a "Special Declaration in the Interest of National Self-Esteem, Unification and Prosperity," in which he committed the nation to improve relations with the Soviet Union, China and other socialist states. It was hoped that by improving relations with North Korea's socialist allies, these nations could be convinced to use their good offices to nudge North Korea toward opening its society to the outside world and instituting reforms, thereby becoming a more responsible member of the world community.

The first socialist nation with which the Republic of Korea normalized diplomatic relations was Hungary, in February 1989. By August 1991, Seoul had achieved normal ties with all of the nations of Eastern Europe in less than 30 months. Diplomatic relations with Mongolia were normalized in March 1990. China and the Republic set up trade offices with consular functions in early 1991 and established full diplomatic relations in August 1992. In December 1992, South Korea and Vietnam established full diplomatic relations.

The normalization of diplomatic relations with the Soviet Union and China influenced the peace and stability of the Korean Peninsula as well as expanded the nation's economic and diplomatic horizons. Exchanges with the Soviet Union began in earnest with its participation in the Seoul Olympic Games in 1988. After Korea and the Soviet Union established consular offices in each other's capital in early 1990, the presidents of the two countries agreed in principle to establish diplomatic relations at a summit in San Francisco in June 1990, and relations were finally established on September 30, 1990. Two summit meetings followed relatively quickly: the first in Moscow in December 1990 and the second on Korea's Chejudo Island in April 1991. These meetings established a firm foundation for exchanges and cooperation in a wide variety of fields.

The Korean-Chinese relationship is distinctive because for many centuries China exercised a dominant influence over the region from her position at the center of the Northeast Asian order of international relations. Beginning in the late 19th century, the entire Asian continent, including China, became a stage for competition among the imperialist nations. This period was followed by the communization of China and the Cold War. China occupied a central position in the Communist structure, and the Republic served as a front-line democratic nation, setting the stage for continued bilateral confrontation.

Two developments paved the way for substantial cooperation between the Republic of Korea and China. One was China's turn toward openness and pragmatism in the late 1970s, and the other was the enhanced national strength of Korea that sprang from continuous economic growth. Contacts between the two countries began to proliferate after China attended the 1986 Asian Games in Seoul. Trade between Korea and China has increased rapidly since the 1988 Seoul Olympics, reaching US$8.2 billion in 1992. China thus became Korea's third largest trading partner, and Korea became China's seventh largest. A trade agreement between Korea and China took effect in February 1992, and as a result, experts estimate that two-way trade will reach about US$10 billion by the end of 1993.

The normalization of relations between Korea and China on August 24, 1992, has and will have a major influence on the peace and stability of the Korean Peninsula in particular and Northeast Asia in general. This is illustrated by the PRC's role in trying to help influence North Korea to alleviate international concern over its suspected nuclear development program. While in Seattle to attend the APEC Leaders Economic Meeting, President Kim Young Sam and Chinese President Jiang Zemin met on November 19, 1993, and discussed the North Korean issue, bilateral economic cooperation and the emerging role of APEC.

The Road to Unification

With the end of the Cold War, a wave of openness, reconciliation and cooperation swept over the world. A ripple of that wave has also reached the shores of Korea. Taking advantage of the spirit of the times with the Northern Diplomacy, the Republic successfully coaxed North Korea to return to the negotiating table.

There is great pressure on North Korea to adopt a policy of openness toward the outside world despite the possible deleterious impact on its ability to maintain its political system and transfer of power. The North faces both serious economic difficulties and diplomatic isolation in the wake of the normalization of relations between South Korea and the Soviet Union and China. The first sign of increased openness in the North was the abandonment of the unrealistic insistence that South and North Korea share a seat in the United Nations. South and North Korea, thus, were able to join the United Nations simultaneously in September 1991. In contrast to the past, China and the Soviet Union not only did not veto the South's application, but actually supported its position, the Soviet Union actively and China implicitly.

The Republic of Korea's efforts to promote unification through prime ministerial talks with North Korea, finally bore fruit in February 1992, when the Agreement on Reconciliation, Nonaggression and Exchanges and Cooperation Between the South and the North (the Basic Agreement) and the Joint Declaration of the Denuclearization of the Korean Peninsula were put into effect. These agreements lay the foundation for peaceful coexistence between the two halves of the peninsula. Under the agreements, three committees and five commissions have been set up: the South-North Exchanges and Cooperation Committee, Political Committee and Military Committee and the South-North Joint Commission for Economic Exchanges and Cooperation, and for Social and Cultural Exchanges and Cooperation, the Joint Military Commission, the Joint Nuclear Control Commission and the Joint Reconciliation Commission. Liaison Offices have also been set up in P'anmunjŏm.

Suspicions that North Korea is pursuing a nuclear weapons development program have attracted international concern and remains a problem that must be solved with the highest priority, both for the sake of peaceful unification and for the peace and stability of Northeast Asia and the world. Efforts to allay these misgivings, however, have had disappointing results. North Korea has not shown any intention of abiding by the provisions of the Joint Declaration of Denuclearization by abandoning its nuclear reprocessing facilities and assenting to South-North mutual nuclear inspections.

The Republic of Korea intends to pursue a determined diplomatic initiative to gain the support of nations in the region for peace on the peninsula. It will also strive to set the stage for unification by pushing for the implementation of the Basic Agreement and the Joint Declaration of Denuclearization.

International Economic Relations

In the wake of the Cold War, a distinct trend toward regionalism emerged. The North American Free Trade Area took an effect from 1994 and European integration is growing closer. Thus North America, Europe and East Asia, each producing a quarter of the World's GNP, are all becoming trade blocs, edging the world toward economic polarization. The importance of the economic factor in international relations has increased since the end the Cold War. Nations have become more interdependent economically which, in turn, has tended to increase friction.

Countries like the Republic of Korea which have pursued export-led growth find themselves facing a very different international economic landscape than in the past. Korea has mostly traded with the advanced countries—the United States, Japan and the European Community. This often caused friction over trade imbalances. As Korea has gradually increased its trade with developing countries, however, the share of its trade with advanced countries has gradually decreased.

To the extent that the advanced countries remain key to trade and crucial as partners in industrial science and technology, Korea will have to endeavor to minimize friction by opening its markets to the same extent that developed countries' markets are open, starting with industrial goods and agricultural products and extending to the service market as well. Korea will continue to try to achieve expanded, balanced trade and increased technological cooperation with the advanced nations.

The Republic of Korea's trade with developing countries and the nations of Eastern Europe will continue to expand as long as Korea's economy and trade continue to grow and as long as its industrial structure continues to become more technology-intensive, which tends to make Korea's economy more complementary with theirs. Once Korea has completed its industrial restructuring, it will be able to make a greater contribution to international economic development by accelerating cooperation with the developing countries on the basis of comparative advantages and complementarity.

The pace and pattern of Korea's future economic growth will be heavily influenced by the Uruguay Round Final Act which will bring new rules to world trade. It will also be affected by the possible introduction of new international environmental restrictions under the auspices of the United Nations Conference on Environment and Development (UNCED).

The Uruguay Round Final Act will basically provide for a comprehensive reduction in tariffs and a general removal of non-tariff trade barriers, a crucial step in the global movement toward free trade. Korea relies heavily on trade to keep its economy running and therefore participates actively in these negotiations to promote a global free trade system that will deter protectionist, discriminatory trade policies and practices.

Due to heightened concerns over the pollution of the earth's environment, the June 1992 UNCED—or Earth Summit—drove home the message that continuous economic development must not be allowed to harm the environment, which sustains us all. At the conference, there was a sharp confrontation between the advanced and developing nations over the issue of how to allocate the burden of responsibility for protecting the earth's environment. As a newly-developed country, Korea participated in all sessions of the UNCED, playing an intermediary role in this conflict. Koreans were particularly proud of their contribution to the adoption of the Rio Declaration and Agenda 21. They helped expedite agreements on the issues of the voluntary transfer of environmental protection technology possessed by governmental entities and the protection of similar technology belonging to the private sector against abuse of property rights.

International Peace and Cooperation

In September 1991, the Republic of Korea joined the United Nations as a full member and, in this capacity, has actively participated in multilateral diplomatic activities and made contributions commensurate with its standing in the international community. Even before joining the U.N., however, Korea was active in the United Nations specialized agencies, such as the International Monetary Fund (IMF), the International Bank for Reconstruction and Development (IBRD), the United Nations Industrial Development Organization (UNIDO) and the United Nations Educational, Scientific and Cultural Organization (UNESCO), as well as the GATT and other key inter-governmental bodies. Korea has also taken a leading role in strengthening international cooperation in the field of drug abuse control. It has helped to launch the Goodwill Ambassadors Program

adopted by the U.N. International Drug Control Program as part of activities for the U.N. Decade Against Drug Abuse.The program aims to enhance public awareness of the problem and to reduce the demand for illicit drugs. Korea hosted the 18th session of the Meeting of Heads of National Drug Law Enforcement Agencies, Asia and the Pacific, in Seoul in September 1993.

When it was admitted into the United Nations, Korea stepped up efforts to expand its role. In 1992, Korea became a member of several important U.N. bodies, such as the Commission on Crime Prevention and Criminal Justice, the Governing Council of the United Nations Development Program (UNDP), The Commission on Human Rights and the Committee for Program and Coordination. At the 47th session of the General Assembly in October that year, Korea was elected to the U.N. Economic and Social Council, one of the principal U.N. organs, along with the Security Council and the General Assembly, and the only global body with an extensive mandate governing most economic and social matters. These memberships provide Korea with a better opportunity to make its voice heard in the process of decision-making on various economic and social issues, including the environment, energy, food, poverty, population, refugees, human rights, narcotics and crime prevention.

At the ECOSOC session in January 1993, Korea was elected a vice-president, even though it was only a new member and, in the same year, also became the chairman of the ECOSOC Social Committee. Korea was also elected to the Commission on Sustainable Development, a new commission established under the ECOSOC in February 1993 to coordinate and monitor the activities taken to implement Agenda 21 and follow-up on the UNCED. It is considered the most important body in the field of environment and development.

The Republic of Korea is also engaged in other U.N. activities. For example, it is active in the First Committee and the Special Political Committee of the General Assembly which deal with political and security issues, such as conventional and nuclear arms reduction and peacekeeping. In 1992, Korea was elected an executive member of the Board of Governors of the International Atomic Energy Agency for the eighth time since 1957.

In other ways, Korea is also increasing its role in the international political and security arenas. For example, Korea joined the coalition efforts during the Gulf War early in 1991, in accordance with a United Nations resolution establishing an international force. Korea provided assistance in the form of a military medical team and a transportation unit, as well as providing financial assistance for the coalition forces and for restoration projects in countries that suffered damage. Korea intends to actively participate in the rapidly-expanding U.N. peace-keeping operations.

Developing countries often face serious problems because they lack experience in preparing economic plans, in procuring necessary investment capital and in executing the economic policies necessary for sustained economic growth. Korea's developmental experience, therefore, can be of direct help to such nations. Korea had begun helping developing countries already in the 1960s, when it invited small numbers of trainees and dispatched a few specialists overseas. After 1975, when the economy had reached impressive levels, Korea began to provide increased assistance in a variety of forms: grants of machinery and materials, free construction technology, Economic Development Cooperation Fund (EDCF) loans and direct personnel assistance, especially through the Youth Volunteer program. Korea also provided assistance to developing countries through multilateral organizations such as the IMF, IBRD, ADB and nearly a dozen other international financial organizations. Korea also regularly pays its share of the operating costs of the United Nations, the GATT and other organizations, a share that increases annually.

In 1992, the Republic of Korea invited 8706 persons for training in Korea and sent 556 specialists and 25 medical missions and taekwondo teams abroad. It provided direct grants of machinery and materials exceeding US$100 million and gave another US$200 million in loans through the EDCF. In April 1991, Korea created the Korea International Cooperation Agency (KOICA) under the Ministry of Foreign Affairs, to consolidate the provision of assistance to developing countries. Korea annually contributes about US$100 million in official developmental aid (ODA). As a percentage of GNP, this amount is less than the average provided by the member nations of the OECD's Developmental Aid Committee (DAC); however, Korea's contribution is impressive considering the short period of its economic development, its limited natural resources and its relative lack of technology.

The Republic of Korea is committed to the pursuit of cultural exchanges to enhance bilateral friendship and understanding and to contribute to global reconciliation and cooperation. Korea also wants to introduce Korean traditional art and culture abroad, and supports overseas Korean studies programs as well as numerous academic conferences and athletic exchanges. In December 1991, the Korea Foundation was established to coordinate and support international cultural exchanges.

New Diplomacy

To effectively cope with international and domestic changes, the new Administration has decided to pursue a New Diplomacy as part of its efforts towards the creation of a New Korea. In May 1993 Ministry of Foreign Affairs laid out five areas which will be emphasized in this New Diplomacy: globalization, diversification, multilateralism, regional cooperation, and future-orientation.

The globalization of Korea's foreign policy will entail a greater emphasis on such universal values as democracy, freedom, welfare and human rights. In the belief that an ethics-based foreign policy is not necessarily too idealistic to be realistic, the Republic will try to promote these ideals and values internationally and strengthen ties with like-minded countries, while also promoting security and other national and regional interests.

By foreign policy diversification, it is meant

that the Republic will try to expand its foreign relations in all areas, concentrating on economic, trade, environmental and cultural affairs. It will try to outgrow its excessive preoccupation with national security, although security will continue to be a critical concern. In recognition of the changing international environment, Korea will reach out more energetically to all nations, while maintaining close ties with traditional friends. Multilateral ties will be pursued with the members of the Association of Southeast Asian Nations (ASEAN), the European Community, Latin America, the Middle East, and Africa.

The need for the Republic to be actively involved in regional cooperation stems from the near certainty that the Pacific Rim countries will play a leading role in the 21st century. The Republic will seek to develop a broad Pacific economic structure, chiefly through the Asia-Pacific Economic Cooperation (APEC) forum. Regarding security, the Republic will deepen the ROK-USA alliance, while pursuing multilateral security cooperation in the Asia-Pacific region in general and in Northeast Asia in particular.

One of the key distinguishing characteristics of the New Diplomacy is its focus on the future. While the new foreign policy entails diplomatic endeavors to deal with problems stemming from the continuing national division, the New Diplomacy will also deal with the diplomatic aspects of the eventual unification of the land and the post-unification era. Consequently, one task of the new foreign policy is ensuring that the international community fully understands the Republic of Korea's position and policies to induce reform and openness in North Korea and also enlisting international support and help. It is hoped that through these efforts, North Korea will institute reforms and become a responsible member of the international community, thereby bring peace and prosperity to the Korean Peninsula.

UNIFICATION POLICY

Background

The Korean Peninsula was unified under the Shilla Kingdom in A.D. 668, making it a single political entity with a common language and culture.

Because of the geopolitical situation in Northeast Asia, however, by the end of the 19th century Korea had become an arena where the interests of major powers created constant, sometimes violent, confrontation. After their victories in the Sino-Japanese War in 1895 and the Russo-Japanese War in 1904-5, Japanese stepped up their aggressive maneuvers involving Korea and formally annexed the peninsula in 1910.

In the years before and after Korea fell victim to Japan's imperialism, the Korean people sought to resist the Japanese both inside and outside the country. Their effort culminated in the March First Independence Movement in 1919, which aroused international sympathy and moral support. With this as a turning point, the Provisional Government of the Republic of Korea was established in Shanghai as the nerve center of the independence struggle against Japan.

From the closing stages of World War II, the struggle for freedom from Japanese colonialism drew the attention of the world powers to Korea. The leaders of the United States, Britain and China agreed in the 1943 Cairo Conference that after the surrender of Japan, Korea would become an independent state. This was reaffirmed by the 1945 Potsdam Declaration, and subsequently by the Soviet Union, which declared war against Japan.

But the fate of Korea was reversed overnight. At the Yalta Conference in 1945 the leaders of the United States, Great Britain and the Soviet Union in 1945 reached a secret agreement that included the division of the Korean Peninsula at the 38th parallel in order to facilitate the disarming of Japanese military forces—the Soviet Union occupying the area north of the 38th parallel and the United States that to the south.

In accordance with this agreement, the Soviet Union, which entered the war against Japan only eight days before the Japanese surrender, promptly dispatched armed forces to the region north of the 38th parallel. They were equally prompt in establishing their own military government, which eventually helped establish the North Korean Communist regime. The Soviet move into the Korean Peninsula could be identified with its postwar policy in Eastern Europe, and at the same time reflected Russia's traditional expansionist policy in East Asia. The United States still maintains that the 38th parallel was not intended as a political demarcation, but as a temporary expedient to facilitate military operations. Whatever the real motive, the Soviet Union made the best use of this circumstance, making the line one of political confrontation and establishing a satellite state north of the parallel, while eliminating opposition nationalist forces one by one.

At the time, the commander of the U.S. army south of the 38th parallel asked his Russian counterpart to reconsider the Russian move to enforce a military government in the North, an issue that was not resolved through a conference of military commanders. A conference of the foreign ministers of the three powers was convened in Moscow on December 21, 1945, which came up with an agreement that Korea would become independent after five years under the joint trusteeship of the United States, Britain, the Soviet Union and China. With this agreement as authority, the Joint Commission of the United States and the Soviet Union was convened in Seoul in March 1946 to assist in the establishment of a unified government of Korea. The meeting ended without reaching a conclusion due to opposition by a majority of the people and excessive demands on the part of the Soviet Union.

At this juncture, on August 26, 1947, the United States proposed the reconvening of the contracting powers of the so-called Moscow Agreement, but the proposal was thwarted due to Soviet rejection. Recognizing the fact that efforts to resolve the Korean question within the framework of the Moscow Agreement were futile, the United States decided to bring the question to the United Nations, thus initiating the beginning of Korea's relations with the world community.

The United Nations, on November 14, 1947, adopted a U.S. resolution which called for a general election under the supervision of a U.N. commission. A nine-member United Nations Temporary Commission arrived in Korea on January 12, 1948. However, the Soviet military commander in the North refused to comply with the U.N. resolution and denied the U.N. Commission access to the northern part of Korea. Under such circumstances, the U.N. General Assembly on February 26, 1948, reaffirmed its resolution of November of the previous year, and adopted a new resolution calling for elections in areas accessible to the U.N. Commission.

The first elections in Korea took place on May 10, 1948, only in the area south of the 38th parallel. A National Assembly was elected and adopted a constitution on July 12. On August 15 the Government of the Republic of Korea was inaugurated, while a Communist regime headed by Kim Il-sung was set up in the North. The Republic, recognized by 38 countries, including the United States, filed an application for admission to the United Nations on January 29, 1949, which was rejected because of a Soviet veto.

The division of the Korean Peninsula, originally intended as an operational expediency for the two occupation forces to facilitate the disarming of a vanquished enemy, has persisted, causing needless suffering for the Korean people.

Korean War and Geneva Conference

The perpetuation of the division of Korea in 1948 had different meanings for the peoples of the South and the North. To the people of the Republic of Korea, it was a situation they had to accept although one which they had no desire to maintain. What most concerned the Republic of Korea was the fear of communization of the whole peninsula. Their attitude was that they would rather live divided temporarily than unified under Communism.

On the other hand, the division of Korea ran counter to North Korean design. The regime in the North felt it had been denied a good chance to extend its control over the South. The North had already established a full-fledged army by February 1948, and its strength soon reached 200,000 regular soldiers in contrast to the small numbers of the South Korean constabulary.

The ultimate objective of North Korea's unification policy was to take over South Korea by military means. In order to pursue that objective, the North Korean regime improved its military preparedness through negotiations with the Soviet Union on the one hand, and attempted to undermine the Republic of Korea Government by a peace offensive and by subversive means on the other. In the face of unremitting Communist pressure, the Republic of Korea Government tried to insure its security. However, the peace and security that South Korea sought was illusory. On June 25, 1950, less than a week after North Korea had made another "peaceful unification" proposal, it launched a full-scale invasion of South Korea and started a war that was to continue for three years.

To repel the unprovoked aggression, the United Nations, led by the United States, quickly took steps to organize a collective police force and come to the aid of the South. The war was finally brought to a cease-fire in July 1953, with the conclusion of the Armistice Agreement between the U.N. Command and the North Korean and Chinese Communist forces. This failed to bring about a unified Korea, leaving the country divided as before along a 4-kilometer-wide and 249 kilometer-long Demilitarized Zone (DMZ).

The Armistice Agreement called for a conference to seek a peaceful settlement of the Korean issue, and the Geneva Conference opened on April 26, 1954. It was made up of 19 powers: the 16 United Nations members which had sent troops to Korea (minus South Africa), plus the Republic of Korea, on the one hand, and North Korea, Communist China and the Soviet Union on the other.

The debate at the Geneva Conference uncovered three key issues that the two sides could not agree on: 1) the authority and competence of the United Nations on the Korean question; 2) the principle of free elections, and 3) the withdrawal of foreign troops. The Republic of Korea and its allies recognized the authority and competence of the United Nations to deal with the Korean issue, insisting that the world body should have the primary role in bringing about a settlement. They also argued for the stationing of U.N. forces in Korea until the mission of the United Nations had been accomplished by the creation of a unified, independent, and democratic Korea. North Korea, the Soviet Union and Communist China rejected these views. They argued that the only acceptable formula was one in which Koreans would be left to solve their own problems free from "outside interference." They demanded that all foreign troops withdraw from Korea prior to elections. The Republic of Korea and the United States advocated elections under U.N. supervision, proportionate to the population of the whole of Korea. North Korea and its allies advocated international supervision and South-North equality.

Since the impasse over these three issues was not resolved, the Republic of Korea and its allies decided to adjourn the conference. On June 15, 1954, they issued a "Sixteen-Nation Declaration on Korea," acknowledging that the Geneva Conference had been in vain.

After the break-up of the Geneva Conference, the basic responsibility for the Korean question automatically returned to the United Nations. At its Ninth General Assembly on December 11, 1954, it approved a report on the Geneva political conference and reaffirmed that the aim of the United Nations was to create through peaceful means a unified, independent and democratic Korea. The 10th General Assembly on November 29, 1955, reaffirmed this principle and urged North Korea to accept the proposal.

The Beginnings of Dialogue

During the 1960s, South Korea held the policy that it was dangerous to compromise with the Communists and that it would be unwise to try and deal with them from a position of weakness. A precondition to dialogue was economic development. In the 1970s, after a steady success in developmental efforts, the Park Chung Hee

People gathered at the KBS studios to participate in a family search campaign held by the network in 1983.

Government made a dramatic change in policy. This was hinted at in a Liberation Day address on August 15, 1970, when President Park called for a *bona fide* competition with the North and expressed willingness to suggest further measures to gradually remove various artificial barriers between the two sides. This has come to be known as the August 15 Declaration.

It was not until a full year later, however, that any progress toward communication was made. On August 12, 1971, the president of the Republic of Korea National Red Cross (ROKN-RC) proposed a South-North Red Cross conference to discuss a campaign to search for relatives scattered in the two halves of the Peninsula. Surprisingly, P'yŏngyang accepted the proposal. The first preliminary meeting was held on September 20, and seven full-dress meetings were held between August 29, 1972, and July 10, 1973.

The start of the Red Cross meetings was followed by another surprising development in May 1972, when President Park secretly sent Yi Hu-rak, director of the Central Intelligence Agency, to P'yŏngyang for four days to confer with President Kim Il-sung and other North Korean leaders on ways to ease tension on the Korean Peninsula and to eventually unify the country. Kim Il-sung reciprocated by sending his personal envoy, Pak Sŏng-ch'ŏl, also secretly, to Seoul a few weeks later.

A South-North Joint Communique on the agreements reached through these high-level intra-Korean discussions was issued on July 4, 1972. Among other things, the communique called for peaceful unification without outside intervention; national reconciliation transcending differences in ideologies and institutions; steps to ease tension; the stopping of mutual abuse and slander, the prevention of inadvertent military incidents; an early and successful conclusion of the South-North Red Cross Conference and a hotline telephone service between Seoul and P'yŏngyang. It also called for the formation of a high-level South-North Coordinating Committee (SNCC) to implement the aforementioned agreements, improve intra-Korean relations and resolve the question of unifying the country on the basis of the agreed principles.

The SNCC was officially inaugurated in November 1972, following meetings in P'anmunjŏm, P'yŏngyang and Seoul between its designated co-chairmen. This was followed by three plenary sessions held alternately in Seoul and P'yŏngyang before North Korea suspended dialogue on August 28, 1973.

From the beginning, two contrasting attitudes were in evidence in the Red Cross talks. North Korea stressed the importance of political discussions, maintaining that political and humanitarian issues could not be separated. In their view, humanitarianism could not exist unless it was supported by nationalism and meant to solve problems ultimately aimed at achieving national unification. South Korea claimed it was both possible and desirable to separate political and humanitarian matters. The Red Cross talks should tackle only humanitarian issues while economic, political and cultural exchanges should be settled by the SNCC.

North Korea attempted to turn the Red Cross talks into a political forum. At the second full-dress meeting held on September 13, 1972, its delegation insisted that the talks should proceed, "on the basis of freedom and democracy." For this purpose, at the third talks held on October 24, 1972, it formally proposed a resolution saying "a favorable climate should be constituted in South Korea by eliminating all social, political and statutory obstacles to the talks." The essence of North Korea's demand was a call for the abrogation of South Korea's Anti-Communism Law and National Security Law. In the previous month, Kim Il-sung had stated that the enactment of these two laws was "an open provocation" against North Korea. South Korea was adamant in rejecting this proposal, arguing that North Korea was mixing humanitarian matters with political matters and meddling in South Korea's internal affairs. These issues subsequently served to stalemate the full-dress talks.

The issue of mutual non-interference in internal affairs clearly divided the two sides. North Korea never hesitated to touch upon South Korea's internal affairs and attempted to manipulate them whenever possible. North Korea attributed its decision to discontinue the South-North dialogue to South Korea's internal affairs in August 1973.

The SNCC meetings also revealed a distinct difference in basic approaches to the solution of problems created by the division of the country. South Korea favored a gradual, functional, step-by-step approach and stressed the need for mutual psychological readjustment. North Korea stressed a "once and for all" approach. Its rationale was that the division of Korea was causing unbearable misfortune and suffering for compatriots in the South and constituted a national calamity for the entire Korean people, impeding unified development of Korea society.

The Opening and Suspension of South-North Dialogue

The South-North Red Cross Conference, which had been held alternately in Seoul and P'yŏngyang with the goal of resolving the problems of the dispersed families in the two halves of the Peninsula, was suspended after its seventh meeting held in P'yŏngyang in July 1973. The South proposed to the North that a preliminary contact immediately resume the deadlocked Red Cross conference.

As a result of repeated appeals by Seoul, the two sides agreed to dispatch delegates to P'anmunjŏm and held a total of seven meetings during 1973-1974. In accordance with an agreement made through these meetings, the South and North began the first working-level meeting of the Red Cross Conference in July 1974, and held 25 meetings until these talks were broken off by North Korea in 1977. Likewise, meetings at the SNCC vice-chairman level were held 10 times between 1973-1975 with the aim of resuming the SNCC talks suspended after a third meeting in 1973. This effort also was scuttled unilaterally by the North. The telephone hotline between Seoul and P'yŏngyang was also cut off by North Korea in the wake of the axe murders of two American military officers at P'anmunjŏm on August 18, 1976.

Since such intra-Korean dialogues during the 1970s as the South-North Red Cross Conference and the South-North Coordinating Committee were halted, contacts between Seoul and P'yŏngyang have been made only sporadically. In February 1979, Seoul proposed a vice-chairman level meeting of the SNCC in P'yŏngyang to revive the broken SNCC talks. The North ignored this offer. Instead, they dispatched representatives of the Democratic Front for the Unification of the Fatherland (DFUF) to P'anmunjŏm. They met with South Korean counterparts three times until those contacts were broken off in March 1979. In the same year, meetings between the South-North Table Tennis Associations were held four times with the goal of sending a single intra-Korean team to the 35th World Table Tennis Championships in P'yŏngyang. These meetings were also broken off by North Korea which rejected the South's bid to participate in this international meet.

As 1980 started, the South-North working-level meeting was held at P'anmunjŏm in February 1980 to arrange a South-North Prime Ministers conference. A total of 10 meetings were held until they were disrupted in September the same year. As usual, no agreement was reached through these meetings.

Efforts by the South to Continue Dialogue

Since the South-North dialogue was suspended by unilateral decisions of the North, South Korea has repeated its appeals to reopen the deadlocked talks. After the assassination of President Park Chung Hee in 1979, the newly inaugurated government of President Chun Doo Hwan pursued a more aggressive unification policy. On January 12, 1981, President Chun proposed an exchange of visits by the top leaders of South and North Korea with the goal of providing a breakthrough for the restoration of mutual trust and the prevention of fratricidal war, thereby leading to peaceful reunification. On June 5, 1981, President Chun again offered to meet Kim Il-sung, the leader of North Korea, at any place and at any time chosen by P'yŏngyang to discuss all questions raised by both sides. In this proposal, President Chun expressed his hope to open contacts with exchanges in the areas of sports and culture, economic cooperation and postal services between the two sides of Korea, if the North was not prepared to open its country.

On January 22, 1982, President Chun promulgated a comprehensive plan for unification, namely the Democratic Reunification Formula for National Reconciliation. Under this formula, a Korean Unification Council would be formed with delegates from both halves of Korea who could represent the views of the people. The council also would be charged with the task of writing a constitution for a united democratic republic. Such a constitution could then be adopted through referendums or general elections held throughout the Peninsula to establish a unified legislature and government, thereby establishing a unified country.

In order to facilitate this formula, the South proposed a Provisional Agreement on Basic Relations to normalize the deadlocked South-North dialogue and suggested seven specific provisions. These provisions called for relations based on the principle of equality, the abandonment of all forms of military force in settling issues, recognition of each other's existing political order and social institutions, ending the arms race and military confrontation, opening each other's society through various forms of exchange and cooperation, respecting each other's bilateral and multilateral treaties and agreements concluded with third countries, and establishing liaison offices in Seoul and P'yŏngyang.

Likewise, the Republic of Korea urged the North to agree to a summit meeting to discuss candidly all of the above issues. However, North Korea's Kim Il, chairman of the Committee for Peaceful Unification of the Fatherland, rejected Seoul's proposals in a statement issued on January 26, 1982, describing them as political philosophy ignoring reality. On February 1 of the same year, the South proposed to the North a package of 20 projects with the goal of opening each other's society, realiz-

ing cooperation and easing tensions. This also was rejected.

Rejecting all other ROK proposals aimed at unification, the North issued a statement in the name of the Committee for Peaceful Unification of the Fatherland on February 10, 1982, calling for a joint conference of 100 politicians, 50 from each side, to discuss North Korea's unification formula centered on a confederation. In this statement, the North unilaterally selected 50 persons it said could represent the South at the proposed joint meeting.

Despite North Korea's obvious attempt to obstruct intra-Korean dialogue, the Republic of Korea continued its efforts to reunite the divided land. On February 25, 1982, the Minister of the National Unification Board suggested to the North that high-level talks, attended by nine delegates from each side and headed by a minister-level official, be held to discuss the issues of holding a summit meeting between the South and the North and organizing a Korean Unification Council. On January 18, 1983, the South renewed its proposal to North Korea for a summit meeting and listed four issues to be discussed: easing tension and preventing war on the Korean Peninsula; jointly reviewing the unification formula of both the South and the North; halting excessive competition in the international arena, and creating an international milieu conducive to unification.

Ignoring the South's repeated proposals to discuss steps for unification, North Korean authorities demanded that tripartite talks be held between Seoul, P'yŏngyang and Washington. In a letter sent to Seoul on January 10, 1984, the North also insisted on signing a peace treaty between the United States and North Korea and a non-aggression pact between the South and the North. The proposed treaty would replace the Korean War Armistice Agreement, and was seen as an attempt to effect the withdrawal of U.S. military forces from the South.

For all practical purposes, the P'yŏngyang proposal called for two bilateral negotiations, not tripartite talks, and was aimed at upsetting the military balance between the South and North by bringing about the removal of the American military presence.

The North had made an earlier proposal for tripartite talks, but it came on October 8, 1983, only one day before a North Korean terrorist bombing attack on a South Korean presidential delegation in Rangoon, Burma, that killed 17 South Korean government officials, including four cabinet ministers. North Korea relayed its proposal to hold tripartite talks to the United States through the People's Republic of China with the aim of diverting attention from its scheduled terrorist attack in Rangoon. The tripartite talks proposed by the North were a fraudulent peace initiative by North Korea. The Republic of Korea, thus, suggested to North Korea that intra-Korean talks be held in which unification itself and numerous related problems could be solved by Koreans.

The Second Evolution of South-North Dialogue

On March 30, 1984, the North Korean Olympic Committee proposed to the South that sports talks be held to discuss the formation of a single Korean team for the 23rd Olympic Games in Los Angeles, a proposal the Republic of Korea had made in 1981. The South agreed to hold the intra-Korean sports talks, thereby resuming the first official South-North contact in four years. Although the South-North sports talks were convened three times between April and May the same year, this contact was also unilaterally broken off by the North.

In a press conference on August 20, 1984, President Chun proposed to the North bilateral trade and economic cooperation between the two Koreas with the aim of hastening national reconciliation and joint prosperity. The South offered to provide the North with technological and material assistance free of charge with the aim of contributing to North Korea's economy.

On September 8, North Korea offered to send relief goods to the South to aid victims of flooding. Although relief activities had been virtually completed and there was no need for such support, the president of the Republic of Korea National Red Cross (ROKNRC) accepted the offer in the hope it would help to improve relations.

Soon after the delivery of the materials, the ROKNRC proposed the resumption of a full-dress meeting of the South-North Red Cross Conference to discuss the question of reuniting families and other humanitarian issues, which had been suspended for 12 years. The government also proposed an intra-Korean economic meeting to discuss trade and other cooperation.

As a result, the first intra-Korean economic meeting was held on November 15, and a preliminary Red Cross meeting was held on November 20, 1984, both at P'anmunjŏm. In spite of minor differences, a surprisingly quick agreement was reached at the first economic meeting on possible items to be traded, areas of economic cooperation and operational procedures.

At the preliminary Red Cross session, the two sides agreed to resume holding full-dress meetings, the next one in Seoul. They also prepared a five-point agenda, and set the size of the delegations at 84 from each side. Although there was some disagreement on working procedures related to the opening of the eighth full-dress meeting, they were ironed out through compromise. The two sides agreed to hold the second economic meeting at P'anmunjŏm on December 5, 1984, and the eighth full-dress Red Cross meeting in Seoul at a time to be established later.

On November 27, however, the North unilaterally postponed the economic talks until sometime in 1985. The postponement was triggered by a November 23 incident at P'anmunjŏm in which 20 to 30 North Korean security guards crossed the Military Demarcation Line and opened fire at a Soviet defector. In the shootout, a South Korean soldier was killed and an American serviceman wounded. Several North Koreans were killed or wounded. As a result of the incident, North Korea claimed the atmosphere was not suitable for dialogue.

Subsequently, it was decided to hold the economic talks on January 17, 1985, and the full-dress Red Cross meeting in Seoul on January 23. However, on January 9, North Korea unilaterally postponed these talks indefinitely, giving as an excuse the routine annual Korea-U.S. joint military exercise, Team Spirit.

The North's postponement of the economic and Red Cross talks came only a few hours before President Chun renewed a call for a South-North summit to expedite dialogue in all appropriate fields and achieve a further breakthrough in intra-Korean relations. He also renewed a proposal to exchange high-level resident liaison missions to facilitate South-North exchanges and cooperation pending unification.

First Practical Achievement

In March, following Team Spirit, South Korea again proposed reopening the two meetings, and it was finally agreed to hold the economic talks on May 17 and the Red Cross talks on May 28. At the second economic talks, the Republic, in line with the agreements reached at the first meeting, made concrete proposals for trade. The North refused to discuss concrete agreements and instead proposed a deputy prime minister-level committee meeting be held. The meeting closed on a less optimistic note than the first, with only an agreement to meet again on June 20.

On June 5, 1985, in a meeting with the Advisory Council on Peaceful Unification Policy, President Chun expressed hope that North Korea would participate in the 1986 Seoul Asian Games and the 1988 Seoul Summer Olympics. In a Liberation Day address on August 15, he again urged North Korea to promptly agree to a top leaders meeting and other measures to normalize intra-Korean relations.

By the end of September 1985, four sessions of economic talks had taken place at the truce village of P'anmunjŏm. Plenary Red Cross Conference meetings also had been held in Seoul and P'yŏngyang alternately, leading to an agreement to exchange home visit groups and performing art troupes between September 20-23. For the first time since the end of the Korean War, sizable numbers of private citizens crossed the Demilitarized Zone in both directions with official approval. Though limited in scale, the visitors exchange was the first practical outcome of a South-North dialogue conducted on an on-and-off-again basis for 15 years.

This was followed by the 10th plenary Red Cross Conference meeting in Seoul on December 3, 1985. Two working-level intra-Korean meetings were held on July 23 and September 25, 1985, to pave the way for a South-North interparliamentary conference. Athletic officials from the South and the North met in Lausanne, Switzerland, in October 1985, and again in January 1986, under the sponsorship of the International Olympic Committee. This was an attempt to induce North Korea to participate in the 1988 Summer Olympics in Seoul. They agreed to hold a third athletic meeting on June 11, 1986, again in Lausanne.

On January 20, 1986, North Korea unilaterally postponed all scheduled South-North meetings, again using as an excuse the annual Team Spirit exercise scheduled for February. This affected the sixth round of economic talks slated for January 22, the 11th meeting of the Red Cross Conference planned for February 26-27 in P'yŏngyang and the third preliminary meeting to arrange for an interparliamentary conference on February 18. In response to requests from the South to resume the deadlocked intra-Korean talks, the North proposed to the South some new topics for intra-Korean talks. This included a call for tripartite military talks on June 17, 1986, a South-North high-level political and military meeting on December 30, 1986, and multinational arms reduction talks on July 23, 1987. The North insisted that the newly proposed South-North meetings be held prior to resuming the earlier deadlocked South-North talks. On April 24, 1987, however, the North issued a statement unilaterally announcing its decision to halt all existing intra-Korean talks.

While insisting on solving political and military problems prior to resuming the South-North dialogue, the North demanded tripartite talks between the United States and the two Koreas with the goal of breaking off South-North overtures. On November 29, 1987, the North perpetrated a terrorist bombing attack on a Korean Air flight that killed all 115 people aboard. This reinforced further the international terrorist label given North Korea for the Rangoon bombing and demonstrated North's Korea's intent to raise a security threat in the Republic of Korea, in order to disrupt or abort the 1988 Seoul Olympic Games.

Turning Point in South-North Relations

At his inaugural address on February 25, 1988, President Roh Tae Woo declared his determination to bring about reconciliation on the Korean Peninsula by peacefully cooperating with North Korea in line with the people's yearning for an end to the division of the land. The Sixth Republic endeavored actively to redefine the North not as an adversary involved in competition and confrontation with the South, but as a member of the same ethnic family to be included in a national community seeking common prosperity on the basis of mutual trust, reconciliation and cooperation. President Roh took the lead in revitalizing national self-confidence in political and economic development, spurred by the successful staging of the 1988 Seoul Olympic Games, with the goal of building an era of reconciliation and cooperation between the South and the North. In addition, the Government opened the door so that people working in every sector could voice their viewpoints on unification, thus constructing a platform to reach a national consensus. It also implemented various policies to create a turning point for improved South-North relations, thereby hastening the pace of national unification.

Despite a series of unification proposals from the South, no progress was made because of North Korea's intransigence. However, on July 7, 1988, in compliance with rising hopes for unification, President Roh announced the Special Declaration in the Interest of National Self-Esteem, Unification and Prosperity, considered to be the most feasible unification proposal to date. It was seen as especially timely in view of the changing international situation and the shifting domestic environment, both of which created conditions favorable to reunification. The essence of the July 7 Declaration can be categorized into three general points: (1) the South will no more regard North Korea as an adversary but as a member of one ethnic community; (2) the South will endeavor to move the North from its self-imposed policy of isolation and help North Korea actively take part in the international community as a responsible member; (3) the South will continuously carry out its policy to increase mutual cooperation and reconciliation between the South and the North. The spirit of the July 7 Special Declaration, which marked a major turning point in the conduct of establishing the unification and diplomatic policy toward North Korea by defining it not as an adversary but as a member of a single ethnic family, was adopted as a basic principle of the Korean National Community Unification Formula declared by President Roh in 1989. With this new unification policy, the Republic of Korea continuously urged the North to resume the existing South-North contacts and to hold a summit meeting with the aim of expeditiously solving pending problems.

After proposing a summit meeting without pre-conditions to North Korea in his address delivered on the 43rd National Liberation Day on August 15, 1988, President Roh emphasized the prompt realization of such a meeting. In an address delivered at the General Assembly of the United Nations on October 18 of the same year, President Roh pointed out some specific subjects to be discussed in a summit meeting and outlined the importance of such a meeting.

As the year 1988 began, Kim Il-sung, leader of North Korea, proposed a South-North joint conference in his New Year's message and sent letters to 50 South Koreans, unilaterally chosen by the North, to convene a preliminary meeting for the conference. North Korea's call for a South-North joint conference could not be seen as a genuine proposal, but as deceptive propaganda with the goal of blaming the tension between the two Koreas on the South. One of the main reasons why North Korea proposed a South-North joint conference was to split public opinion in the South, thereby upsetting South Korean society and bringing about social chaos.

To that end, the North induced radical students in the South to propose a South-North students meeting with the aim of destroying a national consensus on unification.

Broken off in 1985, the preliminary contacts for interparliamentary talks finally were resumed in 1988. It had taken two years and 11 months for the two sides to resume such moves, but contact was made seven times in 1988, clearing several obstacles to interparliamentary talks. However, an eighth preliminary contact, scheduled for February 10, 1989, was indefinitely postponed by the North again in protest against the annual ROK-U.S. joint military exercise Team Spirit. Instead, the North sent a letter to the Prime Minister of South Korea on November 16, 1988, in which it proposed a high-level political and military meeting. As a response to this proposal, the South proposed a preliminary meeting to arrange high-level official talks, headed by the prime ministers of each side. The South told the North discussions could include ways to establish mutual trust and ease tension between the two sides. The North agreed to the proposal, and, as a result, the first and the second preliminary meetings to arrange high-level official talks were held at P'anmunjŏm in February and March 1989. As before, however, this contact ran into difficulty from the start due to the Team Spirit issue raised by North Korea. The talks stalled prior to a third preliminary meeting scheduled for April 12, 1989. The North then denounced the Republic of Korea's decision to prosecute the Rev. Mun Ik-hwan, who had made a secret visit to the North without permission from the Seoul Government, using it as an excuse to break off the preliminary talks.

In March 1989, South-North sports talks were held twice to discuss the formation of a single team to take part in the 11th Asian Games in Beijing, China. In these meetings, the two sides agreed to use "Arirang" as the official song of the South-North single national team and cleared several obstacles. However, this dialogue also was postponed unilaterally by the North.

Despite North Korea's bid to use intra-Korean talks for its political purposes, the Republic of Korea continued all-out efforts to normalize the frustrated South-North dialogues and urged the North to consider such contacts more seriously. Intra-Korean talks, including the South-North Red Cross Meeting, ceased for nearly four years, resumed in October 1989 and proceeded until North Korea broke them off in 1990 with charges about a non-existent concrete wall south of the DMZ, and the Team Spirit exercise as another excuse.

The preliminary meeting to arrange for a high-level talks, to be headed by the prime ministers, on the other hand, fared much better. They, too, were resumed in October 1989 and a final agreement was reached at the eighth session on July 26, 1990.

The historic initial round of High-level Talks between South and North Korea convened in Seoul on September 4, 1990. An additional seven rounds of the "Prime Ministers' Talks," as they are commonly called in the South, followed, with the last being held in P'yŏngyang in September, 1992. The venue alternated between Seoul and P'yŏngyang.

As these talks could hardly be more meaningful, they will find a prominent place in the history of the South-North Dialogue. Delegations headed respectively by the prime ministers of South and North Korea met officially, the first time in 45 years of national division that talks had occured at such a high level. Whatever the talks ultimately achieve, the simple fact that they were held at all is of monumental consequence.

South-North relations fell into a stalemate in early 1991. The Gulf War broke out in January, and the ROK-U.S. Team Spirit military exercise followed soon thereafter. North Korea announced the indefinite postponement of the fourth round of prime ministerials, which had been slated for P'yŏngyang on February 25, 1991.

The North later rescheduled the delayed fourth round for August 27, 1991, but a *coup d'etat* erupted in Moscow on August 19th, causing the North Koreans once again to postpone the talks, using a minor outbreak of cholera in the South as an excuse.

The much-delayed fourth round of Prime Ministers' Talks finally got underway in P'yŏngyang on October 24, 1991. In a bold stroke aimed at achieving a breakthrough in the talks, the South tabled a proposal for a basic agreement, a comprehensive document addressing in broad outlines the full range of major South-North issues, reconciliation, nonagression, and exchanges and cooperation.

Pursuant to a request by the North at the first round of Prime Ministers' Talks, working level contacts were held on three occasions to discuss the U.N. membership issues. The North's position was founded on its so-called "Korea is one" policy and called for South and North either to join the United Nations and share a single seat or to defer joining the U.N until after unification. The South asserted that the North's call for the two sides to share a single U.N seat was illogical, an unrealistic idea that could never be realized. The South favored simultaneous South and North entry into the United Nations, but the North continued to oppose this approach vigorously. During the working level contacts, a frustrated South Korea announced that if the North continued to oppose simultaneous membership, the South would join the United Nations unilaterally.

The North abandoned its call for sharing a single U.N. membership in May 1991, choosing in the end to go along with simultaneous South-North entry into the world body. Both joined the United Nations on September 17, 1991. U.N. membership is an inevitable phase the two sides must experience on the path to unification and marks a new point of departure for South-North peaceful coexistence.

Opening an Era of South-North Reconciliation and Cooperation

On December 18, 1991, President Roh stated publicly that there were no nuclear weapons in the Republic of Korea. "Not a single nuclear weapon exists in South," the President said. President Roh had urged the North to join in arms reduction and the denuclearization of the Korean Peninsula the previous month, on November 8, 1991.

The sixth round of Prime Ministers' Talks was held in P'yŏngyang on February 18, 1992. The two prime ministers signed not only the basic, bilateral document proposed initially by the South, the Agreement on Reconciliation, Nonaggression, and Exchange and Cooperation (also known as the Basic Agreement), but also signed a Joint Declaration of the Denuclearization of the Korean Peninsula (also known as the Joint Declaration). This latter instrument 1) forbids the manufacture, possession, or use of nuclear weapons; 2) restricts the use of nuclear energy to peaceful purposes only; 3) commits each side not to possess facilities for enriching uranium or for reprocessing nuclear fuel; 4) commits each sides to simultaneous, mutual nuclear inspections; and 5) establishes the South-North Joint Nuclear Control Commission.

As stipulated in the Basic Agreement and the Joint Declaration, the two sides were to undertake a series of negotiations to agree on details of execution and compliance with these two fundamental agreements. Starting in March, 1992, the various bodies established and defined in the Basic Agreement and the Joint Declaration began to hold ad hoc meetings. These bodies were the Political Committee, the Military Committee, the Exchanges and Cooperation Committee, and the Joint Nuclear Control Commission.

The seventh round of High-level Talks was held in Seoul on May 5, 1992. The prime ministers of South and North officially approved the agreements creating and providing for the operation of the Military Committee and the Exchanges and Cooperation Committee, and agreements creating and providing for the operation of a Liaison Office at P'anmunjŏm. The two sides also agreed to form and operate the Reconciliation Committee.

In the wake of the seventh round of prime ministerials, the various committees convened or their co-chairmen met on no fewer than 26 occasions. The committees were negotiating subsidiary agreements for detailed implementation of the Basic Agreement. This effort was successful, and Basic Agreement's three subsidiary agreements were signed at the eighth

The Prime Ministers of South and North Korea exchanging an intra-Korean agreement on September 17, 1992.

round of High-level Talks held in P'yŏngyang on September 17, 1992. The three subsidiary agreements addressed, respectively, Reconciliation, Nonagreession, and Exchanges and Cooperation. Four South-North joint commissions were also established during the eighth round talks: the South-North Joint Economic Exchanges and Cooperation Commission, the South-North Joint Social and Cultural Exchanges and Cooperation Commission, the South-North Joint Military Commission and the South-North Reconciliation Commission. The purpose of the commissions is to put the fundamental Basic Agreement and its three subsidiary agreements into actual practice. The two sides agreed that the commissions would hold their first meetings in November 1992.

Thus, it was September 1992, before the Basic Agreement, the Joint Declaration of Denuclearization and the Basic Agreement's three subsidiary agreements were all adopted and put into effect. The paper chase was over; the time for practical application had arrived. This was a first giant step toward independent,

peaceful liquidation of a sad history of national partition over nearly five decades of friction and confrontation.

After its July 7, 1988 Special Declaration of intent to improve relations with North, the Government of the Republic of Korea adopted follow-up measures such as a seven point economic exchanges plan on October 7, 1989, the Special Act Governing Intra-Korean Exchanges and Cooperation enacted on August 1, 1990, and the Law Establishing a South-North Cooperation Fund. These steps together formed the legal foundation and support base for systematic South-North exchanges and cooperation.

Under the provisions of these laws, 569 North Koreans have visited the South, and 678 South Koreans have visited the North as part of sports teams or performing arts troupes. Citizens of South and North have contacted each other on 496 other occasions, including reunions of family members separated by the South-North division and meetings held while attending international academic conferences.

Twenty-five billion won went into the South-North Cooperation Fund in 1991 and another 40 billion Won in 1992. The fund will continue to grow in the future and will provide financial support for South-North exchanges and cooperation.

From the initial opening measures adopted on October 7, 1988, to the end of 1992, officially-approved South-North trade developed as follows. North Korea exported goods to the South on 822 occasions for an aggregate amount totaling 408 million dollars. South Korea exported goods worth 42 million dollars to the North on a total of 85 occasions. Thus, two-way, official trade totaled 450 million dollars over that time. Most of this trade took place through third-party countries, but the two sides succeeded in late 1992 in conducting direct trade in a number of items, including agricultural products and Chinese medicines.

These various successes in reconciliation and cooperation faced reversal once again on March 12, 1993, when North Korea suddenly announced its intention to withdraw from the Nuclear Non-proliferation Treaty (NPT). The North's abrupt action followed the IAEA's decisions to conduct special inspections of two North Korean nuclear installations which are widely suspected of serving a secret nuclear weapons program. It will be difficult to expect any real or important progress in South-North relations so long as North Korea does not retreat from its intent to withdraw from the NPT and so long as the North fails to allay international suspicions about its nuclear weapons development program.

Keynotes of the New Administration's Unification Policy

On February 25, 1993, a new government headed by President Kim Young Sam was inaugurated with the popular support of the people, the first civilian democratic administration in 32 years. The inauguration of this new Administration provided the foundation for a genuine national consensus on the best policy for unification.

In hopes of making a significant improvement in relations with the North, the new Administration is following a unification formula based on the perception that the North is not an adversary, but a partner for dialogue and cooperation. Despite efforts at improvement, relations between the South and the North have become strained due to mounting suspicions over the North's nuclear arms development. Moreover, the abrupt declaration by the North on March 12, 1993, that it was withdrawing from the Nuclear Non-proliferation Treaty aroused serious concern in the global community, especially in Northeast Asia.

Following the adoption of a resolution by the Security Council of the United Nations urging the North to promptly resolve the issue of its nuclear arms development, as well as two rounds of talks with the United States, North Korea announced that it was suspending its decision to withdraw from the NPT and would resume negotiations with the International Atomic Energy Agency concerning the latter's inspection of suspected nuclear facilities in the North. In addition, it also announced that it would respond to the repeated call of the South to resume talks on how to substantially implement the Joint Declaration of Denuclearization.

In subsequent negotiations with the IAEA, however, the North flatly refused to even discuss special inspections of its suspected nuclear facilities. Furthermore, it turned down the South's call to resume talks on mutual inspection of nuclear facilities and instead proposed to exchange special envoys with the South, thereby attempting to side-step the nuclear issue.

True to its firm belief that dialogue with the North must be continued in some format, the South accepted the North's call for working-level meetings to discuss an exchange of special envoys, and an initial round of working-level talks were held on October 5, 1993, some nine months after the suspension of dialogue. The South and the North have since met twice more on October 15 and October 25 at P'anmunjŏm, yet there is still no agreement.

No tangible progress in negotiations for sub-

stantial reconciliation and cooperation will be possible, however, until and unless the North agrees to accept special inspections of its nuclear facilities by the IAEA and assumes a sincere attitude in negotiations with the South. Furthermore, mutual nuclear inspections must be undertaken in accordance with the Joint Declaration of the Denuclearization of the Korean Peninsula.

A Three-stage Approach to Unification

The unification formula of the Kim Young Sam Government has been devised to ensure peace. It rules out the use of force even though unification is an urgent task. This is deemed to be realistic and logical given the utter destruction that would result from a modern war.

Unification must guarantee the well-being of all of the Korean people, not their destitution.

To ensure a peaceful and orderly unification process, the new Administration has designed a three-stage unification formula. It consists of a stage of reconciliation and cooperation, a stage of a Korean commonwealth and a final stage of a unified Korea-one nation and one state.

During the initial stage, the two parts of Korea would begin cooperative endeavors while working to lessen the hostility and distrust between them. Exchanges and cooperation in various fields would be initiated.

During the stage of the Korean commonwealth, there would be a substantial level of exchanges and other forms of cooperation, and peace would be institutionalized. During this stage, the two Koreas would begin to reestablish a sense of national community and could expect to reap the benefits of coexistence with greater prosperity for all.

The final stage of unification would be reached when Korea becomes one nation and one state. The North and the South would be completely integrated into a single political entity.

This gradual approach to unification based on reconciliation and cooperation reflects the spirit of the Agreement on Reconciliation, Nonaggression and Exchanges and Cooperation Between the South and the North (the Basic Agreement) which became effective in February 1992.

Stage One: Reconciliation and Cooperation

During this stage, the South and the North would learn to cooperate with each other and reconcile their differences by seeking confidence-building measures to overcome the hostility and distrust which deepened during the Cold War era. To pursue these objectives, the two sides must be realistic in recognizing that two political entities exist on the Korean Peninsula: each must be willing to coexist and accept the other as a partner in the pursuit of prosperity for all, rather than as an enemy to be destroyed.

Despite the fact that the Basic Agreement respects the principle of coexistence, the relationship between the two states has never reached a satisfactory level of reconciliation and cooperation. More is required than mutual recognition. The two sides must take concrete measures to restore trust. These can include exchanges and other forms of cooperation in various fields. During this stage, it would be essential to build up popular support. In the past, South Koreans have been divided on this issue, but because the Kim Young Sam Government enjoys unquestioned legitimacy, it is able to win full public support.

Stage Two: A Korean Commonwealth

As trust between the South and the North is built up through exchanges and cooperation, it will be necessary to institutionalize peace between the two parts of Korea also. This would set the stage for a Korean commonwealth.

In this arrangement, the South and the North would form a common sphere for national life, leading to the development of social, cultural and economic communities. At this stage, South-North joint bodies would be created to discuss various alternative ways of integrating the two states. The issue of what specific bodies the commonwealth would have to perform what functions would be decided by agreement between the two areas of Korea.

Our basic idea is to establish a council of the Presidents of the South and the North and a South-North Ministerial Conference as regular bodies to progressively remove elements of heterogeneity between the two parts of Korea. It would also be advisable for representatives of the national legislatures of the South and the North to get together to draft the constitution for a unified Korea.

In pursuing this stage to unification, a spirit of sharing and cooperation would be indispensable. This would be conducive to exchanges and other joint activities between the South and the North to promote coexistence and mutual prosperity.

Stage Three: One Nation and One State

By this stage, the council of representatives of the South and the North would have completed the process of writing a constitution for a unified Korea through democratic methods. A unified government and a unified legislature would be established through national elections under the new constitution. The new institutions would take the necessary legislative and administrative actions to merge the separate governmental organizations and institutions into single entities under the unified government, thus completing the process of unifying the peninsula into one nation and one state.

The establishment of a unified government, however, would not necessarily mean the automatic completion of national integration. There would be inevitable complications resulting from the long division. For the full benefits of unification to be felt, the two economies must be successfully integrated and socio-cultural harmony restored between the two parts of the nation, in addition to political unification.

The Three Pillars of the Unification Policy

The Kim Young Sam Government has set forth three pillars for the implementation of its unification policy: a democratic national consensus, coexistence and coprosperity and national well-being.

First, the new Government is a genuinely democratic government elected by the people. The broad public support for the first civilian government since 1961 gives this administration an advantage that other administrations have not enjoyed. Second, in pursuing unification, the South Korean Government will try to promote coexistence and coprosperity with the North and will not try to isolate or contain it. Finally, in achieving full unification, the Government will pay less attention to ideology and political system but will rather stress the achievement of national well-being. In this context "national well-being" embodies the universal values of freedom, welfare and human dignity.

These three pillars must be erected in sequence. A national consensus is the basis for achieving coexistence and coprosperity which in turn will be followed by the attainment of national well-being when full unification has been achieved.

Democratic National Consensus

A democratically achieved consensus is the first pillar of national unification. In his inaugural address, President Kim emphasized, "what is needed is not emotionalism but a reasoned national consensus on achieving this crucial goal." On the one hand, a national consensus on this issue will strengthen the unification process and on the other, it will weaken the effectiveness of the North Korean tactic of forming a united front to undermine the South Korean Government. It will also, in the long run, help induce North Korea to respond positively to the peaceful overtures of the South Korean authorities.

Because the question of political legitimacy plagued previous administrations, they had to deal with rampant social conflict and confrontation. The North was able to readily take advantage of such conflicts. The Administration of President Kim, however, enjoys unquestioned legitimacy which is the foundation for a national consensus. Due to full public confidence in the Government, the authorities and the people are able to work hand-in-hand to achieve unification step by step. Furthermore, the government is able to accommodate both liberal and conservative views and thus can implement its unification policy more effectively.

A national consensus on unification is the first pillar which must be erected before the others. Without such a consensus, it would be impossible to achieve coexistence and coprosperity or national well-being with the North.

Coexistence and Coprosperity

"Coexistence and coprosperity" mean that the South and the North should coexist and seek freedom and affluence, discarding confrontation and antagonism. This process would begin with the South and the North recognizing each other and respecting each other's existence. Despite ideological and institutional differences, each side should respect the other and accept the other as a partner in dialogue and in cooperative efforts and renounce the intent to destroy the other.

To achieve this both sides must learn new ways of thinking and behaving and accept their differences. In other words, it is essential that they both shed their Cold-War mentality and adapt to a new reality. When the South and the North learn to coexist, they would then be able to seek coprosperity. Living together in poverty is not acceptable; existing together without freedom is not worthwhile. When the two sides agreed to coexist, they would be able to promote economic exchanges and other forms of cooperation, leading to mutual prosperity.

This process should not just involve the authorities. Athletes from the South and the North could organize exchanges of teams and players; academicians could exchange information and their expertise; businessmen could exchange resources and students could share their learning, ambitions and dreams. Nevertheless, the Government must play the principal role in solving the vital issues affecting the destiny of individual citizens and the Korean people as a whole. This is its inherent responsibility.

The aim of coexistence and coprosperity excludes a policy of isolating or containing the other side. With this in mind, it is the policy of the new South Korean Administration to not only encourage but assist North Korea to end its isolationism and participate in the international community as a viable member. It also excludes unification by absorption.

National Well-being

Ensuring the well-being of the whole nation is the ultimate goal of unification. This will be attained when the entire nation can enjoy freedom, a decent standard of living and full human rights. National well-being is thus the core value.

The Korean people all aspire to live in a unified state guaranteeing freedom, public well-being and human dignity. In fact, these are universal values appreciated by the whole global community.

Chronological Review of South-North Dialogue

*1970

August 15, 1970—President Park Chung Hee, in a Liberation Day address, calls for peaceful competition in development, construction and creativity between the South and the North.

*1971

August 12, 1971—Dr. Ch'oi Tu-sŏn, president of the Republic of Korea National Red Cross (ROKN-RC), proposes to the North Korean Red Cross (NKRC) that the Red Cross societies in the two sides of Korea jointly initiate a campaign to search

for the families dispersed throughout the South and the North.

August 14, 1971—The NKRC announces its acceptance in principle of the ROKNRC proposal for the family search campaign.

September 20, 1971—First preliminary meeting of the South-North Red Cross Conference opens at P'anmunjŏm.

*1972

May 2, 1972—President Park secretly sends, as his emissary, Yi Hu-rak, director of the Central Intelligence Agency, to P'yŏngyang, where Yi meets with Kim Il-sung in an attempt to create and operate an intra-Korea body for dialogue between the two sides.

May 29, 1972—P'yŏngyang secretly sends Pak Sŏng-ch'ŏl to Seoul in return for Yi Hu-rak's visit.

July 4, 1972—Seoul and P'yŏngyang announce the historic South- North Joint Communique, in which the two sides vow to cease slander and defamation of each other and to promote exchanges. They also agree to create a South-North Coordinating Committee (SNCC) and to open a direct Seoul-P'yŏngyang telephone line.

August 11, 1972—The preliminary meeting of the South-North Red Cross Conference ends.

August 29, 1972—The first full-dress meeting of the South-North Red Cross Conference opens in P'yŏngyang.

September 12, 1972—The second full-dress meeting of the South-North Red Cross Conference opens in Seoul.

October 12, 1972—The first meeting of the co-chairmen of the SNCC opens at P'anmunjŏm.

November 2, 1972—The second co-chairmen's meeting of the SNCC opens in P'yŏngyang, and adopts an agreement on the formation and operation of the South-North Coordinating Committee, and an agreement on the suspension of propaganda broadcasts against each other.

November 30, 1972—The SNCC is formally inaugurated and holds its first meeting in Seoul.

*1973

March 10, 1973—The first Executive Council meeting of the SNCC opens at P'anmunjŏm.

June 10, 1973—P'yŏngyang renews propaganda broadcasts across thetruce line, violating the propaganda suspension agreement.

June 23, 1973—President Park declares the Special Foreign Policy for Peace and Unification, in which he calls for peaceful coexistence between the South and the North pending national unification, and discloses his willingness not to oppose P'yŏngyang's entry into the United Nations if it does not unfavorably affect conditions for peaceful unification.

July 10, 1973—The seventh full-dress meeting of the South-North Red Cross Conference opens in P'yŏngyang; the NKRC rejects the ROKNRC proposal that the two sides exchange groups of visitors to ancestral tombs in the South and the North. No date is set for the next meeting.

August 28, 1973—Kim Young-ju, P'yŏngyang's co-chairman of the SNCC, announces P'yŏngyang's boycott of the South-North dialogue.

November 28, 1973—The first South-North delegates' meeting is held to discuss the resumption of full-dress South-North Red Cross talks.

December 5, 1973—The first vice-chairmen's meeting is held to discuss resumption of the deadlocked SNCC meeting.

*1974

January 18, 1974—President Park proposes, in a New Year press conference, the conclusion of a South-North nonaggression agreement.

May 29, 1974—The delegates meeting of the South-North Red Cross Conference winds up seven rounds of contacts, and agrees to hold working-level meetings of the Red Cross talks.

July 10, 1974—The first working-level meeting of the South-North Red Cross Conference is held.

*1975

May 29, 1975—The P'yŏngyang-side notifies Seoul that it has decided to put off indefinitely the 11th vice co-chairmen's meeting of the SNCC originally slated for May 30, 1975.

*1976

March 31, 1976—The ROKNRC proposes a meeting between the chief delegates of the two sides to discuss a solution for the deadlocked Red Cross talks.

August 18, 1976—North Korean soldiers commit the axe slaying of two American army officers at P'anmunjŏm.

August 30, 1976—North Korea unilaterally severs the Seoul-P'yŏngyang telephone line.

*1977

January 12, 1977—President Park reiterates his proposal for the conclusion of a South-North nonaggression agreement and offers grain to the hunger-stricken North Korean people.

February 11, 1977—At the 21st Red Cross working level meeting, the Seoul side suggests that if P'yŏngyang cannot agree to the holding of the 8th full-dress meeting in Seoul, it be held at P'anmunjŏm. P'yŏngyang rejects this new offer.

July 22, 1977—Dr. Min Kwan-shik, Seoul's acting co-chairman of the SNCC, denounces P'yŏngyang's establishment of a 322-kilometer economic sea zone.

*1978

March 19, 1978—P'yŏngyang unilaterally postpones the 26th working-level Red Cross talks that were to take place on March 29.

June 23, 1978—President Park proposes the creation of a consultative body for the promotion of South-North economic cooperation.

*1979

January 19, 1979—President Park Chung Hee, in a New Year news conference, calls on North Korea to resume the stalemated South-North Korean talks between responsible authorities "at any place, at any time, and at any level" without any preconditions.

January 23, 1979—In the name of the Central Committee of the Democratic Front for the Unification of the Fatherland (DFUF), North Korea proposes to convene an all-Korea national convention in early September.

February 17, 1979—Dr. Min Kwan-shik, Seoul's acting co-chairman of the SNCC, meets in P'anmunjŏm with North Korean representatives of the DFUF in the first South-North contact in a year and three months in an attempt to open the way for the resumption of the long-stalled dialogue between the two halves of the Korean Peninsula.

February 27, 1979—The first South-North table-tennis meeting is held to discuss formation of a single intra-Korean team to take part in the 35th World Table Tennis Championship Games in P'yŏngyang.

March 7, 1979—Dr. Min Kwan-shik meets with the North Koreans for a second time in P'anmunjŏm. Dr. Min states that the DFUF is not an acceptable negotiating partner and calls for the normalization of the SNCC.

July 1, 1979—President Park Chung Hee and President Jimmy Carter of the United States propose the convening of a "meeting of official representatives of South and North Korea and the United States" to seek means to promote dialogue and reduce tension in this part of the world.

July 10, 1979—P'yŏngyang officially rejects three-way talks through a radio broadcast.

August 15, 1979—President Park calls on North Korea anew to reopen the South-North Red Cross talks and to accept the offer made by the Republic of Korea either to hold talks between responsible authorities of the two sides or to hold tripartite talks including the United States.

*1980

January 12, 1980—North Korea proposes a South-North prime ministers' conference.

January 24, 1980—Prime Minister Shin Hyun-hwak of the Republic of Korea accepts a North Korean proposal to hold a South-North prime ministers' meeting.

February 6, 1980—The first South-North working-level officials' meeting is held to arrange a South-North prime ministers' meeting.

*1981

January 12, 1981—President Chun Doo Hwan proposes to North Korea an exchange of visits between the top leaders of the South and the North.

June 19, 1981—Cho Sang-ho, president of the Korean Olympic Committee, proposes the formation of single intra-Korean teams to take part in the 1984 Los Angeles Olympics and the 1982 New Delhi Asian Games and suggests the convening of an intra-Korean sports delegates meeting.

*1982

January 22, 1982—President Chun outlines the Formula for National Reconciliation and Democratic Unification in which he proposes the formation of a Korean Unification Council with participants from the two sides who can represent the views of the people, and that the Conference be charged with the responsibility of writing a constitution for a unified democratic republic.

February 1, 1982—Minister of National Unification Son Chae-shik proposes, as a follow-up to President Chun's proposal, 20 pilot projects which could be easily implemented and which, if implemented, would greatly ease tension.

February 25, 1982—The Republic of Korea proposes to hold a high-level delegates meeting in Seoul, P'yŏngyang or P'anmunjŏm within the month of March.

August 15, 1982—President Chun declares the opening of the Republic to compatriots living in the Communist bloc, including North Korea, and that their free and safe travel will be absolutely guaranteed.

*1983

February 1, 1983—Minister of National Unification Son Chae-shik proposes the convening of a conference of representatives of South and North Korean authorities, political parties and social organizations to discuss all problems raised by both sides.

June 1, 1983—President Chun proposes that North Korean delegates attend the 70th Conference of the Inter-Parliamentary Union Seoul was to host the following October.

October 9, 1983—North Korean army officers bomb President Chun's official entourage in Rangoon, Burma killing 17 and wounding 12.

*1984

January 10, 1984—P'yŏngyang repeats a proposal for tripartite talks among Seoul, Washington and P'yŏngyang to discuss unification.

March 30, 1984—P'yŏngyang proposes the formation of intra-Korean teams to take part in the 23rd Olympics and other future international sports events.

April 2, 1984—The Korean Olympic Committee (KOC) in a message to the North agrees to the convening of a sports meeting and suggests it be held on April 9.

April 9, 1984—North Korea unilaterally walks out of the first session of the South-North sports talks.

May 4, 1984—Juan Antonio Samaranch, president of the International Olympic Committee (IOC), proposes that South and North Korea hold sports talks in Lausanne, Switzerland, under the auspices of the IOC.

May 25, 1984—The third session of the intra-Korean sports talks is held.

June 2, 1984—The North Korean Olympic Committee announces a boycott of the Los Angeles Olympics.

August 20, 1984—President Chun, in a news conference, offers trade and economic cooperation with North Korea and offers to supply technology and commodities free of charge.

September 8, 1984—North Korea offers to send relief goods to the South to aid victims of flooding.

September 14, 1984—The president of the ROKNRC accepts the North Korean offer of aid for flood victims.

September 29-October 4, 1984—The NKRC delivers relief goods comprising 50,000 bags of rice, 500,000 meters of cloth, 100,000 tons of cement and 14 kinds of medicine to the ROKNRC through P'anmunjŏm and the ports of Inch'ŏn and Pukp'yŏng.

October 12, 1984—The Republic of Korea Deputy Prime Minister Shin Pyŏng-hyŏn proposes South-North economic talks.

October 16, 1984—North Korea agrees to the South's proposal for economic talks.

November 15, 1984—The first intra-Korean economic meeting is held and agreements are reached on possible items to trade, areas of economic cooperation and operational procedures.

November 20, 1984—An intra-Korean Red Cross meeting is held to discuss the holding of the eighth full-dress Red Cross meeting and agrees to hold the next in Seoul at a time to be established by telephone contact.

November 27, 1984—North Korea postpones the second intra-Korean economic meeting scheduled for December 5 until sometime in 1985.

December 14, 1984—North Korea, in a telephone message, agrees to hold the second intra-Korean economic meeting on January 17, 1985, and the eighth full-dress Red Cross talks in Seoul, January 22-25, 1985, as suggested by the South.

*1985

January 9, 1985—North Korea unilaterally postpones both the economic and the Red Cross talks indefinitely with the excuse of the annual U.S.-ROK joint military exercise, Team Spirit.

May 17, 1985—The second session of South-North economic talks is held and it is agreed to meet again on June 20.

May 27-30, 1985—The eighth plenary session of the South-North Red Cross talks is held in Seoul. An agreement is reached to hold the next session in P'yŏngyang on August 26-29 and also to exchange groups of hometown visitors and art troupes in the future.

June 20, 1985—The third session of the South-North economic talks is held and an accord is reached on adopting agreements on the promotion of goods exchanges and economic cooperation and the establishment of a South-North economic cooperation body headed jointly by deputy-prime-minister-level officials.

July 15, 1985—Working-level delegates to the South-North Red Cross Conference meet to discuss concrete methods and procedures for conducting the agreed exchange of hometown visitors and art troupes and agree to have a second meeting on July 19.

September 20-23, 1985—Groups of hometown visitors and art troupes are exchanged between Seoul and P'yŏngyang via P'anmunjŏm; of 50 visitors from the South, 35 meet 41 relatives from the North, and of 50 North Korean visitors 30 meet 51 relatives from the South.

October 8, 1985—The first session of the South-North sports talks under the auspices of the IOC is held in Lausanne, Switzerland.

*1986

January 20, 1986—A North Korean group of chief delegates to the economic, Red Cross and sports talks issues a joint statement postponing all South-North dialogue with the 1986 Team Spirit (joint ROK-U.S. military exercise) as an excuse.

January 22, 1986—The North Korean chief delegate to the inter-parliamentary talks notifies Seoul of the indefinite postponement of the third preliminary session of talks.

June 17, 1986—North Korea proposes tripartite military talks between Washington, Seoul and P'yŏngyang.

November 28, 1986—Minister of Construction Yi Kyu-ho of the Republic of Korea proposes South-North talks dealing with water resources.

*1987

January 11, 1987—P'yŏngyang proposes a high-level political and military meeting between the South and North.

January 24, 1987—Seoul urges the North to resume the deadlocked South-North dialogue, and proposes a summit meeting between the South and North with the goal of discussing political and military issues.

March 17, 1987—Seoul suggests that a South-North prime ministers' meeting be held to discuss the exchange of water resources.

March 30, 1987—North Korea proposes the holding of a minister-level meeting as a preliminary to opening a prime ministers' meeting.

April 24, 1987—North Korea unilaterally halts the existing South-North dialogue and claims that South Korea is responsible.

July 14, 1987—The fourth South-North sports meeting is held in Lausanne, Switzerland. The International Olympic Committee proposes to the North in its final conciliation efforts that five Olympic events be held in P'yŏngyang. The IOC urges the North to give its response to this proposal by August 30, 1987.

July 23, 1987—North Korea proposes multinational military talks to facilitate step-by-step arms reduction.

August 3, 1987—The Republic of Korea proposes a South-North foreign ministers' meeting.

August 6, 1987—The North suggests a tripartite foreign ministers' meeting between the United States, the Republic of Korea and North Korea.

August 11, 1987—The vice president of the North Korean Olympic Committee proposes the fifth South-North sports meeting in Lausanne, Switzerland. He demands that six events of the Seoul Olympics be allocated to the North.

August 17, 1987—Kim Chong-ha, president of the Korean Olympic Committee, sends a letter agreeing to the conciliation move by the IOC.

November 11, 1987—North Korea decides to send letters to the political parties and the people of all sectors in the South in its joint meeting of the Council for the Peace and Unification of the Fatherland and the Central Committee of the Democratic Front for the Unification of the Fatherland. The North proposes five steps toward national unity, including the establishment of democratic government on their terms and the abolition of anti- communism in the South.

November 29, 1987—North Korea carries out a bombing of Korean Air flight 858, killing all 115 persons aboard.

*1988

January 1, 1988—In his New Year's message, Kim Il-sung, President of North Korea, proposes a series of South-North meetings to discuss multinational arms reduction talks, and calls for a halt of Team Spirit, an annual joint US-ROK military exercise.

January 12, 1988—The North Korean Olympic Committee announces its decision to boycott the 1988 Seoul Olympic Games.

January 15, 1988—Concerning a series of South-North meetings proposed by North Korea, a government spokesman for the Republic of Korea demands that the North apologize for the North Korean bombing of the Korean Air flight and urges the North to create a milieu for talks.

February 25, 1988—President Roh Tae Woo, in his inaugural speech, declares a policy seeking conversation, coexistence and cooperation with North Korea.

June 3, 1988—Prime Minister Lee Hyun-jae proposes a South-North high-level officials' meeting, headed by a minister-level official, with the goals of facilitating personal exchanges and resuming the existing South-North dialogue.

July 7, 1988—President Roh Tae Woo announces the Special Declaration in the Interest of National Self-Esteem, Unification and Prosperity.

July 9, 1988—The National Assembly of the Republic of Korea adopts a resolution urging the North to take part in the Seoul Olympic Games.

July 16, 1988—Son Sŏng-pil, president of the North Korean Red Cross, rejects the South's proposal to hold working-level officials' meetings of the Red Cross talks.

July 17, 1988—A spokesman for the North Korean government rejects the South's offer to hold an educational officials' meeting between the South and the North.

August 1, 1988—The Speaker of the National Assembly of the Republic of Korea proposes a preliminary contact for South-North interparliamentary talks.

August 15, 1988—President Roh Tae Woo proposes a South-North summit meeting in his address commemorating National Liberation Day.

August 19, 1988—The first preliminary contact for South-North interparliamentary talks is held.

October 18, 1988—President Roh Tae Woo proposes in an address delivered at the 43rd General Assembly of the United Nations the establishment of a Peace City in the Demilitarized Zone, the holding of a South-North summit meeting and a Northeast Asian Peace Council.

October 19, 1988—North Korea demands a halt to the South's military exercise as a precondition for a South-North summit meeting.

November 16, 1988—Yi Kŭn-mo, prime minister of North Korea, proposes to his counterpart, Lee Hyun-jae, Prime Minister of South Korea, the holding of South-North high-level political and military talks headed by a deputy prime minister-level official.

December 21, 1988—Kim Yu-sun, president of the North Korean Olympic Committee, proposes that South-North sports talks be held at the end of February to discuss the formation of single intra-Korean teams to take part in the Beijing Asian Games.

December 28, 1988—Kang Young-hoon, Prime Minister of South Korea, proposes the holding of a preliminary meeting in early February to prepare for South-North high-level officials' talks headed by the prime ministers of both sides.

*1989

February 8, 1989—A spokesman for the North Korean delegation to the preliminary contact for South-North interparliamentary talks notifies the South of the postponement of the eighth preliminary contact until after the Team Spirit exercise ends.

March 9, 1989—The first South-North sports talk is held concerning the Beijing Asian Games.

April 11, 1989—North Korea notifies the South of the postponement of the scheduled third preliminary meeting for South-North high-level officials' talks from April 12 to April 26.

April 17, 1989—North Korea notifies the South of the postponement of the rescheduled third preliminary meeting for South-North high- level officials' talks from April 26 to July 12.

April 17, 1989—North Korea notifies the South of the postponement of the scheduled third South-North sports talks from April 18 to July 18.

May 31, 1989—Son Sŏng-pil, president of the North Korean Red Cross, proposes a Red Cross working-level officials' meeting on June 16 with the goal of discussing the second exchange of hometown visitors and art troupes.

June 26, 1989—South Korea proposes to the North the holding of the eighth preliminary contact for South-North interparliamentary talks on July 11.

September 11, 1989—President Roh Tae Woo declares a Korean Community Unification Formula in his special address delivered at the opening ceremony of the National Assembly.

September 16, 1989—South Korea proposes to the North the third preliminary meeting for South-North high-level officials' talks on October 12.

September 27, 1989—The first meeting of a South-North Red Cross working-level delegates' contact is held.

November 20, 1989—The sixth meeting of a South-North Red Cross working-level delegates contact is held. Delegates agree in principle upon the size of home visiting teams and the details of broadcasting the art troupes' performances.

November 27, 1989—The seventh meeting of a South-North Red Cross working-level delegates contact is held with a view towards endorsing an agreement made in the previous meeting. However, the two sides fail to sign it for political reasons, thereby aborting the talk.

December 1, 1989—The fifth South-North sports talk is held. In this talk, the song and flag of South-North single teams for the Beijing Asian Games scheduled for September 1990 are decided.

December 20, 1989—The fifth preliminary meeting for South-North high-level officials' talks is held. The official name and the number of participants in the talks including their entourage are decided.

*1990

January 1, 1990—North Korean President Kim Il-sung, in his New Year's speech, proposes the holding of a South-North high-level political conference.

January 10, 1990—President Roh Tae Woo, in a New Year's press conference, urges the prompt holding of a South-North summit meeting.

January 31, 1990—The sixth preliminary meeting for South-North High-level Officials' Talks is held at P'anmunjŏm.

February 7, 1990—The ninth session of South-North Sports Talks is held, but the North unilaterally suspends all channels of the on-going South-North dialogue on February 8, 1990, using the annual Team Spirit military training exercise in the South as its excuse.

March 3, 1990—The Defense Ministry of the Republic of Korea announces discovery of the fourth invasion tunnel dug by North Korea.

July 5, 1990—North Korea announces it will unilaterally open the northern part of the truce village of P'anmunjŏm.

July 20, 1990—President Roh Tae Woo of the South proposes a five-day span of grand intra-Korean exchange over the National Liberation Day (Aug. 13-17).

July 26, 1990—An agreement to hold South-North High-level Talks is signed at the eighth preliminary meeting for the talks held at P'anmunjŏm.

September 4, 1990—The first South-North High-level Talks are held in Seoul.

October 9, 1990—The South Korean team enters North Korea via Beijing for a South-North soccer match (Oct. 11, in P'yŏngyang).

October 16, 1990—The second South-North High-level Talks are held in P'yŏngyang.

October 21, 1990—The North Korean team enters Seoul via P'anmunjŏm for the second round of the South-North soccer matches (Oct. 23, in Seoul).

November 9, 1990—The third round of the South-North working-level officials' meeting is held at P'anmunjŏm to discuss entry into the United Nations.

November 29, 1990—The first round of the South-North sports talks for sports exchanges and formation of a single intra-Korean team to take part in major international games is held at P'anmunjŏm.

December 8-13, 1990—33 people from the North enter Seoul via P'anmunjŏm to participate and perform a 1990 Year-End Unification Traditional Music Concert.

December 11-14, 1990—The third South-North High-level Talks are held in Seoul.

*1991

January 1, 1991—In his New Year's message, Kim Il-sung, President of North Korea, proposes the holding of a conference for political negotiation towards national unification.

February 12, 1991—The fourth round of South-North Sports Talks is held at P'anmunjŏm.

February 18, 1991—Kim Sang-hyŏp, president of the ROK Red Cross, proposes the holding of the 11th South-North Red Cross Talks.

February 18, 1991—North Korea's delegation to the South-North High-level Talks announces the indefinite postponement of the fourth round of the talks.

March 25-May 9, 1991— A South-North unified national team is formed and competes in the 41st World Table Tennis Championship tournament.

May 6-June 28, 1991—A unified South-North national team is formed and competes in the sixth World Youth Soccer Championship tournament.

May 27, 1991—The North Korean Foreign Ministry declares the North's intention to join the United Nations.

July 11, 1991—Prime Minister Yŏn Hyŏng-muk of North Korea proposes in a letter to the South that the fourth round of South-North High-level Talks be held on August 27, but with preconditions.

July 15, 1991—Choi Ho-joong, ROK Deputy Prime Minister and Minister of National Unification, publicly asks the North to cooperate in holding a Grand March for Unification.

September 17, 1991—South and North Korea concurrently join the United Nations.

October 10-25, 1991—The fourth South-North High-level Talks are held in P'yŏngyang, where a written agreement on major issues, reconciliation, nonagression, and exchanges and cooperation between South and the North is signed.

November 8, 1991—President Roh Tae Woo announces the Initiative for Denuclearization and Peace on the Korean Peninsula.

December 10-13, 1991—The fifth South-North High-level Talks are held in Seoul, and the two sides agree on the South-North Agreement on Reconciliation, Nonaggression and Exchanges and Cooperation.

December 18, 1991—President Roh Tae Woo declares that no nuclear weapons exist in South Korea.

December 26, 1991—The South and the North provisionally sign the Joint Declaration of the Denuclearization of the Korean Peninsula.

*1992

February 7, 1992—Agreement on the organization and operation of committees for the South-North High-level Talks is provisionally signed.

February 18-21, 1992—The sixth South-North High-level Talks are held in P'yŏngyang and the Agreement on Reconciliation, Nonaggression and Exchanges and Cooperation between the South and the North (the Basic Agreement), the Joint Declaration of the Denuclearization of the Korean Peninsula and the Agreement on the Organization and Operation of the Committees for the South-North High-level Talks are signed and take effect.

March 9, 1992—The first meeting of the South-North Political Committee is held at P'anmunjŏm.

March 13, 1992—The first meeting of South-North Military Committee is held at P'anmunjŏm.

March 14, 1992—An Agreement on the organization and operation of the South-North Joint Nuclear Control Commission is discussed and provisionally signed.

March 18, 1992—The first meeting of the South-North Exchanges and Cooperation Committee is held at P'anmunjŏm.

March 19, 1992—The agreement on the organization and operation of the South-North Joint Nuclear Control Commission takes effect.

March 19, 1992— The first meeting of the South-North Joint Nuclear Control Commission is held at P'anmunjŏm.

April 9, 1992—North Korea's Ninth Supreme People's Assembly ratifies the nuclear safeguard agreement.

May 5-8, 1992—The Seventh South-North High-level Talks are held in Seoul.

May 18, 1992—The South-North Military Committee, the South-North Economic Exchanges and Cooperation Committee and the South-North Social and Cultural Exchanges and Cooperation Committees are organized and membership rosters are exchanged. The South-North liaison office begins operation at P'anmunjŏm.

June 16-17, 1992—The South and North agree in Paris on a "Proposal for a System to Transliterate Hangul into Roman characters," concerning a Romanization system to represent the Korean native script

June 30, 1992—The sixth meeting of the South-North Joint Nuclear Control Commission is held at P'anmunjŏm.

July 19-25, 1992—North Korean Deputy Prime Minister Kim Tal-hyŏn visits Seoul at the invitation of Deputy Prime Minister Ch'oe Kak-kyu. Kim tours industrial sites such as Daewoo Auto and P'ohang Iron and Steel and meets with President Roh on July 24th.

July 21, 1992—The seventh meeting of the South-North Joint Nuclear Control Commission is held at P'anmunjŏm.

August 15, 1992—President Roh Tae Woo makes the following points in a speech to commemorate Liberation Day: 1) It will be impossible to expect real progress in South-North relations until suspicions about the North Korean nuclear development program have been allayed; 2) The South regrets that the planned exchange of performing arts troupes and members of families separated by national division did not occur; and 3) The South wants regularly scheduled exchanges of visits between separated family members.

August 24, 1992— The Republic of Korea and China establish full diplomatic relations.

August 26, 1992— The seventh meeting of the South-North Military Committee is held at P'anmunjŏm.

August 28, 1992— The seventh meeting of the South-North Political Committee is held at P'anmunjŏm.

August 31, 1992—The eighth meeting of the South-North Joint Nuclear Control Commission is held at P'anmunjŏm.

September 1-6, 1992—Representatives from South and North attend the third round of discussions at the "Women's Role in Asian Peace" conference held in P'yŏngyang.

September 3, 1992—The seventh meeting of the South-North Exchanges and Cooperation Committee is held at P'anmunjŏm.

September 5, 1992—The eighth meeting of the South-North Military Committee is held at P'anmunjŏm.

September 17-18, 1992—The eighth round of South-North High-level Talks is held in P'yŏng-yang. The two sides adopt three subsidiary agreements related to the Basic Agreement and reach the following agreements: 1) To establish the Joint Reconciliation Commission; 2) To hold in November the first meetings of the Joint Reconciliation Commission, and the Social and Cultural Exchanges and Cooperation Commission; and 3) to hold the ninth round of High-level Talks in Seoul during the period December 21-24, 1992.

October 6-9, 1992—A joint civilian and governmental survey team travels to North Korea to inspect the Namp'o Light Industrial Park, preparatory to expediting a South-North joint venture on the site.

October 22, 1992—The ninth meeting of the South-North Joint Nuclear Control Commission is held at P'anmunjŏm October 27, 1992—North Korea announces that it will boycott scheduled elements of South-North dialogue—November's joint commission meetings and December's High-level Talks—if the Team Spirit military exercise is held in early 1993.

November 11, 1992—The 10th meeting of the South-North Joint Nuclear Control Commission is held at P'anmunjŏm.

November 27, 1992—The 11th meeting of the South-North Joint Nuclear Control Commission is held at P'anmunjŏm.

December 10, 1992—The 12th meeting of the South-North Joint Nuclear Control Commission is held at P'anmunjŏm.

December 17, 1992—The 13th meeting of the South-North Joint Nuclear Control Commission is held at P'anmunjŏm.

December 21, 1992—North Korea boycotts the High-level Talks in Seoul and breaks off the dialogue, using the excuse of the ROK-U.S Team Spirit joint military exercise.

*1993

January 25, 1993—The 14th meeting of the South-North Joint Nuclear Control Commission is held at P'anmunjŏm.

March 12, 1993—North Korea announced that it will withdraw from the Nuclear Non-Proliferation Treaty, the first nation ever to do so.

January 25-February 6—North Korea refuses to allow International Atomic Energy Agency (IAEA) inspectors onto two sites which the IAEA suspects are connected to the North Korean nuclear weapons program but North Korea insists are military sites. The refusal sets off an international crisis over the issue of whether North Korea had made or is making an atomic bomb.

February 10—The IAEA demands that North Korea open two suspected nuclear sites to "special inspection" or face possible U.N. sanctions. This is the first time the IAEA has called for a special inspection.

February 13—North Korea rejects special inspections.

March 12—North Korea announces that it will withdraw from the Nuclear Non-Proliferation Treaty, the first nation ever to do so.

March 19—In a conciliatory gesture to induce the North to resume dialogue, the South Korean authorities allow 76-year-old Li In-mo to travel to North Korea for "humanitarian reasons." Li is a North Korean guerrilla/agent who was first captured in 1952 and after serving two lengthy prison sentences, was finally freed in 1988 although he never renounced Communism.

May 11—The United Nations Security Council passes a resolution calling on North Korea to reconsider its withdrawal from the Nuclear Non-Proliferation Treaty and honor its nonproliferation obligations

May 20—South Korean Prime Minister Hwang In-sung sends a letter to North Korean Premier Kang Song-san, proposing vice-minister-level working meeting to discuss the nuclear issue and other related questions

May 25—North Korean Premier Kang replies to South Korean Prime Minister Hwang, proposing a vice-minister-level meeting to discuss an an exchange of special envoys to prepare for a South-North Summit meeting.

June 2—The United States and the DPRK (North Korea) hold a high-level meeting at the U.S. mission to the United Nations to discuss the nuclear issue and the possibility of improved ties. The U.S. is represented by Robert Gallucci, Assistant Secretary of State for Political and Military Affairs, and the DPRK by Kang Sok-ju, first Vice-

Minister of Foreign Affairs.

June 4— The United States and North Korea hold a second high-level meeting in New York

June 10—The United States and North Korea hold a third high-level meeting in New York

June 11—In a Joint Statement following the fourth and last U.S.-DPRK high-level meeting in New York, North Korea says it has "decided unilaterally to suspend as long as it considers necessary the effectuation of its withdrawal from the Treaty on the Non-Proliferation of Nuclear Weapons ."

July 14—The United States and North Korea resume their high-level talks, meeting this time in Geneva.

July 16—The United States and North Korea hold a second high-level meeting in Geneva.

July 19—In a Joint Statement following the third and last U.S.-DPRK high- level meeting in Geneva, North Korea agrees to resume negotiations with the IAEA on nuclear inspections and reopen North-South talks. The two sides agree to meet again in two month to discuss outstanding matters related to the nuclear issue and to lay the basis for improving overall relations.

August 4—ROK Prime Minister Hwang In-sung sends a telephone message to North Korean Premier Kang Song-san calling for the reopening of the South-North Joint Nuclear Control Commission on August 10.

August 9—The North Korean Central Broadcasting System broadcasts a statement by the North Korean spokesman to the South-North High-Level Talks, rejecting the August 4 suggestion to reopen the South-North Joint Nuclear Control Commission and saying that if the South wants to resolve the nuclear issue it must discontinue nuclear war exercises, accept an exchange of presidential envoys and discontinue cooperation with the international community on the issue.

August 14—A spokesman for the National Unification Board issues a statement calling on North Korea to resume the deadlocked South-North Joint Nuclear Control Commission and saying "we are keeping the doors to dialogue wide open."

August 17—A White House official says that U.S.-DPRK high-level talks have not been scheduled because North Korea had not met the conditions.

October 1—The 37th General Meeting of the International Atomic Energy Agency passed a resolution urging North Korea to cooperate immediately with the IAEA and open up suspected nuclear sites to inspection.

October 4—After a series of proposals and counter-proposals that began on May 20 and 25, South Korean Prime Minister Hwang In-sung agreed with North Korean Premier Kang Song-san to hold vice-minister- level talks on October 5 to discuss an exchange of envoys.

October 5—No progress is made at the first South-North working-level meeting to prepare for an exchange of special envoys.

October 15—No progress is made at the second South-North working-level meeting to prepare for an exchange of special envoys.

October 25—At the third South-North working-level meeting to prepare for an exchange of special envoys, North Korea tables a draft agreement in response to an earlier draft submitted by the South and some progress is made in discussions.

November 1—The United Nations General Assembly passes a virtually unanimous resolution urging North Korea to cooperate with the International Atomic Energy Agency in fully implementing the Nuclear Non-Proliferation Treaty and the Nuclear Safeguards Agreement.

November 3—The North Korean chief delegate to the working-level talks to arrange for an exchange of special envoys says that P'yongyang will boycott the meetings because of "dangerous" remarks it alleged the ROK Defense Minister had made in a T.V. interview.

November 23—At a joint press conference with President Bill Clinton after the ROK-U.S. summit meeting in Washington, D.C., President Kim Young Sam says "we agreed to make a thorough and broad effort..." to solve the nuclear issue.

December 3—Kang Young-hoon, president of the Republic of Korea National Red Cross, sends a telephone message to his North Korean counterpart, proposing resumption of Red Cross talks to arrange for reunions of families separated in the South and the North.

NATIONAL DEFENSE

History of National Defense

For thousands of years, Korea's geopolitical location at a convergence point of surrounding powers has attracted covetous attention and periodic invasions. China's Han, Liao, Yüan, Chin and Ch'ing dynasties, and finally Japan, invaded Korea. The land was devastated and lives and property were destroyed. At times, Korea's sovereignty was usurped and its culture was plundered by invaders.

However, these foreign invasions and oppressions never succeeded in crushing the tenacious will of the Korean people to maintain their territorial and ethnic integrity. The Koreans have always been aware that the nation must stand so that the people may survive. This awareness has been demonstrated on numerous occasions—in the heroic death of Admiral Yi Sun-shin in 1592 in a naval engagement with invading Japanese forces, and in the valiant uprisings of the civilian populace in the face of foreign invaders. An unyielding spirit of independence was amply displayed by the volunteers, independence militias, and the Restoration Army in heroic armed struggles against the Japanese Imperial Army in Siberia, China and at home during Japan's colonial rule.

When Korea was liberated from Japan in 1945, there was a fervent desire among Koreans to create an adequate defense capability of their own in the light of the bitter experiences of the past. On January 15, 1946, the National Constabulary was established in the area south of the 38th parallel under the U.S. military government. The constabulary consisted largely of Koreans who had military experience in the Japanese or Chinese armed forces or in the Korean Restoration Army in China. The constabulary was to become the nucleus of the National Defense Forces created on August 15, 1948, when the Government of the Republic of Korea was inaugurated.

At that time, the total strength of the army consisted of five divisions comprising 15 regiments, 1,403 officers and 49,087 men. These troops were engaged primarily in the mopping up of communist guerrillas in South Korea.

The North Korean Communist regime, which had been secretly sending small guerrilla forces into South Korea, began early in 1950 to dispatch armed guerrillas in larger numbers across the 38th parallel along the T'aebaek mountain range. Then came North Korea's full-fledged invasion on June 25, 1950, which marked in blood the most tragic chapter in Korean history: a fratricidal war.

On that day, the North Korean army crossed the dividing line, spearheaded by 242 Russian-built T-34 tanks and supported by an air cover of 211 Russian-made aircraft. The invading army took Seoul in three days, and in about 40 days its advance units had reached the Republic's last defense perimeter along the Naktonggang River near the southern tip of the peninsula.

The South Korean military, together with United Nations forces sent under a U.N. mandate to help repel the aggressors, managed to regroup and prepared to launch a counteroffensive. The combined forces made a daring landing at Inch'on on September 15, 1950, and with their supply route cut, the enemy began to retreat on all fronts.

U.N. forces recaptured Seoul on September 28, 1950, and advanced as far as Hyesanjin near the Amnokkang (Yalu) River by November. At that point, the Chinese Communists committed nearly 30 divisions to the war, and bitter, see-saw fighting went on for months before the front was stabilized along the 38th parallel, roughly the same line where North Korea had launched its invasion.

After two years of difficult, often frustrating, negotiations, the U.N. Command finally managed to sign an armistice agreement with the communist side on July 27, 1953.

By that time, the Republic of Korea Army, which had been made up of only eight divisions at the outbreak of the war, had increased to a force of 600,000 strong. That strength level has been maintained since. The growth process of South Korea's defense forces from the beginning has been that of a series of trials and challenges by North Korean forces.

In the early 1960s, the Republic of Korea Defense Forces began to build on the foundations of a self-reliant capability. During that decade, South Korean troops were sent to take part in the war in Vietnam. The experience gained by that expeditionary force has given the South Korean military an increased sense of confidence. Furthermore, acting in response to a relevant United Nations resolution, the Republic of Korea dispatched a medical support contingent and an air force transport support team to aid in the Gulf War.

Now, more than 40 years after their creation, the Armed Forces of the Republic of Korea have demonstrated they are firmly resolved to defend the nation, single-handedly if necessary.

ROK Armed Services

Army

Military deployment in Korea is determined by the geopolitical location, topographic conditions and the political reality of national division. The main elements of the ground forces are of necessity concentrated along the Demilitarized Zone (DMZ), where the armed forces of the South and North confront each other across the four-kilometer wide truce line.

The ROK Army deployed along the 250-kilometer long DMZ is determined to defend the present truce line and the capital at all costs, based on a strategy of "victory at the first encounter." This strategy is formulated against North Korean strategy of a preemptive surprise attack.

The present-day ROK Army is equipped with 155mm field artillery pieces, 8-inch self-propelled guns, Honest John missiles, Hawk missiles, TOW missiles, and Vulcan and Oerlikon guns. In 1950, 75mm field artillery represented its heaviest firepower. Today, this defensive power is prepared to meet North Korean tank assaults and aerial offensives, and the ROK armed helicopter force is considered an excellent assault arm.

Welfare facilities for officers and men of the Army are continually being improved and expanded, and technical training is given to men on active duty to enable them to adapt to

The Army of Republic of Korea.

civilian life after discharge.

Navy

The Korean Coast Guard, created in 1945, became the basis for the Korean Navy, that was organized at the time of the establishment of the Republic of Korea Government. The Korean Navy, like the Army, has grown as a result of the Republic's efforts to deal with North Korean aggression.

Since then, the ROK Navy has strengthened its combat capability by constantly increasing its tonnage. The Navy, which started with a few PT (patrol-and-torpedo) boats, acquired escort destroyers and combat destroyers in the 1960s, and a fleet of LVT's (landing vehicle and tracks), helicopters, and high-speed patrol boats in the 1970s, and 150 combat vessels, 40 support ships and 2 submarines (*Ichŏn, Changbogo*) in the 1990s. The Navy will be equipped with a total of 8 submarines by 1998. The Navy is capable of launching sea-air operations on its own.

The Korean Marines, created April 5, 1949, quickly gained the nickname "Devil Hunters." They acquired valuable experience and a reputation as a strike force in the Vietnam War. The Marines now function as the principal striking force in the entire system of national defense, and are ready to conduct amphibious operations. They are charged primarily with the defense of five islands off the west coast and the capital itself.

Air Force

The Air Force was formed from the National Constabulary's Reconnaissance Unit in October 1949. It started with a handful of L-4 and L-5 light planes and 10 C-4 propeller-driven noncombat aircraft. The Air Force was only eight months old when it was called upon to engage the numerically superior air force of North Korea. In the course of the war, the Air Force received a number of F-51 Mustangs from the U.S. Air Force and flew a total of 8,276 sorties. About 40 pilots flew more than 100 sorties each.

While the North Korean Air Force, which was destroyed in the initial stages of the war, attempted to rebuild its air strength, the ROK Air Force began switching to jet aircraft. After the introduction of a small number of F-4 Phantom fighter-bombers in 1969, the Air Force kept expanding with C-123 cargo carriers, and later F-5D/E/F and F-16 fighters.

The Republic of Korea's air defense network now has established a double warning system in anticipation of a surprise raid from North Korea. The so-called radar gap, or blind spot, has been eliminated with an early-warning system and all air-warning points are interconnected with a microwave communications system.

Today, the ROK Air Force is striving to improve its capability through constant development of its air defense doctrine and by carrying out training maneuvers in conjunction with the Navy and Army.

Defense Capability

Threat from the North

At times, in some quarters, questions have been raised as to whether the threat from North Korea is real or imagined. The obvious answer is that the threat is real.

As has been made clear many times, the fundamental policy of the Republic of Korea toward the question of national unification is that there should first be genuine peace. On the other hand, North Korea has made clear its ultimate goal of unifying the land through armed force. Its basic strategy is to consolidate North Korea as a base for revolution in the South, pending the moment when it will create a second front deep inside South Korea with guerrilla forces and launch a decisive thrust across the truce line.

Based on this strategy, North Korea adopted the Four-point Military Guidelines in 1962 and has been concentrating on a military buildup since then. In November 1970, North Korea declared at the Fifth Congress of the Korean Workers' Party that "our war preparations are

The Air Force of the Republic of Korea.

now complete." In a determined bid to communize all of the Korean Peninsula, North Korea has unceasingly built up its arms. In 1980 alone, the North drastically bolstered its military manpower and equipment, creating more offensive units and deploying special warfare forces in the forward area near the DMZ.

Despite this belligerent attitude, the fundamental position of the Republic that peace must be consolidated on the peninsula remains unchanged, along with the determination that any renewed aggression or adventure by North Korea must be deterred at all costs.

North Korea, however, has continually resorted to provocative actions since the signing of the Armistice Agreement in 1953. The North Koreans have violated the terms of the agreement on more than 76,000 occasions on land and sea and in the air. Remembered vividly are the brutal axe-murders at P'anmunjŏm on August 18, 1976; the shooting down of an unarmed U.S. helicopter in 1976; the tunnels under the DMZ discovered in November 1974, March 1975, October 1978 and March 1990, along with the frequent infiltration of spy boats and the violations of air space.

The disclosure at the Sixth Congress of the Korean Workers' Party in P'yŏngyang in October 1980 of the planned power succession from Kim Il-sung to his son, Kim Jong-il, added another element. A new, hawkish force loyal to

the younger Kim began to raise its voice within the party. The increasingly belligerent position of that group posed still another threat to peace and stability on the Korean Peninsula.

North Korea also has shown on numerous occasions that it would not hesitate to use terrorism to carry out a policy of animosity against the South. One shocking example was the bomb attack against a South Korean presidential delegation in Rangoon, Burma, in 1983. No less heinous was the bombing of Korean Air flight 858 in November 1987 by North Korean terrorists killing all 115 persons abroad.

Well aware of the strong security links between the Republic of Korea and the United States, the North Koreans have also tried the ploy of calling for tripartite peace talks in an effort to drive a wedge between Washington and Seoul. During the 1980s, the North from time to time agreed to open contacts as proposed by the South to deal with various issues, including steps toward peace and unification. Consistently, however, the authorities in the North broke off such contacts or refused to follow through with their participation.

At the same time, North Korea sought to strengthen its ties with the Soviet Union, bringing in modern new armaments such as MIG-23 and MIG-29 fighter planes, Scud surface-to-surface missiles, and SA-3 and SA-5 surface-to-air missiles.

The North also has accelerated its production of tanks, armored vehicles, artillery pieces and submarines. North Korea also possesses hundreds of tons of chemical weapons, which are forbidden by international law, and has conducted military exercises involving such materials.

The assessment of this grim record leaves little doubt as to whether the threat from the North is real or imagined.

In the latter half of the 1980s, the North Korean Army reorganized its mechanized army corps and artillery corps and placed them in forward areas near the demilitarized zone. The Supreme Commander of the People's Army issued an order for "battle readiness."

While building up its conventional forces, North Korea has also been conducting a propaganda war against the South in order to instigate a so-called "revolutionary war." The North Korean Army has organized special forces units which can infiltrate the South simultaneously by air, sea and land. For that purpose, North Korea smuggled in a number of U.S.-made helicopters of the same type used by South Korea.

In the mid-1980s North Korea secretly embarked on a program to develop nuclear weapons. In mid-1992 an IAEA inspection team verified that North Korea had a nuclear reprocessing facility and possessed the other crucial technology requisite for manufacturing nuclear weapons.

Moves by the North Korean military indicate it is prepared for war and is capable of carrying out a war characterized by a combination of conventional and unconventional warfare, a preemptive strike and blitzkrieg tactics. The North could use conventional forces to make direct strikes along the DMZ, instigate guerrilla warfare by infiltrating armed agents into the South, and launch terrorist activities, such as assassination or arson, by infiltrating the South through third countries. The third method could be aimed at disrupting international events held in the Republic of Korea.

Primary Concern

Under these circumstances, of primary concern for the ROK is the nurturing of a defense capability to adequately counter possible aggression by North Korea. South Korea must maintain a military balance with North Korea so that it can repulse any North Korean attack. Without keeping a defense level equal or superior to North Korea's, the armistice cannot be maintained nor can peace be sustained.

It should be noted that the present truce in Korea is possible not because it is guaranteed by the superpowers, but because the combined military force of the Republic of Korea and the United States matches that of North Korea. Koreans are convinced, in light of the Vietnam lesson, that a resumption of the South-North dialogue as an initial step toward unification cannot be expected unless South Korea's continued desire for dialogue is backed by a strong defense posture.

The Republic of Korea is working to build and maintain a military power balance vis-a-vis North Korea that will prevent an outbreak of war first, and be sufficient to defend itself if necessary.

Defense Industry

In the early 1970s, South Korea embarked on the development of a defense industry. In December 1971, following the U.S. decision to pull its 7th Infantry Division out of Korea, the Government proclaimed a "state of national emergency," calling, among other things, for the domestic production of military equipment. In 1973, the Law on Military Supplies was enacted under which various measures were taken to foster and support defense industries. The steps included the creation and operation of a support fund, provision of subsidies, taxational privileges, contractual favors and a defense fund-raising drive. With the fall of South Vietnam in 1975, the defense tax system was introduced to accelerate the development of defense industries.

As a result of these measures, Korea, which

was unable to produce even rifles until the early 1970s, successfully developed missiles and multi-firing rockets by 1978. In the same year, preparations were completed for the production of M-48A3 and M-48A5 tanks, identical in performance to the M-60A1 tanks of the U.S. Army.

South Korea now is able to mass produce such crew-served weapons as mortars, recoilless guns, Vulcan anti-aircraft guns and grenade launchers, along with ammunition, mines and grenades. It also is prepared to produce 105mm and 155mm caliber guns, 106mm recoilless rifles and TOW missiles on a large scale.

In addition to these basic firearms, the Korean arms industry manufactures heavy hardware such as armored equipment, armored personnel carriers and amphibious vehicles. Since 1977, 500MD helicopters, nicknamed "black-eared kites," have been produced in large quantities. A Korean-built destroyer, *Ulsan-ham*, was put into service in March 1980. With the Second Force Modernization Program, which began in 1982, Korea entered a stage where it could produce up-to-date F5F fighter-bombers through a joint venture with the U.S. The Republic of Korea plans to push forward with its Korean Fighter Project during a five-year span from 1994 to 1999. The project will provide the ROK with tactical fighter aircraft equivalent to the MIG 23/29.

South Korea also has been deploying the K-1 or "88" tank, a domestically produced and modified version of the M60A1, since 1987 to replace the M-48 series tank.

The defense industry has developed on the basis of, and in conjunction with, a series of national economic development plans and the Heavy and Chemical Industries Development plan, utilizing fully the civil industrial facilities of the country.

Basic Tactical Concept

Tactical concepts related to the defense of the Republic of Korea have repeatedly been the subject of intensive study and discussions between South Korean and American military leaders and strategists. Entering into the 1990s, the United States, under treaty agreements with the Republic, still maintained a force of 36,400 personnel in South Korea in 1992. There was general agreement that the U.S. military presence served as an effective deterrent, helping to discourage possible aggressive moves by North Korea.

It long has been recognized and emphasized by military planners that the location of the capital city of Seoul, the country's political, economic, cultural and educational center, being only 40 kilometers from the DMZ was a critical factor. In addition to the relatively short distance any attack from the North would have to cross, North Korea has long-range firepower capable of reaching 70 kilometers to strike targets, a capability that could put the central areas of South Korea in danger.

This threat called for a defense posture that could react immediately with massive concentrations of firepower directed on an enemy from the beginning of hostilities, seizing the initiative and turning back any advances that might have been made in the opening round of engagement. Military commanders emphasized that new strategy calling for the destruction of an enemy force before it could reach Seoul had replaced the older conventional defense concept based on an initial retreat.

The new outline was in complete agreement with the established tactical principles of authorities in Korea's Ministry of Defense, who asserted that the present frontline must be held and maintained and the capital city defended at all costs.

National Security Capability

In 1968, there were signs of increased North Korean provocation. On January 21, North Korea sent a well-trained commando unit to attack Chong Wa Dae, the presidential residence in Seoul. The attack was halted, but later that year there were two infiltrations of communist guer-rillas at Ulchin and Samch'ŏk along the east coast. In the early 1970s, there were unmistak-able indications of the eventual collapse of anti-communist South Vietnam.

Under these circumstances, the Republic of Korea was awakened to the reality that its defense was primarily its own concern and that dependence on allied support without self-reliant efforts could spell disaster. That realization led to the organization of the Homeland Reserve Forces and the incorporation of students and other civilians in that organization in 1975. That measure constituted an all-out defense posture, encompassing the armed forces, government officials and the civilian populace. It contributed to the general awareness of the joint responsibility for national defense and to reaffirming the national resolution to defend against a North Korea attack. This outlook recognizes that modern warfare involves the totality of the nation's abilities and resources, not merely the capabilities of its armed forces.

The establishment of a complete national security set-up in this manner was an expression of determination to insure security and the right to survive by means of the Republic of Korea's own ability and resources.

Homeland Reserve Forces

The Homeland Reserve Forces, since their formation on April 1, 1968, have engaged in the defense of the country, and, at the same time, helped to propel the *Saemaŭl Undong*, or New Community Movement. The command system of the reserve forces is subject to the regular army, and their training and education are all conducted by regular army members. Compared with the 200 hours of training a year of the Laborer and Farmer Red Guard units in North Korea, the number of training hours of the ROK Reserve Forces is 100 hours a year for first combatants and 68 hours a year for regional combatants.

The reserve forces are made up of reserve officers, warrant officers, non-commissioned officers and soldiers as well as volunteers. Before 1971, the organization and formation of the reserve forces came under the control of regional division commanders. Now, however, the reserves are the responsibility of the Office of Military Manpower Administration and regional forces are organized by township administrative heads. The organization of the Workplace Reserve Forces is the responsibility of the heads of work places.

Civil Defense Corps

A Civil Defense Corps unit is organized in every community in accordance with the provisions of the Basic Law on Civil Defense promulgated in July 1975. The Civil Defense Corps is charged with the responsibility of protecting the lives and property of the people in times of enemy attack or other situations affecting the public peace and order. Principal activities include air raid defense, prevention of disasters and protection, rescue and rehabilitation in times of disaster, and other civil defense activities auxiliary to military operations.

All male citizens between the ages of 20 and 50, who are not in the Homeland Reserve, are legally obliged to serve in the Civil Defense Corps. Members of government agencies, policemen, firemen and civilian personnel working for the armed services are exempted from this service.

The Civil Defense Corps units are organized at various work places as well as in each community. By the end of 1991, there were about 5 million members across the country including 4.4 million in the community units.

Civil Air Raid Defense Training

Beginning in early 1972, the 15th day of each month was designated Civil Defense Day with all government and civil offices, factories and other designated sectors carrying out air raid defense exercises. Since the spring of 1983, the exercises have been held on days announced by Civil Defense authorities. On the day of the exercise, sirens and bells signal the nature of the emergency by predetermined code. The training, conducted under the command of the Civil Defense Headquarters, includes countermeasures such as rescue and medical aid in the wake of conventional, atomic, biological and chemical attacks. Members of the Civil Defense Corps also engage in such duties as relaying messages, guarding important installations, sheltering victims and firefighting.

Military Power Balance

Comparison between South and North Korea

Although both its population and economy are smaller, North Korea maintains a military force numerically superior than South Korea's. This has been attributed in large part to the fact that the North began its military build-up 12 years ahead of South Korea and received military aid from both China and the Soviet Union.

It also has been emphasized that North Korea has devoted 24 percent of its gross national product to military spending, the highest level in the world, while South Korea has been allocating about 4 percent of its GNP to defense. P'yŏngyang has long strained its resources to maintain a wartime military-industrial system, making it difficult for the South to redress the military imbalance.

As of 1992, North Korean troop strength stood at 1,010,000, or 1.5 times that of South Korea. The North had more than 3,700 tanks, 2.3 times that of the South, and 9,800 field artillery pieces, double the number of the South. With 1,620 aircraft, including 850 combat aircraft, North Korea's air force outnumbered South Korea's by 1.3 times.

North Korea started the Korean War in 1950 in the hope of communizing the entire peninsula, and its basic military strategy has been the same ever since. In the immediate wake of the Armistice Agreement in 1953, the North began to rebuild its military strength in a renewed pursuit of the same policy. In 1962, rearmament efforts in the North were greatly stepped up when the Four-point Military Guidelines, including "the arming of the entire people," were adopted. North Korea has since been rapidly expanding its military forces.

Committed to a policy of peaceful unification, the Republic of Korea has emphasized economic development and the improvement of living standards more than armaments. In addition, the United States was tending toward a reduction of its military presence in the Asian-Pacific region following the end of the war in Vietnam. As a result, it was as late as 1974, or 12 years behind the North, that the Republic of Korea embarked on an armed forces modernization program.

While prospects for catching up with the North are good, it will require more time. The dramatic growth of the Republic's overall economy has made South Korea's GNP ten-fold that of the North, although the two economies were similar in size in the 1960s. If the South maintains its military expenditure at the current rate of 4 percent of the GNP, it will attain 80 percent of the military strength of the North by the middle of 1990s, even if North Korea continues to allocate 24 percent of its GNP to military spending. Full equality will be achieved by the early 2000s if present courses are maintained.

Population

In population, South Korea outnumbers North Korea two to one, which leaves little problem maintaining military manpower. In North Korea, there is one soldier for every 24 inhabitants, which entails difficulty in keeping up manpower levels. This is resolved by enforcing extended military service on the populace—7 to 10 years for the army, 10 years for the navy, and 3 to 4 years for the air force. The North attempts to augment its regular fighting forces with paramilitary organizations such as the Pacification Corps, the Laborer and Farmer Red Guard units and the Young Red Guard. The authorities in the North also have completed various measures necessary for prompt wartime mobilization and for attaining other strategic objectives through tight regimentation of the civilian population.

The maximum manpower to be mobilized for military service in time of war generally is considered to be about 24 percent of the total

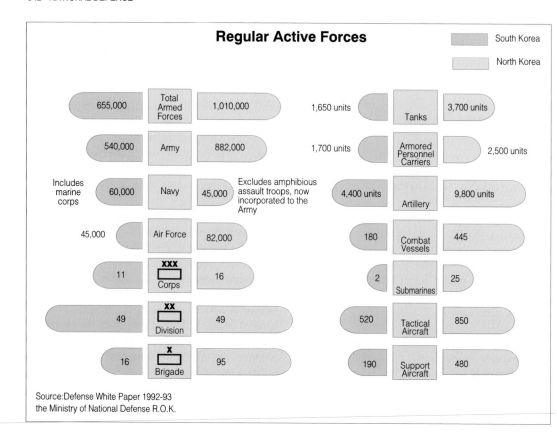

Regular Active Forces

South Korea
North Korea

		South Korea		North Korea
655,000	Total Armed Forces	1,010,000	1,650 units	Tanks	3,700 units
540,000	Army	882,000	1,700 units	Armored Personnel Carriers	2,500 units
60,000 (Includes marine corps)	Navy	45,000 (Excludes amphibious assault troops, now incorporated to the Army)	4,400 units	Artillery	9,800 units
45,000	Air Force	82,000	180	Combat Vessels	445
11	XXX Corps	16	2	Submarines	25
49	XX Division	49	520	Tactical Aircraft	850
16	X Brigade	95	190	Support Aircraft	480

Source:Defense White Paper 1992-93
the Ministry of National Defense R.O.K.

population of a country. As of 1992, the military manpower of South Korea, including paramilitary troops, represented about 14 percent of the total population, whereas that of North Korea accounted for approximately 20 percent. The ratio is comparable to the extent Germany mobilized during the time of World War II.

Army

As of 1992, South Korea has a 540,000-man army, comprised of 2 mechanized divisions, 21 infantry divisions, 2 surface-to-air (SAM) brigades, 7 special forces brigades, and 2 anti-aircraft artillery brigades.

In North Korea, ground troops have been increased sharply in the past several years so that they now total about 882,000. The North Korean army comprises 26 infantry divisions, 5 mechanized divisions, 2 armored divisions, 7 armored brigades, 9 independent infantry

brigades and 250 artillery battalions. North Korea strives to further increase the firepower and mobility of these units, which are mostly offensive oriented. In particular, the existence in North Korea of a large number of special warfare units—22 brigades, including three amphibious commando units and an airborne unit—may well point to the intention of P'yŏngyang to create a situation ripe for invasion.

Navy

The basic character of both North and South Koreas' navies is coastal defense. North Korea has 25 submarines, 4 frigates, 18 OSA and KOMA-class high-speed patrol boats, 32 large patrol craft, 167 FAG, 170 FAG (T), and 90 *Nampo* landing craft. South Korea has 11 destroyers, 11 frigates, 11 corvettes, 52 large patrol craft 8 MSC-268/294 coastal minesweepers 32 landing ships and 2 submarines (*Ichŏn, Changbogo*). South Korea also has a marine corps, while North Korea does not.

The South Korean Navy has fewer naval craft, but they are heavier and more seaworthy than their North Korean counterparts. The South recently has increased the number of anti-submarine patrol aircraft and patrol boats in its navy.

Air Force

North Korea's Air Force has approximately 850 combat aircraft, which constitute 28 fighter wings and 3 bomber wings. The principal craft are 290 MIG-15 and MIG-17s, and 92 MIG-19s. It also has 46 MIG-23s, 120 MIG-21s, 20 SU-7s, and unknown numbers of SU-25s and MIG-29s, which are its newest and best. Its bomber wings are comprised of obsolete IL-28s.

As of 1992, the South Korean Air Force had 520 combat aircraft, which constituted 18 fighter-bomber squadrons, 190 support aircraft and 580 helicopters. Three of the squadrons together deploy 60 F-4Es and F-4Ds, and 20 F-16s, while 13 squadrons have 250 F-5A/B/E/Fs, F-86Fs, and another two squadrons have 30 RF-5As and S-2A/Fs.

In terms of quantity, North Korea has 1.3 times as many war planes as South Korea. The quality of the South Korean Air Force, however, has improved markedly due to the introduction of newer sophisticated planes in the early 1970s under the Force Improvement Program. In addition, the presence in South Korea of U.S. Air Force units manned by highly seasoned pilots helps offset the numerical superiority of the North Korean air force.

Paramilitary Units

Paramilitary forces are essential for the defense of rear areas. North Korea has a total of 6 million paramilitary troops, composed of the Pacification Corps, the Laborer and Farmer Red Guard units, the Young Red Guard and the Armed Reserve Guard.

All members of the Laborer and Farmer Red Guard units and the Young Red Guard are armed with individual firearms, while training units possess crew-served weapons. The strength of these reserve forces is comparable to 23 to 25 lightly armed regular divisions.

In South Korea, there are 4 million men in the Homeland Reserve Forces, which have been further strengthened by incorporating the Civil Defense Corps. South Korea's paramilitary force is numerically superior to North Korea's, but in terms of firepower and equipment, the South lags behind the North.

Assessment

A comparison of the military strength of the two contending parties cannot be made accurately on the basis of manpower, military organization and equipment. Account also must be taken of the consolidated reactive power of each side based on motivation and morale of the public, support capability of the rear areas, quality of intelligence and communications, and, above all, the skill and integrity of commanders.

However, on the basis of the superficial comparison of quantitative military strength between the two sides in Korea, it may be concluded that greater and accelerated efforts are necessary for South Korea to acquire sufficient strength to maintain a military balance vis-a-vis North Korea and to deter the latter's aggression.

What is of extreme importance in the evaluation of South-North military strength is not the relative military inferiority of South Korea, but the possibility of any weakening of its deterrent capability, thereby inviting a recurrence of the tragedy of 1950. It is for these reasons that the Republic of Korea requires, and has striven to acquire, a resolute determination and an all-out national security capability to deter North Korean aggression. It is also for these reasons that the U.S. military presence in Korea is necessary. Tilting of the existing power balance in Korea by premature withdrawal of U.S. troops could invite a North Korean attack on South Korea.

The time has come for the Republic of Korea to insure its own national security by attaining overall superiority in national resources and capabilities, and by establishing an all-out defense posture. South Korea currently enjoys wide economic superiority over the North, and this could become a decisive factor in shaping long-range peace in Korea. South Korea's open, free economy, with its great potential for further development, stands in sharp contrast to North Korea's closed, totalitarian economy. The economic gap between the two undoubtedly will widen in the future, proving to be a favorable factor for the Republic of Korea.

South Korea's developing economy, the strength and morale of its armed forces and the determined will of its people provide the basis for optimum assurance of security. In this respect, the steady growth of a defense industry which has reached a stage where it can mass produce most arms requirements is of particular significance.

Behind this remarkable growth there is the shared effort of the people of the Republic, encompassing on the military side the modernization of hardware, rigorous training, rising morale and the enhancement of military doctrines adapted to Korean national traits, geopolitical conditions and culture.

The armed forces of the Republic of Korea stand ready to defend the country in crisis, creating and maintaining a lasting peace on the peninsula and preserving the heritage of the nation.

The Navy of the Republic of Korea.

FINANCE

The Financial System

The Financial System in the Public Sector

The activities and functions of the financial system in the public sector can be divided into two parts—general government and public enterprises. The general government sector can be further classified into the central government sector and the local government sector.

The general account, 18 special accounts and 33 government management funds together constitute the central government sector. The local government sector includes general and special accounts for the Special City of Seoul, five major cities and nine provinces, and financial accounts for counties and cities under each provincial government.

The general account executes all of the administrative functions of the Government, including the operation of the revenue raising activities, the operation of the various ministries, and the majority of the economic and social development activities of the Government. The fiscal investment and financing special account covers the investment and subscription to public enterprises and funds, domestic credit activities of the Government, and the management of government foreign borrowing. Other special accounts are established for specific projects, whose revenues are earmarked for particular expenditures. The general account usually aids these other special accounts, in spite of the principle that their expenditure is to be self-financed.

Four enterprise special accounts are organized essentially along departmental lines. They are national railroad, communication service, procurement, and grain management special accounts. The transactions of these four accounts and two public enterprise funds are closely related to those of the central government so that a consolidated approach is appropriate for evaluating the impact of fiscal poli-

Structure of the Public Sector

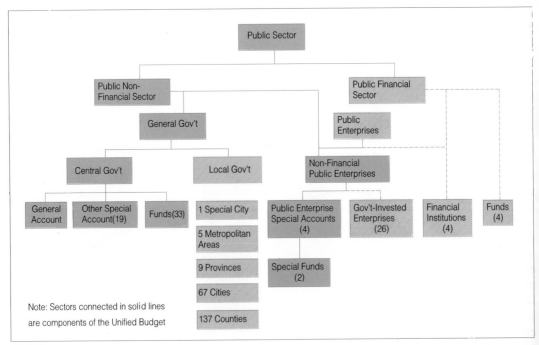

Note: Sectors connected in solid lines are components of the Unified Budget

cies.

The 26 government-invested enterprises, in which the Government has an equity share, are not included in the government budget accounts because their operations are financially independent of the central government.

Thirty-five government funds set up for specific government objectives are in operation through primarily net lending. The activities of these funds do not need to be deliberated and approved by the National Assembly. Thus, the operations of these funds are more flexible than those of G/A or S/A. Several of the funds are especially important in terms of their contribution to the overall public sector deficit.

Since 1979, the Government has monitored the budget through a unified budget system in accordance with the International Monetary Fund's model laid out in "A Manual on Government Finance Statistics." The total amount of the unified budget, including the general account, 22 special accounts, and 35 government management funds, totals 45,246 billion won (excluding intra-government transactions), accounting for 19.7 percent of the gross national product (GNP) in 1992.

Relations Between Central and Local Government Finances

Finances for the central government and 219 local governments including the Special City of Seoul, five major cities, and provincial and county capitals are systematically linked. First, a local administrative body collects local taxes within the scope of the taxation law which stipulates all details related to local finances, such as the creation of local taxes, the designation of taxpayers subject to local taxes, the determination of tax rates and the standard assessment of taxation.

Second, local bonds, when floated to supplement local finances out of the official budget, are issued only with the authorization of the central government. The size of the issuance and applications of the local bonds are strictly limited to the original purpose for which the local bonds are issued. Third, the central government finances local governments in the form of subsidies, constituting a statutory 13.27 percent of the internal tax revenue, and also grants to supplement local finances for special purposes, such as the repayment of local bonds. The central government also finances an additional 11.8 percent of the internal tax revenue for education.

In addition to central government subsidies and grants, government aid from the national treasury is specially funneled to local governments for use in government-sponsored local projects. Since decisions to aid certain local governments are at the discretion of the central government, they can be used as a tool to supervise and control local governments financially, and thus reflect a weakness in the autonomy of local governments over local development.

The Current Financial Situation

Financial Size

Ratio of Expenditures to GNP

(percent)

	1975	1980	1985	1990	1992
Total	24.6	28.7	28.1	27.8	34.2
Central Gov't	21.0	23.2	20.6	19.2	19.7
(General Account)	(15.2)	(17.4)	(17.0)	(16.3)	(14.1)
Local Gov't	3.5	5.4	7.5	8.6	14.5

As a nation's economy expands and income increases, it is common for the level of the public's financial burden to increase. The ratio of Korea's total finances to GNP stood at about 28.7 percent in 1991, up from 24.5 percent in 1975. In particular, local spending has grown remarkably, while the general account of the central government has remained relatively stable at 16-18 percent, reflecting the Government's monetary tightening policy in the 1980s. Meanwhile, the ratio of tax burden has steadily increased to 19.4 percent of GNP in 1992.

Structure of Revenue in the General Account

Approximately 95 percent of all revenues in the general account depend on taxes. As such, Korea's general account is relatively less dependent on non-tax revenue than that of more advanced countries. Temporary national taxes, such as defense and education taxes, are increasingly bearing their share of total tax revenues at present. In 1992, the internal tax revenue made up 89.7 percent of total tax revenues.

It is particularly noticeable that foreign loans, which constituted a considerable portion of total government revenues in the 1960s and 1970s when economic development was rapid, decreased significantly in the early 1980s. The nation's finances are now being maintained at a healthy level by slowing the issuance of government bonds, which have made up for revenue shortages in the past.

In comparison, for most foreign countries, the general account depends on tax revenues for 70-80 percent of its total revenues, while the remaining revenues are supplemented by public

Composition of Tax Revenues

(percent)

	1975	1980	1985	1992
Internal Taxes	62..0	55.4	57.6	83.6
Customs Duties	11.0	11.5	12.0	9.1
Defense Surtaxes	3.8	12.9	12.8	0.5
Education Surtaxes			2.5	-
Monopoly payment	8.3	7.7	6.4	-
Total	(8.52)	(87.5)	(91.3)	(93.2)
Non-Tax Revenues	14.8	12.5	8.7	6.8

Revenues by Source

(billion won)

	*1990	**1992	Change	
			Amount	Rate(%)
National Taxes	26,847.5	32,172.1	5,324.6	19.8
Internal Taxes	19,130.2	28,856.0	9,725.8	50.8
Customs Duties	2,765.4	3,153.2	387.8	14.0
Defense Surtaxes	4,430.6	162.9	Δ4,267.7	Δ96.3
Education Surtaxes	521.3	-	Δ521.3	Δ100
Monopoly Payment	-	-	-	-
Non-Tax Revenues	1,026.3	1,455.8	429.5	41.8
Carry-Over	3,430.8	906.2	Δ2,524.6	Δ73.6
Total	30,278.3	34,534.1	4,255.8	14.1

Source: Ministry of Finance.
*At the end of 1990, U.S. $1 = 760 won
**At the end of 1992, U.S. $1 = 788 won

bonds.

Total revenues in 1992 were set at 34,534.1 billion won compared with 30,278.3 billion won in 1990, an increase of 4,255.8 billion won.

Internal taxes were estimated at 28,856 billion won, an increase of 50.8 percent from 1990.This accounts for 83.5 percent of total revenues, making it the main source of budget revenues. Although there is no tax revision, the anticipated economic growth will raise taxes.

Customs duties increased by 387.8 billion won; compared with 2,765.4 billion won in 1990, this is a 14.0 percent increase.

Structure of Expenditures
in the General Account

Total expenditures in 1992 were set at 33,362.5 billion won, up 21.6 percent compared with 27,436.8 billion won in 1990.

Inflexible expenses have increased 32.1 percent to 18,945.3 billion won, making up 52.3 percent of the total general account expenditures in 1990 and 56.8 percent in 1992. This high ratio is one of the major characteristics of the Korean budget.

The defense expenditure has increased 25.8 percent to comprise 25.9 percent of the total general expenditure. General grants to local governments have increased 42.1 percent in accordance with the fixed ratio of 13.27 percent of internal tax revenue.

The contingency reserve has also risen 12.5 percent to 293.9 billion won. It is ascribed to the increase in contingency reserves in case of natural disasters.

As Table   indicates, the expenditure on development was 14,417.2 billion won in 1992, an increase of 10.1 percent from 1990.

Total expenditures in FY'92 were 33,362.5 billion won. The share of defense expenditures was 25.9 percent, while the shares of education, economic development, general administration, and social development expenditures were 19.4 percent, 18.6 percent, 12.5 percent and 9.7 percent respectively.

The ratio of economic development expenditures to total expenditures has gradually declined, except for 1992, while on the other hand, the ratio of social development expendi-

Expenditures by Major Expenses

(billion won)

	*1990	**1992	Change	
			Amount	Rate(%)
Inflexible expenses	14,340.4	18,945.3	4,604.9	32.1
Defense	6,856.2	8,625	1,768.8	25.8
Grants to Local Gov'ts	2,764.7	3,927.8	1,163.1	42.1
Personnel Expenses	4,458.2	6,098.6	1,640.4	36.8
Contingencies	261.3	293.9	32.6	12.5
Development	13,096.4	14,417.2	1,320.8	10.1
Total	27,436.8	33,362.5	5,925.7	21.6

*At the end of 1990, U.S. $1 = 760 won
**At the end of 1992, U.S. $1= 788 won

Source: Ministry of Finance.

Expenditures by Function

(percent)

	1975	1980	1985	1992
General Administration	11.3	9.7	10.1	12.5
Defense Expenditures	28.8	35.6	30.6	25.8
Education Expenditures	12.7	17.3	20.1	19.4
Social Development Expenditures	6.7	6.3	6.3	9.7
Economic Development Expenditures	26.6	21.5	16.1	18.6
Unallocable Grants to Local Gov'ts	7.7	6.3	8.1	11.8
Repayment of Debt & Others	6.2	2.7	8.1	7.2
Total	100.0	100.0	100.0	100.0

Source: Ministry of Finance

tures has increased, especially in the field of medicare and medical insurance. However, compared with other countries, expenditures for social welfare projects are still insufficient.

The Influence of Finance on the National Economy

The Influence of the Government Budget on the Currency

In the process of performing its inherent financial procurement and management function, the government influences the monetary supply. In the course of securing financial sources to cover budget deficits, the government can trigger currency expansion. In the unified budget, the following elements cause currency expansion: government debts from the Bank of Korea and from city banks; spending from government savings; and loans to, and investment in, city banks from the investment account.

Government Consumption and Savings

The concept of government consumption includes the cost of personnel and supplies. All fixed capital formations related to the national defense are included in government consumption. Government savings are the balance of ordinary revenue minus ordinary expenditures.

Table indicates that government consumption was 10,247.6 billion won, or 6.1 percent of GNP in 1990, a 19.7 percent increase since 1989.

With increases in the government consumption taken into account, government savings were to reach 6,674.3 billion won, up 27.7 percent from 1989.

Government Consumption and Savings

(billion won)

	*1989	**1990	Difference between 1989 and 1990	
			Amount	Percentage
• Gov't Consumption	8,564.2	10,247.6	1,683.4	19.7
(Percentage of GNP)	(6.0)	(6.1)	(0.1)	(0.1)
• Central Gov't	7,810.5	9,487.8	1,677.3	21.5
• General Account	7,784.9	9,182.1	1,397.2	17.9
• Others	25.6	305.7	280.1	1,094.1
Gov't Savings	5,135.7	7,434.1	2,298.4	44.8
(Percentage of GNP)	(3.6)	(4.4)	(0.8)	(0.8)
• Central Gov't	5,227.1	6,674.3	1,447.2	27.7
General Account	5,075.5	6,973.1	1,897.6	37.4
Others	151.6	-298.8	-450.4	-297.1
• Non-Financial Public Enterprises	-91.4	759.8	851.2	931.3
Enterprise Special Accounts	81.6	-297.5	-379.1	-464.6
Funds	-173.0	1,057.3	1,230.3	711.2

*At the end of 1989, U.S. $1 = 679 won
**At the end of 1990, U.S. $1 = 760 won

Source: Ministry of Finance

Government Investments

Investments in the government sector, or the formation of government fixed capital, include all capital formation, except expenditures for land purchase and capital transfers. Defense-related expenses, which are considered as consumption, are excluded from government capital formation, while increases in grain inventory and the grain management fund are regarded as government investments.

Government investment in 1992 totaled 3,388 billion won, up 7.8 percent since the previous year.

The percentage of the Government's fixed capital formation against the GNP, when compared with that of other countries, is generally higher than that of advanced countries. This reflects the Government's effort to make up for capital shortage in the private sector, even though the Government's total expenditures are smaller than those of the other countries.

Basic investments by the government sector are steadily increasing to strengthen the bases for economic growth by expanding financial loans from special accounts and curtailing direct financial support from the general account.

Financial loans from the fiscal investment and financing special account were raised to about 1,232 billion won in the 1992 budget, a sharp boost from the 330 billion won level in 1984.

In principle, these financial loans are supplied to projects whose beneficiaries are able to repay principal and interest. Among the projects receiving these government loans are those aimed at improving farming and fishing household incomes and general living conditions, and those related to railroad, subway, and water supply and drainage. Financial loans are made to projects when financial resources for public investment to improve national welfare cannot be supplied through hiked fees, or when high risk requiring a long period for return on investment is involved, such as technological development projects.

The Fiscal Investment and Financing

At the start of FY 1988, the fiscal investment and financing special account (FIFSA) was founded for some development projects which had been previously financed by the general account. This special account absorbed the government fund management special account and a variety of different funds from sales of state-held stocks in state-

Government Investment

(billion won)

	*1989	**1990	Difference between 1989 and 1990	
			Amount	Percentage
Gov't Investment	1,706.1	1,854.8	148.1	8.7
(Percentage of GNP)	(1.2)	(1.1)	(-0.1)	(-0.1)
• Fixed Capital Formation	1,633.1	1,972.4	339.3	20.8
· Central Gov't	1,388.8	1,614.4	225.6	16.2
· Non-financial Public Enterprises	244.3	358.0	113.7	46.5
• Increase in Stocks	73.0	-117.6	-190.6	-261.1

*At the end of 1989, U.S. $1 = 679 won
**At the end of 1990, U.S. $1 = 760 won

Comparison of Central Gov't Expenditures against GNP

(percent)

	Fixed capital formation against GNP		
	Total(A)	Central Gov't(B)	B/A
Korea (1988)	28.8	1.4	4.9
Japan (1985)	27.7	0.9	3.2
U.S. (1987)	17.9	0.3	1.7
U.K. (1986)	16.9	1.0	5.9
W.Germany (1987)	19.3	0.4	2.1
France (1987)	19.4	1.0	5.1

Financial Loans Supplied by Sector

(100 billion won)

	1984	1986	1988	*1990	**1992
Development of Farm and Fishery Products	815	1,859	4,341	2,920	1,590
Support for Small and Medium Industries	100	420	2,900	4,110	3,050
Technology	20	100	270	-	-
Transportation	1,889	2,427	1,997	7,453	5,700
Electric Power & Energy Resources	30	284	312	104	137
Housing & Environment	398	520	2,419	1,019	1,304
Other	50	50	430	492	535
Total	3,302	5,660	12,649	16,099	12,316

*At the end of 1990, U.S. $1 = 760 won
**At the end of 1992, U.S. $1 = 788 won

Source: Ministry of Finance

Function of Fiscal Investment and Financing Special Account

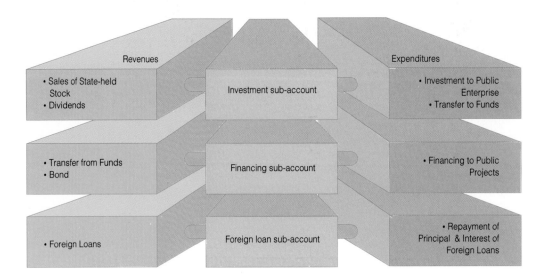

Operation of Investment Account in FIFSA

(billion won)

	*90 Budget	**92 Budget	Change Amount	Change Rate(%)
(Revenues)				
-Transfer from General Account	1,826.5	1,147	△679.5	△59.2
-Sales of State-held Stocks	-	2	2	100
• Korea Electric Power Corp.	-	-	-	-
-Dividends etc.	95.1	135	39.9	42
Total	**1,921.6**	**1,283.9**	**△637.7**	**△49.7**
(Expenditures)				
-Equity Subscription	672.6	427.8	△244.8	△57.2
• Korea Highway Corp.	84.1	98.5	14.4	
• Korea Housing Corp.	522.0	248.5	△273.5	
• Small and Medium Industry Bank	-	5.0	5.0	
• Other Gov't-Invested Enterprises	66.5	75.8	9.3	
-Subscription for Funds	1,243.3	856.1	△387.2	△45.2
• Grain Mng't Fund	880.0	300.0	△580.0	
• Rural Area Dev't Fund	85.2	-	△85.2	
• Foreign Exchange Stabilization Fund	--	-	-	
• Nat'l Housing Fund	-	-	-	
• Other Funds	278.1	556.1	278.0	
-Administration Cost	5.1	0.03	△5.07	△170

*At the end of 1990, U.S. $1 = 760 won
**At the end of 1992, U.S. $1 = 788 won

Source: Ministry of Finance

Operation of Investment Account in FIFSA

(billion won)

	*89 Budget	**90 Budget	Change Amount	Change Rate(%)
(Revenues)				
-Transfer from General Account	152.5	289.0	136.5	89.5
-Trust from Public Funds	1,103.5	790.0	-313.5	-28.4
• Postal Insurance & Deposits	100.0	130.0	30.0	
• Civil Servants Pension Fund	203.5	170.0	-33.5	
• Petroleum Business Fund	460.0	100.0	-360.0	
• National Pension Fund	340.0	390.0	50.0	
-Collection of Loan Principal and Repayment	494.7	530.4	35.7	7.2
Total	**1,750.7**	**1,609.4**	**-141.3**	**-8.1**
(Expenditures)				
-Agriculture and Fishery	267.3	292.0	24.7	9.2
-Transportation and Communication	660.6	745.0	84.4	12.8
-Small and Medium Industries	373.0	411.0	38.0	10.1
-Housing & Local Community Dev't	236.7	5.9	-230.8	-97.5
-Living Environment	138.1	95.9	-42.2	-30.6
-Power and Electricity	-	10.4	10.4	-
-Others	75.0	49.2	-25.8	-34.4

*At the end of 1989, U.S. $1 = 679 won
**At the end of 1990, U.S. $1 = 760 won

Annual Deficit in the Unified Budget

(billion won, %)

	1982	1983	1984	1985	1986	1987	*1988	**1989
Deficit	-2,222	-951	-923	-713	-65	260	1,642	-19
Percentage of GNP	(-4.2)	(-1.5)	(-1.3)	(-0.9)	(-0.1)	(0.2)	(1.3)	(0.0)

*At the end of 1988, U.S. $1 = 684 won
**At the end of 1989, U.S. $1 = 679 won

Source: Ministry of Finance

invested or funded enterprises. Presently, it consists of an investment account from stock sales, a financing account from the government fund management special account, and a foreign loan account.

The special account is aimed at the continued, rather than one-time, use of the sales of stocks in government invested corporations for investment and financing to some projects. Revenue in the investment account is comprised of transfers from general account, sales of stocks and transfer from other special accounts. In 1992, the investment account invested 1,283.9 billion won in the Korea Highway Corp., the Korean Housing Corp., the Small and Medium Industry Bank, and other funds such as the grain management fund and the national housing fund.

Major sources in the financing account are public funds such as the civil servants pension fund and the national pension fund, founded in 1988. With these sources, the Government makes loans to government agencies, public corporations, special accounts, and local governments. Fiscal financing is provided in various fields. Allocation of funds is made with the objective of enhancing public policy, especially in the fields of agriculture and fisheries, transportation and communication, and small and medium industries.

Government Efforts
for Sound Fiscal Policies

Structural weaknesses in the Korean financial system have resulted in chronic budget deficits as the money supply was expanded excessively, partly to meet the rapidly increasing demand for funds needed for industrial development in the 1960s and 1970s. Bureaucratic inertia, waste, and inefficiency in the past have been partly responsible for these structural weaknesses.

Since 1981, drastic measures have been taken to establish a healthy financial structure to overcome perennial problems and respond to newly arising circumstances. Drastic budget balancing measures have stressed the reduction of financial deficits in order to back up economic management aimed at stabilization, improve productivity despite limited financial sources, and eliminate inefficiency which cropped up during the high growth period.

Realizing that a chronically inflationary economy could not be restructured without the combined efforts of the Government, household economies, and businesses, the Government was determined to wipe out all sources of misappropriation and waste. Several measures were taken to rectify financial deficiencies.

First, a zero-base budget system was devised, by which the previous year's projects or similar ones were started on a zero-base or blank-basis in the new budget without giving consideration to the previous year's budget allocations or previous priorities, and to re-evaluate the significance, priority or fund allocation for ongoing projects from the zero point. The introduction of the new zero-base system has slowed inflation considerably.

During the high-growth and high-inflation period, the budget was organized on the basis of the previous year's budget. Additional budget allocations, exceeding the economic growth rate by 20 or 30 percent, were almost automatically made. As such, the new budget simply carried over the previous year's allocations with the addition of unnecessary secondary appropriations. The zero-base budget system has eliminated this waste and inefficiency, and has

restructured the national budget to increase the possibility of achieving a balanced budget.

Second, attempts have been made to balance the general account by limiting expenditures to available revenues. Moreover, government spending has been increased at a rate below the projected rate of economic growth. Also, to mitigate inflationary pressure arising from liquidity growth resulting from sustained balance-of-payments surpluses, the Government raised the ceiling on the issuance of treasury bills. As a result, the chronic budget deficits were changed into a surplus in 1987.

Recent Direction
in Financial Management

From the 1960s to the early 1980s, the major emphasis of national budgets was placed on supporting economic development, thus contributing to sustained rapid economic growth. However, this policy emphasis led to widening budget deficits and caused other difficulties in budgetary operations. In 1982, the Government launched efforts to balance the budget. Since then, it has also undertaken budgetary reforms designed to assure sound budgetary management and to maintain economic stability.

The shift in fiscal policies helped stabilize domestic prices and hence alleviate inflation-induced income disparity, and eliminate inefficiencies in various sectors of the economy. The result has been a strengthened foundation for fostering economic and social conditions conducive to improving national well-being.

As the level of national income continues to rise, thanks to sustained high economic growth, there have been increasing demands from the people for an improved quality of life. To meet these demands greater government efforts were made to reform various existing economic and social institutions.

Moreover, sustained balance-of-payments surpluses in recent years have resulted in external demands for market opening and have added to inflationary pressure. This changing economic environment points to the need to adopt a more flexible fiscal policy.

To respond to these recent developments, the

future fiscal policy needs to emphasize outlays for expanded welfare programs for rural people and low-income families, while adhering to sound budget policies. A substantially greater portion of budgetary resources also will be assigned to investments aimed at accelerating relatively lagging sectors and facilitating balanced development among different geographical regions. These changes conform to the ongoing democratic reforms and the growing emphasis on local economies that have prevailed since the inauguration of the Sixth Republic.

More specifically, to help augment budgetary revenues of local governments and thus invigorate local economies, in 1989, the tobacco sales tax was converted from a national tax to a local tax. In addition, a road construction and maintenance special account will be established to expand investment in road construction projects necessary to strengthen provincial infrastructure.

The national budget will also stress support for the start-up and technology development of small and medium-sized industries to contribute to the ongoing industrial restructuring needed to strengthen the competitiveness of Korean industry and foster economic growth potential. At the same time, the budget will provide active support for measures strengthening diplomacy and national security to respond to changing circumstances and bolster law enforcement activities.

The Banking System

Introduction of the Banking System

The introduction of a modern banking system into Korea dates to the beginning of Japan's domination of the country. In 1878, the First National Bank, a Japanese bank, opened a branch office in Pusan, the port city nearest to Japan. It engaged in modern banking practices, including the issuance of bank notes. Japanese banks soon opened a network of branches in Korea.

A bank called the Bank of Korea was found-ed in 1909 to function as a central bank. It took over the legal right to issue bank notes from the First National Bank, which, until that time had been the only bank authorized to issue notes under a government commission. In 1911, following Korea's formal annexation by Japan in 1910, the Bank of Korea was renamed the Bank of Chosun. It initiated monetary reforms and replaced the currency with new Bank of Chosun notes. Following this, numerous commercial and specialized banks were established under Japanese colonial domination. Of them, the Chosun Industrial Bank, established in 1918, was especially notable as it played a major role in medium and long-term financing in close cooperation with other institutions established to support Japanese colonial rule.

In addition to the Bank of Chosun and the Chosun Industrial Bank, the Korean banking structure prior to liberation in 1945 included two commercial banks (the Chosun Commercial Bank, later renamed the Commercial Bank of Korea, and the Choheung Bank), the Chosun Savings Bank and the Federation of Financial Association. The Chosun Savings Bank was a subsidiary of the Chosun Industrial Bank and channelled its funds largely into Japanese government bonds and the Chosun Industrial Bank for long-term financing. The Federation of Financial Associations specialized in loans to farmers and small businesses.

Establishment of a New Banking System

The sudden separation of the Korean economy from the Japanese economic system in the wake of liberation produced serious dislocations. During the three years preceding the inauguration of the Republic of Korea in August 1948, political instability and crippled economic conditions created runaway inflation fed by a continuously increasing money supply. Confronted with such economic disorder, the newly established Government soon recognized that the existing financial system was inadequate for the new economic situation and ill-equipped to combat galloping inflation. This resulted in the drafting of new central and general banking statutes. The drafts were approved by the National Assembly in April 1950, and a new central bank, the Bank of Korea, came into being on June 12, 1950. Upon its establishment, the Bank of Korea initiated a number of policies to combat inflation and drafted the General Banking Act, under which commercial banks were to be reorganized. The implementation of the General Banking Act, however, was delayed until August 1954.

The Korean War (1950-53), which broke out less than two weeks after the establishment of the Bank of Korea, created disastrous new problems. After the cease-fire, the primary task facing banks was the financing of the necessary industrial and agricultural projects for economic rehabilitation. For this purpose, the Korea Development Bank was established in 1954, with capital wholly paid by the Government, and in 1956, the Federation of Financial Associations was reorganized into the Korea Agriculture Bank.

Reorganization of the Banking System

Following the military revolution of 1961, a series of measures was undertaken to promote the development of the economy. The Government launched the First Five-Year Economic Development Plan in 1962, and, at the same time, reorganized financial institutions to finance the development plan more efficiently. In 1961, a major portion of the equity capital of commercial banks was transferred to the Government, and the Bank of Korea Act was amended in 1962 to render the monetary policy of the Bank of Korea more effective.

In the early 1960s, the Government also introduced various specialized banks to facilitate financial support for underdeveloped or strategically important sectors: the National Agricultural Cooperatives Federation, the National Federation of Fisheries Cooperatives, the Small and Medium Industry Bank, and the Citizens National Bank. Later in the 1960s, the Korea Exchange Bank and the Korea Housing Bank were established. In 1983, the National Livestock Cooperatives Federation was added to complete the present setup of specialized banking institutions.

Meanwhile, the commercial banking system was restructured to meet the changing needs of the economy. Provincial banks were introduced with the prime objective of supporting regionally balanced development. In conjunction with the rapid increase in external trade volume and the internationalization of the economy, foreign banks were allowed to open branch offices.

Development of Non-Banking Financial Intermediaries

Toward the end of the 1960s, the Government recognized that the existing banking system was not able to meet the surging need for investment funds for further economic development. Confronted with this problem, the Government tried to diversify the sources of investment funds by introducing various non-banking financial institutions and by fostering the securities market.

Near the end of the 1960s, the Korea Development Finance Corporation, a private development financial institution, later renamed the Korea Long Term Credit Bank, was incorporated as a long-term financial institution. The Export-Import Bank of Korea was established to facilitate financial support for exports and overseas investment. With the promulgation of the Presidential Emergency Decree in 1972, designed to induce unorganized curb market funds into the organized financial market, investment and finance companies were introduced to engage in short-term dealings in papers issued by business firms. Mutual savings and finance companies, specializing in receiving installment savings and extending small loans to be repaid in installments, were formed from what were formerly pseudo-financial companies. In 1974, merchant banking corporations were introduced to induce foreign capital and supply medium and long-term funds for business.

The securities market has also grown rapidly since 1972, as the result of a series of supportive measures to promote investment in securities and to encourage enterprises to go public. Late

Shares of Financial Institutions

(Unit: Percent)

	Loans				Deposits			
	'71	'76	'84	'92	'71	'76	'84	'92
Deposit Money Banks	79.2	74.4	56.5	44.5	84.9	78.1	53.8	36.2
Non-Banking Financial Institutions	20.8	25.6	43.5	55.5	15.1	21.9	46.2	63.8
Development Institutions	10.1	10.7	11.4	7.8	1.2	0.7	0.5	4.8
Savings Institutions	8.8	6.5	10.8	31.8	10.5	10.7	16.7	31.7
Investment Companies	0.2	6.7	15.3	6.7		7.1	17.7	14.3
Life Insurance Companies	1.7	1.7	6.0	9.2	3.4	3.4	11.3	13.0

Source: Ministry of Finance

in the 1970s, various institutional arrangements were made to ensure the sound operation of the market. These included the strengthening of the underwriting function of investment trust companies and the establishment of the Securities and Exchange Commission and the Securities Supervisory Board. Internationalization of the securities market also has progressed steadily since 1981, when the Government formulated a plan to open the securities market by the early 1990s.

Until 1992 foreign investors were able to invest in Korean securities through indirect vehicles such as country funds, beneficiary certificates and overseas securities issued by domestic companies exclusively for foreign investors. Since 1992, foreign investors have been able to invest directly in Korean securities.

These non-banking financial intermediaries have grown rapidly, thanks to the relatively higher interest rates they are permitted to apply and to the fact that they were given more independence than banking institutions. The share of non-bank financial intermediaries in terms of deposits increased from 15.1 percent in 1971 to 63.8 percent in 1992. The increase in the share of investment and finance companies was particularly significant.

Recent Developments in the Financial Market

The successive government-led economic development plans were responsible for Korea's remarkable economic development in the 1960s and 1970s. At that time, there was little capital, a lack of natural resources, a large population, a low level of savings, and the economy was small in scale and simple in structure, making government control highly effective. However, as the economy grew larger and more complex, government control became increasingly inefficient. Thus, in the early 1980s, wide-ranging structural adjustments were begun to shift from government management to a market-oriented system. These policies were aimed at enhancing economic efficiency by assigning a greater role to the market mechanism and by promoting competition in every sector of the economy. In line with this, various measures for liberalization and promotion of competition in the financial sector were taken.

In a major effort to liberalize the banking sector, the Government turned over the ownership of four national commercial banks to private hands: the Hanil Bank in 1981, the Korea First Bank and the Bank of Seoul and Trust Company in 1982, and the Choheung Bank in 1983. With the Commercial Bank of Korea having already been turned over to private hands in 1972, the denationalization of all five leading commercial banks was completed. Among specialized banks, the Korea Exchange Bank was privatized in December 1989. Along with the denationalization of the commercial banks, the General Banking Act was revised toward the end of 1982 to give banks a freer hand in dealing with their own managerial affairs while boosting

Financial Institutions in Korea

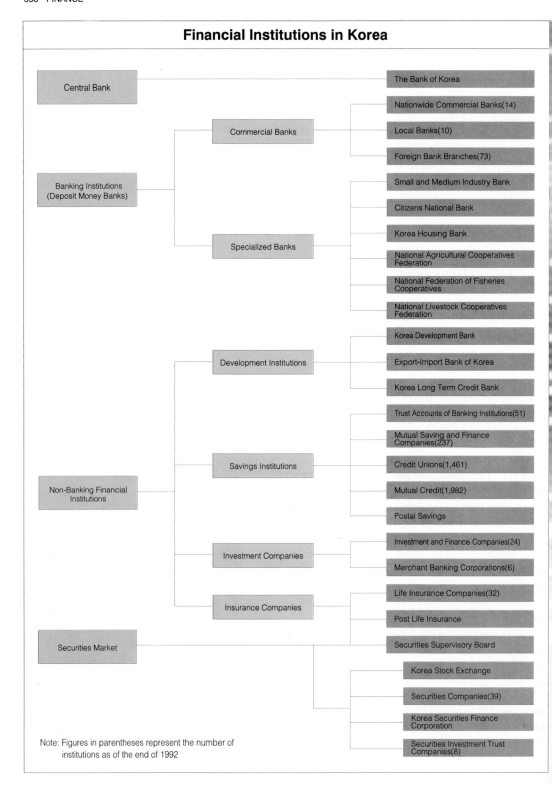

Central Bank — The Bank of Korea

Banking Institutions (Deposit Money Banks)
- Commercial Banks
  - Nationwide Commercial Banks(14)
  - Local Banks(10)
  - Foreign Bank Branches(73)
- Specialized Banks
  - Small and Medium Industry Bank
  - Citizens National Bank
  - Korea Housing Bank
  - National Agricultural Cooperatives Federation
  - National Federation of Fisheries Cooperatives
  - National Livestock Cooperatives Federation

Non-Banking Financial Institutions
- Development Institutions
  - Korea Development Bank
  - Export-Import Bank of Korea
  - Korea Long Term Credit Bank
- Savings Institutions
  - Trust Accounts of Banking Institutions(51)
  - Mutual Saving and Finance Companies(237)
  - Credit Unions(1,461)
  - Mutual Credit(1,982)
  - Postal Savings
- Investment Companies
  - Investment and Finance Companies(24)
  - Merchant Banking Corporations(6)
- Insurance Companies
  - Life Insurance Companies(32)
  - Post Life Insurance

Securities Market
- Securities Supervisory Board
- Korea Stock Exchange
- Securities Companies(39)
- Korea Securities Finance Corporation
- Securities Investment Trust Companies(8)

Note: Figures in parentheses represent the number of institutions as of the end of 1992

their public accountability by setting upper limits on the ownership of bank stocks per shareholder. At the same time, regulations on the internal management and operations of banks were simplified and drastically reduced in number.

In order to increase the independence of banking institutions in fund operations, direct credit controls through credit ceilings on individual banks were replaced with indirect controls through the management of bank reserves. In 1982, preferential loan rates by commercial banks were abolished and a system by which banks are allowed to charge different rates based on the credit worthiness of the borrower was introduced in January 1984. As a first step toward the liberalization of interest rates, the ceilings on inter-bank call rates and the issuing rates of unsecured corporate bonds were lifted. In December 1988, interest rates on loans of banks and non-banking financial intermediaries were deregulated along with those on deposits with long maturities.

To provide a more competitive financial environment, five new national commercial banks, the Shinhan Bank, the Boram Bank, the Donghwa Bank, the Dongnam Bank, and the Daedong Bank were established in the 1980s. Among the five newly opened banks, two of them (the Dongnam Bank and the Daedong Bank) specialize in financing small and medium sized firms. Also in 1982, entry barriers were substantially lowered for such non-banking financial institutions as investment and finance companies and mutual savings and finance companies. As a result, the number of financial institutions increased sharply.

In addition, business boundaries between financial institutions have been adjusted. Since 1982, the ancillary and peripheral functions of commercial banks have been diversified to include the sale of commercial bills, credit card accounts, sales of government and public bonds on repurchase agreements (RPs), factoring, investment trusts, mutual installment savings and negotiable certificates of deposit (CDs). As for non-banking financial institutions, commercial papers (CP) were introduced for investment and finance companies and merchant banking

corporations in 1981, and for large securities companies in 1984. The cash management account (CMA), a Korean version of the money market funds in the United States, was introduced in 1984 for investment and finance companies and merchant banking corporations. Mechanization, including computerization, has enabled financial institutions to supply more sophisticated financial services, such as on-line deposit and withdrawal systems, cash dispensers, and night depositories.

To motivate domestic banks into improving their banking practices and managerial skills, the government has allowed 34 additional foreign bank branches to open in Korea since 1981, bringing the total number of foreign bank branches to 73. A number of discriminatory restrictions on foreign bank branches in the domestic financial market have been ruled out. In 1985, they were permitted to make use of the rediscount facilities of the Bank of Korea for export financing and to enter the investment trust business. Since 1986, they have been entitled to make use of the rediscount facilities for call loans.

Bank Supervision

The supervision and guidance of banks is carried out by the Bank of Korea Act and the General Banking Act. Accordingly, the Office of Bank Supervision and Examination of the Bank of Korea, which is subject to the instructions of the Monetary Board, is in charge of the supervision and regular examination of banking institutions.

Monetary and Credit Policy

Overview

Monetary policy in Korea, as elsewhere, is exercised principally through three related and complementary instruments which affect the reserve position of banking institutions: changes in the terms and conditions of rediscounts, open market operations in specified securities, and changes in reserve requirement ratios.

Until the 1970s, monetary policy relied mainly on a reserve requirement policy and other direct measures to control monetary aggregates and domestic credit. In particular, from 1978 to 1981, the fixing of credit ceilings for individual banks was the main instrument of monetary control. But in 1982, it was decided to give banking institutions a freer hand in their own portfolio management. Direct credit control through credit ceilings for individual banks was replaced with an indirect control system under which rediscount and reserve requirement policies could be utilized.

Rediscount Policy

As in other countries, the monetary authorities can raise or lower interest rates on central bank loans to control the credit operations of banking institutions. The changes in the rediscount rates have, however, had only limited influence on the volume of bank credit. With a chronic excess demand for bank credit, banking institutions tend to depend extensively on borrowings from the Bank of Korea. Accordingly, the traditional interest rate policy mechanism of the central bank, through which a change in rediscount rates ultimately affects business demand for bank credit by bringing about a change in the loan rates of banking institutions, has not functioned well in Korea.

The emphasis of rediscount policy has, therefore, been placed on determining rediscount ratios and the availability of funds depending upon the bills presented from loans and rediscounts. The Bank of Korea supplies credits to banking institutions either by rediscounting commercial bills or by extending loans on the collateral of selected financial assets of banks. Commercial bills issued and or accepted by eligible enterprises, or guaranteed by the Korea credit guarantee fund, are eligible for rediscounts for which the Bank of Korea sets the rediscount ratio.

In addition, general loans are available for banks which have participated in preferential financing or have fallen temporarily short of reserve funds. The rate of interest charged for the loans to supplement reserve deficiencies assumes the character of a penalty rate.

Open Market Operations

The Bank of Korea is authorized to buy or sell in the open market securities representing government obligations, other securities fully guaranteed by the Government, and monetary stabilization bonds issued by the bank.

Monetary stabilization bonds, as enacted in the Bank of Korea Act and actually introduced in 1961 as special negotiable obligations of the Bank of Korea, have played an important role in controlling the reserve positions of banking institutions. The Bank of Korea may issue the bonds in the open market under terms and conditions determined by the Monetary Board, the supreme policy-making organ of the Bank of Korea, and may repurchase them before maturity, depending upon monetary and credit conditions. As a practical matter, the bank has issued and repurchased the bonds at rates of discount similar to the interest rates on time deposits of a comparable maturity.

Recently, attempts have been made by the Bank of Korea to create an environment conducive to open market operations in the literal sense. Though limited in size and frequency, the bank now and then auctions the monetary stabilization bonds to the general public, including non-banking financial intermediaries.

Reserve Requirement Policy

Another monetary instrument is the fixing and altering of the minimum reserve requirement ratios banking institutions must maintain against their deposit liabilities. The ratios may not exceed 50 percent, but in a period of pronounced monetary expansion, the Bank of Korea is authorized to impose marginal reserve requirements according to which banking institutions must hold minimum reserves of up to 100 percent of any increase in deposits.

At present minimum reserve requirement ratios range from 3.5 to 11.5 percent, different rates being applied to different forms of deposits. Up to 25 percent of the reserve requirements may be held in cash. In case the reserves of banking institutions fall short of the legal reserve amount, the institutions concerned must pay the Bank of Korea a penalty of 1 percent of the amount of the average deficiency during each half-month period.

Along with the rediscount policy and open-market operations, changes in the reserve requirement ratios are frequently employed when controls on credit volume are called for, and this has now and then brought about relatively high reserve requirement ratios.

High levels of required reserve ratios, however, have reduced the profitability of banks and often were alleged to be one of the causes leading to the chronic failure of banks to maintain required reserves. In many cases when banks were not able to meet the required reserves and had to pay penalties, the Bank of Korea extended them general loans so that they could make up the reserve deficiency, thereby weakening the effectiveness of the instrument. Taking this problem into consideration, the ratios were lowered on several occasions from 1980.

In an effort to reinforce the reserve requirement policy and also to develop a new instrument similar to open market operation instruments, the stabilization account system was introduced in 1967. Under this system, the Bank of Korea is empowered to require banking institutions to deposit a certain amount in the account. The system is identical to a required-reserve system, but it can have an effect similar to open market operations. Funds deposited in the account are not regarded as reserve requirements and interest is paid on them. Because the operation of the account can be conducted selectively and flexibly with attention being paid to the reserve position of each bank, the account has frequently been manipulated since its introduction.

Interest Rate Policy

Prior to December 1988, when interest rates on loans and deposits with long maturities were deregulated, maximum interest rates on each type of loan and deposit of banking institutions were set by monetary authorities. However,

reflecting the excess demand for funds in the financial market, the maximum interest rates actually have tended to be considerably lower than the rates prevailing in the money market, and this in turn has caused the actual interest rates on bank loans and deposits to be at the same levels as the maximum rates.

The interest rate reform in 1965 is a case in point. At that time, the interest rate on time deposits was raised from 15 percent to a high of 30 percent per annum to lay a foundation for maximized mobilization of domestic savings urgently needed to finance economic development projects. The interest rate on general loans, however, was set at 26 percent per annum, four percentage points lower than the rate on deposits with a comparable maturity, in an effort to alleviate the excessive interest burden on enterprises. To prevent the profit conditions of banking institutions from being adversely affected by this so-called "negative margin," the Bank of Korea paid interest on bank deposits with the Bank of Korea from October 1, 1965 to March 31, 1966.

With inflation rates declining in the latter half of the 1960s, interest rates were gradually lowered until the maximum rates on time deposits and general loans were set at 12.6 percent and 15.5 percent per annum, respectively, in August 1972, almost the same level as before the interest reform in 1965. This lowering of interest rates was effected to alleviate the interest burden of businesses and to increase the price competitiveness of export goods.

Since 1978, the market force has become more important in the operation of the interest rate policy. Interest rates, which had remained virtually at the same level since 1975, were raised by four percentage points in 1978 and by six early in 1980 to 24 percent for one-year time deposits and 25 percent for general loans. This was done in an effort to reduce the inflationary pressure aggravated by the second oil shock and to enhance the efficiency of the function of interest rates in resource allocation. As prices stabilized from the latter half of 1980, however, interest rates were lowered again in several steps by as much as 16 percentage points, and at the end of 1982 stood at 8 percent for one-year

Changes in Maximum Interest Rates of Banking Institutions

(Unit: Percent Per Annum)

Effective from	Nov. 8, 1980	Apr. 4, 1981	Nov.30, 1981	Dec.29, 1981	Jan.14, 1982	Mar.29, 1982	June.28, 1982	Jan.23, 1984	Nov.5, 1984	Dec. 5, 1988	Mar.26, 1993
Deposit											
Time Deposits	19.5	19.5	17.4	16.2	15.0	12.6	8.0	9.0	10.0	10.0	8.5
Installment Savings Deposits	19.5	19.5	17.3	16.2	15.0	12.6	8.0	9.0	10.0	10.0	8.5
Savings Deposits	12.3	12.3	14.4	14.4	14.4	12.0	8.0	6.0	6.0	5.0	3.0
Loans											
Loans for Exports	15.0	15.0	15.0	15.0	12.0	11.0	10.0	10.0	10.0	.	.
Discounts on Bills	20.0	20.0	18.0	17.0	16.0	14.0	10.0	10.5	11.5	.	.
Overdrafts	22.0	21.0	19.0	17.0	16.0	14.0	10.0	10.5	11.5	.	.
Term Loans	22.0	22.0	20.0	19.0	18.0	16.0	10.0	10.5	11.5	.	.

Source: Ministry of Finance

time deposits and 10 percent for general loans.

In January 1984, an important beginning toward step-by-step interest rate deregulation was made as a narrow band from 10 to 10.5 percent was introduced to permit banks to charge different rates based on borrowers credit worthiness. As a first step toward enlarging the scope of free markets, the ceiling on inter-bank call rates was also lifted. Reflecting the need for more efficient allocation of funds through market mechanism, interest rates on loans were completely deregulated in December 1988. Meanwhile, liberalization of interest rates on deposits was limited to deposits with long maturities in order to prevent an excessive and abrupt shift in funds among deposits and financial institutions. As of March 1993, interest rates for time deposits and installment savings deposits were at 8.5 percent, while the rate for savings deposits stood at 3.5 percent.

Direct or Selective Credit Controls

An important feature of the Korean monetary policy had been that in addition to the indirect instruments mentioned earlier, monetary authorities were equipped with a wide range of direct or selective credit control instruments. They included the power to fix ceilings on the aggregate outstanding volume of loans, to approve in advance individual loan applications made to banks in excess of a specified amount in periods of pronounced monetary expansion, and to establish general guidelines on the efficient allocation of banking funds.

Fixing credit ceilings for each banking institution was widely used, along with prior approval of bank credit, to repress galloping inflation during and immediately after the Korean War. It has been resorted to frequently even after the interest rate reform in 1965 when the indirect credit control system began to play a major part in attaining the monetary target. During the period from 1977 to 1981, for example, a ceiling was set on the domestic credit expansion of each bank to put a curb on excessive monetary expansion. With the progression of financial liberalization, however, the emphasis of monetary control has shifted from direct credit control to indirect control, using the conventional monetary policy instruments. The change in policy direction has been especially pronounced since the late 1980s.

As for guidelines on the efficient allocation of banking funds, the pertinent regulations prepared by the Monetary Board in 1962 and revised in 1982 encourage banking institutions to operate in a manner more conducive to the development of the national economy. Banking institutions are discouraged from making loans to nonessential sectors such as businesses producing luxuries or those which foster speculation. At the same time, each commercial bank is required to extend at least 35 percent of its loans (80 percent for provincial banks) to small and medium firms.

ECONOMY

Overview of Economic Development

Korea's economy has made an outstanding performance despite unfavorable initial conditions for development, such as limited natural resources, a narrow domestic market, negligible domestic savings and a lack of development experience.

Since Korea launched its first five-year development plan in 1962, real GNP has expanded by an average of more than 8 percent per year. As a result, Korea's GNP grew from $2.3 billion in 1962 to $295 billion in 1992, and per capita GNP increased from a meager $87 to $6,700, all at current prices.

In addition, Korea's industrial structure has been drastically transformed. The manufacturing sector enlarged its share of the GNP from 14.3 percent in 1962 to 27.3 percent in 1992. Korea's commodity trade volume increased from $500 million to $158.4 billion at current prices, and the ratio of domestic savings to GNP grew from 3.3 percent to 34.9 percent during the same period.

The development Korea has experienced is even more remarkable in view of its record up until the early 1960s. For most of its long history, Korea had been economically backward. Few significant industries developed in Korea before independence from Japan. Soon afterward, the economy was devastated by the effects of the 1950-53 war, followed by a long period of recovery.

Thus, as late as 1961, Korea suffered from many of the difficulties facing less developed countries today. In addition to its extreme poverty, population was growing by three percent annually, and unemployment and underemployment were pervasive. Domestic savings were negligible; Korea had no significant exports and depended on imports for both raw materials and most manufactured goods.

Over and above these problems, the country still lacked the critical requirement of leadership as a basis for growth. Throughout the 1950s, the Government failed to provide stability and direction in domestic affairs. Under these conditions it was impossible to mobilize the creative energy of the Korean people to build an economy.

Policy Initiatives of the 1960s

The Start of Growth

Change began in the early 1960s when Korea launched its first five-year plan. At that time, the Government had to decide between two alternative approaches to economic development: an inward-looking strategy based on import substitution or an outward-oriented strategy emphasizing exports and participation in the world economy. Korea chose the latter approach because of its poor natural resource endowment and small domestic market. Given the country's long tradition of isolationism, the decision was remarkable, but it was well suited to the potential of the Korean economy.

The essence of the outward-looking development strategy was to promote exports of light manufactured goods, where Korea had a comparative advantage. As it implemented this strategy, the Government depended heavily on the market mechanism. For example, to mobilize domestic savings the Government allowed commercial banks to raise their interest rates to as much as 26 percent per year. After the Government took that step in 1965, savings deposits in Korean banks nearly doubled annually for three consecutive years. To encourage the inflow of foreign investment, the Government enacted a comprehensive Foreign Capital Promotion Act, whereby it underwrote the risk borne by foreign investors.

As part of its strategy to promote exports, the Government devalued the Korean won by almost 100 percent and replaced the previous multiple exchange rate system with a unified exchange rate. It also provided short-term export financing, allowed tariff rebates on materials imported for re-export use, and simplified customs procedures. These policy changes eliminated the previously existing bias against the export sector, enabling Korean exporters to do business as if they were operating under a free trade regime.

The Government's new development strategy also affected its attitude toward imports. Realizing that it was inefficient for Korea to insist on self-sufficiency in major grains, the Government allowed large-scale imports of such grains for the first time. In addition, it shifted from a "positive list" of import controls to a "negative list" system. This system emphasized the need to prove that items required import protection, rather than showing that they did not. It marked the first step toward liberalizing imports.

The Government's outward-looking strategy did not receive complete acceptance in Korea at first. Many conservative economists felt that it could even endanger national independence through excessive reliance on foreign capital. Indeed, foreign capital made up 83 percent of total Korean investment in 1962, and it was not until late in the decade that Korea raised its exports enough to attain a creditable debt servicing capability. Yet the alternatives were even less acceptable. During the 1950s, Korea had depended on grants-in-aid and concessionary public loans, mainly from the United States, which financed imports and domestic projects. While useful in the short run, it would have been ultimately destructive for Korea to become dependent on such aid for its long-term development.

Policy Results

Results of the outward-looking policy were astonishing. Between 1961 and 1971. Korea's exports rose more than 36 percent per year in real terms. Real GNP grew by an annual average of 8.7 percent. This growth was accompanied by some inflation, but price rises were modest compared to those in the following decade. Wholesale price increases during the 1962-1971 period averaged 12.0 percent per year.

This performance was not due entirely to the Government's policy orientation, because there were at least three other factors working to Korea's advantage. First, Korea was fortunate to have a well-educated population. For centuries, the Korean people have placed a high value on education. By the early 1960s, the literacy rate was close to 80 percent, and today literacy is almost universal in the age group below 50. This heritage of respect for learning has made Korea one of the most literate countries in the world, contributing to labor efficiency.

Second, the outward-looking strategy would not have succeeded without Korean entrepreneurs, who had the energy and dedication to exploit new opportunities. In this respect, Korea benefited from a large pool of highly trained managerial manpower. Many Korean college graduates obtained advanced degrees in developed countries, and the military also was a source of managerial talent and experience. Many retired officers made successful transitions to managerial careers in private business. Third, the international economic environment of the 1960s boosted Korea's development. Throughout the decade, the volume of world trade was expanding by nearly 8 percent annually, the level of trade protectionism was relatively low, and world economic growth had not yet been hampered by serious shortages of oil or other major raw materials.

Shifting Policy Emphasis in the 1970s

In the early 1970s, this positive environment worsened in a number of areas. In 1971, the Nixon Administration reduced the U.S. troop level in Korea by about one-third, a decision seen as the beginning of an eventual withdrawal of all U.S. forces. As a result, the Government resolved to develop the defense industry so that Korea could stand alone if necessary.

Another highly significant development in 1971 was the demise of the Bretton Woods monetary system. For a quarter century, that system had ensured relative stability in exchange rates and international trade. Nevertheless, it was widely considered to encourage protectionism because it dissuaded trading nations from adjusting their payment balances via exchange rate modifications. The advent of a flexible exchange rate system, however, failed to reverse the trend of protectionism. On the contrary, restrictions on trade increased. Many industrial countries were unwilling to undertake the neccessary structural adjustments and imposed trade restrictions instead, worsening fluctuations in exchange rates and payment balances.

The worldwide commodity shortage of 1972-73 and the quadrupling of oil prices in 1973-74 also hit Korea hard. The oil price increases in particular forced Korea to respond quickly to an alarming deterioration in its trade balance. Similarly, significant price rises for imported grains meant further pressure on the balance of payments, supporting the argument that Korea should achieve self-sufficiency in major food grains.

As a result, the Government modified its outward-looking development strategy by emphasizing import substitution. Korea's reaction divided into three categories: restructuring the composition of commodity exports in favor of more sophisticated, higher value-added products; diversifying its trading partners; and increasing domestic agricultural production. As it carried out this shift in strategy, the Government intervened extensively in the functioning of the market mechanism.

To upgrade the composition of its exports, Korea turned to the heavy and chemical industries. Already an important priority of the third five-year plan (1972-76), these industries received greater emphasis because of the changes in the external environment. In 1973, the Government announced its Heavy and Chemical Industry Development Plan, which set forth an accelerated development schedule for technologically sophisticated industries. In order to finance faster development of heavy and chemical industries, the Government established a National Investment Fund. This mobilized public employee pension funds and a substantial portion of private savings in regular banking institutions.

Investments in new industries produced sig-

nificant results, and the country soon developed successful undertakings in electronics, ships and other fields. The ratio of ship exports to total Korean exports, for example, rose from 0.06 percent in 1973 to 16 percent in 1984. However, the Heavy and Chemical Industry Development Plan had a number of negative side effects throughout the economy. Because the projects in question often had long payback periods, the Government set low interest rates for loans from the National Investment Fund. These rates, together with overly optimistic projections of world trade growth, led to excessive investment in several capital intensive industries, such as power generation equipment, heavy machinery, and diesel engines. Many firms accumulated excessive debt loads.

In addition, the sharp demand for low-interest loans swelled the domestic money supply. At the same time, the low interest rate policy made banks less able to offer interest rates high enough to attract savings, impeding the growth of that sector of the economy. Finally, producers of light manufactured goods found themselves losing competitiveness during the 1970s because the Government's emphasis on creating new industries was depriving existing ones of investment funds.

Korea's efforts to diversify its markets were directed to all regions, and achieved considerable success in the Middle East and Europe. The Middle East's share of total commodity exports rose from 1.8 percent in 1973 to 11.7 percent in 1976, and the European percentage went up from 11.8 percent to 17.5 percent. There was, however, little progress in the Latin American and African markets.

An important aspect of market diversification was the growth of the construction industry. Particularly in the Middle East, Korea sold construction services as well as goods. Gross earnings from construction contracts in the region totaled almost $15 billion by the end of 1978, and about 122,000 Koreans were employed on Mideast projects by that time.

Despite the invaluable experience these projects provided for Korean workers and firms, the immediate consequences of the Middle Eastern ventures were a mixed blessing. The departure of a large number of skilled workers pushed up domestic wages, which were already under some pressure because of the growing demand for skilled workers by heavy industry. As a result, the wage differential between skilled and unskilled workers widened during the decade. In addition, the sudden surge in remittances from the Middle East expanded the domestic money supply, providing another stimulus to inflation.

In order to improve the balance of income between urban and rural workers, the Government initiated the self-help Saemaŭl Movement to improve productivity and living standards in rural areas, and adopted a grain price support program. These programs were successful in raising crop yields and rural income and in reducing the imbalance in Korea's standard of living. Nevertheless, the grain price supports were extremely costly to the Government, leading to substantial budget deficits, also contributing to inflation. Price supports encouraged the production of grain at a time when consumption was shifting toward non-grain foods. As a result, the program contributed to an imbalance in the demand and supply of agricultural goods.

Policy shifts in these areas did, however, produce impressive results: GNP growth between 1972 and 1978 averaged 10.8 percent annually, and the annual growth rate from 1976 to 1978 reached 11.2 percent. The share of heavy and chemical industry products in total exports rose from 21.3 percent in 1972 to 34.7 percent in 1978. However, this progress came at the cost of high inflation. Wholesale price rises accelerated to nearly 18 percent each year from 1972 to 1979, compared to about 12 percent between 1962 and 1971. In addition, Korea's industrial structure was distorted by over-investment in heavy industries and under-investment in light industries, and government controls distorted prices and stifled competition. At the same time, real wages were increasing faster than productivity, weakening export competitiveness.

Recession and Reform

By 1979, the Government realized the dangers posed by these imbalances. Accordingly, it began a broad stabilization program designed to control excess liquidity, realign credit priorities, eliminate price distortions, and promote competition. This program had positive effects on prices, but its results were soon negated by a series of external and internal shocks. OPEC's second round of oil price increases nearly doubled Korea's oil import bill in only 12 months, and the resulting worldwide recession limited exports.

The death of President Park Chung Hee in October 1979 caused worsening political and social instability, which reduced investment and consumer spending and weakened the resistance of employers to high wage demands. Further economic damage was inflicted by a bad harvest in 1980. As a result of all these factors, Korea's economic performance in 1980 was the worst in more than 20 years. The economy contracted by 5.2 percent during the year, wholesale prices soared more than 38 percent and the current account deficit grew to $5.3 billion, the highest in Korea's history.

This critical economic situation obviously called for decisive policy responses, and in late 1980, with the establishment of a new Government under the leadership of President Chun Doo Hwan, corrective action began. The reforms launched at that time still are at the center of Korea's economic policies. They focus on three major areas: price stability, continued economic growth, and improved income distribution.

The importance of price stability is obvious, especially in light of Korea's experience during the 1970s. If the country is to allocate its resources efficiently, it must depend upon the operation of the free market rather than on the centralized government decisions of the past. However, such free-market allocation is possible only if inflation is low enough to avoid price distortions.

Korea's need for high growth is obvious as well. During the 1980s, the work force expanded by about 2 percent per annum, bringing about 320,000 new workers into the job market annually. In order to create jobs for these new workers, GNP must grow by 7-8 percent annually. Furthermore, if Korea is to maintain its high defense expenditures and to develop social welfare, its economic growth must continue.

In the field of income distribution, Korea is committed to ensuring that all its people benefit from the nation's growth. In addition, there is a widely perceived need to demonstrate that the free-market approach to economic development is superior to the strategies followed by the Communist regime in the North. To achieve these objectives, the Korean Government has worked to liberalize its external economic policies and promote competition in all sectors of the domestic economy.

External Policy Reforms

On the external front, Korea has dramatically increased the openness of its market. As late as 1979, only 68 percent of all products could be imported without prior government licensing. The Government has steadily increased this import liberalization ratio and in 1989 it reached 94.8 percent.

A similar liberalization program has cut tariff rates across the board. Duties on manufactured goods have shown the sharpest declines, falling from 31.8 percent in 1980 to 12.1 percent in 1989 and to a scheduled 6.2 percent in 1993.

Korea also has been liberalizing its foreign investment regulations, allowing foreign investors greater access to opportunities in Korea and helping to reduce the Korean economy's reliance on borrowing. Since September 1980, foreign investors have been allowed a 100 percent equity share in many industries. In 1984, the Government opened the door for investment further by adopting a "negative list" system of investment approval. The negative list system shortens and simplifies the approval process for projects which are not included on the negative list.

The Government, has annually reduced the number of industries on the negative list, trimming it from 34 percent to 20 percent of all industries in 1988. The manufacturing sector, in particular, is almost completely open to foreign investment with all but 2 percent of the industries liberalized.

Internal Reforms

Korea's external policy changes have been accompanied by reforms in the internal economic structure. The Government's new policies have focused on stabilizing prices and increasing the balance of the economy.

In its quest to maintain price stability, the Government worked to lessen inflationary pressure in all economic sectors. It instituted tight monetary and fiscal policies, bringing annual M2 growth down from 27 percent in 1980 to 8 percent in 1984. The Government also held down spending increases and froze the budget entirely in 1984. This emphasis on reduced spending, along with reforms in the budgeting system, eliminated the expansionary influence the Government had repeatedly exercised on the nation's money supply. Beginning in 1983, the government sector had a deflationary effect on the money supply.

A chronic source of inflation during the 1970s was real estate speculation, which diverted scarce capital to unproductive uses and forced up land prices to exaggerated levels. Since 1980, the Government has fought this economic abuse. A series of controls on real estate transactions has made speculative purchasing easier to spot, as has the computerization of all land ownership records and the improvement of the apartment purchase system. Problems persisted into the late 1980s, however. Meanwhile, the Government attacked cost-push inflationary pressures. Promoting increased business productivity and restraining wage increases, it sought to end the vicious cycle of high prices and high wages. It also kept closer track of demand and supply trends for major agricultural goods which allowed it to import when necessary to avoid price jumps. The success of these efforts was aided by the worldwide decline in commodity prices and by good agricultural harvests.

In 1980, the Government established a formal fair-trade system for the first time in Korea. The

Monopoly Regulation and Fair Trade Act discourages market domination and abuses by existing monopolies and oligopolies. In addition, the fair trade system forbids industrial associations from taking actions that limit competition, and stresses accuracy in advertisement. A related act sets forth subcontraction standards to improve cooperation between large and small businesses, backing up these standards with penalties and other corrective measures. The range of industries covered by fair trade regulations has been steadily expanded over the last ten years, and enforcement has been consistent and strong.

In another measure aimed at attaining economic balance, the Government has promoted the nation's small and medium industries. These industries had suffered from low investment, weak marketing facilities, and outdated technology, preventing them from taking advantage of their ability to thrive on small orders of diverse products. To exploit this growth potential of these industries, the Government has supported their modernization by increasing the availability of loans and by promoting technology transfers and research.

Government measures also have improved the market information network for smaller firms and have streamlined their marketing and distribution channels. By encouraging small firms to serve as parts suppliers to larger firms, the fair trade system has given particular benefit to that sector of the economy. Helped by all these factors, small businesses have taken an increasingly important role in the economy, generating jobs and strengthening the country's competitiveness.

To overcome the inefficiency caused by discriminatory support to specific industries, the Government has revamped its system of economic incentives. The new system gives uniform support to all industrial sectors for manpower training and technology development and through assistance in finding markets and developing sales networks.

Economic Performance in the 1980s

It did not take long for Korea's economy to benefit from these policy reforms. In 1981, the economy bounced back from its contraction the year before to record 6.6 percent growth, and wholesale inflation declined to barely half of its rate in the previous year. The current account deficit shrank $0.7 billion, to $4.6 billion, helped by a $3.5 billion increase in commodity exports, and unemployment fell.

This progress continued throughout the rest of the decade. Real GNP growth from 1982 through 1988 averaged 10.5 percent per year, and inflation in both the wholesale and the consumer sectors was well below 5 percent annually after 1982. The trade account turned to surplus in 1986, and the amount of current account surplus reached 14.2 billion dollars in 1988. During this period the economy generated about 2.8 million new jobs, and the unemployment ratio sank to the unprecedented level of 2.5 percent in 1988.

Economic Structure

The expansion of the Korean economy was accompanied by dramatic changes in its structure. The mining and manufacturing sector grew much faster than the agricultural sector between 1962 and 1988. As a result, the share of agriculture in Korea's GNP dropped from 37.0 percent in 1962 to 10.8 percent in 1988. The agriculture, forestry and fisheries sector accounted for 63.1 percent of all jobs in 1963, but this percentage fell to 19.7 percent in 1988. The mining and manufacturing sector grew to make up 34.4 percent of GNP, up from 16.3 percent in 1963, and jobs in this sector swelled to 28.5 percent of Korean employment from 8.7 percent in 1963.

The makeup of Korea's manufacturing sector also was transformed. During the 1960s and early 1970s, Korea based its growth on light industries making wigs, footwear, textiles and other labor-intensive products. Reflecting this concentration on labor-intensive industries, the por-

External Debt and Assets

(US$100million)

	1990	1991	1992
Total external debt (A)	317	391	426
External assets (B)	253	272	317
(External exchange holdings)	(148)	(137)	(172)
Net external debt (A-B)	64	119	109

tion of total investment going to manufacturing increased slowly, from 19.3 percent in 1954-60 to 19.8 percent in 1961-72. The share allocated to utilities and transportation facilities rose from 23.9 percent to 34.9 percent, however, giving entrepreneurs the advantage of a better infrastructure in producing and distributing their goods.

In the 1970s, the share of investment coming into the manufacturing industries again showed only a slight rise, despite initiation of the drive to develop heavy industries. Manufacturing sector investment edged up to 20.7 percent of the total from 1973-76, but fell to 19.1 percent from 1977-81. These relatively low figures reflect the large increase in overall investment, particularly in services, during the decade. The 1977-81 figure also shows the dampening effects of high inflation and the 1980 recession on business investment. Investment in agriculture, meanwhile, increased to 8.8 percent of the total from 1973-76, but it dropped to 7.5 percent in 1977-81.

Throughout Korea's development, the country's investment has exceeded its domestic savings. As a result, it has relied on foreign savings to make up the difference. Foreign savings equaled about 7 percent of GNP in the first half of the 1960s, rising to 9.3 percent in 1970. Since 1986, the situation has been reversed and Korea now records more savings than investment by 8 percent of GNP. In the early 1960s, Korea obtained much of its foreign savings from United States aid, but such aid was phased out during the decade in favor of loans. Trade credits made up the majority of Korea's capital inflow during the 1960s and 1970s, compensating for chronic trade deficits. The U.S. and Japan provided most of the public and private

lending to Korea during this period.

In more recent years, as Korea gained a favorable credit rating, it has turned increasingly to bank loans, bond issues and other sources of capital. In 1985, such long-term funding exceeded short-term loans for the first time.

An inevitable consequence of Korea's need for foreign savings has been its accumulation of a large foreign debt. At the end of 1985, Korea owed $46.8 billion to creditors in other countries, making it the fourth largest debtor in the world. However, both total and net amounts of foreign debt outstanding began to lessen in 1986 owing to self-sufficiency in financing investment. Reducing foreign debt gradually and accumulating external assets through the promotion of exports on credit and overseas investment, Korea was expected to become a new creditor country very soon.

Foreign investment in Korea made up only a small fraction of capital inflow in the 1960s and 1970s. However, investment liberalization and economic performance attracted a rising level of investment during the 1980s. In 1989, foreign investment totaled $1,090 million on an approval basis.

External Trade

Expansion of Korean exports since 1961 has far exceeded even the most optimistic projections of that time. Between that year and 1992, exports of Korean goods rose from $60 million to $76.6 billion, showing one of the highest growth rates of any country in the world. Similarly, as the country has developed and as its society has become more sophisticated, imports have soared from $400 million in 1961 to $81.8 billion in 1992.

The composition of exports reflects both the light industrial origins of Korea's growth and the effects of the heavy and chemical industry development program. The single largest export category as of 1991 was textiles, maintaining the predominant position it had held for years. Electronic products made up the second largest export category, followed by machinery, automobile, footwear and iron and steel. A particularly promising export item has been automo-

Exports and Imports by Commodity Group

(In million U.S.dollars)

	Exports			Imports		
	1980	1988	1992	1980	1988	1992
Total	17,504.9	60,696.5	76,631.5	22,291.8	51,810.6	81,775.3
Food & Live Animals	1,152.7	2,379.6	2,118.5	1,797.0	2,298.7	4,096.8
Beverage & Tobacco	124.2	131.2	77.4	84.9	87.2	243.4
Crude Materials & Inedibles (except fuels)	331.2	691.6	1,072.6	3,632.3	7,749.0	8,314.9
Mineral Fuels, Lubricants & Related Materials	46.4	584.4	1,742.3	6,659.6	5,986.3	14,636.1
Animal & Vegetable Oils & Fats	12.8	2.8	6.5	118.5	174.7	269.1
Chemicals	754.7	1,878.7	4,454.9	1,800.3	6,271.8	7,667.6
Manufactured Goods Classified by Material	6,251.9	12,645.0	18,490.8	2,449.6	7,970.4	11,898.4
Machinery & Transport Equipment	3,555.4	23,458.1	32,547.4	5,000.5	18,241.8	28,965.7
Miscellaneous Goods	5,229.1	18,729.6	15,883.2	687.3	2,878.9	5,227.4
Not Classifiable	46.5	195.5	237.7	61.8	151.8	455.8

Source: Office of Customs Administration

biles. Korean cars are now sold in Canada, the United States and many other countries.

The United States has for years been Korea's biggest export customer, taking 35.3 percent of the country's exports in 1988. Japan followed with 19.8 percent and the EC accounted for 13.4 percent. Korean industries have continued working to diversify their markets, and have recorded significant sales to Canada, Hong Kong, Australia, Latin America, and the Middle East. The Middle East in particular became a valuable market for Korean commodities during the 1970s, but the decline in oil prices during this decade has cut opportunities for Korean exporters there.

Because of Korea's lack of natural resources, crude oil and raw materials make up well over half of its total imports. In 1988, for example, Korea imported $3.7 billion of oil and $24.2 billion of other raw materials, out of a total import figure of $51.8 billion. Other major import items include transportation equipment, particu-

Composition of Export and Import Markets by Principal Country

(percent)

	Exports			Imports		
	1980	1988	1992	1980	1988	1992
Total	100.0	100.0	100.0	100.0	100.0	100.0
U.S.A.	26.3	35.3	23.6	21.9	24.6	22.4
Japan	17.4	19.8	15.1	26.3	30.7	23.8
Hong Kong	4.7	5.9	7.7	0.4	1.1	1.0
Taiwan	1.2	1.5	3.0	1.4	2.1	1.6
Indonesia	2.1	0.7	2.5	2.2	1.7	2.8
U.K.	3.3	3.2	2.4	1.4	1.8	1.7
Germany	5.0	3.9	3.8	2.9	4.0	4.6
Others	40.0	29.7	41.9	43.5	34.0	42.1

Source: Office of Customs Administration
Note: Customs Clearance Basis

larly ships and aircraft, machinery, and electric and electronic products. The machinery industry is developing rapidly, but Korean firms must still import much of their specialized or highly sophisticated machinery.

Korea also remains a significant consumer of imported grain. From a 1970s average of about $500 million per year, Korea's grain imports soared to $2.1 billion in 1981 alone. Although grain imports slackened after that year, Korea purchased $1.7 billion in imported grain in 1988.

Japan was Korea's most important supplier of imports in 1988 with Japanese goods making up 30.7 percent of the import total. The geographical proximity of Japan has always given its producers an advantage in sales, delivery, and service in the Korean market. The United States, which supplies both raw materials and sophisticated capital goods to Korea, held a 24.6 percent share of the Korean import market in 1988. Other major exporters to Korea are the oil-producing nations of the Middle East and Southeast Asia, as well as Australia, a source of grain and coal. European firms still have a fairly small market preference in Korea, providing only about 11.7 percent of the nation's 1988 imports.

Present Status and Future Prospects

Current Economic Situation

Since Korea launched its economic development in 1962, it has experienced an average growth rate of 8 percent or more per year for the past 30 years. This remarkable performance is attributed mainly to the effective combination of the abundant, high-quality labor supply with cheap foreign capital and technology under government-guided systems.

However, these advantages are diminishing due to rapid changes in the domestic and international environment. Although Korea continues to pursue outward-oriented economic development, the international trading environment has developed unfavorably. Protective measures by the advanced countries have increased in an

Major Economic Indicators (1988-1992)

Year	'88	'89	'90	'91	'92
GNP Growth[1] (%)	12.4	6.8	9.3	8.4	4.7
Private Consumption[1] (%)	9.8	10.9	10.3	9.2	6.4
Equipment Investment[1] (%)	13.0	15.2	18.4	12.8	-0.8
Construction Investment[1] (%)	13.8	18.5	29.1	11.2	-2.6
Consumer Prices[1] (%)	7.2	5.0	9.4	9.3	4.5
Housing Prices[1] (%)	13.2	14.6	21.1	-0.5	-5.0
Land Prices[1] (%)	27.5	32.0	20.6	12.8	-1.3
Nominal Wage Increases[1] (%)	15.5	21.1	18.8	17.5	15.2
Real Wage Increases[1] (%)	7.8	14.6	9.4	7.1	8.5
Current Account (US $ billions)	14.16	5.06	-2.18	-8.73	-4.53
Trade Balance (US $ billions)	11.45	4.60	-2.00	-6.98	-2.15
Export Growth[1] (%)	28.4	2.8	4.2	10.5	6.6
Import Growth[1] (%)	26.3	18.6	13.6	16.7	0.3
M2 Growth[2] (%)	18.8	18.4	21.2	18.6	18.4
Yields of Corporate Bonds[3] (%)	13.7	15.4	18.5	19.0	14.0
Call Rates[3] (%)	11.2	14.2	15.0	17.4	13.5

Note: 1) The figures indicate percentage changes from the end of the previous year

2) Averages

3) As of the end of the year

Source: Economic Planning Board

effort to solve growing deficits in their balance of payments and to protect declining industries. Regionalism, which entails economic cooperation among neighboring countries, has expanded as well. In addition, China and other Asian countries, which have abundant human resources and access to technology from the developed countries, are threatening Korea's market share in every corner of the world.

Furthermore, a wave of market liberalization has extended to the financial, service, and environmental sectors. Domestically, Korea has undergone democratization at a breathtaking pace since the middle of 1987. Thus, the government-led economic management of the past no longer guides the economy. Democratization has ignited strong and violent labor disputes as well as tremendous wage hikes which have far exceeded rises in productivity; For the past 5 years, wage hikes have averaged 18 percent per year. In addition to excessive wage hikes, high financial costs, excessive administrative regulation of business activities, and low social overhead capital investment have been major deadlocks afflicting industrial competitiveness and entrepreneurship. Furthermore, the sudden increase in disposable incomes has induced private overconsumption and speculation.

However, there have been some positive developments. One of the most noticeable improvements was in government social-welfare programs. Faced with Korea's altered socioeconomic environment, the government has expanded these programs, which include regional medical insurance, the national pension plan, a minimum wage, etc.

Nevertheless, overall Korea's entry into the 1990s was crippled by a deterioration of its balance of payments and inflation. The current-account balance, which had shifted from chronic deficits to surpluses after 1986, again reverted a deficit in 1990. Inflation, as measured by the consumer price index, reached nearly 10 percent in the early 1990s.

In light of these serious economic changes, the former Administration adopted an austerity program as of the second half of 1991. This program effectively stabilized prices and reduced the size of the current-account deficit.

Specifically, the consumer price index rose in 1992 by only 4.5 percent, compared to nearly 10 percent in 1991, and 1992's current account deficit was half of l991's.

However, this economic stabilization policy in addition to the combination of the aforementioned factors plunged the Korean economy into a "state of stagnation." The growth of exports to advanced countries, such as the United States and Japan, slowed down and the GNP growth rate fell in 1992 to 4.7 percent, the lowest level since the 1980s. And facility investment fell by 7.0 percent during the second half of the year, compared to the corresponding period the year before. The reluctance of investors to invest due to low profitability and the consequent lack of capital resulted in the bankruptcy of many small and medium-sized firms.

Thus, most Koreans were deeply concerned about the future of the Korean economy and felt the need for drastic reforms to revitalize the economy and nurture its competitiveness.
reviewed at that time, the Government decided

Towards a New Economy

Economic sluggishness, particularly since the third quarter of 1992, made economic revitalization the first priority of the new Administration of Kim Young Sam, who came into office on February 25, 1993. It was apparent that the current economic problems of Korea needed to be approached differently, since the various institutions which had been established under the government-guided systems of the earlier developmental years were no longer contributing to and instead were impeding further development and economic growth. With the realization that these institutions were anachronistic in the light of the new civilian, democratic rule and the rapidly changing international economic environment, a new source or engine of growth needed to be developed for the revitalization of the economy.

Accordingly, President Kim Young Sam proposed the building of a New Economy, as part his overall plan for the creation of a New Korea. In the proposed New Economy, the voluntary participation of individuals and private initiatives supplant government guidance and control. As the first step, the new Administration implemented the 100-Day Plan for the New Economy, a number of short-term measures for the revitalization of the economy. This was followed by the announcement of A Five-Year Plan for the New Economy; this plan elaborated on how the New Economy is to be constructed by economic reforms, which include budgetary, banking, and administrative reforms. In another major step, the President announced the implementation of the real-name financial transaction system on August 12, 1993.

Short-term Measures:
The 100-Day Plan for the New Economy

Revitalization of the Economy;

In light of the fact that the new Administration considered revitalization of the economy as its most important task, the following measures comprised the 100-Day Plan for the New Economy.

1) Investment Boosting
—The Government tried to induce lower interest rates by cutting rediscount rates and other regulated interest rates by pursuing flexible monetary policy
—Extended the maturity of usance bills drawn for the purchase of imports used to manufacture products for exports
—Expanded loans for the purchase of machinery and extended tax credits for facility investments
—Began the early implementation of 1993 fiscal projects.

2) Structural Improvement of Small and Medium-sized Firms
—The government created a US $1.75 billion fund, derived mostly from budgetary savings, in order to help small and medium-sized companies purchase one another's products as well as accelerate their structural adjustement
—Removed the ceiling for the discount of commercial papers issued by small and medium-sized firms, and allowed them to use properties owned by others as collateral for bank loans in order to alleviate the financial difficulties of small and medium-sized firms
—Tried to make institutions more accessible to small and medium - sized firms.

3) Deregulation of the Economy
In an effort to promote private initiative in the business sector, the Government eliminated a variety of governmental regulations and removed obstacles to fair competition. As a result, of the 1,079 business restrictions reviewed at that time, the Government decided to ease or abolish 757 items. Moreover, ad hoc committees continue to review other cases in order to further ease restrictions on business activities.

4) Promotion of Technology Development
The Government established supportive institutions and improved the foreign investors' climate in order to promote technological development. In particular, the scope of land acquisition by foreigners and borrowing privileges of foreign-invested enterprises were expanded.

Such a package of short-term measures for economic recovery would normally shake price stability. However, it was believed that a small increase in the money supply would not have a large impact on price levels because overall demand had contracted and the rate of plant operation was relatively low. Furthermore, the Government tried to minimize price increases through the careful monitoring of the prices of daily necessities. The Government has also continued to strictly enforce regulations curbing speculation through the improvement of land-tax assessments, heavier property taxes for multiple homeowners, and other measures.

Most important, the active participation of all of the economic agents in pain-sharing is necessary to address the current economic problems. President Kim Young Sam emphasized this point in his inaugural speech as well as his special address to the people on March 19. To escape the vicious wage-prices spiral, every economic agent has been urged to take part in the government's efforts to stabilize the economy.

Mid- and Long-term Policy Directions

The ultimate objective of economic policy is

to enhance the quality of life through employment stabilization and higher real incomes. Real income can be increased through price stability and increases in productivity, which can be made possible by enhancing the quality of labor and increasing investments. However, the achievement of these goals also requires the evolution of supporting institutions; reform and advancement of such institutions will guarantee the free activity of companies and the equitable distribution of economic rewards.

What follows are salient features of the core reform measures of the Five-Year Plan for the New Economy;

1) Reform of the Tax System

The problems of the former tax system were a low capital-gains tax, rampant tax evasion, and outright tax exemption for preferred groups which encroached the equity and neutrality of taxation. Therefore, the reform of the tax system is aimed at enhancing the equity of the tax burden, reducing distortions in resource allocation and increasing work incentives. Such reforms will include the introduction of a comprehensive taxation of income, the reinforcement of the tax administration and the minimization of tax exemptions. The necessary increase in government expenditures will be funded by a higher per capita tax rate, which will be raised from 19.4 percent in '92 to 22-23 percent in '98.

2) Reform of Government Expenditure

First, the new Administration will reduce the portion of personnel costs, grants to local governments, and defense spending, which currently account for more than two-thirds of the government budget. The savings from the reduction in the aforementioned expenditure will be allocated to priority sectors for future nation-building.

Second, it will expand the size of public finance in order to reinforce the social infrastructure and to meet the basic needs of the people such as housing and environmental needs among others.

Third, it intends to streamline or merge overlapping accounts as well as change the budgetary structure in order to enhance the self-regulation and flexibility of various government agencies. In order to pursue national objectives consistently, the annual fiscal guidelines will be transformed into mid-term fiscal programs.

3) Reforms of the Financial Sector

First, the Government will ease regulations in the financial sector in order to nurture its competitiveness. Specifically, it will allow more freedom in the selection of the heads of commercial banks as well as phase out policy loans for commercial banks.

Second, it will gradually introduce an indirect monetary control policy as well as improve existing financial structures by developing a credit-rating and accounting system. Furthermore, it will induce specialization and enhancement of financial institutions and strengthen the supervisory function of financial institutions for the sound and stable management of assets.

Third, it will establish the necessary framework for real-name usage in financial transactions.

4) Reforms of Administrative Regulations

Regulations which impede free and innovative economic activities such as restrictions regarding new entry into certain industries, the establishment of enterprises, production & technology and prices should be alleviated. On the other hand, regulations regarding the environment and health care have been and will continue to be adjusted and rationalized. Administrative procedures and practices will also be improved.

Some factors underlying the recent economic sluggishness and fall in exports since the third quarter of 1992 are the diminishing will to economize and an overly narrow pursuit of individual and group interests. Reforms of the economic consciousness are based on the recognition that individual self-interest must be pursued within the context of community membership in order to promote new economic development. Although every economic agent is urged to participate in these movements, individuals must continue to take the initiative.

The tasks which must be performed during the current planning period can be categorized as follows;

1) Enhancing Growth Potential
— Strategy for industrial development;

The industrial development strategy will focus primarily on the enhancement of growth potential through the continuous improvement of the competitiveness of the manufacturing industry. It will emphasize the transformation of the current industrial structure into a technology- and information-intensive one. An energy and resource development strategy that includes securing a stable source of energy and natural resources, developing alternative energy sources and raising the efficiency of energy usage will be established. To reinforce the structural integrity of the export industry, the industrial development strategy will cover not only the improvement of the institutions of the trust-guarantee and insurance system of exporters but also the simplification of export procedures. In addition, there will be an increased involvement by the private sector in making industrial policy and development strategy decisions.

— Strategy for technology development

The Government plans to promote the development of necessary industrial technology as well as up-to-date technology. To make the environment favorable for technology development, it will continue to expand investment in research and development from 2.1 percent in '92 to 3-4 percent in '98 as well as strengthen financial support for technology development. Furthermore, it will create incentives for research and promote cooperative research efforts among the industrial sector, universities and research institutes.

— Fostering small-and medium-sized firms

The engine of future industrial development is to be found in the prosperity of small and medium-sized firms. Thus, the enhancing of growth potential will include the full-scale promotion of small and medium-sized firms. The Government intends to promote not only closer links between large enterprises and parts suppliers (i. e., small and medium-sized firms), but also cooperative links and interactions among small and medium-sized firms. Furthermore, it will help their internationalization by supporting the development of joint brands and designs as well as technology transfers from advanced small and medium-sized companies. It will also introduce various incentives for local small and medium-sized firms that reflect the special characteristics of their locality. In addition, the policy with regard to the fostering of small and medium-sized firms will primarily focus on enhancing "autonomy and competition" rather than implementing the "protection and physical incentives" of past authoritarian regimes.

— Strategy for developing the information industry

The Government plans to upgrade the strategic information industry to the level of the advanced countries by 2001 and make all industries information-oriented. In this light, core strategic plans will be established and implemented in information- machinery, software and data-communication industries. To some extent, the Government is trying to augment domestic demand in the information industry through the public sector's purchasing of domestically-produced computers and software. In particular, it will give financial assistance and tax credits to the infant data-processing industry. Furthermore, it plans to enact "the fundamental law for the promotion of information activities," which includes government investment, standardization of related industries and the protection of intellectual property rights.

— Improvement of vocational training system

The Government will increase the number of industrial high schools and encourage large companies to build more vocational training centers. In addition, it intends to procure qualified teachers and create retraining programs for teachers in other fields. The public training center will train women and the elderly as well as facilitate occupational changes.

— Improvement of the land-use system

Land prices in Korea, despite current downward stabilizing trends, are still high. This is attributed mainly to real-estate speculation and regulations restricting land utilization. Access to land for industrial and housing sites must and will be facilitated. Specifically, the Government will make it easier to develop marginal farmlands and useless forests. In addition, supplementary anti-speculation measures will be implemented in order to curb land price hikes.

— Expansion of social overhead capital

This scheme will lower the distribution costs of firms and improve imbalances in regional development. Specifically, further investment will be made on roads, railways, harbors and airports. However, these will proceed in order of priority to guarantee links between the various means of transportation. The Government is planning to raise funds for facility investments by introducing private capital and investing jointly with the beneficiaries of these investments.

— Redefinition of laborer and employer relations

In light of the rapidly-changing economic realities, the Government will revise labor-related statutes. The revisions will target working conditions such as wages and working hours, the activities of labor unions and the dispute-resolution system. The Government will provide the foundation for establishing rational institutions and practices between laborers and employers through a joint commission composed of laborers and employers. Furthermore, it will provide welfare funds for workers, introduce an employment- insurance program by 1995 and strengthen prevention of and compensation for industrial disasters.

— Establishment of fair competition and managerial innovation

Most Korean firms face fierce competition in the domestic and international environment as internationalization advances. Thus, the Government is in the process of creating an institutional framework in order to make firm management and industrial organizations more efficient.

First, it will try to reduce the concentration of economic power and precipitate competition by regulating abuses of dominant large enterprises, multi-national firms and monopolistic importers. Second, it will transform the managerial structure of firms by reducing excessive ownership concentration, enlarging the autonomy of professional managers and improving the financial independence of firms. Furthermore, it will develop various institutions to ensure fair competition.

— Implementation of a new agricultural policy

The Government will rearrange the priorities of fiscal investments for structural improvement in rural areas. Investments in production facilities for "Agricultural Promotion Areas," mechanization and automation of farming, training in modern farming techniques and technological innovations for high-quality products will be preferred. In addition, it will also develop income sources such as agricultural-product-processing plants and rural sightseeing areas. Farmers and their associations will also play an instrumental role in implementing the new agricultural policy.

2) Strengthening Internationalization

— Adjusting to changes in the international economic environment

The Government is trying to advance the economic management system in order to prepare for membership in the Organization of Economic Cooperation and Development, a promising institution for economic cooperation among advanced countries. To open the domestic market effectively, the Government will formulate a plan for allowing foreign investments as well as repeal most of the remaining import-curbing measures regarding, for the most part, agricultural products. Furthermore, it will continue to make every effort to actively deal with protectionism and regionalism by increasing cooperative relations with advanced countries such as the United States, the European countries and Japan, etc.

—Enhancement of economic interaction and cooperation between South and North Korea

The Government will adhere to a consistent policy regarding economic interaction and cooperation between the South and the North under the unification policy, which is based on national consensus. The first step is to increase commodity exchanges between the two Koreas through the opening of a direct trade route as well as an economic counseling office in P'anmunjŏm. In addition, economic cooperative projects will be launched according to their feasibility and importance. The Government

Macroeconomic Projections during the Five-Year New Economic Plan Period

	'91	'92	'93	'94	'95	'96	'97	'98	'93-'98
GNP growth,%	8.4	4.7	6.0	7.1	7.2	7.1	7.0	7.0	6.9
Per capita GNP, US$	6,518	6,749	7,306	8,196	9,339	10,716	12,305	14,076	14,076[2]
Increase in producer prices,%	4.7	2.2	1.8	1.8	1.7	1.6	1.5	1.4	1.6
Increase in consumer prices,%	9.3	6.2	4.9	4.3	3.7	3.6	3.2	2.9	3.7
Increase in GNP deflator,%	11.2	6.3	5.3	5.3`	4.8	4.5	4.1	3.8	4.6
Current account balance	-8.7	-4.6	-1.4	0	0.9	2.1	3.7	5.3	5.3[2]
(US$ billions)									
Exports[1] (US$ billions)	69.6	75.1	82.3	82.3	99.3	110.1	122.6	136.3	136.3[2]
Rate of increase,%	(10.2)	(7.9)	(9.5)	(9.5)	(10.2)	(10.9)	(11.3)	(11.2)	(10.4)
Imports (US$ billions)	76.6	77.3	81.3	81.3	95.8	105.3	116.1	128.1	128.1[2]
Rate of increase, %	(17.5)	(1.0)	(5.1)	(5.1)	(9.3)	(9.9)	(10.2)	(10.3)	(8.8)

Note. 1) On a balance-of-payments basis

　　　2) In terms of 1998 current market prices

Source: Economic Planning Board

intends to cooperate in the fields of science, technology, health and environment. Furthermore, it is confident that such efforts can expand to become joint economic efforts in the international community.

3) Enhancing the Living Environment
—Easing housing shortages

The Government will stabilize housing prices and supply on average 500,000 to 600,000 housing units per year from 1992 to 1998, thereby increasing the rate of house-ownership to 90 percent by 1998. The public sector will continue to provide housing mainly to the urban poor, who face serious housing shortages in metropolitan areas. Therefore, it will support housing development for the urban poor and improve their financial status by facilitating their access to the public housing fund.

—Improving the environment

The Government, in light of the national desire for a clean environment, will harmonize economic growth and environmental protection. First, it will induce the industrial sector to lower its energy consumption and more carefully evaluate the environmental impacts of potential development projects. Second, it will not only

promote environmentally-clean technology development, but also the waste-processing and recycling industry. Third, it will expand investments in environmental infrastructure and contamination-prevention facilities. The Government will continue to actively and willingly conform to the worldwide environmental conservation trends in order to contribute to the preservation of the global environment.

—Alleviating metropolitan traffic congestion

The Government will stress the expansion of public transportation, such as subways and buses, in order to ease the current traffic congestion in metropolitan areas. In addition to considerable investments in transportation facilities, it will attempt to limit demand for cars by encouraging car pooling and legally requiring car-owners to maintain parking spaces.

—Improving social welfare

The Government will redefine the existing categories of insurance: the National Pension Program, medical insurance and industrial- disaster insurance, because of the need for greater coverage. It will expand the coverage of the National Pension Program; the plan of its scope

Social Indicators under the Five-Year New Economic Plan

	1990	1992	1993	1998
Population (1,000 persons)	42,869	43,663	44,056	46,033
(Growth) (%)	(0.93)	(0.91)	(0.90)	(0.86)
Life expectancy (years)	71.3	71.9	72.2	73.9
Population per doctor	1,006	896	855	701
Population per bed	429	387	371	310
Housing supply (%)	72.1	76.0	78.5	89.9
Piped water supply (%)	78.4	80.6	81.7	87.0
LNG supply (1,000ton)	2,316	3,481	4,255	8,208
Farm household income (10,000 won, per month)		120.9	133.7	224.7
Household acreage (ha)		1.26	1.29	1.44
Road pavement (%)	71.5	80.8	87.0	100.0
Telephone supply (per population of 100)	31.0	80.8	87.0	100.0
Expressway (km)	1,551	1,600	1,602	2,062
Railway (km)	6,435	6,496	6,507	7,050
Subway (km)	144	147	156	432

Source: Economic Planning Board

expansion will be prepared to include farmers and fishermen by 1994. The current medical insurance system will be improved to better suit new welfare needs. Furthermore, it will encourage firms to expand child day-care facilities and participate in welfare projects.

—Protection of consumers and improvement of the distribution network

The Government will extend the consumers' sovereignty by providing information about commodities and services. It also strives to prevent and compensate for consumer injury caused by the usage of goods. It will promote the freedom of enterprises through the easing of regulations on investments and the expansion of financial support in the distribution sector. Furthermore, the Government intends to continue to reinforce distribution networks in order to promote price stability and industrial competitiveness as well as improve freight distribution and information for circulating goods.

The Real Name Financial Transaction System

On August 12, 1993, the President took a decisive step toward revitalizing the economy and eliminating corruption by announcing the implementation of the long-anticipated real-name financial transaction system. In the past, it had been possible to open accounts and conduct business transactions under false names, directly and indirectly fostering institutionalized corruption and illegal financial dealings. Deeming this reform as the most important in the creation of a New Korea, the President announced this action in a Presidential Emergency Order, stating that the real-name system was essential for cutting the dark link between politics and business.

All accounts under false names were to be switched to real- name accounts within the following two months. however, it was decided that the composite income tax on profits from financial transactions would not be levied until the computer system of the Office of the National Taxation Administration was ready, and furthermore, taxation on revenues accruing from stock dealings would not be enforced until the end of President Kim's five-year term, in order to lessen the impact this reform would have on the stock market. While acknowledging that this and other reforms would be accompanied by initial pains and hardship, the President stated that this change was done with popular consensus and would lead to a healthier economy and a more prosperous society-the New Korea envisioned by him.

INDUSTRY

Overview

Since the launching of the First Five-Year Economic Development Plan in 1962, the Korean economy has maintained almost 9 percent of GNP growth rate amually annually. This rapid growth was accompanied by structural transformation from subsistence agriculture to modern manufacturing. Given the limited size of the domestic market, planners found it necessary to adopt an export-oriented industrialization strategy. Foreign capital in Korea played the dual function of financing import requirements for rapid industrialization and of supplementing the scant domestic capital available for investment. After nearly a quarter of a century of rapid development, however, the Korean economy achieved self-reliance in capital formation and balance of payments. With the formulation and implementation of the First Five-Year Economic Development Plan, focused and vigorous attention was given to industrialization. The goal established for the first plan was "a reversal of the decelerating trend in growth of the economy over the past several years." The plan focused on laying a foundation for industrialization, and it seems to have had a positive effect in initiating and accelerating structural readjustment of the country's industry. Figure 1 shows the changes in the industrial structure since 1966.

The share of primary industries in the total industrial structure decreased from 34.8 percent in 1966 to 23.5 percent in 1976 and to 7.6 percent in 1992. On the other hand, the share of secondary industries increased from 20.5 percent in 1966 to 27.7 percent in 1992. Tertiary industries also held their ground, with a share of 64.7 percent in 1992 compared with the 44.7 percent recorded in 1966 and 48.1 percent in 1976.

Structural change is also reflected in the composition of export commodities. Exports of manufactured goods comprised 62.4 percent of the total in 1966 and thereafter the portion increased substantially, to 86.0 percent in 1971, 89.8 percent in 1976, and 95.7 percent in 1992. Heavy and chemical product exports made rapid

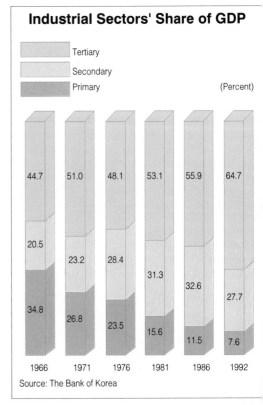

Industrial Sectors' Share of GDP

Tertiary
Secondary
Primary   (Percent)

Year	Tertiary	Secondary	Primary
1966	44.7	20.5	34.8
1971	51.0	23.2	26.8
1976	48.1	28.4	23.5
1981	53.1	31.3	15.6
1986	55.9	32.6	11.5
1992	64.7	27.7	7.6

Source: The Bank of Korea

strides to occupy a larger and larger share of export composition. The portion of heavy and chemical products in the export mix increased to 62.8 in 1992 from 15.3 percent in 1966, primarily as a result of increases in production of steel, electronics, machinery and transport equipment, and chemicals. Under the policy of economic development planning aimed at modernization and attainment of a self-supporting economy, the first (1962-66), second (1967-71), third (1972-76), fourth (1977-81), fifth (1982-86) and sixth (1987-91) five-year plans were successfully implemented.

For the first time in two decades, however, a negative GNP growth rate of minus 5.7 percent was recorded in 1980. This sudden drop can be attributed to a number of causes, including global stagnation caused by increasing oil prices, high interest rates, increased protectionism imposed by developed countries on imports of Korean goods, a poor domestic agricultural crop, and a rising won-U.S. dollar exchange rate.

After 1980, the Korean economy recovered its vitality; from 1980 to 1991 the GNP increased 8.4 percent annually. The sixth five-year plan (1987-1991) was revised in 1988 because economic performance during 1987, the first year of the five-year plan, far exceeded the original projection, and because political democratization and the subsequent demand voiced by different segments of society made the adjustment of macroeconomic management and the priorities of economic policy inevitable. The sixth five-year plan was carried out successfully and Korea embarked on new five-year plan, looking forward to the 21st century.

In Korea, economic prosperity is not far off. This country is one of the best examples that economic development can be accomplished without sacrificing national defense or social stability. The country has grown rapidly and will continue to progress steadily.

Manufacturing

Steel Industry

Prior to the 1970s, the Korean steel industry was composed of small ironmaking and rolling facilities equipped primarily with electric-arc furnaces. Until 1972, the steel industry suffered not only from structural imbalance due to inadequate ironmaking and steelmaking capacity, but also from small-scale production facilities and poor technology. The self-sufficiency rate in steel in Korea continued at a low 23 percent.

In 1973, the first stage construction of an integrated steel mill, Pohang Iron & Steel Co., Ltd. (POSCO), was completed with an annual capacity of 1.03 million tons of crude steel, and other expansion soon followed. In 1992, Korea's annual crude steel production capacity was 31.5 million tons, consisting of 9.1 million tons at POSCO's Pohang works, 11.4 million tons at the company's new Kwangyang works and 11.0 million tons at electronic-arc furnaces.

Korea's steel production continues to increase steadily with the growth of steel-consuming industries. Total crude steel production

Korea's Share of World Steel Production

(Crude steel, million tons)

	World Total	Korea	Percent
1970	595.4	0.5	0.1
1980	716.4	8.6	1.2
1991	734.4	26.1	3.6
1992	714.0	28.1	3.9

Output of Finished Steel Products

(million tons)

	'80	'90	'91	'92	Annual average Increase rate (1980-1992)
Long Products	3.2	8.7	10.1	11.4	11.2
Flat Porducts	4.5	13.2	14.9	18.0	12.2
Total	7.8	22.9	25.3	29.7	11.8

Steel Supply & Demand Forecast (Crude Steel)

(million tons)

	'89	'90	'91	'92
Total Demand	26.0	29.1	34.2	34.0
Production	21.9	23.1	26.1	28.1
Shortage	4.1	6.0	8.1	5.9

in 1992 was 27.8 million tons, representing 3.8 percent of the total world steel production.

At the same time, the Korean steel industry has shown impressive progress in incorporating new technology into the steel making process and in producing finished products. The continuous casting ratio in the production of semi-finished products has increased to a level of 96.4 percent. Finished products output in 1992 was 29.7 million tons, resulting in an average annual increase of 11.8 percent since 1980. The portion of flat products, particularly cold-rolled products, also has increased significantly.

The Korean domestic steel demand increased rapidly during the 1980s, reflecting the rapid growth of steel-consuming industries such as automobile production, electronics, industrial machinery, and ship-building. Also contributing to demands for steel in the 1980s was the special need in the construction of large sporting arenas for the Asian Games in 1986, and the 1988 Seoul Olympics.

Total steel consumption for 1992 was 25.2 million tons, reflecting an average annual increase of 11.6 percent since 1980. Per capita crude steel consumption in 1992 was 580kg, a level higher than the 500kg average per capita consumption of other industrialized countries.

As the Korean economy continues to expand and becomes more highly sophisticated in structure, it is expected that steel consuming industries will grow rapidly, and that Korean total demand will reach 34.3 million tons in 1993.

Nonferrous Metals

Despite its importance as a supplier of basic materials to related industries, the nonferrous metals industry remained largely undeveloped until the mid-1960s. Since then, a notable expansion of production facilities has been achieved in this sector through the implementation of six five-year economic development plans. Led by the rapid increase in demand resulting from development of heavy and chemical industries, Korea has become a producer of electrolytic copper, zinc, lead and aluminum ingots. At the end of 1992, Korea's production of electrolytic copper reached 207,000 tons, zinc ingots 254,000 tons, and lead 84,000 tons.

Production capacity has also increased in recent years. Production capacity of electrolytic copper reached 225,000 tons per year at the end of 1992. Production capacity of zinc ingots reached 300,000 tons at the end of 1992. Young Poong Co., Ltd. expanded its production capacity to 100,000 tpy and Korea Zinc Co., Ltd. expanded its production capacity to 200,000 tpy. Production capacity of lead reached 156,000 tpy in 1992. The Korea Zinc Co., Ltd., installed new lead smelting facilities with 80,000 tpy in 1992.

Demand for nonferrous metals also continues to increase, in line with production increases in related industries. From 1982 to 1992, domestic demand for electrolytic copper increased at an average annual rate of about 13.4 percent, while production increased at a rate of 8.0 percent. As a result, in 1992, demand was 366,000 tons while production amounted to only 207,000 tons or only 56.5 percent of demand. In zinc, supply met demand, as demand for zinc ingots was 257,000 tons while production was 254,000 tons. Between 1973 and 1990, aluminum ingots

Production Capacity and Demand of Four Major Nonferrous Metals (1992)

(1,000 tons)

	Annual Capacity	Domestic Demand
Electrolytic Copper	225	366
Aluminum Ingots	-	390
Zinc Ingots	300	317
Lead Ingots	156	181

Demand and Supply of Four Major Nonferrous Metals (1992)

(1,000 tons)

		Electrolytic Copper	Aluminum Ingots	Zinc Ingots	Lead Ingots
Demand		366	390	317	181
	Domestic Demand	352	377	257	173
	Export	14	13	60	8
Supply		366	390	317	181
	Production	207	-	254	84
	Import	159	390	63	97

were produced exclusively by Aluminum of Korea Ltd., which had an annual capacity of 17,500 tons. However, Aluminum of Korea Ltd. was forced to interrupt production in March, 1990 because of high costs. Demand for aluminum increased rapidly at an annual average rate of about 17.8 percent from 1982 to 1992. Demand for lead ingots in 1992 reached 173,000 tons, while domestic demand increased at an annual average rate of about 16.1 percent from 1982 to 1992. The demand for lead ingots is expected to continue to grow in line with an expanding automobile industry.

The industry's heavy dependence on imported raw materials has pushed up production costs, and supplies of raw materials are not stable. It is hoped that domestic resources can be exploited more fully, and that imports of raw materials can be handled smoothly through economic cooperation with resource-rich countries. In addition, the industry must pay special attention to pollution control problems in line with the present worldwide movement toward environmental protectionism and energy conservation.

Machinery Industry

Industrial Machinery

A dull national economy caused production of industrial machinery in Korea to decrease 8.2 percent in 1992, to 8,368 billion won. Exports of industrial machinery, meanwhile, increased 3.2 percent, to 1,894 millionU.S.dollars. The following chart tracks Korean exports of industrial machinery.

The basic role of the industrial machinery industry is to supply the production facilities in every industry; therefore the industrial machinery industry plays an important role in determining national competitiveness. However, Korea imports about 50 percent of all its industrial machinery; this low self-sufficiency in industrial machinery is the main reason for Korea's trade deficit. In this sector, the trade deficit in 1992 amounted to about 10 billion U.S dollars.

The Government will implement the following policies to promote competitiveness in the industrial machinery industry. First, the localization of machinery will be increased by emphasizing the local production of parts and components to decrease the trade deficit. Second, focus will be placed on technological development to meet new demands in manufacturing facilities, such as the environment and automation sectors. Third, the long-term need to develop capital goods will be emphasized.

Machine Tools

The production of Korean machine tools has increased rapidly as a result of the expansion of domestic markets. Active capital investment as well as the positive implementation of economic development plans have provided the machine tool industry with wider domestic markets and a solid foundation for further growth.

Demand for machine tools soared during the past decade because many machine tool users modernized their facilities and increased productivity following the Government's declaration of support for heavy and chemical industrialization in 1973. Accordingly, demand for machine tools rose an average 26.1 percent per annum from 1975 to 1992.

Though domestic demand has increased considerably, the quality of locally produced tools has remained inferior to those produced by advanced countries. Local production also is limited both in size and variety. As a result,

Export of Industrial Machinery

(In million u.s. dollars)

	1975	1980	1988	1992
Exports of industrial machinery	77	369	1,204	1,894
Total exports of machinery	275	1,413	8,191	12,027
Total exports	5,427	17,505	60,696	76,632

approximately 67.3 percent of the demand for machine tools has so far been met by imports.

With the development of related industries, the domestic demand for machine tools recently has shown a pattern of rapid change, moving from low to high-grade products and from general to specialty machine tools. The demand for N.C. (numerical control) machine tools and transfer machine tools has increased rapidly as businesses are increasingly turning to them to enhance precision and productivity.

Domestic production also has shown an upward trend with diversification growing at an annual average rate of 27.1 percent from 1975 to 1992. The major domestic products are general-purpose machinery and low-grade N.C. machines such as lathes, boring machines, milling machines, planes, grinding machines, N.C. milling machines and machining centers.

Since N.C. lathes were first developed on a trial basis by the Whacheon Machinery Works Co. in 1976, machining centers, N.C. milling machines, laser processing machines and transfer machines have been developed by the Daewoo Heavy Industries Co., the Se-il Co., the Hyundai Motor Co., and a number of other firms.

Taking into account the rapid economic development of Korea and positive government support, prospects for the machinery industry throughout this decade are quite favorable. The domestic sufficiency ratio for machine tools, which was 58.7 percent in 1992, is projected to reach nearly 68.0 percent in 1996. The export ratio in this industry should also increase from 14.6 percent in 1991 to 24.0 percent in 1996.

Electronics

Korea's electronics industry has developed rapidly, from the simple assembly of transistor radios in the early 1960s, to the current sophisticated fabrication of state-of-the-art memory chips.

Korean product lines already include even more sophisticated consumer products such as digital televisions, videotext, LCD televisions, 45-inch color televisions, video cameras, projection TVs, and laser disc players. As a result of a steady emphasis upon research and development, Korea's electronics industry has narrowed the gap in technological expertise with advanced countries to a relatively narrow margin.

In 1992, Korea became one of the five largest electronics producing nations. Production exceeded U.S. $33 billion, while total exports topped U.S. $20 billion. As a result, the electronics industry emerged as the largest export sector in Korea. While the major export items now are consumer electronics with modest levels of technology, such as televisions and VCRs, high-tech products including computers and telecommunications equipment are increasingly important.

Despite its rapid progress, the Korean electronics industry faces serious challenges due to

Supply and Demand in Electronics Induatry

(Unit: million in U.S.$)

		1970	1980	1992	Annual average increase rate(%)		
					'70 - '80	'80 - '92	'70 - '92
Demand	Export	55	1,964	20,682	43.2	21.7	30.9
	Domestic Demand	133	2,154	28,589	33.0	24.0	27.6
	Total	188	4,118	49,271	36.8	23.0	28.8
Supply	Production	106	2,852	37,621	39.0	24.0	30.6
	Imports	82	1,266	11,650	33.3	20.3	25.3

Source: Electronic Industries Association of Korea

Korea is now a leading producer of semiconductors.

growing protectionism abroad coupled with decreasing profitability. A substantial number of smaller firms were forced to cut back their operations after 1989 or face bankruptcy. This was due to a decline in export profitability generated by the appreciation of the won against the dollar by more than 15 percent and the domestic cost-push factor created by widespread labor disputes and sharp wage hikes.

With minimal natural resources and a comparatively small domestic market, focus has long been on the electronics industry as the domestic sector with the greatest potential for helping Korea join the ranks of the advanced countries. The abundance of skilled and highly educated workers is one of the nation's primary assets and has contributed greatly to the industry's development.

Transition from Consumer Appliances to Industrial Equipment

The Korean electronics industry is moving quickly from an emphasis upon consumer appliances to higher value-added industrial equipment. Of the U.S.$33.6 billion in production in

1992, about U.S.$7.3 billion is attributable to industrial electronics, a 12 percent increase over the previous year. Also noteworthy was the successful growth of the parts and components sector. State-of-the-art semiconductors, including 1M D-RAMs and 4M D-RAMs, became popular both at home and abroad due to their high quality.

Facing the declining competitiveness of consumer electronics, Korean manufacturers are putting emphasis upon upgrading quality and developing higher value added consumer electronics items such as CDPs, camcorders, large size CTVs, 4HD hi-fi VCRs, etc.

In production capacity, Korea ranks second in the world for VCRs, microwave ovens, facsimiles and videocassette tapes, and third for color televisions and telephone sets.

Diversifying Suppliers and Buyers

The Government's effort to diversify both the suppliers and customers of the Korean electronics industry is paying off. The new trend was strengthened also by the industry's own effort to reduce its dependence on Japanese suppliers and

U.S. buyers. Due to sluggish demand, exports to the US and Japan showed minimal increase while exports to the developing countries such as Southeast Asia, the Middle East and Latin America increased rapidly.

In 1992, electronic parts and components accounted for 50.7 percent of the total electronics exports, followed by consumer electronics at 28.8 percent and industrial equipment at 20.4 percent.

Consumer Electronics

In the 1970s, the Korean consumer electronics industry maintained annual growth rates that averaged 47.2 percent in terms of product value. Since the beginning of the 1980s, however, the industry has experienced somewhat slower growth because of a sluggish world economy and protectionist tendencies in developed countries. In response, the industry has shifted from simple assembly and quantitative growth toward qualitative growth through the domestic production of parts and materials and indigenous technological development.

With its continuous growth throughout the 1970s and 1980s, Korea's consumer electronics industry has become significant, both domestically and internationally, and is expected to grow as an export-leading industry.

However, many problems remain to be solved. These include underdevelopment of the associated parts and materials industries, growing protectionism in world trade, Korea's small domestic market and a weakening of Korea's international price competitiveness due to rising wages and the appreciation of the won.

Industrial Electronics

The current technological level of the Korean industrial electronics industry remains low in comparison with the consumer electronics industry. However, as the industrial structure develops, so will the industrial electronics industry. Since the middle of the 1980s, Korean electronic firms have accelerated their efforts to move toward high-tech computers, telecommunications, and factory automation areas. Since 1981, the industry has grown at an annual rate of 34 percent and its share of the total electron-

ics industry has grown from 13 percent in 1981 to 19.8 percent in 1992.

The most prominent success is found in the computer industry. Despite its short span, Korea's computer industry has grown remarkably, sparked by soaring PC exports. Since 1989, however, due to fierce price competition in the export market, the Korean PC industry has lost ground in the export market and faces

Structural adjustment

Total telecommunication equipment production has been growing steadily, encouraged by the Government's ambitious telecommunications policy and continued R&D investment by large business groups. The upgrading of the TDX-1, a locally developed digital public switching system, was pursued in order to open the era of an integrated services digital network (ISDN).

Other important industrial electronics include copiers, facsimiles, calculators, and radio communications equipment. Home, office and factory automation equipment also is an important aspect of the country's move towards an automated society. Factory automation and robotics, in particular, have become an increasingly important area for most business conglomerates. Industrial robots are used widely for production of virtually all electronics items from parts and components to consumer products such as VCRs.

Precision Machinery and Instruments

The precision machinery industry is both labor and technology intensive. It is high in value added per employee, consuming small energy and a comparatively small outlay of capital. These characteristics combine to make the industry a likely candidate for success in developing countries, where skilled labor is plentiful. As such, its consistent development as a strategic export industry is expected.

In 1992, domestic production supplied 50.1 percent of total demand. Imports increased from $12 million in 1970 to $465 million in 1980 and $2,292 million in 1992. The largest share of the imports (73.1 percent) were measuring apparatus and medical appliances. Clocks and watches accounted for 7.8 percent of the imports and optical instruments 17.4 percent.

As Korean clock, watch, optical lens and spectacles technologies have reached the international level, these products have been well received in overseas markets with 36.0 percent of the total production exported. Such items account for 59.4 percent of the total production of the entire precision machine industry and 47.5 percent of its total exports.

World demand for such products is expected to increase at the same time that this and other labor-intensive industries are declining in advanced countries. Exports of watches, clocks and binoculars have increased annually by 15 percent and measuring apparatus by 22 percent. Accordingly, the Korean precision machinery industry has bright prospects and is expected to develop as a major export industry.

Many of these products are purchased at home by people with high living standards, and as Korea's per capita income increases, demand for these products should continue to expand. Production is expected to increase at 25 percent

Motor Vehicle Production

(1,000 tons)

Year	Total(unit)	Passenger Cars	Commercial Vehicles
1970	28,819	14,487	14,332
1975	37,179	18,398	18,781
1980	123,135	57,225	65,910
1985	378,162	264,458	113,704
1990	1,321,630	986,751	334,879
1991	1,497,818	1,158,245	339,573
1992	1,729,696	1,306,752	422,944

Source: Korea Automobile Industrial Cooperative Association

per year through 1995. Production amounted to a total $1.1 billion in 1990 and will increase to $1.8 billion in 1995, at 1990 current market prices.

Automobiles

Early in the 1980s, the Korean car industry policies aimed at stimulating and improving an

As of 1992, Korea has exported over 456,000 motor vehicles to over 160 countries around the world.

One of the largest shipbuilding facilities in the world located at Ulsan, Kyŏngsangnamdo province.

auto industry depressed by worldwide economic stagnation resulting from two oil shocks. Since then, Korean automakers have begun to invest heavily in expansion of facilities and to enter into technical assistance agreements with foreign auto and parts makers.

Annual production increased from 378 thousand units in 1985 to 1,729,696 units in 1992. In early 1986, Korea's biggest automaker, Hyundai, began to export its subcompact Pony Excel to the United States, the world's largest automobile market. Along with exports, domestic demand for automobiles has increased sharply since 1987, as a result of an improved standard of living. In 1992, domestic sales made up 1,268,374 units.

The combined production capacity of all Korean automakers was 637,000 units including 486,000 passenger cars in 1985, and increased to 2,600,000 units including 1,800,000 passenger cars by the end of 1992.

Korean automakers are now working to develop fuel efficient cars and high technology for some auto parts in order to better compete with automakers in advanced countries.

Shipbuilding Industry

Until the 1960s, Korea's shipbuilding industry was involved mostly in the production of inner coastal fishing boats and other small vessels for domestic use. It was not until the Hyundai Shipyard, one of the largest shipbuilding companies in the world, was completed in 1974, that any substantial shipbuilding was undertaken.

In the early 1980s, Korea became one of the world's largest shipbuilding countries, offering various shipbuilding services including ship repair and conversions, yachts and offshore structures. The industry's exports totaled $4.11 billion in 1992, about 5.4 percent of the nation's total exports.

The rapid and successful growth of the ship-

Production and Export of Newly Built Ships

Year	Production(thou.G/T)	Exports(mil.US$)
1976	684	298
1979	525	519
1982	1,426	2,813
1986	2,715	1,816
1988	3,360	1,763
1991	3,941	3,615
1992	4,567	3,778

building industry has been mainly due to a strong competitiveness created by diligent, abundant and skilled labor and by modern facilities. Its excellent delivery record also has attracted shipowners from all over the world.

Continued efforts are being made to maintain and strengthen Korea's shipbuilding industry as an internationally competitive endeavor. Further growth will depend on how well shipbuilders effect improvements at all levels including technology, productivity, labor, and capital.

Chemical Industry

Petrochemicals

Korea's petrochemical industry has made remarkable growth throughout its short history of 20 years, in tandem with rapid national economic growth.

Korea has three petrochemical complexes with a total annual capacity of 3,255,000 MTA based on ethylene, the fifth largest capacity in the world. The first is the Ulsan Petrochemical Complex, located in the southeastern part of the peninsula, which boasts two naphtha crackers with a total ethylene capacity of 805,000 MTA. The second is the Yeochun Petrochemical Complex, located in southwestern Korea, which has five naphtha crackers with a total ethylene capacity of 1,750,000 MTA. The third is the Daesan Petrochemical Complex located in the middle of the west coast. Daesan contains two naphtha crackers with a total ethylene capacity of 700,000 MTA. With the facility expansion of naphtha crackers, production capacities of derivatives are also increasing greatly.

Major resins such as PS and PVC have been produced since about 1965. Production of major synthetic resins, including LDPE, HDPE, PP, PVC, ABS, PS, amounted to 4,807,000 MTA in 1992.

Synthetic fiber raw materials have been produced since 1972. In 1992, the output of major synthetic fiber raw materials, including caprolactam, AN, TPA/DMT and EG, amounted to 1,828,000 MTA. Production of synthetic rubber, including SBR and BR, amounted to 208,000 MTA.

As for supply, Korea imported the majority of its petrochemicals up to the late 1980s because local production capacity could not meet domestic demand. But with the completion of new plant and expansion projects underway since the late 1980s, Korea is now self-sufficient and has a sizable excessive capacity, except in certain products like AN, EG, and etc.

The demand for petrochemicals in Korea has

Supply and Demand for Major Petrochemicals

(In thousand tons)

	1980	1985	1989	1990	1991	1992
Production	990.0	1,737.4	2,814.2	3,140.2	4,961.2	6,843
Import	415.6	869.6	1,140.1	1,275.4	1,160.7	956
Export	119.6	272.2	216.7	381.3	1,099.2	2,150
Consumption	1,286.9	2,334.8	3,739.9	4,034.3	5,022.7	5,649

Note : 1) Major petrochemicals : Thermoplastics (ldfe, hdpe, PP, pvc, ps, abs), Synthetic fiber raw materials (Caprolactam, an, tpa, dmt, eg)
Synthetic rubber (SBR, BR)

2) Consumption : Production + Import - Export

soared. Demand for petrochemicals in the 1970s increased by an average 20 percent per year, more than double the GNP growth rate. In the 1980s, the demand fell, only to soar again, establishing a high growth of average 15 percent per year, 1.5 times the GNP growth rate.

The prospects for Korea's petrochemical industry are not so bright even though this industry has grown rapidly in supply and demand for the past 20 years. The future rate of demand is not expected to increase at past rates due to dullness of economic growth and difficulty in developing new uses of processed products for major synthetic resins. On the other hand, due to greatly expanded capacity by completion of new facilities and expansion projects, the imbalance of supply and demand, especially in case of synthetic resins, is serious, and has emerged as a main issue for the Korea petrochemical industry.

Thus, Korea's petrochemical industry is actively pursuing the development of the export market as well as creating new demand in the domestic market to solve the oversupply problem.

Chemical Fertilizer

The chemical fertilizer industry, a leading sector in the chemical industry in the 1960s, realized self-sufficiency in the latter half of that decade.

The Chungju Fertilizer Co. began operation in 1961 as Korea's first chemical fertilizer producer. Its initial capacity was 85,000 tons of urea per year, and in 1968 its capacity increased to 115,000 tons. The Honam Fertilizer Co., the industry's second-largest company, was constructed in 1962 and expanded in 1969 from an original production of 85,000 tons to 123,750 tons per year of urea. The Yŏngnam and Chinhae chemical companies, each with annual capacities of 84,000 tons of urea and 180,000 tons of compound fertilizer, opened in 1967. In the same year, the Korea Fertilizer Co. went on line with a 330,000 ton urea capacity.

The chemical fertilizer industry grew into a comprehensive undertaking through the expanded production of co-products or by-products in the 1970s.

The domestic production of chemical fertilizer has increased consistently since 1968 to meet more than 90 percent of the domestic demand. The industry recorded its highest production level in 1992 with 1,709,000 nutrient tons, of which nitrogen accounted for 930,000 tons. Also produced were 473,000 tons of $P_2 O_5$ and 306,000 tons of $K_2 O$.

The increasing domestic consumption of fertilizer has had a noticeable impact in agricultural productivity. Part of the demand for potash as a finished fertilizer has been met by imports.

Fertilizer nutrient consumption in Korea showed its first decrease in 1979 and declined the next year, also. Consumption totaled 1,307,000 nutrient tons in 1992, 771,000 tons of N, 266,000 tons of $P_2 O_5$ and 270,000 tons of $K_2 O$.

Although Korea's primary fertilizer exports are urea, exported since 1968, and compound fertilizers, exported since 1970, fused magnesium phosphate and ammonium sulfate also have been exported. Exports were suspended in 1974 to give priority to domestic supply, but were resumed in 1976.

The export of all chemical fertilizers rose to its highest level in 1984 with 663,000 nutrient tons, but declined to 397,000 nutrient tons in 1991. The total exports of Korean-made fertilizer reached 474,000 nutrient tons ($173,526,000) in 1992, to 12 countries including Thailand, Vietnam and the Philippine.

In 1988, the Government decided to open the domestic fertilizer market to imports in order to make up any shortfall in local production. Government regulations permit only licensed fertilizer manufacturers and the National Agricultural Cooperative Federation to import fertilizers. Imports amounted to 100,000 nutrient tons in 1992.

Raw Materials

As all Korean fertilizer plants use naphtha as the raw material for ammonia production, the industry was affected severely and its international competitiveness was weakened by oil price hikes. Naphtha, indispensable in Korea as natural gas is unavailable, is supplied from oil refineries in the country. However, after

Overall Supply and Demand for Fertilizer Elements

(thousand nutrient tons)

	1981	1982	1983	1984	1985	1986	1987	1988	1989	1990	1991	1992
Production	1,202	1,278	1,227	1,393	1,412	1,374	1,592	1,702	1,646	1,648	1,572	1,709
Import	-	53	7	-	-	-	10	12	67	78	78	100
Export	401	497	590	663	593	514	522	582	411	461	397	474
Consumption	838	860	746	796	817	903	987	1,120	1,276	1,288	1,238	1,307

Imports : Agricultural Use

Source : Ministry of Trade, Industry and Energy

Production of Fertilizer Elements

(thousand nutrient tons)

	N	P_2O_5	K_2O	Total
1981	680	343	179	1,202
1982	627	447	204	1,278
1983	595	458	174	1,227
1984	685	493	215	1,393
1985	686	493	233	1,412
1986	657	480	237	1,374
1987	726	502	284	1,512
1988	901	488	313	1,702
1989	885	447	314	1,.646
1990	867	454	327	1,648
1991	861	411	300	1,572
1992	930	473	306	1,709

* Source : Ministry of Trade, Industry and Energy

Consumption of Fertilizer Elements

(thousand nutrient tons)

	N	P_2O_5	K_2O	Tatal
1981	474	499	165	838
1982	447	220	193	860
1983	405	174	167	746
1984	441	182	173	796
1985	454	188	175	817
1986	491	217	208	903
1987	542	237	209	987
1988	679	238	203	1,120
1989	755	283	238	1,276
1990	778	272	238	1,288
1991	744	259	234	1,238
1992	771	266	270	1,307

* Source : Ministry of Trade, Industry and Energy

Namhae Chemical Corp. and Korea Fertilizer & Chemicals Co. converted its ammonia processing from naphtha to LPG early in 1992, consumption of naphtha dropped precipitously.

Other raw materials, such as sulphur, rock phosphate, and potash, are all imported. In 1992, 1.57 million tons of rock phosphate, 482,000 tons of sulphur, and 607,000 tons of potash were imported.

On the other hand, the domestic industry has mostly relied on its own supplies of ammonia since 1961 when the Chungju Fertilizer Co., Ltd., was completed. Recently, however, it began to make use of foreign manufactured materials because of their relatively cheap prices compared with local ones. The ammount reached 571,000 tons in 1992.

The major consumers of rock phosphate are the Namhae, Chinhae, and DongBu Chemical companies, the Kyunggi Chemical Industry Co. and the Pungnong Co. Most of the raw materials have been provided through long-term supply contracts with foreign joint venture partners. Both the Kyunggi and Pungnong companies import rock phosphate and potash but have no stable procurement contracts and are thus vulnerable to price fluctuations.

Ceramics Industry

Cement

Since its modernization under the First Five-Year Economic Development Plan in 1962, Korea's cement industry has maintained vigorous growth, expanding into one of the country's key industries.

At the end of 1991, production capacity stood at 42,104 thousand tons per annum with total output reaching 38,335 thousand tons and supplying domestic demand at 44,218,000 tons, and exports at 1,671,000 tons. Compared with 1962, this shows an increase in production capacity of 57.8 times, and output 48.5 times.

Until 1972, the cement industry made little effort to maximize production facilities, which were considered sufficient to meet domestic demand. In the early 1970's, the industry was faced with the problem of overproduction, due in part to the intensive expansion of production capacity. From 1973, domestic demand rose drastically due to a new construction boom, reaching 8,435,000 tons in 1975, an increase of 10.2 percent over the previous year, and exports hit 2,463,000 tons.

From 1976 through 1979 the Korean economy expanded rapidly, partly due to the overseas construction boom, and with it, domestic demand for cement grew. With the strong demand for cement both at home and abroad, cement producers began to expand their production capacities.

With increased production capacity and a decrease in domestic demand from 1980 through 1982, the producers made efforts not only to export cement to overseas markets, but also to switch from oil to coal to lower production costs. Early in 1983, however, this situation reversed. Thanks mainly to soaring economic growth, domestic demand for cement skyrocketed.

From 1988 through 1991 the cement industry grew rapidly due to the booming construction industry. In 1988 domestic demand increased to 26,202,000 tons, twice what it had been in 1980. In 1990 the domestic demand increased by 20.5 percent compared to the previous year, and in 1991 it jumped to 44,218,000 tons, over 1,000 kilograms of annual per capita consumption. This was mainly a result of high levels of activity in the domestic construction industry, for social infrastructure, housing supply programs, and commercial structures. In order to meet the exploding domestic demand, cement exporting was limited, but in such a way as not to negatively influence long-term overseas markets. Since then the industry has expanded production capacity to reach 47,760,000 tons in 1992.

Up to now, through persistent efforts, the cement companies have not only expanded the production capacity but also promoted a plan for the construction of cement silos nationwide to meet the increasing demand for bulk cement

Increase in Clinker Production Facilities

(in thousand tons)

	Capability of Production Facilities(A)	Production(B)	Rate of Operation(B/A)
1962	728	733	100.7
1966	1,782	1,832	102.8
1970	6,919	6,266	90.6
1974	10,100	9,333	92.4
1976	12,977	12,448	95.9
1978	15,785	15,545	98.5
1980	22,185	17,115	77.2
1982	23,463	19,062	81.2
1984	23,463	20,433	87.1
1986	29,863	22,482	75.3
1988	29,863	27,416	91.8
1990	33,109	29,281	88.4
1991	42,104	34,999	83.1
1992	47,760	38,999	81.7

Source : Ministry of Trade, Industry and Energy

Production Capacity of Cement Companies

(in thousand tons)

Company	1990	%	1991	%	1992	%
Ssangyong	13,494	37.5	13,494	32.1	14,995	31.4
Dongyang	5,030	14.0	7,538	17.9	7,538	15.8
Hanil	4,465	12.4	4,465	10.6	6,016	12.6
Hyundai	2,904	8.1	2,904	6.9	4,884	10.2
Asea	4,146	11.5	4,146	9.8	4,146	8.7
Sungshin	4,079	11.4	4,079	9.7	4,703	9.8
Halla	1,188	3.3	4,818	11.4	4,818	10.1
Koryo	660	1.8	660	1.6	660	1.4
Total	35,966	100	42,104	100	47,760	100

Source : Korea Cement Industrial Association

and to boost the efficiency of transportation. They also are gradually replacing old facilities with new, more efficient ones.

Pottery and Porcelain

Korea has been famous as a producer of exquisite ceramics since ancient times. However, it was not until the the 1960s that a ceramics industry in the modern sense of the word began to develop.

Thanks to increased national income and a domestic housing boom in the latter half of the 1960s, the manufacturing of construction-related ceramic items, such as tiles and sanitary ware, became active. With the emergence of tableware and novelty items in the 1970s, the ceramics industry began to diversify.

Production capacity greatly increased, from 112,000 tons in 1973 to 1,000,000 tons in 1992, while exports, led by tableware and novelty

Cement Supply and Demand

(in thousand tons)

Year	Supply				Demand		
	Total	Production	Import		Total	Domestic	Export
			C/E	C/K			
1962	970	790	180	-	977	977	-
1966	2,074	1,884	190	-	2,073	1,902	171
1974	8,838	8,838	-	-	9,531	7,655	1,876
1978	15,733	15,467	266	-	16,365	14,496	1,869
1980	15,573	15,573	-	-	17,582	13,173	4,409
1982	17,912	17,912	-	-	19,899	14,301	5,598
1984	20,359	20,359	-	-	21,683	18,976	2,943
1986	23,225	23,225	-	-	24,792	20,387	4,405
1988	28,995	28,995	-	177	29,797	26,202	3,595
1990	35,758	33,375	2,183	1,558	35,938	33,986	1,952
1991	45,438	38,335	7,103	103	45,889	44,218	1,228
1992	48,052	42,650	5,402	-	47,564	46,517	1,047

Source : Ministry of Trade, Industry and Energy

Note : Imported clinker is used in production activities and accordingly, included under "Production"

items, went from U.S.$13 million in 1973 to U.S.$66 million in 1992, accounting for 0.09 percent of total national exports.

In 1992, there were 80 main manufacturers in the pottery and porcelain industry. By item, they may be classified into four groups: 41 manufacturing tile, 26 tableware, 8 novelties and 5 sanitary ware.

The tile sector began to grow early in the 1970s, producing mostly mosaic types. In 1973, 53,000 tons, or 61 percent of the total tile output was exported. However, tile exports have since suffered a drastic decline as the industry no longer has a competitive edge over industries of other developing countries. As a result, most output is now consumed domestically.

The development of the tableware industry suffered a slowdown due to the emergence of plastic and other products. However, with improvement in quality, tableware has emerged as a major export item since the latter half of the 1970s. Approximately 68 percent of the total output worth U.S.$227 million was exported in 1992.

Domestic demand for sanitary ware has sharply increased as a result of the introduction of Western-style housing and fixtures. More

than 63,000 tons of sanitary ware were produced in 1992, 99 percent of which went to domestic consumption.

Novelty items began to be produced in Korea as late as the 1970s, and production has grown at a rapid rate due largely to increasing overseas demand.

Textile Industry

Spurred by the Government's export policy during the period of industrialization since the 1960s, Korea's textile industry has grown to be a major part of the Korean economic scene.

Textiles in 1992 accounted for 7.9 percent of total manufacturing production, 10.7 percent of total manufacturing sector employment and 20.5 percent of total exports.

Korea is one of the world's top 10 textile producers in terms of facilities and exports. While relatively low priced, Korean textile products are considered of top quality and enjoy a high reputation in world markets.

The textile industry in Korea in 1992 showed a 8.8 percent increase in production compared with the previous year. Textile exports in 1992 increased by 1.5 percent from 1991, but the

The Position of the Textile Industries

Classification	1980	1989	1990	1991	1992
Production in Manufacturing sector Billion Won(value added)(A)	14,426	40,543	44,216	47,966	50,469
Production in Textile Sector Billion Won(value added)(B)	2,363	3,885	3,800	3,657	3,980
Ratio B:A %	16.4	9.6	8.6	7.6	7.9
Total Export Million US$ (A)	17,505	62,378	65,016	71,870	76,632
Textile Export Million US$ (B)	5,014	15,197	14,670	15,478	15,710
Ratio B:A %	28.6	24.4	22.6	21.5	20.5
Employment in Manufacturing Sector Thousand Persons (A)	2,955	4,840	4,847	4,936	4,673
Employment in Textile Sector Thousand Persons (B)	729	676	544	537	501
Ratio B:A %	24.7	13.8	11.2	10.9	10.7

Export Source : Ministry of Trade, Industry and Energy

Korea's textile industry is striving to remain internationally competitive by modernizing plants.

share of total exports decreased to 20.5 percent, from 21.5 percent in 1991.

By item, textile goods totaled U.S.$7,789 million, fabric $6,460 million and fiber and yarn $1,461 million in 1992. Exports to the United States totaled $3,442 million, a decrease of 2.6 percent over the previous year. Exports to Japan totaled $2,819 million, down 6.3 percent, while exports to the EC totaled $1,697 million, an decrease of 18.6 percent from 1991.

Korea's textile imports in 1992 amounted to $4,001 million, down 1.4 percent from the previous year. Of this amount, imports from the United States totaled $574 million; from Japan, $714 million; and from China, $972 million; all together representing 56.5 percent of all textile imports.

The bulk of Korea's raw cotton imports comes from the United States. Chemical fibers, yarns and fabric are largely imported from Japan and China, while most raw wool is imported from Australia.

Korea's textile exports are facing increasingly strong protectionism in advanced countries and rising competition from developing countries. Therefore, the textile industry in Korea is not expected to show significant progress in the future.

Chemical Fibers

Korea's chemical fiber production facilities rank fifth in the world with a total production of 1,582,200 M/T as of the end of 1992. At that time, the industry was composed of 18 companies and employed 19,373 persons, 3.9 percent of the total employment of Korea's textile industry. Domestic consumption reached 22.3 percent of total production and exports accounted for the remaining 77.7 percent in 1992.

Domestically produced raw materials for chemical fibers in 1992 accounted for 67.5 percent of domestic consumption, although the remaining 32.5 percent is still imported. In this respect, Korea's chemical fiber industry faces problems obtaining a stable supply of raw materials.

Spinning

As of the end of 1992, production facilities for Korea's spinning industry totaled 4,735,000 spindles of which about 3,521,360, or 74.4 percent, were for cotton spinning. Worsted spinning accounted for 20.8 percent of the total production facilities, or 983,715 spindles, while approximately 4.8 percent, or 172,979 spindles, were for spinning wool.

183 companies were involved in cotton spinning, worsted spinning, and woolen spinning. The spinning industry employed 70,100 persons, accounting for 14.0 percent of the total empoyment in the textile and clothing industries in 1992.

Weaving

Korea's fabric industry in 1992 maintained 144,301 weaving looms, of which 88,843, or 61.6 percent, were filament looms. Cotton weaving looms totaling 42,451 accounted for 29.4 percent of the total facilities.

Exports of fabrics in 1992 accounted for 41.1 percent of total textiles and clothing exports, reaching 6,460 million dollars. The Korean fabric industry was composed of 3,000 companies and employed 72,200 persons in 1992.

Garments

Korea's garment industry in 1992 consisted of 7,285 companies, making up more than 50 percent of total textile operations, while 225,000 people, 45 percent of total textile employment, were in the garment field.

The garment industry in 1992 maintained a total of 283,000 sewing machines. Of these, 65 percent or 183,950 were lock-stitch machines, and the remaining 35 percent a variety of special machines. Exports of clothing in 1992 accounted for 41.3 percent of Korea's total tex-

tile exports.

Dyeing and Finishing

The dyeing and finishing industry in 1991 is one of the more rapidly modernizing sectors of Korea's textile and clothing industry. Large scale improvements are underway to modernize facilities and production.

Korea's dyeing and finishing industry employs 61,158 persons or about 9.8 percent of the total employment in the textile and clothing industry, and 49 percent of the dyestuffs is supplied domestically and 5 percent is imported.

To foster the development of the dyeing and finishing industry and the special dyeing and finishing industry, special dyeing and finishing complexes have been constructed since 1980, and the specialization and systematization of the dye-finishing industry has been encouraged. The Taegu Dyeing Industry Complex, which was constructed in 1980, currently houses 111 companies, and 68 companies are operating in the Panwol Dyeing and Finishing Industry Estate, which was reconstructed in 1983.

Other Manufacturing Industries

Sugar Refining

The sugar refining industry has maintained steady growth by overcoming many obstacles since 1953, starting out as an import substitute industry in order to meet domestic demands. Refined sugar began to be exported in 1962 and has a reputation for quality.

At present, the total sugar refining capacity of three plants is 1,290,000 tons per annum, an increase of six times in comparison with that of 1962. This output covers the range of all domestic demands for food, beverages, and other industries. More than 70 percent has been used for domestic consumption and the remaining 30 percent exported to many countries around the world during the past five years.

The sugar industry in Korea is entirely dependent on imported raw sugar. More than 80 percent of the raw sugar has been imported from the main exporting countries in Asia and Oceania since 1981. Total imports of raw sugar reached 1,237,000 tons in 1992.

Paper

The Korean paper industry has made considerable progress with activation of related industries, and also has established new facilities and expanded others to cope with the increase in paper demand. Gradually it has begun to emerge as an exporter.

There were about 130 paper producing companies at the end of 1992 in Korea, with a total production capacity of 6,008,000 M/T. Exports in 1992 reached U.S. $465,799,000 (633,000 M/T), representing 11.6 percent of the year's total paper output.

Among the principal raw materials for paper making, the self-sufficiency rate of groundwood pulp was 76.3 percent, but chemical pulp reached a self-sufficiency rate of only 9.6 percent.

If the paper industry is to be competitive in the growing export market, products of high quality and diversity, developed technology and expansion of production capacities are a must.

To ensure long-term and stable supplies of principal raw-materials, it is necessary to pursue the expanding of facilities by the establishment of locally incorporated firms with foreign partners in resource-rich countries.

Rubber Goods

The rubber goods industry in Korea may be divided into three categories: rubber footwear manufacturing, tire and tube manufacturing, and industrial rubber manufacturing. Of these, rubber footwear and tires have been the industry's leaders and have shown remarkable growth.

The production capacity of rubber footwear increased from 185 million pairs in 1975 to 500 million in 1992. Output increased from 147 million pairs in 1975 to 360 million in 1992.

In 1992, the production capacity for tires stood at 45.7 million, and output has increased to 29.8 million from one million pieces in 1971. Korea now has three tire plants with relatively large-scale capacities. The footwear and various other rubber products industries are made up largely of small-scale firms.

The industry depends on imports for all the natural raw rubber it consumes. The proportion of synthetic rubber consumption, including SBR, to the total was 36 percent in 1977 and 61 percent in 1992. Imports of natural and synthetic rubber reached almost 418,000 tons, equivalent to U.S. $464 million, in 1992.

Mining

The Korean mining industry has experienced considerable growth in production and consumption since the First Five-Year Economic Development Plan was launched in 1962.

Explorative reports show the country's reserves of some metallic and most non-metallic mineral resources are relatively plentiful. In par-

Production of Major Minerals

Minerals	Grade	Unit	1970	1975	1980	1985	1990	1991	1992
Gold	Au 99.9%	M/T	1.6	0.4	1.3	0.4	1.2	1.1	1.4
Lead	Pb 50.0%	"	32.0	24.3	23.1	19.4	29.7	25.3	27.3
Zinc	Zn 50.0%	"	48.0	91.8	113.6	91.5	45.6	44.1	43.8
Iron	Fe 56.0%	"	571.0	644.0	618.9	668.1	298.3	221.5	221.5
Tungsten	Wo3 70%	"	3.7	4.4	4.9	4.6	2.5	1.4	0.4
Talc	Any Grade	"	83.9	92.9	204.7	194.2	181.7	170.6	149.9
Kaolin	"	"	194.6	513.2	577.8	658.3	1,446.3	1,755.2	1,856.6
Limestone	"	"	9,104	16,904	28,024	35,135	48,806	59,297	65,508
Pyrophylite	"	"	120.1	323.0	514.5	738.3	557.6	573.2	602.6
Quarzite	"	"	259.4	265.5	291.2	871.6	1,451.8	1,626.9	1,870.2

Source:Ministry of Trade, Industry and Energy

ticular, the tungsten ore reserve is known as one of the most abundant in the world. In addition, good supplies of non-metallic minerals such as limestone, talc, pyrophylite, kaolin and silica, categorized as essential raw materials, are all available.

Because of the growing demand for minerals resulting from rapid industrialization, the country's mining promotion policy has stressed boosting mineral production. Accordingly, the production of lead ore has increased since the 1960s. However, the production of zinc and iron ore began declining in the latter half of the 1980s, and the output of tungsten ore also decreased rapidly in the 1990s due to changes in demands and prices in the international market. The production of gold, talc, kaolin, phyrophylite, limestone and silica have increased steadily.

Until the mid-1960s, approximately 60 percent of all mineral resources produced in Korea were exported and the remainder consumed at home. With rapid industrialization in the 1960s, however, mineral demand started to grow and now a large portion of metallic and non-metallic mineral resources must be imported.

As production of some raw materials is not sufficient to meet domestic demand, the Government established a plan for the long-term supply of those major minerals through 2001.

Energy Industry

Electric Power

Since electric power is one of the most important factors in the development of a country's economy, in the 1960s the Government placed emphasis on the development of the electric power industry, designing a series of the five-year power development plans (1962-66, 1967-71).

In 1961, the Government established the Korea Electric Power Corporation (KEPCO), merging existing companies in charge of the production and distribution of electric power, and launched the First Five-Year Power

Development Plan in 1962. With the successful accomplishment of that plan, marked progress was seen in the electric industry. Generating facilities were expanded by 420 megawatts with the completion of eight planned projects. This rise in generating capacity resulted in a removal of restrictions on power use which had been in force since 1945.

The soaring demand for electricity caused by rapid industrialization and rising living standards, however, put pressure on the power supply, and restrictions were reset in June 1967.

The Government then worked out the Second Five-Year Power Development Plan, after several readjustments, expanding the planned capacity by allowing private electric companies to participate in developing electrical energy.

During the Third Power Development Plan period (1972-76), the Tonghae and Honam electric companies were taken over by KEPCO. Kyung-In Energy Co. continued to operate its oil-fired power plants, providing electricity to KEPCO. As the third power development plan called for diversification of power-generating resources, the government-run Industrial Sites and Water Resources Development Corporation was established in 1974 to construct hydro-electric power plants. Two nuclear power plants were commissioned in 1978 and 1982 to meet Korea's increasing energy needs and to reduce dependency on imported oil. An investment of 814,783 million won (about U.S. $1.7 billion) was used to develop power plants during this period. The basic objective of the fourth power plan (1977-81) was to complete rural electrification. Towards this end, a series of rural power development plans begun in 1965 was completed in 1978, with the minor exception of several mountainous areas and remote islands.

Between 1982 and 1985, four coal-fired plants, two nuclear power plants, two LNG plants and one pumped-storage station were commissioned to meet the increasing electricity demand and reduce reliance on oil. In 1992, generating capacity reached 24,120 megawatts, 49.5 percent more than that of 1985.

In the last two years, peak demand has increased sharply. Accordingly, the long-term power development plan established in 1989 was revised in 1991 in response to the current situation. The Government set the goal of expanding power generating facilities to 20,962 megawatts by 1991, but that target was achieved two years early, reaching 20,997 megawatts in 1989.

Korea's power development program involves the substitution of nuclear and coal energy for petroleum. According to the new plan (1991-2006), generating capacity will be increased from 24,120 MW in 1992 to 58,669 MW, in 2006, which breaks down into nuclear plants (23,229 MW), coal-fired plants (17,760 MW), LNG combined cycle plants (9,980 MW), and oil-fired plants (1,731 MW) and others (5,969 MW). If construction of nuclear power plants goes smoothly, the Korean electric power industry is likely to enter the nuclear age by the year 2000.

Power Generating Facilities

At the end of 1992, there were 37 thermal power plants, 31 hydropower stations, nine nuclear units and two pumped storage plants in operation. In December 1985, the Samnangjin pumped storage power plant began operation with a rated generating capacity of 600 MW. It took six years and cost 153,200 million won (about U.S.$187 million) to construct this plant. The plant was expected to cushion maximum demand in the Yongnam area at peak hours. In addition to the increase in power generating facilities, expansion of power transmission and distribution systems has also been considerable. Transmission lines totalled 20,477 km in 1992, an increase of 178.3 percent, or 13,121 km, over 1972, attributable to a rise in high-voltage transmission lines for 154 kilovolts. Actual available capacity has been greatly enhanced since 1976 due to the use of 345 kilovolt cables.

The rate of power loss in transmission and distribution fell from 22.3 percent in 1962 to 5.78 percent in 1992.

Supply and Demand

The energy resources used for power generation in Korea include petroleum, anthracite coal, bituminous coal, hydraulic power and nuclear energy. Of these resources, petroleum, which mostly depends on imports, plays the leading role. Petroleum made up almost 40.1 percent of all energy resources used as generating fuels in 1992.

The Government has attempted to subsitute non-petroleum energy for petroleum energy, and has promoted the installation of nuclear power plants and coal-fired plants. The Government has established nine nuclear power plants using natural or enriched uranium as fuel. The ratio of nuclear power to total electric power generated reached 43.2 percent in 1992.

With rapid economic development and industrialization, the demand for electric power increased by an annual rate of 22.3 percent during the 1962-71 period, 16.5 percent per year for the 1972-76 period, 12.3 percent per year for the 1977-81 period, 9.7 percent per year for the 1982-86 period, and 12.4 percent for the 1987-91 period, almost double the rate for developed countries. Consumption of electric power also soared. Total electric power sales increased to 115,224 million kilowatt hours in 1992, from 1,189 million kilowatt hours in 1961.

Total power generated in 1992 amounted to 130,963 million kilowatt hours, ten times that of 1972; of that total, 43.2 percent of all electricity

Major Indicators in Electric Power System

	Unit	1987	1988	1989	1990	1991	1992
Power Sales	GWH	64,169	74,317	82,192	94,383	104,374	115,224
Power Generation	GWH	73,992	85,462	94,472	107,670	118,619	130,963
Peak Demand	MW	11,039	13,658	15,058	17,252	19,124	20,438
Rate of Reserve	%	51.5	18.7	18.7	8.3	5.4	6.4
Installed Capability	MW	19,021	19,944	20,997	21,021	21,111	24,120

Source : Ministry of Trade, Industry and Energy

Power Generating Facilities

(Unit : Megawatts)

	Hydro	Thermal	Nuclear	Total
1961	143	224		367
1966	215	554		769
1972	341	3,541		3,872
1976	711	4,009		4,810
1982	1,202	7,836	1,266	10,304
1984	1,202	11,073	1,916	14,191
1986	2,225	11,070	4,766	18,060
1988	2,236	11,043	6,666	19,944
1990	2,340	11,065	7,616	21,021
1991	2,445	11,050	7,616	21,111
1992	2,498	14,006	7,616	24,120

Power Generating Facilities in 1992

(Unit : megawatts)

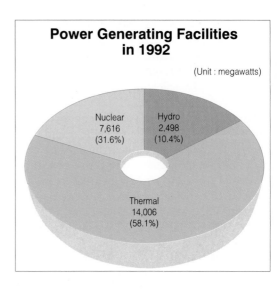

Nuclear 7,616 (31.6%)
Hydro 2,498 (10.4%)
Thermal 14,006 (58.1%)

Length of Transmission Lines

(Unit : Kilometer)

	345KV	154KV	66KV	22KV	Total
1962	-	603	1,958	2,858	5,419
1972	-	1,768	3,003	2,585	7,356
1978	1,348	5,124	4,334	185	10,991
1981	2,097	6,381	4,483	98	13,059
1984	3,180	7,547	4,414	32	15,172
1986	4,203	8,497	4,389	12	17,101
1988	4,924	9,346	4,301	12	18,583
1990	4,935	10,609	3,877	11	19,432
1991	4,941	11,189	3,721	-	19,851
1992	5,259	11,631	3,579	-	20,469

Source : Ministry of Trade, Industry and Energy

Electric Power Generated and Purchased

(Unit : Million Kilowatt hours)

	Hydor	Thermal	Nuclear	Sub total	Purchased	Total
1962	702	1,276	-	1,978	-	1,978
1972	1,368	8,518	-	9,886	1,953	11,839
1981	1,701	32,829	2,897	37,427	2,779	40,206
1984	1,698	39,206	11,792	52,696	1,111	53,807
1986	2,590	32,073	28,311	62,973	1,722	64,695
1988	2,361	40,400	40,101	82,862	2,600	85,462
1990	3,738	46,562	52,887	103,187	4,483	107,670
1991	3,154	55,004	56,311	114,469	4,150	118,619
1992	3,347	66,144	56,530	126,021	4,941	130,962

The bulk of Korea's power development program involves the substitution of nuclear and coal energy for petroleum. If Korea's nuclear power plant construction plans go smoothly, its electric power industry will enter the nuclear age in the year 2,000.

Anthracite Coal Production

(thousand tons)

	Total	DHCC*	Private Mines
1975	17,593	4,574	13,019
1980	18,624	4,786	13,838
1986	24,253	5,218	19,035
1988	24,295	5,222	19,073
1990	17,217	3,988	13,229
1991	15,058	3,846	11,212
1992	11,970	3,624	8,346

*) Dai Han Coal Corporation

Source : Ministry of Trade, Industry and Energy

was generated by nuclear power, or 56,530 million kilowatt hours. Such progress was ascribed to the Government's positive support for power development through the successive series of five-year power plans.

The power reserve ratio for peak demand has been improved from the level of minus 9.8 percent in 1962 to 20.0 percent in 1979, and to 6.4 percent in 1992.

Coal Mining

Anthracite is Korea's major coal resource and, as no liquid energy resources have been discovered and hydraulic energy resources are

Scale of Coal Mines

(number of mines)

Scale (thousand tons/year)	1981	1983	1985	1986	1987	1988	1989	1990	1991	1992
More than 500	10	9	10	10	10	10	9	8	9	7
300-500	7	2	4	4	5	5	4	4	2	3
100-300	22	26	27	31	28	29	17	16	12	7
50-100	22	29	35	33	35	40	35	25	21	12
Less than 50	158	280	285	283	285	263	267	162	126	86
Total	219	346	361	361	363	347	332	215	170	115

Source : Korea Institute of Energy Resources, Yearbook of Energy Statistics, 1992

Anthracite Coal Consumption by Sector

	Total	Residential & Commercial	Electric Utilities	Industry	Others
1975	15,945(100)	13,613(85.4)	1,349(8.5)	643(4.0)	340(2.1)
1980	20,830(100)	18,037(86.5)	1,865(9.0)	708(3.4)	220(1.1)
1983	21,670(100)	18,960(87.5)	2,074(9.6)	518(2.4)	118(0.5)
1985	25,339(100)	23,100(91.2)	1,778(7.0)	353(1.4)	108(0.4)
1986	26,928(100)	24,250(90.1)	2,285(8.5)	277(1.0)	116(0.4)
1987	26,327(100)	23,587(89.6)	2,444(9.3)	206(0.8)	90(0.3)
1988	25,641(100)	22,926(89.4)	2,407(9.4)	209(0.8)	99(0.4)
1989	22,843(100)	20,054(88.0)	2,483(10.7)	214(0.9)	92(0.4)
1990	20,979(100)	18,779(89.5)	1,983(9.5)	171(0.8)	46(0.2)
1991	17,181(100)	14,996(87.3)	2,070(12.0)	115(0.7)	-
1992	13,077(100)	11,069(84.6)	1,945(14.9)	63(0.5)	-

Source: Ministry of Trade, Industry and Energy

poor, it has been the country's major energy resource as well. But it was only in the 1960s that its exploitation was begun in earnest. In order to meet the sharp increase in energy demands due mainly to the rapid industrialization during the five-year development plans, the Government took a series of measures to promote coal production. The promulgation of the provisional Coal Development Law in December 1961, providing for unifying small private coal mines, was one of these measures.

As a result, the coal mining industry made great progress in all aspects during the first half of the 1960s. The number of mines in operation increased from 131 in 1960 to 177 in 1964, and employees increased from 24,661 to 37,047 in the same period. Output increased to 12,436 thousand tons in 1967, about double 1962's output.

Such increases in coal production made it possible to change the fuel consumption pattern from firewood to anthracite. The share of coal in energy consumption rose from 36.9 percent in 1962 to 42.9 percent in 1967, while that of firewood dropped from 51.9 percent to 30.6 percent during the same period.

The coal mining industry, however, began to decline in the latter half of the 1970s because coal production was unable to meet rapidly increasing demands for energy. The production of anthracite peaked at 12,436 thousand tons in 1967. The Government adopted a new energy policy calling for the substitution of oil for anthracite.

After the first oil crisis in 1973, the Government was forced to reconsider the coal industry, and offered subsidies and tax exemp-

tions to spur development of coal energy. Output of coal then increased by 10 percent per year from 1973 to 1975. Production in 1975 totalled 17.6 million tons, much greater than demand. From 1977, however, demand for coal increased each year, and production of 18.2 million tons in 1979 did not meet domestic demand.

In 1980, as the consumption of petroleum products decreased, the production of 18.6 million tons of coal also failed to meet demands, so 2.7 million tons of anthracite were imported in 1980. Since the second half of the 1980s, the demand for coal has decreased rapidly due to a drop in oil prices. As a result, the share of coal in total energy consumption dropped to 5.2 percent in 1992, from 21.9 percent in 1985. When the international oil market is volatile, coal development is pushed more vigorously to minimize dependence upon imported energy sources. Government loan funds were offered through the Korea Mining Promotion Corporation, and financing was made available for coal stockpiling during the off-season to avoid price fluctuations.

The coal mining industry is a typical labor-intensive industry in which labor costs comprise nearly 50 percent of the total cost.

The number of employees in the coal mining sector was about 32,561 in 1991. The wage level of miners is comparatively high. In recent years, however, miners are leaving their jobs each year because of the risky and difficult nature of the work.

As an aftermath of the first and second oil crises, the importance of energy self-sufficiency was fully recognized, spurring domestic coal

Anthracite Demand Prospects

	1992	1993	1996	Average Annual Growth Rate %
				1993 - 1996
Households & Commercial Facilities	11,230	10,121	7,558	- 9.2
Power plants	2,000	2,000	2,000	-
Industry & Others	90	75	90	-7.2
Total	13,320	12,196	9,648	-7.5

development. Accordingly, the Government decided to continue the structural adjustment of local industry with regard to insufficient indigenous resources and the diminishing price advantage of coal against oil energy. The Government plans to support the development of large-scale remunerative coal mines while encouraging the shutdown of non-economic small mines.

Oil Refining

The refining industry in Korea was launched with the completion of a facility in Ulsan in 1964 as a joint venture between the Korean Government and the Gulf Oil Co. of the United States. This refinery, Korea Oil Corporation (now Yukong Limited), went into operation with an initial capacity of 35 thousand barrels per stream day (BPSD).

With completion of the first and second five-year economic development plans, petroleum demand skyrocketed. The increase in petroleum demand forced construction of four more refineries. Kukdong Oil Company's refinery was built with 100 percent Korean capital and came on stream in 1966.

Three more joint venture refineries with foreign oil companies have been constructed since then: Honam Oil Refinery Co., Ltd., a partnership between Caltex Petroleum Corp. of the United States and the Lucky Group which went on stream in 1969; Kyung-In Energy Co. Ltd., owned by the Korea Explosives Group, and Unoco. Ltd., of the United States, in 1971; and Ssangyong Oil Refining Co., Ltd., originally incorporated under the name of Korea-Iran Petroleum Co., Ltd., in a joint venture between Ssangyong Cement Industrial Co., Ltd., of Korea and the National Iranian Oil Co. (NIOC) in 1980. Of these five refineries, Honam is still affiliated with Caltex, and Saudi ARAMCO joined Ssangyong's oil refinery in 1991. Five refineries now are in operation and their total capacity is 1,675,000 BPSD as of the end of 1992, more than 47 times that of 1964.

Total production of petroleum products increased from 4.8 million barrels in 1964 to 503.3 million barrels in 1992. Until the middle of the 1970s, Korean refiners were unable to meet domestic demand for fuel oil and petrochemical feedstock. Following the completion of the Yŏchŏn Petrochemical Complex in 1979, however, they were able to meet the abrupt increase in demand for naphtha. This resulted in the expansion of the national refining capacity from 580,000 BPSD in 1978 to 1,675,000 BPSD in 1992.

Increase in the domestic supply of petroleum products brought a change in the pattern of energy consumption. Until the first half of the 1960s, coal was a major energy source, but domestic coal production failed to meet the increasing energy requirement. Accordingly, the Government after 1967 switched from coal to petroleum as the major energy source. As a result, in 1969 petroleum accounted for 40.1 percent of total primary energy consumption and coal 32.8 percent, while in 1992, petroleum energy amounted to 62.2 percent of total primary energy consumption. The total consumption of petroleum products in 1992 reached 518.1 million barrels, or 7.3 times of 1970.

The domestic consumption of petroleum products, both as a fuel and as a raw material, increased more than 20 percent per year from 1967 to 1979. During the latter half of the 1970s, the rapid increase in the consumption of oil products was due fundamentally to the greater convenience of that fuel. From 1980 to 1982 the consumption of petroleum products decreased due to negative economic growth in 1980, energy conservation efforts, and diversification from oil to other energy sources.

The consumption of oil products for non-energy purposes has shown a greater increase rate than that for energy purposes. Demand for oil as a raw material increased by some 20 percent per year during the 1964-85 period while that for energy oil showed an average annual increase rate of 15.5 percent. The higher increase rate for non-energy oil was due mainly to the expansion of the fertilizer and petrochemical industries. In particular, the demand for naphtha grew rapidly after the construction of three fertilizer plants in the 1960s, the Yŏchŏn Petrochemical Complex in 1979, and the Sosan Petrochemical Complex in 1990. Thus, the share of non-energy oil of total oil consumption

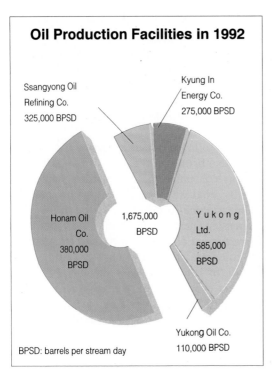

Oil Production Facilities in 1992

Ssangyong Oil
Refining Co.
325,000 BPSD

Kyung In
Energy Co.
275,000 BPSD

Honam Oil
Co.
380,000
BPSD

1,675,000
BPSD

Yukong
Ltd.
585,000
BPSD

Yukong Oil Co.
110,000 BPSD

BPSD: barrels per stream day

increased from less than one percent in the early
1960s to 6.2 percent in 1975, 14.1 percent in
1985 and 19.7 percent in 1992.

This increase in demand for naphtha was satisfied by domestic supply from 1970 to 1979,
but imports of naphtha increased after 1980. In
1992, the import volume of naphtha reached
50.2 million barrels, or about 50.8 percent of
total naphtha consumption.

Crude Oil

As Korea has not found any domestic source
of oil, all crude oil has been imported, mostly
from the Middle East. Crude oil imports have
increased in response to consumption. Import
volume rose to 509.4 million barrels in 1992
from 5.8 million barrels in 1964, more than an
89-fold increase. The import value of crude oil
increased abruptly in the 1970s, due mainly to
the two oil crises. In 1981, the import bill for
crude oil reached US$6.9 billion but was
reduced to US$4.8 billion in 1985, thanks to the
drop in international oil prices, in spite of an

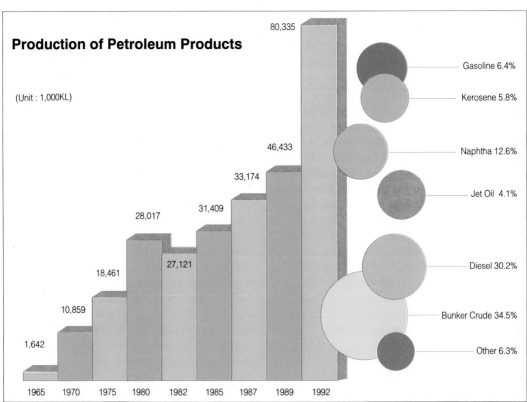

Production of Petroleum Products

(Unit : 1,000KL)

80,335
46,433
33,174
31,409
28,017
27,121
18,461
10,859
1,642

1965   1970   1975   1980   1982   1985   1987   1989   1992

Gasoline 6.4%
Kerosene 5.8%
Naphtha 12.6%
Jet Oil 4.1%
Diesel 30.2%
Bunker Crude 34.5%
Other 6.3%

Source: Ministry of Trade, Industry and Energy

An offshore oil-drilling rig made in Korea.

A petrochemical complex in Ulsan.

increase in import volume. The amount increased again to 9.4 billion dollars in 1992 due to increased import volume.

From the beginning, Korea has been heavily dependent on two Middle Eastern countries, Saudi Arabia and Kuwait, in importing crude oil. This brought about a difficult situation during the second oil crisis, and since then much effort has been made to diversify sources of crude oil in order to cushion another possible oil shock. As a result, import sources of crude oil were gradually expanded. In 1992, 133,588 thousand barrels or 33.5 percent was imported from Saudi Arabia, 52,775 thousand barrels or 13.2 percent from Iran, 33,436 thousand barrels or 8.4 percent from Indonesia, 26,103 thousand barrels or 6.5 percent from Malaysia, 51,155 thousand barrels or 12.8 percent from Oman, and the remaining 102,247 thousand barrels or 25.6 percent from Ecuador, Brunei, Mexico and other countries.

Prospects

As Korea has no proven oil resources, the government has adopted various policies for maximum utilization of domestic energy sources and for the reduction of dependency on imported oil on a long-term basis.

In spite of remarkable achievements in the construction of nuclear, hydroelectric, and coal-fired power plants and the introduction of liquefied natural gas since 1986, it is expected that Korea will rely upon petroleum as its essential source of energy through out the 1990s.

In order to meet the growing demand for middle distillates, the government has been formulating plans to upgrade facilities, import middle distillates, and increase light petroleum production. Along with these plans, the nation has placed strong emphasis on the economic stockpiling of crude oil as well as of finished products.

AGRICULTURE, FORESTRY AND FISHERY

Agriculture

In the late 1970s, political leaders became concerned with maintaining a healthy and expanding agricultural industry, partly because of the chronic shortage of foodstuffs suffered by the country. But self-sufficiency in food grains was a difficult and expensive policy goal due to limited land and underdeveloped technology. Since then, Korea has become more self-sufficient with regard to food grains. Policies have included an active government price support program, an agricultural research and development program, and plans for improving the rural infrastructure. Additional policies to promote self-sufficiency have included the promotion of farm mechanization, the improvement of farm technology through irrigation and drainage, the extensive use of modern farming techniques, the use of water management and the application of developed fertilizers. In particular, the Government has taken on the task of accumulating an adequate supply of Korea's major crops, rice and barley, which are the principal grains of the Korean diet.

Rice Production

In 1965, rice accounted for 53.7 percent of the total grain production. By 1980, its share had risen to 66.7 percent, and in 1991 and 1992, its shares were 86.3 percent and 85.9 percent, respectively.

Due to the dominance of rice in Korean agriculture, policies pertaining to rice have been particularly important to both food and farm policies.

To achieve self-sufficiency in rice production, active government policies have been implemented. Major programs to increase rice production included the efficient control of disease and insects, the improvement of soil fertility and development, water management, and the development and use of high-yielding varieties of rice. Thanks to these efforts, Korea has achieved self-sufficiency in rice.

Rice production over the last thirty years, in fact, has been so successful that problems of overproduction and overstock have arisen in recent years, causing concern among policymakers. For example, the 1971 introduction of the high yield rice variety *T'ongil* led to a continuous increase in rice production so that by 1990, the average yield of *T'ongil* rice per 10 ares (1,000 square meters) had risen to 500kg, a more than 20 percent increase over the common varieties. Therefore, recent policies have aimed at reducing rice production by decreasing the planting of the indica-japonica hybrid, and since 1991, government procurement of *T'ongil* rice has been discontinued. As a result of these policies, the supply and demand of rice has been balanced in recent years.

Production of Wheat, Barley and Other Crops

Wheat and barley are also major food crops in Korea. Although extensive research has been undertaken on ways to increase their production in order to meet the demands of a growing population, wheat and barley production have continued to decrease. This has mainly been due to

Grain Production in 1992

(milled basis)

	Total Production	Cultivated Area	Yields/10a
Unit	1,000 M/T	1,000 ha	Kg
Total	6,206	1,478	-
Rice	5,331	1,157	461
Barley and Wheat	315	103	260
Soybeans	212	135	168
Potatoes	243	50	622
Miscellaneous	105	33	440

Source: Ministry of Agriculture, Forestry and Fisheries

their low profitability for farmers, and to the labor and technical constraints of double-cropping on rice paddy lands. An examination of the supply and demand situation reveals that while barley is approximately self-sufficient, wheat is not. Consumption of milled wheat has increased due to a shift towards Western-style tastes, and most of the milled wheat is imported from the United States.

Soybeans are one of the most important staple food crops and are mainly used for soy paste, soy sauce, and bean sprouts. All soybean varieties grown on farmers' fields in the early 1930s were local collections, but varietal development by artificial hybridization was begun in 1958. The release of a newly-developed variety called *Kwangkyo* in 1969 caused the yield of soybeans to increase rapidly to 2 tons per hectare. Since then, eight more soybean varieties have been released to farmers. As a result, the soybean yield has tripled in the last three decades.

A 200 percent increase in corn yield during the last two decades is a good example of successful varietal improvement. Corn yield in Korea was about 0.6 tons per hectare in 1962, when corn research was initiated. As new varieties, along with new cultivation techniques, were developed and disseminated, corn yield gradually increased, reaching about 3.4 tons per hectare in 1991.

Total grain production is expected to show a slight decline due to a decrease in cultivated acreage despite significant strides in the development of agricultural technology.

Fruit Production

With its four distinct seasons, large fluctuations of temperature and humidity, and adequate precipitation, Korea has favorable conditions for fruit production. Many kinds of fruits—apples, pears, peaches, mandarin oranges, grapes and sweet persimmons are produced in Korea. Korean fruits, especially apples and pears, are known to fruit lovers around the world for their sweet taste and flavor. Apples and pears are, in fact, two of Korea's major agricultural export products. The Fuji apple, one of Korea's representative varieties, is characterized by juicy, crunchy pulp and a pleasing flavor. Korea's Shingo and Mansamgil pears are big, round and contain a large quantity of sweet juice.

In 1992, the production of apples, peaches and grapes was concentrated in Kyŏngbuk province, where, respectively, 68.8 percent, 41.5 percent and 35.4 percent of these fruits were produced. Mandarin orange production was concentrated in Chejudo, an island province off the southern tip of Korea.

Korea's fruit production steadily increased throughout most of the 1980s due to efforts to enhance quality and to diversify variety. To encourage cultivation and export, special programs were implemented to expand orchards, provide new technology, construct storage facilities and improve the marketing structure.

Total fruit production increased between 1991 and 1992 from 1,729,000 tons to 2,090,000 tons. Apple production rose 28.2 percent, to 695,000 tons, and pear production increased 6.0 percent, to 175,000 tons. Tangerine production also soared from a record high of 556,000 tons in 1991 to 719,000 tons in 1992.

Vegetable Production

Vegetable production has increased rapidly since the 1970s for several reasons. Consumer demand for garden products has continuously

Fruit Production

(Unit: 1,000 M/T)

	Total	Apple	Pear	Peach	Orange	Grape	Others
1980	833	410	60	89	161	57	56
1990	1,766	629	159	115	493	131	239
1991	1,729	542	165	122	556	149	195
1992	2,090	695	175	116	719	146	240

Source: Ministry of Agriculture, Forestry and Fisheries

Vegetable Production

(Unit: 1,000 M/T)

	Total	Chinese Cabbage	Radish	Red Pepper	Garlic	Onion	Others
1980	7,676	3,158	2,023	125	253	275	1,842
1990	8,677	3,373	1,761	133	417	407	2,586
1991	8,609	2,731	1,559	141	481	530	3,167
1992	8,700	2,600	1,500	172	465	810	3,153

increased in recent years due to expanding incomes. Farmers have diversified their upland crops to grow various kinds of vegetables. Production has increased due to successful implementation of special programs, and due to the high profitability of vegetables to farmers.

Sixteen percent of farmer's total agricultural income came from vegetable production in 1992. Chinese cabbage, radishes, onions, garlic and red pepper comprised 63.8 percent of the total vegetable production, with Chinese cabbage alone accounting for about 29.9 percent. The nation's overall vegetable production increased from 8.6 million tons in 1991 to 8.7 million tons in 1992. The production of most vegetables, with the exception of garlic, increased in 1992. Red peppers and onion production rose about 22.0 percent and 52.8 percent, respectively, primarily due to favorable growing conditions in 1992.

Livestock

Status of Output and Direction of Production

In 1991, the production of livestock accounted for 24.3 percent of all production in the agri-cultural sector, and its value amounted to U.S.$ 5.6 billion (based on 1991 market prices).

Cattle production contributed toward 30.0 percent of the total value of livestock production, while pork and poultry production contributed 31.0 percent and 12.0 percent, respectively.

Meat output has risen annually on a rising wave of consumer demand. In 1992, total meat output was 933 million tons, a 15.9 percent increase over the previous year. This amount can be broken down to 100 million tons of beef, 601 million tons of pork, and 232 million tons of chicken.

The total head count of cattle raised in 1992 was 2,527,000, an 11.4 percent increase over the previous year. With a total of 613,000 farm households engaged in raising cattle, this works out to approximately 4 head of cattle per farm household. 5,463,000 pigs and 73,324,000 chickens were raised in 1992.

Status and Direction of Consumption

Consumption of meat products increased along with the rise in national income and changes in dietary patterns. In 1992, meat consumption increased by 10.8 percent from the previous year, reaching 1,041,000 tons. Total consumption broke down to 224,000 tons of

Number of Livestock and Poultry

(Unit: 1,000 head, 1,000 birds)

	1980	1985	1990	1991	1992
Number of Cattle	1,541	2,923	2,126	2,269	2,527
- Korea (beef) Cattle	1,361	2,533	1,622	1,773	2,019
- Dairy Cattle	180	390	504	496	508
Hogs	1,653	2,853	4,528	5,046	5,463
Chickens	40,999	51,081	74,463	74,855	73,324

Source: Ministry of Agriculture, Forestry and Fisheries

Production and Consumption of Livestock Products

(Unit: 1,000 M/T)

	Beef		Pork		Chicken		Milk	
	Production	Consumption	Production	Consumption	Production	Comsumption	Production	Consumption
1980	93	100	235	242	90	91	452	412
1985	117	120	345	346	126	126	1,006	972
1990	95	177	507	511	172	172	1,752	1,879
1991	98	221	499	511	207	207	1,741	1,869
1992	100	224	601	585	232	232	1,816	1,919

Source: Ministry of Agriculture, Forestry and Fisheries

beef, 585,000 tons of pork, and 232,000 tons of chicken. Beef consumption in particular showed explosive growth in 1992, impelled by temporary overconsumption. Consequently, beef imports increased to 132,000 tons in 1992.

Consumption of milk and eggs also has increased annually. In 1992, 1,919,000 tons of milk and 424,000 tons of eggs were consumed.

Chicken consumption as well has been increasing because of the recent boom in the fast food business.

Rural Restructuring

Since the early 1980s, the Government has implemented several medium and long-term rural restructuring policy packages to tackle agricultural problems that have arisen during the fast economic growth. A new plan focused on improving productivity and enhancing competitiveness through modernization and mechanization has been implemented since 1992. This plan stresses the revitalization of rural communities, the development of market-oriented agriculture and the diversification of crops.

The goal of the plan is to expand the scale of farm operations, sustain agricultural production and transfer land to young full-time successors. The specified sub-plans of the program aim to: (1) achieve economies of scale by relaxing limits on farm size, providing long term credits and developing infrastructure, (2) expand and strengthen job training and employment programs for those who want to leave farming or hold multiple jobs, (3) diversify the structure of the rural economy including rural industrialization, (4) provide special retirement programs and social welfare programs, (5) improve rural living conditions, education, medical services, roads, water supply and sewage systems.

In 1992, the first year of the new Restructing Plan, the Government successfully undertook 92 projects to enhance competitiveness and to revitalize the rural community, by budgeting 2,721 billion won for these projects, 53 percent more than in F/Y 1991.

Forestry

Forests cover about 65 percent of Korea's total land area, or about 6,468,000 hectares. However, forest land per capita is only 0.2 hectares, a bare one-quarter of the world average.

Forest land in Korea is classified into national, public and private forests. National forests make up about 21 percent of the total forest area, public forests about 8 percent, and forests under private ownership about 71 percent. The total stock volume stands at 257.3 million cubic meters, and the average stock volume per hectare is estimated at 40 cubic meters.

The typical type of forest in Korea is the coniferous forest. Coniferous forests constitute about 46 percent of the total forest while deciduous, mixed forests and other forests constitute 21 percent, 30 percent, and three percent, respectively. The major tree species in Korean forests are red pine, Korean white pine, larch and oak.

Forestry Management

In a highly populated and land-limited country such as Korea, the forest serves many functions: it supplies forest products, provides public recreational areas, stores precipitation, maintains ground water and prevents soil erosion.

Therefore, forests are indispensible for the maintenance of a high quality of life. In order to effectively preserve and develop the forests, the forest land has been divided into reserve and semi-reserve forests, based upon on-site inspections by the Government. Reserve forests are managed for the purposes of land conservation, timber production, scientific research, historic and cultural preservation and for other public benefits. Semi-reserve forests provide farmlands, grasslands or industrial lands.

In order to enhance forest resources and promote public benefits, forests are managed through the government's long-term forest management plan, which includes developing forest roads, improving self-sufficiency of timber and achieving a balance between conservation and development of forest resources.

The Government has implemented a 10-year plan for forestry resources development for the years 1988-1997 designed to reforest denuded lands. A total of one million hectares is to be reforested under the plan, which calls for the designation of forestry development promotion zones and the provision of technical guidance for forestry land owners. Although denuded forests were reforested between 1973 and 1987, Korea still depends on foreign sources for timber. At the same time, there is also an increasing demand for the conservation of the environment and for outdoor recreation. The main goals of the 10-year plan, therefore, are maximizing the efficiency of forestry utilization, building a foundation for forestry management, creating forestry income sources in rural areas and improving the multiple public benefits from the forests. The Government plans to implement a series of 10-year forestry development plans so as to attain over 50 percent self-sufficiency in the supply of timber by the 2030s.

Export and Import of Forest Products

Korea was one of the world's largest plywood exporting countries in the late 1970s. Even in 1992, Korea produced 1,123,000 cubic meters of timber. Forest products that were exported consisted primarily of plywood and sawn products, wood products, stone products, chestnuts and mushrooms. Recently, the quantity of chestnuts and mushrooms being exported has rapidly increased.

However, despite the large proportion of forest area to total land area, most of the wood industries in Korea have relied largely on foreign raw materials. Of the wood used in Korea in 1992, for example, 88 percent was imported from overseas; thus a stable supply of raw materials has been quite important. The major imported products have traditionally been logs, bamboo and rosin. Since the end of the 1970s, however, key products such as round logs became difficult to acquire from abroad due to the emergence of resource nationalism among timber exporting countries. The installation of new facilities and the expansion of Korea's plywood industry were consequently discouraged.

Currently, the development of domestic resources and the management of a stable supply of raw materials are the most important targets for Korea's forest products industry.

Imports of Forestry Products

(Unit: million U.S.$)

	Logs	Lumber	Plywood	Other	Total
1980	858	7	14	33	912
1985	479	28	5	117	629
1990	990	167	226	309	1,722
1991	1,041	228	358	367	1,994
1992	919	250	351	383	1,903

Source: Ministry of Agriculture, Forestry and Fisheries

Overseas Forest Development

As mentioned above, forest poducts imported by Korea have traditionally been logs, bamboo, stone and rosin. Logs have been the largest import item and filled 87 percent of the total wood demand in Korea. The major exporting countries to Korea have been Malaysia, Papua New Guinea, the U.S.A, Chile and New Zealand. To ensure a stable supply of timber, private enterprises have launched timber development projects with government support in some of these countries, such as Malaysia, Papua New Guinea, the U.S.A., as well as other countries including Indonesia, the Russian Federation, the Solomon Islands and Fiji.

To further ensure adequate and timely supply of sawlogs from overseas, Korean end users of sawlogs have been endeavoring to develop forestry resources overseas, and in 1993 alone two Korean firms launched reforestation projects: one in Australia and the other in Vietnam. Domestic end users of sawlogs including manufactures of plywood and chipboard also plan to set up factories in foreign countries with rich forestry resources, and plan to develop a total of 300,000 hectares of overseas forestry by 2020, so as to secure annual supply of 6,000,000 square meters of sawlogs for use in Korea.

Fishery

Because fish is a major part of the Korean diet, the fishing industry has been very important to the Korean people. As personal incomes have grown, fish consumption has also increased. In 1991, about 49 percent of Korea's animal protein was supplied by fishery products. A total of 2,983,000 tons of fishery products was produced by 470,000 fishery household members.

Up until the early 1960s, the Korean fishing industry was limited to coastal fishing. However, with the development of aquaculture and of the deepsea fishing industry in the 1970s, the structure of the Korean fishery industry diversified, and Korea is now one of the major

fishing nations in the world. Although catches by coastal, off-shore and inland fisheries have shown few changes over the past ten years, catches by shallow sea aquaculture and deep sea fisheries have increased.

However, the Korean fishing industry now faces serious concerns because of the introduction of 200-mile Exclusive Economic Zones by many coastal nations, intensified fishing regulations for resource management, the financial burden of fishing permit fees, the decline of fishing resources and increased labor costs. In addition, imports of fishery products have accelerated since the early 1980s, and the total amount of imports in 1991 was 10 times higher than that of the early 1980s.

To develop the fishing industry, several policies have been introduced to improve fishing ports, fishing facilities and the processing of fisheries products. Recently, special policies for improving the environment for fisheries and for enhancing artificial reefs have also been undertaken.

Coastal Fishing

Korea's peripheral waters contain a mixture of warm and cold waters, thereby giving Korea's fishery industry a comparative advantage in fisheries production and in the variety of available fish species. Up until the mid-1970s, coastal fishing increased due to modernization of fishing methods. But the rate of coastal fishing catches has decreased since then. In 1992, catches from coastal fishing fleets totaled 1.3 million tons, 43.6 percent of the total catch.

Deep Sea Fishing

Korean deep sea fishing began with tuna fishing in the Indian Ocean in 1957. Since then, tuna fishing, squid fishing and trawling have all been successful, and production steadily increased until the late 1970s.

At that time, however, the enforcement of international maritime laws forced the deep sea fishing fleets to face a great deal of international restrictions. In particular, in 1977, the USA and the Russian Federation proclaimed 200-mile

Exclusive Economic Zones, prompting many other nations to enact similar zones to preserve their own fish resources. This inevitably led to reductions in the fishing areas and resources open to Korean fishermen.

These nations also demanded expensive fishing permit fees, reciprocal economic aid, the landing of catches at their ports for processing or export and other restricting measures. Korean overseas fishing fleets thus found themselves in a very unfavorable position.

Korean deep sea catches currently consist of Alaska pollack (40.9 percent), squid (24.3 percent) and tuna (31.5 percent).

Cultivation Fishery

Cultivation fishery is an industry in which fish fry are produced and reared under careful observation, released into a natural environment, and then caught for consumption.

Cultivation fishery has primarily been implemented at fishery cultivation centers run by the national government. Currently, eleven cultivation centers are engaged in fishery cultivation. These centers undertake technology research for the production, release and reproduction of fish fry.

Aquaculture

The aquaculture sector of the fisheries industry carries great importance because it accounts for 26 percent of Korea's total production and 16 percent of its value, an importance which has increased since the introduction of 200-mile Exclusive Economic Zones. Thanks to technical innovation, fish culture has been rapidly expanding, and the application of fish culture techniques has diversified into various species groups over the last decade.

To further develop this sector and to efficiently implement the coastal development plan, the Fishery Act was revised in 1991. The revised Fishery Act aims to improve the productivity and quality of aquaculture products.

Inland Water Fisheries

Inland water makes up 1.5 percent of the total area of Korea. But inland-water aquaculture production is becoming more common. Production stood at about 34,241 tons in 1992. Aside from providing places for fisheries production, inland water fisheries also provide places for recreation.

International Fishery Trade

Since 1962, the export of fisheries products has increased. But relative proportion of fisheries exports to total exports has been decreasing. In the 1960s, fisheries exports amounted to 20 percent of total exports. In 1992, it represented only 2.3 percent of the total national exports, or about U.S. $1.5 billion. Products for export include tuna (31.2 percent), live and fresh fish (21.2 percent), frozen products (28.7 percent), seaweed and pickled products (9.5 percent) and other miscellaneous products (21.5 percent).

Imported fisheries products have doubled in the late 1980s and stood at about U.S. $506,487,000 in 1992. Almost half of total imports consist of raw materials for re-export. The Government has liberalized the import of 253 species of foreign fisheries products.

Exports of Fisheries Products

(Unit: million U.S.$)

	Fresh Fish	Seaweed	Tuna	Frozen	Canned	Others	Total
1980	128	58	352	103	28	202	871
1985	279	97	328	124	55	87	970
1990	328	156	475	202	85	267	1,513
1991	349	156	513	272	95	258	1,643
1992	356	156	504	160	99	243	1,518

Source: Ministry of Agriculture, Forestry and Fisheries

TRANSPORTATION AND COMMUNICATIONS

Transportation

Introduction

Koreans have long enjoyed traveling, and with the marked improvement in the standard of living over the last few decades, there has been a corresponding increase of people taking to the roads. During the summer vacation season and on the eve of traditional holidays, inter-city bus terminals and railroad stations bustle with people heading for their favorite resorts or their homes in the provinces.

Korea is relatively small and its population density is among the highest in the world. Due to a rather short history of modern transportation, it is only recently that railway and highway networks have been fully developed, and there is continuous demand for rapid improvement of transportation systems. The constant excessive loads of both passengers and cargo have called for vast investments in the expansion of existing facilities and the opening of new routes and transport systems.

To cope with the growing volume of passenger and cargo traffic, ambitious projects have been drawn up for the transportation sector in the successive Five-Year Economic and Social Development Plans. The latest projects include the laying of high speed railway tracks, the extension of subway lines in Korea's two largest cities, Seoul and Pusan, highway network expansion, provincial road paving, and an increase in ships for coastal and ocean service. Planning has required careful consideration of energy resources, with particular attention to the alleviation of economic pressure from oil imports and the search for more energy-efficient systems.

A railway was first introduced to Korea at the turn of the 20th century. During the 35 years of Japanese colonial rule, a rudimentary rail network was formed to link major cities with cites where raw materials were produced. After liberation in 1945, the nation had little time to improve its transportation facilities before the three-year Korean War devastated much of the railway system.

Postwar reconstruction work quickly restored the railroads, and locomotives and coaches were imported with foreign aid. Until the first five-year development plan was launched in 1962, however, expansion and improvement of the railway network remained insignificant. Even the ambitious five-year plans put more emphasis on road transportation until the early 1970s.

During the first five-year plan period, railroad passenger transportation volume grew at an average annual rate of 10 percent. But with the opening of the nation's first superhighway, the Seoul-Inch'ŏn Expressway in 1968 and the Seoul-Pusan Expressway two years later, passengers were diverted to the new highways in substantial numbers. As a result, 25.1 percent of passengers were carried by railroad and 24.0 percent by highway in 1976. Although the railroad traffic share has been increasing gradually, reaching 26.8 percent in 1992, private cars have taken over a growing share of transportation volume in recent years as more and more people can afford to own automobiles.

Overall Transportation Situation

Overall, the increase in traffic volume in Korea has actually surpassed the economic growth rate. During the past two decades, annual domestic passenger transportation volume has grown more than 8.9 times from 1,656 million persons in 1966 to 14,948 million persons in 1992. Domestic cargo volume increased 6.4 times during the same period, from 59.7 million tons in 1966 to 411 million tons in 1992.

Even greater increase rates were recorded in international air and surface transport volumes during the period, as foreign trade expanded sharply from almost nothing in the 1950s to export worth over $71.8 billion in 1991. Statistics show that Korean and foreign air and sea carriers transported a meager 1,998,000 people and 52,472,000 tons of cargo to and from Korea in 1976. The figures swelled to 11,595,000 passengers and 286 million tons in 1992.

Reflecting the fast pace of economic growth, the number of automobiles in the country has increased sharply since the late 1980s. After passing the 1,113,430 mark in 1985, the number of motor vehicles grew an average of 25 percent each year, The figure jumped to 4,247,816 in 1991, and to 5,230,894 in 1992. Of the 1992 figure, passenger cars numbered 3,416,000; buses 484,000; trucks 1,261,000; and special cars 25,000.

Land Transportation

Expressways

The 29.5km Seoul-Inch'ŏn Expressway, completed in 1968 at a cost of 3.49 billion won (about $9 million at that time), was the first modern highway to be built in Korea. The four-lane route cut the travel time between the capital city and Korea's second largest port, Inch'ŏn, from one full hour to less than 20 minutes.

The dedication of the 428km Seoul-Pusan Expressway in July 1970 marked another great stride forward in the nation's efforts to expand and modernize its transportation network. The four-lane arterial road, which runs diagonally across the entire length of the country, passes through such industrial and urban centers as Suwon, Ch'ŏnan, Taejŏn, Kumi, Taegu and Kyŏnjugju. The 79.5km branch route from Taejŏn to Chŏnju was completed in December 1970.

In 1973, a two-lane 358km southern coastal route connecting Chŏnju with Pusan via Kwangju was completed, speeding up transport of the area's agricultural products. The industrial city of Ulsan was linked to the expressway network with the construction of the 14.3km Onyang-Ulsan artery in November 1974. Next came the Suwon-Kangnŭng Highway stretching 201km, across the rugged T'aebaeksan Mountain Range in Kangwon-do province. With its highway's dedication in 1975, the eastern coastal area, rich in mineral deposits and marine products as well as tourist attractions, was drawn much closer to the nation's economic centers.

A 30km east coast route between Tonghae and Kangnŭng was connected to the Suwon-Kangnŭng Highway at the same time. Taegu was linked to Masan Port in Kyŏngsangnam-do province, which has a large free export zone, by

an 84km expressway opened in late 1977.

In 1981, the two-lane Pusan-Masan Highway was expanded to four lanes, and the `88 Olympic Highway, a 175.5km road connecting Kyŏngsang-do and Chŏlla-do provinces in the southern region, was built between 1981 and 1984.

The four-lane Chungbu Highway, a 145.3km road connecting Seoul and Taejon via Chŏngju, was constructed between April 1985 and December 1987, thereby sharing the ever increasing traffic volume of the Seoul-Pusan Expressway. By the end of 1992, the total length of the nation's highways reached 1,600 km.

As the overall volume of traffic grew rapidly in the early 1980s, construction of the two-lane Chung-ang Highway, which spans a total of 280km between Ch'unchŏn and Taegu passing in central Korea, was started in October 1989. A 114.5km long four-lane highway circling Seoul is under construction.

The Korea Highway Corporation (KHC), established in 1969 to take charge of the management of the nation's expressway system, is responsible for maintaining expressways, collecting tolls and opening new routes. According to KHC statistics, total of 309 million vehicles used the expressways under its care in 1991, giving the state-run corporation an annual revenue of 400.6 billion won (about $500.7 million).

During the first few years after the opening of Korea's first expressway, passenger vehicles were dominant on the new roads. Since 1972, however, there has been a growing percentage of freight trucks. In 1989, the share of vehicles on all expressways was 70.1 percent passenger cars, 8.6 percent buses and 21.3 percent trucks.

Railroad

In 1889, the first railroad line in Korea, the Kyŏng-in line linking Seoul and Inch'ŏn, was established. The Kyŏngbu line, running 445km between Seoul and Pusan was completed in 1905. Major trunk lines were formed in the shape of an "X" when the Honam line and Chung-ang line were opened in 1914 and 1942 respectively. Currently, total trackage is

Railroads and municipal subways are being expanded, with a high-speed rail system slated to link Seoul with Pusan in 2002.

6,462km with 846km double-tracked.

In 1963, the Korean National Railroad (KNR) was established as a separate government agency from the Ministry of Transportation.

The KNR is headed by an administrator who oversees six general agencies: the Planning and Management Office, the Transportation Bureau, the Engineering Bureau, the Rolling Stock Bureau, the Electrical Bureau and the Finance and Accounting Bureau. There are also five regional bureaus, a railroad college, a training center, and a laboratory and research institute.

The KNR now employs 37,800 people and operates four types of passenger trains: Pidulgi, T'ong-il, Mugunghwa, and Saemaŭl. In addition, the KNR sells through tickets between the KNR and Japanese Railways, which allow travelers from Korea and Japan to utilize a "railroad-ferry-railroad" connecting system with a single ticket.

For managerial improvement, the Government plans to convert the KNR into a public corporation by no later than January 1996 and is currently preparing the measures

necessary for this step, including the revision of pertinent regulations and a personnel reorganization.

To make railroads the leading means of transport in medium and long distance usage in Korea in the 21st century, the government established the Korean Highspeed Railroad Construction Corporation to build new electrified high speed lines, including the Seoul-Pusan and Seoul-East Coast lines. The corporation is now working on such practical matters as finance, optimum alignment and evaluation of alternatives for system selection.

The KNR is also engaged in three projects begun in 1991: the improvement of established major trunk lines, the augmentation of transportation capacity in the Seoul suburban area, and the construction of electrified lines from Seoul to Kwach'ŏn, Bundang and Ilsan.

In the future, the KNR plans to increase the transportation capacity of industrial lines and to restore the Kyŏngŭi and Kyŏngwon lines to prepare for future cooperation between North and South Korea.

Subway Systems

With the dedication of Seoul Subway Lines No. 3 and No. 4 on October 18, 1985, Seoul had the eighth longest subway system in the world with a total length of 120.7 km. Line 1 (7.8 km with nine stations), which opened on August 15, 1974, runs northeast to southwest through the downtown area. It is connected with the National Railway to the suburbs Suwon, Inch'ŏn and Ŭijŏngbu. Line 2, which runs 57 km through 48 stations, has a circular route that connects all major commercial and residential districts on both sides of the Han-gang River. Lines 3 and 4 cross each other like the letter "X," while Line 5, which is under construction, will traverse east to west for 52 km when completed in 1994. Three additional subway lines are currently under construction, to be completed during this decade. With its fully automated ticketing and fare collecting system, the Seoul subway carries about 3.7 million passengers a day, accounting for 21.2 percent of total traffic volume. The entire subway has the newest facilities, and stations are decorated in a combination of traditional motifs and contemporary designs.

Pusan, the second largest city in Korea, began laying subway tracks in 1981. Route No. 1 became operational in 1985, and route No.2 is scheduled to be completed in 1997.

Air Transportation

Korea's two air carriers currently serve 44 air traffic centers in various parts of the world, as part of Korea's expanding airline industry. The country's first airline was operated by the government and called Korean National Airlines. In 1969, management was turned over to private hands and renamed Korean Airlines. Later the name was changed to Korean Air (KAL), and the carrier now serves points in Asia, the Middle East, Europe, North America, South America and North Africa. Asiana Airlines (AAR), the country's second private airline, was established in 1988 and serves Asia and the U.S.A.

The growth of KAL, the national flag-carrier, has been rapid since its formation, recording an average 12 percent annual increase in passenger transportation volume.

In 1992, KAL carried 8,952,000 passengers on its domestic lines and 11,257,011 on international flights. Cargo services also have grown impressively, particularly since the opening of American routes in 1971. KAL and AAR planes now fly to 14 cities in Japan: Tokyo, Osaka, Fukuoka, Nagoya, Niigata, Sendai, Sapporo, Kagoshima, Nagasaki, Kumamoto, Okayama, Hiroshima, Okinawa and Oita. The national flag carrier's operations reach Los Angeles, New York, Chicago, San Francisco, Honolulu, Anchorage, Toronto and Vancouver in North America and Sao Paulo in South America. On Southeast Asia and Pacific routes, KAL flights go to Hong Kong, Manila, Bangkok, Guam, Saipan, Singapore, Kuala Lumpur, Jakarta, Bombay and Sydney. Middle East routes cover Jeddah and Bahrain, while European destinations include Paris, Frankfurt, London, Amsterdam, Zurich, Moscow, Vienna and Rome.

Seoul's growing importance in international air traffic can be attributed to a number of factors, including the hosting of the 1988 Olympics, Korea's geographic location, and expanding relationships in the fields of diplomacy, trade and culture. Many foreign airlines have been attracted by the proximity to impor-

Merchant Fleet and Cargo Handling Capacity

(Unit: Index Numbers)

	1968	1971	1976	1981	1986	1989	1991	1992
Cargo Handling Capacity (Thousand ton)	11,964	19,507	34,000	87,423	150,676	189,926	248,365	258,000
Vessel Tonnage (Thousand gwt)	294	1,043	3,139	6,309	7,294	8,797	9,645	9,770

tant markets and have opened regular services to and from Korea. As of 1992, the number of foreign airlines operating into Korea had reached 25.

In recent years the Government has made large investments in expanding and improving airport facilities. New installations at Kimpo Airport, the main air center serving the capital city, make it capable of handling 10.9 million passengers and 1.4 million tons of cargo annually.

There are three international airports in Korea: Kimpo in Seoul; Kimhae, which serves the large southern port of Pusan; and Cheju Airport on the island off the southern tip of the peninsula. Domestic airports include those in Kwangju, Taegu, Ulsan, Pohang, Sachŏn, Yechŏn, Mokpo, Yŏsu, Kangnŭng, Sokcho, Chinju and Kunsan.

The Korea International Airports Authority, established in 1980, has the responsibility of managing and operating the three international and 12 domestic airports as well as the Civil Aviation Training Center. It will also oversee the construction of a new international airport on Yŏngjongdo island, just west of Seoul. in 1998, that will meet the ever-growing traffic demands in Seoul.

Marine Transportation

In a country like Korea which depends on export-oriented policies to achieve economic growth, an adequate merchant fleet is essential for development. Until the early 1970s, Korea's merchant fleet was inconsequential, and the volume of seaborne trade carried by national flag vessels was insignificant. The Government established the Korea Maritime and Port Administration (KMPA) in 1976 in order to promote the marine transportation industry.

As a result of integrated government and private efforts to expand the national fleet, by the end of 1992 Korea had ships totalling 9.8 million gross tons. Korean ships travel trade routes through Asia to North and South America, Europe, Australia, the Middle East and Africa. The nation's cargo volume has increased sharply as foreign trade has expanded year after year. Total cargo volume in 1992 stood at 286 million tons, 90 million tons of which was transported by national flag carriers.

Since ports are intersections of overland and marine transportation, expansion of harbor facil-

Trade Volume and Transport volume of Korean Vessels

(In million M/T)

	Trade Volume	Transports by Korean Vessels	Percentage
1965	6.0	1.8	30.2
1970	22.4	5.5	24.4
1975	41.3	13.4	32.5
1980	94.0	46.4	49.4
1985	133.0	62.3	47.2
1989	204.0	80.2	39.3
1991	263.0	90.0	34.2

Source: Korea Maritime and Port Administration

Air Passenger and Freight Traffic

Unit: thousand persons, thousand tons

		1966	1970	1975	1980	1985	1988	1991	1992
Number of Passengers	International	131	398	1,566	2,922	4,382	6,353	10,476	11,257
	Domestic	192	917	906	1,480	3,467	6,297	12,505	14,555
	Total	323	1,315	2,472	4,402	7,849	12,650	22,981	25,812
Freight	International	7	25	97	191	333	508	901	837
	Domestic	1	4	5	13	67	111	208	241
	Total	8	29	102	204	400	609	1,109	1,078

Source: Ministry of Transportation

ities is essential to handle increasing cargo volume. Korea has invested large amounts in expansion and improvement of harbor facilities since 1962. These improvements have facilitated rapid growth. By the end of 1992, Korea's total cargo handling capacity reached 258 million tons per year, 28 times more than the 1961 level of nine million tons.

By 1993, Korea's total cargo volume is expected to reach 299 million tons. To transport cargo smoothly, a total tonnage of 10 million G/T will be necessary, and it is expected that the nation's ship building industry will make a significant contribution to fleet expansion. The annual cargo handling capability is also set to increase.

Communications

The telegraph service from Seoul to Inchon, the first modern communications service in Korea, was established on September 28, 1885. The introduction of this service gradually replaced fire signaling, which had been the main communications method. Telephone service was first introduced in 1902. The international telephone service between Seoul and Bongchun, China was available in 1924. However, the actual basis for the development of Korean communications infrastructure was provided in 1961 with the beginning of the Five-Year Telcommunications Plans, which were part of the First through Fourth Five-Year Economic Development Plans.

Infrastructural facilities for communications were expanded in the following stages: first, a land subscription wireless mobile telephone was opened in 1961. This was followed by the introduction of semi-electronic switching M10CN in 1978. Second, two satellite communication earth stations were established in 1970 and 1977, repectively. Third, a coaxial carrier circuit, a long-distance communications network, between Seoul and Pusan was opened in 1975.

Up until the early 1980s the most crucial task for the communications business was to promptly and efficiently satisfy the immense communi-

cations demand following in the wake of economic development. Also, the chronic telephone backlog and the low standard of telephone service were the subjects of public complaint and hindered national development as well.

As a result, the Government designated the Ministry of Communications to be in charge of the public telecommunications business in order to resolve various obstacles which were accumulating throughout all aspects of communications management. As the first corresponding measure, the Ministry of Communications separated policy-making tasks and business operations by establishing the Korea Telecommunications Authority in 1982, and the Data Communications Corporation (DACOM) in 1991.

The separation of tasks allowed the Ministry of Communications to concentrate on communications policies. Since 1982, the Ministry has invested much in facilities, and promoted advanced technology development in order to resolve chronic telephone backlogs and to modernize the telecommunications sector, which lagged behind those of developed countries. As a result, Korea became the tenth nation in the world to develop an electronized switching system with the introduction of the TDX-1 in 1986. With this development, Korea can provide additional 1 million communications line facilities annually. In particular, the number of telephone facilities exceeded 10 million lines in 1987, completely resolving the telephone backlog, and Korea entered the era of one telephone per household. As of the end of 1992, the number of facilities was 19 million, and the number of subscribers was 16 million. Korea is now the ninth nation in the world to possess such extensive facilities. The telephone distribution rate also increased from 10.4 sets per 100 persons in 1982 to 35.7 sets in 1992.

Furthermore, the Government permitted competition in all aspects of the VAN service sector in July 1990, in order to firmly establish competition in the communications business. The Government also introduced competition to the international telephone sector in December 1991, forming a duopoly system. In addition, competitors for providing mobile telephone sevice were selected for different regions, and

The Korean satellite "Uribyŏl 2" *carrying out telecommunications and broadcasting.*

their business operations were permitted beginning in August 1992. Competitors for providing mobile telephone services will also soon be selected. Korea entered the executing stage of competition with the establishment of such measures. The objectives of these measures are to introduce stimulation and creativity in the private sector so that competitive strength will increase in the communications industry.

The private use of radiowaves was restricted in many ways in order to protect against the use of communications in upholding the different political systems of South and North Korea. Inevitably, this hindered the use of radiowaves and its technology development, leading to regulation-oriented operation of radiowaves and its technology development, including: frequency management, permission and review of radio stations, and operational supervision. However, in 1980, radiowave use was gradually deregulated following the demand to stimulate the highly advanced information transmission functions required by radiowave media. As a result of the high frequency development, the number of radio stations increased from 30,723 in 1982 to 502,285 as of the end of 1992. This is an annual average increase of 33 percent. The number of radio station employees increased from 72,384 in 1982 to 164,633 as of the end of 1992. In particular, the paging sector, which was first introduced with one million circuit capacity, rapidly increased to 2.5 million circuits as of the end of 1992. The cellular mobile telephone service was first introduced to metropolitan areas, including Seoul, Anyang and Suwon, with 3,000 circuits, increasing to 514,000 circuits as of the end of 1992, demonstrating the ever increasing popularity of mobile communications.

In the broadcasting communications sector, business to expand the broadcasting network was promoted from 1982 to 1985 in order to meet the rapidly increasing demand of TV, following the introduction of color TV. This resulted in increasing the TV view rate from 66 percent to 91.6 percent. As a result of actively promoting measures to stimulate the broadcasting sector, new broadcasting stations were established towards the end of the Sixth Five Year

The use of cellular phones and computer modems is rapidly increasing in Korea.

Telecommunications Plan, from 1987 to 1991. These new stations include Pyŏnghwa Broadcasting Corporation, Buddhist Broadcasting System, and Traffic Broadcasting System. These initiations are the contributing factors to the turning point of Korean broadcasting stations. Also, with the introduction of character multiplex broadcasting service, the Ministry actively promoted new types of broadcasting methods such as high definition TV broadcasting, FM multi-broadcasting, and integrated wire broadcasting. Furthermore, the Government is proceeding with plans to launch KOREASAT, a broadcasting/communications satellite, towards the middle of 1995. This launching is in line with the existing plans for communications/broadcasting business. In addition, the launching of KOREASAT will resolve the difficulties in viewing caused by uneven frequency delivery, and provide high-tech communications service such as high quality broadcasting service.

The communications industry achieved a surprising success by completely satisfying the basic communications demand in the 1980s. In the 1990s, however, communications demands are becoming more advanced and diverse with the rapid development of communications technology. Also, the information/communication industry is oriented towards information production and distribution. This industry is expected to contribute to new employment opportunities, create added value to the communications sector, and play a crucial role in economic activities in the future. The developed countries are concentrating on fostering this industry, and its importance is increasing day by day.

Corresponding to its increased significance, the Ministry plans to consistently expand basic communications facilities during the Seventh Five-Year Telecommunications Plan (1992-1996). In addition, plans to modernize communications networks and to construct an Integrated Services Digital Network (ISDN) will be expedited. Moreover, services in the information/communications sector will be improved by settling fair competition systems in the communications industry and be distributed to the public by standardizing communications call rates between different regions. Also, the Ministry plans to foster and support related industries.

The Ministry aims for the following in the local communications facilities sector: 1) continue satisfying demands for telephone stations; 2) improve call quality; and 3) replace mechanical switching systems with digital switching systems by 1995 in order to construct intelligent communications networks.

In particular, 9.202 million switching circuits will be provided during the Seventh Five-Year Telecommunications Plan so that the number of circuits will increase from 2.014 million in 1992 to 24.753 million by the end of 1996. Also, the Ministry plans to completely replace the existing paper insulated cable with Foam Skin cable, which has superior transmission qualities, in order to improve the quality of subscriber line route facilities.

In the long-distance call facilities sector, the Ministry plans to annually supply 401,000 circuits for switching facilities,and 493,000 circuits for transmission line facilities.Also, the following will be promoted: digitalizing toll switching facilities, installing optical cable transmission lines among administrative organizations, and constructing optical cables near highway roads. Moreover, the Ministry aims for the early construction of a satellite communications network. Following this objective, leased satellite service through INTELSAT has been provided since 1992. From 1995, the domestic satellite Mugunghwa will provide the satellite communications service.

In the international communications facilities sector, 10,856 circuits for international switching facilities will be supplied during the Seventh Five-Year Telecommunications Plan. In 1992, the facilities were converted to full electronic international switching facilities. Also, more international gateways will added to the existing one in Seoul. The second international gateway will be established in 1994 also in Seoul. Pusan International Gateway will be established in 1994. By 1996, the construction of Taejŏn International Gateway will be completed.

In the satellite communications facilities sector, the second satellite communications earth station for DACOM was newly established from 1991-1992 through the INTELSAT system. During the same period, an earth station for restoring international communications in times of emergency, will be constructed in Bo-eun. In 1994-1996, a small-scale earth station (C-Band) for IBS will be newly established in the Seoul and Taejon areas. In 1995, a coastal earth station will be constructed in Keum-san through the INMARSAT operated satellite by the end of 1993, and will be used to communicate with vessels in the Indian Ocean region. A satellite communications earth station for air vessels will be constructed in 1995 and operated in the same region. Along with the satellite communications facilities, marine optical cable will be used to expand international transmission lines.

Also, the Ministry plans to realize the digitalization the communications network at an early stage in order to construct the Integrated Services Digital Network. Therefore, the Ministry will establish an ISDN model suitable for domestic circumstances and improve and develop a Public Services Telephone Network (PSTN). As a final objective, the ministry will construct a foundation for a Broadband Integrated Digital Network (B-ISDN), which can accommodate moving pictures. This plan will proceed in connection with the plan to construct a cable TV network.

Such directions for advancing the communications network can be summarized into the following: first, the modernization and expansion of service areas for transmitting and exchanging various composite media; second, the privatization of communications made possible by micro-cell mobile communications and the development of portable communications through private numbers; third, the development of intelligent communications networks which allow users to receive various services.

In order to correspond to both domestic and international environmental changes, the Ministry will continue to establish the necessary environment for the development of domestic communications industries. Also, during the Seventh Five-Year Telecommunications Plan,

A collection of Korean stamps.

Korea Telecom will be authorized to continue its monopoly of the local telephone business, which needs large scale investment in facilities, in order to increase its international competitive strength. Moreover, competition was introduced to the international telephone service sector as of December, 1991. With this basis, measures to gradually introduce competition to the long distance telephone service sector and the mobile communication sector, which are small in investment scale and rapidly changing in technology, are being reviewed.

Postal Service

Korea's postal service has played a significant role in modernizing the country for one hundred years, since its inception in 1884. Keeping pace with the economic growth of the country, the postal system has grown remarkably into what it is today.

Korea has been associated with the Universal Postal Union's activities since it was admitted to the union in 1900. Korea is now prepared to take a more active part in the work of the UPU along with other members of the world postal community.

As of the end of 1992, there were 3,422 post offices operating throughout the country, meaning at least every myŏn (a group of several villages) was being served by one post office.

In 1992, postal mail volume amounted to about 2,850 million items, and most of the letter-post items were delivered by the next working day, although delivery to remote villages might require two to three working days. The volume of mail is constantly growing, with an average rate of increase of about 10.6 percent per year.

The efficiency of mail operations has greatly increased since the introduction of the five digit postal code in July 1970, and the standardization of envelope sizes in January 1974. The revision of the former postal code into six digits was effected in February 1988, to make it more adaptable to the mechanization of mail operations. Mechanization of mail operations is being expanded and optical character reading machines are being installed at the Seoul Mail Center as a part of the policy to increase the efficiency of mail operations. More machines for mechanization of mail operations will be installed at major post offices in larger cities in the future.

To meet the special needs of customers, International Express Mail Service which can provide next day delivery service to specific cities of major countries and the Intelpost (Bureaufax) Service are also being provided. Presently the EMS has networks with 92 countries.

Postal Saving and Insurance Services

All post offices across the nation offer postal savings, postal life insurance, postal money orders and postal giro services. The postal savings and insurance business got off to a modest start in 1983. Such business transactions, however, have increased remarkably over the past several years. The number of postal savings accounts passed the 11 million mark as of the end of 1992, and the number of insurance policy holders totaled more than one million.

To provide the public with postal saving and insurance services of first-rate quality, the Ministry has brought into operation an on-line computer banking network linking 2,700 post offices throughout the country. Almost all of the on-line banking terminal machines are manufactured locally. A new on-line postal savings service called the Integrated Passbook System began operation in October, 1985. Cash dispensers also are in operation at major post offices.

SCIENCE AND TECHNOLOGY

History of Science

Iron technology entered Korea from China during the fourth and third centuries B.C. at a time when China's influence on Korea was significant. Iron quickly replaced bronze as the main metal for making both weapons and tools.

Generally speaking, science in Korea developed under the influence of China until the 19th century, and the development of Korean science depended on the combination of external stimulation and influences, and internal needs. As in other fields, Korea imported and then modified Chinese science and technology, to better suit local needs and conditions. This more often than not resulted in new inventions and discoveries.

Ancient Chinese achievements were notable in the fields of mathematics, astronomy, meteorology, magnetism, mechanical engineering, civil engineering, gunpowder, textiles (especially silk), paper-making, printing, ceramics, agriculture, and medicine. Not so well-known is the fact that early Korea achieved almost equal success in nearly all of these areas as well. In particular, Korean astronomy, printing, and ceramics, though all originally based on techniques imported from China, were in some ways more advanced than their Chinese counterparts.

The earliest Korean educational institution, called *T'aehak* (Great Learning), was established in A.D. 372 and modeled after similar Chinese institutions. In 682, during the Unified Shilla period (668-935), a similar school, *Kukhak* (National School), was established. These schools taught the Chinese language and Confucian classics exclusively and were intended mainly to train prospective government officials. These early Korean educational institutions survived or were succeeded by similar institutions until the late 19th century. Adoption of Chinese government and educational institutions, though in highly modified form, stimulated the growth of Confucian scholarship among the upper classes in Korea.

Traditional Confucian education maintained that to be a man of noble character was an end in itself, not a tool for any professional pursuit. The goal of Confucian education was to create a perfect man, not a professional, and this perfect man was required to think in a way suitable to a man of noble character, not a practical man. Accordingly, there was no desire for the development of natural science and technology among the ruling class. Astronomy and calendar-making, which had special interest for the government, however, showed significant development, as did medicine and agriculture.

Successive Korean dynasties were sensitive to the phenomena of the heavens, and developed astrological concepts linking the security and safety of the royal family and the country to such phenomena. These astrological concepts, along with the development of agriculture, contributed to the development of astronomy and meteorology. At first, Korean astronomy developed as a branch of Chinese astronomy; since Chinese astronomy after the Han Dynasty stressed calendrical studies, Korean astronomy at first proceeded along similar lines. However, the Koreans developed their own scientific methods of astronomy and weather observations and data processing.

Technological developments during the Three Kingdoms period (57 B.C.-A.D. 668) are exemplified in the construction of the Ch'ŏmsŏngdae Observatory, the Sŏkkuram Grotto, and beautiful metalwork, especially the bronze bells, as well as the oldest surviving printed scroll of the *Dharani* Scripture. The Ch'ŏmsŏngdae Observatory, built in A.D. 647 and standing 9.17 meters in height, is probably the oldest observatory still remaining in East Asia. As an astronomical observation center of the Shilla Kingdom (57 B.C.-A.D. 935), it served as the standard of the meridian.

Another well-known symbol of the cultural attainments of the Shilla Kingdom is the artificial cave temple, Sŏkkuram. Its geometrical design, beautiful sculptures, and architectural plans represent the essence of the arts and sciences of ancient Korea. Sŏkkuram is an artificial structure built around a dome and comprised of stone structures of circular, triangular, hexagonal, and octagonal shapes, which required a high degree of mathematical and engineering knowledge.

The creative techniques and metallurgical

skills of the Shilla artisans are demonstrated by numerous Buddhist bells. In their attempts to make these large bells, a combination of the *chung* and *to* bells of ancient China, the Shilla artisans endeavored and finally managed to find the perfect bronze alloy suitable for their casting. It was a zinc-bronze alloy, which was a mixture of copper, zinc, tin, lead, and other metals. Chinese experts of the time observed, "Persian copper is good for making mirrors, and Shilla's is good for making bells."

Also highly illustrative of the excellence of Shilla technology were their printing techniques. The printed scroll of the *Dharani* Scripture, discovered in a pagoda at Pulguksa Temple in 1966, was printed by woodblock, possibly between 704 and 751. Since it proved to be the oldest woodblock printing, it can be assumed that Korea was a pioneer in the development of woodblock printing and that Shilla printing techniques might have been instrumental in making the Japanese Million Pagoda *Dharani* Scripture possible.

The technology of Koryŏ (918-1392) was based largely on the tradition and heritage of Shilla. Koryŏ's level of science and technology is illustrated in its astronomical observation activities, the development of woodblock printing, and the superb technique for making the exquisite inlaid ceramics known as Koryŏ celadon.

The astronomy of Koryŏ is distinguished by the development of observational procedures, as well as by the creation of a more accurate calendar. Koryŏ observation records are notable for being independent, accurate, and long-standing. It is noteworthy that all the observation records of the eclipses of the sun (132 occurrences), of comets (87 occurrences) and especially of sunspots (34 occurrences) during the years from 1024 to 1383 are shown in intervals of eight to 20 years. The calculating table of the *Shou-Shi* calendar, compiled by Kang P'o in 1343, shows that Koryŏ astronomers were familiar with the theory of *Shou-Shi* in calculating a calendar with highly advanced methods. The length of the year that they calculated corresponds with the modern value up to the sixth decimal place.

The development of woodblock printing in Koryŏ was motivated by the wish to repel external enemies, the Khitan and the Mongols, with the spiritual help of Buddha. The resulting work, the famous *Tripitaka Koreana*, is the oldest and greatest achievement of this art still extant.

Koryŏ celadon earned fame for its artistic beauty and quality. Produced entirely for the aesthetic enjoyment of the aristocracy of that kingdom, they are characterized by a unique inlaying technique which was greatly admired by contemporary Chinese scholars.

Another major technological accomplishment during the Koryŏ period was the invention of metal printing type, sometime between the late 12th century and the early 13th century. The movable metal type was not developed further, however, because of the attachment of the people of that time to the beautiful woodblock printing.

Signs of original and creative endeavors were also found in various fields of national life in the early part of the Chosŏn Dynasty (1392-1910). In 1403, King T'aejong ordered his men to make bronze printing type in spite of opposition from his courtiers. Existing copies of books printed with the 1403 bronze type are in no way superior to the woodblock printing of the Koryŏ era, and the casting of bronze type must have been much more time-consuming than the carving of woodblocks. The additional expense in time, money, and labor was not worth the results. This project served as a matrix for the development of the renowned Chosŏn printing of the next era, however.

Astronomical research continued as well. The Royal Astronomical Observatory (*Sŏun-gwan*) compiled statistical meteorological data gathered from outposts in the provinces, counties, and towns for more than 400 years, until the downfall of the Chosŏn Dynasty in 1910.

Many new observational devices, such as armillary clocks, simplified armillary spheres, automatic water clocks, jade clepsydras, and sundials, were installed in the Astronomical Observatory in Kyŏngbokkung Palace. With these new devices, research was modernized, leading to the development of a much more accurate calendar. Many important astronomical

Chŏmsŏngdae, an ancient observatory in Kyŏngju (A.D.647)

Copper-alloy type, dating from the reign of King Sejong (r.1419-50)

books and articles, the combination of the practical results of observations and theories, were published. In the medical field, an 85-volume collection of various herb prescriptions, *Hyang-yak Chipsŏngbang* (Compilation of Native Korean Prescriptions) was published in 1433. This collection presented for the first time a systematic study of Chosŏn's medical science on a thoroughly academic basis. In 1445, after three painstaking years of research, the 365-volume *Ŭibang Yuch'wi* (Classified Collection of Medical Prescriptions) was published.

There also was the invention of rain gauges and water marks during the reign of King Sejong (r.1419-50), accompanied by the perfection of methods to measure precipitation. These developments resulted from efforts of Chosŏn scientists and scholars to obtain a statistical understanding of Korea's erratic seasonal rainfall distribution.

But, as in China, there was no attempt to develop theoretical studies of astronomy and meteorology in the Chosŏn period. Astronomers and meteorologists were lower-level officials of government offices whose work was related to the observation of the heavens and weather. The purview of these officials was of necessity limited to practical subjects related to astronomical and weather observations, leading to no theoretical or creative work. The origin of Korean science can be found in the technical tradition of craftsmen who passed down their practical experience and skills from generation to generation. They attached importance to empirical research, rather than theoretical research, resulting in the development of technology but not any systematic or theoretical methods.

Korean scientific tradition, which reached its apex in the days of King Sejong, remained at a standstill until the 17th century, when Western science and technology, which offered a new prospect and orientation, were introduced.

This 17th century sundial replica is based on the original from the reign of the King Sejong.

Contact with Western Science

Christianity and the science and technology of the Western world found their way into China, Japan, and Korea in the 17th and 18th centuries. Western religion and science presented formidable challenges to the established systems and orders in these three Asian countries whose societies were based on the tenets of Confucianism. Western science and technology proved to be more advanced, as demonstrated in the Western military victories during the Opium Wars of 1840-42.

The first Western work to reach Korea was Matteo Ricci's map of Europe which was brought to Korea by Yi Kwang-chŏng in 1603, one year after its publication in Peking. This was followed by several copies of other maps drawn by Ricci. Many more were to follow. In 1630, the Korean envoy to China, Chŏng Tu-won, became acquainted with Johannes Rodriguez, an Italian priest in Peking.

Rodriguez presented Chŏng with books on astronomy, the calendar, geography, and also a telescope, an alarm clock, and a cannon, all of which were presented to the king upon Chŏng's return home.

In 1720, the Korean envoy to Peking, Yi Im-yŏng, met two Jesuits, Koegler and Saurez, who were supervisors of the royal astronomical observatory in Peking. He received books from them on scientific subjects and read them diligently. He was particularly impressed by Ricci's *Outline of Arithmetic* and took a keen interest in Western science. Numerous other Korean envoys visited the Catholic cathedral in Peking, and a small but steady stream of Western works on religion and science, translated into Chinese, began to flow from Peking to Seoul. All of this Western learning made a considerable impression on Korean scholars.

It is regrettable, however, but significant that the only practical result of this knowledge was a calendar reform in 1654, following the example of the Chinese. Western knowledge in the 17th and 18th centuries remained a mere intellectual curiosity, with little or no effect upon government or society.

In the latter half of the 19th century, Korea, known in the West as "the Hermit Kingdom," was fully exposed to the challenge of Western civilization, as Catholicism, steamships, and Western industrial products made massive inroads into the country. Western steamships equipped with guns and other arms showed up from time to time in the waters off the coast, posing a grave threat to national defense.

In 1876, Korea discarded the extreme isolationist policy it had pursued up until that time and opened its doors to the world by concluding a treaty of amity with Japan. This was followed by treaties of commerce and navigation with the United States, Great Britain, and Germany in 1882 and with France in 1886.

On the domestic front, an enlightenment movement was launched to develop the country by importing Western culture, especially technology. In 1894, the Kabo Reforms were announced as an attempt to modernize the administrative and social systems of the country. After the Kabo Reforms, education was modernized with the establishment of government-run elementary schools, middle schools, normal schools, and foreign-language schools. "Knowledge is power" was a maxim that was common among learned people in those days. Many politicians, who were active in the enlightenment movement, began to devote themselves to the education of young people. By 1910, when Korea was annexed by Japan, about 3,000 private schools had been established throughout the country. These schools taught Western science, history, geography, political science, law, arithmetic, and algebra. The 50 years that followed was a period during which Korea made little or no progress in terms of science and technology, due to oppressive Japanese policies at first, and then post-liberation disarray culminating in the Korean War of 1950-53.

From 1945, the year Korea was liberated from Japanese colonial rule, through to the 1950s, Korea remained in a period of preparation. There was only piecemeal transplanting of advanced science and technology from more advanced countries, and a very gradual development of scientific and technological education to train much needed manpower. The 1960s, when Korea's First Five-Year Economic Development Plan was launched, marked a turning point in the development of science and technology. The importance of science and technology to the process of rapid industrialization was fully recognized, and the nation pushed ahead with their development, in line with the successive five-year economic development plans.

As a result, investments in science and technology have increased markedly over the years. The Government has made systematic efforts to develop science and technology by realigning relevant policymaking mechanisms and administrative machinery. The inauguration of the Ministry of Science and Technology (MOST) in 1967, perhaps the first such institution in any developing country, cleared the way for this realignment.

Science and Technology Development

Role of Science and Technology

Science and technology have been important instruments in effecting national development policy since the early sixties, and as a consequence, science and technology policy has been implemented in line with Korean economic policy.

The main features of Korea's science and technology strategy to support industrialization can be separated into three stages. In the first stage, in the 1960s, the main development goal of industry was to lay a foundation for industrialization through the development of import-substitute industries, expansion of light industries, and support for producer goods industries. The science and technology strategy was to strengthen scientific and technical education, to build up the technological infrastructures, and to promote foreign technology imports. During this period, the Ministry of Science and Technology, a central government body, was established to undertake scientific and technological development. The Korea Institute of Science and Technology (KIST), a comprehensive industrial technology research institute, was inaugurated in 1966. The following year, in 1967, the Science and Technology Promotion Law was enacted.

In the second stage, in the 1970s, the science and technology strategy aimed at strengthening technical and engineering education in the heavy and chemical industry fields, improving the institutional mechanism for adapting imported technology, and promoting research to meet industrial needs. These strategies were to support the government's efforts to expand the heavy and chemical industries. In line with these strategies, government-supported specialized research institutes were established in the fields of machinery, shipbuilding, marine science, electronics, electricity, etc. The Technology Development Promotion Law and the Engineering Services Promotion Law were also enacted. In the course of industrialization,

Outline of Strategy

Period	Industrialization	Science and Technology
1960s	· Develop import substitute industries · Expand export-oriented · Support producer goods industries	· Strengthen S&T education · Deepen scientific and technological infrastructure · Promote foreign technology imports
1970s	· Expand heavy and chemical industries · Shift emphasis from capitals · Strengthen export-oriented industry competitiveness	· Expand technical training · Improve institutional mechanism for adapting imported technology · Promote research applicable to industrial needs
1980s	· Transform industrial structure to one of comparative advantage · Expand technology intensive industries · Encourage manpower development and improve productivity of industries	· Develop and acquire top-level scientists and engineers · Perform national R&D projects efficiently · Promote industries technology
1990s	· Adjust industrial structure and improve productivity · Promote balanced regional development	· Develop basic science, high technology and social welfare technology · Expand science and technology resources and promote efficiency

the manufacturing sector has expanded substantially and contributed extensively to Korea's economic growth. Since the mid-1970s, the industrial structure has expanded extensively.

In the third stage, in the 1980s, Korea's industrial policy was directed to transforming the industrial structure into one with a comparative advantage, to expanding technology-intensive industries such as machinery and electronics, and to encouraging technical manpower development and enhancement of productivity. To this end, in the science and technology fields, Korea has continuously sought the development and acquisition of high level scientists and engineers by adopting an extensive policy which includes the reinforcement of graduate school education, the expansion of overseas training programs, and the repatriation of experts abroad. This leaves an important task facing the country in the 1990s, to maintain the current growth rate and in particular to further enhance the efficiency of the maunufacturing sector.

To promote the productivity of research and development, joint efforts among R&D institutes, universities, and industry have been strengthened in the implementation of select large-scale R&D projects, and at the same time, joint research programs and joint ventures with other countries have been stressed. By strengthening indigenous R&D capabilities and introducing advanced technology from abroad, the Government has localized the key industrial technologies.

Outline of Science and Technology Policy

The Korean Government, recognizing the importance of science and technology to the country's development, has formulated and implemented science and technology development policies in an organized manner. Since the launching of the First Five-Year Economic Development Plan in 1962, science and technology development has been deliberately and systematically integrated into development planning to provide Korea with the means for reaching its overall development targets. Particularly, the Government has placed heavy emphasis on the promotion of science and technology by taking concrete steps to push ahead with science and technology policy programs that will benefit the general public, with the intention of realizing the people's visions and hopes. The primary policy directions emphasize "creation" rather than "imitation," developing selected high-tech areas toward the 21st century, strengthening science programs for the younger generation, and securing stable financial resources for R&D investment.

For an effective science policy and institutional infrastructure, Korea's policy on science and technology development concentrates on the following points.

First, the Government will continuously pursue a technology-led policy, allowing science and technology to play a leading role in promoting socio-economic development. For this purpose, available resources are to be allocated for the promotion of science in a preferential manner, attracting high caliber manpower to the science and technology fields by improving the social condition for these fields. As for existing policies and systems which are liable to be easily diversified or altered, they will be restructured in order to ensure consistency and comprehensiveness for the sake of technological innovation. In addition, the Presidential Science and Technology Advisory Committee, consisting of representatives and experts from industrial, academic, and scientific fields, operates in accordance with Article 127 of the Constitution to recommend the most desirable science and technology policies to the President.

Second, the Government has placed special emphasis on the securing and nurturing of groups of creative scientists and high caliber technological manpower in order to meet the rapidly increasing demand for R&D, both in the public and private sectors. As of 1991 the total number of qualified scientists and engineers stood at 76,252 representing 17.6 persons per 10,000 people, showing that Korea is still short of high-caliber manpower. To alleviate this shortage, the Government, together with the private sector, will pursue the development of effective training in science and technology-related fields in higher education. In accordance with long-term projections of high-level scientific and technological manpower requirements, Korea will try to secure a total of 150,000 scientists and engineers, or 30 persons per 10,000 people, by the year 2001. Among these scientists and engineers, 15,000, or 10 percent, will be tapped as top-level scientists capable of carrying out leading roles in their respective R&D fields. To this end, the Korean Government will try to improve higher science and engineering education, expand overseas training programs for advanced study, and also increase repatriation of Korean scientists and engineers from abroad.

Third, the Government has drastically increased R&D investment, thereby making remarkable achievements since 1980. The budget for science and technology has been increased by about 15 percent annually over the past eight years, while public enterprises, including telecommunications and electrical power companies, are encouraged to set aside a sizable portion of their income for technology development. Along with this, the private sector has also rapidly augmented their R&D investment by about 20 percent annually, aided in large part by various government incentive programs. As a result, the total amount of R&D expenditures jumped from $418 million in 1981, or 0.64 percent of the GNP, to $5.46 billion in 1991, or 2.02 percent of the GNP. However, more extensive funding will be required if Korea is to upgrade its science and technology to the level of advanced countries by the turn of the century. Therefore, the Government has set the goal of boosting R&D investment to 4.0 percent of the GNP in 1998, and to over five percent in the year 2001.

Fourth, the Korean Government also has undertaken national R&D projects which normally could not be pursued by industry alone since 1982, in order to develop the key industrial technology for Korea's industrialization. The criteria for selecting national projects include their technology intensiveness, international comparative advantage, conservation of energy and resources, growth potential, and contribution to social development. Among these projects, industry-oriented projects have been carried out through the joint efforts of industry, public institutes, and the Government, while those projects of public interest, such as energy and resources development and health and environment related projects, have been undertaken by the public sector itself. In response to the trend of the ever-increasing R&D scale and sophistication, the Government is responding systematically by carrying out national R&D projects with increased investment.

Fifth, in order to utilize R&D resources effectively, which are not sufficient in absolute scale, and to push ahead with policies systematically, the Korean Government redefined the roles of government-supported R&D institutes, universities and private enterprise in carrying out R&D activities. The R&D capability of universities and private enterprise was nominal in the 1960s, with most R&D activities being conducted by government-supported institutes. This has changed drastically, particularly in the 1980s. Private businesses have established their own in-house R&D facilities, greatly enhancing R&D capability, while universities have also enlarged their R&D capacity by allocating more expenditures for R&D. In this trend, universities pursue basic science, while private institutes undertake R&D for commercialization. Government-supported institutes play the role of a bridge linking universities and private institutes, and are also responsible for the areas which private institutes cannot afford due to heavy financial burden and high risk, along with

commonly based technology areas having a great impact on socio-economic sectors.

Sixth, in order to foster the industrial technology development, the Korean Government provided various incentives to private enterprise, which must play the leading role in the process of industrial technology development in a free market economy. In the case of proprietary technology, the Government provided indirect incentives to the private sector under the principle of competition. Meanwhile, in the case of generic technology, the Government extended direct as well as indirect support to the private and public sectors under the principle of cooperation.

Following these two basic principles, the Government recommends that large scale companies establish at least one research center per company, while small and medium companies are encouraged to organize research and development consortia in related fields. For this purpose, various incentives are provided through tax exemptions, special depreciation, financial grants, availability of long-term low interest development loans, and government procurement, among others. As a result of this incentive system, Korea has witnessed a remarkable increase in the number of private research institutes from 52 in 1980 to 1,445 in January 1993, and research consortia from none to 68 in the same time period. In addition, in order to adapt to the new policy direction towards autonomy and market opening under the free market principle, the Government will minimize controls and restrictions on industry. Korea will virtually liberalize technology inducement, revise the protectionist measures for the local innovator and extensively overhaul laws and regulations related to science and technology to increase autonomy.

Seventh, Korea has strengthened international technical cooperation in order to meet the rising tide of internationalization of technology development. To better cope with the growing interdependence of the world economy, Korea has been expanding both bilateral and multilateral international cooperation activities, especially since 1980. As of the end of 1992, the Korean Government had exchanged 25 scientific and technical cooperation agreements with foreign countries, while holding science minister meetings regularly. Furthermore, 72 international joint research projects have been in full swing with financial support from the Government amounting to $6.3 million in 1992. In the spirit of mutual benefit and utility, the Government will make continuous efforts towards the exchange of researchers, the exchange of technical information, joint R&D programs and active participation in international cooperative programs. In addition, Korea intends to increase technical assistance to developing countries to share Korea's experiences and technologies for common prosperity.

Eighth, one of Korea's major policy directions is the regional dispersion of technology development domestically. The Government has established industrial complexes in major regions of the country since the 1970s, while actively promoting the construction of Taedŏk Science Town along with new technology-based industries in the vicinity. The Government also plans to construct other specialized research parks in major industrial areas throughout Korea, forming a nationwide technobelt where full utilization of manpower, technology, and information is possible through networking of telecommunication systems, transportation and utilities.

Last, a climate favorable to the development of science and technology has been a major policy goal for laying a solid foundation for science and technology. Accordingly, the Government, with the cooperation of the academic and industrial communities and the mass media, has launched a nationwide science movement whose main objectives are to create an environment in which the general public can apply scientific principles to daily living and to instill in youth an exploratory attitude in science with a spirit of rationality, efficiency, and creativity. The Government also plans to launch a science movement designed to enhance the ability of the people to adapt to a modern industrialized society, thereby providing a strong foundation for national development.

Long-range Plan of Science and Technology Toward the 2000s

The Korean Government has set the ambitious goal of becoming a developed country by the year 2000. For the realization of this goal, the Ministry of Science and Technology has prepared a "Long-range Plan of Science and Technology Toward the 2000s".

With its limited available resources, Korea realizes the difficulty of competing against advanced countries in every field simultaneously. Therefore, Korea will select its areas of comparative advantage, based on certain criteria, and focus intensively in these areas with all of its capabilities. Based on this strategy, the Government has categorized science and technology areas into the following five groups.

The first group includes those areas which are economically feasible from a short-term viewpoint, such as informatics, fine chemicals and precision machinery. The next group encompasses areas where the possibility of medium-term success is high, including bio-technology and new materials. Public welfare areas such as the environment, health and welfare constitute the third group. The fourth group is made up of oceanography and aeronautics, where the future prospects are promising in the medium and long-term. The last group, or those showing short, medium and long-term prospects, is comprised of basic science and engineering, providing the basis for development in all sectors of science and technology.

For effective implementation of these five groups, the Government will pursue the following strategies. The first is the strategy for "specialization", by which technology development will be specialized in specific fields with the limited available resources Korea has for R&D. The next is the strategy for "cooperation" in the development of technology—the systemizing of R&D capability by constructing a cooperative research system among industry, academia and research institutes. Third, the strategy for "internationalization" of R&D will be pursued in order to overcome the limitations of domestic R&D capabilities. Fourth is the strategy for "localization," the formation of a research and development network across major regions of the country. Finally, Korea will push ahead with the strategy of "autonomy", by which the private sector will enjoy a free hand in benefiting from the market mechanism.

By applying these strategies in harmony and balance, the Government will accelerate the nation's science and technology innovation in order to realize Korea's target of joining the ranks of advanced countries by the turn of the century.

Recently, the Korean Government has been preparing a "Seven-Year Plan for High-Technology and Industry Development" in which policy priorities will be placed in strategic fields such as the information industry, machatronics, new materials, bio-engineering, fine chemicals, new energy, space technology, ocean engineering, and welfare technology.

Research and Development in Korea

Institution Building for R&D

In the early stages of industrialization, the Korean Government focused on institution building for the R&D infrastructure, as demonstrated in 1966 with the establishment of the Korea Institute of Science and Technology. This institute was charged with the responsibility of covering a broad spectrum of activities in applied research, including project feasibility studies, technical services for small and medium industries and engineering studies on a pilot

plant scale. The Government decided to establish an institute for science education that would meet the need for high-level scientists and, as a result, in 1971, the Korea Advanced Institute of Science was inaugurated. In 1989, this institute was renamed the Korea Advanced Institute of Science and Technology (KAIST).

In the 1970s, the Government established other specialized industrial research institutes related to machinery, metals, electronics, nuclear energy, resources, chemicals, telecommunications, standards, shipbuilding, marine science, etc. The Government, finding it inefficient to operate these small-scale institutes, decided in 1981 to make them optimal size for better utilization of research staff and equipment.

Sixteen research institutes supported by various government agencies were integrated into nine major institutes supervised by the Ministry of Science and Technology. Finally, after the Government reassessed the capability and function of the institutes, some institutes were reorganized for the effective promotion of research and development.

Along with these government-supported institutes, private companies are finding it necessary to establish their own R&D institutes in order to meet the ever-increasing international competition and to be able to participate in the technology-intensive high-tech industries. The Government encourages the establishing of R&D institutes through tax incentives and financial support.

National R&D Projects

In the course of industrialization efforts during the 1960s and 1970s, R&D activities and

Annual Investment for National R&D Projects

(In million U.S. dollars)

Sector \ Years	'82	'83	'84	'85	'86	'87	'88	'89	'90	'91	Total
Government	18	28	26	35	58	64	82	98	128	141	678
Industry	8	17	13	19	53	58	51	53	107	83	462
Total	26	45	39	54	111	122	133	151	235	224	1,140

Source: Ministry of Science and Technology

technical improvements in vulnerable fields were the major tools in bridging the technological gap. Recently, however, successive technical innovations in advanced countries and the interdisciplinary nature of large-scale R&D programs have shown that a more systematic approach, more advanced technology, and a higher level of technical information are required for the success of R&D programs. To cope with these needs, the Government initiated national research and development projects in 1982 in which industry, research institutes and the Government jointly carried out specified research projects by forming centers of excellence in each field. Projects in this category are large-scale R&D projects, which need to be given the highest priority for the long-run economic and social development, and which cannot be implemented by industry alone. Knowledge-intensive and resource-saving technologies which also enhance comparative advantage in international competitiveness have been highly favored.

Promotion of Basic Science

The Government places utmost emphasis on research in basis science, the very foundation of technological innovation. This is to stimulate Korea's own creative capability for science and technology development, breaking from the stage of mere imitation and improvement of foreign technologies.

As a concrete step toward this policy, the Government endeavors to create a vitalizing climate for basic science research activities at universities, which have enormous potential. The Government is establishing Science Research Centers (SRC) and Engineering Research Centers (ERC) at universities around the country in order to support R&D activities and the common utilization of major advanced R&D facilities.

In addition, funds for basic research will continue to increase, as well as the proportion of basic research among total R&D funds, ultimately reaching more than 20 percent.

Concurrently, the Government has promulgated the "Basic Science Promotion Act" to establish a government-supported system for basic science research, which includes a stable supply of R&D funds.

Scale of Research and Development

As of 1991, there were 2,352 R&D related institutes in Korea, which included 188 public research institutes, 221 at universities, colleges and junior colleges, and 1,943 belonging to private enterprises. Researchers totaled 76,252, or 17.6 persons per 10,000 people. The total R&D investment stood at 5.46 billion US dollars, or 2.02 percent of the GNP. To meet the increasing demand for science and technology, the Government is planning to expand and strengthen the present small scale of R&D so that R&D investment will increase to 4.0 percent in 1998. The ratio between public and private sector R&D investment was 50:50 in 1982, and 20:80 in 1991. In addition to this quantitative expansion, the Government will improve R&D management, lay a stronger R&D foundation through basic scientific research, and train highly qualified scientific and technological man-

R&D Expenditures

(In million U.S. dollars)

Expenditures \ Years	'81	'86	'90	'91
R&D expenditures	526	1,865	4,676	5,466
Government	290	434	909	1,072
Private	236	1,431	3,767	4,394
Proportion of GNP(%)	0.81	1.77	1.95	2.02
Ratio(Government to private)	55:45	23:77	19:81	20:80

Source: Ministry of Science and Technology

Researchers at Taedŏk Science Town.

power to support R&D expansion. In 2001, R&D investment will be boosted to over 5 percent of the GNP, and the ratio of R&D personnel from the 16.4 persons per 10,000 people as of 1990, will increase to 30 persons per 10,000.

Science Towns

Taedŏk Science Town

The blueprint for the Taedŏk Science Town was completed in December 1973. It was constructed to serve as the apex for the transfer of technologies developed by research institutes and universities to the end users in industry. After 20 years of construction, the town is now the very center of science and technology in Korea.

The objectives of the town were established by the Ministry of Science and Technology (MOST) and include: 1) to create a foundation in science and technological development for joining the ranks of the advanced countries in 21st century; 2) to foster closer links between research institutes of academia and industry

through the effective placement of government-funded research institutes, universities and private research institutes ; and 3) to establish a pollution-free science garden city with cultural facilities. With these goals in mind, MOST commenced construction of the town, which can accommodate 60 research institutes.

The total area of the town is 27.6 million square meters; 50 percent, or 14 million square meters, will be used for education and research facilities; 42 percent, or 11.4 million square meters, will be left in a more or less natural state ; and 8 percent, or 2.2 million square meters, will be used as a residential area.

The notice duration under the Law on Establishment and Development of Industrial Areas, which was introduced to facilitate the construction of the research complex, expires at the end of 1993. After that, the Urban Planning Law will be applied to the buildings and facilities of the town. Additionally, a Research Town Management Law (provisional name) will be enacted to limit development that might undermine efforts to establish a comfortable research environment.

At Taedŏk Science Town, numerous high-tech products in different fields have been developed for improving the quality of life in the present and future and to increase the industrial productivity. Following are some major items that have been developed at the Science Town.

Computer: TICOM (Tightly Coupled Multi-Process System), the main computer for the National Administration and Information System Technology for Cultural Property Restoration

Semi-conductors:16 Meg D-RAM chips
64 Meg D-RAM chips

Automation: Intelligent and Mobile Robots

Advanced materials:
High Performance Shape-memory Alloys
Artificial Diamonds
A New Manufacturing Process of Poly-crystalline Silicon

Health, Medical service: Intra-ocular Lens
Radioactive Isotopes used to detect cancer
Transdermal Delivery of Insulin
High Sensitivity and Accuracy Diagnostic Kits for detecting AIDS

Energy: Amorphous Silicon Solar Cells
Crystalline Silicon Solar Cells
Photo-voltaic System for Isolated Islands

Biotechnology: Interleukin II, an anti-cancer drug

Transportation: Magnetic-Levitation Train

Other Regional Science Towns

In response to the constantly increasing demand for technology development, the Government will forge ahead with its strategy of creating an infrastructure promoting science and technology innovation region by region, resulting in balanced national development. Towards this end, while Taedŏk Science Town is in its final completion stage, the Government is also currently constructing Kwangju Science Town in the southwest, where an exchange and full utilization of manpower, technology, and information will be available, thereby linking research, education, and industry. Also, local governments are planning to construct four science towns which will have similar functions to Kwangju Science Town in Pusan, Taegu, Chŏnju and Kangnŭng, construction beginning in 1993. These science towns will be increased to form a nationwide techno-belt by linking telecommunication systems, transportation, and utilities.

Industrial Technology Development

Support for Industrial Technology Development

In addition to efforts to establish the institutional infrastructure and to develop manpower, the Korean Government has emphasized the development of appropriate industrial technology. Under the Technology Development Promotion Law, promulgated in 1972, industries are provided various tax incentives and financial support, as follows;

—tax exemptions for technology development reserve funds —tax exemption for 10 percent of the costs of investment in R&D equipment and the adaptation of new technologies;

—special depreciation for 90 percent of the initial investment in testing and research facilities;

—direct financial grants in conjunction with national projects; and

—long-term, low-interest technology development funds.

In order to promote industrial technology development, the Government will foster a competitive environment and attitude, one voluntarily and fairly created by each enterprise based on the principles of autonomy and competition, with minimized governmental control and restrictions. Meanwhile various measures for the promotion of technology development will be expanded in an efficient manner.

Promotion of Private Research Institutes

To promote technological development in the industrial sector, the Government recommends that large companies establish one research center per company while small and medium companies are advised to organize research consortia by specific fields. Tax privileges and government funds have been extended to private research institutes as well as government-funded research institutes to carry out joint national projects. Researchers at private research institutes are allowed the same military conscription exemption as those at government-funded research institutes.

Support for Small and Medium Industries

The Government provides small and medium industries with financial and technical support. To reinforce weak areas commonly faced by most small and medium industries, technical consultation service by researchers and the dissemination of the latest technological information will be increasingly provided to improve existing technology.

The newly established Korea Academy of Industrial Technology will actively help industries to solve technical problems with its highly trained staff and abundant technological information. In addition, a technology guidance support system consisting of qualified researchers from government-funded research institutes will be expanded for small and medium industries. At the same time, financial support from the Small and Medium Industry Bank will be increased.

In order to expand the industrial structure, strengthen the international competitiveness of Korean goods and research and development in business, and promote commercialization of new technologies, the Government authorized the establishment of venture capital corporations. Since the end of 1974, numerous venture capital corporations have been in operation to offer technical and financial support for venture businesses in the development of new technolo-

gies, investigations, surveys, consultations, andarrangements.

The Korea Technology Advancement Corporation (KTAC) was established in 1974 to link research organizations with businesses and entrepreneurs by converting research and development into practical applications. In 1981, the Korea Technology Development Corporation (KTDC) was established for the financial support as well as improvement of existing technologies. In 1991, the Government enacted a special law for the establishment of the Korea Technology Banking Corporation (KTB), which was inaugurated in July 1992. Presently, more than 50 similar corporations are in operation.

Promotion of Cooperative R&D

Given Korea's limited R&D resources, it is necessary to systemize and maximize R&D resources. For this, the government encourages the formation of research consortia to strengthen cooperative R&D activities.

In the future, the Korean Government will promote R&D by the sharing of manpower, funds, information, and facilities for effective use of resources; encourage cooperative research between academia, industry and institutes; and broaden the scope of cooperative research through national R&D projects.

Along with this, the manpower exchange system will be expanded in order to promote the dissemination of R&D results. The Academia-Research-Industry Cooperation Center, a central information exchange forum for scientists, is now in operation at Taedŏk Science Town.

Promotion of the Engineering Industry

During the course of industrialization since the 1960s, most major industrial plants have been constructed with foreign loans on a turnkey basis, which allows almost no opportunity for local engineers to participate in major engineering projects. Due to this lack of practical experience, Korea's engineering standards failed to improve.

To remedy this weakness, in 1973 the

Engineering Firms

(As of Dec, 1992)

Type of Engineering	No. of firms	Engineers
Plant Construction	16	2,475
General Construction	24	3,641
Specialized	525	6,159
Individual	158	158
Total	723	12,433

Government enacted the Engineering Service Promotion Law, which encourages domestic engineering services, particularly by supporting small scale firms. Since then engineering firms have been growing in quality and quantity. In 1992, 723 engineering firms with which 12,433 highly educated engineers are associated were registered with MOST. The technology capability of these firms does not yet meet international standards in feasibility studies, project management and other disciplines. However it is estimated that they are able to meet international technological standards in basic design, detailed design, and supervision work.

Engineering firms still face restricted participation in active engineering projects due to the strict provisions of the Engineering Service Promotion Law. Therefore, the Government has been endeavoring to revise the Engineering Service Promotion Law and other regulations to provide engineering firms with technological competition through the abolition of regulatory articles. The new law, when enacted, will help promote technological capability in engineering industry, and improve the quality of life and welfare of the Korean people.

Promotion of Information Industry

Korea's information industry is moving into competitive world markets, and with the goal of being in the top five countries in the world in software technology, Korea is making all-out efforts to develop enabling technologies and cultivate high caliber manpower in the field.

The Government has begun to support large scale research projects to develop certain funda-mental technologies such as software engineering tools, artificial intelligence, and systems software, all of which are being carried out in a collaborative manner by public research institutes, private industry, and universities.

Despite the fact that computer programming is a relatively new industry in Korea, it was determined to be necessary for Korea—as well as for its trading partners—to provide copyright protection for computer programs. This is provided under the Program Protection Act, effective from July, 1987, while protection for computer programs copyrighted in foreign countries is effective from October, 1987, upon Korea's accession to the Universal Copyright Convention.

The Government is planning the establishment of five National Key Computer Networks, with one of its sub-systems being the Academic and Research Network. The Korea Academic and Research Network connects more than twenty major national research institutes, most of the major universities and a number of private research centers, facilitating computing power sharing and information gathering and distribution. The Government designated the System Engineering Research Institute (SERI) as the central organization in charge of the operation of these computer networks, and a core institute for science and technology information services.

The Government has keen interest in computer system safety, protection from computer related crimes, and protection of private information stored in computer systems, and has taken countermeasures into account accordingly.

Nuclear Energy

Nuclear Related Organizations in Korea

Nuclear development in Korea began in 1957 when Korea joined the IAEA, which was followed by the establishment of the Office of Atomic Energy in 1959. This office was reorganized as the Atomic Energy Bureau under the

Ulchin Nuclear Power Plant.

newly established Ministry of Science and Technology (MOST) in April 1967. MOST, whose function is to promote and coordinate science and technology in general, also serves to research and develop the use and application of energy as well as to regulate nuclear safety.

Another branch of the central Government, the Electric Energy Bureau of the Ministry of Trade, Industry and Energy (MOTIE), draws up basic plans for nuclear power development and supervises the construction and operation of nuclear plants.

By the revision of Atomic Energy Law in May 1986, the Atomic Energy Commission (AEC) was reorganized under the Office of the Prime Minister, and its members were also upgraded to minister level. The AEC has between 5 to 7 members; the standing members are the ministers of MOST & MOTIE, the president of KEPCO, the Deputy Prime Minister as chairman, and remaining members nominated by the President. The major function of AEC is to deliberate and resolve important matters on the use of nuclear energy and safety.

The Korea Atomic Energy Research Institute (KAERI) is a government-supported national nuclear research and development institute established in 1959 to serve as a center for promoting the peaceful use of nuclear energy in Korea. KAERI carries out extensive R&D pro-grams related to nuclear fuel design, nuclear safety, reactor engineering, and radio-isotope (RI) applications, as well as undertaking fundamental research.

The Korea Institute of Nuclear Safety (KINS) was established as an independent nuclear regulatory organization on February 4, 1990. The objective of KINS is to protect individuals, society, and the environment from radiation hazards as a consequence of nuclear activities, and to review the reports concerning the construction and operation of nuclear power plants.

The Korea Electric Power Corporation (KEPCO), a state-run corporation, is the only electric utility in Korea. The function of KEPCO is, as a utility, to supply cheap electricity of good quality to customers and take a leading role in encouraging the development of the nuclear industry such as architect/engineering (A/E) and the localization of equipment and materials. KEPCO created Korea Power Engineering Co.(KOPEC) in 1975 in order to increase A/E capability. One of the other KEPCO subsidiaries co-shared with KAERI is the Korea Nuclear Fuel Co (KNFC), subsidiary which has produced 200 tons of nuclear fuel for PWRs annually since 1989.

As the equipment manufacturer related to nuclear components, Korea Heavy Industries and Construction Co.(KHIC) has already been

Status of Nuclear Power Plants

Item		Reactor Type	Capacity (Mwe)	Manufacturer		Commercial Operation
				Reactor	T/G	
Kori	Unit 1	PWR	587	Westinghouse	GEC	1978.4.29
	Unit 2	PWR	650	Westinghouse	GEC	1983.7.25
	Unit 3	PWR	950	Westinghouse	GEC	1986.9.30
	Unit 4	PWR	950	Westinghouse	GEC	1986.4.29
Wolsŏng	Unit 1	PHWR	678.7	AWCL	NEI Parsons	1983.4.22
	Unit 2	PHWR	700	AECL/KHIC	KHIC/GE	(1997.6)
Yŏnggwang	Unit 1	PWR	950	Westinghouse	GEC	1986.8.25
	Unit 2	PWR	950	Westinghouse	GEC	1987.6.10
	Unit 3	PWR	1,000	KHIC/CE	KHIC/CE	(1995.3)
	Unit 4	PWR	1,000	KHIC/CE	KHIC/CE	(1996.3)
Ulchin	Unit 1	PWR	950	Framatome	Alssthom	1986.8.25
	Unit 2	PWR	950	Framatome	Alssthom	1987.6.10
	Unit 3	PWR	1,000	KHIC/CE	KHIC/CE	(1998.6)
	Unit 4	PWR	1,000	KHIC/CE	KHIC/CE	(1999.6)

Source: Ministry of Science and Technology

nominated and supported by the Government not only for manufacturing reactor and turbine-generator components but also for supervising plant construction.

Nuclear Policy and Development

Peaceful Use of Nuclear Energy

Korea became affiliated with the International Atomic Energy Agency (IAEA) to promote the peaceful use of nuclear energy in August 1957. Since then, bilateral or trilateral agreements related to the application of safeguards have been signed with the IAEA, the US, France, Canada, Germany, and Australia, while the Nuclear Non-Proliferation Treaty (NPT) was ratified on April 23, 1975.

The Government has established and maintained a national safety system for nuclear material and other materials subject to NPT safeguards. These materials are not only used only for peaceful purposes, but have also been verified by IAEA fullscope safeguard activities for all nuclear facilities in Korea.

In line with this, President Roh Tae Woo declared in November 1991, that "Korea will use nuclear energy only for peaceful purposes." This was followed with an announcement of the Republic of Korea non-nuclear policy, ensuring no manufacture, possession, storage, deployment, or use of nuclear weapons. Korea also assured that all the peaceful uses of nuclear R&D activities have been and will be carried out through international cooperation for mutual interests.

Nuclear Power Program

Korea currently operates nine nuclear units, including one heavy water reactor (PHWR) and eight pressurized light water reactors (PWR). The total nuclear installed capacity was 7,616 MWe at the end of 1991, which accounted for about 36 percent of the total installed generation capacity and which supplied a little over 47 percent of the total electricity generation. By 2006, the Korean Government plans to bring another 18 units on line, including one PHWR, four PWRs currently under construction, and 13 units that have yet to be specified. Under this program, Korea will be able to keep the capacity of its own nuclear power plant facilities at about 40 percent of total electricity generation capacity.

Nuclear Research and Development

Korea has a 30-year history in nuclear research and development. Until the late 1970s, it focused on research and development of radioisotope utilization and radiation applications in the fields of agriculture, medicine, and industry. Studies on reactor physics and material properties were also conducted, mainly by using TRIGA Mark II and III research reactors.

Ever since the first nuclear power project in Korea was undertaken in the early 1970s, the nuclear power program has grown steadily. From the beginning of the 1980s, the major direction of nuclear R&D was changed from theoretical nuclear research to practical nuclear power technology development.

Through active participation of R&D projects in nuclear power plants, self-reliance in nuclear power technology will be better achieved by the turn of the century. With this in mind, technology for the design and manufacture of CANDU fuel was developed by KAERI with extensive technical cooperation with Atomic Energy of Canada Limited (AECL). Based on this successful experience, KAERI is jointly carrying out NSSS design and engineering work for PWR plants with Combustion Engineering (C.E.) of the U.S., high burn-up PWR fuel design with Siemens/KWU of Germany, and NSSS design for the CANDU plant with AECL of Canada.

Nuclear Safety

Nuclear Safety Status

As Korea's nuclear power plant program expands to meet increasing energy demands, the safety of these nuclear power plants becomes an important issue. For a successful nuclear power plant program, safety of these plants at all stages of development including site selection, design, manufacturing, construction, commissioning, operation, and decommissioning must be assured. Nuclear safety is extremely important to safeguard the health of plant employees and neighbours and to protect the environment from possible radiation hazards.

The nuclear regulatory procedures in Korea were made from a combination of those of the U.S. and Japan. The first step is licensing on construction permit. The environmental impact report and the preliminary safety analysis report prepared by the owner are forwarded to the KINS via the Government for review and comments by the experts of the KINS, and then are approved by the Government following AEC deliberation. An operation license is also issued following a review of the final safety analysis report and technical specifications prepared by the owner.

Regulation and Licensing Procedures

Enforcement and regulation of the Atomic Energy Law is provided by a prime ministerial ordinance which details the provisions commissioned by the Atomic Energy Law and the Enforcement Decree of that Law. Specific requirements are imposed through this enforcement regulation.

The current regulations stipulate three licensing stages for the nuclear power plant; siting and limited work authorization, the construction permit, and the operating license. The regulation also requires that any person or authority wishing to construct and operate installations for nuclear energy in Korea is required to obtain a licence from the Ministry of Science and Technology. Before issuing a license to the utility, the MOST requires sufficient information from the person or organization to show that the required technical, health, safety, and security standards stipulated in the Prime Ministerial Ordinance are met and maintained.

Build-up of Regulatory Capability

Because the introduction of nuclear power plants in Korea raises concerns about nuclear power plant safety, regulations and licensing procedures are in place to assure the licensee complies with established nuclear safety standards. Many analysis, evaluation, research and development activities are also being continued to provide additional information and guidance in the regulatory work. Currently, Korea depends mainly on foreign nuclear technology.

As KAERI, KOPEC and other nuclear industries in Korea increase their engineering design capabilities, the Korean Government hopes to achieve 95 percent self-reliance in nuclear power plant design and construction technology by 1995. MOST, together with KINS, must improve the regulatory and licensing capabilities as well as unify the regulations to meet Korean regulatory requirements and needs. These will be streamlined with the advancement of capabilities in engineering design.

Challenges for Advanced Technology

Background

The vision of Korea in the 21st century is to become a member of the ranks of the advanced countries. To join this group, it is necessary for Korea to strengthen her potential industrial development capability and to overcome domestic and international hurdles that hinder social and economic progresses.

But the growth of the Korean economy is stagnating due to bottlenecks, and the future seems rather uncertain. Internal problems are the main culprits, but the overall economic environment is also quite unfavorable for Korea.

Korea is in the midst of an economic slump and faces a large trade deficit. Labor costs are rising every year, and accordingly, Korea is losing its international market share in the light industries. Korea is also experiencing difficulties in the heavy industries in competing with advanced countries because of inferior high technological capability.

In light of the December 1993 conclusion of the Uruguay Round talks led by the advanced countries to open up world markets, further market opening will take place in the near future. But developing countries who lack capital, technology and high-tech manpower cannot compete with advanced countries in all areas. From this view point, Korea's current situation seems very unfavorable.

Advanced countries have spent and continue to spend great effort in developing high technology, and mutual cooperation among the advanced countries is not uncommon. Now is the time for Korea to join in international technology cooperation to overcome its insufficient R&D capability and to acquire such high technology. However, in order to become a self-reliant and advanced country, Korea must also independently strengthen its industrial and technical capabilities. To achieve this goal, the Korean Government has prepared a plan to advance science and industrial technology to the level of advanced countries in the 21st century.

Formation of Highly Advanced

National Projects

The Korean Government has launched a "Highly Advanced National Project" (HANP) plan to select and develop strategic industrial technology requiring nationwide R&D investmest which should be self-reliant.

For this purpose, a selection and planning task force was established to guide the project at the national level. When HANP is completed in 2000, specific industries are expected to gain competitiveness and respond promptly to the rapidly changing world market.

To achieve success with HANP, Korea must resolve the problems of insufficient investment, insufficient manpower and the insufficient accumulation of high technology in science, public, and industrial technology. In terms of R&D investment, manpower, and accumulation of high technology, a great technological gap exists between Korea and advanced countries. It will be nearly impossible for Korea to catch up with advanced countries in every technological fields.

Therefore, the strategy for elevating the technological level is very clear. Technology will be emphasized rather than science. To achieve this goal, the limited national resources should and will be concentrated on a few critical technologies.

Two categories of HANPs were selected. The first group, called "Products Technology Development Project," concerns the technologies for specific products. These are technologies for high technology products which have or will have in the future substantial shares in the industrial world market, and in which fields Korea will have the capability to compete with advanced countries in early 21st century. The second category, called "Fundamental Technology Development Project," concerns core-technologies which are absolutely necessary in advancing the economy, society and human life, and must be self-supported. However, it is believed that it will be impossible to manufacture products or complete the projects under this category by the year 2001. According to the criteria of these two categories, 14 HANPs were selected.

Policies for Implementing HANP Projects

In Korea, national R&D programs are basically controlled by the Ministry of Science and Technology and the Ministry of Trade, Industry and Energy. MOST is mainly responsible for basic and fundamental technology development, while MOTIE is in charge of industrial technology development. Other related ministries such as the Ministry of Communications and the Ministry of Environment also participate in the R&D projects of related technologies.

However, the involvement of several ministries in R&D programs without explicit policy and coordination has caused an overlap of R&D investments in some specific areas by different ministries, and in some cases the investment amount was too small to undertake large R&D projects.

To overcome these problems, HANPs are supported by all government ministries and agencies with inter-ministrial cooperation and coordination, and will be carried out under the cooperative activities of national R&D systems that include universities, industries as well as government-supported research institutes.

Because the time horizon of HANPs stretches up to the year 2001, Korea must have long-term R&D plans for the coming decade. The biggest obstacles are the lack of R&D investment and manpower. Several measures have been considered to increase R&D investment based on ministry-wide activities. But manpower development for high-tech industries cannot be accomplished within a short time period. The available and capable manpower in Korea will be utilized in carrying out HANPs and in initiating manpower deveopment programs based on forecast demand. But this will not be sufficient to accomplish the set goals.

In this setting, the Korean Government is pushing forward a new science and technology policy for the internationalization of R&D in carrying out HANPs. For example, the involvement of foreign experts is strongly recommended for HANPs from the planning stage. Also, internationally recognized foreign experts can evaluate the R&D planning results for each HANP.

Especially, MOST will invest up to 20 percent of HANP R&D budgets for international joint R&D activities to achieve their targets and to increase R&D performance. Active international exchange programs for researchers will also be promoted.

To implement this global R&D strategy, the Korean Government will amend some related regulations to permit participation of foreign researchers and related experts in Korea's national R&D projects and to vitalize R&D activities of government-supported research institutes. In particular, active technological cooperation with advanced countries such as the United States, Japan, and European countries will be realized in the near future.

Korea is facing a new international environment. The world is becoming borderless, while world competition is becoming more severe every day. To become a technologically self-reliant country, Korea must focus its indigenous capability on the priority areas and utilize foreign sources of R&D and technology. The coming decade will decide Korea's destiny for the 21st century.

Creating a Climate for Science and Technology

A climate favorable to the development of science and technology has been a major policy goal in order to lay a solid foundation for science and technology. As mentioned before, the Government, with the cooperation of the academic and industrial communities and the mass media, has launched a nationwide science movement whose main objective is to create an environment in which the general public can apply scientific principles to daily living with a spirit of rationality, efficiency and creativity. This science movement has provided a strong foundation for national development.

In its efforts to realize the ideas and goals of the movement, the following activities have been effected:

—operation of exhibition halls in the National Science Museum;
—operation of science film libraries;
—publication of science and technology book lets;
—lectures on science for housewives and stu dents;
—The National Science Exhibition and Invention Contest;
—technical guidance for farmers and fisher men;
—The National Personal Computer Contest;
—establishment of the Young Astronauts Korea (YAK); and
—activation of mass media.

Thus, the exploratory spirit of youth in science will be encouraged in order to expand the foundation for future science manpower development while enhancing the ability to adapt to a modern industrialized society.

In this regard, the new international-level science museum will be devoted to collecting, preserving, studying and exhibiting materials in the fields of science, technology, industry, and natural history. The main functions of the museum will be to propagate scientific and technical knowledge and to promote a scientific way of living for the general public.

The Taejŏn International Exposition

Korea hosted the Taejŏn Expo '93 for a full 93 days, 10 hours a day, seven days a week, from Saturday, August 7 to Sunday, November 7, 1993. The mammoth EXPO exhibit was held in Taejŏn City, 150 km south of Seoul. The EXPO organizers chose an apt theme for the first EXPO in a newly-industrialized country: "The Challenge of a New Road to Develop-

ment." Two subthemes pointed to the competing demands of modern science: "Traditional and Modern Science and Technology for the Developing World," and "Towards an Improved Use and Recycling of Resources."

A total of 108 countries and 33 international organizations, together with foreign enterprises and research institutes, participated making this the broadest-based specialized exposition ever held. Over 14 million people visited EXPO site from all over the word. With such spirited international participation, it is hoped that the EXPO has been successful in fostering greater cooperation and information exchanges around the world. While the EXPO was an extravaganza featuring science and technology to be sure, but EXPO also emphasized economic, cultural, and social events as well, furthering international goodwill at many levels.

More than one billion dollars was spent in preparing for EXPO, but the city reaped rewards in permanent facilities and in the good will of the many visitors. EXPO has cemented Taejŏn's place as the science capital of Korea, a claim already sustained by Taejŏn's role as the hometown of Korea's remarkable Taedŏk Science Town.

It is hoped that Taejŏn Expo '93 amply rewarded its guests of every size, whether nations, international organizations, and business concerns sponsoring pavilions or young people coming to see the scientific wonders. As the EXPO emphasized practical science education, it is hoped that young people exposed to EXPO's technical marvels learned about modern civilization's basic debt to science.

Taejŏn Expo '93, however, also boldly told the whole story. EXPO spelled out how rapid industrialization scars the environment. EXPO not only challenged its young visitors to expand the frontiers of science and technology, but also challenged them to develop benign technologies that will allow mankind to improve their financial and spiritual lot while preserving for their children the environment bequeathed to them by their forebears.

EDUCATION

Historical Review

In Korea there is an old saying: "One should not step even on the shadow of one's teacher." That adage, emphasizing the degree of respect traditionally accorded teachers, has long been a guiding principle in Korean education. While there have been changes in the educational system, as in other sectors of society, much of the old tradition remains.

Education in Pre-modern Period (Fourth-19th Centuries)

It generally is taken for granted that Koreans attach great importance to education, a view that has held true for many centuries and continues in this modern age. According to history, formal education in Korea began in the Three Kingdoms period (57 B.C.-A.D. 668) under the influence of the Chinese educational system. As in other countries, including China, it was available only to boys of the upper classes.

It was in A.D. 372 that a state-operated institute for higher education known as *T'aehak* (National Confucian Academy) was established in the Koguryŏ Kingdom (37 B.C.-A.D. 668). A similar institution for higher education named *Kukhak* (National Confucian College) was set up in the Shilla Kingdom (57 B.C.- A.D. 935) about three centuries later in A.D. 682.

Shilla also had a unique training system for the *Hwarangdo* ("Flower of Youth Corps"), the elite youth of the aristocratic class. The *Hwarangdo* proved instrumental in unifying the Korean Peninsula in the seventh century. The Paekche Kingdom (18 B.C.-A.D. 660) also emphasized education and produced numerous scholars in various academic disciplines, many of whom made important contributions to the flourishing early Japanese culture.

Higher education in all these kingdoms tended to be focused on the study of Chinese classics of Confucian orientation. Although the succeeding Koryŏ Dynasty (918-1392) adopted Buddhism as its state religion, Confucian studies continued to have a major influence on academic circles and the educational system. The institutionalization of the civil service examination in the mid-10th century set the pattern for educational reform, by directing the role of education toward preparing young men for public service.

Koryŏ founded a state institution for higher education called *Kukchagam* (National University) in A.D. 992 in its capital, Kaesong. It was also about that time that the central government began to dispatch scholars to provincial areas to implement education for local residents.

Buddhism gradually declined and so did the central government. The founders of the Chosŏn Dynasty (1392-1910) turned to Confucianism as the source of basic principles for national politics, ethics and social institutions. Chosŏn's highest educational institution was *Sŏnggyungwan* (National Confucian Academy), which also served as the center of Confucian studies. On the secondary level were two kinds of schools: *haktang* in the capital of Hanyang (today's Seoul) and *hyanggyo* in villages. Private schools called *sŏdang* carried out elementary education.

Education in the old aristocratic society was mainly considered an institution for preparing young men for future public service. Examinations in the Chinese classics were the major criteria for qualification. This tradition survived as the backbone of education until the late 19th century, when Korea opened its doors

Educational Institutions in Ancient and Pre-Modern Age

Classification / Dynasty	Public Institutions Higher	Public Institutions Middle	Private Institutions Middle	Private Institutions Lower
Koguryŏ	Taehak (372)*			Kyŏngdang
Unified Shilla	Kukhak (682)*			
Koryŏ	Kukchagam (992)*	Haktang, Hyangkyo	Shib-i-do (12 Schools)	Sŏdang
Chosŏn	Sŏngkyunkwan (1398)*	Haktang, Hyangkyo	Sŏwon	Sŏdang

* means the year of establishment
Source: The History of Education in Korea

to Western civilization and the powerful tide of modernization.

Advent of Modern Schools

Korea actually experienced the budding of a strong movement for modernization in the late 17th to 18th century. A group of young scholars banded together to search for practical ways to utilize academic knowledge for the cause of modernizing the country. Their scholarship and thought became known as *Sirhak* or "Practical Learning."

Those pioneering young scholars had become disillusioned by the impractical theoretical discussion that dominated conservative academic circles. They sought practical values in all disciplines of learning, including history, politics, economics, the natural sciences and humanities, and attempted to utilize them in building a modernized nation. Of special note is the fact that they tried to draw lessons from the experience of Ch'ing China, which had learned a great deal from its contact with the West.

The waves of Western culture and modernization that reached the coast of the "Hermit Kingdom," as Korea was known to the West, were powerful enough to move King Kojong to issue an edict in 1882 upholding education as one of the "pillars" of the nation and opening the doors of state-operated schools to citizens of all classes. *Yugyŏng Kongwon*, which was Korea's first school in a modern sense, was established in 1886. It employed American teachers who taught English with the aid of interpreters.

The contribution made by Western Christian missionaries to the early development of modern education in Korea can hardly be overestimated. The first missionary school, Paichai Haktang, was founded in 1886 by a mission group from the North Methodist Church led by Henry G. Appenzeller. A boy's high school, Kyungshin, was established in 1887 by a Presbyterian group. Ewha Haktang, which was set up in 1886 by a Methodist mission group, was Korea's first school for girls. Five other missionary schools were founded in major cities in the following years, and all contributed great-

A sŏdang, *or private elementary school, as depicted by Kim Hong-do, a leading artist in the mid-18th century.*

ly to the growth of modern education.

The 1900s saw a mushrooming of private secondary schools founded by Koreans, most of them wealthy aristocrats who realized the importance of education in the critical period leading to Japan's annexation of Korea in 1910. The most notable of these were Posŏng, Yangjŏng, and Whimoon in Seoul, and Osan in P'yŏngyang for boys; and Sukmyŏng, Chinmyŏng, and Tongdŏk for girls in Seoul.

American Christian missionaries particularly contributed much to the development of higher education in Korea, founding Chosŏn Christian College (which later developed into Yonsei University) in Seoul in 1905, and Sungshil College in P'yŏngyang in 1906.

The development of modern education as a basis for national development was disrupted by the Japanese colonial rule, which lasted 35 years from 1910 until the end of World War II. Although the number of public schools increased substantially during the colonial period, the education provided by these schools fell far short of the rising aspirations of Koreans. Educational opportunities were limited to a small number of Koreans: primary schools accommodated only 30 percent of all school-age children, only one out of 20 or so enrolled in secondary schools, and very few attended college.

Post-Liberation Period

Korea's liberation from Japan in 1945 marked a turning point in the history of education. As the country underwent a transition from totalitarian rule to democracy, a primary concern was to provide everybody with equal educational opportunities.

The period from 1945 to 1970 witnessed a dramatic expansion of education. In spite of the widespread destruction and economic suffering brought about by the Korean War (1950-53), Korea succeeded in virtually eliminating illiteracy. During the 46 years following liberation, the number of schools increased from 3,000 to nearly 19,693 and the number of students rose from 1.5 million to 11.5 million, about one fourth of the total population. Today, every child of elementary school age is offered a free education in accordance with the compulsory education system.

Such a rapid expansion was naturally accompanied by problems, the most serious being a deterioration in the quality of education. This was caused in part by the superficial imitation of the education systems in some advanced countries. As the 1960s drew to a close, Korea's educators turned their attention to these problems and several projects were launched to improve the curriculum and the methods of instruction. Most notable among these was the abolition of the middle school entrance examination in 1968, the adverse effects of which had long been recognized. During the next five years, the proportion of primary school students advancing to middle schools rose from 55 to 75 percent. Such a change contributed not only to raising the educational level of the people but also to the production of trained workers required for industrialization. However, the new system of admitting students on a district basis led to widening diversity in individual abilities within a single class, presenting a new problem in education.

In recognition of the needs for educational reforms, the Charter of National Education was promulgated in 1968. The charter emphasized the philosophical aspect of education to help people achieve a firm national identity and develop respect for history and tradition. It also stressed the development of creativity and a pioneering spirit to revitalize national strength and to pursue common prosperity. The charter stressed a balance between tradition and development and between the needs of the individual and the needs of the nation.

The 1970s brought a period of great national endeavor for modernization. Education played a vital role in this sweeping national movement by developing human resources. Technical education was increasingly stressed as demands for technicians increased sharply. But industrialization brought about an inevitable gap between cities and rural villages. The Saemaŭl (New Community) Movement initiated by the Government helped farmers improve their living standards by advocating a spirit of self-reliance, diligence and mutual cooperation.

Of all the innovative efforts made in the field of education in the early 1970s, the Elementary and Middle School Development Project (E-M Project) undertaken by the Government was of special importance. The project's goal was to improve the quality of primary and middle school programs through the revision of educational objectives, curricula and teaching methods. Under this project, competition was abolished in the recruitment of high school students for the purpose of normalizing middle school education, which had largely been focused on preparations for entrance examinations.

Efforts to improve higher education were made at the same time with long-term goals. The Higher Education Study Committee was formed in 1972 to analyze problems and needs and formulate a development plan. This led to the introduction of pilot programs for strengthening professional training in selected institutions. The aim was to better prepare college students for their future in a fast-moving industrial and technological society. Engineering colleges were urged to reinforce specialized education required for regional development.

Another important achievement during this period was the inception of new forms of education such as correspondence schools. This was primarily aimed at providing young workers and adults of all ages with the opportunity to receive a college or high school education.

The year 1980 saw the successful implementation of a bold educational reform—the abolition of private tutoring—which had been one of the most controversial issues in education. Enthusiasm for education, coupled with a feverish rush to the so-called "first-rate" colleges, had precipitated the widespread practice of private tutoring. However, that practice had resulted in a financial burden for parents and had undermined regular school education. The Government, recognizing the undesirable effects, proclaimed a legal ban on private tutoring and changed the college entrance system.

In accordance with this policy, the Government has administered a state examination for all high school graduates wishing to attend college or university since 1981. The scores from this written test, uniform for all students, and high school records are combined to determine the qualification of a student to enter a certain college or university. The system prohibits individual colleges and universities from conducting their own entrance examinations. Beginning from 1994, a student's high school achievements will be weighted 40 percent or more in the admission screening procedure. Each school will decide individually how much weight will be given to the college academic aptitude test assigned and administered by the state and its own independent admission test in its admission procedures.

Legal Basis and the Goals of Education

The goals of education are manifested in the Constitution and the Charter of National Education. Article 31 of the Constitution promulgated in 1987 reads as follows:
1. All citizens shall have the right to receive equal education according to their ability.
2. All citizens shall have the duty of ensuring that all children under their protection receive a primary education, and that this education is regulated by law.

3. Compulsory education shall be free.
4. Independence, professionalism, political impartiality and college autonomy in education shall be guaranteed in accordance with the provisions of law.
5. The state shall promote lifelong education.
6. Fundamental matters pertaining to the educational system, including in-school and lifelong education, administration, finance, and the status of teachers shall be determined by law.

The basic directions and objectives of education are specified according to these provisions in the Education Law. Section I of the Education Law provides the following general rules:

Article 1: Education shall, under the great ideal of *hongik-ingan* (benefits for mankind—the founding spirit of the first kingdom in Korean history), aim to assist all people in perfecting their individual character, developing the ability for an independent life and acquiring the qualifications of citizens capable of participating in the building of a democratic state and promoting the prosperity of all humankind.

Article 2: In order to achieve these aims, the following educational objectives shall be set up:
a. Development of the knowledge and attitudes needed for a sound cultivation and sustenance of health and the cultivation of an indomitable spirit.
b. Development of a patriotic spirit for the preservation of national independence and enhancement of an ideal for the cause of world peace.
c. Transmission and development of national culture and contribution to the creation and growth of world civilization.
d. Fostering of a truth-seeking spirit and the ability of scientific thinking for creative activity and rational living.
e. Development of a love for freedom and of respect for responsibility necessary to lead a well-harmonized community life with the spirit of faithfulness, cooperation and understanding.
f. Development of an aesthetic sensibility to create and appreciate arts, enjoy the beauty

of nature, and utilize leisure effectively for a joyful wholesome life.

g. Cultivation of industriousness and dedication to one's work in order to become a competent producer and wise consumer.

Article 8 stipulates the right to receive basic education by stating, "Every person shall be entitled to receive a primary education of six years."

With the acceleration of modernization from the 1960s, Korean society was dominated by an overwhelming tendency to pursue change and progress at the expense of traditional values. The country already had witnessed a sudden disruption of old ways and customs caused by the massive influx of Western culture and technology. Such discontinuity of tradition brought about much confusion in the general system of values. It became necessary to determine a philosophical and ideological background for national endeavors towards modernization and to reinstate the traditional values as worthwhile resources of wisdom and knowledge for modern times. It was in this social context that efforts were made to redefine the ideals and goals of education in the form of the Charter of National Education proclaimed in 1968.

Educational System

Organization Framework

The organization of educational administration consists of three layers of administrative authorities, namely: the Ministry of Education, local offices of education on the provincial level, and those on the county levels.

The Ministry of Education is the central authority responsible for discharging the Constitutional mandates for education. It makes policies in regard to education and science, takes actions for the implementation of policies, publishes and approves textbooks, directs and coordinates subordinate agencies for planning and policy implementation, and supports and supervises local educational agencies and national universities.

The Ministry of Education is headed by the Minister of Education, who is a member of the Cabinet Council. He is assisted by a Vice Minister. The Ministry is divided into three branches, each headed by an assistant minister, five bureaus and 25 sections. In addition, 27 professional directors are responsible for the affairs of professional concerns, which remain independent of branches or bureaus.

Subsidiary organizations under the direct supervision of the Minister include the Korea History Compilation Committee, the National Institute of Educational Research and Training, the National Institute of Educational Evaluation, and the Appeal Commission for Teachers.

In response to heightening concern for diverse needs of local education and the skills they require, local offices of education distinct from the general administration have been established in six municipalities and nine provinces, as well as in counties and equivlent adminstrative areas. These offices make decisions regarding education, art and science pertaining to the respective local area.

Each local office has a board of members elected by the local council, which makes decisions regarding educational matters pertaining to the respective local area. Decisions are made through such a procedure that provides for compromise between public opinion and professional views, separate from political influence.

The office term of a board member is four years. Each administrative district has a representative on the board. By setting the minimum number of board members at seven, it ensures that the board functions properly, even if the local office of education covers a small administrative area and falls short of the required number of board members.

A superintendent represents the executive branch of the local board of education, which is responsible for the administration of education, art and science. The superintendent has a right to call the board of education into session and send bills to local parliaments. Elected by winning more than half of the members' votes, the superintendent serves four years. As of 1992, there are 15 local offices of education in special

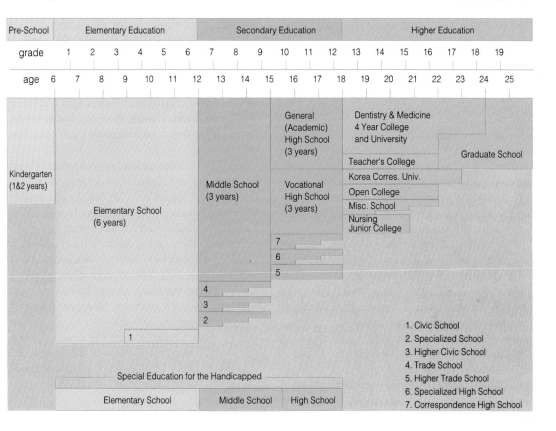

Pre-School	Elementary Education						Secondary Education						Higher Education					

grade 1 2 3 4 5 6 7 8 9 10 11 12 13 14 15 16 17 18 19

age 6 7 8 9 10 11 12 13 14 15 16 17 18 19 20 21 22 23 24 25

General (Academic) High School (3 years)

Dentistry & Medicine 4 Year College and University

Graduate School

Teacher's College

Kindergarten (1&2 years)

Middle School (3 years)

Vocational High School (3 years)

Korea Corres. Univ.

Open College

Misc. School

Elementary School (6 years)

Nursing Junior College

7

6

5

4

3

2

1

1. Civic School
2. Specialized School
3. Higher Civic School
4. Trade School
5. Higher Trade School
6. Specialized High School
7. Correspondence High School

Special Education for the Handicapped

Elementary School | Middle School | High School

cities and provinces. At the county level, there are 179 local offices of education.

To assist the Minister of Education in the formulation of educational policies, two advisory councils exist, namely: the Advisory Council for Educational Policy and the Council for Higher Education.

Financing of Education

The financing of education is centralized, and government grants constitute the largest component of the entire budget.

The budgets drafted at the provincial and county levels are sent to the Ministry of Education for initial review and approval. The Ministry incorporates them into its own budget, which it submits to the Economic Planning Board for review and adjustments. These adjusted budgets are subject to approval by the Cabinet Council before they are included in the agenda of the National Assembly as budget proposals for final review and approval.

The budget of the Ministry of Education varies from one year to another, but generally accounts for some 22.8 percent of the total government budget, which is about 3.2 to 3.4 percent of the GNP. The Ministry has been shouldering financial burdens beyond its management in recent years, due to the rapid increase in the number of students and the expanding scale and diversity of educational activities in general. The most notable increase has been recorded in the funding of compulsory education. A legislative act allocating 12.98 percent of the total internal revenue for the financing of compulsory education was temporarily suspended in 1973, and appropriations thereafter fell short of the minimum requirement. Since 1977, however, the proportion of annual education budgets to the GNP has been higher than 3 percent, and their proportion to the total government budget has exceeded 22.8 percent.

The educational budgets are jointly met by

the central government and local authorities with the former bearing 78.2 percent and the latter 21.8 percent. The central government remains in the position to decide the general educational policy.

The educational expenditures of the provinces include direct expenses for provincial educational programs and the salaries of personnel employed by primary, secondary and special schools. Parents pay a small portion of the expenditures incurred for the instructional materials supplied to pupils. Except for these expenses, the costs for elementary education at public schools are met by public funding.

Most costs of higher education in national and public colleges and universities are borne by the Government. Tuition and entrance fees paid by students meet only a small portion of the total expenditures. Private colleges and universities are financed by foundations and student payments, but the Education Law stipulates the granting of subsidies to private institutions for research projects and programs for expanding and improving facilities for education in science and technology.

School System

The general school system in Korea is comprised of primary, lower secondary, higher secondary, and higher education. These correspond to primary school (first to sixth grades), middle school (seventh to ninth grades), high school (tenth to twelfth grades) and junior college, college and university (two to four years post-high school). Primary school provides six years of compulsory elementary education to children between the ages of six and 11. Middle school offers three years of lower secondary education to those aged 12 to 14. High school offers three years of higher secondary education to students aged 15 to 17. High school graduates can choose to apply to a two-year junior college or a four-year college or university to receive higher education.

High schools are generally divided into two categories, general and vocational. Correspondence schools are included in the former, while agricultural, commercial, fishery,

and technical high schools are included in the latter. There are a limited number of schools of the so-called "comprehensive" type offering both general and vocational courses.

Institutes of higher learning include two-year junior and vocational colleges and four-year colleges and universities. Both the teachers' colleges and colleges of education offer four-year courses.

Parallel with the general school ladder system are the trade and higher trade schools at the secondary level which provide highly specialized vocational training. Civic schools, originally intended to offer literacy programs, now provide elementary and secondary level education mostly for financially underprivileged students. With compulsory education requirements extending to the sixth grade, however, these schools have been gradually disappearing.

There are special schools offering elementary and secondary education for the deaf, blind and other physically and mentally handicapped. Preschool education is provided by kindergartens.

School Education

The school system in Korea follows a 6-3-3-4 ladder pattern. As noted earlier, it is comprised of primary school, lower secondary school, higher secondary school, and junior college (two-year post-high school) and college or university.

Pre-School Education

Preschool education is not included in the formal school system. However, its importance justifies attention in relation to the formal school system. Kindergarten is the main facility for preschool education in Korea.

As of 1992, there were 8,498 kindergartens enrolling 450,882 children, accounting for 40 percent of the children four to six years of age. The completion of two or four-year courses of study at the college or university level in either nursing or preschool education is required for kindergarten nurses.

Kindergartens place no importance on academic pursuits, their main objective being the all-round development of the child. Within this framework, kindergartens seek to provide children of preschool age with an environment conducive to sound physical and emotional development as well as self-reliance.

To cope with the increasing demand for preschool education, the Ministry of Education recently began experimenting with the idea of opening kindergartens affiliated with existing primary schools in large cities where there is much competition in kindergarten enrollment. The Ministry expanded kindergarten facilities to admit up to 54 percent of all children of kindergarten age in 1993.

Primary Education

Although relevant legislation was enacted in 1948, primary education for children aged six to 11 was not made compulsory until 1953 because of the post-Korean War rehabilitation. The Constitution stipulates in Article 31 that it is the responsibility of all parents and guardians to ensure a primary school education for their children aged six to 11 and that this education is free.

Primary school enrollment showed a sharp increase from 1952, reaching a peak of more than five million in 1971. The increase in student enrollment during those years pushed some individual school enrollments as high as 10,000 or more, with more than 90 pupils crammed in a classroom in some schools. Many schools found it necessary to operate classes in two or even three shifts daily. This situation has been improved in all respects. As of 1992, there were 6,122 primary schools throughout the Republic of Korea, with 4,560,128 pupils accommodated in 114,290 classes and staffed by 138,880 teachers. Primary school teachers must be graduates of a four-year teachers college.

Article 93 of the Education Law states that the goal of primary school education is to teach the fundamentals necessary for a successful civic life. Article 94 of the same law lists the following objectives of primary education: (1) to improve the student's ability to correctly understand and speak the national language

Preschool education.

needed in daily life; (2) to improve the student's moral rectitude, sense of duty, and the ability to cooperate in improving relations among individuals, groups, and nation; (3) to improve the student's ability to rationally observe and deal with natural phenomena occurring in daily life; (4) to develop the student's ability to lead an independent life by providing him with fundamental skills of practical use in future occupations and daily activities; (5) to enable the student to understand and deal with the quantitative relationships which are necessary for daily life; (6) to develop in the student an appreciation for music, fine arts, literature, etc., and (7) to ensure that the student develops daily health habits. To fulfill these objectives, the basic curriculum for primary school education is composed of eight principal subjects: moral education, Korean language, social studies, arithmetic, natural science, physical education, music, and fine arts. In the first and second grades, some of these subjects are taught in combined courses and practical arts are added from the fourth grade. The current primary school curriculum was established by the Ministry of Education in 1987.

Secondary Education

Secondary education is divided into the lower secondary (middle) school and the higher secondary (high) school. Each is a three-year course.

Middle School

Upon completing primary school, children in the 12-14 age bracket are allowed to enter middle school for the seventh to ninth grade courses.

The number of middle school students showed an impressive rate of growth in recent decades. The percentage of primary school graduates advancing to middle school increased from 58.4 percent in 1969 to 98.5 percent in 1992. There are 2,539 middle schools across Korea with a total enrollment of 2,336,284 as of 1992.

Since the abolition of entrance examination in 1969, admission to middle school has been made through a lottery assignment administered on a zone basis, which gives the applicants no choice. This equalizing measure eradicated distinctions between so-called inferior and superior schools so that all primary school graduates could have equal access to all middle schools located in their respective school zones. There have been contrasting reactions to the system, however, because it was initiated without consideration of how to instruct students of diverse intellectual capacities who are put in the same class together.

Article 101 of the Education Law presents the following objectives for middle school education: (1) to provide the student with the knowledge and skills needed to become a responsible member of a democratic society; (2) to teach the student the basic knowledge and skills for specific occupations, cultivating respect for work and proper conduct and developing the ability to recognize one's individual aptitude in choosing a career; (3) to develop the student's capacity for critical thinking and responsible decision making, and (4) to improve the student's physical well-being. The middle school curriculum is composed of 12 basic or required subjects, elective subjects, and extracurricular activities. Technical and vocational courses are included in the elective subjects to ensure a productive relationship between education and occupation.

High School

The high school entrance examination system was revised in 1974 to effect a lottery assignment on a zone basis for applicants who have passed the qualifying state examination. The revision, which abolished examinations governed by individual schools, has had the desired effect of "equalizing" high schools and has brought about a marked increase in the number of middle school graduates advancing to high schools. The total high school enrollment in 1992 stood at 2,125,573 in 1,886 schools employing a total of 96,342 teachers and instructors. High schools are largely divided into two categories, general and vocational.

General High School: The revised high school entrance examination system was implemented in five major cities on an experimental

General Conditions of Schools, 1992

Classification	Number of Schools	Number of Classes or Departments	Number of Students	Number of Teachers
Grand Total	19,680	234,063	11,150,650	403,282
Kindergarten	8,498	15,561	450,882	21,107
Elementary	6,122	114,290	4,560,128	138,880
Middle School	2,539	48,042	2,336,284	95,330
General High School	1,058	26,470	1,313,081	57,358
Vocational High School	677	16,922	812,492	38,984
Special School	103	1,938	20,646	3,014
Civic School	1	3	150	4
Civic High School	10	26	448	80
Trade School	1	1	23	3
Trade High School	25	442	21,422	605
Miscellaneous School (Middle school course)	8	95	5,258	168
Miscellaneous School (High school course)	26	537	21,831	885
Junior College	126	1,538	404,996	8,518
Teacher's College	11	350	16,504	719
College & University	121	4,315	1,070,169	37,287
Graduate School	335	3,418	96,577	-
Miscellaneous School (Undergraduate courses)	19	115	19,759	340

* The number of professors in Graduate School is included in each college and univ.

basis and applied later to all schools across Korea. One of the most notable results of the new system in its initial stage of implementation was a drastic increase in the number of students enrolling in general high schools. In 1974, the first year of implementation, the number of students in general high schools was recorded at 530,177, representing an increase from 411,106 in the previous year. The number further rose to 932,605 in 1980 and to 1,313,081 in 1992. Article 104 of the Education Law states that the goal of high school education is to provide advanced education in general and technical disciplines. Specific objectives are listed in Article 105. They are the following: (1) to extend the results of middle school education; (2) to improve the student's capacity to understand and make judgments about the nation and society, and (3) to improve the student's physical well-being and ability to plan and manage his own life.

The curriculum consists of 27 subjects to be taught over a three-year period, allowing the principal of each school extensive latitude in deciding elective subjects.

Vocational High School: Those completing middle school may proceed to vocational high schools. These schools provide a more specialized program for vocational training. Schools in this category include eight major types: (1) agricultural, (2) technical, (3) commercial, (4) trade, (6) marine, (7) comprehensive, and (8) arts. As of 1992, there were 47 agricultural high schools, 127 technical high schools, 225 commercial high schools, nine fisheries and marine high schools and 240 comprehensive high schools, totaling 648 altogether. Their total enrollment in 1992 was 812,492:31,853 in agricultural, 200,920 in technical, 358,762 in commercial, 7,482 in fisheries and marine, and

186,451 in comprehensive schools.

Applicants for vocational high schools must be middle school graduates and are required to take a preliminary examination administered at the provincial level. Those who pass this examination are tested again by the individual schools and those failing this main test are given a chance to enter academic high schools through the lottery system without taking another examination.

The curricula of these schools are of various types, usually consisting of 30 percent general education courses and 70 percent vocational courses with equal emphasis on theory and practice. The minimum number of course units to be completed during the three-year duration is 204. In general, the first year is devoted to learning general subjects while vocational subjects occupy greater proportions of the program in later grades. Before graduating, all students are required to complete an apprenticeship ranging from one to three months.

Higher Education

There are four categories of institutions for higher learning: (1) colleges and universities with four-year undergraduate programs (six-year medical colleges), (2) two-year junior vocational colleges, (3) four-year teachers colleges, and (4) miscellaneous schools of collegiate status with two to four-year courses, such as nursing schools, theological seminaries, etc.

In accordance with the Education Law and the relevant presidential and ministerial decrees, all institutes of higher education, whether public or private, come under the supervision of the Ministry of Education. The Ministry exercises control over such matters as student quotas, qualifications of teaching staff, curriculum and degree requirements and general education courses.

About 80 percent of all Korean institutes of higher education are private. Nevertheless, the appointment of presidents and members of the board of trustees is subject to approval by the Ministry of Education. The minimum qualifications for teachers are specified by the Law for Educational Public Officials.

Institutes of higher education have a high degree of autonomy in organizing courses. One legal stipulation, however, is that studies should include a general and liberal education program, consisting of such basic subjects as Korean language, at least two foreign languages, introduction to philosophy, cultural history, general theory of science, and physical education.

There were only 19 institutes of higher education in the entire Korean Peninsula at the time of national liberation in 1945. In 1992 the number in Korea was reported to be 626 (including 494 private institutes) with a total of 1,982,510 students and 48,265 faculty members.

Entrance Examination

Colleges and universities in Korea operate under strict enrollment limits. Because of the difference in college admission quotas and the number of applicants, each school year produces a large number of repeat applicants who add to the intensity of competition for college admission. This disparity has been continuously widened because the rate of increase in the number of high school graduates has far surpassed that of college openings.

In the past, an applicant for college admission had to pass two examinations. The first, strictly based on high school curriculum, was a qualifying test selecting about twice the number of college openings available. Only those who passed this preliminary test could apply for the second examination given by individual colleges and universities.

The college entrance examination system underwent drastic reform in 1981. The main entrance examination was abolished and a new system was introduced that combined scholastic achievements in high school and the score obtained in a nationwide qualifying examination to determine the applicant's eligibility for admission. In the admission process, the current ratio of weight given to a student's high school scholastic achievements and the qualifying examination score is 30 : 70, but the proportion for the former will rise gradually, according to education specialists. From 1994 high school achievements will be given greater weight—at least 40 percent—and a university-offered

A graduation ceremony at a university.

Students of Junior Colleges by Course, 1992

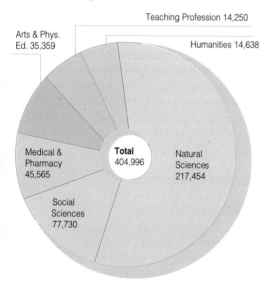

Teaching Profession 14,250

Arts & Phys. Ed. 35,359

Humanities 14,638

Medical & Pharmacy 45,565

Total 404,996

Natural Sciences 217,454

Social Sciences 77,730

examination will be another stage to go through in addition to SAECE (the Scholastic Achievement Examination for the College Entrance), a personality test and aptitude test. The new system will give each university greater latitude in determining eligibility for entrance.

Junior Vocational College

Junior vocational colleges, which developed from the former five-year technical colleges for middle school graduates, have increased sharply in recent years. As of 1992, there were 126 junior vocational colleges with a total enrollment of 404,996 students across Korea. These schools are grouped into agricultural, technical, nursing and sanitation, fisheries, marine and arts. Most offer two-year programs, but fisheries and marine junior colleges provide an additional six-month course for navigation practice. Nursing colleges have three-year programs.

The curriculum for junior vocational colleges emphasizes laboratory practice and on-the-job training. These institutes are gaining public recognition because of their increasing role in supplying skilled manpower required for industrialization and economic development.

College and University

Colleges and universities offer four or six-year courses, the latter including medical and dental colleges. College education aims to train young people to search for the truth, to find methods for applying their findings toward the development of the nation and society, and to prepare them for leadership roles in society.

Colleges and universities have shown great

Students of colleges & Universities by Course, 1992

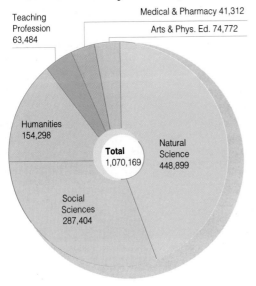

Teaching Profession 63,484

Medical & Pharmacy 41,312

Arts & Phys. Ed. 74,772

Humanities 154,298

Total 1,070,169

Natural Science 448,899

Social Sciences 287,404

quantitative growth in the present decade. At present, there are 121 colleges and universities attended by a total of 1,070,169 students.

A student who has completed 140 credit units is awarded a bachelor's degree (except in medicine and dentistry). There are over 25 fields of study or departments, such as literature, theology, fine arts, music, law, political science, economics, business administration, commerce, physical science, home economics, physical education, engineering, medicine, dentistry, traditional Asian medicine, public health and nursing, pharmacology, agricultural science, veterinary medicine, and fisheries.

The college curricula consist of required courses and electives. Required courses must be finished by every student to graduate. Elective courses are left to the student's discretion, providing minimum credit unit requirements are met.

The required courses consist of general education subjects and specialized subjects. The general education subjects include national ethics, Korean language, philosophy, culture and history, introduction to the natural sciences, and physical education. In addition, the student must select more than one subject (exclusive of

one's specialized subjects) from the following:

1) Humanities: philosophy, ethics, literature, history, psychology, logic, sociology, religion, pedagogy, cultural geography and anthropology;

2) Social Sciences: the constitution, law, political science, economics, psychology, anthropology, pedagogy, history, sociology, statistics and home economics;

3) Natural Sciences: mathematics, physics, chemistry, biology, geology, astronomy, anthropology and home economics.

Graduate School

The Education Law stipulates that a university must have at least one graduate school offering in-depth research-oriented courses for graduate students who aspire to pursue academic or professional careers.

As of 1992, the total enrollment in graduate courses provided by universities across Korea was 96,577, including 80,417 working for master's degrees.

The minimum requirement for a master's degree is 24 credits, normally achieved in four semesters by day students and five semesters by night students. The minimum requirement for a doctorate is 36 credits, which usually takes three years to earn. Proficiency tests in two foreign languages are additionally given to Ph.D. candidates.

Teacher Education

Pre-Service Education

There are two types of teacher education institutions in Korea: teachers' colleges for training elementary school teachers, and colleges of education for training secondary school teachers, both offering four-year programs. There are 11 teachers' colleges, one in each province, all of which are national. Colleges of education are either national or private, the main difference being that the national colleges offer various advantages in addition to relatively lower tuitions. Graduates of national colleges of education and teachers' colleges are obligated to teach at designated schools for a prescribed period of time.

Some ordinary four-year colleges and universities offer specialized teaching courses, completion of which entitles the graduate to teach in middle or high school. Another way to obtain a teacher's license is for graduates of four-year colleges or universities to pass the teacher qualification examination.

In- Service Training of Teachers

In growing recognition of the importance of in-service teacher training, a law was enacted in the mid-1960s to establish training centers at both the elementary and secondary levels. In 1992, 17 universities opened affiliated in-service training institutes for secondary school teachers and 13 national teachers' colleges operated similar institutes for elementary school teachers.

Since 1985, two local in-service teacher training institutes have been constructed each year with the goal of providing training facilities for in-service teachers only. As the result, there were 13 local in-service teacher training institutes in 1992 and two more are under construction. Local in-service teacher training institutes will be utilized as a center for training teachers.

Every year about 20,000 teachers receive qualification training to be certified for promotion to higher grades, and an additional 43,000 teachers receive a short period of refresher training to revitalize their professional work on education. The programs for qualification training consist of courses totalling more than 180 hours with allocations of 10 percent for general education, 16 percent for an introductory education course and 74 percent for subject matter. For refresher training, a minimum of 60 hours are required.

In addition, Seoul National University's College of Education runs a training institute for educational administration which offers a six-month intensive program for principals of both elementary and secondary schools. Korea University of Education's Integrated Training Institute for Teachers gives an intensive training program to teachers with the aims of increasing professionalism in education and preparing teachers to take a lead in such areas as the development of teaching and learning materials, instructional design and teaching methods.

Special Education

Special education in the modern sense was begun in Korea by an American missionary named R.S. Hall, who established a school for the blind in 1894 in P'yŏngyang. Similar projects were undertaken during the following decades by a number of social and charitable organizations to educate the handicapped. The schools for the blind were nationalized in 1945, and they incorporated secondary courses in 1947. A special teacher training course was opened in 1950. Finally, the Law for the Promotion of Special Education was enacted in 1977.

The Education Law provides that one or more special schools be established in each of the special cities and in each province. Although public awareness of the importance of special education is still inadequate, the number of schools for the handicapped has increased steadily. The number of special schools rose from 28 in 1969 to 57 in 1980. As of 1992, there were 103 institutions for special education across Korea with a total enrollment of 20,646. They include 12 for the blind, 20 for the deaf and mute, 13 for the physically handicapped, 58 for the mentally retarded, and one for the sufferers of Hansen's disease (leprosy).

In addition to general education, these schools offer skill programs designed to prepare physically handicapped children for productive jobs. The Ministry of Education sponsors an annual skills competition and job placement programs. The former is aimed at providing disadvantaged children with opportunities to demonstrate their skills in as many as 40 different vocational areas, and encouraging them to learn skills so that they will be able to earn their own living in the future. The winners in the skills competition are presented awards and chances to acquire better jobs. Job placement programs serve to increase the employability of handicapped persons.

Vocational education.

Non-Formal Education

The Non-Formal Education Law was enacted in 1982 and revised in 1990. The law defines the basic directions of non-formal education, the roles and responsibilities of concerned organizations, interrelationships among these organizations, and other matters pertinent to the management and support of education conducted outside formal educational institutions.

Non-formal education in Korea is divided into two types. One is a kind of para-institutional education for youths and adults who have not had the full benefit of formal education. The other is designed to provide short-term technical or refresher courses to those who are already employed or in the non-student population.

Non-formal education in its early stages emphasized literacy campaigns, civic education, agricultural extension study, and adult education. It was usually carried out by social organizations. But with the successful implementation of economic development plans which have brought significant changes in all aspects of

Korean life, non-formal education became more diverse in nature and skill training programs emerged as its main thrust.

Institutional Non-formal Education

Youths wishing to advance to or resume regular courses in formal education can take preparatory courses at civic schools, higher civic schools, trade schools, higher trade schools and air and correspondence high schools or colleges.

Civic and Higher Civic Schools

Civic schools offer a range of education comparable to a regular primary school for those who have not completed primary school. The courses are from one to three years. Schools of this type were popular during the early post-liberation years as a large portion of the population had not received regular school education. As primary school education has become universal, however, there has been a marked decrease in the number of people needing education of this kind. Consequently, the number of civic schools fell from more than 1,400 in the late 1950s to 69 in 1970. There were five of these schools in 1980, and only 1 in 1992.

Higher civic schools are designed to serve primary or civic school graduates who failed to advance to middle school, so they offer curriculum corresponding to that of regular middle schools. The courses are from one to three years.

The need for civic schools of this type has also diminished markedly since the 1970s with the increased availability of regular middle school education. Many of the existing higher civic schools were changed to either regular middle schools or high schools. The number of higher civic schools decreased from 323 in 1960 to 127 in 1980, and to 10 in 1992.

Trade and Higher Trade Schools

Trade schools and higher trade schools offer programs for job-oriented knowledge and skills. The courses are from one to three years. Graduates of primary schools, civic schools, or the equivalent are eligible for admission to trade schools. Admission into a higher trade school is limited to graduates of three-year trade schools, regular middle schools, and the equivalent.

Some trade and higher trade schools are operated by large business corporations or industrial establishments to meet training needs of training their own employees. Subjects taught at these schools include farming, engineering, commerce, fisheries, housekeeping, cosmetology, and hairdressing. All are designed to prepare the students for work after graduation.

Correspondence Education

The concept of an "open university" became a reality in 1972 with the establishment of the Correspondence College. This provides working youths and adults with four-year, post-high school courses in home economics, business administration, agriculture, elen_ ary education, and public administration. Thirty-minute lectures are broadcast over the radio every day and learning materials are provided for all courses offered.

Twenty-three colleges have been designated as collaborating institutions for this program. Their facilities are open to students of the Correspondence College to assemble for testing and other activities for a two-week period during summer vacation and during winter vacation. The number of students taking correspondence courses in 1992 totalled 303,760, most of whom were employed.

Eleven correspondence high schools affiliated with regular high schools were opened in 1974. The program has continuously expanded so that in 1992 there were 49 correspondence schools with 23,515 students. They cover all requirements of the regular high school curriculum, giving lectures both on radio (313 days per year) and in classes (26 days). By passing a government-administered examination, graduates of these schools are credited with the same qualifications as regular high school graduates.

The textbooks are prepared by the Korean Educational Development Institute and classroom facilities, and teachers are provided by the collaborating high schools.

Tuition for correspondence courses averages one third of regular high school tuition. Only radio broadcasts have so far been used for lectures, but plans are being made to use television as well.

Special Classes for Working Youths

Night classes for working youths began in 1977 at secondary school facilities located near large industrial establishments, with their employers paying part of the tuition. These classes have assisted young workers in getting an education and have helped employers by boosting the morale and efficiency of workers. As of 1992, there were a total of 10,030 businesses participating in these special class programs benefiting 47,698 workers.

Non-Formal Education Outside Institutions

Government agencies and private organizations provide various training courses ranging from special vocational skills to techniques in the arts in order to assist youths and adults in their job performance.

The Status of Nationwide Libraries, 1992

(In thousand won)

Classification	Libraries	Staffs	Seats	Collection of Books	Clients	Volumes in Circulation	Budget
Total	1,160 (13,488)	7,840 (2,464)	511, 790 (980,798)	48,581,333 (40,401,734)	106,232,521 (36,082,274)	50,755,870 (38,243,590)	99,080,754 (12,980,508)
Central National Library	1	239	4,089	1,437,991	1,226,364	1,797,909	5,585,575
National Assembly Library	1	256	526	622,864	66,367	190,733	2,360,716
Public Library	174	2,976	107,137	5,830,094	20,083,414	16,110,470	38,598,064
College & Univ Library	304	3,031	264,184	32,412,920	77,935,451	28,665,394	38,222,884
High School Library	318 (3,278)	266 (1,252)	110,166 (393,110)	2,785,616 (12,455,020)	4,176,998 (12,923,944)	1,429,296 (7,269,618)	745,462 (6,272,834)
Middle School Library	42 (3,896)	12 (1,014)	7,216 (269,268)	238,344 (2,979,926)	250,184 (6,965,164)	117,678 (8,059,432)	23,058 (2,256,708)
Elementary School Library	70 (6,314)	44 (198)	7,794 (318,420)	351,824 (24,966,788)	543,284 (16,193,166)	387,682 (22,914,540)	94,652 (4,450,966)
Special Library	250	1,016	10,678	4,901,680	1,950,459	2,056,708	13,450,343

* The figures in ( ) indicate the data by item with respect to the number of reading rooms.

Vocational Training Centers

Vocational training centers are usually set up in vocational high schools and industrial establishments to offer short-term job training to high school graduates. The primary purpose of these centers is to equip young people with specific work skills to enable them to earn a living.

The programs offered include farming, factory work, housekeeping and retail sales. The period of training ranges from three months to one year and classes are conducted mainly during the evening. A majority of these centers use the existing school facilities.

Students Service Corps

This program organizes student volunteers for visits to rural communities to help with farming and environmental improvement projects. These activities, which are usually undertaken by college students during vacations, contribute to the mutual understanding between urban and rural communities.

Private Institutes

Private institutes offer group instruction as well as single lessons on a great variety of subjects, including general academic subjects, skills, arts, and sports. Private lessons conducted by individuals in such fields as musical instruments, painting, and acting also fall within this category of education.

Adult Education Classes

These classes are designed for the general public to strengthen cooperative ties between schools and local communities, and to encourage good habits such as diligence, conservation, frugality, and saving. Classes are conducted mostly at primary schools during the winter in rural villages, and in the spring or autumn in urban communities, at a time convenient to residents.

The subjects taught at these classes often reflect the needs of the individual community. They include social ethics, family rituals simplified to suit today's lifestyle, flower arranging, knitting, dressmaking, and practical farming methods.

The National Central Library in Seoul.

Public Libraries

Libraries play an important role in social education. There are three principal types: public, school, and special. Public libraries must meet the informational needs of the public and stimulate the cultural development of the communities they serve. Many public libraries receive financial support from both the central Government and the municipal or provincial administrations, and are subject to their direction and supervision.

School libraries are encouraged to open their doors to the public when practicable so that they can increase their function as an important link with the community. There are also numerous private libraries, reading circles, and mobile libraries in cities and villages across the country, helping to raise the general cultural standards of the people.

Research Institutes

In response to the growing complexity of educational problems and the heightening demands for major reforms in educational system, educational research has gained in intensity leading to the birth of the following research institutions.

Central Educational Research & Training Institute (CERTI)

CERTI is a subsidiary component of the Ministry of Education which is primarily responsible for: (1) training of school supervisors, educational researchers, elementary, secondary school principals and general administrators; (2) research and evaluation for the continual improvement of training programs; (3) development and distribution of training materials to local training institutes and assistance in their efforts to improve training programs. There are 19 kinds of task-related programs intended to enhance the professionalism of trainees in their area of concern.

National Board of Educational Evaluation (NBEE)

NBEE is a subsidiary component of the Ministry of Education at the national level. The institute has sought to raise the social credibility of education by seeking and developing evaluation and measurement tools. NBEE serves the following specific functions:

1. Development of nationally standardized examinations for entrance to high schools and universities.
2. Evaluation of academic achievement of students in all school levels.

3. Research on evaluation methodology and provision of advisory and consultative services to schools.

Korea Educational Development Institute (KEDI)

KEDI is an independent, autonomous, and government-funded research and development organization charged with the following activities:

1. Comprehensive and systematic research and development activities on goals, content and methodology of education.
2. Formulation of policy alternative and the development of long and mid-term educational development plans.
3. Production of TV and radio programs and improvement of teaching and learning results by tapping the potential advantages of broadcast media in the educational process.
4. Dissemination of research findings and hosting of forums to give exposure to research findings.

Korea Institute for Research in Behavioral Sciences (KIRBS)

KIRBS is a private organization seeking to apply the theories of behavioral sciences to the solution of human and social problems. Since human behavior is categorized into various aspects of human life, KIRBS conducts research in the following areas:

1. Research related to the instructional process and development of materials to enhance the effectiveness of teaching and learning.
2. Research on psychological and attitudinal factors that affect the management of educational systems in order to enhance the effectiveness of system management.
3. Development of educational programs that facilitate the growth of children in linguistic and intellectual development and social maturity.
4. Development of aptitude testing tools.
5. Provision of counseling services regarding child development, aptitude development, academic achievement, and socialization.

Municipal and Provincial Education Research Centers

There are 14 educational research centers, each in an independent city and province, aimed at addressing problems involved in teaching and learning, and producing and disseminating audio-visual materials and teaching aids. In addition, they provide counseling services for teachers regarding instruction, host workshops and forums and provide training, all intended to enhance the teaching skill of teachers.

Educational Research Institutes Attached to Universities

These institutes conduct research on specific topics or issues commissioned by the Ministry of Education, Korea Trade Association and Korea Research Foundation. The university's grant or subsidy and the contributions of sponsoring organizations comprise the main source of revenue.

National Academy of Arts

The National Academy of Arts was inaugurated in 1954 with a view towards the renewal of institutional support for the development of the nation's cultural heritage and enhancing the status of artists (Culture Preservation Law No. 17). It also serves in a consultative capacity to the government regarding issues that affect the development of traditional cultures.

National Academy of Science

The National Academy of Science was inaugurated in 1954 in order to renew institutional support for the development of sciences and enhance the status of scientists. It also serves as a consultant to the Ministry of Education regarding scholarly works, science, language and culture, and awards scientists and writers who have distinguished themselves by scholarly works.

Academy of Korean Studies

The Academy of Korean Studies was established by the government in 1978 with the objective of carrying out in-depth studies in the heritage of the Korean nation. The academy sponsors research projects on Korean history, philosophy, education, society, literature, arts and various other aspects of traditional Korean life and culture. It opened graduate courses in Korean studies in 1980.

National History Compilation Committee

The National History Compilation Committee was established in 1945 and is under the direct control of the Ministry of Education. The committee conducts research on national history, compiles and publishes Korean history-related materials and collects various types of data and materials related to national history.

The committee is composed of 15 experts on Korean history. It deliberates and decides on matters related to the compilation of national history and data collection. Its administrative structure is composed of three offices: the General Service Division, the Historiographic Office, and the Research Office.

Research and Academic Institutions

There are about 600 research and academic organizations throughout the country, covering humanities, social sciences and natural and applied sciences.

The Korea Research Foundation

The Korea Research Foundation was founded in 1980, to support and coordinate various types of academic research activities of the nation. To support academic activities, it also runs an academic information network linking major research institutes and university libraries, provides for international exchanges of scholars and promotes joint research projects under bilateral agreements with foreign institutes. The major component of international exchange activities is the development of Korean studies at foreign institutes of higher learning and research. In addition, it engages in youth exchange programs and cultural events, designed to develop better understanding and cooperation between countries.

The Korean Council for University Education

The Korean Council for University Education is an organization composed of the presidents and deans of 124 colleges and universities across the nation. The council conducts independent research for the development of college and university education. Research on the higher education system, exchange of professors and academic information among institutes are its major functions.

International Exchange

With the expanding exchange of people and information in all academic and professional fields, the number of Koreans studying abroad has been constantly increasing in recent times. One reason is that the national endeavor for economic development and industrialization requires highly specialized manpower. Another factor boosting international exchange of education has been the growth of Korean communities abroad.

In response to the increasing demand for international exchange of education, the Ministry of Education supports exchange programs administratively and financially. The categories covered by international exchange programs are varied, including inter-governmental programs, overseas studies, invitation of foreign scholars and students, youth exchanges and scholar exchanges.

Inter-governmental Programs

The Korean Government has established bilateral agreements with more than 60 countries concerning programs intended to effect reciprocal exchanges of information, mutual understanding and cooperation between different peoples. Likewise, the Korean Government has participated actively in exchange programs promoted by international organizations. One example is its relationship with UNESCO, which has undertaken several programs to promote international understanding and provide information services on the nation's cultural heritage and foreign cultures. It also has hosted international forums and training programs. The

National Commission for UNESCO has served as an agent and facilitator for the exchange of academics, professionals and students.

The Korean Government encourages and supports the development of Korean studies at overseas institutes of higher learning by providing grants for staff development and lectures, facilitating the exchange of academics, financing research and publication and supplying materials. At present, 173 universities and research institutes in 36 foreign countries are associated with the development of Korean studies.

Area studies concerning Asia, the Middle East, Europe, North America, Central and Latin America and Africa are gaining momentum at higher educational institutes in Korea. Foreign languages presently offered are English, Japanese, Chinese, German, French, Russian, Spanish, Italian, Portuguese, Dutch, Swedish, Malay-Indonesian, Arabic, Thai, Hindi, Turkish, Persian, Vietnamese, Swahili, Czechoslovakian, Yugoslavian, Rumanian and Polish.

The Government sponsors refresher programs abroad which enable professors to keep up with the advancing frontiers of science and technology. From 1978 to 1992, a total of 3,121 professors were beneficiaries of this program.

Korean Students and Scholars Abroad

Regulations governing overseas education have been liberalized in recent years, contributing to the fast growth in the number of Korean students going abroad for advanced study at their own expense or with government or public funding. Eligibility for overseas study, earlier limited to college students and graduates, now is extended to high school graduates.

Previously, overseas study generally depended on the student's personal funds or scholarships offered by foreign schools and foundations. The situation has changed considerably as government scholarships have increased both in kind and in the number available.

In proportion to the increasing number of students studying abroad, opportunities are being expanded for teachers and college professors to travel abroad to enhance their competence through first-hand observation of up-to-date academic achievement in foreign countries.

Foreign Students and Scholars in Korea

The Ministry of Education's scholarships are available for foreign students who wish to study in Korea for advanced degrees or in connection with short-term language and study tour programs. Foreign students in countries with which Korea has diplomatic relations are eligible for the scholarships. Generally, it takes three or four years to obtain master's and doctoral degrees. The Korea Research Foundation is responsible for the administration, monitoring and evaluation of the scholarship programs. It also provides economical lodging, informational and other services to make the studies productive and worthwhile.

The number of foreign students enrolling in Korean colleges and universities, though small in comparison with that of Korean students studying abroad, has been increasing steadily in recent years. A total of 1,989 foreign students attended Korean universities and colleges in 1992. The number of foreign professors and scholars residing in Korea, either on invitation from Korean universities and colleges or under financial grants from foundations, was 413 in 1992.

Youth Exchanges

Youth exchanges have been carried out under bilateral agreements with the United States, Japan, Malaysia and Saudi Arabia. The purpose of these exchanges is to give young people the opportunity to know and cooperate with each other on the principle of mutual understanding.

Youth exchange programs initiated by the Government are now implemented by government-affiliated agencies, such as the Korea Federation of Youth, the National Commission for UNESCO and the Korea Research Foundation.

SOCIAL DEVELOPMENT AND QUALITY OF LIFE

Population

Rapid demographic transition, along with sustained socio-economic development, have resulted in unprecedented human resource development in Korea. A look at Korea's population structure shows the number of those of productive age, namely 15 years old and above, rose from 24,751,000 in 1980 to 32,831,000 in 1992, when the total population has expanded steadily in pace with the diversifying social structure.

Throughout the period of rapid economic development, a high priority has been placed on human resource development. Efforts are being made to ensure sustained manpower development in order to better meet demands for specialized manpower in an industrialized society. At the same time, labor-intensive industries and vocational training are being expanded to provide employment opportunities to the working populace. Korea has long demonstrated a level of educational attainment comparable to that of advanced countries. Even today, the educational level in Korea is still regarded as one of the world's highest, at least in quantitative terms, suggesting that high priority is continuously being placed on education in Korea.

Despite various administrative and tax devices to discourage such action, migration from rural areas to cities has been excessive. This unwelcome trend has increased the population of the country's two largest cities, Seoul and Pusan, from 14 percent in 1960 to 33 percent in 1990. Including other cities, the urban population also jumped from 28.0 percent in 1960 to 74.4 percent in 1990.

This concentration has given rise to a number of serious urban problems. To cope with these, the Government has prepared a long-term manpower development plan aimed chiefly at discouraging heavy concentrations of people in large cities and ensuring population dispersion in the provincial areas. To do this, it is initiating the relocation of economic activities in the provincial areas and ensuring balanced land development. The fostering of provincial cities, the construction of cities near industrial estates, and the improvement of countrywide transportation, communications and service facilities are part of this effort.

Manpower Development

Due to rapid economic growth and an improved industrial structure, the problem of unemployment has virtually been overcome in Korea. Manpower shortages even arose in some industrial sectors during the brisk business period of 1977- 78.

Due to the decline in birth rate, the elevation of income levels and the trend of avoiding the "3D" (dirty, dangerous, difficult) jobs, however, the Korean economy has been experiencing a serious labor shortage, especially in production workers for the manufacturing industry for the past 3-4 years.

It has become an important task for the Government to supply the manpower necessary to back up stable economic activity. With a view to matching manpower supply and demand, various employment policies have been executed and various vocational training opportunities have been opened. Those who seek new jobs or want to change their jobs are provided with vocational guidance services, such as vocational aptitude tests and counselling. Placement services are being promoted to improve worker's job security through employment security agencies throughout the country. These agencies are linked to one another through up-to-date computer data bases.

To train technical manpower and expand employment in preparation for the advent of an advanced industrial society, manpower development programs focus on the better utilization of educated or trained manpower. Also emphasized are the improvement of working conditions and environment, including the fostering of a constructive dialogue between labor and management, and the revitalization of labor unions at the industrial level. To foster the heavy and chemical industries and to promote export industries, efforts have been made to ensure the qualitative improvement and increased sophistication of skilled and technical manpower.

The vocational training system can be divided into public and private training. Public training is mainly conducted by the Korea Manpower Agency (KOMA) under the supervision of the Ministry of Labor. Other governmental institutions also conduct vocational training to meet sectoral needs. KOMA training focuses on basic trades, new technology trades and advanced skilled manpower. Private vocational training consists of in-plant training offered by companies and authorized training conducted by individual or non-profit bodies. The former is conducted to meet the specific needs of the enterprises and the latter is conducted with approval from the Ministry of Labor.

In 1991, vocational training was provided for 25,950 people through public training and 67,553 people though private. In 1993, it is expected that 31,000 will receive public vocational training with another 126,000 receiving private.

In order to increase employment opportunities, policies have concentrated on the development of skilled-labor intensive industries and on increasing scientifically and technically-oriented manpower through the expansion of vocational and technical training. Junior vocational colleges, which developed from the former five-year technical colleges for middle school graduates, have increased sharply in number in recent years. As of 1992, there were 126 junior vocational colleges with a total enrollment of 404,996 students across Korea. In an effort to obtain qualified vocational teachers, the engineering education system at state-run colleges and universities has been improved to diversify vocational training, and the departments of vocational high schools have been further subdivided to better cope with specialization in industry and the professions. Technical classes have been introduced in middle and high schools to improve the adaptability of graduates seeking employment. At the same time, emphasis has shifted from government programs to in-house training by industries. As a result in 1992, authorized vocational training

institutes numbered 115 and in-house training centers about 260. To encourage such training, the tax system was revamped to provide benefits for the purchase of training equipment and other expenses. Efforts also were made to improve the quality of teachers, including the upward readjustment of teachers' salaries and improvements in the curricula. Of equal importance were such things as expanded training for career advancement, the training of the elderly and the handicapped, and the establishment of a rational system for job placement.

Housing

Fueled by an expanding population, a chronic housing shortage persists in Korea in the face of sharply rising demand. Factors contributing to this include heavy migration to the cities, a trend toward nuclear families, and the superannuation of existing dwellings. Overpopulation and spirals in land prices in the big cities have led to an imbalance in the distribution of housing between urban and rural areas. As of 1992, the nationwide housing supply ratio stood at 76.0 percent.

The Government has worked out various policy measures to meet the increased housing demands as part of its economic development plans As a result, housing production increased from a 65,000 unit annual average during the first five-year plan (1962-1966) to an average of 477,000 during the sixth five-year plan (1987-1991). Investment in the housing sector more than tripled, from 1.5 percent of the GNP to 4.7 percent over the same period.

There have also been substantial improvements in the quality of housing; nonetheless, housing remains a major problem. The core of this problem is an acute shortage, defined as the difference between the number of houses and that of households.

The new Korean Constitution, as amended in 1987, proclaims that every citizen is entitled to adequate shelter as a basic right. It specifically mandates the Government to develop comprehensive housing plans and programs to improve conditions for all.

Accordingly, the Government introduced an ambitious housing program extending until 1992. It aimed at building two million units of housing over a five-year period from 1988-1992. This goal has been accomplished very succesfully with a 128 percent increase in housing construction as compared with the previous five years. The number of newly-built housing units over the five years went up to 2.7 million, improving the housing supply ratio from 69.2 percent in the year of 1987 to 76.0 percent in 1992. This rapid increase in the housing supply somewhat alleviated the shortage in urban areas and contributed to stabilizing sharply rising housing price.

For the lowest income households, the Government has taken responsibility for supplying public rental housing at reasonable rents. Low monthly rents are set for the lowest 20 percent of the income bracket. The Government allocated as much as four trillion won, equivalent to five billion U.S. dollars, to construct 190 thousand units over the next five years. The public rental housing program is intended to provide not only decent housing for the poor, but also the opportunity for job training and employment.

For the next income bracket, which ranges from the lower 20th to 40th percentile, the Government has provided small apartment units with various subsidies such as public housing finance, tax and land provisions. The Government depends largely on private initiative to supply most housing for middle and higher income families. Various regulations, legal and administrative, have been under study in order to stimulate private housing construction.

The proclaimed aims of the housing policy in the next ten years are relieving the housing shortage and stabilizing housing prices. To attain this goal, the Government will maintain a housing construction rate of 500-600 thousand units of housing construction annually through various policies.

Health and Medicine

Medical Benefits

Since the latter half of the 1970s, medical security, in the form of medical insurance and medical aid, has been expanded to cover a substantial portion of the population. In 1992, the number of persons covered by medical security reached 41,325,395 persons, or 93.9 percent of the total population.

Because of a long-standing policy of laissez faire, however, Korea's medical supply system and medical resources were insufficient to meet the sharply rising needs engendered by the development of the medical security system. Therefore, to supply low-cost quality medicine to all people, efforts were made to establish an effective medical supply system through the reasonable distribution and supply of medical resources. To ensure the qualitative improvement of health and medical programs, efforts were made to develop more effective means of hospital management.

Present State of Health and Medicine

The health of the Korean people as a whole has improved substantially, as noted in the indices chart. This is related directly to the qualitative improvement of diet, the rise in living standards and the development of health and medical programs, all prompted by the rapid economic growth of the 1970s.

The incident rates of communicable diseases have declined sharply; however, there have still been some cases of cholera in endemic areas recently. The incidence of tuberculosis has declined markedly, but the number of positive germ carriers or contagious persons is decreasing at a negligible rate. The incidence of intestinal worm infection also has declined sharply.

People are using medicines with growing frequency, and the share of medical costs in the total household expenditures has increased accordingly. In 1963, the medical expenses of an urban family averaged 2,280 won or 2.7 per-

Major Health Indices

Item	1970	1976	1979	1985	1988	1991	1992
Health							
Birth rate (per 1,000)	30	24.3	23.7	19.7	16.51	15.6	-
Natural population growth rate (per 1,000)	21.0	17.7	17.5	13.5	9.7	9.7	-
Mortality rate (per 1,000)	8.5	6.6	6.2	6.2	5.93	5.8	-
Life expectancy (age)	65	67.4	68.2	69.0	70.4	71.3	-
Child mortality (0-4 years, per 1,000)	45.5	38.0	42.0	13.3	12.4	12.8	-
Maternal mortality (per 10,000)	8.3	5.6	4.2	3.4	3.2	3.0	-
Nutrition							
Calorie intake (per day, per person)	-	1,922	2,097	1,935	1,935	1,989	-
(Comparison with recommended 2,111 calories)	(-)	(91.1)	(99.3)	(91)	(91)	(87.5)	-
Protein intake (grams per day)	-	60.4	69.6	75	79.3	83.6	-
Animal protein (grams per day)	-	12.2	22.2	31	49	38	-
Medical resources & utilization							
Population per physician	1,773	1,732	1,554	1,235	1,005	837	786
Population per nurse	1,796	553	417	698	551	453	429
Population per hospital bed	909	796	610	426	348	302	288
Utilization of hospital beds (%)	58.4	55.6	62.9	61.6	71.1	80.7	77.3

Source: Ministry of Health and Social Affairs

cent of its total spending and that of a rural family 1,893 won or 2.4 percent. In 1990, however, this average jumped to 5.3 percent of an urban family and 6.4 percent in rural family.

Development of Health and Medicine

Attempts have been made to establish a system to provide equal medical benefits for all. First, in keeping pace with the expansion and development of the medical security system, the restructuring of the countrywide medical network into several medical zones was planned and implemented. In such a way, 2,039 primary health care posts were established under each of the existing 268 health centers and 1,333 health subcenters. This required special training for nurses or midwives so that they could provide preventive medical and first aid services in remote doctorless areas.

Also, with this restructuring, the clinical function of general hospitals and clinics, whose operations had been left on their own, were clearly defined and medical charges adjusted to serve public interests.

Second, to ensure a rational supply of health and medical personnel and rectify the heavy concentration of medical resources in the urban areas, efforts were made to enable specialists to handle secondary and tertiary treatment at hospitals and general hospitals and to restrict the practices of general practitioners.

Third, to cope with the lack of a comprehensive health information management system and the insufficiency of the current systematic health indices, health statistical programs were developed and a statistical worker assigned to each health center. An overall health survey and a survey of medical costs were to be conducted every five years.

Public Health Management

Various projects have been implemented to promote public health. First, the Government has actively propagated adequate health information and implemented preventive programs for infectious and non-infectious diseases, thereby clearly enhancing the general level of public health and reducing communicable diseases drastically. The nutritional status of the Korean people has improved remarkably. Koreans now consume more animal protein and less grain due to rapid economic growth. However, certain nutritional elements such as calcium and vitamin A are deficient in the diets of some youth and some pregnant women, suggesting a need for nutritional guidance to the general public.

Second, Korea began implementing a family planning program in 1961. As a result, the natural population growth rate has been reduced from 3.0 percent in 1960 to 0.91 percent in 1992. Korea has entered into the final population equilibrium state, the last stage of demographic transition. A national maternal and child health (MCH) program aims at improving the level of national health by means of prenatal care for pregnant women as well as health care services for preschool children. MCH activities include delivery care, regular check-ups and immunizations for infants, and MCH education, with the work partly done by public health centers and health workers and partly done by private clinics and hospitals. The safe delivery rate has risen to 98 percent thanks to national medical insurance plans and MCH programs, but the infant mortality rate remains at 12.8 per 1,000 births, which means that still more effort should be exerted to improve MCH programs.

Third, the incidence of major, acute, communicable diseases has been decreasing and that of non-communicable diseases increasing due to increased life expectancy, economic development and changes in the socio-cultural environment. Recently non-communicable diseases such as cancer, cerebrovascular disease, and cardiovascular disease have caused a large share of all deaths. Accordingly, the Government has begun a nationwide non-communicable disease control program, placing primary emphasis on public education for the prevention of cardiovascular diseases. To help control cancer (malignant neoplasm), the most common cause of death in Korea, the Government is setting up the National Cancer Institute which will be responsible for national cancer control and patient management programs.

Mental health is the other important health problem in the non-communicable disease category. The Government is expanding specialized hospitals like the National Mental Hospital and facilitating the rehabilitation of mental health patients. The Government enacted the Mental Health Act which insures the rights of mental disease patients and establishes comprehensive care and control of them.

Social Security

Insurance and Relief Programs

Korea's social security system consists of two categories: insurance programs based on the Social Security Law, and public relief programs or free grants. In the first category are benefits for medical, business suspension, unemployment, old age, industrial accident compensation, family allowance, child delivery and bereaved family and funeral payments. The social security programs can be supplemented, if necessary, with social welfare and other related programs.

Because of Korea's socio-economic situation, the scope of coverage is divided into the insurable income bracket and those eligible for public relief. Under the policy, various welfare systems have been introduced which are to be expanded and developed step-by-step in a manner adaptable to socio-economic developments. In this way, the creation of an effective social security system is being promoted by the integration and adjustment of various welfare programs.

Socio-Economic Background: Living standards have improved markedly due to the rapid economic growth of the 1970s. At the same time, this fast growth and industrialization have given rise to an assortment of social problems, such as extreme income gaps and a widespread imbalance of development among regions and industries.

The deterioration of socio-economic conditions, especially price spirals, economic slowdown and thr increase of unemployment, prompted by the 1973 and subsequent oil shocks, added further to the need for broad welfare programs.

With the successful implementation of fifth five-year economic development plan, demand for welfare programs and the expansion of

State of Social Security Programs

(As of December, 1992)

Programs	Scope	Coverage	Beneficiaries	Relevant Office
1.Social Insurance				
a. Medical insurance	All employees and self employed except for those persons covered by medical aid, assistance program	Disease, injury,	40,779,149	Ministry of Health & Social Affairs
b.Industrial accident compensation insurance	Workers of workshops with 5 or more employees (154,820 workshops)	Disease, injury, disability, death	7,058,704	Ministry of Labor
c.National pension	All citizens	Old age, disability, death	5,012,159	Ministry of Health & Social Affairs
d.Special profession pension insurance	Public officials, military servicemen, private shool	Old age, disability, death	798,000	Ministries of Gov't Administration, National Defense, and Education
e.Seamens insurance	Seamen	Old age, disability, death		Maritime & Port Administration
f.Severance allowance system	Workers of workshops with 10 or more employees	Severance allowance		Ministry of Labor
2. Public Relief a.Subsistence care				
Care at home	Persons, as defined by Law on Subsistence Care	Food, fuel, educational and funeral expenses	338,000	Ministry of Health & Social Affairs
Care at facilities	Persons accommodated at social welfare facilities under Law on Subsistence Care	Food,fuel,clothing educational and funeral expenses	83,000	Ministry of Health & Social Affairs
Care of the needy	Persons with low incomes, as prescribed by Law on Subsistence Care	Educational expenses,Cash Loans, Vocational Training	1,580,000	Ministry of Health & Social Affairs
b.Medical care	Economically incapable persons, needy persons, and persons accommodated at facilities as defined by Law on Subsistence Care, persons subject to veterans assistance, etc.	Disease, injury	2,878,684	Ministry of Health & Social Affairs
c.Veterans assistance	Wounded veterans and policemen, bereaved families of fallen servicemen and policemen, those who had rendered outstanding contribution to the nation's independence,defectors from North Korea, etc.	Subsistence, medicine, etc	132,000	Office of Veterans Administration
3.Social Welfare service				
Care at 730 Facilities	Persons accommodate at facilities for the aged, physically handicapped persons,childrens welfare,etc.	Subsistence, medicine,etc.	77,749	Ministry of Health & Social Affairs, Office of Veterans Administration
4.Disaster Relief	Victims of disasters	Emergency relief, etc.		Ministry of Health & Social Affairs

Source: Ministry of Health and Social Affairs

employment opportunities have risen in many sectors. The imbalance in income distribution has led to poverty consciousness, a phenomenon that has spurred the establishment of a social security policy to create a balance and equilibrium between economic and social developments. In this direction, the medical aid and insurance systems began expanding in 1977, and the National Pension Law, enacted in 1986, also has been enforced since 1988. Efforts were concentrated on the expansion of social welfare policies to bolster the public relief of those unable to support themselves due to old age, disability and other causes.

State of Social Security: In Korea, the history of active social security programs dates back to 1963, when the Social Security Law was enacted. The key devices provided by this law were social security and public relief programs. The law also called for the providing of social welfare services through supplementary programs.

Types of Insurance: A number of insurance laws have been enacted to facilitate various social insurance programs. They include the Civil Service Pension Law legislated in 1960, Seamens' Insurance Law of 1962, the Law on Insurance for Compensation of Industrial Disability, the Medical Insurance and the Military Pension Laws of 1963, the National Welfare Pension and Private School Teachers Pension Laws of 1973, the Civil Service and Private School Teacher-Employees Medical Insurance Law of 1977, and the National Pension Law of 1986.

The scope of these insurance systems has been expanded steadily. In particular, the Medical Insurance, the National Pension System and the Industrial Accident Compensation Insurance entered full-fledged operation.

Public Relief: Public assistance has been extended to the needy and feeble, such as the elderly and those disabled due to injury, mental illness and physical handicaps.

Public relief activities in the form of subsistence, income support and medical care were based on the Law on Subsistence Care, the Military Relief and Compensation Law of 1961, societies from July 1989, more than 94 percent

and the Disaster Relief Law and the Law on Special Care of Persons Who Rendered Meritorious Services to the Nation, both legislated in 1962. The Temporary Law on Self Support Guidance, legislated in 1968, provides wage-distribution projects for needy persons. The legislation of the Law on Medical Care in 1977 has, along with the expanded medical insurance program, provided the groundwork for the consolidation of the medical security system. As a further relief measure, needy families have been subsidized with household fuel expenses and the entire cost of school fees for their children attending middle school.

Other Social Welfare Systems: Other social welfare services are intended to subsidize the subsistence and promote the welfare of such socially disadvantaged persons as children without support, the elderly, physically and mentally handicapped persons, and mother-child families. Demand for these types of services are increasing with the changes in social patterns brought about by industrialization and urbanization, and the increased aged population. However, this area still remains largely in the hands of private agencies, with the Government subsidizing food expenses.

Medical Insurance

Although medical insurance was legislated in 1963, only a few pilot programs were carried out before 1976, when laws were revised. With these revisions, large industries were obligated to have their employees covered by medical insurance beginning in July 1977. The medical insurance system has since been expanded to cover the workers of all businesses employing five or more people. As of 1992, a total of 5,359,957 persons in 154 industrial establishments and their 10,775,948 dependents were benefiting from the medical insurance system.

In addition to the employee medical insurance societies, there were six medical insurance societies for the self-employed, established in 1981 as pilot projects for those living within a designated area who were not eligible for other types of medical insurance. With the implementation of medical insurance for self-employed

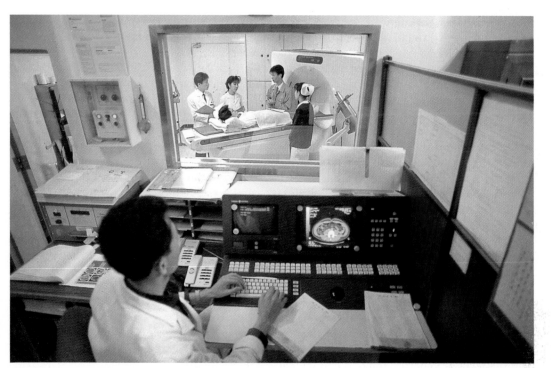

Korean hospitals are now equipped with state-of-the art facilities.

of Koreans were covered under some type of program.

In January 1977, the Medical Insurance Law for Civil Servants and Private School Teachers and Employees was enacted to provide medical insurance benefits for public officials and employees of private schools. The law was expanded in 1980 to cover the dependents of career military servicemen. To ensure its efficient management, the Medical Insurance Management Corporation was founded as a special corporation.

The monthly insurance premiums for members of the employee medical insurance societies are 3 to 8 percent of their monthly wage. The premium for public servants and employees of private schools was 4.6 percent of their salaries. Premiums for those working in remote mountainous or offshore island areas and the dependents living in Korea of those working abroad are reduced by half. The premiums for the self-employed depend on their income level and size of family.

Medical insurance benefits are in kind or cash. Benefits in kind include payments for examination and treatment, provision of medicine or other medical supplies, surgical operation or other treatment, accommodation at medical facilities, nursing and transportation. Benefits in cash are to cover funeral expenses and maternity allowance, etc.

In the case of public officials and private school employees, medical insurance provides funeral expenses in amounts determined by law. Health check-ups also are covered as benefits in kind.

The medical insurance system presently is operated on a three-tier basis: employee medical insurance societies, medical insurance societies for the self-employed, and the Medical Insurance Management Corporation for public officials and employees of private schools. However, the medical insurance system is still being expanded step by step, and by the early 1990s coverage for the entire population is expected. At that time, the managerial system of medical insurance will be integrated to further increase the effect of risk dispersion.

In other words, the employee medical insurance system was expanded in scope to cover employees in businesses employing five or more workers from 1988, and insurance for the self- employed expanded to all regions. As of July 1989, almost all eligible persons were covered under the medical insurance system.

The number of medical institutions participating in medical insurance programs as medical care providers reached 47,255 across the country in 1992, including 236 general hospitals, 369 hospitals, 6 dental hospitals, 12,629 clinics, 6,708 dental clinics, 269 midwifery clinics, 19,295 pharmacies, 3,628 health centers, 53 herb doctors' hospitals and 4,062 herb doctors' clinics.

Industrial Accident Compensation Insurance

Begun as compulsory social insurance under the Industrial Accident Compensation Insurance Law enacted in 1963, this insurance service has expanded steadily in the range of application and the level of benefits. Industrial Accident Compensation Insurance is the oldest and leading social security program designed to insure workers against industrial accidents.

At the time of implementation of this law in 1964, the program was applied to businesses with 500 employees or more, and 81,798 workers in 64 businesses benefited from the program during this early stage. In response to economic development, the program was expanded to cover businesses with five employees or more, except for certain agriculture, forestry, fishery and service operations. Participation in the insurance program is mandatory for mining, manufacturing, construction, utility and hygiene service, transportation, and warehousing and communication enterprises employing five or more workers. It now covers 7,058,704 workers in 154,820 work places.

The owner of a business automatically becomes insured by law. Those not included in the above category may become an insured by application and with the approval of the Minister of Labor. The insured should report and pay the insurance premiums at the beginning of each year. Premiums are determined by the total amount of wages of the workshop multiplied by business premium rates decided on the basis of accident rates over the past three years.

A worker whose business is subject to insurance application can request insurance benefits in case of an occupational accident even if the business has an established insurance relationship. Compensation for an occupational accident is generally dependent on whether or not the accident occurred during or in the course of employment under the supervision of the employer. An injury not due to such an accident, or an injury or disease not specifically presecribed, may lead to a claim for medical insurance. In 1992, a total of 107,435 workers suffered occupational accidents and received 931,564 million won (US$1,164 million) in insurance benefits.

Medical care benefits cover the total amount of medical care expenses if the care is provided at insurance facilities established by or at medical institutions designated by the Minister of Labor.

If the relevant injury or disease can be cured in three days, medical care benefits shall not be paid. That expense is born by the employer under the Labor Standard Law.

The scope of the medical care benefits are as follows: (1) diagnosis; (2) provision of pharmaceuticals, medical treatment materials, artificial limbs and other prosthetic devices; (3) treatment, operations and other remedies; (4) hospitalization in medical facilities; (5) special nursing in medical facilities; (6) transportation to a new medical institution for further treatment; (7) other matters to be determined by the Minister of Labor.

Sick pay shall be an amount equivalent to 70 percent of the average wage for a period in which the employee cannot work because of medical care.

Disability benefits are paid according to disability grades, either in the form of a disability compensation annuity or lump-sum disability compensation. Disability grades are classified into 14 grades for 133 items. Whether the disability compensation is distributed in annuity or lump-sum is determined by the beneficiary except in grades 1-3. A totally disabled worker included in grades 1-3 receives an annuity only. The amount of disability compensation annuity for the first year may be paid in advance in a lump-sum according to the choice of the beneficiary. If the beneficiary of a disability compensation annuity dies and the total of the annuity already paid is less than the lump-sum disability compensation, the balance is paid to the beneficiary's survivors in the form of a lump-sum payment.

Survivor's benefits shall be in the form of either survivors' compensation annuity or lump-sum survivors' compensation.

The lump-sum survivors' compensation shall amount to the equivalent of the average wage for 1,300 days.

If an employee has not recovered within two years after commencing medical treatment and is included in totally disabled grades, an injury-disease compensation annuity of 70-90 percent of average wage is given to the employee so long as such condition continues.

Funeral pay is an amount equivalent to the average wage for 120 days.

Pension Insurance

In the area of Korean old-age income security, private sector workers are covered by the National Pension Plan (1988) and public sector employees are covered by three pension plans: the Civil Servant Pension Plan (1960), the Military Personnel Pension Plan (1963), and the Private School Teacher's Pension Plan (1975).

National Pension : The Korean National Pension Plan applies, compulsorily, to all workers between the ages of 18 and 59 who are working at establishments with 5 or more workers. The self- employed, including farmers and fishermen, can be insured voluntarily. The number of persons covered was 5,021,000 as of the end of 1992.

The insured are entitled to monthly payments or lump-sum refunds. The monthly pension benefits available include an old- age pension, a survivor's pension, and a disability pension. The old-age pension is payable at age 60 to persons with at least 15 years of contributions. If a person with at least one year of coverage becomes disabled as a result of sickness or injury, a dis-

ability pension is payable in accordance with the degree of disability. Survivor pensions are payable on the death of an insured person or old-age pensioner. A lump-sum refund is payable to a person with less than 15 years of contributions.

Financing of the plan is shared equally by three sources: employers, employees, and the Retirement Payment Reserve which is funded by the Working Standards Act. The contribution rate is 9 percent. In the first 10 years of the plan, however, reduced rates apply—three percent from 1988 to 1992 and six percent from 1993 to 1997.

The National Pension Plan is administered by the National Pension Corporation under the general supervision of the Ministry of Health and Social Affairs.

Public Relief

As of 1993, the number of persons requiring subsistence support stood at more than 2,001,000 or 4.5 percent of the population. This included 83,000 accommodated at facilities, 338,000 given support at their homes and 1,580,000 destitute. Although the number of needy persons has declined with the increasing economic growth, the number receiving support remains about the same because the income ceiling of those eligible for public relief has been raised.

As of 1993, those accommodated at relief facilities were provided with 456 grams of rice, 114 grams of polished barley and 700 won for side dishes per person per day. Additional provisions are 1500 won in fuel costs per person per month, 351,000 won in tuition per student per annum and 250,000 won in funeral expenses for the dead. Subsistence support at home consisted of 341 grams of rice and 85 grams of polished barley per person per day, 21,300 won in side dish expenses, another 9,300 won in fuel expenses per person per month, and 351,000 won in tuition fees per student per annum. The efficiency of public care will be increased by differentiating the amount of relief cash depending on areas and the number of family members. The entire amount of the minimum required living cost is to be provided to those accommodated at social welfare facilities.

In a move to foster self-support among the needy, cash loans within a 7,000,000 won (US$ 8,750) limit are provided for about 6,000 households. The loans are repayable over five years at an annual interest of 6 percent with a grace period of 5 years. Recipients are selected by mayors or county commissioners at the recommendation of township heads. In addition, there are plans to provide 3 to 12 months of vocational training to about 15,000 youths of needy families. After such training, jobs are to be arranged for them through local labor offices.

Medical care is directed toward those in the low-income bracket, veterans, disaster victims and government-designated "human cultural treasures." Under the medical care program, the state bears the entire medical expenses of persons economically inacapble. For low-income people, the state provides for all out- patient expenses and half of the in-patient charges, the remaining half being borne by the patients themselves. Even the 50 percent borne by patients comes from the Medical Aid Fund for repayment on an installment basis.

The medical care program is based on the Law on Medical Care legislated in 1977. About 2,879,000 persons were eligible for the benefits of the program, in one way or another, as of 1990. For the effective implementation of medical care, the country has been divided into 57 clinical zones with a total of 16,027 medical institutions specially designated for the program: 15,445 public or private primary medical institutions, 576 secondary institutions and 12 tertiary institutions.

Through the medical care program, funds have been established within the provinces and six major cities to be disbursed by city, county and ward governments. The nation provides 80 percent of the Medical Care Fund and provincial administrations the remaining 20 percent. For Seoul, however, the funding is divided 50-50 between the state and the Seoul municipality.

In 1988, a cumulative total of 36,102,000 persons received medical aid, about six million of them in-patients. The average number of treatment days per patient has been increasing steadily.

Under the Military Relief Programs, public assistance is extended to about 149,544 families of fallen or disabled veterans and 2,303 families of those who have rendered meritorious services to the nation. Aid includes compensation in cash, educational aid for children and vocational training. Those beneficiaries able to work are provided with special funds for the purchase of farm lands or with some business funds in soft-term credits. In 1985 alone, a total of 4,154 families received such special funds.

In addition, soft-term loans are provided to homeless beneficiaries for use in building, purchasing or renting homes. Recipients of such loans numbered 4,400 in 1985. Homeless beneficiaries also are given priority in the distribution of public housing. A total of 352,244 wounded veterans continued to receive full medical care at veterans' hospitals, and disabled veterans are supplied with various complementary services.

Plans have been made to provide a firmer base for their self- support by expanding the range of those entitled to compensation, giving them additional payments for old age in amounts equivalent to 50 percent of their basic pensions, and increasing the amounts of various relief allowances.

The expansion of educational assistance and the enlargement of vocational training programs has been planned. Assistance is to be additionally extended to unassisted families, numbering approximately 8,500 who own and operate their own businesses. If any of those eligible for veterans relief are in urgent need of farming, schooling or medical aid, loans are provided with repayment over three years. Relief programs for retired servicemen are also to be expanded.

Social Welfare Services

The major emphasis of social welfare has been placed on children, the disabled, the elderly and women who need special care. As of 1992, a total of 21,293 children were accommodated at 278 facilities throughout the country. There were 6,902 households headed by children with a total number of 13,985 children. There were 956,000 needy disabled persons, of which 13,180 were accommodated at 136 facilities; 1,890,000 persons aged 65 or over, or 4.5 percent of the population.

The Government has increased public support for child welfare facilities, providing vocational training at 15 public training facilities and carrying out job-placement campaigns to help older children become self-reliant. The Government also has provided subsidies for living and educational expenses of children who are heads of households. Counseling for children was provided by 383 counselors at child guidance centers nationwide. A nationwide network for finding missing children was set up in 1986. Despite the traditional value placed on blood relationships in family succession, it has been the policy of both governmental and private organizations to encourage adoption by Korean families rather than allowing children to be adopted by foreigners.

With the overall revision of the Disabled Welfare Law in 1989, a welfare system for the disabled has been established, medical rehabilitation programs strengthened, and welfare centers for the disabled expanded. The Government has promoted the welfare of the disabled by developing and enforcing various measures for reducing their economic burdens. The National Rehabilitation Center was constructed and now is in operation. The Government also has taken over from the Red Cross the program to provide such items as artificial limbs, hearing aids and wheelchairs to the disabled poor.

Government authorities have joined with the private sector to ensure that the disabled have a fair opportunity to reach their full potential. The Government's Directive on the Promotion of the Employment of the Disabled was designed to encourage industries to employ the disabled. At the private level, the Korean Society for Rehabilitation of the Disabled conducts various programs to train the disabled and obtain jobs for them. To promote equal opportunities for disabled persons, restrictive provisions in existing laws have been amended. Public facilities for the disabled have been expanded.

As for the welfare of the elderly, a major emphasis has been placed on increasing respect for senior citizens. Schools and mass media have been drafted into the cause and one week of the year has been designated to honor the elderly. The Government annually honors filial sons and daughters-in-law and typical traditional families as a way to encourage time-honored values. A system was introduced in 1980 in which people aged 65 or older can use some public facilities free of charge and others at a discount. These include public transportation, parks and public baths. In addition, free health examinations have been given to the elderly since 1983 in accordance with the Aged Welfare Law. The Government will place more emphasis on the establishment of facilities to take care of the physical and mental needs of the elderly rather than just relying on residential facilities. The number and types of nursing homes will be increased.

Welfare programs for women are aimed at helping female heads of families, runaway women, unmarried mothers, women exploited by places of entertainment and other needy women. Support for maternal and child welfare facilities has been strengthened, as well as support for vocational training programs for young girls who run away from home, unmarried mothers and other needy women. There are 372 counselors throughout the country who provide guidance for women employed for entertainment purposes and runaways. There also are vocational training facilities where such women can stay and receive professional training and moral education.

The Korean Women's Development Institute was established in 1983 with strong government support. It is aimed at promoting women's welfare through research on women's problems and training programs. Together with the National Committee on Women's Policy under the Prime Minister's office, which systematically and comprehensively reviews government policies affecting women, the Women's Development Institute is playing a leading role in promoting and enhancing the status of women.

Environmental Protection and Pollution Control

Evolution of Environmental Policy in Korea

Korea achieved rapid economic development during the last three decades as a result of the successful implementation of its five-year economic development plans. At that time, national policy was to attain such development through rapid industrialization.

Therefore, all national resources were mobilized for this industrialization, while the environment deteriorated, becoming one of the serious social problems of the 1970s. At the beginning of the 1980s, when the national economic policies turned out to be successful and living standards of the people rose, needs for national environment protection policies became more evident.

A new article proclaiming the people's environmental rights was included in the national constitution in 1980 along with the establishment of the Environment Administration (upgraded to the minister level in January 1990). Subsequent environmental laws were strengthened to enforce regulations already existing but badly neglected.

In the fifth five-year economic development plan, begun in 1982, a phrase was adopted that called for "balance and harmony between economic development and environmental conservation." Under the newly-stated national policy, various environmental programs and projects were undertaken.

While stimulating environmental awareness through public relations activities, the Government developed and implemented policies for the improvement of air quality in municipal areas, the improvement of water quality in rivers and lakes, and the proper disposal of industrial and municipal wastes. The organizational basis for environmental administration was improved significantly with the establishment of six regional environment offices.

Also contributing to this effort was the establishment of such semi-government agencies as the Korea Resource Recycling Corporation and the Environment Management Corporation.

Building on this organizational foundation, a number of dynamic programs were launched. They included the production of low pollution cars and unleaded motor fuel, the construction of desulfurization plants by major oil refinery companies, and the preparation of large scale landfill sites for wastes from metropolitan areas. All of this contributed to the maintenance of a fair environmental quality in air and water during the 24th Seoul Olympiad in 1988. With the establishment of the Ministry of Environment in 1990, the Government formulated a five-year environmental improvement plan, which aims at increasing the harmony between development and environment.

It is obvious that as the economy continues to grow and the people achieve higher living standards, the need for a better environment will increase dramatically. To meet this ever growing demand, more policy emphasis will be placed on environmental conservation and improvement.

Environmental Programs and Projects

The basic objectives of the government environmental policies are to achieve high quality of life standards for the people through an environmental administration that is open to the public and encourages public participation. An important part of this is the carrying out of public relations activities that will develop and increase environmental awareness. Second, efforts will be made to induce industries to treat pollutants generated in their production process in accordance with the polluter-pay-principle. Third, steps will be taken to facilitate implementation of an increased number of basic environmental regulations.

To elaborate on the plans for carrying out these programs and policies:

1) Continued Environmental Awareness Activities

Conservation of the environment cannot be attained by government regulation alone. It requires the combined efforts of the people, industries and government bodies, all well informed of the importance of and need for environmental protection.

The Ministry of Environment, therfore, has put strong emphasis on raising public environmental awareness, carrying out various informational measures through the mass media facilities of television, radio and newspapers. Along with this, educational programs have been developed to improve environmental knowledge in primary and secondary schools. Social education programs also reflect the increasing importance of protection of the environment. In conjunction with these actions, such private organizations as the Korea Environmental Preservation Association and other social interest groups such as consumer protection organizations have been and assisted in carrying out their own activities in the field of environmental awareness and protection.

2) Improvement of Environmental Impact Assessment Procedures and Review of Development Projects

Korea started to implement an Environmental Impact Assessment (EIA) system in 1981. In 1987, the Environment Ministry amended and expanded the Environmental Preservation Law.

These moves included private development activities, which had previously been excluded, in the category of development activities for environmental impact assessment.

The existing law concerning EIA is the Basic Environmental Policy Act (BEPA), which was promulgated in August 1990. In an amendment of the Act, categories of projects subject to the EIA procedure were added and the integration of public opinion became obligatory to the EIA procedure.   Since adoption of the EIA system, various studies have been carried out for the development and dissemination of environmental assessment methods and technologies.

3) Abatement of Air Pollution

Korea has undertaken various policies to pro-

gressively reduce the sulfur content of oil. The legal sulfur content in Bunker C oil has been reduced to 1.6 percent, and in diesel fuel, to 0.4 percent. In July of 1993, the limits will drop further to 1.0 percent for Bunker C oil and 0.2 percent for diesel fuels destined for metropolitan areas. In accordance with this new policy, major oil refineries are drawing up plans to construct de-sulfurization facilities by the year 1995. Supplying natural gas to the major power plants and to gas consumers in and around the Seoul metropolitan area, started in 1988, has also contributed to a decline in sulphur dioxide concentration in Seoul. By the year 2000, natural gas will be supplied to all major cities throughout the country.

The Ministry of Environment will continue to gradually strengthen emission standards up to the level of developed countries by the end of 1999. For the control of motor vehicle emissions, current emission standards require all gasoline-powered vehicles produced since 1988 to be equipped with a catalytic converter that relies on unleaded gas. In addition, regulations prohibit the production of leaded gasoline from January 1993 and recent amendments to the Air Act call for gradually more stringent standards.

4) River Clean-up Activities

Following the extensive effort to clean up the Han-gang River, which flows through Seoul, prior to the 1988 Olympic Games, activities got underway to restore the water quality of all rivers, numbering about 4,000 throughout the country. With the Minister of Environment in charge, regional and local governments were given specific functions to carry out these programs. In line with this program, 195 watersheds were classified for the application of different water quality standards. Special measures were prepared for dealing with severely polluted streams flowing through municipal or industrial areas to restore them in a short period of time. Environmental authorities also decided to establish water quality standards for lakes and reservoirs.

5) Marine Pollution Control

A master plan was developed for the protection of water quality at 63 of the country's coastal areas. It included various measures of minimizing pollutants from inland areas and for responding to oil spills. Special measures also have been provided for marine parks and coastal areas especially vulnerable to pollution.

6) Waste Management

The most important goals in waste management are (1) minimizing volume, (2) providing for safe treatment, and (3) recycling wastes to the greatest degree possible. The Government has carried out construction of plants for night soil treatment and for hazardous industrial wastes, as well as a major coastal landfill site for Seoul. The metropolitan landfill project required an investment of 350 billion won, the equivalent of US$500 million over the period from 1987 to 1992.

7) Hazardous Chemical Management

The safe management of hazardous chemicals has not been achieved in Korea. As a result, risks to human health as well as to the environment exist in handling and using pesticides, chemical fertilizers and other materials. The Government has developed stronger procedures for intensive reviews and inspection of hazardous synthetic chemicals. The regulation of toxic chemicals also has come under more stringent rules and regulations.

Consumer Protection

Overview

Consumer protection came to Korea in the 1960's, introduced by private organizations who promoted Korea's consumer movement. The Government joined in the effort in 1980, passing the Consumer Protection Act. Progress continued apace with the amendment of the Act in 1986 and creation of the Consumer Protection Board in 1987. The 1990s have ushered in a new, mature stage in the history of Korean consumerism.

Broadly speaking, consumer protection in Korea rests on a foundation provided by the Consumer Protection Act, while the main players in the consumer protection arena include national and local government agencies, organizations specializing in consumer affairs, businesses, and consumers themselves. Each player executes functions and roles in support of consumer protection, and together they guarantee the basic rights of the Korean consumer.

The Consumer Protection Act

The Consumer Protection Act is the warp and woof of the legal foundation of consumer protectionism in Korea. The Act stipulates seven basic consumer rights, delineates the roles of national and local governmental agencies in protecting consumer rights, and specifies what is required of industry in this regard.

The Consumer Protection Act also stipulates the roles and functions of private consumer protection organizations, provides for establishment of the Consumer Protection Board, details its mission and organizational structure, and directs the establishment of the Consumer Dispute Settlement Committee (CDSC) under the Consumer Protection Board.

Government Policies on Consumer Protection

The principal agency involved in consumer protection is the Economic Planning Board's Price Policy Bureau. The Economic Planning Board operates the Consumer Policy Deliberation Committee, which creates detailed consumer protection policy. The Minister of the Economic Planning Board himself chairs the Consumer Policy Deliberation Committee, whose members include the director or Minister of other interested central administrative agencies, consumers, business executives and experts on consumer affairs. The Committee acts as the supreme policy decision-making government agency. Its other key functions include deciding matters related to drafting and revising laws and regulations pertaining to consumer protection, establishing the annual package of consolidated consumer protection measures, enacting the various laws and regulations which guide industry's actions to protect the consumer, and deliberating other key items of consumer protection policy.

As an example of the Committee's work, listed below are extracts from the 1993 package of key consumer protection measures generated by the Consumer Policy Deliberation Committee: 1) Bolster efforts to provide merchandise information to the consumer to guarantee essential buying information. 2) Prevent potential loss or damage to the consumer before the purchase, and fully recompense the consumer if he suffers loss or damage after purchase. 3) Develop consumer protection policies appropriate to today's era of internationalization and openness. 4) Bolster consumer protection measures aimed specifically at the provincial consumer. And 5) nurture the consumer's ability to reach free solutions. Each level of local government shall form a Consumer Policy Deliberation Committee and shall formulate its own package of regional consumer protection measures, using the package of measures provided by the central Government's Consumer Policy Deliberation Committee as a foundation but accommodating regional circumstances and conditions. Local committees shall generate and implement whatever measures are necessary to protect the regional consumer.

The Korean Consumer Protection Board

Stipulations of the Consumer Protection Act created the Consumer Protection Board and gave it the task of improving the Government's consumer protection measures professionally and with more precision. The Board is located in the capital city of Seoul, has 260 employees, and as of 1993 had not yet established regional branches. Its key components include the departments of Consumer Research, Consumer Testing and Evaluation, Research and Suryey, Consumer Safety, Consumer Redress, Consumer Education, and Publication and Distribution. The Board also operates a Dispute Resolution Committee to rule on consumer disputes.

The first key function of the Consumer Protection Board is consumer research. The Board conducts research to generate recommendations to improve the quality of life for consumers and to improve the laws, regulations, and systems which together support national policy designed to bolster protection of the consumer. The recommendations will then be reflected in the Government's consumer protection policies.

The second key function of the Consumer Protection Board is consumer evaluation and testing. The Board conducts periodic inspections of all consumer goods used in everyday life, checking on quality, performance, and safety. The results of these inspections are provided to satisfy the consumer's right to know and to aid the consumer in making purchasing decisions. Evaluations and tests are conducted with equipment on the cutting edge of technology and in a most strigent process, but are nevertheless eminently fair and objective.

A third key function of the Consumer Protection Board is consumer redress. When the consumer is involved in a dispute over merchandise or service, the Board may intervene to ensure that the business involved agrees to appropriate compensation for the consumer. If an agreement between the consumer and the business has not been reached after 30 days, the consumer may request that the Consumer Protection Board's CDSC consider the case. The CDSC is composed of a chairman and six other members, who are selected from the legal community, the academic community, and from directors of organizations representing both industry and consumers.

The Committee reviews a case by listening to representations made both by the consumer and the business concerned and then renders a ruling. If both parties agree with the ruling, the case is considered settled. Rulings issued by the Committee are regarded as legally binding as judgments rendered in a court.

A fourth key function of the Consumer Protection Board is conducting research, surveys, and investigations and distributing the information so accumulated. The Board investigates losses suffered by consumers, checking into the real prevailing situation in all kinds of commodities, services, marketing procedures, marks and labels, advertising practices, unfair sales and promotion means, unfair trade practices, and inflated promises, in order to ensure consumer protection. The Board monitors hospitals and drug stores across the country , collecting information of all types of consumer losses. The results of the research, surveys, and investigations are furnished to consumers and also communicated to relevant governmental administrative agencies in an effort to ensure that the lessons learned are reflected in national consumer policy.

A fifth key function of the Consumer Protection Board is conducting consumer education and publishing. The Board divides education related to consumer protection into two board categories, education for consumers and education for businesses. Education for consumers includes programs for students, professors, and government authorities, and aims at raising consciousness about the consumer's basic rights.

Professional instructors focus especially on fostering in consumers a willingness to challenge and on instilling the knowledge required to prevent losses to the consumer. Education for business involves technical training on consumer protection issues and is directed at executives and those involved in consumer relations.

Among the publications issued by the Consumer Protection Board is the *Sobija Sidae*, or "Consumer Era," a monthly newsletter detailing the projects and achievements of the Consumer Protection Board; the semi-annual academic journal, *Research in Consumerism*; and the English language quarterly, *The Consumer's Newsletter*, which provides information on developments in the consumer protection field within the Republic of Korea.

The Consumer Protection Board also maintains periodic contacts with key countries on the American continents, Europe, and in Asia, exchanging consumer information and other materials and participating in the international flow of developments in the consumer protection arena. The Board also works to maintain exchanges with international consumer protection organizations, such as the IOCU.

Private Consumer Organizations in Korea

The Consumer Protection Act guarantees the basic right of Korean consumers to organize consumer organizations and to be active therein. These organizations are composed of private citizens who themselves promote consumer rights, consumer protection, and consumer advantages. Stipulations of the Consumer Protection Act specify that private consumer organizations may undertake authorized functions that include: making recommendations regarding consumer protection measures generated by agencies of national and local government; conducting consumer investigations, inspections, and testing of consumer goods and services; conducting research and development on consumer issues; and educating the consumer and providing consumer consultation services and consumer information. The private consumer organizations play a lead role in consumer campaigns. They stand at the forefront of actions taken in Korea to support the growing global interest in environmental protection, trash recycling, resource conservation, and other active consumer movements. The private organizations also perform a tremendous service to society by monitoring firms who pollute air and water and push harmful merchandise on consumers.

Eleven private consumer organizations are registerd with the Economic Planning Board and receive government subsidies. Seven of these have chapters organized across the nation and play a leading role in regional consumer protection activities. These seven are the YWCA, the YMCA, Korean Federation of Housewives' Clubs, the National Conference of Housewives for the Betterment of Home Life, the Korean Women's Association United, the Citizens' Alliance for Consumer Protection of Korea, and the Consumer Union of Korea.

Status of Korean Women

In the traditional society of Korea, woman's role was confined to the home. Women were required to follow the Confucian virtues of subordination and endurance, while denied opportunities to participate in political and social activities. Their major function was to give birth to offspring to preserve the family line, and women served to maintain the order of the family under the extended family system. In terms of both social status and hierarchy, women were inferior to men. Regardless of social status, social institutions and the custom of avoiding the opposite sex did not permit women to be involved in non-family affairs.

The situation began to change, however, thanks to the beginning of educational opportunity for women that followed the opening of the country to the outside world in 1880s. Educated women engaged in arts, teaching, and religious work, as well as enlightening other women on the problems of poverty and illiteracy.

The self-awakening of women led to their national awakening under Japanese colonial rule, and women took part in the independence movement with no less vigor and determination than men. A liberation movement calling for human rights for women also began to emerge.

With the promulgation in 1948 of the Republic of Korea Constitution guaranteeing equal rights for both sexes, women began to obtain equality under law. Having been given the right to vote, to be elected and to assume public duties, women were able to participate in the country's major policy making processes.

Although these changes were ultimately in requital for the stand and actions of women in the struggle for the country's independence and enlightenment, it could be said that suffrage for Korean women came relatively easily compared to their western counterparts who acquired the franchise only after long struggle.

In line with the successful implementation of six five-year development plans since the early 1960s, Korea has achieved remarkable economic growth. Export-oriented industries required a large female labor force. As society diversified and the educational level of women was raised, demands for skilled and professional women increased.

Despite the increase in the number of women engaged in social and economic activities, it has not been easy to resolve women's problems arising from traditional values and social institutions.

Women and Development

As a result of the country's industrialization, there has been vast change and development in much of Korean society. The impact of this social transition has been especially strong on Korean women, who have experienced role expansions through changes in the traditional family structure, the traditional value system and the employment structure. In addition, the expansion of the educational opportunities for women has contributed to the development of women's capabilities and the raising of their social consciousness.

Internationally, the proclamation of the International Women's Year by the United Nations in 1975 and succeeding international events have encouraged Korean women to address issues on women and development. Korean women began to actively demand solutions to women's problems at the national decision making level. They felt that policies to improve the status of women could not be effective unless they were concerned with development of women as a whole. Therefore, there was strong demand for setting up pertinent national agencies or structures for women's development.

In response, the Government established two special organizations: the Korean Women's Development Institute (KWDI) and the National Committee on Women's Policies in 1983.

The doors are open to women's participation in national development through these two organizations, whose mandates are to establish long-term master plans for women's development and to carry out policy-oriented research and activities to integrate women's development plans into national development plans.

National Efforts for Women

Administrative Organizations

The systematic administration of women's affairs began with the establishment in 1948 of the Women's Bureau of the Ministry of Social Affairs. The bureau was reorganized into the Women's Bureau of the Ministry of Health and Social Affairs in 1955, and then incorporated into the Family Welfare Bureau of the same Ministry in 1981.

Handled by the Family Welfare Bureau are the establishment and coordination of programs for women's welfare, guidance for women's welfare facilities, relief projects for needy women, vocational training for women, life improvement projects, guidance and fostering of women's organizations, and matters of international cooperation relevant to women. The Women and Juveniles Section is responsible for such activities in the provincial and city administrations. Recently the Government decided to rearrange local administrative organizations for women. In 20 cities and 36 districts with a population greater than 100,000, Women and Juveniles Sections were enlarged to Divisions of Family Welfare in January 1988.

In July 1988, the Divisions of Women and Juveniles in 14 major cities and provinces were expanded to Bureaus of Family Welfare, headed by 14 women officials, to handle a variety of problems faced by women, juveniles and the elderly. As the demand for family welfare administration rapidly increased, the Family Welfare Sections of 32 cities and 137 counties were enlarged to the Divisions of Family Welfare in order to care for disadvantaged children, women and elderly in April 1991. Women have been appointed as chiefs of those divisions.

There were 15 Family Welfare Bureaus and 260 Family Welfare Divisions in Korea by early 1992. Meantime, the Ministry of Labor established the Women and Juveniles Protection Office in 1970, the designation of which was changed to the Women and Juveniles Division in the Labor Standard Bureau in 1981. At the same time the Women's Guidance Office was established. This office is responsible for the special protection of female and juvenile workers, the education of women workers, and welfare programs and cultural activities for women workers.

The National Committee on Women's Policies

The National Committee on Women's Policies was established in December 1983, under the authority of the Prime Minister's Office. It is in charge of deliberating and coordinating national policies concerning women. It focuses especially on providing basic plans and integrated policies for women's development and coordinates the policies of various administrative organs concerning women. It also assesses government policies aimed at increasing employment for women, expands women's social participation and promotes the general status of women.

The Prime Minister presides over meetings of the committee. Half of the members—ministers of relevant ministries and the president of the KWDI—are permanent and the rest are chosen from experts of women's issues.

In 1984, the committee asked the KWDI to carry out two basic and long-range projects—a master plan for women's development, and a guideline for the elimination of discrimination against women. The KWDI accomplished the projects. and the committee adopted them as government policies, thereby opening a channel for the first time for women to reflect their interests and needs in policy making at the national level.

In February 1988, the newly launched Administration appointed Cho Kyŏng-hŭi Second State Minister for Political Affairs to formulate and implement policies concerned with women's affairs. At present, Kwŏn Youngja, former president of the KWDI, is in charge of the ministry.

Korean Women's Development Institute

The Korean Women's Development Institute (KWDI) was established April 21, 1983, as part of the national machinery to formulate comprehensive studies of women's issues and to reflect its findings in government policies. Many women's organizations have played a significant role in bringing KWDI into existence; as a result of these efforts, the law proclaimed by the National Assembly in 1982 called for the establishment of an organization to promote women's welfare and expand women's social participation.

The major functions of the KWDI are: research and study on women's issues; education and training to fully develop women's capabilities; active utilization of women's resources, and collection and dissemination of information on women. It is fully financed by the government.

Since the launch of KWDI, it has carried out various research projects and action programs for women's development. Noteworthy among these works are the master plan for women's development, the guideline for the elimination of discrimination against women, and participation in the planning process of the Sixth Five-Year Economic and Social Development Plan's Women's Development Sector. The institute also accomplished the "Long- term Perspective on National Development Toward the Year 2000: Women's Development Perspective."

Women and Education

In early Korea, women's education was confined to the home. Only men were given any formal education, while women performed the duties of looking after the home and bearing children to maintain the family line.

The first edification for women in the country, "Instructions for Housewives," written in 1435 by Queen Sohye(sohye),wife of King Tŏkjong of the Choson Dynasty (1392-1910), outlines a code of conduct for housewives based on Confucian norms of a traditional society, calling on women to become affectionate mothers and good-natured wives. However, the emergence of the *Sirhak* (Practical Learning) in the middle of the 17th century and the *Tonghak* (Eastern Learning) in the late 19th century resulted in an expansion of the ideology of human rights and equality regardless of social classes and sexes. This ideological base led to gradual changes in traditional norms and the woman's role. Meanwhile, Western civilization began to be introduced into Korea through missionaries around the 1880s.

Consequently concepts of modern education started to take root, and attention was paid to women as well as men. The country's first newspaper, *Tongnip Shinmun* (Independence News, published by the Independence Club), called on the government several times to recognize the importance of women's education and to establish schools for girls.

Formal education for women began with the Ewha Haktang, Korea's first school for women, which was inaugurated in 1886 with the enrollment of only one girl student. Confucian culture and the national policy of isolation that dominated Korean society at that time made it difficult to establish and operate girls' schools. Christian missionaries, however, managed to set up a number of middle schools such as Chŏngsin and Paewha Girls' Schools in Seoul, and Sungŭi Girls' School in P'yŏngyang.

It was after the political reform of 1884 that Korea established public schools under a new educational system. The 1884 reform move recognized the need for education of women, but the school decree that was proclaimed had provisions for male schools only. The Adoration Society, founded in September 1898, with the objective of establishing and operating a girls' school financed by membership fees, released in the same month "A Letter on Girls' School Facilities." This document was considered the country's first declaration of the rights of women with respect to education in that it was aimed at not only establishing a girls' school, but also at attaining equal rights for both sexes.

Hansŏng Girls' High School, Korea's first public school for women, was established in 1908. In April of that year, the government promulgated the Girls' High School Decree, stipulating as its objective, "to teach high school education, skills and arts essential for women." This was the first legal provision for women's education since private education began in Korea.

The Republic of Korea Constitution pre-

Number of Students by Education Level in 1992

	Total	Male	Female	Female Composition
Kindergarten	450,882	236,541	214,341	47.5%
Elementary School	4,560,128	2,355,499	2,204,629	48.3%
Middle School	2,336,284	1,200,765	1,135,519	48.6%
High School	2,125,573	1,113,168	1,012,405	47.6%
College & University	1,491,669	1,012,225	479,444	32.1%
Graduate School	96,577	72,778	23,799	24.6%
Total	11,061,113	5,990,976	5,070,137	45.8%

Source: Ministry of Education

Number of Higher Education Students by Major Study in 1992

	Total	Male	Female	Female Composition
Humanities	154,298	78,287	76,011	49.3%
Social Sciences	287,404	229,898	57,506	20.0%
Natural Sciences	448,899	357,803	91,096	20.3%
Medical & Pharmacy	41,312	26,360	14,952	36.2%
Arts & Physical Education	74,772	32,653	42,119	56.3%
Teaching Profession	63,484	23,853	39,631	62.4%
Total	1,070,169	748,854	321,315	30.0%

Source: Ministry of Education

scribes that "all citizens shall have the right to receive equal education in accordance with their capabilities." Thus, one of the basic rights of citizens is to be accorded educational opportunities irrespective of sex, age or class.

The average number of years of education in 1990 was registered at 10.01 years for males and 8.22 years for females. A six-year primary school course has been compulsory since 1949 when the Education Law was adopted. As early as the 1960s, more than 90 percent of all children, boys and girls, eligible for schooling were enrolled in primary schools.

Entrance rate of primary school graduates to middle school was 99.5 percent for girls and 99.6 percent for boys in 1992, and the entrance rate of middle school graduates to high school in the same year stood at 94.4 percent for girls and 96.2 percent for boys, showing a small margin between male and female. The ratio of high school graduates entering higher education in 1992 was 62.5 percent for females and 33.9 percent for males. Of total enrollments in colleges and universities in 1992, women accounted for 30.3 percent.

As in Western countries, the number of female teachers in Korea has increased. The proportion of women teachers in 1992 stood at 52.4 percent in primary schools, 47.7 percent in middle schools, 23.2 percent in high schools and 20.5 percent in colleges. These figures represent a continuous increase over previous years, but it is to be noted that the number of female teachers dwindles as the level of education advances.

To correct this situation, it is considered necessary that more women be promoted to administrative positions of responsibility, that measures be worked out to reduce current male dominance at higher educational institutions, and that sexually discriminatory contents and expressions in curricula be eliminated. Further efforts must be made to provide both sexes with equal opportunities in education and employment. To meet these requirements, the Ministry of Education directed the 5th School Curriculum Study Council to review sexual discrimination in the curricula. Accordingly, contents of textbooks being used in schools were revised on principles of equality between sexes beginning in 1989.

Technical crafts for male students and home economics for female students were merged into one subject, offered to both boys and girls in middle and high schools since 1987. Along with the revision of curricula, efforts are being made to change teachers' sex-biased teaching attitudes.

In an effort to meet the increased demand for skilled manpower in the wake of the industrialization of the 1970s, vocational high schools provide education and training in more than 90 courses. Girls account for 53.2 percent of the enrollment in vocational high schools, but in technical high schools, the proportion of girls was only 2.8 percent, while in commercial schools it was 80.6 percent in 1992. These figures show there still are traditional prejudices against girl students seeking to choose the technical course and new technologies.

The most popular non-formal education for women in urban areas is general education. Various institutes are engaged in such education for women. They include educational facilities attached to women's organizations, public welfare facilities, educational institutes operated by the media, college institutes, primary and secondary schools, community development centers and institutes run by public libraries. Non-formal educational programs for women consist of skills (53 percent), population and family life (19 percent), languages and culture (18 percent), and services for others (10 percent). Women's welfare centers in special cities and provincial capitals conduct various programs designed to improve the education of women so that they may elevate their social standing and

contribute more to social development. Since 1975, the Ministry of Labor has been operating educational programs for working women in industrial complexes with large numbers of workers. Educational programs designed to raise the social consciousness of women also are provided by specialized organizations and religious groups.

Non-formal education for women in rural areas centers on women's guidance programs. In educational activities conducted rural women's societies emphasis is put on subjects designed to teach new farming techniques, solve rural problems, improve the quality of life, instruct in family planning and develop better sanitation methods. Guidance for such activities is provided by the Ministry of Health and Social Affairs, the Office of Rural Development, and National Federation of Agricultural Cooperatives and the Family Planning Society.

Women and Economic Activities

The participation of women in social activities today is at a higher level than ever before, especially in economic fields. It is a well-known fact that the remarkable economic growth Korea has achieved in the past three decades owes much to the female labor force in the manufacturing sector. Women are expected to make an even greater contribution to future economic development in view of the changing structure of industry and employment.

The economically active population rate among the country's female population 15 years old and over showed a sharp increase from 26.8 percent in 1960 to 45.7 percent in 1975, but fell to 38.4 percent in 1980, and then moved up to 47.3 percent in 1992. The decline in women's participation in economic activities in the latter half of the 1970s was attributed to the economic recession in the wake of the oil crisis.

Women's economic participation is greater in farm households than in non-farm households. The figures in 1992 stood at 64.4 percent in farm households and 44.4 percent in the non-farm households. In the rural areas not only was the percentage of economically active women greater in general, but the percentage showed a

Age Distribution of Women Employees in Manufacturing in 1992

(Thousand Persons, Percent)

	Total	15-19	20-24	25-29	30-34	35-39	40-44	45-49	50-55	55-59	60 and over
1966	322	29.0	24.0	10.3	8.1	7.6	6.5	4.8	3.3	2.1	1.9
1970	520	39.1	27.5	7.1	5.5	5.6	4.7	3.4	1.9	1.2	0.9
1975	835	44.3	29.8	6.0	4.1	4.6	3.9	2.6	1.4	0.6	0.3
1980	1,012	37.4	37.0	6.2	4.4	4.5	4.2	2.8	1.4	0.7	0.3
1985	1,353	15.7	27.4	12.5	9.8	9.5	8.9	7.0	4.1	2.6	2.1
1990	2,050	7.0	21.9	13.0	15.0	11.7	10.5	7.6	6.0	3.6	3.7
1991	2,058	7.0	20.8	11.6	14.8	13.2	10.7	7.5	6.4	4.3	3.7
1992	1,917	5.5	19.0	11.3	14.9	13.6	11.5	7.8	7.5	5.0	4.1

Source: National Statistical Office

Distribution of Employed Women by Occupation

(Thousand Persons, Percent)

	Pro., Tech., Workers Related			Adm. & Managerial Workers			Clerical & Related Workers			Sales Workers		
	(A) Total	(B) Female	B/A (%)	(A) Total	(B) Female	B/A (%)	(A) Total	(B) Female	B/A (%)	(A) Total	(B) Female	B/A (%)
1966	224	46	20.5	69	1	1.4	340	37	11.0	850	300	35.3
1970	323	74	22.9	96	3	3.1	591	101	17.0	1,023	344	33.6
1975	417	105	25.2	102	4	3.9	844	197	23.3	1,317	475	36.1
1980	531	162	30.5	134	2	1.5	1,203	400	33.3	1,531	540	35.2
1985	1,090	317	29.1				1,729	597	34.5	2,313	1,070	46.3
1990	1,301	553	42.5	267	11	4.1	2,337	937	40.0	2,616	1,243	47.5
1991	1,413	623	44.0	299	12	4.0	2,467	1,033	41.8	2,717	1,218	47.3
1992	1,570	718	45.7	329	13	4.0	2,178	1,099	40.4	2,812	1,330	47.3

	Service Workers			Agri., Forestry Workers & Fisherman			Production & Related Workers, Transport Equipment Operators & Laborers			Others		
	(A) Total	(B) Female	B/A (%)	(A) Total	(B) Female	B/A (%)	(A) Total	(B) Female	B/A (%)	(A) Total	(B) Female	B/A (%)
1966	426	240	56.3	4,525	1,559	34.4	1,528	355	23.2	2	1	50.0
1970	679	386	56.8	5,148	2,135	41.5	2,193	526	24.0	89	7	8.0
1975	816	465	57.0	6.190	2,296	47.3	2,891	808	27.9	105	1	1.0
1980	895	459	51.3	4,768	2,151	45.1	3,570	925	25.9	1	0	0
1985	1,622	996	61.2	3,686	1,611	43.7	4,530	1,245	27.5	-	-	-
1990	2,007	1,223	60.9	3,270	1,494	45.7	6,238	1,882	30.2	-	-	-
1991	2,125	1,298	61.0	3,081	1,393	45.2	6,474	1,861	28.7	-	-	-
1992	2,117	1,345	61.8	3,000	1,380	46.0	6,316	1,724	27.3	-	-	-

Source: National Statistical Office

Distribution of Employment by Sex and Industry

(Thousand Persons, Per cent)

	Female				Male			
	Total	Agriculture, Forestry & Fishing	Mining & Manufac-turing	Soc. & Other Services	Total	Agriculture, Forestry & Fishing	Mining & Manufac-turing	Soc. & Other Services
1963	2,674	68.7	7.0	24.3	4,988	60.1	9.7	30.2
1970	3,578	57.2	12.0	30.6	6,167	46.5	15.6	37.9
1980	5,222	39.0	22.3	38.7	8,462	31.0	22.7	46.3
1984	5,535	30.2	22.9	46.9	8,894	25.2	25.0	49.8
1988	6,771	22.9	29.2	47.9	10,099	19.1	28.0	52.9
1990	7,341	20.4	28.0	51.6	10,695	16.8	26.8	56.4
1991	7,508	18.6	27.5	53.9	11,068	15.4	26.6	58.0
1992	7,609	18.2	25.2	56.6	11,312	14.5	25.7	59.8

Source: National Statistical Office

sharp increase among women in their 30s and above. This indicates that the rural areas suffered a shortage in the labor force as males and young girls migrated to the cities and industrial areas, and the gap created was filled, in large part, by middle-aged housewives. This reflects a feminization of farming labor during a period of rapid industrialization and urbanization.

In cities, the participation of married women in economic activities has shown a gradual upturn, due to a number of factors. First, women are receiving more education than before, and so do not start working at such early ages, and the gap is filled by middle-aged women. Second, increased living standards and educational expenses for children prompt housewives to earn money to supplement their husband's incomes. Third, women have a stronger desire to take part in social activities and are able to adapt themselves to careers more readily than their predecessors.

In addition to the quantitative increase in women's economic activities, there has been a structural change in female employment. About 18.2 percent of women workers were engaged in primary industry, 25.2 percent in secondary industry and 56.6 percent in tertiary industry in 1992. The female proportion engaged in primary industry has declined in recent years in contrast with increases in the secondary and the tertiary sectors.

A great number of women (25.2 percent) are found in the manufacturing sector, but coming in next, the farming and fishing sectors still absorbed 18.2 percent of women workers in 1992. About 80 percent of female workers in the manufacturing sector are employed by textile, clothing, electric and electronic industries, which have led the nation's exports since the 1970s. Most of them are young and unmarried, so that women aged 15 to 24 account for 24.0 percent of the female labor force in the manufacturing industries in 1992.

A similar trend is seen in the occupational distribution of women workers. The distribution is gradually moving away from a heavy concentration in farming to production, sales and service occupations.

The clerical area has shown a conspicuous increase in women workers in the past two decades. Women in clerical occupations accounted for 14.4 percent of the whole female work force in 1992 in comparison with 1.5 percent in 1966. These jobs, however, seem to continue to be dominated by young, unmarried women workers since unmarried women constitute an absolute majority in clerical work.

The proportion of female employees in professional, technical and administrative jobs increased from 1.5 percent in 1960 to 9.6 percent in 1992, indicating that the level of education acquired by women has been upgraded due to increased educational opportunities. However, this rate of increase needs to be accelerated in order to respond to the increasing number of women graduates from schools of higher education.

The level of education acquired by women at work shows great improvement in recent decades. However, social and cultural conditions are still unfavorable for even women of higher education in regard to participation in economic activities.

Official statistics indicate that women workers are still facing sexual discrimination in the labor market in the form of restrictive recruitment practices, lower wages, and limited opportunities for promotion. In an effort to alleviate such discrimination, the Equal Employment Opportunity Act was established in 1987, and came into force on April 1, 1988. The act guarantees basically equality between men and women in employment, and special provisions for pregnancy and maternity with one-year child care leave as well as 60 days paid maternity leave. The act also imposes upon employers the duty to provide child care facilities in work places. The Equal Employment Opportunity Act was amended in March 1989 in order to effectively enforce the Act. The terms of discrimination, equal pay for equal work, and strengthened penalties were provided for in this amended Act. The Government incorporated a plan for women's development in the Sixth Five-Year Economic and Social Development Plan launched in 1987. Envisaged under the plan were the establishment of nursery facilities at job sites and the introduction of a child care leave system under which female employees could leave to rear their infants and then return to their jobs. As of 1992, 20 day care centers have been established at workplace. However, the total number of day care centers was 4,089 in 1992, including national and public day care centers, private day care centers and family day care centers. Regarding child care leave, about 61 percent of companies employing 300 or more female workers have implemented the system in 1992. The Seventh Five-Year Economic and Social Development Plan, launched in 1992, has various programs for improving the status of women in the fields of education, employment, cultural and social activities, social welfare and international cooperation.

Studies also are underway for the expanded employment of women on a part-time basis. If

Educational Attainment of Employed Women by Occupation in 1992

(Thousand Persons, Percent)

	Total		Under Primary School		Middle School		High School		College and University	
	Number	%	Number	%	Number	%	Number	%	Number	%
Total	7,609	100.0	2,799	100.0	1,427	100.0	2,600	100.0	784	100.0
Pro., Tech., & Related Workers	718	9.4	31	1.1	16	1.1	196	7.5	476	60.6
Adm., & Managerial workers	13	0.2	2	0.1	2	0.1	5	0.2	3	0.4
Clerical & Related Workers	1,099	14.4	10	0.2	46	3.2	865	33.3	177	22.5
Sales Workers	1,330	17.5	375	13.4	305	21.4	575	22.1	75	9.6
Service Workers	1,345	17.7	519	18.5	379	26.6	415	16.0	33	4.2
Agri., Forestry Workers, Fisherman and Hunters	1,380	18.1	1,185	42.3	143	10.2	48	11.8	4	0.5
Production & Related workers	1,724	22.7	676	24.2	535	37.4	495	19.1	17	2.2

Distribution of Employed by Age and Industry in 1992

(Thousand Persons, Percent)

	Total	Age Group							
		Total	15-19	20-24	25-29	30-39	40-49	50-54	55+
Total	7,609	100.0	4.1	16.6	10.6	24.4	19.7	9.0	15.6
Agri., For., & Fishing	1,384	100.0	0.1	0.7	2.4	13.4	0.4	18.2	44.8
Mining	4	100.0	0	25.5	0	0	50.0	25.0	25.0
Manufacturing	1,917	100.0	5.6	19.1	11.3	28.5	19.3	7.5	8.7
Electricity, Gas & Water	9	100.0	11.1	33.4	22.2	11.1	11.1	11.1	0
Construction	164	100.0	7.8	25.5	5.5	18.8	19.4	10.3	12.7
Trade, Restaurants and Hotels	2,240	100.0	4.0	13.7	9.7	29.2	24.8	8.1	10.5
Transport, Storage and Communication	91	100.0	8.8	39.5	13.2	19.8	11.0	4.4	3.3
Financing, Insurance, Real Estate and Business Services	446	100.0	8.5	31.5	13.9	21.3	13.6	4.7	6.5
Social & Personal Service	1,354	100.0	4.1	26.7	18.8	24.1	14.1	5.0	7.2

Source: National Statistical Office

such social and institutional support were provided, women would be able to offer a more specialized and stable labor force in a wide range of fields and make a further contribution to their society and country.

Women and Politics

Under the Constitution of the Republic of Korea promulgated in 1948 in which equal rights for both sexes were declared, women have enjoyed equal rights with men before the law, having been given the right to vote, to be elected, to assume public duties and to affiliate with political parties.

Exercising equal rights with men, women have so far participated in 14 general elections to choose legislators, 14 presidential elections and six national referenda. Of eligible women voters, 80.6 percent used their right to vote in the presidential elections, while 85.1 percent of eligible men voted. In the general elections, 72.9 percent of eligible women voted while 76.6 percent of men voted. It is to be noted that the women's vote increased from 70.5 percent in the 1963 general elections to 70.9 percent in the 1992 general elections, registering an increased political awareness on the part of women voters.

A total of twelve women have so far been appointed as cabinet members since the inauguration of the Republic of Korea in 1948. Im Yong-shin served as the first Minister of Trade and Industry between 1948-9. In 1993, the new Administration appointed three women as ministers. Former KWDI president Kwon Young-ja was appointed as Second State Minister for Political Affairs, the lawyer Hwang San-sung as Minister of Environment, and a newspaper editor Song Jung-sook as Minister of Health and Social Affairs. Of a total of 837,582 civil servants in 1991, 24.5 percent were women, of whom 59.7 percent were teachers and faculty members in public schools. The higher the rank, the smaller the number of positions held by women is. Only 1.6 percent of civil officials of rank 5 and above were women in 1991.

Women who have served as legislators total 63, of whom only 25.4 percent have been elected from electoral districts. The remaining 74.6 percent occupied seats in the National Assembly as the result of the national representation system. In the 14th National Assembly launched in

May 1992, only three of a total of 299 are women, that is 1.0 percent. The number of women judges and lawyers has increased in recent years. The first Korean woman who succeeded in the 1951 examinations for higher government officials in the judiciary department was Yi T'ae-yŏng. She was succeeded by five more women in the 1970s and 68 more during the 1980s.

The proportion of women among political party members shows a sharp increase in recent years as does the actual number of women party members. In the ruling Democratic Liberal Party the ratio of men to women among party members is 6 to 4. The opposition Democratic Party has a woman member on the eight-member supreme council. Efforts are being made to increase the number of women members in influential decision-making party organs, including educational programs designed to upgrade the leadership and political consciousness of women party members. Women and Welfare

Welfare programs for women are aimed especially at female heads of families, runaway women, unmarried mothers, women employed for entertainment and other needy women. Support for maternal and child welfare facilities has been strengthened as has support for vocational training programs for young runaway girls, unmarried mothers and other needy women. The Government has put special emphasis on the protection of fatherless families. There are 33 facilities for maternal and child protection to provide fatherless families with accommodations, basic living costs and services. In April 1989, the Mother-Child Welfare Law was enacted to support fatherless families and unwed mothers and came into effect later that year. Throughout the country, 334 counselors provide guidance for women working in entertainment places and for runaways in 1991. There are also vocational training facilities where such women can stay and receive professional training and moral education. A draft for revision of the Prohibition Law of Prostitution is under enactment to make rehabilitation more effective. As the number of working mothers with children under six years of age is increas-

ing, the problem of creating enough child care facilities is becoming a key issue in both welfare services and working conditions. As the proportion of the aged in the population and the number of dependent elderly also rises, problems concerning these older people are also emerging as a significant social issue. Of those 65 years of age and older in the population, women accounted for 61.9 percent in 1990. Therefore, services for aged women who have economic, psychosocial and family problems require special attention under the social welfare policy. Since its establishment in 1983, the Korean Women's Development Institute has aimed at promoting women's welfare through various research projects focused on women in general as well as on special target groups. It also engages in the formulation and revision of laws and institutions promoting the welfare of women.

Women and Health

Women's health and the involvement of women in health care are essential to the health of everyone. Women not only have special health problems relating to pregnancy and childbirth, but they also customarily have major responsibility in caring for family members and their health. In modern society, with increased participation of women in the labor force, the issue of maternity protection is emerging as a significant concern of the Government, employers and trade unions.

Some indicators relating to women's health show that the average life expectancy in 1990 was 66.92 for males and 74.96 for females. The ratio of women of child-bearing age (15-49) formed 46.7 percent of the total female population in 1970 and 57.1 percent in 1990, while the total fertility rate decreased from 4.5 in 1970 to 1.6 in 1990. More than 90 percent of married women experience conception and delivery. Clinical delivery increased from 32 percent in 1977 to 85.8 percent in 1986, while home delivery dropped from 64.2 percent in 1977 to 12.9 percent in 1986. The rate of expectant mothers receiving prenatal care has increased from 75.9 percent in 1980, to 93.8 percent in 1986, and the

An increasing number of Korean women are pursuing professional careers.

average number of visits for prenatal medical checks increased from 3.9 in 1980 to 5.9 in 1986.

The maternal mortality rate per 10,000 persons decreased from 5.0 in 1976 to 4.2 in 1980 and to 3.0 in 1990. The infant mortality rate (0-4 years) stood at 12.8 per 1,000 in 1990.

Women's health has improved markedly in recent decades due to economic growth, an improved public hygiene, better nutrition, and expanded medical facilities. The National Health Insurance Program which expanded its coverage for all from July 1, 1989, has contributed significantly to the improvement of women's health care. As a protective measure for the health of both mother and child, the Mother-Child Health Act was enacted in 1973 and revised in 1986. Under the newly revised act, a Maternal and Child Health Care Pocketbook system was put into effect in February 1987. Under this system, local administrative offices issue a medical check-up pocketbook to pregnant or nursing mothers which guarantees medical examinations on a regular basis, pre and post- natal care, and safe delivery. Newborn babies also receive free vaccinations.

Women's Organizations

The first women's organization in Korea was the *Sunsŏng* (Adoration) Society. Formed in 1896, it established and operated the Sunsŏng Girls' School. The Korean women's movement at that time was linked to the country's independence movement and was strongly motivated to emancipate women from ignorance through education as a means of building a strong nation and maintaining independence. Women took part in the national debt payment drive of 1907, a nationwide campaign to pay back debts Korea owed to Japan, by organizing the Women's Society for the Payment of National Debts. This is considered to have been the first time women participated in a tangible way in the politics of the country. The *Kŭnuhoe* (Society of the Rose of Sharon's Friends) was organized in 1927 as an arm of the women's liberalization and independence movement. As the first nationwide women's organization, this body took the initia-

tive in protecting women's rights and economic interests by advocating the elimination of social and legal discrimination, the abolition of early marriages, the guaranteeing of freedom in marriage and the elimination of discriminatory wage levels for women workers.

A number of women's organizations came into being in the wake of Korea's liberation from Japanese colonial rule in 1945. They included the Women's League for National Construction, the Women's Society for the Promotion of Independence and the Korean Women's National Party. As social stability increased in the latter half of the 1950s, various women's social and cultural groups emerged as well, leading to the formation in 1959 of the Council of Women's Organizations. It was aimed at presenting a consolidated women's voice and also at promoting exchanges between Korean women's organizations and foreign organizations. Registered women's organizations numbered more than 71 in 1992. It is believed that the number surpasses 2,200, including unregistered organizations.

Reflecting the political and social conditions of the times, Korean women's organizations first concentrated their efforts on soliciting women's participation in social campaigns. As women's activities diversified in the 1960s and 1970s, Korean women began to better understand the unique nature of the women's movement. Priority has been given in recent years to active participation in local government, and the fostering of women's awareness of social problems such as environmental issues and the consumers movement.

Women's organizations are engaged in a wide range of activities in accordance with the objectives of their establishment. Included among them are the education of adult women to develop their abilities and make constructive use of their leisure time; social campaigns aimed at reinforcing the consciousness of women and improving their social standing; counseling designed to resolve women's problems arising from family conflicts; revision of the Family Law which contains sex-discriminating provisions, and consumer protection drives tackling problems that have arisen in the process of industrialization and economic development. Also included are volunteer activities aimed at contributing to community development and increasing self-respect among women; international activities promoting the exchange of information and experience with international bodies and women's organizations overseas; social and friendship promotion activities, and projects to train women leaders.

Women and Culture

During the Chosŏn Dynasty, some outstanding women artists produced distinguished works despite the constraints in learning opportunities. In the 16th century, Lady Shin Sa-im Dang, the mother of Yi Yul-gok, one of the most famous philosophers in the period, was an outstanding calligrapher, painter and poet. In the 18th century, court literature began to claim a significant position in the cultural history of Korea. *Hanjungnok* (The Diary of a Princess) was written by the wife of Crown Prince Sado, and *Inhyŏn Wangbijŏn* (The Story of Queen Inhyŏn) was another famous work from that period.

The introduction of Christianity, with its teachings of liberty and equality, in the late 19th century provided women with an exposure to modern thought and an opportunity to pursue social and cultural activities. On the strength of the women's cultural movement begun in the early 1920s, women became active in literature, arts and education. As a result, today's women are no less active than men in cultural functions. However, of a total of 134 members of the Korea Academy of Sciences, only two are women, while 11, or 18 percent, of the 60 members of the Korea Academy of Arts are women.

The Federation of Artistic and Cultural Organizations of Korea, a pan-national entity encompassing men and women of letters and arts, had 10 organizations and 60,405 members at the end of 1989. The federation was headed by a woman three times during the period of 1984-1990. Women engaged in artistic activities are many and no less outstanding than men in their reputation at home and abroad.

From the 1980s, a noticeable change has been seen in women's movement. Some women's

organizations have pursued an alternative culture instead of male-dominated culture. In the fields of literature, drama, movies, arts and even in daily life, they have tried to change the existing patriarchal culture towards a more egalitarian society.

Korea's first woman journalist was Ch'oe Ŭnhŭi, who started her career in 1924. She has been followed by a number of women working for newspapers. In 1992, males accounted for 86.4 percent and females for 13.6 percent of all journalists. Female journalists in newspapers stood at 14.4 percent of the total, in radio and television broadcasting stations 12.3 percent, and in news agencies 8.5 percent. There are several women editors and overseas correspondents.

Women and Sports

With the promulgation in 1966 of the Sports Promotion Law and construction of the Korea Amateur Sports Association Training Academy and the Korea Amateur Sports Association building, sports circles were invigorated and this was accompanied by a rapid development in women's sports activities. Female athletes take active part in sports at the national, professional and school team level.

Korean women athletes continue to distinguish themselves in the international competition. Korea's women's volleyball teams have distinguished themselves in the international arena, winning a bronze medal at the 1976 Summer Olympics in Montreal. Korea's women's basketball teams were runners-up in the 1967 World Women's Basketball Championships held in Prague and in the 1984 Summer Olympics in Los Angeles. In table tennis, a women's doubles team won a gold medal at the 1988 Seoul Olympics. Korean women have been outstanding in archery, too, winning gold and bronze medals at the Los Angeles Olympics, and gold, silver and bronze medals at the Seoul Olympiad. Women athletes won six gold medals at the Barcelona Olympics, half of Korea's total of 12, garnering gold medals in shooting, judo, archery, badminton and handball competitions. The number of women mountaineers too has increased sharply in recent years, and a women's team succeeded in scaling one of the highest peaks in the Himalayas.

Saemaŭl Undong

Introduction

Saemaŭl Undong, Korea's new community movement, came into being in the early 1970s aimed initially at improving the quality of life in rural areas.

Two successful five-year development plans covering the period from 1962-1971 had seen rapid progress in urban localities, but with farmers in the countryside lagging far behind. The late President Park Chung Hee sought to remedy this situation by putting forward the Saemaŭl Undong idea in 1970, and starting the first experimental projects in 1971. As part a nationwide campaign to promote better living and a new work ethic among farmers, the guidelines for the Saemaŭl movement were summed up in the slogan "diligence, self-help and cooperation."

With about 35,000 village units involved, the movement over the past two decades has been termed a remarkable success, one that has made a dramatic contribution to the living environment in rural regions. Soon after its establishment among the people in the countryside, efforts began to extend the movement to urban and industrial sectors. Various action programs were started centering on such things as keeping neighborhoods clean and beautifying the environment voluntarily in traffic control campaigns.

Basic Concept

From its start, the Saemaŭl Undong has been envisaged as a "hands-on" effort, emphasizing actual practice rather than rhetoric.

In its first steps in 1971, the Government decided to subsidize extensive projects in rural villages by distribution of cement. About 300 bags of cement were distributed to each village taking part, with the provision that the cement should not be divided among individuals or used for private purposes, but should be devoted to common interest projects.

The response of the farmers was greater than had been anticipated. In many cases, villagers added their own capital goods and labor to the distribution program with the aim of quickly accomplishing the selected projects. This undertaking was termed an outstanding success with about 16,000 of 35,000 villages responding in what was described as a "very active" manner.

Achievement

Soon approximately 20 kinds of rural development projects were undertaken in the drive to improve living conditions and to increase income in rural areas under the Saemaŭl movement. These included an important village road expansion plan designed to improve access and accelerate the movement of people and goods. In the past, village roads linked to local public roads generally were narrow and winding and often lacked bridges. Under the Saemaŭl campaign, most of the 35,000 participating villages launched projects to straighten and widen roads so vehicular traffic could be handled more easily.

Bridge construction also was undertaken, with about 65,000 built in the period between 1971 and 1975.

As a result, motor vehicles, ox carts, push carts and motor tillers could reach the villages and most individual farmhouses except for those located on remote islands.

Another project called for the renovation of farmhouse roofs. In 1971, more than 80 percent of the 2.5 million farmhouses across the country had rice-straw thatched roofs that had to be replaced every winter season, a process calling for a great deal of work. As cement tiles and slate became more available in the early 1970s, it was recognized that the annual replacement of the thatch roofs was uneconomical as well as wearying.

Renovation programs were carried out and by the end of 1977, almost 100 percent of the farmhouse roofs were switched to cement tile or

Young farmers learning advanced technology for dairy farming.

slate construction. The appearance of rural villages was altered, and there were some complaints that one aspect of "quaint" beauty had been lost. For the people who lived and worked in the rural areas, however, the change was practical one that saved money and labor.

Also starting early in the Saemaŭl movement was the countrywide distribution of a newly developed, high yield rice that boosted production of that grain dramatically during the 1970s. In the period from 1971-1977, the national average rice yield rose from 3.5 to 4.9 tons in polished rice per hectare.

The emphasis on cooperation in rural areas has carried over to rice production, and it is quite common to see work teams made up of 20 to 30 farmers participating in a joint endeavor. Usually, the rice seedbed is made in one location for all members instead of having individual seedbeds scattered in several localities.

Also carried out jointly is the grain variety selection, the work of growing healthy seedings, transplanting, application of fertilizer and insecticide, weeding, irrigation and harvesting.

Factors in Success

The success of the Saemaŭl movement has been attributed to three key factors.

First, there has been a continuous supply of qualified village leaders as a result of institute training at various levels. In January, 1972, 150 village leaders, one from each county, entered the Saemaŭl Leaders' Training Institute located at Suwon as its first trainees. Since then, most local officials and many high-ranking officials from the central Government have received the same training with the goal of heightening their understanding of local problems. The program was extended to include businessmen, university professors, judges, legislators, journalists, religious leaders and others. In 1988 alone, a total of 21,000 leaders from various social sectors went through the Saemaŭl training course. They included 13,024 village leaders as well as people from industrial plants and factories.

A second factor has been the spread of the Saemaŭl from its original rural environment to include those from other walks of life. Using the same principles of diligence, self-help and cooperation, various action programs have been undertaken for city dwellers. Along with helping to clean and beautify the city environment, there have been programs to boost reforestation, preserve nature, combat pollution and aid resort areas.

The third important factor has centered on the assurance of appropriate guidance with a minimum amount of material assistance from local governments, along with cooperation between pertinent ministries. This has required the prompt demonstration and distribution of professional knowledge and knowhow on income enhancement, environmental clean-up and project implementation.

International Cooperation

In addition to its domestic achievements, the Saemaŭl Undong has developed into an international model, and people from many countries have come to study and share in its plans and experiences. In particular, many developing countries in Asia, Latin America and Africa have shown keen interest, often directly introducing principles for use in their own development programs. Foreign colleges and universities and other academic circles have made careful studies of the Saemaŭl Undong and its possible application in their home environment.

By the end of 1989, a total of 864 foreigners from 47 countries had visited Korea to undergo regular training courses with Korean Saemaŭl leaders. Many more came to study or observe the movement.

Future Directions

While hailed as a success from its start in 1971, the Saemaŭl Undong still faces new challenges and the attainment of new goals. Amid the rapidly occurring changes and developments of today's world, efforts should be made to guide the future Saemaŭl movement in new directions, including the serious problems of over-population in urban areas and housing shortages.

Also facing future leaders is the need to ease the conflict and strife between different regions and classes caused by the unfair distribution of the rewards of economic growth.

Future directions and policies of the Saemaŭl movement also must be oriented to usher in a prosperous, confident year 2000 with appropriate cultural activities, plans and programs for the conservation and protection of the environment in both rural and urban areas, and for further building the overall quality of life.

MASS
COMMUNICATIONS

Newspapers

Historical Background

Modern Newspaper Pioneer

The first privately published, modern newspaper to appear in Korea was the *Tongnip Shinmun* (The Independent), established in 1896 by Dr. Sŏ Chae-p'il (Philip Jaisohn), a medical doctor and independence leader educated in the United States. Dr. Sŏ published his newspaper from an office on the premises of the then Paichai Hakdang, presently Paichai High School.

The *Tongnip Shinmun* printed 300 copies of four tabloid pages three times a week. The first three pages were printed entirely in *Han-gŭl*, the phonetic Korean alphabet, and the last page in English. It had bureaus in Inch'ŏn, Suwon, Kanghwa, P'aju, Pusan, Songdo, Wonsan and P'yŏngyang. The first issue came out on April 7, 1896, which was declared Newspaper Day in 1957 and has since been observed as a holiday by the Korean press.

Dr. Sŏ was a young, reform-minded member of pro-Japanese political group called *Kaehwadang* in the declining years of the Chosŏn Dynasty. In 1884 his political faction staged an unsuccessful coup d'etat against an incumbent government made up largely of conservative pro-Chinese politicians. Dr. Sŏ fled to the United States, where he became an American citizen, married an American woman and studied medicine at George Washington University.

After the fall of the pro-Chinese group, he returned home in 1896 to devote himself once again to Korea's modernization. He obtained a sizable grant from the government and founded the *Tongnip Shinmun* as a vehicle aimed at reforming the political and social systems by enlightening the masses.

When the pro-Chinese faction regained power in 1897, Dr. Sŏ was again forced into exile in the United States. Following his departure, the paper was published under a caretaker management, but finally folded in December 1899.

Dr. Sŏ remained in the United States and worked for the independence of Korea throughout the Japanese occupation. He returned home in 1947 after liberation, served briefly with the U.S. military government in Seoul, then returned to the United States and died there in 1951.

A now famous editorial in the first issue of the *Tongnip Shinmun* read in part: "We propose to become a spokesman for the entire Korean people. We will inform the people about what the government does, and communicate to the government about how the people fare." The *Tongnip Shinmun* was a newspaper in a truly modern sense.

Earlier Publications

There were earlier types of Korean newspapers. Records show that a news sheet called *Kibyŏlji* was published as far back as A.D.692. In 1392 the royal court issued the *Chobo* (Court Gazette) to communicate to the people government information such as court announcements, appointments, transfers and dismissals of officials.

In 1578, a group of civic leaders in Seoul began a brief experiment with a private news bulletin patterned after the *Chobo*, also called *Chobo*. For the next two centuries, intermittent attempts were made to publish private newspapers, but they were unsuccessful, largely because they lacked the blessing of the court. It was only in the latter half of the 19th century that newspapers in the modern sense of the word appeared.

In 1883, a group of progressive reformers in the government began publishing an official gazette entitled the *Hansŏng Sunbo*. The paper, using only Chinese characters, was printed three times a month by the newly-formed Office of Culture and Information. The *Hansŏng Sunbo* published not only government bulletins, but also general political, economic and foreign news. As the official gazette, its aim was to "enlighten the people" under the direction of the progressives, who were aligned with the Japanese.

After the abortive progressive coup of 1884, the conservatives, who were aligned with the

Chinese, attacked and burned the office of the *Hansŏng Sunbo*. The paper had survived for a year.

In 1886, the Office of Culture and Information revived the *Hansŏng Sunbo* as a weekly, renaming it the *Hansŏng Jubo*. It used a mixture of Chinese characters and *Han-gŭl*. However, with the abolition of the Office in 1888, the weekly also ceased publication.

The First Daily

The first modern newspaper to publish on a daily basis was the *Maeil Shinmun*, which was established in April 1898. The editor was Syngman Rhee, who later became the first President of the Republic of Korea. This daily newspaper championed the reform of domestic politics, modernization of the country and preservation of independence against moves by foreign powers. It printed four pages daily using *Han-gŭl* and was headquartered in a rice wholesaler's shop in the midst of the present-day Namdaemun market. The newspaper survived for one year.

Toward the turn of the century, foreign powers competed for positions of strength in Korea, but the Japanese established dominance following the Sino-Japanese and Russo-Japanese wars. During the Russo-Japanese War (1904-1905), the Japanese commander initiated prior censorship of all Seoul newspapers. Shortly thereafter, the Japanese enforced a military police system in Korea in an attempt to suppress freedom of the press, assembly and association of the Korean people.

Despite such circumstances, another daily newspaper, the *Daehan Maeil Shinbo*, was started in 1904. In an effort to avoid press suppression, the newspaper appointed Ernest T. Bethell, special correspondent of the London Daily News in Seoul, as president-publisher and continued its resistance to Japanese military domination. British subjects at that time received special treatment in Korea because Japan had concluded a military alliance with Great Britain in 1902. The *Daehan Maeil Shinbo* exerted considerable influence among the Korean people, but this was to be short lived.

In a stronger move toward the colonization of Korea, Japan forced a protectorate treaty on it in 1905, granting the Japanese virtual control of the Korean Government. One of the stipulations of the treaty was that all Korean diplomatic relations would be handled through the Japanese Government.

The *Daehan Maeil Shinbo* and other Korean newspapers fought desperately against the treaty, but lost to the tough policies laid down by the Japanese. Bethell and many Korean journalists were subsequently indicted by Japanese authorities, and the *Daehan Maeil Shinbo* was suppressed in 1905.

The Japanese then promulgated a press law in 1907 as a measure to ensure a press favorable to their actions in Korea. Japan annexed Korea in 1910, bringing the Chosŏn Dynasty to an end. The *Daehan Maeil Shinbo* was sold to Japanese interests.

Dark Journalistic Days

In what amounted to the first dark age of Korean journalism from 1910 to 1920, no newspapers were allowed to be published except organs of the Japanese Government. Fighters for Korean independence, however, continued the struggle abroad. publishing the *Kongnip Shinmun* and *Shinhan Minbo* in San Francisco, the *Shisa Shinbo* and *Kukminbo* in Honolulu and the *Daedong Kongbo* and *Haecho Shinmun* in Russia.

With the treaty of annexation, the immigration of Japanese to Korea increased rapidly. One result was that a total of 30 newspapers were published by the Japanese in Korea—16 dailies, 4 tri-weeklies, 6 weeklies and 4 monthlies. No Korean newspaper was allowed to publish except the *Maeil Shinbo*, the mouthpiece of the Japanese Governor-General in Korea.

Following the end of World War I in Europe, U.S. President Woodrow Wilson went to the Paris Peace Conference, where he proclaimed his principle of self-determination for foreign-dominated nations. In Korea, the most dramatic and tragic event demonstrating Korean resistance to Japanese imperialism was a nationwide uprising on March 1, 1919. Known as the

March First or Samil Independence Movement, it was put down harshly by the Japanese authorities.

In view of these developments, the Japanese Government sought to calm the outraged anti-Japanese feeling of the Korean people by moving from all-out suppression toward appeasement. In that climate, three leading newspapers—the *Dong-A Ilbo*, the *Chosun Ilbo* and the *Shisa Shinmun*—came into being in Korea. All published privately, the three papers entered into commercial competition as business enterprises in the early spring of 1920. The *Dong-A Ilbo* and the *Chosun Ilbo* have become the most respected and longest-lived newspapers in Korea.

The *Dong-A Ilbo* introduced the first rotary press in Korea in 1921, and organized a newspaper club called *Mumyŏnghoe*. The *Chosun Ilbo* first published both morning and evening editions in 1924, and ran the first comic strip seen in Korea. The paper also devoted space to women's news. The first convention of newspapermen in Korea was held in Seoul in 1925 with the participation of 700 journalists from across the country.

The Japanese Governor-General stepped in again, however, to suppress these developments and the growing influence of the Korean journalistic society.

From 1926 to 1940, both the *Dong-A Ilbo* and the *Chosun Ilbo* were suspended four times. Newspaper sales were prohibited 587 times between 1926 and 1932. A total of 1,729,478 copies of newspapers were confiscated in 1927, another 877,959 in 1928 and 761,647 in 1929.

The Japanese Governor-General banned the use of the Korean language in schools in 1938, and a second dark age of Korean journalism began in 1940. The *Dong-A Ilbo*, the *Chosun Ilbo* and other Korean newspapers were ordered to suspend their operations indefinitely. Following the Japanese attack on Pearl Harbor and the surge of the war in the Pacific, the suppression of the Korean press became even more intense.

Liberation and the Korean Press

The Allied victory in 1945 brought World War II to an end and liberation, independence and freedom to Korea. Within weeks, no fewer than 68 newspapers sprang up, some of them published by communists. To curb their operations, which were seen as a threat to internal security, the U.S. Army Military Government in Korea (USAMGIK) in 1946 promulgated Ordinance No. 88 providing for the registration and licensing of publications. As a result of this action, many leftist papers were closed. The founding of the Republic of Korea in 1948 led to a further decline of the leftist media, and it had faded completely by the time the Korean War broke out in 1950.

After the 1960 student uprising that led to the fall of the Syngman Rhee Government and brought about the Second Republic, Ordinance No. 88 was abolished. Almost unlimited press freedom followed, and there was a dramatic surge in the number of newspapers, news agencies and periodicals that began operations. The count of newspapers more than doubled to 85, press services soared, and innumerable periodicals made their appearance.

That period of unbridled growth and turbulence was ended, however, by the military revolution of 1961 that saw Park Chung-hee, an army general, come into power.

The military government instituted a number of strong press policies and controls. The registration of newspapers and news agencies was enacted into law, and only 34 papers and six agencies managed to survive.

During the 1970s, the Korean press underwent severe trials in the midst of a delicate political situation in and around the peninsula. Concern for national security brought about by the 1970-71 partial pullout of U.S. forces and President Park's August 15, 1970 declaration initiating efforts for achieving peaceful reunification with the North resulted in many restrictions on the press.

Following Park's assassination in October 1979, there again were sweeping changes that affected the press. Strictures continued through much of the early 1980s, but freedom of the press was one of the eight points that Roh Tae Woo, then a presidential candidate, included in his Declaration of Democratic Reforms issued June 29, 1987. After Roh was elected President and the Sixth Republic was launched, a new growth in freedom of expression was hailed as one of the most impressive changes brought about by the new Administration. Many new newspapers and magazines began publication.

As of March 1993, there are 103 daily newspapers in Korea. Of them, 68 are general papers, 18 economic papers, 2 English-language dailies, 1 Chinese-language daily and 3 sports and entertainment papers. There also are six other specialized daily newspapers. Of these, 54 are published in Seoul, while the others are regional vernacular dailies.

The *Dong-A Ilbo* (*ilbo* meaning daily news and shinmun meaning newspaper), *Chosun Ilbo, Joong-ang Ilbo, Hankook Ilbo, Seoul Shinmun* and *Kyunghyang Shinmun* were the six national dailies being published when the Sixth Republic was inaugurated. The *Han-Kyoreh Shinmun, Segye Ilbo* and *Kookmin Ilbo* started publishing in or after 1988 and are distributed countrywide. All are privately owned, except for the *Seoul Shinmun*, the controlling stocks of which are owned by the Korea Broadcasting System (KBS).

The two English-language dailies also are privately owned. The *Korea Times* is published as a sister paper of the *Hankook Ilbo*, and The *Korea Herald* is owned by several business firms including the *Daenong* Group. Both are morning newspapers.

Most of the national dailies print 186 pages a week, and most of the provincial papers 100 to 140 pages. They normally print 24 pages a day seven days a week.

Korean newspapers have continued their practice of withholding information on the exact number of copies they print. Circulation traditionally has been guarded jealously as a business secret. Unofficial but reliable statistics put the combined circulation of newspapers throughout the country at 13 million at the end of 1992. That represented 31 copies per 100 people, more than triple the UNESCO standard of at least 10 newspaper copies per 100 inhabitants.

The Korea Audit Bureau of Circulation (KABC) was established formally on May 31, 1989, to audit and confirm the standardized statements on circulation and distribution date reported by newspapers, magazines and other periodicals which carry commercial advertisements. Newspaper circulation has grown steadily in Korea and so has the volume of advertisement. Chief revenue sources for newspapers are subscriptions and advertising. The ratio between them presently is about 3:7.

The *Chosun Ilbo* and the *Dong-A Ilbo* have each been printing more than one million copies daily with distribution largely on a home delivery basis. The ratio of home delivery compared with street sales is about 90 percent to 10 percent for most national newspapers.

The *Chosun Ilbo* founded March 5, 1920, is the country's oldest newspaper. The *Dong-A Ilbo* was founded about one month later, on April 1, 1920. Both established reputations for their independent and conservative editorial policies. These two dailies and other vernacular national newspapers have played an important role in the shaping of public opinion in Korea.

The *Korea Times* published its first edition November 1, 1950, at the height of the Korean War. It was founded under the auspices of the late Dr. Helen Kim, who was then serving as Director of the Public Information Office. She had temporarily left her post as president of Ewha Womans University to serve in the government. The paper was taken over in 1953 by Chang Ki-young, who later founded the *Hankook Ilbo* and a chain of magazines and specialized newspapers, including a sports daily and a business daily.

The *Korea Herald* was founded August 15, 1953. It originally was named The *Korean Republic*, but the name was changed in 1965. The paper began as a semi-official daily and continued that status until 1978, when it was sold to the Korean Traders Association and later sold again to a number of business firms.

In view of the relative size of Korea and the fact that a centralized form of government has been a tradition, it is considered remarkable that regional newspapers have proved viable. Each province has one or more dailies, largely of local significance.

The typical Korean newspaper consists of 24 pages, having been expanded from eight pages in 1981 to include women's pages and economic sections, and to provide more coverage of special events and features. Front pages usually are devoted to the domestic as well as the international political scene. There also are an editorial page; sections reporting crimes, accidents, features and social affairs; 2-4 pages devoted to culture and cultural events; and several pages of sports.

Newspapers play an important role in politics as providers of information and shapers of opinion. They normally devote more space to political-diplomatic news than any other subject. One survey showed the national dailies devoted 48 percent of their space to such news.

Another study showed that a large majority of people, almost 78 percent of those with higher education, tended to rely on the daily newspaper for their information.

Korean newspapers have made significant investments towards improving press facilities and equipment. Major dailies, for example, have built modern, new buildings and have made major innovations in printing equipment, procedures and methods. Newspaper companies have utilized high-speed rotary presses capable of printing 150,000 copies per hour with multicolor capabilities.

In line with developments on the political and governmental fronts in the fall of 1980, several newspapers, broadcasting companies and news agencies were merged. The action was taken at the urging of the government on the basic of putting the media on a sounder management basis.

News Agencies

With liberation from Japanese imperial rule in 1945, the first Korean news agency, the *Haebang T'ongshin* (Liberation Press) was

established by Korean staff members of the *Domei* News Agency which had been operated by Japanese authorities. Until then, Japanese colonial policy had barred Koreans from setting up their own news agencies. On September 4, 1945, the *Chosun T'ongshin*, or Korea Press, was organized, while branches of the *Domei* News Agency in Seoul and Pusan were reorganized as the *Kukje T'ongshin*, or International Press.

The *Yonhap T'ongshin*, or United Press, was established near the end of 1945 under the control of the U.S. military government. On December 20, 1945, the *Kukje T'ongshin* and *Yonhap T'ongshin* merged to become the now defunct *Hapdong T'ongshin*, or *Hapdong* News Agency.

During the Korean War, the *Chosun T'ongshin* lost its United Press contract to a newcomer, the *Tongyang T'ongshin*, or Orient Press. In 1953, *Hapdong* lost its Reuters contract to another newcomer, the *Segye T'ongshin*, or World Press. *Hapdong* also lost its Associated Press contract in 1962. The emergence of still another newcomer, the *Donghwa* News Agency, which merged with the *Segye T'ongshin* and concluded a contract with the AP, set off keen competition among Korean news agencies. In 1965, *Hapdong* became the first Korean news service to provide English-language coverage to foreign clients in major world cities, including Washington, D.C., New York and Tokyo.

The *Hapdong* News Agency regained its exclusive contracts with Reuters and AP in October 1972 and April 1973. The Orient Press signed an exclusive contract with Agence France Presse in April 1973. At the same time, the *Donghwa* News Agency went into voluntary liquidation due to financial difficulties following the expiration of its contracts with AP and Reuters.

At that time there was a movement for the merger of the three existing major news agencies to strengthen Korea's overseas news activities in light of North Korea's expanding overseas propaganda efforts. A government statement supported such a move in June 1970, but it said the decision should be voluntary by the

three private news agencies concerned.

Not until December 19, 1980, was a merger carried through when the *Hapdong* News Agency and Orient Press were combined to form the *Yonhap* News Agency. Three other small, special interest agencies, the *Sisa* Press, Economic News Agency and Industrial News Agency, were later absorbed into the newly-formed *Yonhap* agency.

The *Yonhap* News Agency, a cooperative of all the Korean news media, was the first of its kind in the country. Its stocks are shared by all daily newspapers and radio and television stations.

The agency has expanded its domestic and foreign news coverage, with a staff of more than 300 reporters, writers and editors in its head office in Seoul and more than 100 correspondents throughout the country. It maintains 13 overseas bureaus with a total of 15 correspondents in Washington, D.C., New York, Los Angeles, Buenos Aires, Paris, Berlin, Brussels, Moscow, Tokyo, Hong Kong, Beijing, Bangkok and Cairo.

As a result of improvements in transmitting facilities, it has become possible for the agency not only to provide foreign and domestic news service to about 500 domestic clients through a computerized system using the Korean alphabet and Chinese characters, but also to transmit an English news service of 5,000 words daily to its 110 overseas subscribers through a relay of communication satellites.

The *Yonhap* News Agency has contracts and news exchange agreements with more than 40 foreign agencies, including AP, UPI, Reuters, AFP, TASS, Xinhua, Kyodo, DPA, ANSA, MTI, Antara and Bernama. It also publishes almanacs in Korean and English, a monthly photo journal and a weekly newsletter in English compiled from major news stories transmitted during the week. There also is a semi-monthly English feature service covering a variety of human interest subjects, including Korean culture, history and industry. Equipped with modern equipment for both transmission and reception, *Yonhap* has become one of the most important channels for international communication in Korea.

Radio

Historical Sketch

Radio broadcasting in Korea started in 1927 when the Japanese established a station in Seoul after two years of experimental broadcasting. This station operated solely as a mouthpiece for Japan's colonial policy until liberation in 1945.

The U.S. military government in Korea took it over in September 1945 and formed the Korea Broadcasting System (KBS). This was the only radio station in the country until 1954, when a privately-owned and operated network, the Christian Broadcasting System (CBS), started educational and religious programs along with news and entertainment broadcasts.

In December 1956, another Christian station, the Evangelical Alliance Mission, inaugurated the Far East Broadcasting Station in Inch'ŏn, transmitting programs in Korean, English, Chinese and Russian for 100 hours a week. The first commercial radio in Korea, the Pusan *Munwha* Broadcasting Station, was set up in Pusan in April 1959. The establishment of a number of private broadcasting companies followed, including the *Munwha* Broadcasting Company (MBC), the *Dong-A* Broadcasting Station (DBS) and the *Tongyang* Broadcasting Company (TBC), all located in Seoul.

MBC began operations in December 1961 with the call sign KLKV and has contributed greatly to the development of commercial radio service in Korea. MBC was followed by two rivals, DBS in 1963 and TBC in 1964. DBS, affiliated with the *Dong-A Ilbo*, covered only Seoul and its vicinity. MBC and TBC, affiliated with the *Joong-ang Ilbo*, had countrywide networks with satellite stations in major provincial cities.

In 1966, the Seoul FM Broadcasting Company put a station into operation marking the beginning of FM broadcasting in Korea. Three other FM stations were set up in 1970, the Korea *Munwha* FM station in Seoul, the Pusan *Munwha* FM station in Pusan and the Korea FM station in Taegu.

The Far East Broadcasting Corporation (FEBC), a non-profit station with headquarters in the United States, was set up in 1972 on Chejudo Island off Korea's south coast for transmitting messages of freedom, peace and hope to Asia.

Two special broadcasting systems also were established in Korea, the Republic of Korea Army Radio and the American Forces Korea Network (AFKN).

The Korean station was established in 1954 to broadcast informational, educational and entertainment programs for ROK armed forces personnel. The American facility began operations in October 1950 to provide news, features and entertainment programs for U.S. military personnel and their families based in Korea.

Present State

The media merger action taken in the fall of 1980 brought about the greatest change in the history of Korean radio broadcasting. The public Korean Broadcasting System (KBS), already the largest network with 20 local stations, took over two of Seoul's four major private broadcasting companies—the *Dong-A* Broadcasting System and the *Tongyang* Broadcasting Company—plus three privately-run provincial radio stations. The Christian Broadcasting System, together with its four provincial stations was directed to specialize in purely evangelical programs. KBS also took over a 65-percent interest in the *Munwha* Broadcasting Company with 19 affiliated provincial stations; but MBC was allowed to continue as a privately-run company.

There also are two special stations—the *Kŭkdong* Broadcasting System and the Asia Broadcasting System—which air special programs designed mainly to carry out Christian evangelism directed to North Korea, the former Soviet Union, the People's Republic of China and Mongolia as well as South Korea.

KBS has maintained an overseas broadcasting network since 1953. With the introduction of two programs in Indonesian and Arabic in 1975 and two programs in German and

KBS Overseas Broadcasting Network.

Portuguese in 1983, the network has broadcasting services in 11 languages. The other languages are Korean, English, French, Chinese, Spanish, Russian and Japanese. Programs are beamed to neighboring countries in the East Asia, to North America, Hawaii, Europe, South-East Asia, the Middle East and South America.

The American Forces Korea Network (AFKN) provides AM and FM radio and television service for U.S. military personnel and their dependents in Korea. Its programs, on the air 24 hours a day, are in English and include a news report every hour.

Another wave of change began to break over Korean broadcasting in 1990. Structural reform was undertaken to adapt to swift changes in the broadcasting environment in order to reach a solution to a number of problems associated with the existing publicly-operated broadcasting system. One reform measure was the emergence of privately-operated broadcasting stations and government-operated stations. Another development was the establishment of a number of specialized broadcasting stations.

The Seoul city-operated TBS (Traffic Broadcasting Station) was inaugurated in June 1990, followed in December by the government-operated EBS (Educational Broadcasting Station). The privately-owned Seoul Radio Station began broadcasting in March 1991, with a target audio region including Seoul and the surrounding areas of Kyŏnggi-do province that comprise the Greater Seoul Metropolitan Area.

There now are a total of 97 radio stations in Korea, including 42 FM stations and one short-wave station. The most popular radio hour is between noon and 1 p.m.; popular programs are news, pop music, serial dramas, classical music, variety shows and sports.

Despite the spread of television in Korea, radio still has an expanding audience. However, the role and function of radio have undergone necessary changes in recent years, due mainly to the influence and popularity of television. One of the important tasks radio must undertake in the years ahead is not to compete with TV, but to search out its own program areas such as news, music and traffic situation reports and develop them to meet the needs of average listeners.

Television

Historical Sketch

Television broadcasting began in Korea in 1956 with the opening of a privately-owned and commercially-operated station in Seoul. That first TV station was destroyed by fire in 1959, however.

On December 31, 1961, the official KBS-TV was inaugurated by the government in Seoul as the first full-scale television service in Korea. A commercial operation, TBC-TV, began broadcasts in December 1964 as a sister station of the *Tongyang* Broadcasting Company, covering Seoul and its immediate vicinity. In the same year, TBC-TV opened a subsidiary station in Pusan to reach the southern part of the country. The *Munwha* Broadcasting Company established Korea's third television station, MBC-TV, in August 1969. It later was expanded to a countrywide network of 19 local stations. As privately-owned stations came on line after 1990 as a result of structural feform, SBS-TV, a private firm, began broadcasting to the Greater Seoul Metropolitan Area in December 1991.

Present State

In the fall of 1980, media merger action was also taken in Korea TV broadcasting field. The Public Korean Broadcasting System (KBS) took over the *Tongyang* Broadcasting Company (TBC).

There are 39 television stations in Korea, and all TV broadcasting is in color. There also is AFKN-TV, operated by the U.S. military in Korea for its personnel and their dependents, which also broadcasts in color.

On weekdays, Korean TV stations operate 10 1/2 hours, from 6 a.m. to 10 a.m., and from 5:30 p.m. to midnight. On weekends, broadcasts are extended to 18 hours, from 6 a.m. to midnight.

When KBS-TV started operations in 1961, there were only about 25,000 television sets in Korea. The number of registered sets exceeded the one million mark in 1973 and reached 2,809,000 by the end of 1976. The number jumped to 5,133,000 at the end of 1978, and went over seven million by the end of 1982.

Statistics reveal that as of March 1993, 9.6 million color television sets had been registered with KBS. Taking unregistered color sets and black-and-white sets into consideration, the total number of television sets is close to 12 million, an average of one television set per household throughout the country.

Peak time for television viewing is from 8 p.m. to 10 p.m. Favorite types of programs include serial dramas, foreign movies, comedy and quiz shows, sports and news, in that order. Students, however, prefer music shows, sports, movies, comedies, quizzes, specials and serial dramas.

Television has become an important mass medium due to its obvious audio-visual appeal and influence. The initial primary function of television has been entertainment, but recently it has placed more emphasis on information and education, making it a more serious competitor for radio stations and newspapers.

Though television has achieved marked success both in quality and quantity, there still are many areas for improvement. Programming is one area that needs immediate attention, and improvement of educational television is another. Television also must be prepared technically for further advances in the age of satellite TV communications. The mass production of transistorized television sets at low cost is another task that requires prompt attention.

In 1984, Korean television networks introduced the "Olympics in the Home" program covering almost all of the Los Angeles Olympic Games competition around the clock. The success of that undertaking gave Korean broadcasting circles added confidence for the giant task of handling the 1988 Summer Olympics in Seoul. KBS was in charge of Olympic TV operations as host broadcaster for the Seoul Games, setting up an elaborate center at its headquarters to meet successfully the needs and demands of domestic and foreign broadcasters.

SPORTS

Marathoner Hwang Young-cho, gold medalist at the Barcelona Olympics in 1992.

Introduction

The development of sports in Korea has been linked closely with the country's economic success, as witnessed by the impressive staging of the Seoul Olympics in 1988.

Over the past several years there has been increased emphasis on the advancement of sports policies along with the construction of all kinds of sports facilities. As a result, sports have become an important part of everyday life for many Koreans, with spectator sports becoming especially popular.

A look at Korea's athletic history shows a long record of active participation in many international events. It also shows some impressive victories, particularly in the fields of soccer, wrestling, boxing and basketball. A Korean runner, Sohn Kee-chung, won the marathon gold medal in the 1936 Berlin Olympics, but he was forced to compete under the Japanese flag because the Korean Peninsula was under the rule of Japan at that time. Korea participated in the international games under its own flag for the first time at the London Olympics in 1948.

Since then, Korean athletes have shown steady improvement as demonstrated by their performances in many events at home and abroad. They won one gold, one silver and four bronze medals in the 1976 Montreal Olympics to rank 19th out of a field of more than 100. In the 1982 Asian Games, Asia's biggest sports festival, Korea ranked third in New Delhi, after the People's Republic of China and Japan, and then placed second in the 1986 Seoul Asian Games, trailing China by only one gold.

In the 1983 World Junior Football Championships in Mexico, the Korean team made a surprising, highly-regarded advance into the semi-finals. Korean athletes have made consistently good showings in boxing, weightlifting and judo, and more recently in wrestling, basketball, football, table tennis, volleyball and archery.

In the Olympiad at Los Angeles in 1984, Korean athletes made their best showing in an Olympics up to that time, ranking tenth in the final medal tally with 6 gold, 6 silver and 7 bronze for a total of 19. That record was, of course, overshadowed in the 1988 Games in Seoul, where Korean competitors ranked fourth in the final gold medal count.

Korean athletes also made a remarkable showing in the 25th Olympic Games at Barcelona in 1992. Korea placed seventh out of 172 countries, garnering 12 golds, five silver and 12 bronze medals. For Koreans, Barcelona was memorable for another reason: Korean athletes won both the first and the last gold medals of the Games. Yo Kap-sun won the Games' first gold medal in the women's 10-meter air rifle competition shortly after the opening ceremony, and marathoner Hwang Young-cho's victory hoisted the Korean national flag atop the center flagpole of the main stadium just before the closing ceremony of the Barcelona Olympiad.

Korea has also played host to many international sporting events over recent years. In 1978, the 42nd World Shooting Championships brought more than 1,300 entries from 71 countries. Those championships, the first ever in Asia, were held at one of the world's five finest shooting sites, the T'aenŭng International Shooting Range, just 45 minutes from downtown Seoul. The Eighth World Basketball Championships for Women were held in 1979 as the first event in the 25,000-seat gymnasium at the Seoul Sports Complex in Chamshil; it too was the first time such a championship had been held in Asia. The Second Asian Swimming Championships and the Eighth Asian Junior Basketball Championships were held in Korea in 1984.

Since 1971, Korea has sponsored the President's Cup Football Tournament annually, contributing to the improvement of soccer skills in Asia by attracting participants not only from the region but also from Europe, Latin America and Africa. In 1980 and 1982, the Seoul Open International Table Tennis Championships were held, and in 1985 an invitational table tennis tournament, the Seoul Grand Prix Masters, attracted players from 10 countries.

In 1985, a year before the Seoul Asian Games and three years before the Seoul Olympics,

Korea was host to a series of international sports events. They included the 3rd Asian Youth Gymnastics Championships, the 33rd World Archery Championships, the 12th Asian Cycling Championships, the 14th World Cup Boxing Championships and the 21st World Cup Bowling Tournament.

The Seoul Asian Games became the largest in the history of this regional sports festival that began in 1951. More than 4,800 athletes from 27 countries took part. Eleven world records were broken and two tied; 98 Asian records were matched or beaten and 223 Asian Games records were bettered. China held on to its Asian Games supremacy in the medal race, taking 94 gold, 82 silver and 46 bronze. Korea placed second, Japan third, Iran fourth and India fifth.

The Asian Games Federation, at a meeting in New Delhi in 1981, selected Seoul as the host city for the 1986 Asiad. In Korean circles, official and non-official, it was recognized that holding the Asian Games would provide an opportunity to demonstrate the country's steady development in all fields along with its potential for becoming an active player on the world stage. The Asian Games served as an important, full-dress rehearsal for the Seoul Olympics that were to follow in two years.

While the Asian Games were a significant event in themselves, broader aspects resulted in more than just the efforts of the organizing committee and sports officials. The Government and the people joined in with great efforts to make the Asiad a resounding success. Construction was pushed to provide the finest facilities for both athletes and spectators along with the most sophisticated electronic and other technical equipment, which would be used in both the regional meet and again later in the Olympics.

As another part of all the developments in the sports movement, Korean college students have also been active at their own levels of competition. They have taken part in the Universiad since 1967, making impressive showings of their discipline and determination.

Seoul Olympics

Dedicated to "Peace, Harmony and Progress," the Games of the 24th Olympiad were brought to a successful conclusion Oct. 2, 1988, in Seoul after 16 days of competition and pageantry.

Colorful ceremonies featuring ancient and modern Korea highlighted the opening and closing ceremonies before enthusiastic throngs.

The Seoul Games were the largest in the history of the Olympic movement at that time, with 13,304 athletes and officials from 160 countries taking part, transcending barriers separating East and West, North and South. Although North Korea and six other countries declined to attend, the competition in Korea was known as the first boycott-free Olympics in 12 years as athletes from the East and West returned to full participation.

The race for Olympic medals was won by the Soviet Union with 55 gold, 31 silver and 46 bronze. East Germany was second with 37 gold, 35 silver and 30 bronze, while the United States placed third with 36 gold, 31 silver and 27 bronze. Ranking fourth in the final gold medal tally and sixth in the overall number of medals was host Korea with 12 gold, 10 silver and 11 bronze. Although Korean athletes had the advantage of home grounds and hometown crowds, their medal harvest came as a surprise even to their most fervent supporters.

The success of the Seoul Games was credited to the all-out efforts made by the officials and people of Korea, working with the International Olympic Committee to achieve in this divided land the goals of peace, harmony and progress.

Following the selection in 1981 of Seoul as the site for the 24th Olympiad, the tireless efforts that had gone into the planning, preparation and actual carrying-out of the 1988 Summer Games resulted in a sports spectacular that brought 30,000 Olympic family members and 300,000 tourists to Seoul.

Construction of the massive Seoul Sports Complex along the Han-gang River, which bisects the capital city, began in 1977 to meet an increasing demand for sports facilities. With the

The lighting of the 1988 Seoul Olympic flame.

successful bid for the 1988 Games, it was to become the center for this heralded international event. The main stadium, with a seating capacity of 100,000, was opened officially in September 1984.

While there were incidents and emotions that marred some aspects of the games—the ugly specter of drugs, charges of professionalism, favoritism and excessive nationalism—by the time the Olympic flame was extinguished it generally was agreed that Korea had staged an outstanding event and that unity and vitality had been restored to the Olympic movement.

Significant contributions to this success were made by the 26,000 volunteer workers who joined in the efforts of Korean organizers and other officials under the Seoul Olympic Organizing Committee; the families that opened their homes to Olympic visitors; the residents who participated willingly in an essential traffic control system, and about 3,180,000 spectators who cheered the athletes from around the world.

Also making an important contribution was the Seoul Olympic Art Festival, which opened one month before the games. It included 30 performing arts presentations and a similar number of exhibitions, academic conferences and film shows. The festival stimulated interest in the Olympics both in and outside Korea, as well as providing a forum for international culture exchange. The participants included top class artists, performing groups and individuals from many countries.

Nearly 900 people from around the world took part in the Seoul Youth Camp held in connection with the Olympics to provide an opportunity for the young men and women to develop friendships and work together for international understanding and stability.

Shortly after the formal closing of the Seoul Olympics, the same sports facilities were used to hold the Eighth Paralympics. This competition, which ran from Oct. 15 to Oct. 24, also was the largest in the history of such events with 3,200 athletes from 61 countries taking part. East bloc countries sent entries to the Paralympics for the first time, joining in the quest for 732 gold medals in 16 sports. The ideals of the Paralympics were expressed in the slogans "Challenge and Overcoming," "Peace and Friendship" and "Participation and Equality."

The president of the International Olympic Committee, Juan Antonio Samaranch, made his first visit to a Paralympics during the Seoul competition and heard an appeal for the participation of disabled athletes in the regular Olympic Games.

In the eyes of many—both at home and abroad—the success of the Seoul Olympics was seen as a giant milestone that moved Korea to stage center among major countries. Linked directly with the country's phenomenal economic strides, the sports spectacle provided a vivid view of the achievements of a country that only a few decades ago had been ravaged by war. *Hodori,* the Korean tiger cub that served as the official mascot of the games, became a symbol of a job done well.

Sports Activities

National Events

The National Sports Festival is held every October for participants from all over the nation. It is a national version of the Olympics and includes 27 categories of events. The festival serves as a springboard for the dynamic development of Korean athletic competitiveness. The meets are held on a rotation basis in all major cities, including Seoul, Pusan, Taegu, Kwangju and Inch'ŏn, making it a truly national competition. The festival is open also to all Korean communities abroad.

The Children's National Sports Festival, held since 1972, is another major event which contributes greatly to the development of the Korean sporting spirit. This sports festival for budding primary and middle school students has produced thousands of talented athletes to represent Korea in future international athletic events, including the Olympics and Asian Games. This children's sports meet annually draws more than 7,000 boys and girls from 15 cities and provinces, and like the National

Sports Festival, is held on a rotation basis in Seoul and other major cities.

The National Winter Sports Festival, held every January, includes figure skating, skiing, ice hockey and biathlon. Seoul has two major ice rinks, the T'aenŭng International Ice Rink and the Seoul Indoor Sports Center. Skiing events take place at Yong-p'yŏng and Taegwallyŏng in mountainous Kangwon-do Province and Ch'ŏnmasan in Kyŏnggi-do Province. Aside from the national competition, there are numerous skiing contests in January and February. Snow-making equipment has extended the Korean skiing season to four months instead of the previous two months.

Another annual event is the National Sports Festival for the Handicapped. Held each year since 1981, it brings together people from over the country and provides the opportunity for them to demonstrate their own special skills. The 13th festival, held in 1993, drew 1,700 participants.

Youth

The number of Korean youths ranging from nine to 24 years of age has increased steadily, reaching 13.6 million in 1991, 31 percent of Korea's total population. Responding to this trend, in June 1991, the Government completed a 10-year plan called the "Basic Plan for Korean Youth'„ and is now implementing many policies to provide hopes and dreams to Korean youth and help them build secure, valuable and meaningful lives.

The Korea Youth Institute was established in July 1989. Various programs were implemented by the Government in order to develop diverse youth programs to meet their unique demand and to guide them, the leaders of the next generation, on the right track.

In addition, various facilities are to be constructed every year with the aim of providing the youths with numerous opportunities for the training of their minds and bodies and to help them enjoy their leisure time. In accord with this, the Government will invest its time and the necessary financial assistance in such projects as youth leadership training, development of

sound programs for youths and a fund-raising campaign for youth education and other related work.

Civic Youth Organizations

The National Council of Youth Organization in Korea has carried out various programs for young people through its 30 or so member organizations since its establishment in December 1965. Some of its main tasks are to increase cooperation between member organizations, train youth leaders and support international exchange programs for youths with the aim of helping sound development.

During the Olympic Youth Camp held in connection with the 1988 Seoul Olympics, a total of 882 young people from 43 countries took part and shared friendships and mutual understanding through such programs as cultural exchanges, entertainment programs and lodging at private residences.

The Boy Scouts of Korea hosted an eight-day, world-wide youth festival, the 17th World Jamboree, in Kangwon-do province's Kosŏng county starting from August 8, 1991. 19,081 scouts from 133 countries around the world attended the jamboree. A total of 110,000 people shared friendship and participated in 37 different kinds of activities, including folk displays and repelling.

The Government formed a World Jamboree Support Committee and provided financial and administrative support to the event, providing management, expenses, medical treatment, sanitation facilities, and transportation, not to mention direct support provided by the 4,500 members of the committee itself. The world's leaders of the 21st century were able to mix and make friends at the 17th World Jamboree despite differences in race, language, religion, and national customs. The jamboree contributed greatly to the sense of international brotherhood of these young men as well as fostering a positive spirit of cooperation.

Facilities

Good playgrounds and equipment are essen-

The Olympic Stadium, surrounded by other sporting facilities in the Seoul Sports Complex.

tial for encouraging sports, turning out first-class athletes and contributing to the general improvement of the health of all.

There are a large number of national athletic facilities in Korea, scattered in civic areas, schools and workplaces, used by local residents and employees. Specifically, there are 127 stadium-size playgrounds, representing 62 percent of all cities and districts, and 111 gymnasiums representing 54 percent.

The Government is planning to construct one playground and one gymnasium per city or district. It also has now opened all Olympic facilities to the public with the goal of increasing interest and boosting sports enthusiasm among the people.

Two facilities playing an important role in these plans and programs are the Seoul Sports Complex and the Olympic Park, both located in southeastern Seoul just south of the Han-gang River.

The Seoul Sports Complex, occupying a land area of 545,000 square meters, was completed in September 1984. It includes two gymnasiums for basketball and boxing, an indoor swimming

pool, a baseball park and warm-up fields. Its highlight feature is the Olympic Stadium, which has a seating capacity of 100,000 and which was the site for the elaborate, colorful opening and closing ceremonies of both the Asian Games and the Olympics, as well as the center for track and field and other competition.

The huge Olympic Park covers an area of 2,175,000 square meters with venue sites occupying 1,674,300 square meters. It includes a velodrome with a seating capacity of 6,000, three gymnasiums with a combined seating capacity of 26,000, an indoor swimming pool that can accommodate 10,000 spectators, and 18 hard-surface tennis courts with seating for 15,000 fans. Also constructed for the Olympics were an equestrian park in the suburbs of Seoul, a regatta course on the Han-gang River and a yachting marina in Pusan, the large port city on the southern tip of the peninsula.

A key training facility for the country's sports competitors is the T'aenŭng Athletes Village located in the eastern outskirts of Seoul. Built on a 7.2-hectare site in the midst of a beautifully wooded area, the village includes a skating rink,

Sporting facilities in the Olympic Park in Seoul.

an indoor swimming pool, a shooting range and gymnasiums for wrestling, boxing and weightlifting. The training camp also has six dormitories that can accommodate 578 persons, billets for foreign coaches, strength-measurement equipment and a medical facility with a dispensary. The camp also houses a coaching academy, where advanced athletic training techniques are studied.

A second training center, a branch of the T'aenŭng Athletes Village, was opened in 1984 in the southern port city of Chinhae. It was designed to facilitate training during the winter season.

Organizations

Korea Amateur Sports Association

The Korea Amateur Sports Association was established July 13, 1920, and existed until it was forcibly disbanded by the Japanese on July 4, 1938. However, after Korea's liberation at the end of the World War II, the KASA was reestablished November 26, 1945.

Some of the major goals of the KASA are to take the lead in uniting the people through sports, inspiring them to be actively involved in sports, discovering talented young athletes as early as possible, and training them to compete in international sports events in the future, thereby bringing recognition in sports to Korea and its athletes throughout the world.

As of 1990, there were 44 amateur sports organizations registered with the Korea Amateur Sports Association.

Korean Olympic Committee (KOC)

The aim of this committee is to promote and spread the Olympic spirit, undertake negotiations with the International Olympic Committee (IOC) and other international organizaions, and conduct affairs pertaining to the dispatch of Korean delegations to the Olympic Games and Asian Games.

Korea has had six IOC members since Yi Ki-bung was first elected to the post in 1955. Kim

Un-yong was elected to the IOC in a meeting in Lausanne in October 1986 to replace Pak Chong-kyu, who died in 1985. The other IOC members have been Yi Sang-paek, Chang Ki-young and Kim T'aek-su, all of whom have passed away.

The Korean University Sport Board (KUSB), affiliated with the International University Sports Federation (FISU), is a special committee of the KOC.

Seoul Olympic Sports Promotion Foundation

The Seoul Olympic Sports Promotion Foundation (SOSFO), expanded from the former National Sports Promotion Foundation, was established on April 20, 1989. About US$430 million, inherited mostly from existing funds from the National Sports Promotion Foundation and profits from the Olympics, were raised as a basic fund to operate the SOSFO.

This foundation is responsible for supporting research to promote national sports and for the expansion of national athletic facilities. It also takes a lead in facilitating the training of athletic leaders and granting funds to enhance the welfare of retired athletes. The SOSFO plays a key role in organizing various activities to commemorate the Seoul Olympics.

Sports Categories

Archery

Archery in Korea dates back to the misty days of pre-history, with the founder-king of the Koguryŏ Kingdom being the first recorded expert archer. From a skill for hunting and warfare, archery has developed into a sport for fun, but its traditional importance is symbolized by the fact that three bow makers have been designated a human cultural properties.

Interest in archery gained sudden enthusiasm when Kim Jin-ho, a young high school girl, won the individual Asian crown in December 1978 in the Bangkok Asian Games and then in July 1979 went on to the 30th World Archery Championships in Berlin to win five out of six gold medals.

Korea garnered one gold and one bronze medal in archery at the 1984 Los Angeles Summer Olympics. At the 24th Olympiad in Seoul in 1988, Korean archers won three gold medals in the men's team, women's individual and women's team events; two silver medals in men and women's individual; and one bronze in women's individual competition. Kim Soo-nyung, already a two-gold medalist in the 1988 Olympics, demonstrated her skill again with two gold medals in the women's team and individual events in the 35th FITA World Archery Championships held in July 1989.

Cho Yun-jung and Kim Soo-nyung won the gold and silver medals in the women's 70-meter individual event at the Barcelona Olympics in 1992. Korea also garnered the women's team gold, making Cho a double gold medalist in Barcelona, and Kim a record Olympic medalist with three golds and one silver. As a result of these successes, Korea is now recognized as one of the strongest nations in the field of archery.

Badminton

Korean badminton got off to a full-fledged start when the Korean Badminton Association was established to promote it as a nationwide sport. The first national tournament was held in December 1957; now there are five national tournaments each year.

In the 1980s, Korean badminton underwent growth in international competition. In 1981 Hwang Sun-ae won the women's singles in the All England Open Championships, one of the major tournaments in the world. Koreans also took two championship titles in the 4th World Badminton Championships at Calgary, Canada.

At the 1988 Olympic Games in Seoul, badminton was a demonstration sport. In Barcelona, where badminton became an official sport of the Olympic Games, Korea won two gold medals in men's and women's doubles. In 1991, Korean won three gold medals at the 7th World Badminton Championships and at the 2nd Sudriman Cup Badminton Championships.

Baseball

Baseball was first played by YMCA staff and students at the German Language Institute in Korea in 1906 and soon became popular. Baseball is one of the leading sports events in Korea, at least in terms of the numbers of spectators, and baseball stadiums in Seoul are always packed with crowds whenever there are professional baseball leagues and nationwide highschool baseball tournaments in weekend. College baseball has been gaining in popularity recently as well. At present, there are eight teams in the Korean Amateur Business Baseball League and there are more than 500 amateur baseball clubs throughout the nation.

In 1982, the Korean team won the 27th World Baseball Championships held in Seoul, upsetting such power houses as the United States and Japan.

A professional baseball league was inaugurated in 1982 with the participation of six teams and has met with much enthusiasm. A seventh team was formed in 1986 and an eighth in 1989.

Basketball

Basketball was brought to Korea in 1903 by an American named Gillet, and by 1920, it was being played nationwide. It is popular among both men and women, and Korean teams have a reputation of being among the best in Asia, although recently they have been receiving a serious challenge from other Asian nations, including the People's Republic of China, which won gold medals in both men's and women's basketball at the 10th Asian Games in 1986.

Nevertheless, Korea has a strong history in basketball, having taken second place at the World Basketball Championships for Women in Czechoslovakia in 1967 and fourth place at the World Championship Games in 1971. In 1979, Korea hosted the Eighth World Basketball Championships for women at the newly dedicated Seoul Sports Complex Gymnasium. Twelve teams participated with the United States winning the gold medal, Korea the silver and Canada the bronze. The Korean women's basketball team won a silver medal in the Los Angeles Olympic Games in 1984, but both the men and women were disappointed by their silver medals in the 10th Asian Games.

As of September 1986, a total of 3,459 registered athletes were taking part in the sport in addition to other students and factory and office workers. There are many basketball facilities scattered across the country, and enthusiasm for the sport extends to primary school students who have their own games.

Boxing

The first recorded boxing match in Korea took place in 1912. Today it is one of the most popular sports in Korea and is watched by millions of fans. There is rigid division between professional and amateur boxing, each having its own association and rules. Nineteen Korean professional boxers have won world titles since Kim Ki-su took the World Boxing Association (WBA) junior middleweight title in 1966, and as of April 1993, Korea held four world titles. Korean pro boxers also held eight of the 15 titles of the Orient Pacific Boxing Federation (OPBF), and a handful of Koreans are pressing for shots at other world titles.

Since the London Olympic Games in 1948, Korean boxers have won three gold, five silver, and eight bronze medals. These include two golds, one silver and one bronze garnered in the 1988 Seoul Summer Olympics.

In the Asian Games, more than half of the boxing championships have been won by Korean boxers. For example, at the Ninth Asian Games in 1982, Korean boxers won gold medals in six different weight divisions and in 1986, Korean boxers swept all 12 weight divisions.

Cycling

Cycling was introduced to Korea at the turn of the century, and the first cycling competition was held in 1906. It became popular in the mid-1910s after an all-Korea Championships in 1913. Cho Duk-heang won a bronze medal at

Professional soccer and baseball, started in 1983 and 1982 respectively, have become two of the most popular sports in Korea.

the World Junior Championships in 1982 and Shin Dae-chul also won a bronze in the individual road race at the Universiad in 1983. In 1985, Korean cyclists swept the 12th Asian Championships with 11 gold medals. Korea placed second at the 15th Asian Championships held in Beijing in 1991 garnering four gold, three silver and six bronze medals, while the younger Koreans won first place at the Junior Championships held concurrently.

There are more than 300,000 people who enjoy speed cycling, but only about 700 are registered with the Korean Cycling Competition League as participants.

Football (Soccer)

The most popular game in Korea is football. First brought to Korea in 1882 by the crew of a British warship, the popularity of the game increased in the 1920s and reached a peak shortly after 1945. Korea is a leader in Asian soccer, having won regional events more often than most other countries, including the gold medal in the 1986 Asian Games.

Korea has hosted the President's Cup Football Tournament annually since 1971, contributing to the improvement of local teams and to the sport across Asia.

In July 1983, in what both Mexican organizing officials and experts called "the biggest upset in the world youth soccer championship history" Korea reached the semi-finals in the 4th World Youth Football Championship by crushing the perennial power house, Uruguay, in the quarter finals. Though they failed to advance to the finals, Korean players earned the admiration of fans around the world by their impressive performance.

Korea and Iraq represented the Asian region in the World Cup Football Tournament held in Mexico in 1986 in which the world's 24 top teams took part. Though they were defeated in the first round, the Korean players made strong showings against Argentina and Italy. In the Rome World Cup in 1990, Korea joined the United Arab Emirates to represent the Asian region, the two consecutive selections serving as testimony to the fact that Korean players have earned their ranking among the world's best.

To increase interest in professional-type football, the semi-professional Korean Super League was launched early in 1983. The league is patterned after the Korean pro baseball league and the pro-football leagues of foreign countries. The Super League was renamed Korean Pro Football League, and consists of six teams.

A number of Korean football stars have joined foreign pro teams. Most notable is Cha Pum-kun, who played for West German teams for about 10 years.

Golf

Before the Korean War broke out in 1950, Korean golfers numbered only 150, and in 1961 the number did not exceed 1,000. Now participation in the "royal and ancient sport" is estimated at 1.5 million people and is expected to grow steadily. With the improvement in the standard of living, golf is no longer regarded as a sport only for the privileged and well-to-do.

At present, there are 77 golf courses in Korea, usually called country clubs, which are managed on a membership system. In the 1986 Asian Games, Korea won a gold in the team event and a silver in the individual event.

Gymnastics

Gymnastics in Korea has moved into a take-off stage. In 1977, Korean girls outscored their Japanese counterparts in the annual high school exchange matches, the first time that the Koreans had defeated the Japanese, who consistently rank high in world gymnastics. Gymnastic techniques are being studied earnestly, and Korea's gymnasts have shown tremendous improvement in recent years, as demonstrated in the 1986 Asian Games, where they won a surprising three gold medals. In the 1988 Seoul Olympics, Pak Chong-hun won a bronze medal, the first Olympic medal for Korea in gymnastics. Yoo Ok-yul won two gold medals in the world gymnastic championships, in 1991 and again in 1992.

Handball

There was little interest in the sport of handball in Korea until the 1986 Seoul Asian Games when the Korean men's team came up with surprising skill and strength to take the gold medal.

Enthusiasm stirred by that performance led to wider participation, increased training and support for handball. That effort paid off handsomely in the 1988 Seoul Olympics, where the Korean women's team won the gold medal and the men's team the silver. The Korean women's team repeated the victory in the Barcelona Olympics defeating Norway in the final.

The increased interest in handball led to the selection of Korea as the host country for the 10th World Women's Championships in November 1990.

Field Hockey

Korean field hockey originated with the traditional Korean sport, *Kyŏkku*, which was played on horseback and in the field from the 11th century. During the Chosŏn Dynasty, it was spread widely among the people and was one of the requirements for selecting high-level warriors.

The first modern hockey tournament was held in December 1947. Since then Korean hockey players have developed rapidly. In the 1986 Seoul Asian Games, both men and women teams won gold medals. The women's team won the silver medal at the 1988 Seoul Olympics and first place in the World Championships held in the Netherlands in March 1989.

Judo

In ancient Korea, martial arts forms called *Subak* and *Kwonbŏp* called for the skilled use of barefists and the whole body. Exported to Japan in the 16th century, they were considered the forerunners of the sport of judo. Japanese judo, the refined and advanced development of the old Korean forms, was reintroduced to Korea in 1907 and has attracted the wide participation of Korean athletes and sports minded men and women.

Judo facilities have been set up in every part of the country. A judo college was established in Seoul and many high schools and colleges have judo clubs.

Korean judoists have turned in outstanding perfomances in Olympic competition and other events. They took one silver and two bronze medals in the 1976 Montreal Olympic Games; two gold medals in the 1984 Los Angeles Olympics; two golds and one silver in the 1988 Seoul Olympic Games, and one gold, one silver and two bronze medals in the 1992 Barcelona Olymiad. They also have won gold medals in the lightweight category in the World Championships and the World Junior Championships.

Mountaineering

The number of Korean mountaineers has skyrocketed in recent years, reaching over five million as of the end of 1992 in comparison with some 40,000 in 1962. At present, there are some 5,000 alpinist clubs throughout the country. Every mountain in the suburbs of a city, especially on weekends, is filled with hikers and mountaineers, including many older climbers in their 60s. Korean enthusiasm for climbing increased sharply when Ko Sang-don reached the rooftop of the world, Mt. Everest, in September 1977. Later, Jang Bong-won climbed the second highest, K-2, in 1986 and the highest, Everest, in September 1988.

Though Korea is a mountainous nation, it has no peak with height of more than 2,800 meters. But the Korean mountains have ample charm and attraction, as they invariably command breathtaking scenery.

Roller Skating

The Korean roller skating population has rolled past the one million mark, a figure compared to only a few hundreds in 1976. The Korea Roller Skating Association, which became affiliated with the Korea Amateur Sports Association in 1980, attributes the boom to the "global phenomenon," rapid urbanization, and a rapid increase in roller skating facilities. Currently there are more than 1,000 roller skating rinks in Korea. Numerous plazas, roadways and playgrounds near apartment complexes provide outdoor facilities for this popular sport.

Shooting

Owing to Korea's large military forces and to favorable topography, shooting has become a popular sport. Rifle contests are featured among military personnel and millions of retired military personnel, while skeet-shooting is largely the province of the well-to-do.

Korea hosted the 42nd World Shooting Championships in 1978, the first time for an Asian nation to take such a role. The T'aenŭng International Shooting Range, the site of the world tourney, has up-to-date facilities and beautiful natural surroundings. The Seoul tournament saw the use of an electronic scoring system for the first time for the 300-meter event.

During the First Asian Ladies and Junior Shooting Championships held in Seoul in September 1977, Korea's shooters won 36 of the 37 gold medals. Korea also successfully hosted the First World Airgun Shooting Championships in 1979. Korean shooters won three gold medals in the 1982 Asian Games and seven in 1986. In the 1988 Seoul Olympics, Cha Young-chul won a silver medal for the first time in the Olympic Games. In the 1992 Barcelona Olympics, Korea garnered two gold medals.

Skating

Winter sports were popular in Korea from the beginning of the 20th century until the division of the country in 1945. Because of climatic conditions, they enjoyed wider popularity in the northern part of the peninsula at that time.

In recent years, however, there has been increased interest in ice skating, both competitive and recreational, in the south despite a shorter winter season. This also has been true for other winter sports activities, but international recognition has come in skating.

An artificial skating rink with a 400-meter

track was built in Seoul in the early 1970s. At the end of the 1980s, a large indoor rink was constructed in the Mok-dong area of Seoul, and quickly became the site for performances by international stars. This renewed interest has resulted in an increase in the number of people going to skating areas for recreation, and in the achievements of Korean skaters in competitive events.

Among the most impressive of these competitors in 1990 was Bae Ki-tae, who won first place honors for combined events at the World Sprint Skating Championships in Troms, Norway, in February. In that same month, he took first place in the 500-meter competition at the World Speed Skating Championships in Innsbruck, Austria. In March 1990, Bae won the gold medals in the 1,000-meter and 1,500-meter and the silver in the 500-meter events at the Winter Asian Games in Sapporo, Japan.

At the first Winter Asian Games in Sapporo in 1986, Korean skaters took one gold, five silver and 12 bronze medals to place third in a field of seven countries. At the 16th Winter Olympic Games in 1992, Korea won a gold for the men's team, and a silver in the 500 meter competition. The Korean men's team won the 1992 World Short Track Championships in Japan, and garnered eight golds in individual races as well.

Skiing

Skiing, which originated in Finland in the Middle Ages as a military skill, was brought to Korea in the 1920s by a foreign missionary. Just a decade ago, it was the sport of only a handful of the well-to-do or youngsters who lived near the hilly slopes of Kangwon-do Province, but in recent years the situation has changed. The number of skiers is increasing annually and is now estimated at about 1,300,000. Ski resorts now are equipped with snow-making machines, which have extended the skiing season to four months—December to March—from the previous two months.

Ssirŭm

Ssirŭm, a form of wrestling, has been popular in Korea since early days. Judging from a mural found in a Koguryŏ tomb, it is believed that *ssirŭm* was originated about 1,500 years ago. The word itself is an ancient one, meaning "competition of man."

Because of the simplicity of its rules, Korean farmers and fishermen delight in this sport. Today, it is part of physical education courses in middle and high schools.

Ssirŭm was a must in the festive programs of the traditional Tano holiday falling on the fifth day of the fifth lunar month, with the winner of the contest accorded the title "Super Strong Man." A big bull was traditionally awarded as the prize.

Ssirŭm used to be played without consideration given to the weight of the contestants, but competition is now by divisions, according to the weight of the wrestler.

The Korea *Ssirŭm* Association has succeeded in generating a nationwide boom in *ssirŭm* by sponsoring the "Top Super Strong Man Competition" three times a year and the "Super Strong Man Contest" by weight division four times annually. *Ssirŭm* has, as a result, become one of the most popular spectator sports in Korea.

Swimming

Before the 1970 Asian Games, interest in competitive swimming was relatively low in Korea. Then two Korean swimmers won three gold medals in that major regional event and enthusiasm developed rapidly. This has been demonstrated by increases in both skill and the number of swimmers.

Various national, regional and international events have spurred the interest in competitive swimming, while swimming for fun and as a means of physical conditioning has become more and more popular with large numbers of the population. During the summer months, seaside and river areas along with outdoor pools are crowded, while a number of indoor pools

Ssirŭm, *traditional Korean wrestling, has gone professional (left); Hyun Jung-hwa, women's singles champion at the 42nd World Table Tennis Championships in 1993 (right).*

make swimming a year-round sport.

A number of promising teenage aspirants are making their debut in this sport each year, and new records are being made and broken every season.

In the 1982 New Delhi Asian Games, Choe Yun-hui, a young junior high school girl, won three gold medals, two for the backstroke. She repeated her performance in Seoul in the Asian Games of 1986, winning two gold medals. Cho Oh-ryun, who captured four gold medals in two Asian Games, succeeded in swimming across the Strait of Korea in 1980 and the English Channel in 1982.

Table Tennis

In recent years, Asian table tennis has received increased attention and acclaim. As in other countries of the region, there is great enthusiasm for the game in Korea. Since it was introduced in the 1920s, Korean table tennis developed year by year, climaxing in 1973 when the Korean women's team won the World Table Tennis Championships in Sarajevo, Yugoslavia.

Since then, Korean women have advanced to the finals of the world championships in 1975, 1977 and 1981, only to be beaten by China. In the 1983 championships, they brought home only one silver medal in the singles event and in 1985 a bronze in the team event.

In the 1986 Asian Games, the Korean team surprised the table tennis world and the "unbeatable" Chinese by winning three of the seven gold medals in the men's singles, men's team, and women's team events. Riding high on a wave of enthusiasm, the Koreans won two gold medals, one silver and one bronze in the 1988 Seoul Olympics. In the 1990 Beijing Asian Games, the men's team and the women's team each took home a gold medal. The Korean women won a gold at the 1991 World Championships as well. After winning five bronze medals at the Barcelona Olympics in 1992, the Koreans followed this up with four medals at the 1993 world Championships, highlighted by Hyun Jung-hwa's gold medal in the women's singles

T'aekwondo

T'aekwondo is a self-defense martial art that has developed in Korea for over 2,000 years. In

T'aekwŏndo, *a Korean martial art and* weightlifting.

recent times, t'aekwondo has become a Korean national sport and has spread swiftly to many foreign countries. Some 1,500 Korean instructors are teaching the sport in more than 100 countries.

In Korea, the T'aekwondo Association has a membership of about 3,500,000, constituting the largest affiliate of the Korea Amateur Sports Association. Kukkiwon is the headquarters of the World T'aekwondo Federation (WTF), located in Seoul. The WTF was officially approved as the world controlling body of the sport by the International Olympic Committee in 1980.

There have been seven world championships since 1973; the first two and the seventh were held in Seoul. The United States, West Germany, Ecuador and Denmark have hosted the other four. The Seventh World Championships in 1985 attracted 776 participants from 63 countries. Korea won seven of eight divisions, which was typical of its performance in all of the world championships.

The World Games under the auspices of the General Asssociation of International Sports Federations (GAISF) has included t'aekwondo in its official program. In the 1981 World Games in the United States, Korea won nine of 10 divisions, and in the 1985 Games in Britain, Korea won seven of eight divisions.

T'aekwondo was adopted as regular event in the 10th Asian Games, and Korea's athletes again demonstrated their dominance by winning seven of eight gold medals. T'aekwondo was a demonstration sport in the 1988 Seoul Olympics, heightening its popularity around the world.

Tennis

Introduced to Korea around the turn of the 20th century, tennis has become a highly popular participant sport for people of all ages. A tennis club was formed in Seoul in 1902. There now are more than 120 private tennis clubs in Seoul area alone, along with a number of others not run for profit. Other tennis facilities often are found as part of the sprawling apartment complexes in southern Seoul and other areas.

Korea's tennis players have reached the level where they can begin to compete in international ranked games. While Korea's women outshone the men in earlier Asian Games, it was the men who excelled in the 1986 Seoul Games, winning four gold medals to the women's one. The men then went on in the same week to defeat Japan for the first time in the Davis Cup regional preliminaries to qualify for the world round.

Track and Field

The track and field competition, considered by many to be the premier events of the international sports scene, was introduced to Korea in the early part of the 20th century. By the 1920s and 1930s, a number of outstanding long-distance runners had been produced, even though a nationwide athletics association was not formed until 1945, when the close of World War II brought an end to Japan's colonial rule.

The track highlight of those early years took place at the 1936 Olympic Games in Berlin, where two Korean runners, Sohn Kee-chung and Nam Sŭng-yong, took the gold and bronze medals for first and third places in the marathon. Because of Japan's colonial domination, however, they were forced to compete under the Japanese flag, not that of their own homeland. Sohn, the gold medalist, was able to recapture some of that denied glory for Korea at the 1988 Seoul Olympic Games when he was the runner designated to make the triumphal entry into the packed stadium bearing the Olympic torch.

The Boston Marathon of 1947 was won by Sŏ Yun-bok, another Korean runner, and Koreans swept first, second and third places in the Boston Marathon of 1950. Hwang Young-cho restored Korea's old fame capturing the gold medal in men's marathon in the 1992 Barcelona Olympiad.

The 1986 Asian Games in Seoul saw Korean athletes take seven gold medals in track and field. Four of them were in men's competition

in the 200-meter run, 800-meter and 1,500-meter events and the long jump.

In the women's events, outstanding performances were turned in by a young Korean woman, Lim Chun-ae, who won gold medals in 800-meter, 1,500-meter and 3,000-meter races.

With world spotlights centering on Korea as a result of the 1986 Asian Games and the 1988 Summer Olympics, Seoul was selected as the host city for the 4th World Junior Athletic Championships in June 1992 with track and field stars from 160 countries.

Volleyball

Volleyball was introduced to Korea in 1917 through the YMCA, and the first national game was held in 1925. The skill of Korean players has improved rapidly since the Fifth Asian Games in 1966, when both Korean men's and women's teams won second places.

The Korean women's volleyball team captured a bronze medal in the Montreal Olympics in 1976, trailing the Soviet Union and Japan. It was the first Olympic medal the Koreans had ever won in a ball game. In 1977 and 1981, Korean girls took the championships in the first and the second World Junior Volleyball Games. In 1980, Korea hosted the first Asian Junior Volleyball Championships and Korean boys and girls both clinched gold medals, defeating pre-tournament favorite Japan. In the 1986 Asian Games, Korea's men won a silver and the women a bronze medal.

Korea's performance in recent years has prompted a number of foreign countries to invite Korean coaches to train their players. They included West Germany, Canada, Mexico, Peru, Argentina, Egypt and some Middle East countries.

Weightlifting

Since its introduction to Korea in late 1920s, weightlifting became popular throughout the country. The Korea Weightlifting Federation was formed in 1936.

When Korea took part in 1948 London Olympics, a weightlifter took a bronze medal, the first time ever for a Korean to win a prize in an international game under the Korean flag. In the Seoul Olympics, Korea garnered one silver and one bronze medal, and in Barcelona in 1992, Korea took one gold medal. The Barcelona gold medalist Chun Byung-kwan won another gold in the World Championships the same year and his compatriots added two more bronze medals.

Wrestling

Wrestling was introduced in Korea in 1935 by a Korean student who had returned home from Japan. It has produced some top-flight participants and drawn an enthusiastic following in both freestyle and Greco-Roman style competition.

Korea took two gold medals in wrestling at the 1984 Los Angeles Olympics and nine in the 1986 Asian Games. In the 1988 Olympics, Korean wrestlers secured two golds, two silvers and five bronzes, and in the 1990 Asian Games, eleven gold medals out of twenty went to Korean wrestlers. In the 1992 Barcelona Olympics, Korea won two gold medals, one silver and one bronze.

Yachting

Yachting was introduced in Korea in 1932 by American missionaries, but was not an active sport until the Korea Yachting Association was formed in 1978. The Association dispatched a Korean team to the World OK Dinghy-Class Yachting Championships held in Sweden in 1980, the Korean yachtmen's first participation in an international yachting contest.

Since Korea has the appropriate natural settings and improved yacht production technology, observers believe yachting will grow both as a leisure and competitive sport. Its popularity was boosted by the construction of a marina in the southern port city of Pusan for the 1986 Asian Games and the 1988 Olympics. Korea won two gold medals in yachting at the Asian Games.

TOURISM

Overview

Rich natural beauty combined with a unique historical and cultural heritage makes Korea a place of delightful discovery for the travelers from abroad.

Spurred by the spectacular Seoul Olympics in 1988, the tourist industry has grown rapidly in recent years. More growth is foreseen as Korea moves to expand its contacts and relationships with all parts of the world.

Foreign tourist receipts in 1992 totaled US$3,259 million, a 4.9 percent decrease from the previous year. The number of foreign visitors increased from 84,216 in 1967 to 3,231,081 in 1992. The number of hotel rooms increased 35 times, from 1,244 in 1963 to 43,401 in 1992.

Tourism officials list 431 hotels across the country that meet international standards for rooms and dining facilities, many of which are part of an international reservations system. In Seoul, there are 11 hotels listed in the super deluxe category. They are the Inter-Continental, Lotte, Lotte World, Shilla, Hyatt Regency, Ramada Renaissance, Hilton International, Plaza, Sheraton Walker Hill, Swiss Grand and Westin Chosun.

The rapid development of Korea's tourist industry is seen as a natural sequel to this country's dramatic economic growth. To support this important industry, the Korean Government enacted a series of tourism promotion laws which resulted in a growth rate of 11.1 percent annually in tourist arrivals in the last decade, and a rate of 23.6 percent in tourist receipts from 1983 to 1992.

The increased number of tourists has outstripped that of other groups of visitors. In 1969, tourists accounted for 30.2 percent of the total, business people 12 percent, people visiting relatives and friends 21 percent and official visitors 21.3 percent. But in 1992, 57.6 percent of foreign arrivals were tourists, 10.9 percent were visiting relatives or friends, 11.2 percent were on business and 0.7 percent were official visitors.

The tourist count in 1970 showed that 32 percent or 55,000 were Americans, with the Japanese making up the second largest group. After that year, however, the number of tourists from Japan began to increase rapidly. In 1992, visitors from the Asia made up 70.7 percent of the total, followed by North and South America, mainly the United States, with 11.2 percent. The influx of Japanese was in large part responsible for the shift in the tourist arrival picture. The increase was attributed to geographic proximity, a similarity of culture and a lesser language barrier, along with increased economic links between Korea and Japan.

The rapid growth in tourism brought increased activity in related sectors such as tour operations, facilities and sites, all boosting the demand for trained, multi-lingual personnel. To help meet such needs, more than 70 universities and colleges offer majors in hotel administration and related tourist fields.

Looking to a continuing expansion of tourism, there have been a number of plans and programs to explore, develop and enlarge tourist resources and facilities in such areas as hotel accommodations, land, sea and air transportation, tourist services, national parks, museums, golf courses and casinos. Governmental financial help for tourism has been extensive and is expected to grow.

Most tourism development and promotion projects are spearheaded by the Korea National Tourism Corporation, which has several multi-million dollar projects under way both in the cities and provinces.

Government regulations are constantly reviewed and revised to accommodate the needs and desires of tourists. Many necessities and souvenir items of both domestic and foreign origin are available tax free. Increasing numbers of tourist guides, proficient in English, Japanese, and other languages, are being trained and employed.

The following is an outline of some of the tourism resources in and around Seoul and throughout the country, as well as transportation and other travel information.

Airlines

Korea is connected with just about every major capital in the world, either with direct flights or with connecting flights at major international airports throughout East Asia. There are about 600 flights in and out of Korea weekly. The following airlines serve Seoul on regular schedules: Aeroflot Russian Airlines, Air France, Alitalia Airlines, All Nippon Airways, Asiana Airlines, British Airways, Cathay Pacific Airways, Continental Airlines, Delta Airlines, Federal Express, Garuda Indonesia Airways, Japan Airlines, Japan Air System, KLM Royal Dutch Airlines, Korean Air, Lufthansa German Airlines, Malaysian Airlines, Nippon Cargo Airlines, Northwest Airlines, Philippine Airlines, Qantas Airways, Singapore Airlines, Swiss Air Transports, Thai Airways International, United Airlines, VASP Brazilian Airlines.

The flight from Tokyo to Seoul takes two hours. Korean and Japanese airlines connect Tokyo, Osaka, Nagoya, Fukuoka, Sapporo, and seven other Japanese cities with Pusan, Seoul and Chejudo Island.

From Hong Kong, passengers can fly direct to Seoul via Cathay Pacific Airways, Asiana Airlines, British Airway, Thai Airways International and Korean Air. Korean Air has opened new routes between Seoul and destinations in Europe, including Moscow, the U.S., and the Middle East.

Since 1963, Seoul has been included in the round-the-world air schedule approved by the International Air Transport Association (IATA). This permits any passenger on a round-the-world ticket to visit Korea at no additional charge.

Domestic air transport service is also provided by Korean Air, connecting Seoul with Taegu, Pusan, Kwangju, Sokch'o, Yŏsu, Chinju, Kangnŭng, Ulsan, P'ohang and Chejudo Island. Korean Air also connects Chejudo with Pusan, Taegu, Kwangju, Chinju, and Yŏsu. A second private line, Asiana, began operating in 1988 with domestic flights and service to cities in Japan, U.S., and Southeast Asia.

Steamship Lines

Several steamship lines provide passenger service to Korea. Among those from the American West Coast are Waterman Steamship, American Pioneer, Pacific Far East, Pacific Orient Express, States Marine and United States Lines.

The Pugwan Ferry travels between Pusan and Shimonoseki, Japan, everyday except Saturday. The Kukche Ferry links Kobe, Japan, with Pusan while the Korea Ferry and the Korea Marine Express serve between Pusan and Hakada, Japan. The Ch'ŏnjin Ferry started serving between Inch'ŏn and Tianjin and Weihai, China. There also are cargo-passenger ships linking Japanese ports with Korea.

Railways Service

The Korean National Railroad runs three kinds of express trains: super, special and regular. Super express trains link Seoul with Pusan, Mokp'o, Kyŏngju, Kwangju and Yŏsu. From Seoul, it takes four hours and 10 minutes to Pusan, four hours and 58 minutes to Mokp'o, four hours and 15 minutes to Kyŏngju, four hours and 10 minutes to Kwangju, and five hours and 45 minutes to Yŏsu. The super and special express trains have dining cars, and Pullman cars are connected to all night express trains. Local trains, which make frequent stops, are also available.

Guided Tour Services

Guided tours around Seoul and other scenic places and historical sites are offered regularly by the Korea Tourist Bureau and other tourist services. A variety of tours are available, including morning, afternoon and night tours, as well as nationwide tours of a week or more duration.

Shopping Guide

Tourists may purchase tax-free souvenir items at any of the hundreds of shops in the

1994 marks the 600th anniversary of Seoul's designation as the nation's capital. Originally Known as Hansŏng during the Chosŏn Dynasty, it was renamed Kyŏngsŏng after the Japanese Annexation in1910, and finally Seoul in 1945.

modern department stores or shopping arcades in Seoul and major cities throughout the country. Prices are fixed.

Among the most popular souvenirs are traditional furniture, lacquerware, brassware, leatherware, ceramics, jewelry, gold, silver and bronze articles, dolls and ginseng.

Artistically designed and expertly crafted jewelry of smoky topaz, amethyst, amber, jade and other semiprecious stones are available at reasonable prices. Lacquerware, produced in many colors and intricately inlaid with silver, brass, or multicolored mother-of-pearl, is especially appealing to tourists. Seoul's East Gate Market is famous for satin, damask, brocade, and other silks.

Currency

Korea's monetary unit is the won, which is easily exchanged for U.S. dollars, Hong Kong dollars, Japanese yen and British sterling as well as other foreign currencies at banks and major tourist hotels. The basic rate of conversion, sub-

ject to change by fluctuation in the market, was about 800 won for one US dollar in mid-1993.

Korea's currency comes in 1,000, 5,000, and 10,000 won bills, and in 1, 5, 10, 50, 100, and 500 won coins.

Seoul: Historic Walled City

Established a hundred years before Columbus discovered the Americas, Seoul, the Korean capital, is an ancient city by New World standards. But compared with the antiquity of Korean history, Seoul is a relatively young.

Once the seat of kings, Seoul now is the hub of the entire nation, with a population of more than 10 million. Its rich ancient culture is readily accessible to visitors. Seoul has been the center of educational opportunities, professional training and leadership in Korea. Living in Seoul still engenders personal prestige, and so, throughout the centuries, young and old have

The photograph is a cityscape of Seoul, today.

converged on the city, taking part in a historical drama staged since the 15th century.

Into Seoul's rich history, a heritage has been woven which is evidenced by palaces, shrines, and monuments found over the city. For both the serious student of Korean history and the casual sightseer, Seoul holds a wealth of lore about Korea and its people. There are few cities in the world where the ultra-modern and the ancient exist side by side in such perfect harmony.

Today, Seoul is a teeming metropolis with many first-class Western-style hotels. English is spoken at many shops, bars, and restaurants. Just a few steps from many hotels in the center of the city is Tŏksugung Palace, which is now a public park. Its ancient tile-roofed throne hall and annex buildings, where the king once received foreign envoys, and two stately Grecian-style buildings are nestled in the shadows of new high-rise office buildings, a perfect example of Seoul's unique blend of old and new.

In the National Museum, located in front of Kyŏngbokkung Palace, the visitor can see priceless treasures of Korea's antiquity. Not far away in Ch'angdŏkkung Palace royal momentoes can be seen, including furnished rooms where Korea's kings and their families once lived. Adjacent to Ch'angdŏkkung Palace is Piwon, the Secret Garden, a lovely expanse of intertwining paths linking wooded slopes, lotus ponds, and pavilions.

Just east of the Secret Garden is Ch'anggyŏnggung Palace, a detached palace in ancient times. It was transformed into an amusement park in the early part of the 1900s, but it has been restored.

Seoul hosts a variety of symphony concerts, operas, and recitals by local and visiting musicians. The Seoul Arts Center in the southern part of Seoul, the Sejong Cultural Center, located on the main thoroughfare in downtown Seoul, the National Theatre in Namsan Park, and the Hoam Art Hall near the City Hall offer a wide range of cultural programs and performances.

Korea House, located near the center of the

Ch'angdŏkkung Palace.

city, is an old-style Korean mansion which provides further insight into Korean traditions and customs. Expertly prepared Korean-style meals are available, as are programs of folk music and dancing. A visit to Korea House is especially worthwhile for those with only a little time to spare.

The Palaces and Seoul's Heritage

Much of Seoul's special lure and charm centers on its palaces, which represent a colorful history of more than 500 years.

For the average tourist on a tight schedule, a half-day visit to one of the palaces can be highly rewarding. The palaces are the most obvious sightseeing attractions in the capital, and all are conveniently located near the downtown area. For a brief moment, a visitor may catch glimpses of Korea's heritage from the worn stone-paved paths, intricately patterned murals, and the clay figures which sit on roof ridges in eternal vigilance, warding off evil.

Palaces

Kyŏngbokkung Palace, located at the north end of Sejongno Street, was first built in 1394, the third year of the Chosŏn Dynasty. It was burned during the Japanese invasion of 1592, and left in ruins until it was rebuilt in 1868. It is located in a 40-acre complex and is comprised of a number of large, impressive buildings. Kŭnjŏngjŏn, the largest palace building, served as the throne chamber and audience hall. Kyŏnghoeru, a spacious, two-story pavilion that seems to float in a man-made pond, served as a banquet hall for royal ministers and diplomatic delegations. Hyang-wonjŏng, nestled in the center of a lotus pond, was the place where royal fami-

Kyŏnghoeru pavillion in Kyŏngbokkung Palace.

ly members enjoyed private occasions. Many of the country's historic stone pagodas and monuments are displayed in various parts of the complex. Also within the walled grounds and of interest to many visitors are the National Museum of Korea and the National Folklore Museum.

A short distance away is *Ch'angdŏkkung Palace*, another favorite tourist spot. Its main gate, Tonhwamun, is considered possibly the oldest gate in the capital city. It escaped the flames when major portions of the palace were burned during the Japanese invasion of 1592. Rebuilt in 1611, the palace was used as the official royal residence until 1910. To the present day, Naksŏnjae, a villa located on the palace grounds, serves as a residence for remaining members of the royal family. Piwon, the Secret Garden, also is a part of Ch'angdŏkkung. A serene woodland covering 78 acres, it was

reserved during the Chosŏn Dynasty for members of the royal family and palace women. It now is open to the public, but only through small, guided tours.

Just to the east of the Secret Garden is *Ch'anggyŏnggung Palace*, where visitors can get some idea of the way of life of the ancient royal family. In the restored palace complex are found well preserved gates and arched bridges from that earlier era. The king conducted affairs of state in a stone courtyard adjacent to the main halls of the palace. Behind the halls are the living quarters for the royal family.

Located across a broad traffic circle from City Hall is *Tŏksugung Palace*, a compound housing traditional Chosŏn Dynasty buildings and some impressive Western-style structures. They include Chunghwajŏn, the throne room or audience hall, and Sŏkchojŏn, a Renaissance style building that was the first of its kind in

Korea. It was in this palace that the Chosŏn Dynasty, which ruled Korea for more than 500 years, drew to a tragic end when Japanese domination brought annexation of the peninsula in 1910. Tŏksugung originally was built as a royal villa to appease a grandson of Sejo, the seventh ruler of Chosŏn, who was passed over twice for the throne. The "Stone Palace," was built at the turn of the century according to a blueprint drafted by a British architect.

In a secluded garden in the heart of Seoul is found Chongmyo, a shrine housing ancestral tablets of Chosŏn Dynasty kings and their queens. On the first Sunday in May, the courtyards and shrine buildings are used for an annual Confucian ceremonial rite that is open to the public. The presentation is enacted by descendants of the royal Yi clan to keep alive the customs and traditions of that period.

Although not a palace site, also of interest in the center of Seoul is *T'apkol (*Pagoda*) Park*, a landmark in the struggle against Japanese colonial rule. It was in this park that the March First Independent Movement of 1919 was launched, a nation wide protest against Japanese domination. Brass plaques along the east side of the park tell the story of the movement and its suppression.

Suburban Seoul

While many of Korea's ancient treasures are located within short distances in Seoul, much to the visitor's convenience, there are many historical and cultural sites and relics in the outskirts of the capital. These include tombs and temples, crumbling fortifications and parts of walls that once surrounded and served to protect the old city.

Outside Seoul

Though Seoul is the center of government, culture, and art, the country's other large cities have much to offer and can provide a different perspective of Korea. These cities, starting with the largest in population, are: Pusan, the southern port; Taegu, the southern apple capital;

Ch'ojijin fortress on Kanghwado Island.

Inch'ŏn, Seoul's port city; Kwangju, the Chŏlla-do region's metropolis; and Taejŏn, Korea's center city.

Historic Kanghwado Island

For those wishing to leave the hustle and bus-tle of Seoul and view some of Korea's pastoral beauty, Kanghwado Island is recommended. Situated on the estuary of the Han-gang River north of Inch'ŏn, this fifth largest island of Korea is rich in history and natural beauty. The road is paved to Chŏndŭngsa, the island's largest temple and one of the 30 major temples in Korea. The driving time from Seoul to the temple is about one and a half hours. Express bus service is also available.

The entire spectrum of Korean history from the hazy era of Tan-gun, the legendary founder of the nation, to the opening of Korea to the Western world can be observed and studied on this island. In the 12th century, one of the major

kilns for making celadon pottery was located on Kanghwado Island.

Numerous fortresses were constructed along the mainland side of the island and a wall was built across the ridges of Mt. Munsusan. Remnants of these fortifications seen today date from the mid-13th century, when Kojong (the 23rd Koryŏ king) fled during the Mongol inva-sion from Songdo, the Koryŏ capital, to the island.

A short distance west of Kanghwa City, amid fields of ginseng, there can be found a prehis-toric dolmen. The remains of at least one more are nearby.

To the south of the city is the island's highest mountain, Manisan. At its summit is an altar believed to have been erected by Tan-gun, the mythical figure said to have established the Korean nation. Ancient records relate that Tan-gun was the son of a heavenly being named Hwanung who, while visiting earth, transformed a bear into a woman and married her. Tan-gun

P'anmunjŏm.

is said to have migrated from his birthplace on Mt. Paektusan south along the Yalu River to P'yŏngyang, where he established Korea's first capital.

On the southern part of the island is the famed temple of Chŏndŭngsa. Circumventing the temple grounds is a 1km fortress wall which was first built, according to legend, in a single day by the three sons of Tan-gun. Many elegant pines, gingko, and flowering cherry trees grace the mountain slopes near the temple. It is believed that a temple was first built in this valley during the early Koguryŏ period when Buddhism was introduced to the peninsula. However, a later temple came into prominence during the late Koryŏ era when Kojong commissioned the carving of the famous 81,258 wood blocks to print Buddhist scriptures known as the *Tripitaka Koreana.* The wood blocks are now preserved at Haeinsa Temple, near Taegu.

They were carved with the fervent prayer that Buddha would come to the aid of the Koryŏ people in driving out the invading Mongols. They are the oldest and best-preserved of any complete Buddhist scriptures in the world. King Kojong died while taking refuge on this island, and his grave can still be seen near Kanghwa City.

Chŏndŭngsa takes its name, which means "Inherited Lamp," from a jade lamp that Chŏnghwagung, the wife of Ch'ungyŏl-wang (the 25th Koryŏ king), presented to the temple. What became of the lamp is unknown.

The temple also boasts three national treasures: a 900-year-old bell of Chinese origin and two buildings, Taeungbojŏn and Yaksajŏn. Under the eaves of the four corners of the Taeungbojŏn are rather curious human figures squatting with their knees under their chins. Each face portrays an anguished look. These

The Korean Folk Village.

carved wooden images are the only ones of their kind in Korea.

P'anmunjŏm: Symbol of a Divided Land

Located only 56.35km from Seoul, P'anmunjŏm is a grim reminder of the 1950-53 Korean War, the armistice that has been in existence for 40 years, and the threat from the North Korean Communists. P'anmunjŏm is where the Korean Armistice Agreement was signed on July 27, 1953 after two years and 17 days of negotiation, 575 major meetings and 18 million recorded words. It is now the domain of the Military Armistice Commission (MAC), the function of which is to supervise the truce.

At MAC meetings, delegates from the United Nations Command and the North Korean and Chinese military, the belligerents of the Korean War, confront each other across a long table, a symbol of the struggle that divided the two sides.

Despite moves toward rapprochement in many parts of the world, tension still prevails at P'anmunjŏm. There have been dangerous outbursts there, including the slaying of two U.S. army officers by North Koreans in August 1976, in what has come to be known as the "axe murder incident."

Tours to P'anmunjŏm can be arranged through the Korea Tourist Bureau with prior notice.

Folk Village—Glimpses into the Past

Korea's Folk Village located 41km south of Seoul near Suwon offers a look at the enchanting rural life of Korea hundreds of years ago. An old gentleman with a slender bamboo pipe in hand and wearing a wide-brimmed horsehair hat can be seen strolling under the low eaves of straw-thatched homes, his flowing *turumagi* coat sweeping through the serene surroundings.

The curious tourist may look into one of the many private homes. On a wooden-floored porch, a woman might be ironing clothes by beating them with two clubs while in the next courtyard another housewife might be spinning silk thread from a small white cocoon simmering in a pot of boiling water.

This village, built in 1973, includes aspects of almost everything uniquely Korean from days gone by. Homes typical of the various provinces of Korea can be identified. In the village square, tightrope walkers, weddings, funeral processions, kite-flying contests, and graceful dance troupes can be seen.

The blacksmith, carpenter, potter, and instrument craftsman can be observed at work in their shops. A *yangban*'s (aristocrat's) house, a watermill and the neat yet humble farmer's home can be entered, and their furnishings inspected.

Don't mistake the young man for a girl just because he has a long single braid hanging down his back. It means he is not married yet and will not cut his hair until his wedding day. A top knot will be formed with the remaining hair, a sign of attainment of maturity which he will want to display by wearing a new horsehair hat.

For the tourist who has only a few days to spend in Korea, a trip to the Folk Village is highly recommended. Most tourist agencies arrange tours.

Shopping

While there have been changes in the Korean shopping scene with more prices fixed and posted, the art of bargaining still can be a valuable skill whether in the crowded marketplaces or a quiet corner of a small shop. Shrewd in the art of salesmanship, the merchant usually wins the battle, though most often the price is reduced and the customer goes away happy. The Korean

way is that neither the buyer nor the seller loses face.

There are a number of major department stores in Seoul and other cities, and it is recommended that they be visited first by any newcomer to get an idea of price ranges. Their prices often are reasonable and fixed. The shopper also can be certain that their merchandise is of good quality.

A network of underground arcades, the newest form of shopping center, branch out from Myŏng-dong and other areas. Subway entrances and underpasses lead to these tunnels of shopping bargains. Clothing, jewelry, records and tapes, even antiques, can be found in the arcades. Not all arcades are underground; some are several stories high, offering shop after shop of bargains.

Silk and silk brocades are two of Korea's best buys, but the shopper should be certain the silk is not mixed with synthetics. But not all synthetics should not be overlooked, for textiles are one of the country's leading exports.

The silk center of Seoul is the East Gate market, a maze of alleys covering huge blocks with thousands of stalls selling colorful fabrics of silk, cottons, and various synthetics.

Though prices have risen over the last few years, amethyst and smoky topaz are considered good bargains as these are mined in Korea. Jewelry stores are found in many places, including department stores and arcades. Again, care must be taken in choosing quality pieces. Gold items in Korea have long been popular as the quality is good, but the price by weight is usually higher than in the United States. Korean gold has a deep yellow luster.

Ginseng in its various forms is another product in great demand. The ginseng grown in Korea is considered the best in the world and brings a high price on the world market. The growing of ginseng and the production of ginseng products are government-controlled. For a foreigner wishing to sample ginseng, the tea in powdered form is recommended, though it has a distinctively earthy flavor.

Bargains in sweaters and other clothing are exceptionally good. Purchased locally at less than half-price, these same items carrying well-known labels are exported to the United States and Europe for sale in many of the large chain stores.

Especially popular are beaded sweaters, which bring high prices in the export markets. Korean tourists in Hong Kong frequently buy such items, not realizing that they originally came from Korea. Custom-made shoes, handbags, and other leather articles are rated high on the list of bargain items in Korea.

Most of the antique stores in Seoul are located in the part of town called Insa-dong or Mary's Alley, though there are a growing number of stores in It'aewon. One can find Buddhist sculpture, Chosŏn and Koryŏ ceramics, old chests, and many other household pieces and other relics of Korea's past. Compared to Western prices, some items can be purchased at a reasonable cost. Ancient Oriental paintings as well as contemporary works are displayed side by side. Prices have skyrocketed over the last few years due to an increasing tourist inflow, especially from Japan, but for those who know the market, good buys in antiques are frequently found. As a word of warning: antiques are subject to government regulation, and the current policy should be thoroughly ascertained before attempting to take an item of great value and age out of the country. Good Korean chests, many with the original brass fittings, are in constant demand among foreigners. Many new chests are being made in imitation of the old style. This is also true of Koryŏ celadons. Kilns near Seoul turn out great numbers of rather good ceramics which copy the celadon treasures found in the country's museums. These modern reproductions of chests and ceramics are often worth buying. The merchants are reasonably honest in telling if an article is genuine or a reproduction.

Lacquerware has historically been a well-developed handicraft. Whether it is a tray or a large wardrobe, the smooth red or black lacquer finish glistening in the light attracts all who appreciate beauty. Often elaborate mother-of-pearl adorns the lacquered surface. This work has to be done completely by hand, making it tedious and time-consuming. Oriental enamelware also has a long history, and in Korea the art is still flourishing. Enameling, too, must be done by hand. Jewelry items in brilliant baked enamel are quite popular.

Good brassware is available at reasonable prices. Items include trivets, candleholders, mugs, lamps, bells and picture frames, as well as an assortment of figurines and household fixtures. Large pieces like beds and chairs can be made to order. The It'aewon shopping district has numerous brass shops, some of which also sell copperware. Shops selling Buddhist paraphernalia are located along Chongno Street, such things as drums, brass cymbals, bells, shaman equipment, temple and funeral decor and lanterns.

Provincial Tours

Chejudo: Island of Fantasy

Chejudo, the largest and most famous of Korea's islands, is situated approximately 97km off the southern coast of the peninsula. It is an island province of about 1,825 square kilometers with a population of 520,000.

Chejudo's principal mountain is Mt. Hallasan, a volcanic cone last active in 1007. At 1,950m, it is the Republic's highest mountain. At least 15 separate lava flows have been identified which have left tunnels, pillars, and other unusual features of quick-cooling basalt. These features have now become objects of tourist interest. At the summit of Mt. Hallasan is a large crater. A round-trip hike to the summit takes about six hours.

Chejudo has become a popular tourist resort for visitors, both foreign and Korean. The flying time from Seoul is only one hour while ferry and air service are available from Pusan to Cheju City, the island's main port. The island is a popular honeymoon destination.

Chejudo has had a turbulent history, and the waves of many cultures have washed ashore in many ways making it both fascinating and different from the culture of the mainland. It first came under government control during the Koryŏ Dynasty in A.D. 938 and later was con-

Fascinating landscapes of Chejudo Island in the four seasons.

quered by the Mongols, who attempted the systematic breeding of cattle and horses.

During the Chosŏn period, a Dutch ship was wrecked on the island's coast and its crew detained for 13 years. Later, one of the seamen, a man named Hendrick Hamel, published a record of his sojourn upon his return to Europe.

Because of the island's remoteness, some primitive practices and beliefs linger on, with shamanistic sorcery still relevant to the local people's way of life. Replicas of primitive stone carvings are sold as tourist objects. Vestiges of a matriarchal society are still noted as the men stay at home to care for their families while women work as divers, gathering shellfish among craggy coastal rocks.

On Chejudo live some of the hardiest women in the world. Working the year round they learn to swim and dive at an early age. The women divers range in age from the early teens to well past 60 years-old and their indifference to winter's frigid blasts and icy water is a legend among visitors. They remain underwater three to four minutes at depths of 12 to 18 meters.

Within Cheju City is Samsŏnghyŏl Hole (Hole of the Three Family Spirits). It is said that on this site appeared three gods named *Ko, Pu,* and *Yang* who are considered the island's forefathers.

On the eastern side of the island are vast meadows suitable for grazing land which have supported Korea's leading livestock breeders through the centuries. An 80,000-hectare ranch located here is rated as one of Asia's best stock farms. Imported breeds have improved Korea's livestock. Historically famous for horse-raising, Chejudo still has over 3,000 horses, some 65 percent of Korea's total 4,600.

Sŏgwip'o is a small town located on the southern side of the island known for its beaches, waterfalls, and oranges. Tourist hotels overlooking the ocean cliffs are a pleasant place to spend a few days. Chŏngbang waterfall rushes over a cliff within view of the town, providing a natural scenic spot.

The mild southern climate is suitable for growing oranges, grapefruit, and tangerines, and Sogwip'o has become the citrus center of the country. Protective rock walls have been built around the orchards to protect the trees from the famous Chejudo winds. In 1965, it was discovered that a high-quality orange could be successfully grafted on the stock of the native thorn-bush variety.

Chungmun resort, about a 20-minute drive west of Sŏgwip'o, is an integrated tourism and recreation center that includes long white beaches and scenic Ch'ŏnjeyŏn Waterfall. Various facilities for sports and recreation along with accommodations are being developed in an area of 420 acres. Existing facilities include first-rate hotels, a golf course, an oceanarium, a botanical garden as well as many other conveniences.

Honoring Admiral Yi Sun-shin

Located at Asan, near the hot springs resort of Onyang, is the country's most impressive shrine. Hyŏnch'ungsa, as it is called, is dedicated to one of the greatest military heroes of history, Admiral Yi Sun-shin, who has been likened to Sir Francis Drake or Lord Nelson of England. When the Japanese fleet defeated the Russian navy in 1905, the Japanese admiral was quoted as saying, "You may wish to compare me with Lord Nelson, but do not compare me with Korea's Admiral Yi Sun-shin . . . he is too remarkable for anyone."

Admiral Yi is credited with the invention of the world's first ironclad warships, called *Kŏbuksŏn,* or "Turtle Ships," with which he defeated the Japanese fleets during the invasions of 1592-98.

At the shrine are preserved Admiral Yi's war diaries as well as some of his personal belongings. Near the shrine stands a gnarled old gingko tree under which the admiral practiced archery during his youth. A replica of a *Kŏbuksŏn* as well as other articles of that period are displayed in a small museum.

Wooded Wonderland of Mt. Sŏraksan

As cooler temperatures come to the Korean Peninsula and autumn foliage begins to turn red and yellow, the scenic peaks guarding the valleys of the Mt. Sŏraksan beckon to Korean and foreign tourists alike. The Sŏraksan Range,

Two different faces of Mt. Sŏraksan.

which is part of the Diamond Mountains, is considered one of the world's most spectacular.

Mt. Sŏraksan located along the eastern coast north of Kangnŭng City, is readily reached by express bus which offers the traveler unsurpassed scenery along the way. An expressway, which passes Wonju, has been completed as far as Kangnŭng, which is the largest city on the coast near the growing resort area. Sokch'o, a coastal town that serves as a gateway to Mt. Sŏraksan, can be reached by air from Seoul in less than one hour. Several tourist hotels are available as well as numerous less expensive inns. During the tourist season, it is recommended that reservations be made through tourist agencies. The Sŏraksan Range is divided into two parts, Inner Sŏrak and Outer Sŏrak. For adventuresome hikers, the valleys of Inner Sŏrak near Paektamsa Temple are still virtually untouched by commercialization. However, Outer Sŏrak, which is no less enchanting, has been more developed. Shinhŭngsa, the main temple, is only a 10-or 15-minute walk from the

tourist hotels. There are several other ancient temples in the region.

Kyŏngju: Legacy of Shilla Culture

The legends of ancient Shilla echo across the years leaving a legacy of beauty and mystery in the valleys surrounding Kyŏngju, an ancient capital where kings and queens reigned for almost a millennium. The achievements of the Shilla people and their devotion to Buddha are evident in the stone images carved on cliff walls and the other stone monuments found throughout the area.

Kyŏngju Valley, the cradle of Shilla culture and site of the Kyŏngju capital from 57 B.C. to A.D.935 , is located in a geographically secluded basin between Taegu and Pusan Expressway. Royal tombs, temple sites with weathered stone pagodas and Buddhist reliefs, and fortress ruins are scattered around the vicinity of this ancient city. Many of the most unique sculptured art objects of Korea's early Buddhist heritage can

Pulguksa Temple, first built in 751, one of the most famous temples in Korea.

be found off the beaten trails and tourist haunts. Recently the Government has started developing the Kyŏngju region into an outdoor museum, and many of the more popular sites can be visited with ease over paved roads.

Kyŏngju is Korea's "culture city" and, for anyone truly interested in delving further into Korean antiquities, a visit to the many sites near this ancient capital is essential. The National Museum of Kyŏngju contains some of the country's finest treasures.

Between 1973 and 1975 several Shilla tombs were excavated under government supervision. Gold art treasures including crowns, pendants and jewelry were brought to light and are now to be found in the museums of Kyŏngju and Seoul. A birch-bark saddle guard, decorated with a painting of a white horse, was discovered in near-perfect condition in a sixth century royal tomb.

The Unified Shilla period carried Korean culture to unprecedented heights. T'ang was one of the most brilliant and prosperous dynasties in all Chinese history, and Shilla's close relationship with T'ang was fruitful both politically and culturally. The *Samguk sagi* (History of the Three Kingdoms) relates that the capital city was copied from that of the T'ang capital with rows of avenues and streets crossing at right angles. All the houses within the city walls were roofed with tile. The estimated population of the capital was one million inhabitants, about nine times the size of today's Kyŏngju (pop. 110,000). A visit to the many ruins can provide the tourist with some idea of the city's magnificence and the height of cultural attainment and excellence in art and learning of the Shilla era about 1,000 years ago.

Pulguksa Temple

Located only a few miles from Kyŏngju city is the largest and most imposing Buddhist temple complex in the area. The Pulguksa Temple was constructed in its present form in A.D.751, and is approached through massive gates over carved granite stairways. The bridges, stairs, terraces and two famous pagodas date from the time of construction, although the wooden buildings in the complex have been destroyed and rebuilt a number of times over the centuries. The most recent restoration took place in the 1970s and duplicated the exact appearance of the temple.

Sŏkkuram Grotto

Built on a mountain above Pulguksa is Sŏkkuram Grotto, housing one of the world's most impressive dedications to Buddha. Dating from about the same period as Pulguksa Temple, the grotto was deserted and ignored by all but the local populace for centuries. Then when it was "rediscovered" in the 20th century, its great granite Buddha and the masterly bas-reliefs of guardian figures were proclaimed the height of East Asian Buddhist art. Placement of the grotto with its domed roof is considered an outstanding engineering feat. A winding road through a scenic forest and hiking paths lead to the site, where the huge seated Buddha gazes toward the sea on the distant horizon.

O-nŭng (Five Tombs)

A grove of pine trees surrounding five earthen mounds is seen when one comes off the Seoul-Pusan Expressway. They are believed to be the tombs of Pak Hyŏkkŏse, first king of the Shilla Dynasty, his queen and three other early rulers of the Pak family.

Ch'ŏmsŏngdae (Stargazing Pavilion)

One of the best-known of Korea's historic remains is Ch'ŏmsŏngdae, an observatory near Panwŏlsŏng Fortress and Kyerim Grove. Built during the reign of Queen Sŏndŏk in A.D.634 , this structure is considered the oldest observatory in the East Asia.

Punhwangsa Pagoda

Listed as a national treasure, this stoneblock pagoda located on the grounds of Punhwangsa Temple ruins is, along with Ch'ŏmsŏngdae, the oldest structure in Korea. This massive pagoda was built in A.D.634 during the reign of Queen Sŏndŏk. It originally had nine stories, though only three remain. It was constructed with slabs of stone which look like bricks in imitation of the Chinese-style brick pagodas. On four sides of the first story are doors flanked on either side by scowling Deva guardians. On the four corners of the platform are sculptured lions, the traditional guards of Buddhist scripture. Near Punhwangsa Temple ruins is the site of Shilla's largest temple, Hwangnyongsa.

Sacred Namsan (South Mountain)

Though broken fragments of Buddhist images, pagodas and other numerous stone temple objects can be found in almost every valley near Kyŏngju, the cultural remains in the more than 20 valleys of Mt. Namsan are the largest in number. The average tourist could not possibly see everything, but the stone relief carvings at Ch'ilburam (Seven Buddha Hermitage) alone are an unforgettable experience. These art objects of a religious heritage are only surpassed by the Buddhist sculptures found in the Sŏkkuram Grotto.

Tomb of Kim Yu-shin

Several Shilla tombs have zodiac animals carved in relief, but the tomb of General Kim Yu-shin is regarded as among the finest. Kim Yu-shin, Shilla's greatest general, served under King Muyŏl and his son Munmu in the seventh century and was instrumental in unifying the peninsula under Shilla. This tomb is located a short distance west of Kyŏngju city. The stone fence surrounding the mound was reconstructed in 1976.

Pomun Lake Resort

A major tourist complex about a 15-minute drive from Kyŏngju city, Pomun Lake has 4 super deluxe hotels, extensive shopping and dining facilities, a golf course, tennis courts, pleasure boats, swimming and even a hotel school. Shuttle bus and taxi service connect downtown Kyŏngju with the resort area.

Paekche's Puyŏ and Kongju

Paekche culture represents a period of almost 700 years from the founding of the kingdom in 18 B.C. until its conquest by Shilla in A.D 660

Pomun Lake Resort, an integrated tourist center, located near Kyŏngju.

Excavations of tomb mounds in Hwangnam-ri (Historic Site No. 40) in Kyŏngju have yielded numerous priceless artifacts. There are 20 tombs, including the tomb of King Mich'u, the largest, the Hwangnam Great Tomb, and the Ch'ŏnmach'ong("Heavenly Horse Tomb").

A bronze incense burner recently excavated at Nŭngsanri *tomb in* Puyŏ, *the capital of Paekche Kingdom(18 B.C.-A.D.660), in Ch'ungch'ŏngnamdo province.*

The two national museums located in Kongju and Puyŏ highlight a visitor's tour of this area of southwest Korea.

Paekche, one of the three kingdoms which rose to power during the first century B.C., had its own unique culture, which is characteristically different from that of Koguryŏ or Shilla. Originally, Paekche established its capital directly south of the Han-gang River in the outskirts of Seoul near the present tourist attraction of Namhansansŏng (South Fortress). Under growing pressure from Koguryŏ, Paekche moved its capital in 475 to the present city of Kongju in Ch'ungch'ŏngnam-do province. Again moving further south in 538, it established its last capital in the city of Puyŏ on the Kŭmgang River. It is believed that the artistic heritage of this kingdom had a strong influence on Japan.

To reach Puyŏ, it is easiest to take the expressway to the Nonsan exit between Taejŏn and Chŏnju. While in Nonsan, it is recommended that the famed Ŭnjin Mirŭk sculpture of Buddha be visited. Located only a few miles from town at Kwanch'oksa Temple, is the largest stone image of Buddha in Korea today.

Puyŏ is a small town. Its museum is located against a hill called Mt. Pusosan which dominates the Kŭmgang River. The stone displays on the museum grounds are fascinating, especially the remains of two memorial steles and a stone tub which have been designated as treasures by the Government. Also a small replica of a Paekche tomb, similar to the ones located in the outskirts of Puyŏ, is seen on the museum grounds.

Mt. Pusosan was at one time the site of the capital's fortress, and many of the ancient pavilions have been reconstructed there. Hours could be spent strolling the many meandering trails and enjoying the panoramic views of the river.

Perhaps the most beautiful of all pavilions in Korea is Nakhwaam, located on a bluff overlooking the Kŭmgang River at a bend called the

The Hallyŏ Haesang National Park, *better known as the* Hallyŏ Waterway, *links the southern coast of the Peninsula and has outstanding scenery.*

Paengmagang River.

Kongju, which served as the Paekche capital until the mid-sixth century, is located north of Puyŏ. On the way, the famous temple of Kapsa on Mt. Kyeryongsan, can be seen. The town is dominated by Mt. Kongsan, where the remains of fortifications are still visible. Two picturesque gates, which were reconstructed during the Chosŏn Dynasty, as well as several pavilions provide a pleasant recreational area for the people of Kongju. There is also a monument honoring the Ming general who aided in the defense of Kongju during the Japanese invasions in the latter part of the 16th century.

A fascinating archaeological display is made up of the relics found in the tomb of King Muryŏng (r.501-524) who was one of the last rulers to reign in the capital of Kongju. His successor moved the capital to Puyŏ. While repairing some Paekche burial mounds on the outskirts of town, workmen accidentally found a mysterious stone wall. Authorities were called in. During the summer of 1971, Dr. Kim Won-yong, one of Korea's most eminent archaeologists, helped bring to the public one of Korea's greatest discoveries of the 20th century, a tomb completely undisturbed since it was sealed in the early sixth century. Hundreds of artifacts which were uncovered are now on display in the national museums at Kongju and Seoul and the tomb, which has been renovated, is open to the general public.

Along the Southern Coast

The southern coastal regions of Korea have long been popular with Korean travelers, but only recently, with the completion of the Honam and Namhae expressways, have these picturesque coastal routes become easily accessible. The areas around Chinhae, Ch'ungmu, Chinju, and Namhae are recommended as highlights of this scenic region.

The southern boundary of the Korean

Peninsula is a sunken coastline which has created an irregular pattern of bays and inlets with more than 400 offshore islands. In addition to the expressway and rail service, the use of the hydrofoil between Pusan and Yŏsu is recommended, as it stops at Sŏngp'o, Ch'ungmu, Samch'ŏnp'o, and Namhae. Reservations for transportation and hotels can be made in Seoul through travel agencies.

Chinhae city is the headquarters for Korean naval activities and should be visited during the cherry blossom season in spring. Ch'ungmu is a traditional seaport of great charm and historical interest, and for someone seeking a quiet place to rest and relax for a few days, it is a particularly good choice. A tourist hotel is situated in a scenic mountain area a few miles from the busy port. The many offshore islands of this port city are rich in tradition relating to Admiral Yi Sunshin, Korea's greatest naval hero, and most of the historical remains are associated with him. The words ch'ung and mu, meaning loyalty and military valor respectively, are derived from the posthumous title conferred on Admiral Yi in 1643.

Located on Nambang, a peninsula jutting into the bay, is a life-size bronze statue of Admiral Yi, considered the oldest in Korea. The sword held by the statue and that displayed at Ch'ungnyŏlsa Shrine show the immense physique of the general.

The shrine of Ch'ungnyŏlsa (meaning "Faithful to King and Country") was first established in 1606. It is now both a museum and shrine dedicated to Admiral Yi. In the inner shrine is an altar, table, and spirit tablet. Visitors can enter with permission from the shrine custodian. The eight relics (Treasure No. 440) on display were gifts to Admiral Yi from a Chinese emperor in honor of his naval victories. They include a 2.13m commander's bugle, a 1.52m sword, a ceremonial sword weighing 30kg, Admiral Yi's seal, and several signal flags.

While in Ch'ungmu one should visit Hansando Island, the site of Admiral Yi's headquarters and where he won his most spectacular naval victory in July 1592. Boats can be rented from the city or tourist hotel. The journey takes about 30 minutes.

Chinju can be reached by air, expressway bus, or train. Though one can stay in town at modest hotels or Korean inns, it is more enjoyable to stay at Lake Chinyang, a newly formed reservoir only a few kilometers from the city. There are many hotels located on a high knoll overlooking the water.

The historic point of interest in Chinju is the old Chinju Fortress, which is situated on the cliffs of the Namgang River. There, one can envision the tragic tale of Non-gae, the patriotic kisaeng, who, in October 1592, leaped to her death from the edge of a cliff holding a conquering Japanese general firmly in her arms.

A large rock is located near Ch'oksŏknu pavilion where the general and Non-gae perished. Called Uirangam (Faithful Woman Rock), it is inscribed with the words: "May the memory of her loyalty be as eternal as the river."

ACKNOWLEDGMENTS

We gratefully acknowledge the cooperation of the experts named below for
contributing original analyses for this
book and for allowing us to quote
extensively from their standard works
of scholarship.

• *Land*

Yi Ch'an, former professor of geography, Seoul
National University (Geography)

Yi Yŏng-no, former professor emeritus, Ewha
Womans University (Flora)

Won Pyŏng-o, professor of biology, director of the
Institute of Ornithology, Kyung Hee University
(Fauna)

Chong Ch'ang-hŭi, former professor of geology,
Seoul National University (Geology,
Earthquakes)

• *People and Language*

Kim Kwang-ŏk, professor of anthropology, Seoul
National University (People)

Yi Ki-mun, professor of linguistics, Seoul
National University (Language)

• *History*

Song Pyŏng-ki, professor of history, Dankook
University

Han U-kŭn, former professor of Korean history,
Seoul National University

• *Belief, Philosophy and Religion*

Pak Chong-hong, former professor of Seoul
National University (Traditional Beliefs, Ancient
Philosophers)

Hong Yi-sŏp, former professor of Yonsei
University (Contemporary Thought)

Chang Pyŏng-kil, former professor of religion,
Seoul National University (Religion)

• *Customs and Traditions*

Im Tong-kwon, professor of folk literature,
Chung-ang University

• *Culture and the Arts*

Yi Ki-baek, professor of Korean history, Hallym
University (The Origin of Korean Culture)

Pak Song-ŭi, former professor of Korean liteature,
Korea University (Classical Literature)

O'Rourke Kevin, professor of English
literature, Kyung Hee University (Literature).

An Hwi-jun, professor of archaeology and art history, Seoul National University (Traditional
Painting)

Yi Il, art critic and lecturer at Hongik University
(Contemporary Painting)

Cho Cha-yong (Zo Za-yong), director of the
Emille Museum (Folk Paintings)

Kim Yang-dong, calligrapher and seal maker
(Calligraphy)

Mun Myŏng-dae, art historian and lecturer at
Dongkook University (Ancient Sculpture)

Kim Pok-yong, art critic and lecturer at Kangwon
National University (Modern Sculpture)

Maeng In-jae, member of Cultural Property
Committee (Ancient Crafts)

Chang Yun-u, professor of applied arts, Sungshin
Women's University (Modern Handcrafts)

Im Yŏng-ju, member of the National Commission
for Cultural Properties (Decorative Patterns)

Chang Kyŏng-ho, senior researcher at the Cultural
Properties Research Institute (Traditional
Architecture)

Cho Yŏng-mu, specialist in urban planning and
architecture critic (Modern Architecture)

Yi Kang-suk, President, The Korean National
Institute of Arts (Traditional Music)

Han Man-young, professor of Korean music,
Seoul National University (Musical Instruments)

Han Sang-u, music critic (Classical Western
Music)

Eleanor King, American dance critic (Traditional
Dance)

Pak Yong-ku, critic of performing arts (Modern
Dance)

Yi Tu-hyŏn, former professor of Korean literature,
Seoul National University (Drama)

Sŏ Chŏng-u, professor of mass communications,

Yonsei University (Movies, Magazines and
Books)
Ministry of Culture and Sports (Cultural Facilities)

• *Constitution and Government*
Kim Pŏn-ung, former professor of public administration, Kook Min University
Chŏng Chŏng-kil, former professor of political science, Seoul National University

• *Foreign Relations*
Ministry of Foreign Affairs

• *Unification Policy*
Kim Hak-joon. professor of political science,
DanKook University
Yun Pyŏng-ik, professor of the Institute of
Political Education for National Unification
National Unification Board

• *National Defense*
To Hŭng-yŏl, professor, National Defense College
Pae Myŏng-ho, former professor, National
Defense College

• *Finance*
Economic Planning Board
Ministry of Finance
The Bank of Korea

• *Economy*
Kim Ki-hwan, former director, Korea
Development Institute
Economic Planning Board

• *Industry*
Research Department, Korea Development Bank
Korea Development Institute
Economic Planning Board
Ministry of Trade, Industry and Energy

• *Agriculture, Forestry and Fishery*
Ministry of Agriculture, Forestry and Fisheries

• *Transportation and Communications*
Kim Myŏng-shik, associate editor the *Korea
Times* (Transportation)
Ministry of Communications
(Telecommunications)

Ministry of Transportation
Ministry of Construction

• *Science and Technology*
Hyŏn Won-pok, science journalist
Ministry of Science and Technology

• *Education*
Korea Educational Development Institute
Ministry of Education

• *Social Development and Quality of Life*
Son Ch'ang-tal, researcher, National Security
Committee, Ministry of Health and
Social Affairs
Kwon Suk-p'yo, former professor of environmen-
tal health, director of the Institute for
Environmental Pollution Research, Yonsei
University (Environmental Protection and
Pollution Control)
Economic Planning Board (Consumer Protection)
Ministry of Construction (Housing)
Ministry of Health and Social Affairs
(Health and Medicine)
Ministry of Labor (Social Security)
Korean Women's Development Institute
(Women's Status)
Ministry of Home Affairs (Saemaŭl Undong)

• *Mass Communications*
Sŏ Chŏng-u, professor of mass communications,
Yonsei University

• *Sports*
Ministry of Culture and Sports

• *Tourism*
Edward B. Adams, educator, writer, and
photographer
Korea National Tourism Corporation

BIBLIOGRAPHY

The following bibliography introduces some 500 publications which may be helpful to readers who seek further information about Korea. The list is limited mostly to recent works published in English, Japanese, French, German and Spanish. It contains some books for specialists, but most are for general readers. For easier reference, entries are arranged alphabetically under the following subject headings: General Works, Philosophy, Religion, Social Science, Pure Science, Technology, Arts, Language, History, and Literature.

• General Works

Adams, Edward B. *Korea Guide.* Seoul: Seoul International Publishing House, 1976.

—. *Seoul: 1988 Olympic Site.* Seoul: Seoul International Publishing House, 1984.

Allen, Horace N. *Things Korean.* Seoul: Royal Asiatic Society, 1980.

Grayson, J. *Taegu Guide.* Seoul: Royal Asiatic Society, 1980.

Holstein, John. *Introducing Seoul.* Seoul: Hollym International Corp., 1993.

Hyun, Peter. *Introducing Korea.* Seoul: Jung Woo Sa, 1979.

Kim Jong-ki. *Seoul: Host City of the '88 Olympics.* Seoul: KBS Enterprises Ltd., 1983.

Kim Tai-jin. *A Bibliographical Guide to Traditional Korean Sources.* Seoul: Asiatic Research Center, Korea University, 1976.

Korea Annual : A Comprehensive Handbook on Korea. Seoul: Yonhap News Agency, 1986-1993.

McMahon, Patricia. *CHI-HOON, A Korean Girl.* Pennsylvania:Caroline House Boyds Mills Press, Inc. 1993.

Popham, Peter. *Insider's Guide to Korea.* Seoul: Seoul International Publishing House,1986.

Rucci, Richard B. *Seoul Shopping Guide.* Seoul: Seoul International Publishing House,1983.

Song ki-Joong. *Basic Glossary of Korean Studies.* Seoul: Korea Foundation, 1993.

Yang Seung-Mok. *Korean Customs and Etiquette.* Seoul: Moon Yang Gak, 1990.

Yang Won-dal. *Korean Ways, Korean Mind .* Seoul: Tamgu Dang, 1982.

Yoo Yu-shin. *Korea the Beautiful: Treasures of the Hermit Kingdom.* Dae Won Press,1987.

• Philosophy

Choi Min-hong. *Comparative Philosophy: Western and Korean Philosophies Compared.* Seoul: Sung Moon Sa, 1980.

—. *A Modern History of Korean Philosophy.* Seoul: Sung Moon Sa, 1980.

Chon Syng-boc. *Korean Thinkers.* Seoul: Si-sa-yong-o-sa, Inc., 1984.

Hong Yi-Sup. *Korea's Self-Identity.* Seoul: Yonsei University Press, 1973.

International Cultural Foundation. *Korean Thought* (Korean Culture Series 10). Seoul: Si-sa-yong-o-sa, Inc., 1982.

Korean National Commission for UNESCO. *Main Currents of Korean Thought.* Seoul: Si-sa-yong-o-sa, Inc., 1983.

Korean Thought and Ethics. Seoul: The Academy of Korean Studies, 1980.

Park won. *Thoughts of a Korean.* Inch'ŏn: Inha University Press, 1978.

Rhee Kyu-ho. *To the Young Korean Intellectuals.* Seoul: Hollym International Corp., 1982.

• Religion

Conze, Edward. *Buddhism: Its Essence and Development.* New York: Harper Torchbook, 1975.

Covell, Alan Carter. *Folk Art and Magic: Shamanism in Korea.* Seoul: Hollym International Corp., 1986.

Daehan Pulkyo Chong Yonhaphoe. *The Teaching of Buddha.* Seoul: Han Jin Publishing Company, 1979.

Hong Jung-shik, et al. *Buddhist Culture in Korea.* Seoul: Si-sa-yong-o-sa, Inc., 1982.

Huhm, Halla Pai. *Kut: Korean Shamanist Rituals.* Seoul: Hollym International Corp., 1985.

Huntley, Martha. *To Start A Work: The Foundations of the Protestant Mission in Korea (1884-1919).* Presbyterian Church of Korea Publishing

House, 1987.

International Cultural Foundation. *Buddhist Culture in Korea* (Korean Culture Series 3). Seoul: Si-sa-yong-o-sa, Inc., 1982.

Keel Hee-sung. *Chinul: The Founder of the Korean Sŏn Tradition.* Seoul: Po Chin Jai Co., Ltd., 1984.

Kim Chang-seok. *Holy Places of the Korean Martyrs.* Lay Apostolate Council, 1986.

Kim Duk-hwang. *A History of Religion in Korea.* Daeji Moonhwa Sa, 1988.

Kim Ki-chang. *The Life of Jesus: Collection of Sacred Paintings.* Seoul: Koung-mi Publications, 1978.

Kim Yong-choon. *The Ch'ŏndogyo Concept of Min.* Seoul: Pan Korean Book Corporation, 1979.

Korean Church Growth Explosion: Centennial of the Protestant Church. World of Life Press, 1983.

Lancaster, Lewis R. *The Korean Buddhist Canon: A Descriptive Catalogue.* Berkeley: University of California Press, 1979.

Lee Kwan-jo. *Search for Nirvana.* Seoul: Seoul International Publishing House, 1984.

Paik Lak-geoon George. *The History of Protestant Missions in Korea, 1832-1910.* Seoul: Yonsei University Press, 1980.

Palmer, Spencer J. *Confucian Rituals in Korea.* Seoul: Po Chin Jai Co., Ltd., 1984.

Yang Han-sung. *The Hye Ch'o Diary Memoirs of the Pilgrimage to the Five Regions of India.* Seoul: Po Chin Jae Co., Ltd., 1984.

Zo Za-yong. *The Life of Buddha in Korean Painting.* Seoul: Royal Asiatic Society and Emile Museum, 1975.

• *Social Science*

Ahn Byong-man. *Elections of Korea.* Seoul: Seoul Computer Press, 1988.

Ahn Chung-si. *Social Development and Political Violence.* Seoul: Seoul National University Press, 1984.

Allen, Horace H. *Things Korean.* Seoul: Royal Asiatic Society, 1980.

Bae Kyu-han. *Automobile Workers in Korea.* Seoul: Seoul National University Press, 1987.

Baek Jong-chun. *Probe for Korean Reunification.* Research Center for Peace and Unification of Korea, 1988.

Baek Kwang-il. *Korea and the United States.* Research Center for Peace and Unification of Korea, 1988.

21st Century: Prospects and Problems. Center for the Reconstruction of Human Society, Seoul: Kyung Hee University Press, 1980.

Chang Dal-joong. *Economic Control and Political Authoritarianism.* Seoul: Sogang University Press, 1985.

Chang Y.S., ed. *Korea-A Decade of Development.* Seoul: Seoul National University Press, 1980.

Chang Y.S. and Peter J. Donaldson., eds. *Society in Transition—With Special Reference to Korea.* Seoul: Seoul National University Press, 1982.

Changing International Environment and Korean Peninsula. Seoul: Kyung Hee University Press, 1988.

Cho Myung-hyun. *Korea and the Major Powers.* Research Center for Peace and Unification of Korea, 1989.

Choi Chong-ki, ed. *Peace and Stability in Northeast Asia: Achieving International Order Without Violence.* Seoul: The Korean Institute of International Studies, 1985.

Choi Sang-su. *Annual Customs of Korea.* Seoul: Seomun-dang Publishing Co., Ltd., 1983.

Chong Chang-nyol, *et al. Economic Life in Korea.* Seoul: Si-sa-yong-o-sa, Inc., 1982.

Chun Kyung-soo. *Reciprocity and Korean Society: An Ethnography of Hasami.* Seoul: Seoul National University Press, 1985.

Chung Chin-wee. *Korea and Japan in World Politics.* Seoul: Seoul Computer Press, 1985.

Chung Chong-wha and J.E. Hoare. *Korean-British Relations: Yesterday, Today and Tomorrow.* American-British Center, Seoul: Korea University, 1984.

Chung Chong-wook. *Maoism and Development.* Seoul: Seoul National University Press, 1988.

Chung Sei-wha. *Challenges for Women.* Seoul: Seoul Ewha Womans University Press, 1986.

The Committee for the Compilation of the History of Korean Women. *Women of Korea: A History from Ancient Times to 1945.* Seoul: Ewha Womans University Press, 1976.

Cook, Harold. *Pioneer American Business in Korea: Life and Times of Walter David Tounsend.* Seoul: Royal Asiatic Society, 1981.

Crane, Paul S. *Korean Patterns.* Seoul: Royal

Asiatic Society, 1986.

Current, Marion E. *Looking at Each Other.* Seoul: Seoul International Publishing House, 1983.

Directory of Korean Trading Agents. Seoul: Association of Foreign Trading Agents of Korea, 1986.

Fisher, James A. *Democracy and Mission Education in Korea.* Seoul: Yonsei University Press, 1970.

Fukuda, Tsuneari. *Future of Japan and the Korean Peninsula.* Seoul: Hollym International Corp., 1978.

Geddes, W.R. *Asian Perspective in Social Science.* Seoul: Seoul National University Press, 1986.

Gibney, Frank. *Korea's Quiet Revolution.* New York: Walker and Company.1992.

Grant, Bruce K. *Korean Proverbs.* Wu Ah Dang, 1985.

Government Legislative Administration Agency of the Republic of Korea, ed. *Current Laws of the Republic of Korea,* I-IV. Seoul: Statutes Compilation & Dissemination Foundation of Korea, 1985.

Grajdanzev, Andrew J. *Modern Korea.* Seoul: Royal Asiatic Society, 1975.

Groth, Alexandar J. *Progress and Chaos: Modernization and Rediscovery of Religion and Authority.* Seoul: Kyung Hee University Press, 1981.

Ha Tae-Hung. *Folk Customs and Family Life.* Seoul: Yonsei University Press, 1983.

—. *Folk Tales of Old Korea.* Seoul: Yonsei University Press, 1984.

—. *Guide to Korean Culture.* Seoul: Yonsei University Press, 1978.

—. *The Korean Nights Entertainments.* Seoul:Yonsei University Press, 1983.

—. *Maxims and Proverbs of Old Korea.* Seoul: Yonsei University Press, 1983.

Ha Young-sun. *Nuclear Proliferation: World Order and Korea.* Seoul: Seoul National University Press, 1983.

Hahm Pyong-choon. *Korean Political Tradition and Law.* Seoul: Royal Asiatic Society, 1971.

Hahn Bae-ho. *Korea-Japan Relations in Transition—Challenges and Opportunities.* Seoul: Asiatic Research Center, Korea University, 1982.

Hahn Bae-ho and Yamamoto Tadashi. *Korea and Japan: A New Dialogue Across the Channel.*

Seoul: Asiatic Research Center, Korea University, 1978.

Han, Kwon, Chun, and Moon. *Water Supply and Sanitation in Korean Communities.* Seoul: Seoul International University Press, 1988.

Han Pyo-wook. *The Problem of Korean Unification.* Research Center for Peace and Unification of Korea, 1987.

Han Sang-bok. *Asian Peoples.* Seoul: Seoul National University Press, 1986.

—. *Korean Fisherman.* Seoul: Seoul National University Press, 1980.

Han Seung-soo. *The Health of Nations: Korean Economy in the 21st Century and Other Economic Columns.* Seoul: Seoul Computer Press, 1985.

Han Sung-joo. *After One Hundred Years: Continuity and Change in Korean-American Relations* (ARC Foreign Policy Studies No.3). Seoul: Asiatic Research Center, Korea University, 1983.

—. *Community-building in the Pacific Region: Issues and Opportunities.* Seoul: Asiatic Research Center, Korea University, 1981.

—. *Soviet Policy in Asia: Expansion or Accommodation.* Seoul: Panmun Book Company, Ltd., 1980.

—. *U.S.-Korea Security Cooperation: Retrospects and Prospects* (ARC Foreign Policy Studies No. 4). Seoul: Asiatic Research Center, Korea University, 1983.

Han Sung-joo and Park Jae-kyu. *East Asia and the Major Powers: From Confrontation to Accommodation.* Masan: Kyungnam University Press, 1975.

Hong Sa-woon. *Community Development and Human Reproduction Behaviour.* Seoul: Korea Development Institute, 1979.

Hong Wan-tack. *Factor Supply and Factor Intensity of Trade in Korea.* Seoul: Korea Development Institute, 1976.

Hong Won-tak and Anne O. Kruegar. *Seoul. Trade and Development in Korea.* Seoul: Korea Development Institute, 1974.

Hyun, Peter. *Darkness at Dawn: A North Korean Diary.* Seoul: Hanjin Publishing Company, 1981.

Il, Sakong. *Korea in the World Economy.* Seoul: Institute for International Economics.1993.

International Cultural Foundation. *Customs and Manners in Korea* (Korean Culture Series 9). Seoul: Si-sa-yong-o-sa, Inc., 1982.

—. *Economic Life in Korea* (Korean Culture Series 8). Seoul: Si-sa-yong-o-sa, Inc., 1982.

—. *Folk Culture in Korea* (Korean Culture Series 4). Seoul: Si-sa-yong-o-sa, 1982.

—. *Korean Folk Tales* (Korean Culture Series 7). Seoul: Si-sa-yong-o-sa, 1982.

—. *Korean Society* (Korean Culture Series 6). Seoul: Si-sa-yong o-sa, 1982.

—. *Legal System of Korea* (Korean Culture Series 5). Seoul: Si-sa-yong-o-sa, 1982.

Ireland, Alley. *The New Korea.* Seoul: Royal Asiatic Society, 1975.

Jang Song-hyon. *The Key to Successful Business in Korea.* Yong Ahn Publishing Co., 1988.

Jang Young-sik. *Econometric Model Building.* Seoul: Yonsei University Press, 1973.

Jeong Gi-nam. *Trade Today of Korea.* Seoul: Overseas Media Corporation, 1984.

Jones, Leroy P. *Public Enterprise and Economic Development: The Korean Case.* Seoul: Korea Development Institute, 1976.

Jong Youl-yoo. *Man's Search for Peace.* Seoul: Kyung Hee University Press, 1985.

Kang Shin-pyo, John Macaloon and Roberto DaMatta. *The Olympics and Cultural Exchange.* Institute for Ethnological Studies, 1989.

Kang Yong-hoon. *Soviet Deterrence Doctrine.* Seoul: Seoul National University Press, 1981.

Kee Sun-byung. *Olympics and Politics.* Seoul: Hyong Sol Publishing, 1984.

Kim Bong-sik, *et al. The Political Economy of Success: Public Policy and Economic Development in the Republic of Korea.* Seoul: Kyung Hee University Press, 1977.

Kim Bun-woong, *et al. Korean Public Bureaucracy.* Seoul: Kyobo Publishing, Inc., 1982.

Kim Bun-woong, David. Bell, and Lee Chong-bum. *Administrative Dynamics and Development: The Korean Experience.* Seoul: Kyobo Publishing, Inc., 1985.

Kim Byung-sung. *Schooling and Social Achievement.* Seoul: Korea Educational Development Institute, 1984.

Kim Chan-jin. *Business Laws in Korea: Investment, Taxation and Industrial Property.* Seoul: Panmun Book Company, Ltd., 1988.

Kim Chuk-kyo. *Essays on the Korean Economy,* 2 vols. Seoul: Korea Development Institute, 1977.

—. *Industrial and Social Development Issues.* Seoul: Korea Development Insitute, 1988.

Kim Dal-choong. *East-West Relations and Divided Nation Problems and the Gorbachev Era.* Seoul: Yonsei University Press, 1988.

Kim Dong-ki. *Management Behind Industrialization: Readings in Korean Business.* Seoul: Korea University Press, 1989.

Kim Haeng-jung. *The Cycle of Maturity.* Seoul: Jung Ang Publishing, 1981.

Kim Hak-joon. *The Unification Policy of South and North Korea.* Seoul: Seoul National University Press, 1978.

Kim Hak-joon. *Korea's Relations with Her Neighbors in Changing World.* Seoul: Hollym International Corp. 1993.

Kim I.K. *Socioeconomic Development and Fertility in Korea.* Seoul: Seoul International University Press, 1987.

Kim Jeh- young. *Toward a Unified Korea.* Research Center for Peace and Unification of Korea, 1987.

Kim Jong-gie. *Development.* Seoul: Korea Development Institute, 1989.

Kim Jong-rim and Pai Sung-dong. *Legislative Process in Korea.* Seoul: Seoul National University Press, 1981.

Kim Jun-yop. *Korea-Japan Relations: Issues and Future Prospects.* Seoul: Asiatic Research Center, Korea University, 1982.

Kim Key-hiuk. *The Last Phase of the East Asian World Order.* Seoul: Royal Asiatic Society, 1980.

Kim Kwang-suk and Park Joong-kyung. *Sources of Economic Growth in Korea, 1963-1982.* Seoul: Korea Development Institute, 1985.

Kim Kyong-dong. *Dependency Iussues in Korean Development.* Seoul: Seoul National University Press, 1987.

—. *Man and Society in Korea's Economic Growth.* Seoul: Seoul National University Press, 1979.

—. *Rethinking Development: Theories and Experiences.* Seoul: Seoul National University Press, 1985.

Kim Ran-soo. *Korean Education in Research Perspectives.* Seoul: Jong-Gak Publishing Co.,1984.

Kim Seung- hwan. *The Soviet Union and North Korea.* Research Center for Peace and Unification of Korea, 1988.

Kim Tae-gon, *et al. Korean Folklore.* Seoul: Si-sa-yong-o-sa, Inc., 1983.

Kim Yong-suk and Son Kyung-ja. *An Illustrated History of Korean Costume,* 2 vols. Seoul: Yekyong Publications Co., Ltd., 1984.

Kim Yoon-tai. *Manpower Projection and Strategies, 1979-1991.* Seoul: Korea Educational Development Institute, 1984.

Kim Young-chul. *Educational Investment and Optimum Unit Cost.* Seoul: Korea Educational Development Institute, 1984.

Kirkbride, Wayne A. *DMZ: A Story of The Panmunjŏm Axe Murder.* Seoul: Hollym International Corp., 1984.

—. *Panmunjŏm: Facts about the Korean DMZ.* Seoul: Hollym International Corp., 1985.

Koh, Frances M. *Oriental Children in American Homes.* New York: East-West Press, 1981.

Korea Year 2000: Prospects and Issues for Longterm Development. Seoul: Korea Development Institute, 1989.

Korean National Commission for UNESCO. *Korean Folklore.* Seoul: Si-sa-yong-o-sa, Inc., 1983.

The Korean Nutrition Society. *Korean Nutrition Resource Data.* Shin Kwang Publishing Co., 1989.

Ku Dae-yeol. *Korea Under Colonialism: The March First Movement and Anglo-Japanese Relations.* Seoul: Royal Asiatic Society, 1985.

Kwak Byong-sun. *Career Awareness in Korean Primary Education Today.* Seoul: Korea Educational Development Institute, 1986.

Kwak Tae-hwan. *In Search of Peace and Unification on the Korean Peninsula.* Seoul: Seoul Computer Press, 1986.

—. *Korean Reunification New Prospectives and Approaches.* Masan: Kyungnam University Press, 1984.

—. U.S.-Korean Relations, 1882-1982. Masan: Kyungnam University Press, 1982.

Kwak Tae-hwan, Wayne Patterson, and Edward A. Alson. *The Two Koreas in World Politics.* Masan: Kyungnam University Press, 1983.

Labor Education and Research Institute. *Economic Development and Military Technical Manpower of Korea.* Seoul: Korea University Press, 1976.

Laws of the Republic of Korea, 3 vols. Seoul: Korean Legal Center, 1983.

Lee Chang-soo. *Modernization of Korea and the Impact of the West.* Los Angeles: East Asia Studies Center, University of California, 1981.

Lee Chung-min. *The Emerging Strategic Balance in Northeast Asia.* Research Center for Peace and Unification of Korea, 1989.

Lee Eun-ho. *Adversary Politics in East Asia.* Seoul: Seoul Computer Press, 1986.

Lee Han-been. *Future, Innovation and Development.* Seoul: Panmun Book Company, Ltd., 1982.

Lee Hong-woo. *Living, Knowing and Education – Essays in the Philosophy of Education.* Seoul: Seoul National University Press, 1985.

Lee Hong-yong. *Applied Economic Research on Livestock Production.* Seoul: Seoul National University Press, 1986.

Lee Jae-chang. *Self-concepts and Values of Korean Adolescents.* Seoul: Korea Educational Development Institute, 1984.

Lee Jay-cho. *Estimates of Current Fertility for the Republic of Korea and Its Geographical Subdivisions: 1959-1970.* Seoul: Yonsei University Press, 1975.

Lee Jung-bock. *The Political Character of the Japanese Press.* Seoul: Seoul International University Press, 1985.

Lee Man-gap. *Ancestor Worship and Korean Society.* California: Stanford University Press, 1983.

—. *Sociology and Social Change in Korea.* Seoul: Seoul National University Press, 1984.

Lee On-jook. *Urban to Rural Return Migration in Korea.* Seoul: Seoul National University Press, 1984.

Lee Suck-ho. *Party-Military Relations in North Korea.* Research Center for Peace and Unification of Korea, 1989.

Lee Won-sul. *The United States and the Division of Korea, 1945.* Seoul: Kyung Hee University Press, 1982.

Lee Yun-sup. *Cognitive Process Factors of Low Achievers.* Seoul: Korea Educational Development Institute, 1984.

Lim Hyun-chil. *Dependent Development in Korea, 1963-1979.* Seoul: Seoul National University Press, 1985.

Mattielli, Sandra. *Virtues in Conflict: Tradition and the Korean Woman Today.* Seoul: Royal Asiatic Society, 1977.

Moon Chang-joo. *The Balance of Power in Asia and U.S.-Korea Relations.* Seoul: Gimm-yo Press, 1983.

Nahm, Andrew C. *The United States and Korea: American-Korean Relations, 1966-1976.* Kalamazoo: The Center for Korean Studies, Western Michigan University, 1979.

New Directions in East-West Relations. East and West Studies, Seoul: Yonsei University Press, 1987.

The Northeast Asian Era and the Roles of Korea, China and Japan in the 21st Century. Institute for Northeast Asian Studies, Seoul: Kyung Hee University Press, 1988.

Oliver, Robert. *Syngman Rhee and American Involvement in Korea, 1942-1960.* Seoul: Panmun Book Company, Ltd., 1979.

Pak Chi-young. *Political Opposition in Korea, 1945-1965.* Seoul: Seoul National University Press, 1980.

Pak Pyong-ho. *Legal System of Korea.* Seoul: Si-sa-yong-o-sa, Inc., 1982.

Pares, Susan. *Crosscurrents: Korean and Western Culture in Contrast.* Seoul International Publishing House, 1988.

Park Chong-kee. *Human Resources and Social Development in Korea.* Seoul: Korea Development Institute, 1980.

—. *Macroeconomic and Industrial Development in Korea.* Seoul: Korea Development Institute, 1980.

—. *Secial Security in Korea: An Approach to Socioeconomic Development.* Seoul: Korea Development Institute, 1975.

Park Choon-ho. *East Asia and the Law of the Sea.* Seoul: Seoul National University Press, 1985.

Park Jae-kyu. *The Foreign Relations of North Korea.* Masan: Kyungnam University Press, 1987.

—. *Nuclear Proliferation in Developing Countries.* Masan: Kyungnam University Press, 1979.

Park Jae-kyu and Joseph H. Ha. *The Soviet Union and the East Asia in the 1980s.* Masan: Kyungnam University Press, 1983.

Park Jae-kyu and Jusuf Wanandi. *Korea and Indonesia in the Year 2000.* Masan: Kyungnam University Press, 1985.

Park Jae-kyu and Kim Jung-gun. *The Politics of North Korea.* Masan: Kyungnam University Press, 1979.

Park Ki-huk. *The Changing Korea Village.* Seoul: Royal Asiatic Society, 1975.

Park Myung-seok. *Communication Styles in Two Different Cultures: Korean and American.* Seoul: Han Shin Publishing Co.,1979.

Park Tae-sun. *Innovation in Higher Education.* Seoul: Yonsei University Press, 1975.

Park, Ungsuh K. *Korea and Her Neighboring Economies.* Seoul: Seoul National University Press, 1988.

Park Won. *Echoes of Korean.* Inch'on: Inha University Press, 1982.

Park Young-hai. *Women of the Yi Dynasty.* Seoul: Sookmyung Women's University Press, 1986.

Regional Cooperation in the Pacific Era. East and West Studies, Seoul: Yonsei University Press, 1988.

The Report of the International Conference on Korean Futures. Seoul: Asiatic Research Center, Korea University, 1975.

The Report of the International Conference on the Problems of Korean Unification (August 24-29, 1970). Seoul: Asiatic Research Center, Korea University, 1971.

The Report of the International Conference on Triangular Relations of Mainland China, the Soviet Union and North Korea. Seoul: Asiatic Research Center, Korea University, 1977.

Resources, Maritime Transport and SLOC Security in the Asia-Pacific Region. East and West Studies, Seoul: Yonsei University Press, 1988.

Rhee Kyu-ho. *Struggle for National Identity in the Third World.* Seoul: Hollym International Corp., 1982.

Rhee Sang-woo. *Security and Unification of Korea.* Seoul: Sogang University Press, 1983.

Rhee Yong-pil. *The Breakdown of Authority Structure in Korea in 1960.* Seoul: Seoul National University Press, 1982.

Rummel, R.J. *In the Minds of Man: Principles Toward Understanding and Waging Peace.* Seoul: Sogang University Press, 1984.

Rutt, Richard. *Korean Works and Days.* Seoul: Royal Asiatic Society, 1978.

Search for Causes of International Conflicts and Ways to Their Solution. Institute of International

Peace Studies, Seoul: Kyung Hee University Press, 1988.

Shim Ui-sup. *Korean Construction in the Middle East.* Seoul: Panmun Publishing Co.,1984.

Shin Jung-hyun. *Japanese-North Korean Relations: Linkage Politics in the Regional System of East Asia.* Seoul: Kyung Hee University Press, 1981.

—. *Northeast Asian Security and Peace: Toward the 1990s.* Seoul: Kyung Hee University Press, 1988.

Shin Young-moo. *Securities Regulations in Korea.* Seoul: Seoul National University Press, 1983.

Song Sang-hyun. *Introduction to the Law and Legal System of Korea.* Seoul: Kyung Mun Sa Publishing Co., 1983.

Suk Joo-sun. *Clothes of the Chosŏn Dynasty.* Seoul: Dankook University Press, 1985.

—. *Hyoongbae.* Seoul: Dankook University Press, 1979.

Swartout, Robert R. *Mandarins, Gunboats and Power Politics.* Hawaii: University of Hawaii Press, 1980.

Synn Seung-kwon. *The Russo-Japanese Rivalry over Korea.* Yuk-Bumb-Sa Publishing, 1983.

Transactions of the Korea Branch of the Royal Asiatic Society (Vols 1-12). Seoul: Royal Asiatic Society, 1985.

Villano, Michael M. *A New Generation of Koreans.* Seoul: Sejong Corp., 1975.

Wang In-keun. *Rural Development Studies: Korea and Developing Countries.* Seoul: Seoul National University Press, 1986.

Whang In-joung. *Management of Rural Change in Korea.* Seoul: Seoul National University Press, 1981.

Wornonoff, Jon. *Korea's Economy: Man-made Miracle.* Seoul: Si-sa-yong-o-sa, Inc., 1983.

Wright, Edward. *Korean Politics in Transition.* Seoul and Seattle: Royal Asiatic Society and University of Washington Press, 1975.

Yim Yong-soon. *Politics of Korean Unification.* Research Center for Peace and Unification of Korea, 1988.

• Pure Science

Keuk Paul-chang. *Separation of Flow.* Seoul: Po Chin Jai Co., Ltd., 1979.

Kim Chang-hwan. *Distribution Atlas of Insects of Korea, 2 vols.* Seoul: Korea University Press, 1978.

Lee Dia-sung. *Geology of Korea.* Kyohak-sa Publishing Co., Ltd., 1987.

Sok Ju-myong. *The Distribution Atlas of Butterllies in Korea.* Seoul: Po Chin Jai Co., Ltd., 1973.

• Technology

Archibald, Anne. *Western Cooking in Korean Kitchen.* Seoul: Seoul International Tourist, 1981.

Choe Yong-tae and Lee Soo-ho. *A Colored Topography of Acupuncture Meridians and Acupuncture Points.* Seoul: Ko Mun Sa, 1975.

—. *Acupuncture and Moxibution Meridians and Points.* Seoul: Ko Mun Sa, 1975.

Choi Byong-hee. *Sericultural Technology.* Seoul: Seoul National University Press, 1978.

Chu Woul-young. *Traditional Korean Cuisine.* Seoul: Kyohak-sa Publishing Co., Ltd., 1985.

Ha Chong-yeon. *Primary Health Care in Korea: An Approach to Evaluation.* Seoul: Korea Development Institute, 1981.

Ha Sook-jeong. *Traditional Korean Cooking.* Seoul: Sudo Publishing, 1985.

Han Chung-hae. *Korean Cooking.* Seoul: Chong Woo Publishing Co., 1983.

Hyun, Judy. *The Korean Cookbook.* Seoul: Hollym International Corp., 1986.

Lee Jang-kyu and Bae Sang-kook. *Korean Acupuncture.* Ko Mun Sa, 1981.

Lee Ki-yull. *Practical Korean Recipes.* Seoul: Yonsei University Press, 1980.

Noh Chin-hwa. *Healthful Korean Cooking: Meats and Poultry.* Seoul: Hollym International Corp., 1986.

—. *Low-Fat Korean Cooking: Fish, Shellfish and Vegetables.* Seoul: Hollym International Corp., 1986.

—. *Practical Korean Cooking.* Seoul: Hollym International Corp., 1986.

—. *Traditional Korean Cooking: Snacks and Basic Side Dishes.* Seoul: Hollym International Corp., 1986.

Rutt, Joan and S. Mattielli. *Lee Wade's Korean Cookery.* Seoul: Hollym International Corp., 1985.

Shin Chung-shill. *Korean Recipes.* Seoul: Seoul

International Publishing House, 1984.

Yoo Tae-woo. *Koryŏ Sooji-Chim: Korean Hand-Acupuncture.* Seoul: Eum Yang Maek Jin, 1983.

• *Arts*

Adams, Edward B. *Art Treasures of Seoul.* Seoul: Seoul International Publishing House, 1979.

—. *Art Treasures of Seoul with Walking Tours.* Seoul: Sam Hwa, 1980.

—. *Korea's Pottery Heritage.* Seoul: Seoul International Publishing House, 1987.

—. *Korean Folk Art and Craft.* Seoul: Seoul International Publishing House, 1987.

—. *Palaces of Seoul.* Seoul: Seoul International Publishing House, 1987.

Choe Hae-chun. Sandae: *The Greatest Folk Performing Art of Korea.* Jeail Publishing Co., 1988.

Choi Sun-u. *Traditional Korean Painting.* Seoul: Si-sa-yong-o-sa, Inc., 1983.

—. *5000 Years of Korean Art.* Seoul: Hyonam Publishing Co., 1979.

Chun Byung-ok. *Decorative Designs in the Houses of the Choson Period.* Po Chin Jai Co., Ltd.,1988.

—. *Traditional Artistic Designs of Korea.* Seoul: Po Chin Jai Co., Ltd., 1981.

Chung Sun-ai. *Flower Arrangement of Korea.* Seoul: Hollym International Corp., 1986.

Chung Sung-gil. *Korea 100 Years Ago in Photographs (1871-1910).* Catholic Press, 1986.

Covell, Alan Carter. *Folk Art and Magic.* Seoul: Hollym International Corp., 1985.

Covell, Jon Carter *Korea's Colorful Heritage.* Seoul: Si-sa-yong-o-sa, Inc., 1985.

Covell, Jon Carter and Alan Covell. *The World of Korean Ceramics.* Seoul: Si-sa-yong-o-sa, Inc., 1986.

The Flavor of Korean Painting. Seoul: Korea Britannica, 1972.

Goo Myong-dok. *Fort Suwon.* Kwangjang Press, 1981.

Ha Tae-hung. *Korean Songs: Folk and Popular Music and Lyrics.* Seoul: Yonsei University Press, 1984.

Howard, Keith. *Bands, Songs and Shamanistic Rituals.* Seoul: Royal Asiatic Society,1989.

Huh Dong-hwa. *Crafts of the Inner Court: The Artistry of Korean Women.* The Museum of Korean Embroidery, 1987.

Hwang Su-yong, *et al. The National Treasures of Korea,* 12 vols. Seoul: Yekyong Publications Co., Ltd., 1985.

Jeon Kyu-tae. *Korean Cultural Potpourri.* Seoul: Seoul International Publishing House, 1988.

Joo Myung-dok. *Korean Tradition As Seen Through Paper Windows.* Seoul: Seoul International Publishing House, 1981.

Kang Bong-kyu. *Traditional Korean Lifestyles.* Samhwa Printing Co., 1988.

Kim Dae-shik. *Complete One Step Fighting Prelude to Sparring: From Beginning to Black Belt.* Seoul: Nanam Publishing, 1985.

—. *Tae Kwon Do: Dynamic Strategic Principles, Movement and Techniques.* Seoul: Nanam Publishing, 1977.

Kim Dong-hwan. *Korean Folk Songs.* Eumak Chunchoo-sa Edition, 1988.

Kim, H. Edward. *The Family of Dolls.* Hyung Mun Publishing Co., 1981.

—. *Korea Beyond the Hills.* Eubyoo Publishing Co., Ltd., 1985.

Kim, John J. *Korean Art Seen Through Museums.* Seoul: Eastern Media, 1981.

Kim Won. *Korean Architecture 11: Kyongbok Palace.* Seoul: Kwang Jang Press, 1982.

—. *Korean Architecture 111: Chongmyo Shrine.* Seoul: Kwang Jang Press, 1982.

Kim Won-yong. *Art and Archaeology of Korea.* Seoul: Daekwang Sorim, 1986.

—. *The Arts of Korea,* 6 vols. Seoul: Dong Hwa Publishing Co., 1979.

—. *Korean Art Treasures.* Seoul: Yekyong Publications Co., Ltd., 1986.

—. *Traditional Korean Art.* Seoul: Si-sa-yong-o-sa, Inc., 1983.

Kim Yong-hwan. *Korean Genre Painting.* Minjok Munhwa Mungo Kanhaeng-hoe, 1988.

Korean Folk Painting. Kyung-mi Publishing, 1980.

Korean Motifs: 1. Geometric Patterns. Ahn Graphics, 1986.

Korean Motifs: 2. Floral Patterns. Ahn Graphics. 1987.

Korean Motifs: 3. Tokkaebi. Ahn Graphics, 1988.

Korean Motifs: 4. Cloud Patterns. Ahn Graphics, 1988.

Korean Motifs: 5. Taeguk.

Ahn Graphics, 1989.

Korean National Commission for UNESCO. *Korean Dance, Theater and Cinema.* Seoul: Si-sa-yong-o-sa, Inc., 1983.

—. *Traditional Korean Art.* Seoul: Si-sa-yong-o-sa, Inc., 1983.

—. *Traditional Korean Music.* Seoul: Si-sa-yong-o-sa, Inc., 1983.

—. *Traditional Korean Painting.* Seoul: Si-sa-yong-o-sa, Inc., 1983.

—. *Traditional Performing Arts of Korea.* Seoul: Seoul Computer Press 1986.

Kowalczyk, Robert. *Morning Calm.* Tokyo: Dawn Press, 1981.

Kwon Yoon-hee. *The Symbolic and Decorative Function of Motifs in Korean Woven Silk Design.* Il Ji Sa, 1988.

Lee Byong-won. *Buddhist Music of Korea.* Jung Eum Sa, 1984.

Lee Hye-kyu. Translated by Robert C. Provine *Essays on Korean Traditional Music.* Seoul: Royal Asiatic Society, 1980.

Lee Kwan-jo. *Korean Countryside: Rhapsody in Nature.* Seoul: Seoul International Publishing House, 1985.

Lim Eung-sik. *Chongmyo Shrine.* Kwangjang Press, 1981.

McCune, Evelyn B. *The Inner Art.* Seoul: Po Chin Jai Co., Ltd., 1983.

McCurdy, John Chang. *Korea Fantasia.* Seoul: Seoul International Publishing House, 1987.

—. *Zen Dance: Meditation in Movement.* Seoul: Seoul International Publishing House, 1985.

Moffett, Eileen F. *Korean Ways.* Seoul: Seoul International Publishing House 1986.

Onyang Folk Museum. *The Folkcrafts of Korea.* Seoul: Kyemongsa, 1980.

Paik Soong-kil. *The Treasure of Sin-an Seabed.* Seoul: Dong Hwa Publishing Company,1983.

Pai Man-sill and Edward Reynolds Wright. *Korean Furniture: Elegance and Tradition.* Tokyo: Kodansa, 1984.

Provine, Robert C. *Essays on Korean Traditional Music.* Seoul: Royal Asiatic Society, 1980.

—. *Essays on Sino-Korean Musicology.* Il Ji Sa, 1988.

Rountree, Charlotte, and Joyce Ryan. *Seoul Sketches: A Visual Narrative of Chosŏn Dynasty.* Seoul: Hollym International Corp., 1985.

Sohn Po-kee. *Early Korean Typography.* Seoul: Po Chin Jai Co., Ltd., 1982.

Suk Joo-sun. *Personal Ornaments in Chosŏn Dynasty.* Seoul: Dankook University Press, 1981.

Song Bang-song. *The Sanjo Tradition of Korean Komungo Music.* Jung Eum Sa 1986.

—. *Source Reading in Korean Music.* Seoul: Korean National Commission for UNESCO, 1980.

Wickman, Michael. *Korean Chests.* Seoul: Seoul International Publishing House, 1978.

Yang Hai-yup. *Die Buddhistische Musik in Korea (La Musigue Bouddhigue en Coree).* Seoul: Seoul National University Press, 1985.

Yi Hye-kyu. *An Introduction to Korean Music and Dance.* Seoul: Royal Asiatic Society, 1977.

Yoon Bok-cha, *et al. Korean Furniture and Culture.* Shinkwang Publishing Co., 1988.

Zo Za-dong. *Guardians of Happiness: Shamanistic Tradition in Korean Folk Painting.* Seoul: Royal Asiatic Society, 1982.

—. *Korean Tiger: An Exhibition of Korean Folk Painting.* Emmille Museum, 1984.

• *Language*

Baek Eung-jin. *Modern Korean Syntax.* Seoul: Jung Min Publishing Co., 1984.

Chang Nam-gui. *Functional Korean.* Seoul: Hollym International Corp., 1989.

Chang Suk-in. *Korean Grammar for International Learners.* Seoul: Yonsei University Press, 1988.

—. *Modern Conversational Korean with Tape.* Seoul: Seoul Computer Press, 1982.

Grant, Bruce K. *A Guide to Korean Characters.* Seoul: Hollym International Corp., 1986.

Huh Woong, *et al. The Korean Language.* Seoul: Si-sa-yong-o-sa, Inc., 1983.

Jones, B.J. *Let's Learn Korean With Cassette Tape.* Seoul: Hollym International Corp., 1986.

—. *Standard English-Korean Dictionary for Foreigners.* Seoul: Hollym International Corp., 1986.

Jones, B.J. and Gene S. Rhie. *English-Korean Practical Conversation Dictionary* (All-

Romanized). Seoul: Hollym International Corp., 1986.

Kim, Jacob Chang-ui. *Pictorial Sino-Korean Characters: Fun with Hancha*. Seoul: Hollym International Corp., 1988.

The Korean-American Educational Commission. *Survival Korean*. Seoul: Seoul Computer Press, 1988.

Lee Chung-min. *Abstract Syntax and Korean with Reference to English*. Seoul: Pan Korea Book Corporation, 1982.

Lee Hong-bae. *A Study of Korean Syntax*. Seoul: Pan Korea Book Corporation, 1970.

Lee Pong-kook and Ryu Chi-shik. *Easy Way to Korean Conversation*. Seoul: Hollym International Corp., 1986.

—. *Let's Talk in Korean*. Seoul: Hollym International Corp., 1986.

Lukoff, Fred. *A First Reader in Korean Writing in Mixed Script*. Seoul: Yonsei University Press, 1982.

—. *An Introductory Course in Korean*. Seoul: Yonsei University Press, 1982.

Park Chang-hai and Park Ki-dawk. *Korean I : An Intensive Course*. Seoul: Yonsei University Press, 1984.

Park Francis T. *Speaking Korean I , II .* Seoul: Myongdo Publishing, 1980.

Park Ki-dawk. *Korean 2: An Intensive Course*. Seoul: Yonsei University Press, 1984.

Park Kyu-soh. *The Methodological Theory and Practice of Korean-English Translation*. Seoul: Hanshin Publishing Company,1986.

Pocket Concise English-Korean Dictionary. Ch'unch'ŏn: Myung Hwa, 1982.

Ree Jung-no. *Topics in Korean Syntax with Notes to Japanese*. Seoul: Yonsei University Press, 1974.

Rhie, Gene S. and B.J. Jones. *Standard Korean-English Dictionary for Foreigners*. Seoul: Hollym International Corp., 1986.

Rucci, Richard B. *Korean with Chinese Characters*, 2 vols. Seoul: Seoul International Publishing House, 1982.

Short-cut Korean. Ch'unch'ŏn: Myung Hwa, 1982.

Song Yo-in. *Topics in Translation Studies*, Seoul: Hanshin Publishing Co., 1984.

Yi Jong-ho. *Hun-Min-Jeong-Eum (Explanation and Translation of the Right Sound for the Education of the People)*. Seoul: Po Chin Jai, Co., Ltd., 1985.

• *History*

Adams, Edward B. *Korea's Kyŏngu: Cultural Spirit of Shilla in Korea*. Seoul: Seoul International Publishing House, 1983.

—. *Palaces of* Seoul: Seoul International Publishing House, 1982.

—. *Through Gates of Seoul: Trails and Tales of Chosŏn Dynasty*, 2 vols. Seoul: Seoul International Publishing House, 1978.

Bartz, Patrica H. *South Korea* London: Oxford University Press, 1972.

Bishop, Isabella B. *Korea and Her Neighbours*. Seoul: Yonsei University Press, 1898.

Clark, Donald N. and James H. Grayson. *Discovering Seoul*. Seoul: Royal Asiatic Society, 1986.

Cook, Harold F. *Korea's 1884 Incident: Its Background and Kim Ok-kyun's Elusive Dream*. Seoul: Royal Asiatic Society,1972.

Covell, Jon Carter. *Korea's Colorful Heritage*. Seoul: Si-sa-yong-o-sa, Inc., 1985.

—. *Korea's Cultural Roots*. Seoul: Hollym International Corp., 1985.

Covell, Jon Carter and Alan Covell. *Korean Impact on Japanese Culture: Japan's Hidden History*. Seoul: Hollym International Corp., 1985.

Deuchler, Martina. *Confucian Gentlemen and Barbarian Envoys: The Opening of Korea, 1875-1885*. Seoul: Royal Asiatic Society 1977.

Fisher, Earnest J. *Pioneers of Modern Korea*. Seoul: Samsung Printing, 1977.

Ha Tae-hung. *Behind the Scenes of the Royal Palaces in Korea: Chosŏn Dynasty*. Seoul: Yonsei University Press, 1983.

—. *Imjin Changch'o*. Seoul: Yonsei University Press, 1983.

—. *Korea –Forty Three Centuries*. Seoul: Yonsei University Press, 1982.

—. *Nanjung llgi –War Diary of Admiral Yi Sun-Shin*. Seoul: Yonsei University Press, 1980.

—. *Samguk Yusa: Legends and History of the Three Kingdoms in Ancient Korea*. Seoul: Yonsei University Press, 1972.

—. *Tales From the Three Kingdoms*. Seoul: Yonsei University Press, 1984.

—. *A Trip Through Historic Korea*. Seoul: Yonsei University Press, 1979.

Han Woo-keun. *The History of Korea*. Seoul: Eul-Yoo Publishing Company, Ltd., 1970.

Henthorn, William E. *History of Korea*. London: The Free Press, 1974.

Hoare, J.E. *The British Embassy Compound, Seoul, 1884-1984*. Korean-British Society, 1984.

Hulbert, Homer B. *The Passing of Korea*. Seoul: Yonsei University Press, 1906.

Hyun, Peter. *Koreana*. Seoul: Korea Britannica Corp., 1984.

International Cultural Foundation. *Upper-Class Culture in Yi-Dynasty Korea*. Seoul: Si-sa-yong-o-sa, Inc. 1982.

Joe, Wanne J. *Traditional Korea: A Cultural History*. Seoul: Chung-Ang University Press, 1972.

Joo Myong-dok. *Fort Suwon*. Seoul: Kwangjang Press, 1981.

—. *Korean Traditions*. Seoul: Seoul International Publishing House, 1981.

Kim, H. Edward. *Korea: Beyond the Hills*. Seoul: Eul-Yoo Publishing Company, Ltd., 1985.

Kim Jong-ki. *Host City of the '88 Olympics*. Seoul: Enterprises Ltd., 1983.

Kim Waren Y. *Koreans in America*. Seoul: Po Chin Jai Co., Ltd., 1972.

King Sejong the Great. Seoul: King Sejong Memorial Society, 1981.

Ku Dae-yeol. *Korea Under Colonialism*. Seoul: Royal Asiatic Society, 1985.

Lee, H. Peter. *Sourcebook of Korean Civilization*. New York: Columbia Univ., 1993.

Lee Ki-baik. *A New History of Korea*. Seoul: Ilchokak, 1984.

Limb Eung-sik. *Kyŏngbok Palace*. Seoul: Kwangjang Press, 1981.

Nahm, Andrew C. *Korea: Tradition and Transformation*. Seoul: Hollym International Corp., 1988.

—. *A Panorama of 5000 Years: Korean History*. Seoul: Hollym International Corp., 1986.

Saccone, Richard. *Korean to Remember*. Seoul: Hollym International Corp., 1993.

Rutt, Richard. *James Scarth Gale's History of the Korean People*. Seoul: Royal Asiatic Society,1967.

Underwood, H.H. *Korean Boats and Ships*.
Seoul: Yonsei University Press, 1979.

Underwood, L. H. *Underwood of Korea*. Seoul: Yonsei University Press, 1983.

Yang Han-song, *et al. The Hye Ch'o Diary: Memoirs of the Pilgrimage to the Five Regions of India*. Seoul: Po Chin Jai Company, Ltd., 1984.

Yoon Tae-hyun. *Historia De Corea*. Seoul: Supeino Munjuawon, 1984.

• Literature

Adams, Edward B. *The Death of Ichadon*. Seoul: Seoul: International Publishing House, 1986.

—. *The Three Good Events*. Seoul: Seoul International Publishing House, 1986.

Carpenter, Frances. *Tales of a Korean Grandmother*. Tokyo: Tuttle, 1973.

Chang Choong-sik. *For the Great Inheritance of Tomorrow*. Seoul: Dankook University Press, 1979.

—. *The Land for the Good*. Seoul: Dankook University Press, 1984.

Chang Dok-soon, *et al. Humor in Korean Literature*. Seoul: Si-sa-yong-o-sa, Inc., 1982.

Chang Wang-nok. *Migrating Birds on the Charles River*. Seoul: Seoul National University Press, 1987.

Chang Yong-hak, *et al. A Respite and Other Korean Short Stories*. Seoul: Si-sa-yong-o-sa, Inc., 1983.

Cho Byung-hwa. *The Fog (Dr. B.H. Cho's Poems and Paintings)*. Seoul: Po Chin Jai Co., Ltd., 1982.

Choi Chung-hee. *The Cry of the Harp and Other Korean Short Stories*. Seoul: Si-sa- yong-o-sa, Inc., 1983.

Choi In-hoon. *A Grey Man*. Seoul: Si-sa-yong-o-sa, Inc., 1988.

Chong Han-sook. *Iyo Island*. Seoul: Si-sa-yong-o-sa, Inc., 1986.

Chun Sang-kook, *et al. Early Spring, Mid- Summer and Other Korean Short Stories*. Seoul: Si-sa-yong-o-sa, Inc., 1983.

Chung Han-mo. *et al. Mainstreams of Contemporary Poetry*. Seoul: The Korean Culture and Arts Foundation, 1978.

Covell, Jon Carter. *Unraveling Zen's Red Thread*. Seoul: Hollym International Corp.,1985.

Daniels, Michael J. *Through a Rain Spattered*

Window. Seoul: Taewon Publishing Company, 1973.

Editorial Department of Poets of the Pacific Countries. *Anthology: Poets of the Pacific Countries*. Seoul: Shimunhaksa, 1985.

Ha Tae-hung. *Folk Tales of Old Korea*. Seoul: Yonsei University Press, 1984.

—. *The Life of a Rainhat Poet*. Seoul: Yonsei University Press, 1977.

—. *Poetry and Music of the Classic Age*. Seoul: Yonsei University Press, 1977.

Hall, Basil. *Voyage of Discovery to the West Coast of Korea and the Great Lou Choo Island*. Seoul: Royal Asiatic Society, 1975.

Han Mal-sook. *Hymn of the Spirit*. New York: Fremont Publications Ltd., 1983.

Han Yong-woon. *Meditations of the Lover*. Seoul: Yonsei University Press, 1980.

Hong, Crown Princess, *Han Joong Nok*. New York: Larchwood Publication, 1980.

Hong Myoung-hee. *Korean Short Stories*. Seoul: Il Ji Sa, 1975.

Hoyt, James. *Songs of Dragons Flying to Heaven: A Korean Epic*. Seoul: Royal Asiatic Society, 1979.

Hwang Sun-won. *The Moving Castle*. Seoul: Si-sa-yong-o-sa, Inc., 1985.

Hyon Joon-shik. *Modern Korean Short Stories*. New York: Larchwood Publication, 1981.

Hyun, Peter. *Darkness at Dawn: A North Korean Diary*. Seoul: Hanjin Publishing Company, 1981.

—. *Korea's Favorite Tales and Lyrics*. Seoul: Seoul International Publishing House, 1986.

International Cultural Foundation. *Humour in Korean Literature* (Korean Culture Series 1). Seoul: Si-sa-yong-o-sa, Inc., 1982.

International Cultural Society. *Lamp Light Ever Burning*. Seoul: Kapin Publishing Company, 1980.

Kim, Agnes Davis. *I Married a Korean*. Seoul: Royal Asiatic Society, 1979.

—. *Unrealized Challenge*. Seoul: Yonsei University Press, 1982.

Kim Dong-gil. *Abraham Lincoln: An Oriental Interpretation*. Seoul: Jung Woo Sa,1983.

Kim Dong-wook, *et al. Korean Culture and Arts*. Seoul: The Korean Culture and Arts Foundation, 1981.

Kim Gi-dong. *The Classical Novels of Korea*. Seoul: The Korean Culture and Arts Foundation, 1981.

Kim Jai-hiun. *Classical Korean Poetry*. Hanshin Publishing Co., 1987.

—. *The Contemporary Korean Poets*. New York: Larchwood Publication, 1980.

—. *Korean Poetry Today*. Hanshin Publishing Co., 1987.

—. *Master Poems From Modern Korea*. Seoul: Si-sa-yong-o-sa, Inc., 1980.

—. *Master Sijo Poems From Korea*. Seoul: Si-sa-yong-o-sa, Inc., 1982.

—. Kim Jai-hiun. *Traditional Korean Verse Since the 1900s*. Seoul: Hanshin Publishing Co. 1992.

—. Kim Jai-hiun. *Unforgettable Love-An Anthology of poems by Kim Sowol*. Seoul: Paikmunsa Publishing Co. 1992.

Kim Jong-won. *Postwar Korean Short Stories: An Anthology*. Seoul: Seoul National University Press, 1974.

Kim, Richard. *The Innocent*. Seoul: Si-sa-yong-o-sa, Inc., 1968.

—. *Lost Names*. Seoul: Si-sa-yong-o-sa, Inc., 1970.

—. *The Martyred*. Seoul: Si-sa-yong-o-sa, Inc., 1985.

Kim So-wol. *Lost Love*. Seoul: Pan Korea Book Corporation, 1976.

Kim Tong-ni. *The Cross of Shaphan*. Seoul: Si-sa-yong-o-sa, Inc., 1983.

—. *Ulhwa the Shaman*. New York: Larchwood Publication 1979.

Kim Yeol-gyu, *et al. The Classical Poetry of Korea*. Seoul: The Korean Culture and Arts Foundation, 1981.

—. *Korean Folk Tales*. Seoul: Si-sa- yong-o-sa, Inc., 1982.

Koh Chang-soo. *Anthology of Contemporary Korean Poetry (Vols. I , II)*. Seoul: Seoul International Publishing House, 1987.

—. *Best Loved Poems of Korea*. Seoul: Hollym International Corp., 1986.

Korean National Commission for UNESCO. *The Cry of the Harp and other Korean Short Stories*. Seoul: Si-sa-yong-o-sa, Inc., 1983.

—. *The Drizzle and Other Korean Short Stories* Seoul: Si-sa-yong-o-sa, Inc., 1983.

—. *Early Spring, Mid-Summer and Other Korean Short Stories*.

Seoul: Si-sa-yong-o-sa Inc., 1983.

—. *Hospital Room 205 and Other Korean Short Stories*. Seoul: Si-sa-yong-o-sa, Inc., 1983.

—. *Loess Valley and Other Korean Short Stories*. Seoul: Si-sa-yong-o-sa, Inc., 1983.

—. *A Respite and Other Korean Short Stories*. Seoul: Si-sa-yong-o-sa, Inc., 1983.

—. *The Road to Sampo and Other Korean Short Stories*. Seoul: Si-sa-yong-o-sa, Inc., 1983.

Ledyard, Gari. *The Dutch Come to Korea*. Seoul: Royal Asiatic Society, 1971.

Lee-chon Seunghi. *Daily Pursuits and Timeless Values*. Seoul: Hollym International Corp., 1978.

Lee Chung-joon. The *Cruel City and Other Korean Short Stories*.
Seoul: Si-sa-yong-o-sa, Inc., 1983.

—. *Home-coming and Other Korean Short Stories*. Seoul: Si-sa-yong-o-sa, Inc., 1983.

—. *New Translations From Korean: A Selection of Modern Korean Literature*. Seoul: The Korean Culture and Arts Foundation, 1982.

Lee Dong-in. *Agony With Pride*. Seoul: Seoul International Publishing House, 1986.

Lee, Grant S. *Life and Thought of Yi Kwang-su*. Seoul: U Shin Sa, 1984.

Lee Jung-young. *Sokdam: Capsules of Korean Wisdom*. Seoul: Seoul Computer Press, 1983.

Lee Kwang-su, *The Unenlightened and Other Korean Short Stories*.
Seoul: Si-sa-yong-o-sa, Inc., 1983.

Lee Mun-yol. *Hail to the Emperor*.
Seoul: Si-sa-yong-o-sa, Inc., 1986.

Lee, Peter H. *Anthology of Korean Literature From Early Times to the Nineteenth Century*. Hawaii: University of Hawaii Press, 1981.

Lee Young-gul, *et al. Paulownia Leaf*.
Seoul: The Korean Culture and Arts Foundation, 1980.

Moffett, Eileen F. *Korean Ways*. Seoul: Seoul International Publishing House, 1987.

Nahm Yong-woo. *Nice to Be Korean*.
Seoul: Lee Woo, 1978.

O'Rourke, Kevin. *The Cutting Edge*.
Seoul: Yonsei University Press, 1982.

—. *Ten Korean Short Stories*. Seoul: Yonsei University Press, 1981.

—. *Tilting the Jar, Spilling the Moon*. Universal Publishing Co., 1988.

—. *A Washed-out Dream*. Seoul: Royal Asiatic Society, 1980.

Price, David. *Between Two Seas*. Seoul: Seoul International Publishing House, 1988.

Rutt, Richard. *Upper-Class Culture in Yi Dynasty Korea*. Seoul: Si-sa-yong-o-sa, Inc., 1982.

Rutt, Richard and Kim Chong-un. *Virtuous Women: Three Classic Korean Novels*. Seoul: Royal Asiatic Society, 1974.

Seligson, Fred Jeremy. *Oriental Birth Dreams*. Seoul: Hollym International Corp., 1989.

Seros, Kathleen. *Sun and Moon*. Seoul: Hollym International Corp., 1985.

Several Phases of Novel and Short Stories. Seoul: The Korean Culture and Arts Foundation, 1978.

Shim Myung-ho. *The Making of Modern Korean Poetry*. Seoul: Seoul National University Press, 1982.

Sim Chai-hong. *Fragrance of Spring*: The *Story of Choon Hyang*. Seoul: Po Chin Jai Co., Ltd., 1970.

Sŏ Chong-ju. *Unforgettable Things*. Seoul: Si-sa-yong-o-sa, Inc., 1986.

Son So-hui. *The Wind from the South*. Seoul: Si-sa-yong-o-sa, Inc., 1988.

Song Yo-in. *The Ferryboat and the Wayfarer*. Seoul: Dongguk University Press, 1987.

Sonu Hui, *et al. One Way and Other Korean Short Stories*.
Seoul: Si-sa-yong-o-sa, Inc., 1983.

Stewart, Ruth. *Wing and Bone*. Seoul: Royal Asiatic Society, 1980.

Suh Ki-won, *et al. Two Travelers and Other Korean short Stories*.
Seoul: Si-sa-yong-o-sa, Inc., 1983.

Underwood, Lillas H. and Leonora H. Egan. *Fifteen Years among the Topknots with Lillie in Korea*. Seoul: Royal Asiatic Society, 1977.

UNESCO. *Wedding Day and Other Korean Short Stories*.
Seoul: Si-sa-yong-o-sa, Inc., 1983.

Wade, James. *West Meets East*.
Seoul: Pomso Publishing, 1975.

Wehry, Whalen M. *The Yobo*. Seoul: Hollym International Corp., 1984.

Zong In-sob. *Folk Tales From Korea*. Seoul: Hollym International Corp., 1986.

—. *A Guide to Korean Literature*. Seoul: Hollym International Corp., 1982.

Index

R